Methods of
Information Integration Theory

Titles in Information Integration Theory

by Norman H. Anderson

Methods of
Information Integration Theory

Norman H. Anderson

Department of Psychology
University of California, San Diego
La Jolla, California

ACADEMIC PRESS   1982
A Subsidiary of Harcourt Brace Jovanovich, Publishers
New York   London
Paris San Diego San Francisco São Paulo Sydney Tokyo Toronto

085340

ACADEMIC PRESS, INC.
111 Fifth Avenue, New York, New York 10003

United Kingdom Edition published by
ACADEMIC PRESS, INC. (LONDON) LTD.
24/28 Oval Road, London NW1 7DX

Library of Congress Cataloging in Publication Data

Main entry under title:

Methods of information integration theory.

(Information integration theory)
Bibliography: p.
Includes index.
1. Psychology—Methodology. 2. Psychological
research. 3. Psychometrics. I. Anderson, Norman
Henry, Date . II. Series: Anderson, Norman
Henry, Date . Information integration theory.
BF38.5.M457 1982 150′.724 82–16273
ISBN 0-12-058102-7

BF
38.5
.A48
1982

Contents

2 Integration Models

3 Special Models and Applications

4 Problems in Model Analysis

5 Monotone Analysis

6 Importance Indexes and Self-Estimation Methodology

7 Sundry Problems in Method

Preface

This volume presents the methodology that has been used in the program of research on information integration theory. As befits an inductive theory, Chapter 1 begins with homely problems of experimental design and procedure. Later chapters take up various integration models and associated problems of data analysis. Many of these problems are more conceptual than statistical, as with goodness of fit in Chapter 4 and importance weights in Chapter 6. This interdependence of method and substantive theory is emphasized in the last several sections of Chapter 7, which consider an integration-theoretical approach to some current issues in cognitive analysis.

The material in this *Methods* volume was originally intended for inclusion in the companion *Foundations* volume. It gradually became clear, however, that a separate volume was needed to allow adequate coverage. This volume is essentially self-contained, but cross-references to the *Foundations* volume are included to provide empirical illustrations of various problems and procedures.

I noted in the preface to the *Foundations* volume that I had wanted to subtitle it, *A Case History in Experimental Science*. This subtitle applies also to the present *Methods* volume, for its contents are part of information integration theory. These methods owe great debts to many previous workers, debts that I have repeatedly emphasized. I believe we have made good progress, but we were beneficiaries of many previous investigators who influenced our work in countless visible and invisible ways. This influence of past work is itself part of the case history theme.

Also part of this case history theme is the negative reaction that our work has often met. This reaction has not been merely natural skepticism and scrutiny of particular issues such as the meaning-constancy hypothesis or the averaging model; rather, it appears to arise from different ways of thinking. Since this has caused continual difficulties, I wish to devote a few comments to it.

Prime illustrations concern the rating method, the analysis of variance, and the concept of weight. Reactions to the rating method are indicated in Section 1.1.1. Our use of analysis of variance in model analysis has been rejected almost out of hand by numerous investigators from the initial studies to the present time. Our conceptual analysis of importance weights has met with similar disapprobation.

These negative reactions may originate in the issue of multiple causation. This issue is basic in psychological theory, and it is the central theme of information integration theory. Previous approaches did not have very good methods for studying stimulus integration, so they tended to focus on substantive issues that could be studied with available methods. These method-issue complexes developed into conceptual outlooks with a conceptual inertia that carried them outside their domain of usefulness.

This difference in ways of thinking may be illustrated by the two main themes of this volume: models and measurement. The role of models is different in integration theory from the most prominent alternative, namely, the various regression–correlation approaches. Standard regression-correlation analysis has important uses, but it is not well-suited for cognitive analysis of multiple causation. Many investigators carried it outside of its domain of usefulness, however, without recognizing that this rested on substantive assumptions that were no longer justified.

On the second main problem, that of measurement, two other outlooks have been popular. Empirical workers have typically ignored the problem or used arbitrary measures, as in standard regression-correlation analysis. This commonsense approach can be useful, and it is the more understandable in view of the disagreements among workers in the field of measurement theory. But this commonsense approach lacks a foundation in substantive theory, so it is often misapplied.

The other popular outlook is the traditional, still dominant view of measurement as a methodological preliminary to substantive inquiry. Functional measurement takes an opposite view, in which measurement is an integral part of substantive theory. The validity of the present methodology rests on the program of empirical research from which it developed, which is summarized in Chapter 1 of the *Foundations* volume. The difference between traditional and present ways of thinking about psychological measurement is epitomized in this empirical research program.

Much of the material in this volume has been scattered across many articles. I hope that this exposition will make this material more available and more useful to research workers. I hope also that it will provide an impetus for further study of many uncertain methodological problems.

Acknowledgments

This book is dedicated to my students, whose work has formed the foundation of information integration theory. First among them are Ann Norman Jacobson and Anita Lampel; their help in the initial investigations of person perception was beyond price. Stephen Hubert and Ralph Stewart also did important work during this initial stage, and James Anderson provided valuable technical assistance.

My students at the University of California, San Diego, have been mainly concerned with exploring new areas. The theoretical developments in decision theory were initiated by James Shanteau, in psychophysics by David Weiss, and in psycholinguistics by Gregg Oden. A foundation of applications in developmental psychology has been provided by Clifford Butzin, Diane Cuneo, and Manuel Leon. Other extensions have been made by John Clavadetscher to perceptual illusions, by Arthur Farkas to equity theory, by Cheryl Graesser to group dynamics, by Michael Klitzner to motivation, by Barbara Sawyers to attitude theory, by John Verdi to moral judgment, by James Zalinski to statistical analysis, and by Lola Lopes to many problems. The work of Donald Blankenship and JoAnn Kahn was also important. It is to these men and women that integration theory owes its breadth.

The theoretical development is also much indebted to work by colleagues at other institutions. Foremost are Martin Kaplan and Clyde Hendrick, who made basic and enduring contributions in the early period, and Michael Birnbaum and Ramadhar Singh, who have done cogent work in many areas. Other contributions, both to theory and method, have been made by Richard Bogartz, Berndt Brehmer, Edward Carterette, Reid Hastie, Samuel Himmelfarb, Wilfried Hommers, Irwin

Levin, Jordan Louviere, Dominic Massaro, Kent Norman, Thomas Os-
trom, Allen Parducci, Charles Schmidt, Joseph Sidowski, Lennart
Sjöberg, Friedrich Wilkening, and Robert Wyer. In addition, I am grate-
ful to Edward Alf, William McGuire, Jeffrey Miller, Miriam Rodin,
Seymour Rosenberg, Paul Slovic, Gordon Stanley, Saul Sternberg, and
Thomas Wallsten for many helpful comments and criticisms, and to
Eileen Beier and Frank Logan for intellectual stimulation.

Many persons already mentioned have made comments on earlier
drafts of this book. Helpful comments have also been made at many
stages in this research program by innumerable persons whose names
cannot be listed here but to whom I wish to express my appreciation and
thanks. I am especially indebted to careful readings by Jerome Busemeyer and to painstaking critiques by James Shanteau. I also wish to
thank Donata Bocko for much patient typing and careful proofing.

Among my teachers, I wish to record my appreciation of Cletus Burke,
David Grant, Carl Hovland, and especially Paul Halmos, whose life and
teaching go hand in hand. In addition, my heartfelt gratitude goes to
four teachers at Milaca High School in Minnesota: Dale Dougherty, Gordon Mork, Nels Tosseland, and Leslie Westin.

I take this opportunity to express my deepest personal appreciation to
Lucille Kirsch, Eileen Beier, Ann Norman, Joan Prentice, Mary Pendery,
and my beloved Margaret. For their love and understanding, I am pro-
foundly grateful. For friendships that have meant much to me in diffi-
cult times, I am grateful to Frank Allen, Lorraine Crawford, Robert
Doan, Agnes Haber, Herb and Lee Kanner, Melvin Kniseley, Anita
Lampel, Wayne Luchsinger, Richard Miller, Thomas Nyquist, Winifred
Riney, Miriam Rodin, and Louise Warner. And to James Alexander,
Lucille Kirsch, and Mary Pendery, I owe more than words can say.

Besides these personal debts are various institutional obligations that
are pleasant to record. The University of California has provided a productive atmosphere for research and teaching. The National Science
Foundation has supported this work since 1962, and I appreciate the
backing of Henry Odbert and Kelly Shaver at critical junctures. My
graduate training at the University of Wisconsin turned me into an
experimentalist, and a postdoctoral fellowship at Yale University sponsored by the Social Science Research Council was important in widening
my psychological outlook. Also notable was a year at the Center for
Advanced Study in the Behavioral Sciences that among other things,
provided a healthy separation from experimental work and started me
on the long path to this book. Above all, I am indebted to the University
of Chicago where, as an undergraduate, I found worlds of which I had
never dreamed.

Experimental Procedures

An integral part of any theoretical development is the network of relations between the verbal statement of the theory and the phenomena that the theory is about. The importance of this network is obvious, but it is often neglected for the verbal or formal structure of the theory. Compared to the intellectual sweep of theoretical analysis, problems of experimental method and procedure often seem dull, obtrusive, unworthy of equal place. But in the inductive view, scientific theory does not exist as an abstract entity, divorced from the phenomena that it is about (Section F1.8.1).[1] The network of relations between the verbal formulation and the phenomena is an organic part of a complete theory. Details of method and procedure therefore deserve no less attention than other aspects of the overall theoretical structure. These aspects of methodology are the major concern of this chapter.

1.1 Rating Response

1.1.1 RATINGS AS LINEAR SCALES

The common rating scale has played a vital role in the development of information integration theory. When this research program was begun, rating methods were held in low regard. Measurement theory was dominated by a concern with choice data and nonmetric methods. This

---

[1]Cross references prefixed by F refer to the companion volume, *Foundations of Information Integration Theory.*

tradition grew from forced-choice methods developed to avoid criterion biases in psychophysics, and especially from Thurstone's development of paired comparisons. As Thurstone (1929) remarked about one rating method,

> Another serious limitation of the method of equal-appearing intervals for which I can offer no solution is that the determinations are undoubtedly affected by the distribution of stimulus values which the experimenter happens to use. . . . Whenever it is at all possible we certainly should avoid the method of equal-appearing intervals and use instead the method of paired comparison or one of its equivalents [pp. 223–224].

Thirty years later, the prevailing view was well summarized by Torgerson (1958), who dismissed ratings with the remark that such data provided "no basis for concluding whether or not the subject was judging on the basis of an equal-interval scale [p. 82]."

This empirical tradition was reinforced by later mathematical developments, most prominently by the work of Coombs (1964) on nonmetric methods and by that of Krantz, Luce, Suppes, and Tversky (1971) on abstract measurement theory. These approaches sought a foundation for measurement that required only rank-order data. The following quotation indicates their outlook on rating scales in psychophysics:

> To the theorist, however, the whole business is a bit hair-raising. To calculate the means of category *labels,* to plot them against physical measures of the stimuli, and then to discuss the form of the resulting function strikes him as close to meaningless. . . . we do not think that the absolute form of the obtained function using the first *k* integers as labels has any meaning [Luce & Galanter, 1963, pp. 264–265].

There was one concerted effort to use numerical estimates as linear scales, namely, Stevens's (1957, 1974) studies with magnitude estimation. But Stevens was more negative about ratings than were the advocates of nonmetric methods.

> The category scale calls for special consideration because it is by far the most common and yet perhaps the least satisfactory form of partition scale. . . . On prothetic continua, the category scale is invariably nonlinear relative to the magnitude scale. . . . Since most scaling problems involve prothetic continua, it seems that category and other forms of partition scaling ought generally to be avoided for the purposes of scaling [Stevens, 1971, pp. 434–435].

> Perhaps the least satisfactory form of partition scale is the category rating scale. . . . On prothetic continua the category scales are invariably nonlinear. . . . The conclusion, then, seems inescapable: For the purposes of

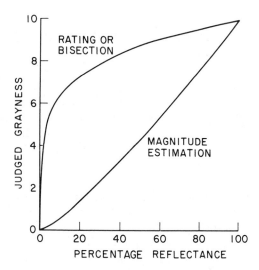

FIGURE 1.1. *Rating and magnitude estimation of grayness of same Munsell chips yield different functions. Magnitude estimation curve is bowed up, corresponding to Stevens's exponent of 1.2 for power function. Rating curve is bowed down, similar to but more strongly than Munsell value curve, as indicated in functional scaling by Weiss (1972, 1975) and Anderson (1976c); see also Figure 3.1.*

serious perceptual measurement, category methods should be shunned [Stevens, 1974, pp. 373-374].

Certainly there was ample reason to avoid ratings. They were known to be subject to several biases, such as the distribution effect mentioned in the preceding quotation from Thurstone (see also Anderson, 1969a; Anderson & Whalen, 1960; Cox, 1980; Eriksen & Hake, 1957; Guilford, 1954, Chapter 11; Jones, 1960; Krantz & Campbell, 1961; Stevens, 1957). These biases would destroy the response linearity needed for analysis of quantitative models.

This problem of bias in the rating method was dramatized by Stevens's (1957) introduction of the method of magnitude estimation. Both methods ask for numerical responses, and subjects find them both easy to use (Section 1.1.7). Introspection gives little indication that the two methods yield very different results.

How different ratings and magnitude estimation can be is illustrated in Figure 1.1. Each curve represents judged grayness as a function of physical reflectance. Magnitude estimation yields a curve that is bowed up (Stevens, 1974, p. 375, 1975, p. 15); ratings yield a function that is bowed down (Section F5.4, Figure 5.3). Such nonlinear relations hold for most sensory dimensions. They also hold for most social stimuli. As

Stevens emphasized, both methods could not be true linear scales. Which—if either—is valid? How can validity be tested?

Successful use of any method of numerical response depends on solving two interlocked problems. The first is to find a validity criterion to assess whether the response measure provides an unbiased linear scale. That is the role of the algebraic rules discussed in Section 1.1.2. The second problem is to find ways to eliminate the various biases to which all numerical response methods are subject. This problem of experimental procedure forms the main content of Sections 1.1.3–1.1.8.

1.1.2 COGNITIVE ALGEBRA

The essential idea of functional measurement is to use algebraic rules as the base and frame for psychological scaling. Algebraic rules can provide the validity criterion that is needed to decide the controversy over rating and magnitude estimation. The logic of this approach is given in Chapters 2, 3, and 5; its psychological structure is illustrated in the following stimulus integration diagram.

Figure 1.2 shows physical stimuli, S_i, that impinge on the organism and are converted by the valuation function, **V**, into subjective or psychological stimuli, s_i. These psychological stimuli are combined by the integration function, **I**, to yield an implicit, psychological response that is then transformed by the response function, **M**, into the observable response measure, $R.^a$

The main concern of functional measurement is with the integration function, which relates the psychological stimuli to the psychological response. In some situations, **I** may be hypothesized to have a simple

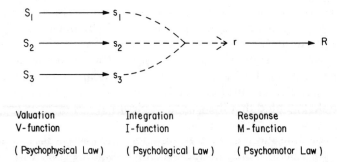

Valuation	Integration	Response
V-function	I-function	M-function
(Psychophysical Law)	(Psychological Law)	(Psychomotor Law)

FIGURE 1.2. *Integration diagram. Chain of three functions,* **V, I,** *and* **M,** *leads from observable stimulus field,* $\{S_i\}$, *to observable response,* R. *Valuation function, or psychophysical law* **V,** *transforms physical stimuli,* S_i, *into their psychological counterparts, represented by subjective values,* s_i. *Integration function, or psychological law* **I,** *transforms subjective stimulus field,* $\{s_i\}$, *into implicit response,* r. *Response function, or psychomotor law* **M,** *transforms implicit response,* r, *into observable response,* R. *(See also Section F1.1.)*

algebraic form, for example, averaging or multiplying. Implicit in such algebraic rules are scales of the stimulus variables and of the response variable. The algebraic rule provides a structural frame for scaling both classes of variables, and separating the **V, I,** and **M** functions.

Figure 1.2 embodies a new way of thinking about psychological measurement. The traditional approach centered on stimulus scaling, which was seen as a methodological preliminary to substantive investigation. That approach was eminently reasonable, for it focused on the first of the three stages in the diagram of Figure 1.2, with the intention of solving them one at a time. However, it was too narrow to provide a base for psychological measurement.

Functional measurement was developed as part of information integration theory and makes measurement an organic component of substantive inquiry. The study of integration involves many-variable stimulus fields, and so all three stages of the diagram must be solved simultaneously. Although simultaneous attack on all three stages may seem forbidding, it turns out to be simple in principle and empirically successful in some situations.

Although functional measurement requires a shift from traditional views, its kinship with previous work and indebtedness to previous workers deserve emphasis. It agrees with Stevens's concern for obtaining numerical response measures. Thurstone's method of paired comparisons may be seen as a precursor of functional measurement and, indeed, as the first true theory of measurement in psychology, for Thurstone's method rested on a formal subtracting model (Section F5.3). Most important is the debt to workers in statistics, who have provided many of the statistical procedures used in this work (see also Section F5.6.1).

But the foundation of functional measurement lies in the experimental studies of algebraic integration rules. The mathematical analyses remain empty until they are embedded in substantive studies. Unless the algebraic rules are shown to hold empirically, there is no measurement. The true foundation for functional measurement lies in the experimental work on cognitive algebra reviewed in the *Foundations* volume.

It should be noted that the empirical picture is not simple. The popular adding rule, in particular, has fared poorly. An averaging rule has had considerable success, but it is nonlinear and nonadditive and yields a simple data pattern only under an equal-weighting condition (Section 2.3). Compounding the uncertainty about the integration rules was the uncertainty about the rating response, for nonparallelism in the observed response is ambiguous if the response scale is not linear. For this and other reasons, the averaging rule and other algebraic rules were not easy to pin down.

It was clear, however, that numerical response measures were potentially efficient. Indeed, they become almost necessary for the study of stimulus interaction and organizing processes. Emphasis was therefore placed on development of methods to eliminate the biases to which the rating method was subject. It is to these mundane problems that the discussion now turns.

1.1.3 DEFINITION AND USE OF RATING SCALES

A rating scale consists of an ordered sequence of response categories that is ordinarily closed at both ends. To use the rating scale requires setting up a correspondence between these response categories and the aggregate of stimuli to be presented. In setting up this stimulus–response correspondence, a special role is played by the two end response categories that ordinarily correspond to the lower and upper ends of the range of stimuli. In this research program, special stimuli, called end anchors, have generally been used to help define this stimulus–response correspondence. These stimulus end anchors are ordinarily made to correspond to the two end response categories. In addition, they define the subjective range of the stimuli. The rating of any particular stimulus can be considered a comparative judgment in which the subjective value of the given stimulus is compared to the values of the two end anchors (Section 3.11). This comparative value is then mapped onto the overt rating scale.

The format most widely used in this research program has been a 1–20 numerical scale (e.g., Section 1.2.1; Anderson, 1962a). The two ends of the scale are ordinarily defined by verbal labels such as "Least Likable" and "Most Likable." Often the numbers are listed in serial order on a card that lies in front of the subject throughout the experiment. The intermediate numbers are not ordinarily labeled, however, and may not even be explicitly presented. Occasionally a 0–10 scale is used instead. Scales with negative numbers are usually avoided because even one error in recording sign could seriously affect the results.

Other investigators have typically used scales with fewer than ten response steps, but that seems risky. Scales with six or seven steps would seem especially susceptible to bias from end effects and distributional effects. The studies that have found strong distributional effects (Section 1.1.6) have almost always employed a small number of steps, a warning against such procedure for model analysis.[a]

There may be an optimal range of from 10 to 20 rating steps. With more than 20 steps, lumping may begin to appear. Subjects typically use a 1–100 scale in round-number fashion so that it has, in effect, no more than 20 steps. Fortunately, people seem to be facile in using rating scales, and scales with different numbers of steps appear to yield equivalent results (e.g., Figure F2.7), at least when the number of steps is not too small.

In some cases, a response scale with verbal labels may be needed. Word labels are risky, however, because words may connote unequal subjective category width and hence cause nonlinear bias if transposed directly to numbers. Alphabetical scales have been used when more than one quality is to be judged and possible interaction among the responses is to be minimized (e.g., Section F4.1.2). It is ordinarily necessary to print the letters in serial order on a card that is continuously visible to the subject. In this form, an alphabetical rating scale can be considered a discrete, graphic scale. Although the letters need to be converted to numbers, recording a letter response is easier than reading a line-mark response.

The best rating format seems to be graphical, and this format is preferred for careful work. Numerical ratings seem at best to suffer from residual number preferences (see Shanteau & Anderson, 1969) that can be substantially reduced with graphic ratings. Graphic scales also have advantages for studies with children. Indeed, such work has suggested that the rating response reflects the operation of a general metric sense, an internalized length scale that develops from reaching movements and other activity in the child's local space (Anderson, 1980a; Anderson & Cuneo, 1978a; Section F1.1.6).

Graphic scales are also useful in serial integration, in which subjects continually revise their responses as new information is received. With a numerical response, each new piece of information might cause an upward or downward shift from the last response number simply because of its positive or negative sign. With a graphic rating, exact memory of the previous response is a lesser problem.

Graphic ratings are often made by locating a pin or slider along an unmarked bar 10 or 20 cm in length, with the pin or slider usually being returned to a neutral position between responses. In most studies, the bar has a scale on the rear that the experimenter reads to the nearest 1 or 2 mm. More convenient is a bar equipped with a graphic readout (Troutman & Shanteau, 1977, p. 48). In some experiments, a computerized graphic rating scale has been used (Oden & Wong, 1973; see Lopes, 1976a,b; Oden & Anderson, 1974). With children, intermediate steps on the graphic scale are usually marked in some way so that the child has a definite target to point at (Anderson & Cuneo, 1978a, Figure 1). A few experiments have used a more tedious alternative in which the subject marks a line on a sheet of paper (e.g., Anderson & Alexander, 1971; Clavadetscher & Anderson, 1977; Massaro & Anderson, 1970).[b]

1.1.4 END EFFECTS AND END ANCHORS

There is no lack of evidence, anecdotal and otherwise, about end effects in rating methods. End effects may occur on the stimulus side because end stimuli are more discriminable than intermediate stimuli. End effects may also occur on the response side. Ceiling effects, for example, refer to suspected nonlinearity near the ends of the response scale. Even joint stimulus–response end effects have been found, as will be noted later.

To help control or minimize such end effects, it has been standard procedure in this research program to use stimulus end anchors. These are stimuli that are mildly more extreme in either direction than are the regular experimental stimuli. In a simple perceptual task, judging heaviness, for instance, the subject would be presented the low end anchor during the instructions and told, "This is the lightest weight you will lift; call it 1." And similarly with the high end anchor, "This is the heaviest; call it 20." The instructions would then continue, "Use numbers between 1 and 20 to indicate weights of intermediate heaviness in the natural way."

One major purpose of stimulus end anchors is to absorb end effects. Since the regular experimental stimuli come from the interior of the stimulus range, they should be affected less strongly by the increased discriminability at the ends of the range than they would be in the absence of end anchors. Again, since the regular response data come from the interior of the rating scale, they should be affected less strongly by response nonlinearities near the scale end points. On both the stimulus and response sides, therefore, the end anchors act to absorb end effects and purify the data. In addition, of course, end anchors provide a stimulus–response calibration.

Some practical aspects of end-anchor usage should be noted. In person perception, it may be inappropriate to assign response numbers to the selected end anchors because subjects may not all agree that they are the highest and lowest. In that case, several presumptive end anchors may be chosen, with the expectation that at least one will work for every subject. Thus, the group of low end anchors would be presented in the instruction period with the comment that "these include some of the lowest you will receive." Alternatively, it may be necessary to preselect anchors separately for each subject (e.g., Shanteau & Anderson, 1969).

In some tasks, stimulus end anchors are not feasible or not desirable. In such cases, it may be possible to simply instruct the subject to stay away from the ends of the response scale. This instruction may be rationalized on the ground that stimuli could be presented that are more extreme than any that will actually be given. This procedure has been used in a few experiments with graphic rating scales (e.g., Shanteau, 1970a, p. 183).

Two details of end-anchor usage deserve mention. First, if the end anchors are too extreme, are perceptually isolated from the experimental stimuli, then the subject may set up a narrow effective response scale in which the usual end effects reappear. For this reason, two or three end anchors, graded in degree, may sometimes be appropriate. Second, repeated presentations of the end anchors may be desirable in order to keep stable the frame of reference, especially with perceptual stimuli.

Stimulus end anchors were introduced on a commonsense basis (Note F2.2.1a; see also Appendix A) and have been continued because they appeared to yield linear response scales. No explicit studies of their mode of operation have been conducted, although this aspect of the response process has considerable theoretical interest.[a] End anchors are not always necessary, and good results have sometimes been obtained without their use. However, omission of anchors can lead to trouble (e.g., Section F2.4.3). Similarly, a minor error in end-anchor usage was the cause of the one-point discrepancy in Figure 4.7.

1.1.5 CONTRAST AND RELATED CONTEXT EFFECTS

The term *contrast* refers to a change in subjective value of a given stimulus away from the value of some contextual stimulus. At the beginning of this research program, the prevailing expectation was for substantial contrast effects in judgment. Contrast was central to Helson's (1964) theory of adaptation level and was widely popularized in the area of social judgment by Sherif and Hovland (1961). Contrast effects were important for two reasons. First, they are a form of stimulus interaction and so have substantive interest as integration processes. Second, they are potentially related to certain biases that would produce nonlinearities in the rating response. Accordingly, the early experiments on integration theory gave considerable attention to assessment of contrast effects.

The outcome of these studies was simple: Genuine contrast was not found outside of the perceptual tasks in which it was well known. Much that had been interpreted as contrast thus appeared to be artifacts of the response language, as had been suggested by other investigators (e.g., Campbell, Lewis, & Hunt, 1958; Stevens, 1958; Upshaw, 1969). This conclusion gained force from the finding that it seemed possible to largely eliminate the response artifacts with the procedural precautions already outlined. Some context effects were obtained, but these generally appeared to result from integration of the context stimuli into the judgment of the focal stimulus.

Contrast as Artifact. Judgment scales are ordinarily relative rather than absolute. As a consequence, the overt response to any one stimulus will in general depend on the range and distribution of the other stimuli that are being judged. To take an extreme case, consider lines judged on a 1–9, Short–Long rating scale. One group judges lines ranging from 6 to 20 inches, and another group judges lines ranging from 20 to 36 inches. Each group will naturally spread its judgments over the whole rating scale. The 20-inch line, which is common to both groups, will therefore be rated high in the first group, low in the second. At face value this is a contrast effect. But to claim that the common 20-inch line is phenomenally different in the two groups is obviously unjustified; the response language itself forces a seeming contrast onto the data. This contrast artifact, which is obvious in this extreme example, arises in other situations in less obvious ways.

D. T. Campbell, who seems to be the first to give this problem proper concern, attempted to demonstrate true contrast beneath the response language artifact. Two of his studies will be considered here. In Campbell, Hunt, and Lewis (1957), subjects judged the quality of definitions of words that had been given by normal and schizophrenic individuals. Judgments were made on a 9-point scale whose ends were defined as "well-organized and normal" and "totally disorganized and eccentric." These definitions had been prerated, and one group received only the better organized definitions, prerated 1–5 inclusive, whereas the other group received only the worse organized definitions, prerated 5–9 inclusive.

The definitions of value 5, which were common to both groups, were rated 6.5 and 3.5, respectively. At face value, the same definition seems to indicate greater mental disorganization to the subjects in the first group. At face value, this is a contrast effect.

But this experiment is very like the preceding example of rating length. The problem that was so obvious for the length judgments reappears in the clinical judgments, and the observed effect must accordingly be suspected of being an artifact of the relative nature of the response language. There is a difference between the two experiments, for the Short–Long scale is basically relative, whereas the rating scale for the definitions had external referents in terms of subjects' previous experience. But the phrase "well-organized and normal" is not absolute, but partly relative, and so the obtained result could be no more than a contrast artifact. If there was genuine contrast, it was confounded with the contrast artifact, as Campbell recognized.

In an attempt to demonstrate true contrast, Krantz and Campbell (1961) obtained numerical judgments of length both with an open-ended rating scale and in inches. They concluded that the apparent contrast was much reduced when subjects judged in inches. If so, that would demonstrate the artifact in the rating data, for the response language can hardly affect phenomenal length.

It does not follow, however, that the apparent contrast remaining with the inch response is genuine. That was the explanation preferred by Krantz and Campbell, but the presence of an artifact in the rating data naturally raises concern that it was also present in the inch response. Although the inch has an absolute physical definition, most subjects have only a rough idea of how long an inch is. Psychologically, the inch response has a relative component, much like the rating scale, and a reduced effect is what is expected under the artifact interpretation. Despite Campbell's focus on the main issue, his evidence does not seem satisfactory.

Indeed, the very magnitude of the apparent contrast effect obtained with the inch response argues for the artifact interpretation. For those subjects who judged lines ranging from 6 to 20 inches, the mean response to the 20-inch line was 17.2; for those subjects who judged lines ranging from 20 to 36 inches, the mean response to the 20-inch line was 12.7. The difference is 4.5. So large a true contrast effect is not believable in the light of what is known about visual perception.[a]

Definitions. The term *contrast* and its sister term *assimilation* originate in the study of perception, where they refer to changes in perceptual value of a focal stimulus, away from or toward the value of contextual stimuli. Such perceptual changes can be demonstrated by sensory comparison. If the index fingers of the left and right hands are adapted in cold and hot water, respectively, they will feel warm and cool, respectively, when placed in lukewarm water.

Central to the meaning of contrast and assimilation is that they refer to real perceptual changes. That was the basic assumption in the cited assimilation–contrast theories, which hoped to set social perception on a solid base of results from classical perception. Unfortunately, there are various effects that masquerade as perceptual contrast or assimilation. The presence of these effects, such as the contrast artifact illustrated in the previous subsection, complicates the theoretical analysis.

Further complications arise from the tendency to use contrast and assimilation in two senses, (*a*) as names for the empirical effects produced by context stimuli and (*b*) as explanations of those effects. With the hope of assimilation–contrast theory that perceptual judgment would provide a theoretical framework for social judgment went a tendency to treat assimilation and contrast as explanations of the very data to which they referred. Even writers who explicitly attempt to use a nominal definition often seem to be trading on surplus meaning in the terms.

By now the terms *contrast* and *assimilation* seem severely compromised for use in judgment theory. Especially to investigators who are not expert in the background literature, how any particular article uses these concepts can be very perplexing. In the present formulation, therefore, the terms *negative context effect* and *positive context effect* will be used as nominal, empirical terms in place of contrast and assimilation. As nominal terms they are intended to refer to observed effects of contextual stimuli without any hidden implications about the causes of those effects. The terms *contrast* and *assimilation* are reserved for their original usage to refer to genuine changes in perceptual value.[b]

Assimilation as Integration. A word should be added on the term *assimilation,* which has a second meaning as integration. This is a legitimate meaning that is sometimes confused with the concept of perceptual assimilation. In a typical example, contextual information is given that bears directly on the response to the focal information. For example, a person may be described by contextual information about group membership or social role and by focal information in the form of personality traits. Stereotypic implications of the contextual information will then be integrated into the overall person impression in the same way as the focal information. Hence the overall person impression will move toward the value of the contextual information. Unless this integration process is recognized, it will seem as though the focal stimuli themselves move toward the value of the contextual information. Nonexistent perceptual distortion may be proffered to explain straightforward integrational assimilation.

Cognitive consistency may thus be derived as a general implication of information integration theory. Essentially the same issue arises in the study of decision commitment effects. These effects may be seen as manipulations that affect the weight of the initial state variable in the averaging model (Section 2.3) rather than as specific processes for maintaining cognitive consistency. This issue is also central in the meaning constancy hypothesis and the halo theory discussed in Chapter F3. Experimental analysis has shown that much of what has been attributed to special consistency processes appears to be more fully understandable in simple informational terms (Section 7.13).

Test with Sequential Dependencies. The following experiment on clinical judgment included a sensitive test for contrast. Subjects rated degree of disturbance of patients described by instances of their behavior in a hospital ward (Anderson, 1962c, 1972b). The contrast hypothesis implies that the rating of each description should be displaced away from the value of the preceding description. The sequence of 45 descriptions was balanced to allow analysis of such sequential effects. This test of sequential dependence is especially sensitive to potential contrast (Anderson, 1959a).

The data, however, were contrary to the contrast prediction: Mean response was greater when the preceding stimulus was severe than when it was mild. Although small, this effect was statistically reliable and a similar effect was obtained in a subsequent experiment with lifted weights, as will be noted later. The interpretation of this positive context effect is uncertain. It might represent genuine assimilation, that is, a true change in perceptual value of the focal stimulus; it might represent a response artifact, such as response perseveration; or it might represent an integration of the preceding stimulus into the judgment of the focal stimulus. In any case, the result disagreed with the contrast hypothesis.

Adding-with-Contrast Hypothesis. A different line of evidence on contrast arose in comparisons between the adding and averaging models. It had been found that addition of mildly favorable information to highly favorable information produced a less favorable response than did highly favorable information alone (Section 5.4), a result that favored the averaging view. However, an adding-with-contrast model could also account for the result: If the mildly favorable information changed value to become somewhat negative—owing to contrast with the highly favorable information—then adding it would decrease the response.

A direct test of this adding-with-contrast hypothesis was obtained by presenting the subject with three personality trait adjectives unrelated except for their contiguity on the slip of paper. After the subject read all three adjectives, the experimenter pointed to one and asked the subject to rate its favorableness as a personality trait. The contrast hypothesis implies that this rating should be displaced away from the value of the other two adjectives. In fact, there was no effect whatever (Anderson & Lampel, 1965), a result that has been corroborated by other investigators (Section F4.1).

Positive Context Effect. Although tangential to the present discussion, the experiment just cited included another condition, in which the three adjectives were related by being said to describe a person. The subject's task was to rate likableness of the person and then rate likableness of a specified adjective on "how much you like that particular trait of that particular person." Unexpectedly, these data showed a large positive context effect: The rating of the single trait was displaced toward the value of the other two traits.

The interpretation of this positive context effect is important for understanding the cognitive processes involved in information integration. At face value, the effect supports the *meaning-change hypothesis* that the specified trait changes meaning and value on being integrated into the overall person impression. That would represent a proper assimilation effect, although cognitive rather than perceptual in nature. The alternative *meaning-constancy hypothesis* interprets the effect as a halo process: The specified trait undergoes no change on being integrated, but the overall impression subsequently affects the overt rating of the specified trait. The extensive study of this question has found little support for the meaning-change hypothesis. Instead, the positive context effect is largely, perhaps completely, a generalized halo effect (Sections F3.2 and F4.1), which supports the meaning-constancy hypothesis.

Test of a Conditioning Hypothesis. Stimuli combined for integration could change one another's values by some kind of conditioning process. To test this conditioning hypothesis, subjects were asked to judge likableness of a person described by an HM (high, medium) or an LM (low, medium) pair of adjectives and, on a later trial, to judge likableness of a person described by the M adjective alone. Since evaluative responses are elicited by both adjectives in the initial paired presentation, the doctrine of association by contiguity implies that each will take on part of the value of the other. The later response to the M adjective alone should thus be more positive if it was initially paired with the H, rather than the L, adjective.

Such an effect was obtained (Anderson & Clavadetscher, 1976; see Section F3.5.4). It did not seem to be true conditioning, however, because it did not increase with additional conditioning trials. Moreover, initial familiarization with the single M adjectives appeared to eliminate the effect. It was suggested, therefore, that the initial presentation induced a constructive process of valuation that could be influenced by context stimuli. Although the effect is neither large nor, perhaps, very important, it has interest as a case in which reasonable evidence for context-induced changes in meaning has been found.

Integration Processes. Not all contextual effects are artifacts of the response measure. Some result from integration of the context stimuli, as in the halo interpretation of the positive context effect. Analogous applications of an integration view have been noted in studies of context effects in lifted weights (Anderson, 1971b), anchor effects in adaptation-level theory (Anderson, 1974a, Figure 10), comparative judgment in geometrical illusions (Clavadetscher, 1977; Clavadetscher & Anderson, 1977; Massaro & Anderson, 1971), as well as in various displacement effects in attitudinal judgment (Anderson, 1971a, pp. 187–190, 1974b, pp. 55–60, 68–81, 1975a; Eiser, 1980, pp. 59–92; Judd & Harackiewicz, 1980; Lopes, 1972). The view that contextual stimuli operate as informational cues in the same way as the ostensible focal stimuli deserves more systematic study.

Recency and Primacy in Social Judgment. In serial integration, the same information can have different effects depending on the order in which it is presented. This effect can be substantial. With only six personality trait adjectives, the HHHLLL and LLLHHH orders of presentation can yield person impressions that differ by almost a full point on an 8-point scale (Anderson & Barrios, 1961).

Such order effects are clearly important in any attempt to study integration processes. Obvious and favorite interpretations have employed contrast and assimilation between the earlier and later adjectives to explain recency and primacy, respectively. Other forms of stimulus interaction, such as distortion, change of meaning, and inconsistency resolution have also been popular (see Anderson, 1974b, pp. 68–81; Sections F2.5 and F3.3).

Because of their importance to integration processes, these order effects received intensive study in the initial stage of work on integration theory. In the tasks that have been studied so far, the outcome seems clear. Primacy and recency result from attentional processes that affect the weights of the information at each serial position. Evidence that the effects are caused by any form of stimulus interaction is notable by its absence.

Recency in Psychophysical Integration. If subjects judge average magnitude of a sequence of psychophysical stimuli, the later stimuli have greater effect. This recency effect is substantial for lifted weights (Anderson, 1967a; Anderson & Jacobson, 1968), loudness (Parducci, Thaler, & Anderson, 1968), and length (Weiss & Anderson, 1969). However, its interpretation was problematical.

One obvious interpretation was in terms of perceptual contrast. In a High–Low sequence, the Low would seem even lower by contrast with the High; in the reverse Low–High sequence, the High would seem even higher by contrast with the Low. These changes in stimulus value would appear as a recency effect in the overall response.

An alternative interpretation is in terms of the weight parameter of the serial integration model (Section 3.6). Recency would reflect greater salience of the later stimuli without any change in their perceptual value.

This problem was studied by presenting sequences of two or three lifted weights and asking subjects to rate the heaviness of one of them (Anderson, 1971b). The heaviness of the weights preceding the judged weight were experimentally manipulated so that any contrast would appear directly in the data. The serial averaging model predicts either no effect from the unjudged weights or possibly a small positive context effect similar to that already noted for the behavior sentences. In fact, the data showed small positive context effects. Similar results have been obtained with psychophysical stimuli by other investigators (see Ward, 1972).

This failure of the contrast hypothesis even with perceptual stimuli is a sobering outcome for judgment theory. Sensory contrast is obtainable in similar tasks (see references in Anderson, 1971b, p. 61), but not much is known about which conditions do and do not produce sensory contrast. So far, however, there seems to be no evidence for contrast in typical integration tasks.

Direct Test for Contrast. One final experimental test for contrast effects deserves mention (Anderson & Leon, 1970). Subjects judged two classes of stimuli, seriousness of crimes and likableness of vegetables. Four single stimuli of one class were presented for judgment at a time, and the subject judged all four at once by placing four flag pins on a 200-mm graphic rating scale. Contrast effects were assessed using a 2 × 5, Context × Test factorial. The two levels of Context each consisted of three stimuli, either from the upper half or from the lower half of the value range. The five levels of Test were single stimuli that covered most of the value range. The context stimuli, it may be noted, are analogous to the anchor stimuli that have been claimed to yield contrast effects in traditional studies of judgment.

The critical question is whether the test stimulus is judged differently in the two contexts. The contrast hypothesis implies that the value of the test stimulus will be displaced away from the value of the context. Hence the test stimulus should be judged lower in the high than in the low context.

Table 1.1 shows the judgments of the vegetable stimuli. There is no sign of any contrast effect: The rating of the test stimulus is virtually identical in the two context conditions. Similar results were obtained with judgments of criminal offenses. A second test for contrast was included in the design by using one stimulus in common to the two

TABLE 1.1
Test for Context Effects

Context	Test stimuli				
	Squash	Tomatoes	Cabbage	Broccoli	Potatoes
High	76	84	98	114	158
Low	75	82	100	112	156

SOURCE: Anderson and Leon (unpublished experiment, 1970).
NOTE: Entries are mean judgments of test stimulus as a function of two levels of context. The high context consisted of corn, carrots, and peas (mean value 143); the low context consisted of beets, turnips, and peas (mean value 89). Data averaged over two replications for each of 22 subjects.

context conditions. Here again, the contrast hypothesis implies that the judgment of this common stimulus will be different in the two context conditions. Here again, no contrast was found.

The present design is especially sensitive to true contrast effects, yet none appeared. Furthermore, since the low and high context conditions correspond to positively and negatively skewed distributions, the data also show that distribution effects can be eliminated. The latter result provides direct support for the argument of Section 1.1.6 that distribution effects need not be a problem. The former result supports the view that the apparent contrast effects reported in judgmental studies are artifacts of response-scale usage. The main conclusion is simple: Contrast is not freely available as an explanatory concept; attempts to use contrast interpretations should first show that the observed effects are not response artifacts.

Comments. It may deserve re-emphasis that genuine contrast effects are common in psychophysical judgment. They appear in illusions (e.g., Anderson, 1970a; Clavadetscher, 1977; Clavadetscher & Anderson, 1977; Massaro & Anderson, 1970, 1971), as well as in various adaptation situations. It seems plausible, therefore, that genuine contrast can also arise with verbal and symbolic stimuli, an outcome that would seem more likely if more extended periods of adaptation were employed.

It is clear, however, that contrast interpretations face severe difficulties. Much of what has been interpreted as contrast is at best confounded with artifacts and noncontrast processes. The present need is for theory and method that are capable of separating these various effects.[c]

1.1.6 DISTRIBUTION EFFECT

The distribution effect is a well-known phenomenon found with ratings. Consider two distributions of stimuli that extend over the same range but have different shapes. One is positively skewed, with a predominance of low stimuli and a long upper tail, and the other is negatively skewed, with a predominance of high stimuli and a long lower tail. If different subjects rate the stimuli from each distribution, the same medium stimulus will under certain conditions be rated higher in the positively skewed distribution.

One interpretation considers this distribution effect to be genuine contrast: The value of the medium stimulus is displaced away from the predominant stimuli to become higher in the positively skewed distribution, lower in the negatively skewed distribution. Another interpretation considers the distribution effect to be a response artifact, analogous to that considered in the previous section and resulting from a similar process. Subjects are assumed to have a tendency to use the available responses with equal frequency, and that would produce the given effect.

The distribution effect is a serious issue for integration studies. Under the contrast interpretation, the value of any to-be-integrated stimulus would depend on which others it was combined with on a given trial and also on the stimuli presented during previous trials. Furthermore, the value of the integrated response would presumably be altered by contrast with the response values on previous trials. All these effects would have to be included in the integration rule—if they are genuine contrast.

On the other hand, if the distribution effect is a response artifact, then it constitutes an undesirable bias. Since the end stimuli in each distribution are rated the same, the two sets of ratings are nonlinearly related. There is a nonlinear response bias, in other words, that should be eliminated. The evidence of Section 1.1.5 supports the response bias interpretation but leaves the problem of how it is to be eliminated.

Fortunately, the rating procedures discussed earlier appear to be reasonably successful at eliminating distribution effects. The end anchors, together with preliminary practice, help establish a stable frame of reference and stimulus–response correspondence before the experiment begins. The use of a moderately large number of steps in the rating scale is intended, among other things, to minimize tendencies to use the response categories equally often. The value of this aspect of procedure has been verified in recent work by Parducci (1982), who found a steady decrease in distribution effects as the number of rating categories increased.

Two lines of evidence from this research program support the claim that the present rating methods can largely eliminate distribution effects. One line of evidence comes from direct assessment and was discussed in Section 1.1.5. The other, no less important, rests on the success of the parallelism and linear fan theorems: That supports the linearity of the response measure and thereby argues against the presence of distribution effects.

This last point deserves emphasis. Under an adding rule, distribution effects, if present, would cause certain systematic deviations from parallelism. Factorial design tends to produce a unimodal distribution of stimulus combinations, with many of intermediate value and progressively fewer toward either extreme. This is no problem, of course, if the response scale is linear. However, tendencies to use the response categories equally often will produce nonlinear distortion of the response and hence of the factorial plot. The response will be displaced outward from the center by an amount that is greatest for the stimulus combinations of intermediate value and decreases progressively toward either extreme. A single straight line in the factorial plot that crosses over the center will thus be distorted toward an ogival form. Parallel curves at different elevations will undergo different distortion and appear nonparallel.

But this pattern of deviation from parallelism is rarely observed. Deviations from parallelism are not infrequent, but they typically have a different shape, often a consequence of differential weighting. An analogous argument can be made for multiplying rules. In this case, factorial design produces a distribution that is skewed, so distribution effects would cause systematic deviations from the linear fan pattern. Thus, the evidence for cognitive algebra is at the same time evidence for the efficacy of the methods employed to eliminate the distribution effects.

1.1.7 THE METHOD OF MAGNITUDE ESTIMATION

The rating method and Stevens's (1957, 1975) method of magnitude estimation seem rather similar. Both ask for direct numerical estimates of subjective values. Subjects find both methods simple and natural. Introspection gives little indication that one method is preferable or that the two typically give different results. How different these results can be was shown in Figure 1.1.

A second illustration of the difference between rating and magnitude estimation is shown in the experiment summarized in Figure 1.3, in which subjects estimated average grayness of two Munsell chips. Since the instructions prescribe an averaging operation, the factorial plot should exhibit parallelism—if the response measure is a linear scale. The

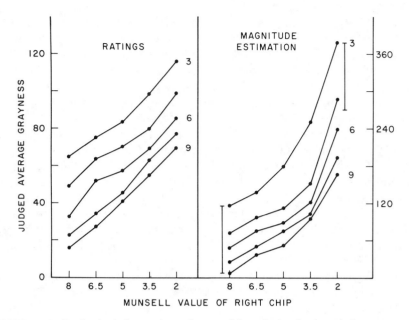

FIGURE 1.3. *Psychophysical averaging task as a validity criterion for numerical response measures. Subjects judged average grayness of two gray chips, with Munsell value of right and left chips listed on horizontal axis and as curve parameter, respectively. Parallelism criterion supports rating method, infirms method of magnitude estimation. (The two equal-length vertical bars in the right panel also illustrate an optical illusion, whereby nonparallel curves look more parallel than they really are; see Note 1.1.7a.) (After Weiss, 1972.)*

rating data (left panel) show rough parallelism, whereas the magnitude estimation data (right panel) show extreme nonparallelism.[a] These data re-emphasize the sharply different results that plausible numerical response methods can yield. They also point up the role of the parallelism property as a validational criterion. Collateral validation is obtainable from stimulus invariance (Note 3.1b).

Such differences in result presumably stem from differences in the comparison structures of the two methods. Ratings locate a given stimulus relative to two standards that ordinarily correspond to the two ends of the rating scale. Magnitude estimation asks for a judgment of the ratio of the given stimulus relative to a single standard (see, e.g., Marks, 1974, p. 40). Ratings thus require two comparisons, whereas magnitude estimation requires only one. In addition, rating responses are ordinarily closed and bounded above and below. In contrast, magnitude estimations can be arbitrarily large integers or arbitrarily small fractions.

Although Stevens did not view the matter in these terms, magnitude estimation might be considered a way of removing the bounds on the rating scale. This is attractive because it potentially eliminates some end effects that can bias the rating method. Unfortunately, another bias seems to have intruded, namely, the diminishing returns bias noted in Section F5.4.[b]

Nevertheless, Stevens's concern with obtaining a numerical, linear response measure was well taken (Anderson, 1975a, p. 476). Linear scales facilitate progress by an order of magnitude compared to rank-order methods. Indeed, linear scales are almost a necessity for studying stimulus interaction and for analysis of nonlinear integration rules. Ratings and magnitude estimation both suffer from various biases, and each may have special areas of usefulness. In some situations, magnitude estimation seems more natural and less demanding of the subject and may provide linear scales. It may also be used as a monotone scale (Section 1.1.9) or together with monotone transformation (Chapter 5). Functional measurement may be applied, in the same way as with ratings, to ascertain linearity and to point to needed improvements in magnitude estimation procedure (see also Sections F5.4 and F5.6.2).[c]

1.1.8 INVALID COMPARISONS OF RATINGS

Rating scales have an arbitrary, relative element that must be allowed for in any attempt to compare two ratings. Subjects tend to fit the given range of stimuli to the available response range. Although this calibrational ability is remarkable and useful, the unit of the response scale is consequently not a fixed quantity but depends, among other factors, on the given range of stimuli. Ratings of two different sets of stimuli may have different units, therefore, so that direct comparison of the response numbers has no more meaning than direct comparison of numbers read from Celsius and Fahrenheit scales (see also Sections 6.1.4 and 7.4).

An illustration of the problem comes from a question that arose concerning the interpretation of the set-size effect (Section F2.4). Suppose that two groups of subjects judge person descriptions using an ordinary Like–Dislike scale without end anchors. For one group, each description contains two trait adjectives of equal value; for the other group, each description contains just one of these two adjectives. Both groups will tend to spread their responses over the whole scale, thereby utilizing the same range of response. Corresponding one- and two-adjective descriptions will, therefore, tend to yield equal ratings. It might seem, therefore, that number of adjectives had no effect, but this is not true. The two groups have adopted a different unit in their scale calibration, and so the rating numbers are not comparable between groups.

This problem cannot be resolved merely by changing to a within-group comparison. If the same subject judges the one- and two-adjective description in separate sessions, the very same problem may arise. The use of the same end anchors in both sessions would reduce, and possibly eliminate, the problem, but this is not guaranteed. It may be generally necessary, therefore, to obtain the ratings under identical conditions. In the preceding example, the one- and two-adjective descriptions would be presented together in intermixed order to a single group of subjects.[a]

1.1.9 VALID USES OF MONOTONE DATA

Many experiments do not require linear scales. Such experiments constitute the bulk of psychological research, in which the goal is to test whether certain stimulus treatments will produce different effects. Under the null hypothesis of no treatment effects, the true response distributions will be identical for the several treatments, regardless of whether a monotone or a linear response measure is used. The response measure cannot produce real differences from nothing. If the true response distributions are identical on one scale, they will remain identical on any transformation of that scale.

The shapes of the distributions are, of course, relevant to the choice of statistical test. Analysis of variance does best, both in power and in effective significance level, with normal distributions. Some distribution-free test might be preferable if the distributions are markedly nonnormal, but this is a purely statistical question about the observed data, and as such can be answered empirically. This question has no necessary connection with that of response linearity, which concerns the functional relation between the observable response measure and an unobservable, theoretical quantity. Indeed, a monotone scale might provide normal distributions and hence the most powerful test. Ironically, in view of the common concern over linear (interval) scales and statistics, monotone scales can be superior to linear scales for parametric statistical procedures.

This point may need emphasis in view of the controversy about using analysis of variance and other parametric tests on monotone data. The source of this controversy was the assertion by Siegel (1956) and others that an essential condition for such tests was that "The variables involved must have been measured in *at least* an interval [linear] scale [p. 19]." For monotone data, only rank tests would be allowed because only ranks, not differences or means, are invariant under monotone transformation. The previous reasoning shows that this assertion is erroneous, as was recognized by statisticians (e.g., Lord, 1953).

There is, of course, a problem in testing interactions because these, in contrast to main effects, can readily disappear or even reverse under monotone transformation. The need to separate these two questions was discussed by Anderson (1961b), who also pointed out that the use of rank tests did not resolve this problem.

The present work is largely concerned with quantitative analysis of functions and models. Many such analyses require linear scales. This is why measurement theory is basic to cognitive algebra. The purpose of this subsection is to make clear that linear scales are not necessary for a large class of psychological experiments.[a]

1.2 Notes on Experimental Procedure

This section outlines various aspects of experimental procedure that have been more or less standard in this research program. These procedures are important for obtaining clean data. They should not be treated as a fixed standard, however, but as a starting point. Each experiment has special requirements that may suggest or require departures from usual procedures, especially as new tasks and new subject populations are explored. These notes describe procedures that have served well in past work but are only guides to experimental methodology.

1.2.1 ILLUSTRATIVE EXPERIMENTS

Various experiments are presented in figures and tables throughout this book to illustrate particular problems of method and analysis. These experiments also illustrate the substantive background to which this discussion explicitly or implicitly refers.

Psychophysical averaging has already been considered in Figure 1.3 of Section 1.1.7, and the analogous task of psychophysical bisection appears in Figure 4.6 of Section 4.1.2. These two tasks also figure in cross-task generality of functional scales of grayness (Figure 3.1 of Section 3.1). Also considered in Section 4.1.2 are experiments on social attribution (Figure 4.2), attitudes toward United States presidents (Figure 4.3), decision theory (Figure 4.4), and area judgments by children (Figure 4.5). Still other tasks are the weight–size illusion (Figure 4.7 of Section 4.2.1), judgments of meals (Figure 6.1 of Section 6.1.2), attitudes in group discussion (Figure 6.2 of Section 6.2.1), and dating judgments based on photographs (Figure 6.3 of Section 6.2.1).

Despite their diverse substantive concerns, most of these tasks share three common characteristics. First, each subject judges a family of stimulus combinations in a within-subject design. Second, the family of stimulus combinations is constructed from factorial design, in which the stimulus variables are under experimental control. Third, the response is numerical, usually a rating.

All three characteristics are important for obtaining statistical precision and power for quantitative analysis. This class of tasks, therefore, has played a central role in the basic experimental work on information integration theory. At the same time, of course, these three characteristics limit the generality of the results, and more general methods deserve consideration. Nonfactorial design has many uses, especially for natural embedding and for uncontrolled variables, and various aspects of nonfactorial design are discussed in Sections 1.3.8, 1.3.9, 4.2.4, 4.3, 6.2, and several sections of Chapter 7. The use of choice data (Section 3.10) and rank-order data (Chapter 5) are also appropriate for many tasks.

Finally, one task deserves separate mention. This is person perception using trait adjectives as stimulus information, which was the main task studied in the foundation work on integration theory. This task has many advantages for cognitive analysis, and it has been important both to theory and to method. The following experiment, which was the first to test the integration model in this task, also illustrates several points of method.

Each subject received sets of three adjectives that described a hypothetical person and rated likableness of that person on a 1–20 scale. A three-factor design was used, with low, medium, and high adjectives as the three levels of each factor. Data from the first two subjects, who received the same person descriptions, are shown in Figure 1.4. Each panel represents one two-factor graph, collapsed over the third factor in the design.

The main feature of Figure 1.4 is the parallelism, which supports an adding-type model. Each subject was run through the complete design once on each of 5 consecutive days, thereby allowing individual analyses of variance for each subject. These analyses showed that the observable deviations from parallelism in the graphs could reasonably be attributed to prevailing response variability. Also of interest is the difference in relative elevation of the middle curve in the two left-most graphs, which shows that the subjective values of the two subjects are nonlinearly related (Section F1.2.1).

Several features of this experiment became more or less standard in subsequent work and are discussed elsewhere in this book. These include stimulus end anchors, given as part of each day's warmup; the 1–20 rating scale; the use of stimulus replication; and the procedures used to control attention. Additional comments, especially on statistical details, are given in Section F2.2.1 and Note F2.2.1a. Experimental ad-

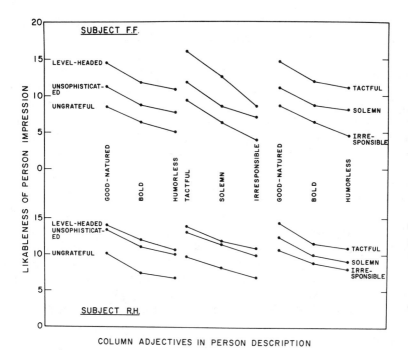

FIGURE 1.4. *Parallelism pattern supports adding-type rule in person perception. Subjects judged likableness of hypothetical persons described by three personality trait adjectives in 3^3 design. Upper and lower layers present the three two-factor graphs for subjects F.F. and R.H., with adjective stimuli listed at margins. (After Anderson, 1962a.)*

vantages of person perception as an experimental task are discussed in Section F1.8.4.

1.2.2 PRELIMINARY PRACTICE

Preliminary practice has several functions. Most important, it allows subjects to develop a frame of reference for the task. The range of stimuli and the response scale are both more or less arbitrary, and some experience is needed to coordinate them (Section 1.1). Practice stimuli are usually chosen to facilitate the development of a frame of reference for stimuli and response. One common start is with the end anchors plus a few intermediate stimuli that span the range. These are typically worked into the instructions, where they can also provide a check on the subject's understanding.

A second important function of preliminary practice is to stabilize stimulus values. Values are not constant properties of the stimulus, as in physics, but are constructed by the organism under task constraints (Section 7.15). Value of a given stimulus will therefore depend on the state of the organism and on diverse aspects of context. A simple example appears in the phrase, "Above Average," which is often used as a verbal quantifier for stimulus dimensions. The value of this phrase is somewhat indefinite, and contextual factors will affect what value becomes operative. For example, subjects might tend to assign a value that is equally spaced relative to the other quantifier phrases, which would increase information transmission. Similar considerations, in lesser degree, may apply to familiar stimuli such as foods or personality trait adjectives.

For studies of integration rules, value changes during practice are generally no problem. The independence assumption requires only that values remain stable once the regular experiment has begun. When the dependence of value on context is itself of interest, it can be studied by varying context systematically within the practice and comparing functional measurement scales obtained after the values have stabilized.

Preliminary practice also helps settle the subject into a stable judgmental set. This has the specific advantage of reducing response variability. It also has the general advantage of yielding more meaningful data since the quality of the data depends on how the subject is engaged to the task. How much practice is required will depend on the demands of the task. The first two experiments on the averaging model used five daily sessions, the first two of which were treated as practice (Anderson, 1962a,c, 1972b). Today that seems excessively cautious. Later work has indicated that a few minutes practice is usually adequate for judgments of likableness and for much perceptual judgment. Other judgments can be more difficult, of course, and may even require special practice sets designed to make the stimulus cues salient (e.g., Anderson & Butzin, 1974).

1.2.3 INSTRUCTIONS

To develop a set of instructions is not usually difficult, at least for most tasks with a normal adult subject population. However, there are a few simple rules that appear to be important. These rules will be set out as part of the following typical instruction format from the present research program. These rules are fairly general, although of course, the format of the instructions depends on the nature of the task. Some examples of instructions are given in Appendix A.

The introductory phase of the instructions has three steps. First, the general idea of the judgment task is given simply and briefly; this orients the subject to the task and provides the idea around which the later detail can be organized. Next, the task is elaborated with a few illustrative stimuli. Then the response scale is introduced.

A general rule is that no detail should be mentioned until it is necessary. Otherwise, it will confuse or distract the subject. This is why the response scale is not ordinarily introduced until the third step, after the idea of the task has become clear. A related general rule, one that beginning researchers usually find hard to follow, is that no detail should be included unless it is really necessary. Important points should generally be stated two or more times, the last time in the final summary.

In the next phase of the instructions, several illustrative stimuli are presented for judgment. These include end anchors plus any stimuli designed to check on the subjects' understanding of the task. Following this, subjects are told that a group of practice stimuli will be presented, during which they should feel free to change their usage of the response scale. These practice stimuli are often preceded and followed by a brief summary of the main points of the instructions. Finally, the regular group of experimental stimuli is presented. In some cases, the first presentation of this group is used as the practice group or even as additional practice.

In some experiments, the same stimulus combination is judged more than once or the same stimulus appears in many different combinations. It seems desirable to tell subjects that this will happen in order to forestall suspicion that tests of memory or accuracy are involved. This instruction is often accompanied by others: that some response variability is perfectly natural; that there is no right or wrong answer; and that subjects should simply give their feeling at the moment. This also provides a natural opportunity to repeat the nature or quality of the dimension of judgment.

Instructions should be written and, of course, labeled and dated. Ad-libbed sections are often appropriate, but their location and nature should ordinarily be indicated in the typescript. The experimenter should be able to read the instructions in a natural way, looking more at the subject than at the typescript.

A vital part of instructions is the inclusion of checks on subjects' understanding. These include stimuli of varied value to check that subjects are using the response scale in a sensible way. Several investigators have independently learned how easily a few subjects can reverse the polarity of a rating scale, even when the labels are plainly visible (e.g., Anderson, 1971c). Test stimuli may also be included to check that subjects are paying attention to the appropriate stimulus dimensions. In addition, it is sometimes desirable, and perhaps should become more common, to require subjects to explain the task in their own words (e.g., Shanteau, 1970a, p. 184, 1974, p. 681), especially when there may be some question about their understanding (Section 7.12).

With child or patient populations, a more interactive mode of instruction is often needed. The experimenter monitors the subject's understanding at each stage of instruction and recycles through that stage, with suitable variation, until understanding is attained. Such interactive instructions can also help by building rapport. Except perhaps for pilot work, however, instructions should virtually always follow a prescribed written outline. When any degree of experimenter–subject interaction is involved, it may be desirable to record some examples on tape. These procedures help ensure that no research assistant will omit some important aspect. And, of course, they provide a sometimes necessary basis for replication, both within and between laboratories.

Most experiments on judgment aim to elicit a quality or dimension of judgment that is already natural to the subjects. With simple perceptual or social judgments, such as loudness or likableness, there is no reason to think that the meaning of the response is sensitive to the instructions. Nevertheless, some meticulousness in instructions is always in order. One reason is to minimize the ever-present possibility of misunderstanding. A second reason is to detect the infrequent, but inevitable, subject who seems unable to perform even very simple tasks. A third reason is to provide a basis for the reader's confidence in the meaningfulness of the published results. A fourth reason is to be able to provide other investigators with adequate detail for replication (e.g., Gollob & Lugg, 1973). And a final reason is that face validity of the response can be incorrect, as instanced in Section 7.12.

1.2.4 PILOT WORK

Pilot work is vital. One main function of pilot work is to develop instructions and procedure. Debugging is almost always necessary, even in a simple variation of an already developed task. It should be standard practice, therefore, to run a few subjects individually and question them about their behavior in performing the task. One useful technique is to run subjects through a reduced set of stimulus trials and then go back to selected stimuli and ask them how they reacted to each one. This may begin in an open-ended manner but should be followed up with more specific, probing questions. Such interrogation seldom tells much about underlying processes (for an exception, see Leon and Anderson, 1974), but it can be valuable in picking up unclarities and deficiencies in instructions and procedure.

Pilot work is also useful for training the experimenter. Even an experienced experimenter needs practice to adjust to a new task, to be able, for example, to read the instructions in a natural way. When an assistant is serving as experimenter, the principal investigator is always well advised to act as a subject before finalizing details. Experimental procedure constitutes a lore, and the experienced investigator will be sensitive to many diverse errors that beginners are prone to. Many of these errors, including some that are obvious to the experienced, will only be detected through personal experience in the experimental situation. In addition, it is highly advisable to have a final, formal session for a complete check on all experimental details. In developing a new task, in particular, pilot work may meander through many phases, and it is surprisingly easy to lose track of important aspects of procedure and design.

Pilot work can be important for selecting or constructing specific levels of the stimulus factors. In moral judgment, for example, stimulus materials may need to be pure forms of certain concepts, such as responsibility or duty, to allow theoretical interpretation. Reaction of pilot subjects can be informative in this respect. Similarly, the stimulus levels should usually cover the range at more or less equal spacing. Both pilot data and direct interrogation can help to accomplish this purpose.

Pilot work is valuable not only to procedure, but also to help determine the experimental design. In many studies, the pattern of results becomes fairly clear during the pilot work. The main experiment is run largely to pin things down and put the results into public form. Besides shaping the main design, pilot work can sometimes suggest added conditions that will help test alternative theoretical interpretations of the expected results.

Finally, pilot work can be helpful in planning the data analysis, for pilot data can be run through some facsimile of the planned analyses. This can be an advisable precaution, especially for an investigator who is not familiar with the analyses to be used.

Students frequently carry pilot work too far, expecting more from it than it can give. As a rough rule, there is not usually much value in running more than two or three pilot subjects to test a given procedure. That is usually enough to raise major questions about procedure that may lead to changes, which are tested, in turn, with another few pilot subjects. Adding a few more pilot subjects under the same procedure is usually a waste of work and time. Instead, it may be preferable to run a substantial number of subjects in each condition as a regular experiment, perhaps of reduced scope, with the expectation that it will be the first of a series, serving in part an exploratory function.

1.2.5 ELIMINATION OF SUBJECTS

Although subject loss is seldom a problem in careful experiments on judgment, the matter does deserve consideration, especially because subject loss can point to shortcomings in procedure.

When there is some apparatus malfunction or some procedural slip by the experimenter, the propriety of eliminating the affected subjects is seldom in doubt. However, the case of deviant subjects can present a dilemma. There will always be an occasional child who seems set on doing something other than the assigned task and an occasional adult whose behavior seems outside the normal range (e.g., Carterette & Anderson, 1979, Experiment 2; Graesser & Anderson, 1974, p. 694). Such subjects might also be eliminated, either on the grounds that they represent a failure of the instructions or on the grounds that their behavior is not properly in the domain under consideration. Both reasons are treacherous, of course, and it can sometimes be painfully uncertain whether or not a subject should be eliminated. Either course of action can introduce a bias. There is no routine resolution to this dilemma, but some relevant considerations will be noted here.

To illuminate the problem, consider the use of a preliminary screening test to eliminate subjects. This limits the subject population and, thereby, the generality of the results, but it does not otherwise introduce bias. Lopes's study of poker (Section F1.5.2), for example, quite appropriately used a screening test to select out experienced players. Again, screening is part of the initial instructions for using the rating scale. A subject who does not rate the practice stimuli in some reasonable way, as occasionally happens with children (e.g., Butzin & Anderson, 1973, p. 532), will not ordinarily be retained.[a]

By analogy, it might be argued that the experiment itself could be used as a screening test. There is a basic difference, however, especially in the canonical randomized experiment in which the aim is to test for significant differences among several experimental conditions. The validity of such tests depends entirely on random assignment, and that can be obtained by making the assignment after the screening test has been given. But the behavior in the experiment itself reflects the action of the specific experimental condition. Eliminating a subject on the basis of this behavior can therefore introduce serious bias.

A different kind of experiment aims at studying some pattern of response on a within-subject basis, as in tests of parallelism. Eliminating subjects on the basis of their behavior during the experiment naturally raises the concern that real deviations from parallelism may have been eliminated. On the other hand, retaining subjects with erratic behavior will increase the error term and so decrease the power of the parallelism test. In some cases it may be helpful to analyze the data two ways, with and without the questionable subjects. There is no easy way to deal with this problem, but it may perhaps be avoided by using some screening test or resolved through individual-subject analysis.

Replication provides a useful way to resolve doubt that arises from subject loss. When moderate doubt is reasonably possible, then it seems advisable to replicate the experiment, perhaps literally but with improved procedure (e.g., Anderson, 1971c) or with extensions to include new conditions.

Finally, there is the absolute rule that all subject loss and elimination must, as a matter of scientific ethics, be fully reported. Perhaps a specific statement on this point should become standard in published articles.

In general, loss of subjects casts an adverse light on experimental procedure and hence on the data. It is the experimenter's responsibility and obligation to develop instructions and procedure that will avoid subject loss. The optimal level of subject elimination need not be zero; there is not ordinarily much cause for concern over elimination of 1 or 2 subjects in 100, and the extra cost to avoid this level of deviance may not be worthwhile. It is important to keep in mind, however, that elimination of some subjects raises a question about the meaningfulness of the data from those that are retained. When the behavior of some subjects shows clear misunderstanding, other subjects may also have inadequate understanding even though this may not be clear in their data. In the last analysis, therefore, it is the adequacy and integrity of the overall experimental procedure that are at issue.

1.2.6 INDIVIDUAL VERSUS BATCH EXPERIMENTS

Subjects should ordinarily be run individually, not in batches. Batch procedure, especially in a classroom situation, can be expected to yield low-grade data. Any moderate number of subjects is likely to include some with low motivation and some with high carelessness. Such subjects can generally be monitored appropriately in individual sessions but not when part of a group. Moreover, group situations are susceptible to distractions that interfere with subjects' understanding of the instructions and attention to the stimulus materials. The importance of attentional factors is illustrated in the work on primacy–recency (Section 7.14).

The main problem with batch running is bias. The increase in response variability caused by batch procedure can be compensated, at least in part, by the increase in number of subjects. Bias, however, can be critical in several ways. For example, application of the parallelism theorem depends on the assumption that the response is a linear scale. However, the precautions used to produce response linearity (Section 1.1) are difficult to apply and to monitor in a group setting. For model analysis, in particular, batch running has little merit.

Bias has an even more serious aspect. Batch running can interfere with subjects' understanding of the instructions. Without reasonable assurance that the subjects understood the instructions, the data may not be meaningful. The problem of meaningfulness can be illustrated by the work of Kahneman and Tversky (1972) on judgmental inference from samples to populations. Arguing from an assumed heuristic of sample-population representativeness, Kahneman and Tversky claimed that responses to single samples would depend almost entirely on the sample proportion, independent of sample size and of population proportion. Although their results seemed to support their claim, quite different results were obtained by Leon and Anderson (1974), who suggested

> The simplest explanation of this difference is that Kahneman and Tversky (1972) failed to make their task clear. Their Ss were run in large classroom groups in 1 or 2 min. of a regular class session, and each S judged only one problem. That the task was not clear is suggested by the fact that about 10% of the Ss had to be eliminated. . . . It hardly seems surprising, therefore, that their Ss might have failed to understand the task and simply interpreted their job as one of judging the sample proportion [p. 34].

Confirmation of this interpretation can be seen in Ward's (1975) results, which showed that subjects do take sample size and proportion into account when the task is made clear to them.[a] As a consequence of such results, the original claims for the representativeness heuristic have had to be abandoned. The fact is, of course, that the original claims rested on defective evidence. When 10% of the subjects have to be eliminated for failure to understand, the adequacy of the experimental procedure comes under suspicion.

Running subjects individually has obvious advantages. The direct experimenter–subject contact improves motivation and reduces casual carelessness. Individual monitoring optimizes instructional aspects and gives the best assurance that subjects understand the task. The disadvantage to individual sessions is expense. Running 60 subjects in one classroom batch is certainly cheaper than running 60 individuals in separate sessions. But group running may be false economy because the meaningfulness of the data may be at stake. The time spent collecting data is typically a small part of the total time of planning and designing the study, analyzing the data, and writing the report. Since the meaningfulness of the conclusions rests on the meaningfulness of the data, it is pennywise to scrimp at this basic level.

The advantages of running two or three subjects at a time could be studied by incorporating group size as a methodological factor in substantive studies. This could often be done without sacrificing the main advantages of individualized sessions. Running two subjects at a time will halve the required number of sessions, a savings of 50%. Further increases in group size show quickly diminishing returns; an increase from four subjects to five yields only a 5% savings. Since the disadvantages of group running would be expected to increase rapidly at four to five subjects, it seems generally unattractive to consider larger groups.

1.2.7 TWO SETS OF STIMULUS MATERIALS

Two sets of stimulus materials have been useful in experimental studies of information integration. One consists of single words, the other of complete paragraphs. These materials are listed in Appendixes B and C and are described here briefly.

Personality Traits. The first set of stimuli is a list of 555 words that describe personality traits; they range from *sincere* to *liar*. In one often-used experimental task, the subject receives a set of several words that are said to characterize a person. The subject's task is to form an impression and judge the person on likableness. Typical instructions are given in Appendix A, and one experiment is summarized in Section 1.2.1.

This task of person perception is basic to human cognition, socially important, and experimentally flexible (Section F1.8.4). The stimuli are single words, simple yet meaningful, and can readily be combined to form a wide variety of descriptions that vary in length, content, and interrelatedness. The task calls on well-learned skills from everyday social interaction and involves basic processes of psycholinguistics and judgment. For these reasons, the task has exceptional potential for cognitive analysis. A variety of experimental questions are considered in the *Foundations* volume, but the potential of this personality trait task is still largely undeveloped.

President Paragraphs. The other set of stimuli is a collection of 220 short biographical paragraphs, of graded value, about 17 United States presidents. These "president paragraphs" are used in studies of social attitudes.

One main purpose in developing the president paragraphs was to facilitate within-subject design in attitude research. Virtually all previous attitude studies had employed between-subject design, which is appropriate for some problems but not for others (see also Section 1.3.1).[a] Within-subject design is in many ways more representative of social attitudes. Within-subject design can also greatly increase experimental efficiency, as illustrated in the power calculation of Section 4.2.2.

A second purpose in developing the president paragraphs was to assess generality of results obtained with the personality adjective task described previously. The paragraphs are substantially more complex than the single words, an issue that is illustrated in Section 7.15. So far, however, the attitude research based on these paragraphs, although much less extensive than the work on person perception, has yielded very similar results.

1.2.8 SINGLE AND MULTIPLE STIMULUS PRESENTATION

Single stimulus presentation, in which one stimulus combination is presented at a time, has been standard procedure in integration experiments. Multiple stimulus presentation also deserves consideration. In multiple stimulus presentation, subjects could be instructed to draw their own factorial graphs or list the corresponding data tables. Factorial graph response is illustrated in the study of intuitive physics in Figure F4.22. This response mode allows subjects to see their own response patterns and makes pattern smoothing possible.

An alternative procedure is to begin with single presentations in the usual manner and add a revision phase in which subjects would have access to all the stimulus combinations at once. This would allow subjects to weed out deviant responses that may have resulted from momentary loss of frame of reference.

One main goal with multiple presentation is to reduce response variability. In addition, the graphic response mode might provide a more sensitive picture of a subject's knowledge. Little is known about the relative merits of the two methods, however, and all that can be done here is to list some of the obvious pros and cons.

One disadvantage of multiple presentation is that it may produce a simple response pattern, such as parallelism, from implicit demand or some other artifact. In addition, multiple presentation introduces comparison processes that may cause unwanted interactions. The experiment of Table 1.1 suggests that contrast may not be important, but salience weighting of dimensions on which two stimulus combinations differ has been observed (Anderson & Butzin, 1978; Anderson & Farkas, 1975; Farkas & Anderson, 1979). Indeed, the opportunity for pairwise comparisons may introduce cancellation strategies that effectively bypass the overall integration (Section F2.3.5).

The relative usefulness of the two procedures will no doubt depend on the tasks they are applied to. Multiple presentation seems a reasonable method for the study of intuitive physics, in which regularity of response pattern is presumably part of subjects' background knowledge. It could also help in the personality adjective task by allowing discrepant responses to be attributed to subjects' beliefs rather than response fluctuation. Existing data, however, provide few clues on the relative merits of single and multiple stimulus presentation.

1.3 Notes on Design

1.3.1 WITHIN-SUBJECT AND BETWEEN-SUBJECT DESIGN

There is no general rule for choosing within-subject or between-subject design, but a few relevant considerations deserve discussion. For testing models, between-subject design has limited value because it lacks power (Section 4.2). Also, between-subject design may be strictly invalid when ratings are to be compared (Section 1.1.8). On the other hand, within-subject design may induce unwanted transfer effects. Some striking examples in applied psychology have been reported by Poulton (1973), and more general discussions are given by Greenwald (1976) and Keppel (1973, pp. 393–400).

In judgment–decision theory, within-subject design can help ensure that subjects understand the task because they can be exposed to a variety of stimulus combinations during instruction. In an illustrative example from social attribution, subjects were asked to judge a person's ability, given information about the person's motivation and actual performance (Anderson & Butzin, 1974). In pilot work, the motivation information had little effect, and subjects appeared to judge only on the basis of performance. This was surprising, for the task scenario was simple and the information was both simple and clear. It seemed inappropriate, however, to conclude that people consider motivation information irrelevant or that they are ignorant of its implications. Although the task was clear to the experimenters, it might be far from clear to the subjects, who find themselves in a novel situation in which a goal is imposed on them externally and verbally. Accordingly, it seemed advisable to rework the experimental procedure to ensure that the motivation information was salient.

Motivation information was made more salient by expanding the instructions to include choice pairs that differed on only one stimulus dimension. For example, both stimulus persons might be equal in performance but differ in motivation. This made salient the motivation information, and the subjects now found the task easy to understand. Within-subject design allows this kind of instruction because a variety of stimulus combinations may be given that facilitate task understanding."

A similar example was mentioned in Section 1.2.6, in which between-subject design led to the conclusion that subjects ignore base rate information in decision tasks. That conclusion was found to be incorrect in later work that used within-subject design and more extended instruction. The shortcoming lay in the experimental procedure, not in the cognitive capabilities of the subjects.

A related issue is that the purpose of the investigator influences the choice of design. To ascertain cognitive capabilities of handling base rate information, within-subject design is appropriate and perhaps essential. However, the neglect of base rate information in the between-subject design just cited may be interesting in itself. Although the task was presented almost as an abstract puzzle, the failure to take account of the base rate information seems surprising, for it was specified and logically relevant. From a logical or normative view, subjects ought to be clear about the task. Further work might employ between-subject design, therefore, to isolate the variables that control task understanding. Such work could have cognitive as well as methodological interest.

The interaction between purpose and design arises even when the investigator is interested in outcome generality rather than process generality (Section F1.8.2). If generalizations to practical, real-world situations are desired, between-subject design might seem more appropriate at first glance. Second glance suggests the opposite. The well-practiced tasks and skills of everyday life are analogous to within-person design. Although between-subject design has important uses, within-subject design seems appropriate for many, if not most, studies aimed at outcome generality.

Many other factors also bear on the use of within-subject and between-subject design. The relative importance of these factors will vary across problems and content areas, moreover, and no general discussion can be given here. In judgment–decision theory, however, two major considerations are the investigator's purpose and the subject's understanding of the task.

1.3.2 POSITION AND CARRYOVER EFFECTS

When a subject goes through a sequence of experimental conditions, two types of transfer effects can arise. *Position effects* refer to transfer that depends on serial position in the sequence, independent of particular conditions. Learning, adaptation, and fatigue would all give rise to position effects. *Carryover effects* refer to transfer that depends on particular experimental conditions. The "gambler's fallacy" and other response patterns in probability learning (see, e.g., Anderson, 1964a) represent carryover effects since the response on one trial depends on the events of the preceding trials.

Position and carryover effects sometimes are of primary interest, as in studies of learning and transfer (e.g., Note 3.6c). Similarly, the theoretical interpretation of the primacy effect in person perception revolved around the question of whether it was a position effect or a carryover effect (Section 7.14). In many judgment–decision tasks, on the other hand, primary interest is in steady-state behavior, and position and carryover effects are generally undesirable.

Steady-state behavior and position–carryover effects may both be of interest in some tasks, as may be illustrated in the case of fair share divisions by children (see Anderson & Butzin, 1978). Most experiments on this issue have presented single trials to each child, using between-subject design. As a consequence, the actual division of the reward will depend on politeness and social constraint. Some children may feel they deserve more yet still divide equally because of politeness and similar social constraints. With further experience in the task, politeness may be expected to wear off and the children's true sense of fairness come to control the division.

Here again, the investigator's purpose governs the choice of design. To study a child's true sense of fair division evidently requires repeated trials, and within-subject design would usually be most informative. If politeness factors are the object of study, on the other hand, it could be a mistake to adapt them out in a practice session or to confound the adaptation with other factors in the regular trials.

A second consideration relates to the desired field of generalization. Some real-life situations involve politeness, as in children's company manners. Other real-life situations involve steady-state behavior with minimal politeness, as in interaction among siblings or playmates. Both kinds of situations are interesting, but they entail different design considerations.

The foregoing considerations illustrate that many design issues are intimately related to the purposes of the investigator. The present research program has concentrated on cognitive analysis of steady-state behavior. For this reason, as well as for reasons of reliability and power, within-subject design has been standard. For much of this work, moreover, position and carryover effects are not wanted. Procedures for handling them are discussed in the remainder of this section.

When position and carryover effects are expected to be small, they may be handled in a simple way that has been fairly standard in this research program. With this method, the stimuli are presented in a different order to each subject. A handy way of doing this is to list the stimulus sets on index cards and shuffle the deck for each successive presentation. The responses can often be recorded directly on the reverse sides of the cards. Whatever position and carryover effects may be present are thus randomly balanced over sequences although, of course, these effects are still present in each particular sequence. In group analyses, therefore, these effects are confounded with subjects and hence go into the error term. Similar procedures can be used in single-subject analyses, although with less confidence because the number of different stimulus sequences is typically small. The deck-shuffling method is not strictly random, of course, but it seems adequate for many experiments. It is widely useful, especially when the number of stimulus sets is moderately large and position and carryover effects do not seem serious.

A more formal version of this method would use a limited number of stimulus sequences as a between-subject factor in the design. Just two sequences, in opposite order, will balance out the linear component of the position effect. A significant difference between sequences would warn of carryover effects, although this two-sequence design is not especially sensitive to them.

If position and carryover effects may be substantial, or if it is needful to show that they are not substantial, then the design should provide for statistical assessment of their magnitude. Latin squares, in which rows correspond to different sequences of stimulus conditions, are useful for this purpose. The Stimulus × Sequence interaction can be broken down into a position component and a square residual.[a] The position component fractionates out the position effects so they are not confounded with stimulus effects. The square residual warns of aggregated carryover effects. Extensions that fractionate out one-step carryover effects are also available, as well as greco-latin squares that allow an additional stimulus to be balanced (Cochran & Cox, 1957). Experimental examples of latin and greco-latin squares are given in Anderson (1964d, 1973b).

Latin-square designs become unwieldly with more than 10 or 15 stimulus conditions because they require as many sequences as stimulus conditions. Also, the square residual, an omnibus test, is not very powerful against isolated carryover effects in larger designs. An alternative approach is to employ sequences constructed to test for specific carryover effects by using whatever background knowledge is available.

1.3.3 MEMORY EFFECTS

Memory for previous responses can lead to carryover effects, especially when the same set of stimuli is presented several times or when the same stimuli appear in several different sets. For convenience, the following discussion will be limited to the personality adjective task. Similar procedures can be used more generally, but there is no guarantee that the outcome will be the same.

Memory effects could be especially troublesome in single-subject design in which several replications of the same stimulus sets are desirable. In Anderson (1962a; see Figure 1.4 of Section 1.2.1), for example, the same 27 sets were repeated in each of five sessions, and it was natural to worry that the subject would begin to fixate on a response over successive sessions. Complete fixation would appear as a complete lack of variability from one session to the next. Partial fixation would appear as a reduction in such variability over successive sessions. The analyses showed little or no such reduction in variability, however, and a similar outcome has been obtained in other experiments. Thus, memory for previous responses to a given set need not be a serious problem.

This fortunate outcome may depend in part on the experimental procedures that have been employed (Sections 1.1 and 1.2), as well as on the specific nature of the experimental task. Other integration tasks may need to be treated more cautiously, especially when the unit stimuli are larger, as when using paragraphs or visual stimuli in place of adjectives.

Memory effects can also arise when the same adjectives are given in different sets. In studies of primacy–recency, for example, the same adjectives are presented in both forward and reverse order. In the initial experiments, a given set of adjectives was presented to a subject in only one order; the reverse order would be presented to another subject to avoid possible memory effects from the given order (Section F2.5.3). Because each subject received sets of both forward and reversed orders, primacy–recency was a within-subject comparison. Nevertheless, because each subject received only one order of a given set of adjectives, primacy–recency was a between-word comparison. The adjectives were equated on the basis of the normative ratings, of course, but that does not equate them for individual subjects. Because of this between-word variability, the data were more variable than was desired.

An opportunity to check out an improved balancing procedure arose during a study of a generalized order effect paradigm (Anderson, 1965b); the relevant data are shown in Figure 1.5 as serial curves that show the effect of each serial position on the person impression. For

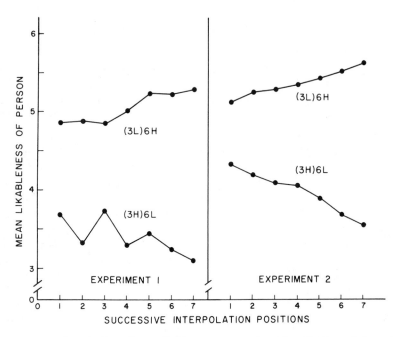

FIGURE 1.5. *Straight-line primacy effect in person perception. Mean likableness judgment as a function of order of presentation. Upper curves represent sequences of three Low and six High adjectives, with the three L's interpolated as a block at each possible point within the sequence of six H's. Upward slope means that the three L's have less effect the later they are interpolated, a primacy effect. Lower curves show similar picture for complementary sequences. Greater regularity of curves in Experiment 2 reflects improved design (see text and Section F2.5.4). (After Anderson, 1965b.)*

present purposes, the important result is that these serial position curves show approximately straight-line primacy in both experiments but are more orderly in Experiment 2 than in Experiment 1. The more orderly curves resulted from the improved stimulus balancing. In Experiment 1, balancing was done as outlined in the preceding paragraph. In Experiment 2, each set of nine adjectives was presented in all seven possible orders to each subject, thus factoring between-word variability out of the error. The gain in precision is evident in Figure 1.5, and the validity of the improved balancing procedure is supported by finding the same pattern of results in both experiments.

A similar problem of memory effects arises in studies of component judgments, in which a given stimulus is judged as a component of several different sets. In the initial work, each subject judged the given adjective in only one set. In later work, each subject judged the given adjective in all the sets. The same pattern of results was obtained in both cases, but the precision of the data was much greater under the stronger balancing procedure (see Section F4.1.5). It is worth adding that the stronger balancing procedure is also simpler.[a]

1.3.4 ATTENTION

The importance of attentional factors in stimulus integration is emphasized by the primacy–recency studies. The same four or six adjectives can give substantially different results, depending on the order in which they are presented. These order effects are very sensitive to experimental specifics and their theoretical significance was difficult to pin down. It now seems clear, however, that they largely reflect differential attention to the words at different serial positions (Section F3.3). That such substantial effects can be obtained with just four or six words shows that attentional factors need careful consideration.

Simultaneous presentation, in which the several stimuli are presented all together, does not avoid the problem of differential attention. The subject ordinarily must process the stimuli in one order or another. This order, even though it is not known, can introduce attentional effects just as in controlled serial presentation.

Equal attention may be facilitated by appropriate procedure. In Anderson (1962a; Section 1.2.1), for example, subjects rated persons described by three trait adjectives. To ensure adequate attention to all three adjectives, the experimenter read the adjectives aloud in reverse order, then handed the index card to the subject, who read the adjectives in the forward order.

An often useful method of controlling attentional factors is to make seriality a formal part of the experimental design. In the foregoing experiment, for example, serial position of the three adjectives on the card corresponded to the three factors in the design. Any remaining position effects were therefore confounded with adjective factors and thereby controlled in the design. Although this design did not include a test for position effects, that was not necessary for any of its purposes. This method of confounding differential attention with serial position has been fairly standard as part of simultaneous presentation procedure.

An alternative way to handle attentional factors is by randomizing temporal or spatial order of presentation within sets (e.g., Anderson & Alexander, 1971). This method seems inadvisable, however, unless the attentional effects are known to be small. Moreover, it would in general be more time-consuming than would the method of confounding.

The essential point of this section can be summarized simply. Attentional factors can have major effects on stimulus integration. When the integration model assumes that the subject gives equal attention to the several stimuli in a given set, it is advisable to adopt experimental procedures that promote equal attention. When attention may be unequal, that should be considered in the experimental design and in the theoretical analysis (see also Section 7.14 and Fiske, 1980).[a]

1.3.5 STIMULUS SELECTION

When there may be a question about possible bias in the selection of stimulus combinations, it is often desirable to use random sampling from some population of stimuli. Stimulus selection bias was of particular concern in the initial tests of the averaging model. Had the sets not been constructed by random choice of adjectives, there would have been some question that the parallelism was not general, but peculiar to the chosen adjective combinations. Of course, random selection has the disadvantage that it may fail to detect model discrepancies that appear in only a small fraction of the stimulus combinations. Subsequent work was accordingly directed at adjective combinations chosen to test for specific kinds of stimulus interaction (e.g., Anderson & Jacobson, 1965; Section F3.4.1).

Some stimulus materials need to be preselected separately for each subject. Food is one such stimulus class because individual differences are so great. A selection of high, medium, and low foods made on the basis of normative data would have limited usefulness. With a preliminary rating of each of a group of stimuli, those stimuli that meet certain specified criteria can be randomly selected to construct stimulus combinations for each subject. Individual selection can be time-consuming, but it can greatly improve efficiency even when it is not strictly necessary. Examples are in Anderson and Norman (1964), Shanteau and Anderson (1969), Butzin and Anderson (1973) and, for a somewhat different need, in Anderson and Alexander (1971).

Simple quantifiers can be convenient for defining factor levels. In Figure F1.16, for example, *honest* defines a factor and its levels are defined by quantifiers such as *somewhat* and *very*. Quantifiers are readily variable in degree, they have maximal commonality over subjects, and they interfere minimally with the qualitative nature of the stimulus dimension. This approach has been widely used, therefore, and in some applications there may be no alternative (e.g., Anderson & Lopes, 1974; Figure F4.17). A useful methodological by-product of an experiment on judged gratitude (Lane & Anderson, 1976) was that bare quantified assertions about intent and outcome yielded the same pattern of response as did paragraph stories. In judgments of marriage satisfaction, similarly, response patterns were the same for actual incidents and abstract quantified dimensions (Section F4.5.2, Note 4.5.2a).[a]

1.3.6 STIMULUS REPLICATION AND GENERALITY

To obtain adequate generality, it is often necessary to use more than one stimulus replication. Studies with verbal or pictorial stimuli, in particular, often involve an arbitrary choice of stimulus materials. Experiments run with just one sample of stimuli would leave more or less uncertainty that the results were peculiar to those stimuli. Replication with even two samples of stimulus materials can go far to assess generality.[a]

In the study of primacy–recency in the personality adjective task, for example, a primacy effect with just one set of adjectives would mean very little. In the initial experiment on this problem, therefore, 48 sets were used, all but 5 of which showed primacy (Anderson & Barrios, 1961). Similarly, in the initial test of the averaging model, six different stimulus replications were used (Anderson, 1962a; Section 1.2.1).

These two experiments also illustrate some of the diverse considerations that can arise in interpreting any obtained differences among stimulus replications. If an integration rule is to be tested, as with the averaging model, then replication differences may merely reflect value differences. A Replication × Row interaction, for example, would merely mean that corresponding row adjectives had different values in different replications. However, the Replication × Row × Column interaction would have theoretical interest since the model implies that it is zero in principle. In this particular experiment, the model tests were actually made separately for each stimulus replication, a practice that has certain advantages.

The primacy–recency experiment presents different questions. The main question was whether the primacy effect would be general across stimulus replications. Since 43 of 48 replications showed primacy, the answer is obviously yes. A rather different question is whether the recency obtained in the other 5 replications was real, and if so why. This question was not pursued, but it could be important. Here, as in many applications, differences among replications may deserve detailed study.

Although differences among stimulus replications deserve careful attention, there is no simple rule for their statistical analysis. Inspection of the separate replications is often most appropriate, whereas other cases require that stimulus replications be included as a factor in the analysis. In some of the specific studies discussed by Clark (1973), stimulus replications could usefully be treated as a random factor, analogous to subjects, in order to allow a statistical generalization to some stimulus population. Unfortunately, Clark's (1973) conclusion that language stimuli should be treated as a random factor "whenever the language stimuli used do not deplete the population from which they were drawn [p. 348]" is far too sweeping. Moreover, Clark's assertion that language stimuli chosen nonrandomly or systematically should be analyzed as though they had been chosen randomly, is not generally appropriate on statistical grounds.

A more serious issue is that attempting to choose stimuli at random in order to allow random-factor analysis is also not generally appropriate. In the psychophysical averaging experiment shown in Figure 1.3, for example, the systematic choice of grayness levels rests on clear background knowledge and would never be left to chance. In studies involving personality trait adjectives and other language stimuli, background knowledge may be less definite, it is true; it is not necessarily less valuable.

Both the preceding studies with trait adjectives employed a joint systematic–random selection procedure. The adjectives were stratified by normative value, as required by the design, and then selected at random within value levels. Random selection was used to avoid bias; random-factor analysis would not be very meaningful if the selection had been nonrandom or systematic, embodying some unknown bias such as bias against inconsistent combinations. Multiple stimulus replications were used to allow assessment of generality, but that can be done with fixed-factor analysis or common sense. In the study of primacy, moreover, random-factor analysis would include real differences among stimulus replications in the error variability, thereby losing power to detect real adjective differences that might deserve individual study. And in the study of the averaging model, random-factor analysis would be virtually irrelevant.

The main flaw in Clark's proposal stems from the basic difference between subjects and stimulus materials. Psychologists are usually interested in the behavior of subjects, not in the behavior of stimulus materials. The stimulus population itself is typically arbitrary. Generalizing from a sample to such a population may mean little, especially when the main inference is extrastatistical, going beyond the stimulus materials to concepts and processes.

It should be recognized, moreover, that a pertinent analysis can always be made by treating stimulus replications as a fixed factor, even when they have been chosen at random. Interactions of replications with other factors will warn that interpretations of main effects may need qualification. This fixed-factor analysis is generally more convenient, more powerful, and more to the point than is random-factor analysis. In most cases, therefore, stimulus materials, including language materials, should be treated as fixed factors.[b]

1.3.7 REDUCING DESIGN SIZE

Factorial designs rapidly become unwieldy as the number of factors increases. To vary four types of information across four levels each requires a 4^4 design. This would not be an especially large sample of stimuli, yet it would yield some 256 stimulus sets, which is around the limit that could ordinarily be expected from a subject in a single session. How to handle experiments that require larger aggregates of stimulus information thus becomes a problem.[a]

Large factorial designs can sometimes be reduced by fractional replication. A fraction of the complete factorial is chosen so that certain higher order interactions are confounded. This procedure has been used in in certain experiments on serial integration (e.g., Anderson, 1964d, 1973c). Shanteau's (1972) paper set a record by reducing a 2^{15} design down to a 2^4 design. Unfortunately, fractional replication is limited in usefulness, as it is only appropriate for linear models. And except for the 2^n designs, it is more or less complicated, especially in the data analysis, and not without dangers from confounding.[b]

Ganging and skipping are often useful. Two pieces of information can be "ganged" by presenting them as a unit pair. Thus, the 4^4 design could be reduced to a 2^4 design by ganging stimuli in pairs for both rows and columns (e.g., Anderson & Farkas, 1973; Weiss & Anderson, 1969). Of course, information about the integration rule for the ganged information is lost. A factor is "skipped" when it is presented at only one level. The amount of information presented can thus be increased without increasing the size of the design itself. Skipping could be useful in studies of information load, for example, although no applications seem to have been made.

Confounding is often useful for controlling minor stimulus variables. If three kinds of stimulus information are used to describe a person, for example, they could be presented in a fixed serial order—spatial or temporal—in every description. This confounds kind of information with serial position. In terms of the serial integration model (Section 3.6), the weight parameter at each serial position is confounded with the weight parameter and scale unit of the information presented at that serial position. In most applications, little or no useful information would be lost.

Another instance of confounding technique is the shuffling method for ordering stimuli noted in Section 1.3.2; it confounds order of presentation with subjects. In the same way, it is sometimes appropriate to confound stimulus replications with subjects. By using a different selection of stimuli for each subject, stimulus variability is confounded with subject variability and both go into a common error term. This is a convenient method for treating stimulus replications as a random factor because it allows the usual repeated measurements analysis. Since this method loses all information about stimulus replications, however, it would ordinarily be used only when there was prior evidence that the differences among stimulus replications could be neglected.

1.3.8 INCOMPLETE DESIGNS

Incomplete designs provide a general way to reduce design size. These designs may be viewed as factorial designs in which a number of stimulus combinations are omitted so that a number of cells in the design are empty. Least squares analysis may be applied to such designs in much the same way as in the ordinary factorial analysis of variance (see Sections 4.3 and 4.4). Since stimulus combinations may be omitted at will, incomplete design offers a flexible method for reducing design size.

Incomplete design has a price, not so much in the computational complications as in information missing from the empty cells. Less constraint is present on the response scale and on the model than would result from complete factorial design. It is thus harder to interpret deviations from, say, parallelism, and easier to overlook them. To appreciate the problem, look at some of the factorial graphs in Section 4.1.2 and imagine that any substantial number of data points are deleted to represent missing cells. The pattern of parallelism or nonparallelism then seems markedly less satisfying. During initial stages of investigation, when response scale and model are more uncertain, incomplete design may thus be inadvisable. Once some measure of confidence in response linearity and in likely integration models has been established, incomplete design promises to be useful.

Analysis of variance is sometimes criticized on the ground that certain stimulus combinations in factorial designs may be strange, meaningless, or otherwise undesirable. If certain stimulus combinations are indeed undesirable, it would certainly be poor practice to use them. Instead, some appropriate incomplete design should be used, together with nonorthogonal analysis of variance (Section 4.3.2).

1.3.9 DESIGN WITH NATURAL ENTITIES

Designs with natural entities can serve two general purposes. First, prior knowledge of the subject can be exploited and studied, especially knowledge in the form of complex processes and skills. Second, greater social relevance can be obtained.

The first goal can be pursued by appropriate choice of task and by treating stimuli as molar units. The personality adjective task of Section

1.2.1 is a good example. Judgments about people require complex processes of valuation and integration that rest on a lifetime of experience. The very naturalness of the task indicates that it taps into a functional judgment system. And although the adjectives may be simple as verbal stimuli go, they still involve complex processing. Treating them as molar units confers important advantages, therefore, and the same holds for more complex stimuli.[a]

The second goal, of social relevance, favors the use of experimental situations similar to those of everyday life. Design within a natural setting brings in added complexities, of course, partly from cost, partly from feasibility. However, it may be possible to tap into ongoing situations and still maintain a needed degree of experimental control.

Marriage provides an ideal natural setting for the study of judgment and decision making. An embedding method would be used to adapt standard judgmental tasks to the context of the individual marriage; for example, one or both members of a couple could be asked to evaluate certain situations based directly on incidents in their marriage. Incidents could include blamable behavior of self or spouse at a party, decisions about children, family budget and purchases, going out, and so forth. These situations would have a real referent but would be chosen to allow experimental manipulation of some stimulus cues. Except for the use of scenarios peculiar to an individual marriage, standard methods and designs of integration theory could be applied. Further discussion and an experimental study of marriage satisfaction are given in Section F4.5.2.

NOTES

1.1.2a. The integration diagram of Figure 1.2 is too simple to hold true in general. The valuation and integration operations are portrayed as distinct, which would not necessarily hold for integration of, say, redundant or inconsistent information. In certain situations, moreover, the integration could be primary, with valuation a subsequent operation that relates the integrated entity to the dimension of judgment (Section F4.5.4). In addition, more than one successive integration process could be involved, with feedback between successive stages. However, the diagram has been helpful in clarifying the structure of the integration–measurement problem (see also Section F1.1).

1.1.3a. Parducci (1982) has verified that distribution effects decrease as the number of steps in the rating scale increases.

1.1.3b. Numerous methodological investigations of rating scales have studied response reliability and amount of information transmitted. These properties have no necessary or likely relation to response linearity. For example, the present use of end anchors to improve response linearity loses the higher reliability of the responses at the ends of the range.

1.1.4a. Anchor stimuli—including end, internal, and external anchors—have been extensively studied in traditional judgment theory but mainly in connection with so-called contrast and assimilation effects. These effects appear to be largely artifacts. Present procedures are intended to avoid them (see Section 1.1.5) although they have intrinsic interest as part of the response operation (Sections 3.11 and 3.12).

Anchor stimuli may affect the response operation by functioning as a reference standard. In Helson and Kozaki (1968), subjects were instructed to judge the actual number of dots in brief stimulus presentations, each preceded by an unjudged anchor. A substantial anchor effect was obtained. For example, the 18-dot stimulus was judged as 15 dots when it followed the 32-dot anchor, as 24 dots when it followed the 4-dot anchor. This result might represent true perceptual contrast, as assumed in Helson's adaptation-level theory, or it might reflect response language effects. The number response is like the inch response discussed in Section 1.1.5 and is subject to the same objections. The data, it may be noted, did not fit Helson's adaptation-level model, but instead followed a comparative judgment model in which the overt response contains both absolute and relative components (Anderson, 1974a, p. 277, Figure 10).

1.1.5a. Relative to the mean judged length of 15 inches, the observed difference of 4.5 inches represents a 30% effect. But contrast effects from the Muller–Lyer and Ebbinghaus figures, which are considered strong illusions, are generally less than 10% (see, e.g., Massaro & Anderson, 1970, Figures 1–3, 1971, Figures 1–2). Even the 15% value for the Baldwin figure obtained by Clavadetscher and Anderson (1977, p. 122) does not approach the 30% value of Krantz and Campbell.

1.1.5b. The need for more careful conceptual analysis appears similarly in the terms *distortion* and *bias* in decision making and social judgment. Because of its influence, the social judgment theory of Sherif and Hovland (1961) may be used to illustrate some relevant conceptual problems. Sherif and Hovland claim that a person's own opinion on an issue acts as an anchor that produces systematic errors in evaluation of statements on that issue. In particular, they claim that statements close to one's own opinion are displaced to lie closer and seem less different than they really are (*assimilation*); statements far from one's own opinion are displaced to lie farther and seem more different than they really are (*contrast*).

An integration-theory interpretation of the so-called assimilation and contrast effects reported by Sherif and Hovland can be given in terms of composite judgmental processes (Anderson, 1971a, p. 190). Two value scales are assumed to underlie the judgments. One value scale represents the location of the statement on a dimension of favorableness-unfavorableness for the issue itself, without regard to subjects' personal preferences. The other value scale represents each subject's personal desirability–undesirability value of the statements. The actual response is a weighted average of the two values for each statement.

This integration analysis provides a straightforward account of the main result claimed by Sherif and Hovland. The critical feature is the personal value scale, for which the valuation function would have the shape of an inverted *V*, reaching a maximum at the subject's own position and becoming negative at farther distances. Statements close to the subject's own position will have high positive value; hence the averaging process will cause them to be judged more favorably than is implied by the first value scale. Statements far from the subject's own position will have negative value; hence the averaging process will cause them to be judged less favorably. This integration explains "assimilation" and "contrast."

Sherif and Hovland (1961, pp. 125ff) mention the possibility of composite judgmental processes, failing to recognize that this approach is inconsistent with their assimilation-contrast theory. This inconsistency is clear in their experiments on anchor effects in lifted weights, which formed the psychophysical foundation for their assimilation–contrast theory of attitudes. The idea of a collateral agree–disagree dimension obviously does not apply to felt heaviness.

A similar integrational approach was suggested independently by Eiser (1971, 1980), who has pursued it in an extended series of experiments. Chapter 3 of Eiser (1980) gives an insightful statement of this position, together with applications to categorization and to stereotypes and attitudes.

From an integration-theoretical view, use of such terms as *distortion, bias, tendency to exaggerate,* and *systematic error* often obscures basic issues. These terms connote deviation from a true position; this position is often left undefined and sometimes has no meaning. Most of the work following Sherif and Hovland (1961) has considered true position as location on the general favorableness dimension, but the existence and measurement of this general scale remain hypothetical. Furthermore, integration of the personal value could result from pervasive integration tendencies, as appears to be the case in the positive context effect noted in the text (see also Section F4.1.8), or from poor instructions (Section 1.2.6) and task difficulty (Section 7.12), which would not properly be called distortion or bias.

Moreover, inaccuracy in judging another's attitude could result from straightforward integration of a nonrepresentative sample of information about the person. Such inaccuracy need involve neither distortion nor tendency to exaggerate; and the term *bias* is correct only in a statistical sense, not in the psychological sense that usually is intended (see also Anderson, 1974b, p. 75, n. 3).

1.1.5c. The extensive literature on contrast–assimilation cannot be covered here, but two additional points deserve mention. First, it seems common sense that people adapt to prevailing social situations such as level of cleanliness or level of violence over extended periods of time. That this has not been definitely demonstrated emphasizes the measurement difficulties involved. Over the short periods of time typical of experimental studies, there is not much basis for thinking that similar adaptation effects are involved. Although the existence of genuine contrast with verbal or symbolic materials remains uncertain, a few investigators have made serious, thoughtful efforts in this direction (e.g., Krantz & Campbell, 1961; Manis & Armstrong, 1971; Simpson & Ostrom, 1976; see also Eiser, 1980, Chapter 3). A comprehensive conceptual and methodological review of this area would be useful.

Second, the effects of relativity in response language are important in social communication even though they may be a perceptual artifact, as has been emphasized by Volkmann (1951), Campbell *et al.* (1958), Upshaw (1969), and others. Because of such language processes, two persons with different experiential backgrounds may come to use the same words to refer to different events. This can produce communicational difficulties even where there is no real difference of opinion (e.g., Anderson, 1974b, p. 75).

1.1.7a. An illusion of nonparallelism is given by parallel lines of varying slope, as illustrated in Figure 1.6. Presumably, the viewer's perceptual judgment is influenced not only by the vertical separation, which is what is ostensibly to be judged, but also by the perpendicular distance between the curves. This perpendicular distance is less for the steeper curves. An averaging rule for integration of the two cues will produce the illusion (see also Clavadetscher & Anderson, 1977; Massaro & Anderson, 1971).

This illusion of nonparallelism complicates visual inspection of factorial graphs. Often it is necessary to use a millimeter scale to measure vertical spread. A helpful device is the inclusion of equal-length vertical bars to make clear the nonparallelism, as illustrated in Figures 1.3 and 4.2.

1.1.7b. Weiss (1980a) found ratings to be statistically more sensitive than magnitude estimations. The validity criteria provided by functional measurement have priority over

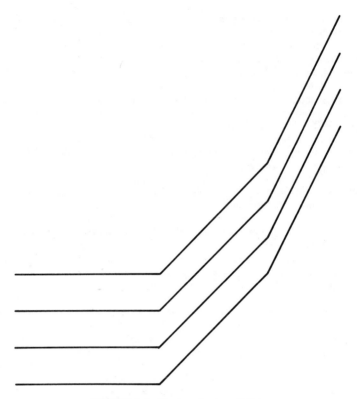

FIGURE 1.6. *Illusion of nonparallelism.*

any such statistical property, of course, but greater sensitivity means greater power in applying a validity criterion such as parallelism.

1.1.7c. Both rating and magnitude estimation appear to have trouble in judgments of loudness. Parducci, Thaler, and Anderson (1968) found a substantial convergence pattern in ratings of average loudness of four successive noise bursts, although this nonparallelism probably involved a response bias, since only six steps were used in the rating scale (Section 1.1.3). Using a 20-point graphic rating scale, Carterette and Anderson (1979) found parallelism for both averaging and differencing of two noise bursts in one experiment, but clear deviations from parallelism in a second experiment. In studies of binaural summation, Marks (1979a,b) found strong convergence with ratings, despite his careful procedure using a graphic scale, but near-parallelism with magnitude estimation (see also Note F5.6.2a). On the other hand, Curtis and Mullin (1975) found marked divergence with magnitude estimation for judgments of average loudness of two tones.

The meaning of this mixed array of results is not clear. One possibility is that unbounded energetic dimensions, such as loudness and brightness (Mansfield, 1976, p. 366), present response problems not found in the main class of integration studies, which typically employ stimulus and response dimensions that are effectively bounded. Another possibility is that the integration follows an averaging rule with greater weighting for more intense stimuli. This rule would perhaps account for the general pattern of results, but no specific tests have been made. In any case, caution is needed in using numerical response methods in loudness studies.

An additional technical difficulty in loudness studies appears in the increasing reliance on monotone transformation to make nonparallel data appear parallel. Almost all this work has used two-factor design with a single score per cell. This is not generally sufficient to prevent transformation to parallelism of data generated by severely nonadditive processes, as shown in Chapter 5 (see also Anderson, 1977b, p. 208; Carterette & Anderson, 1979, pp. 274–276; Note F5.6.2a).

1.1.8a. A similar artifact of between-subject design may be present in studies reporting that subjects are insensitive to information about base rates and predictive validity in certain decision tasks. Of course, within-subject design could also operate by ensuring subjects' understanding of the task (Note 1.2.6a).

1.1.9a. As a specific example, monotone response scales are sufficient for certain questions about integrational capacity. If several variables each have reliable main effects, this suggests they are being integrated. If any one variable has zero true effect, this must hold regardless of the response measure. Of course, a linear response measure is needed to determine the form of the integration rule.

1.2.5a. A preliminary screening test can also reduce error variance. In a study of individual versus group performance (Anderson, 1961a), junior high school students were given a preliminary anagram-type test in their English classroom. They had 15 minutes to make as many words as possible from the letters $i \ w \ m \ r \ p \ a \ c \ o$. The 20% of the students who made five or fewer words were screened out. The rest were stratified into five ability levels on the basis of this screening test performance. This randomized blocks method was effective in reducing error variability, as it was equivalent to doubling the number of subjects. Generality was increased at the same time because the results were found to be independent of ability level.

1.2.6a. Ward (1975) showed that the violations of the representativeness heuristic reported by Leon and Anderson (1974) resulted in part from their use of a within-subject design in contrast to the between-subject design used by Kahneman and Tversky (1972). One main advantage of within-subject design is to make clear the nature of the task by making salient variables that subjects might not otherwise realize are relevant (Section 1.3.1).

Ward (1975), it should be noted, took a somewhat different view, that the violations of representativeness obtained by Leon and Anderson and by himself may have been a demand artifact: "The repeated measures nature of the experiment may make consistency demands on subjects [p. 45]" (see also Section 7.1). The present view is that within-subject design increases the salience of the variables of sample size and population proportion. Their relevance is decided by the subject. Unless subjects understand their relevance to the task, they will not use the variables appropriately.

Fischhoff, Slovic, and Lichtenstein (1979) have corroborated the results of Leon and Anderson (1974) and of Ward (1975). By adopting within-subject design, Fischhoff *et al.* found that subjects could utilize information variables such as base rate to which they had reportedly been oblivious in previous studies that used between-subject design. Similar results have been reported by Birnbaum and Mellers (1981). Fischhoff *et al.* suggest that within-subject design gives a truer picture of subjects' cognitive abilities, an interpretation that agrees with the position of Leon and Anderson.

1.2.7a. The only previous concerted use of within-subject design in attitude research seems to be McGuire's (1964) series of experiments on his inoculation theory. Within-subject design has also been espoused by Ronis, Baumgardner, Leippe, Cacioppo, and

Greenwald (1977), who used both the president paragraphs and another set of stimulus materials. Other attitude studies with the president paragraphs are given in Sawyers and Anderson (1971), Anderson, Sawyers, and Farkas (1972), Anderson (1973b), and Anderson and Farkas (1973).

1.3.1a. Since the possibility that the instructions themselves somehow induce the behavior seems to cause occasional concern, it may be useful to add a few comments on this attribution task (see also Section 7.1). First, it should be clear that if the subject does not already understand that ability is an inverse function of motivation (for fixed performance), nondirective instructions will not artifactually produce that understanding. The fact is, of course, that this task is typical in that it aims to elicit processes and behavior already familiar to the subject. What is not familiar is the experimental setting and scenario, which is why careful instruction is required.

Second, the purpose of the experiment was to study cue integration. Focusing attention on the motivation cue might increase its relative weight, but that has no logical bearing on the integration rule. Indeed, an interesting outcome of this experiment was the lack of formal consistency of the three integration rules that were studied (Section F1.5.6). Of course, for investigations concerned with valuation rather than integration, instructional salience could be more serious.

1.3.2a. The Stimulus × Sequence interaction is calculated in the usual way and has $(a - 1)^2$ df for an $a \times a$ latin square. The sum of squares for position is calculated from the a totals obtained by summing over sequences for each of the a serial positions and has $a - 1$ df; sum of squares and df for square residual are obtained by subtraction.

1.3.3a. Repetition of the same stimulus in different sets can sometimes be avoided by treating each level of a factor as a class of stimuli rather than as a single fixed stimulus. In the personality adjective study cited in the text, for example, each adjective appeared in 9 of the 27 sets. An alternative is to use nine different adjectives chosen from the same value class as the given adjective. This stimulus-replication procedure can avoid memory effects and increase the realism of the task. It may be necessary in some cases, as in the presidents experiments mentioned in Section 1.2.7. This stimulus-replication procedure complicates the design and analysis, however, as illustrated by the necessity for greco-latin square designs in the presidents experiments (e.g., Anderson, 1973b; Sawyers & Anderson, 1971). Since differences among stimulus replications go into the error term, moreover, this procedure may be costly, as is illustrated in Figure 1.5.

1.3.4a. A study by Fiske (1980) helps illuminate the network of interrelations among conceptual and empirical aspects of attention and the model representation. Attention was conceptually related to stimulus informativeness, which was in turn related to stimulus properties of negativity and extremity. At the same time, informativeness was related to the weight parameters of the averaging model. Indexes of negativity and extremity were thereby related to the observed pattern of integrated judgments. Of special interest was the novel use of a behavioral index of weight, namely, subject's viewing time of the individual photographic stimuli. This weight index showed virtually perfect correspondence with weight parameters estimated from the model.

Fiske's experimental design, which was planned to allow assessment of these interrelations, is interesting in several other respects, including the use of a latin square to balance stimulus persons across behavioral situations and incorporation of the initial impression in the estimation of the scale values (Section 2.3.4). Of special interest is her use of normative scale values estimated from one group of subjects to make practicable the weight estimation for the main group of subjects. Although this procedure has certain statistical shortcomings, it can be valuable when theoretical concern shifts from testing and establishing the model to using it as a tool for further analysis (Section 4.4.3).

1.3.5a. One technique is to use a detailed scenario as part of the instruction–practice period in order to develop the subject's conception of the task, with stimuli for the regular judgment trials being given in short form. For example, quantifiers could be used to define levels of dimensions whose nature had been defined in the practice-instruction period. This technique facilitates the collection of a substantial number of judgments within a realistic framework of judgment. This technique could be useful for embedding designs in natural situations (Section 1.3.9).

Quantifiers, it should be recognized, may have nonce values constructed for the task at hand. Quantifier adjectives such as *somewhat*, *very*, and *extremely* are not required to have fixed, universal values; their functional values are derived from the valuation operation associated with the given task and so may depend on task specifics (Sections 1.2.2 and 7.15). The same applies to other verbal, and even to numerical, quantifiers. In particular, due to communicational tendencies to equalize quantifier spacing across the value range, the nonce value of any one quantifier may depend on which other quantifiers are included.

For integration studies, of course, the particular values of the quantifiers are often not important. The capability of using nonce values is thus of advantage to the investigator. It is important, of course, that the instruction–practice period stabilize the value construction, at least for model tests that require constant values across stimulus combinations during the course of the experiment.

1.3.6a. Stimulus generality is one facet of a larger problem faced by every investigator, namely, that the results may be peculiar to task specifics. This problem may be illustrated by the case of the "poop-out effect" accidentally discovered by the writer, in which rats gradually ceased making a shock-avoidance response they had initially learned. This effect was unwanted, since the original purpose was to study long-term latency distributions. It was contrary to prevailing ideas of reinforcement theory, moreover, and so was treated as a fault of procedure. Only after several months of collaboration with Arlo Myers failed to find any experimental conditions that could establish and maintain good avoidance conditioning did avoidance decrement begin to appear as an interesting focus of investigation in its own right. With the help of Ted Coons, a formal experiment was run to pin down the effect and rule out interpretations in terms of general debility and other artifacts (Coons, Anderson, & Myers, 1960). This paper concluded, "Although some unsuspected artifact may still remain, it seems reasonable to interpret the present data as showing a real loss of a proper learned response despite continued 'reinforcement' [p. 292]."

The qualification, "unsuspected artifact," began to seem prudent when a subsequent program of research by the writer and Charles Nakamura at the University of California, Los Angeles, was at first unable to obtain avoidance decrement. Subsequent studies showed that avoidance decrement has a complex dependence on sex of rat, strain and stock of rat, and kind of avoidance task (Anderson & Nakamura, 1964; Nakamura & Anderson, 1962, 1964). Strong individual differences also appeared, with bimodal distributions of avoiders and nonavoiders. Moreover, avoidance decrement did not seem preventable by any number of hopeful variations in shock and time parameters (Anderson, 1969d; Anderson & Rollins, 1966; Anderson, Rollins, & Riskin, 1966; Nakamura & Anderson, 1968). Avoidance decrement seems genuine, therefore, although its interpretation remains a puzzle.

1.3.6b. Clark's (1973) article appropriately criticizes the not-infrequent failure to employ stimulus replication as a basis for generality in language studies. Moreover, his suggestions for use of random-factor analysis are certainly appropriate in some situations. Wike and Church (1976) criticized Clark's article primarily on statistical grounds, but they also emphasized the central role of extrastatistical inference (see also Keppel, 1973, pp. 333–335). It should be added that Clark's recommendation to treat nonrandomly chosen stimuli as random, although it may seem odd, mirrors the generally accepted practice of treating handy samples of subjects as a random factor. However, there is substantive asymmetry between stimuli and subjects, as noted in the text. On the whole, therefore, one might properly rephrase Clark to speak of the language-as-random-effect fallacy.

1.3.7a. A related problem of overly large designs arises when replication is needed to provide an error term for within-individual analyses. Instead of presenting the entire design a second time, it may suffice to present a limited number of stimulus combinations. These replicated cells would then provide an estimate of response variability.

1.3.7b. Cochran and Cox (1957) present a good, fairly extensive treatment of fractional replication. Catalogs of designs are given by Addelman (1962a,b), Addelman and Kempthorne (1961), Connor and Young (1961), and Hahn and Shapiro (1966). The University of California, Los Angeles Biomedical Program P2V may be used to analyze fractionally replicated 2^n designs. A rationale for not testing high-order interactions in high-way factorial designs is given in Anderson (1968e).

1.3.9a. It goes without saying that molar analysis is insufficient for many purposes. The distraction effect in attitude research, in which reduced attention to a message causes increased attitude change, provides an illustrative case in which molecular analysis is needed (Anderson, 1976e, 1981b).

2

Integration Models

This chapter will discuss various models that have been used in general integration theory. For the most part, the formal mathematical analysis is elementary and will not be given in detail. Emphasis will be on practical use, that is, on considerations involved in designing experiments and on statistical problems of estimating parameters and testing the models. The work in this research program has been attentive to statistical problems, but they have been dealt with mainly as need arose within particular experimental investigations. Many of these problems need more systematic study from a statistical point of view. Although the present exposition is oriented toward experimental applications, it is also intended to call attention of statistical workers to these problems.

The simplicity of the present treatment rests largely on the use of numerical response measures. These results are most helpful, therefore, when the observable response is a linear scale, for otherwise deviations from the model have an uncertain interpretation (Sections 7.11 and F1.2.6). The usefulness of these results accordingly rests on the empirical foundation for response linearity provided by the experimental reports reviewed in Chapter F1. The statistical methods can be extended to handle monotone response scales, as shown in Chapter 5. The practical difficulties are greater, however, and the results notably less definite. To avoid these difficulties, it is usually worthwhile to consider procedures that help ensure a linear response, as discussed in Chapter 1.

Notation. Most of this chapter will assume that the stimulus combinations are constructed from a two-way Row × Column factorial design. For simplicity, it is assumed that all cells of the design contain an equal number of observations. Extensions to higher order factorial designs are straightforward. Nonfactorial designs and unequal numbers of observations across cells are not difficult in principle but can be more complicated in practice (Section 4.3.2).

The row stimuli in the design will be denoted by S_{Ai} and the column stimuli by S_{Bj}. Their weights and scale values will be denoted by w and s, with appropriate subscripts. The response to the stimulus combination (S_{Ai}, S_{Bj}) in cell ij of the design will be denoted by R_{ij}. This same symbol will ordinarily be used to denote both the theoretical and the observed responses since the appropriate meaning will ordinarily be clear from context. The symbol e_{ij} will denote response variability and other sources of "error." Thus, the observed response in cell ij is considered as the sum of the "true" response and the error.

Averages will be denoted by the standard bar–dot notation. Row means are denoted by $\check{R}_{i.}$, where the dot indicates that the average has been taken over the column index, j. Similarly, column means are denoted by $\check{R}_{.j}$, and the grand mean by $\check{R}_{..}$.

Schematic notation is occasionally useful for the integration models. In one such notation, the stimulus variables are denoted by the letters A, B, C, ... The two basic two-factor models are then written

$$A + B \text{ and } AB.$$

More complex models are listed in Table 3.1 of Section 3.3. It is also convenient to use the symbol ⊛ to denote a generalized integration operation whose algebraic structure may be unspecified or unknown. Thus the model

$$(A \circledast B) + C$$

implies an additive integration of C with A, with B, and with the compound variable $A \circledast B$, with no assumption about the integration rule for A and B.

Another useful notation uses common language names instead of letters. For example

$$Performance = Motivation \times Ability,$$
$$Punishment = Intention + Damage.$$

In both forms of notation, it is understood that the terms of the model refer to subjective values.

Independence Assumption. The independence assumption states that the parameters of each stimulus have fixed values, independent of what other stimuli it may be combined with. This basic assumption is used, in one form or another, in all model analyses except in the method of component judgments (Section 6.2.4). Two or three aspects of this assumption require amplification.

The concept of stimulus interaction refers to processes that produce changes in stimulus parameters as a function of other stimuli in the combination (see also Section 7.10). In its simplest form, the independence assumption disallows stimulus interaction, and such interactions would generally produce discrepancies from model predictions. If the model passes the test of goodness of fit, this ordinarily is taken as joint support for the model and for the assumption of no stimulus interaction. Indeed, the independence assumption is usually considered part of the model, although the algebraic operation itself may hold even when there is stimulus interaction. If the model fails the test of fit, this may reflect an incorrect integration rule or a failure of the independence assumption. It should be noted, however, that certain kinds of stimulus interaction can escape detection in a test of fit (e.g., Sections 2.1.4 and 2.3.3).

Stimulus parameters may depend on many factors, but some of these dependences are not stimulus interactions in the sense just defined. Stimulus parameters will depend on the specific response dimension and, within that dimension, on the individual organism. They may also depend on the momentary physiological or emotional need state of the organism. These dependences are subsumed under the valuation operation (see Section 7.15) and are not considered interactions within the integration task. Unless otherwise stated, it is assumed throughout that the focus is on a given organism in a given integration task.

Stimulus interactions and context effects can sometimes be incorporated into the model under study. In the averaging model, the relative, or effective, weight parameters do depend on the context, but this interactive dependence becomes a predictive consequence of the completely stated model (Section 2.3). In the model of the positive context effect of Section F4.1.4, the context has a prescribed influence on the judgment of the component. But although these models allow for stimulus interaction, the independence assumption still holds for certain parameters, such as the absolute weights in the averaging model. In general, therefore, the specific meaning of the independence assumption is relative to the particular model under study.

2.1 Linear Models

2.1.1 MODEL AND PARAMETERS

For a two-way factorial design, the linear model can be written[a]

$$R_{ijx} = C_0 + w_{Ai}s_{Ai} + w_{Bj}s_{Bj} + e_{ijx}, \tag{1a}$$

or

$$R_{ijx} = C_0 + \tilde{s}_{Ai} + \tilde{s}_{Bj} + e_{ijx}. \tag{1b}$$

Here R_{ijx} is the xth replication in cell ij. It is expressed as a sum of two stimulus effects, one from the row variable, one from the column variable. To these are added a constant, C_0, which allows for an arbitrary zero in the response scale, and an error term, e_{ijx}, which allows for variability among responses given under the same nominal stimulus conditions.[b] The e_{ijx} are thus random variables and are assumed to have zero expected value. This last assumption rules out statistical interaction terms. It will often be convenient to ignore the error variability and take R_{ij} as the "true" value, and this will generally be done without explicit notice, as already indicated.

In most applications, the R_{ijx} are observed data, but the terms on the right of Eqs. (1) are unknown, to be estimated in the data analysis. The C_0 term, which represents the zero of the response scale, need not be known because it is automatically absorbed into the stimulus values. In general, moreover, the weight parameters are not identifiable, as they are confounded with the unit of the corresponding stimulus scales. Except under special conditions, therefore, $w_{Ai}s_{Ai}$ must be treated as a single parameter denoted by $\tilde{s}_{Ai}$, and similarly for $w_{Bj}s_{Bj}$. The $\tilde{s}_{Ai}$ and $\tilde{s}_{Bj}$ will be called the *gross stimulus values*.

Parallelism Theorem. Analysis of the linear model rests on a simple theorem. To make explicit the assumptions involved in the analysis, the model should be stated in terms of the implicit response, r, which represents the subjective level at which the model applies.

Parallelism Theorem. *Suppose that the linear model holds, so that $r_{ij} = \tilde{s}_{Ai} + \tilde{s}_{Bj}$, and that the observable response is a linear scale of the implicit response, so that $R_{ij} = C_0 + C_1 r_{ij}$. Then the factorial plot of the observable response will exhibit a pattern of parallelism, and the row and column marginal means of the response matrix will constitute linear scales of the subjective values of the stimulus variables.*

The proof is elementary (Section F1.2) and has a straightforward generalization to more than two stimulus variables. Observed parallelism thus supports both premises of the theorem: If either premise is incorrect, parallelism will not, in general, be obtained. There is, of course, a logical possibility that nonlinearity in the response scale could just balance nonlinearity (nonadditivity; see Section 7.10) in the integration rule to yield parallelism.[c] Subject to this qualification, however, observed parallelism accomplishes three simultaneous goals:

1. It supports the linear model.
2. It supports the linearity of the response scale.
3. It provides linear scales of the stimulus variables.

Although simple mathematically, the parallelism theorem is far from simple substantively. Allowing for response variability, which was neglected in the statement of the theorem, is not difficult, as the next section will show. Unless the two premises of the theorem are empirically true, however, the theorem has little relevance. It is important, therefore, to develop procedures that can provide linear response scales, an endeavor beset by many difficulties (Section 1.1). And it is essential to find substantive areas in which the model holds, for the model provides the base and frame for obtaining a linear response scale (Section 1.1.2). Present attention, however, is with statistical problems.

Parameter Estimation. Functional scales of the gross stimulus values, $\bar{s}_{Ai}$ and $\bar{s}_{Bj}$, may be estimated from the marginal means of the factorial data table. The row means, $\bar{R}_{i.}$, are unbiased estimates of the row parameters, $\bar{s}_{Ai}$; similarly, the column means, $\bar{R}_{.j}$, are unbiased estimates of the column parameters, $\bar{s}_{Bj}$. This result is virtually assumption-free, requiring only that each e_{ijx} has zero true mean or expected value. The e_{ijx} may have different variances and different distributional shapes and need not even be statistically independent.

This result follows from the fact that the expected value of a sum is the sum of the expected values. Because the e_{ijx} have zero expected value, the mean of the observed responses in any cell is an unbiased estimate of the true cell response, namely, $C_0 + \bar{s}_{Ai} + \bar{s}_{Bj}$. Hence the observed mean of row i is an unbiased estimate of $C_0 + \bar{s}_{Ai} + \bar{s}_{B.}$, and these constitute a linear scale of $\bar{s}_{Ai}$. Similarly, the observed column means are linear scale estimates of the $\bar{s}_{Bj}$.[d]

Furthermore, the cell entries may be estimated from the marginal means. In terms of the true values, the response in cell ij is the sum of the corresponding row and column means minus the grand mean

$$C_0 + \bar{s}_{Ai} + \bar{s}_{Bj} = C_0 + \bar{s}_{Ai} + \bar{s}_{B.}$$
$$+ C_0 + \bar{s}_{A.} + \bar{s}_{Bj}$$
$$- C_0 - \bar{s}_{A.} - \bar{s}_{B..}$$

In terms of observed values, therefore, the sum of the corresponding row and column means minus the grand mean is an unbiased estimate of the true cell entry. If this estimate is subtracted from the observed cell entry, then the residual is zero except for random variability. Hence the complete factorial matrix of residuals is zero except for random variability if the model is true. This matrix of residuals provides the basis for testing goodness of fit.

Standard statistical theory generally passes over the case just considered to assume equal variances or equal variances plus normality (e.g., Graybill, 1961, p. 226). If the variances are equal, then any linear function of the observations is a linear minimum variance, unbiased estimate of the same function of the true values, regardless of distribution shape (Searle, 1971, pp. 181ff). If the variances are unequal, the estimates are still unbiased, although they will not have minimum variance.

If equal variances and normality are both assumed, much stronger statistical results become available. In particular, valid confidence intervals can be obtained, and the standard analysis of variance F tests can be applied. However, the parallelism property of the factorial graph holds regardless of statistical assumptions, whose role is to augment visual inspection with more objective assessment.

Uniqueness. The preceding estimates of the $\tilde{s}_{Ai}$ and $\tilde{s}_{Bj}$ are on linear scales, unique up to zero and unit. If $(\tilde{s}_{Ai}, \tilde{s}_{Bj})$ is one set of estimates, then $(\tilde{s}_{Ai} - c, \tilde{s}_{Bj} + c)$ is an equivalent set, where c is any constant. The zero point of each stimulus scale is thus arbitrary, although it may be determinable from auxiliary information. Furthermore, since the unit of the response scale is ordinarily arbitrary, it follows that the unit of each stimulus scale is also ordinarily arbitrary.

The gross parameters, $\tilde{s}_{Ai}$ and $\tilde{s}_{Bj}$, are sometimes treated as scale values on the argument that weight parameters are inherently unidentifiable within the general linear model. However, the weight parameters do become identifiable under certain conditions, as when the linear model is actually an averaging model (Section 2.3). Also, weights can be estimated when there is a relation among the scale values of the stimuli across the various factors (e.g., Sections 2.1.4 and 3.6). The distinction between weight and value is real, therefore, and should be maintained even when the two are not separately identifiable.

2.1.2 GOODNESS OF FIT

Graphical Test. A simple and most useful test of the linear model is available by just plotting the raw data. The factorial graph should exhibit the basic parallelism property already mentioned. Mathematically, parallelism follows immediately from Eqs. (1), which imply that the difference between the entries in any two rows is constant across columns, except for response variability. This algebraic constancy is equivalent to geometric parallelism, for which no statistical assumptions are required.

Distribution-Free Tests. Various distribution-free procedures may be applied to get objective statistical tests of goodness of fit. To illustrate the idea, consider the four cells in the upper left corner of a two-way design. These four cells form a 2×2 subdesign that should exhibit parallelism. The deviation from parallelism has the algebraic expression

$$I_x = (R_{11x} - R_{21x}) - (R_{12x} - R_{22x}).$$

A separate value of I_x would be computed for each subject in a repeated measurements design or for each replication in an individual subject design. The model-implied null hypothesis is that the true mean of the I_x is zero. An appropriate test is the signed-ranks test.[a]

This approach can be extended to test the complete matrix of residuals by representing it as a complete set of orthogonal components. Standard orthogonal polynomials could be employed, although other orthogonal decompositions might yield more power. Although these techniques are generally associated with analysis of variance, they are also usable with distribution-free tests. Each component is an unbiased estimate of the same linear function of the true values, as already noted. Because they are orthogonal, the components are statistically independent. Each corresponds to 1 *df* in the complete matrix of deviations, and together they provide a mutually exclusive and exhaustive representation of the residual matrix. Each component may thus be tested in the manner indicated, and multiple comparison procedures (Section 5.4) may be applied to the complete set. In this way, the model can be tested with a bare minimum of statistical assumptions.

Distribution-free tests have had little application in this research program. A major reason is that the assumptions of analysis of variance seem generally well satisfied in the kinds of experiments that have been done. A second reason is that analysis of variance provides omnibus and multiple *df* tests that do not seem to be generally possible with distribution-free tests. Finally, the procedures developed in analysis of variance are remarkably flexible and useful. For these reasons, distribution-free tests will not be considered in detail in this book. It should be emphasized, however, that choice of statistical tests is basically a practical matter, dependent on particular circumstances and on the level of background knowledge about the behavior under study.[b]

Analysis of Variance. There is a simple correspondence between the linear integration model of Eqs. (1) and the linear model used in analysis of variance. In that correspondence, the statistical interaction terms are all zero. The hypothesis that the behavior follows the linear integration model can be assessed with standard tests of these interaction terms.

Analysis of variance requires further assumptions about the distributions of the e_{ijx}: that they are homonormal and either independent or satisfy a sphericity condition for repeated measurements.[c] These distributional assumptions are usually well satisfied in judgmental research, and in any case the analysis of variance is known to be robust against deviations from the distributional assumptions.

Besides the omnibus interaction test, more specific tests of interaction components are also possible. Such tests can increase power by focusing on more likely loci of deviations from the model. In particular, the F test can be applied to 1 df components of the interaction. These 1 df tests require only normality, of course, since the assumption of homogeneity of variance is automatically satisfied in a single sample. Normality is facilitated by the central limit theorem because the interaction components are linear functions of several raw scores. If outlier observations were expected to disturb normality, a trimmed or Winsorized t test might perhaps be justifiable.[d]

Several different cases of the analysis of variance test arise in practice, depending on whether individual or group data are to be analyzed. Somewhat different considerations, both experimental and statistical, are involved in each case. These will be considered next.

2.1.3 DESIGN TYPE

Between-Subject Design. From a statistical standpoint, the simplest design is one in which each subject serves in only one cell of the design, giving, in effect, a single response. That ordinarily guarantees that the responses are statistically independent. Such designs are much used in experimental psychology to avoid unwanted transfer effects among the stimulus conditions.

In studies of algebraic models, however, between-subject designs are rare. They have the serious handicap that all individual differences go into the error term, which is therefore relatively large. With a large error term, the interaction test may have little statistical power, and that gives a weak basis for accepting the null hypothesis that the model is correct (Section 4.2). Accordingly, it is desirable to use each subject in more than one condition. This is often feasible in studies of perception and judgment, where transfer effects are often negligible.

Repeated Measurements Design. The term *repeated measurements design* refers to designs in which each subject responds under all stimulus conditions but the analysis is done on a group basis. The data thus form a three-way, Row × Column × Subjects design, also called a within-subject design. The Subjects factor is treated as random in the statistical analysis, so the error term for the Row × Column interaction is the Row × Column × Subjects interaction.

In repeated measurements design, the responses are not independent but correlated across subjects. Additional assumptions on the covariance matrix of the e_{ijx} are needed to justify the analysis of variance test, which, accordingly, is less robust than with independent responses. For judgment experiments of the kind reported in this book, no reason has arisen to question these additional statistical assumptions. However, a conservative F test can be obtained by reducing the nominal df (e.g., Winer, 1971, Section 4.4; see also Note 2.1.2c), or distribution-free tests that require less restrictive assumptions can be used.

Carryover and serial position effects are a potential problem in any repeated measurements design, so preliminary practice is ordinarily desirable to set the subject's frame of reference. Also, a different random sequence of conditions is often used for each subject to avoid any systematic confounding of carryover and position effects with experimental conditions. In this way, residual carryover and position effects will go mainly into one or another of the error terms (see also Sections 1.3.1–1.3.3).

The repeated measurements design fractionates a major part of the individual differences out of the error term. That includes not merely individual differences in overall response level, which are reflected in the main effect of subjects, but also different weight and value patterns, which are reflected in the interactions of subjects with rows and with columns. This reduction in error variance typically provides a marked increase in the power of the test of goodness of fit and hence a more solid base for accepting or rejecting the model.

Repeated measurements designs are quite useful, therefore, especially in earlier stages of investigation. Serious discrepancies from a model will usually be detected most efficiently in such designs. For firmer validation, however, analysis at the level of the individual subject is desirable.

Mixed Between–Within Designs. Mixed designs allow for both between-subject and within-subject factors. In the attitude study of Figure 4.3, for example, stimulus order was made a between-subject factor, whereas the main factorial design was on a within-subject basis. This not only balances possible carryover and position effects but allows statistical tests for their presence. Similarly, instructions may often be a between-subject factor, as in the inconsistency discounting experiment of Anderson and Jacobson (1965) (see Appendix A). An advantage of mixed designs is that any interaction of between- and within-subject factors has a within-subject error term.

Individual Subject Design. In this case, subjects are individually run through each stimulus condition two or more times, and a separate analysis is performed for each subject. Two methods of analysis are possible, depending on the treatment of the error term.

The first method uses the pooled within-cell variability for the error term, exactly as in the case of independent responses for between-subject design. This method has been widely used, in part because of its simplicity, in part because responses are ordinarily stable across replications in the kinds of experiments that have been studied. Use of this method would be questionable, however, when substantial fluctuations in the stimulus parameters are expected due to changes in the subject's psychological or emotional state, for example, or to extended time periods between replications.

The second method treats replications of the stimulus design as an additional systematic factor. This replications factor might correspond to different sessions, for example, with the subject being run through the complete stimulus design one or more times each session. The complete design would then be a three-way factorial, Row × Column × Replications. Replications would ordinarily be treated as a random factor exactly analogous to Subjects in the preceding within-subject design, so that Row, Column, and Row × Column would each be tested against its own interaction with Replications as error. This analysis has the conceptual advantage of allowing the stimulus parameters to be treated explicitly as distributions (Note 2.1.1b).

The choice between these two methods will depend on the magnitude of any replication effects. The same design can be analyzed both ways, and doing so will help determine which method is more appropriate in various situations. The pooled within-cell sum of squares in the first method is broken down into four sums of squares in the second method: Replications, Replications × Rows, Replications × Columns, and Replications × Rows × Columns. If the first three are substantially larger than the fourth, real changes from one replication to another are implied. The error term from the first method, although having more degrees of freedom, would then tend to be too large. If Replications can properly be considered a random factor, then the three-way interaction would be the appropriate error term for the model test and would, of course, be valid even if there were no replication effects.

Replications will not always be a random factor. In studies of learning and motivation, for example, systematic changes across successive replications may be obtained. The three-way interaction may in some situations provide a rough approximate error term for the critical Row × Column interaction. The main effects of Row and Column are usually trivial, of course; they are built in by the choice of stimuli and are not generally tested.

Regardless of method of analysis, the same experimental precautions are appropriate as for repeated measurements design. Preliminary practice is ordinarily desirable, for it brings the subject near to stable state. Residual temporal trends and transfer effects should be randomized or assessed by including sequence of conditions as an added design factor.

Because individual subject analysis eliminates all individual differences from the error term, it is somewhat more powerful than repeated measurements analysis. Only individual subject analysis is ultimately satisfactory, moreover, because the psychological locus of theory is within the individual organism.

Algebraic Model for Repeated Measurements Design. Certain statistical considerations can be brought out more clearly by presenting a specific model for the repeated measurements design with two systematic stimulus factors and a third factor of subjects. In statistical theory, this model has a standard form that can be written as

$$R_{ijsx} = \bar{\mu}_{...} + \bar{\alpha}_{i..} + \bar{\alpha}_{.j.} + \bar{\alpha}_{..s}$$
$$+ \bar{\alpha}_{ij.} + \bar{\alpha}_{i.s} + \bar{\alpha}_{.js}$$
$$+ \bar{\alpha}_{ijs}$$
$$+ e_{ijsx}.$$

The subscripts i and j stand for the two systematic factors, subscript s stands for subjects, and subscript x for replications within subjects. Each $\bar{\alpha}$ denotes a true value that is averaged over the missing indexes represented by dots.

The first four terms on the right are known as *main effects*. Thus, the $\bar{\alpha}_{i..}$ represent the true effects of the row stimuli, expressed as deviations from the grand mean $\bar{\mu}_{...}$ so that $\Sigma\bar{\alpha}_{i..} = 0$. The same holds for the column means $\bar{\alpha}_{.j.}$ and the subject means $\bar{\alpha}_{..s}$. The main effects ordinarily have little substantive importance. The stimulus levels are ordinarily chosen to produce substantially different effects, and the subject term merely represents individual differences in overall mean response.

Each term in the second row refers to a different two-way matrix of data, averaged over the missing subscript. Thus, $\bar{\alpha}_{ij.}$ denotes the entry in cell ij of the $A \times B$ matrix of true means averaged over subjects. These entries are expressed as deviation scores, residuals after the corresponding main effects have been removed. Specifically, $\bar{\alpha}_{ij.}$ is the residual after

($\bar{\mu}_{...} + \bar{\alpha}_{i..} + \bar{\alpha}_{.j.}$) has been subtracted from the true cell mean. Similar definitions hold for the other two terms. These terms are the two-way interactions.

Primary interest in model analysis is with the $\bar{\alpha}_{ij.}$. The linear integration model of Eqs. (1) implies that $\bar{\alpha}_{ij.} = 0$ for all values of i and j. This null hypothesis is the algebraic equivalent of parallelism and so is central in the test of goodness of fit.

The other two-way interactions both involve subjects. Algebraically they are similar to the $\bar{\alpha}_{ij.}$, but their substantive meaning is different. Thus, the $\bar{\alpha}_{i.s}$ are cell residuals obtained by subtracting ($\bar{\mu}_{...} + \bar{\alpha}_{i..} + \bar{\alpha}_{..s}$) from the true cell means in the $A \times S$ data matrix averaged over B. These residuals thus reflect individual differences in the values of the row stimuli, individual differences in the unit of the response scale, or both; similarly for the $\bar{\alpha}_{.js}$. Since such differences can ordinarily be taken for granted, neither of these two subject interactions has much substantive interest.[a]

The $\bar{\alpha}_{ijs}$ represent the residuals in the cells of the three-way $A \times B \times S$ matrix after the first seven terms have been subtracted out. If each individual subject obeys the linear model, then these residuals are all zero in principle, and any observed residuals represent only response variability. This variability is denoted by e_{ijsx}, which is constrained to have true mean or expected value of zero in each cell of the three-way design.

The foregoing model is entirely algebraic and makes no statistical assumptions. The linear integration model of Eqs. (1) implies the null hypothesis that every $\bar{\alpha}_{ij.}$ term is zero. Testing goodness of fit of the linear model requires a test of this null hypothesis, which may be done with a distribution-free test or with analysis of variance. The selection of error terms is elucidated in terms of expected mean squares in standard texts. The common case in which the two stimulus variables are fixed factors follows two rules.

The first rule is that any systematic source is tested against its interaction with subjects. In particular, the critical $A \times B$ interaction is tested against the $A \times B \times S$ interaction. Similarly, the main effects of A and B are tested against the $A \times S$ and $B \times S$ interactions, respectively. To complete the rule, the grand mean is tested against the main effect of subjects. Although these last three tests would not ordinarily be of interest, they become useful in the general test for nonlinear models of Section 4.4.

The second rule about error terms is that each interaction with subjects may be tested against the replication term, which represents response variability between replications within subjects. These tests, of course, require that two or more replications be obtained for each subject. Of some interest is the test of the $A \times B \times S$ interaction, which provides an additional test of the linear model of Eqs. (1) for the reason already indicated. It should be noted, however, that replication within subjects is not necessary for a model test and may have limited value since the main component of variability is typically between subjects.

An exactly parallel algebraic model applies to individual subject analysis: the s subscript now represents sessions for the given subject; and the x subscript represents replications within sessions, which are assumed to be equivalent except for unsystematic response variability. If the subject's values are expected to fluctuate across sessions, thereby constituting a random factor, then the given statistical tests would apply. If the subject's values are expected to change systematically across sessions, thereby constituting a fixed factor, then the replications term would be used as the error term in all tests. Finally, if the subject's values remain constant across sessions, then all terms with an s subscript have equal expected value and so could be pooled to provide a common error term for the systematic sources.

2.1.4 OTHER CONSIDERATIONS OF DESIGN AND ANALYSIS

Stimulus Selection. The statistical analysis treats the physical stimuli as nominal so no prior scaling is necessary. The analysis does assign values to the stimuli, but these values are derivative from the response metric. The stimuli may, therefore, be chosen entirely arbitrarily.

Of course, the cogency of the experiment does depend on the choice of stimuli. In particular, when the main effect of one variable is small, statistical interactions are likely to be small and unlikely to be detected. It is generally desirable, therefore, to choose a set of stimuli that will cover some substantial range with roughly equal spacing. Pilot work seems to be almost essential for this purpose.

Averaging over subjects in a repeated measurements design is justified by the linearity of Eqs. (1), regardless of how the stimuli are chosen. Different subjects may attach different values to the stimuli, and these values need not even have the same rank order. If each subject's data are parallel, so must be the average. The group test automatically allows for individual differences in stimulus values.

Two Averaging Artifacts. Parallelism is not a sure sign of an adding process. For example, the Height + Width rule of Figure 4.5 could result from averaging over children, some of whom base their response only on the height cue, others only on the width cue. This all-or-none hypothesis can be ruled out fairly simply, however, by obtaining two or more replications and demonstrating significant main effects in individual subject analyses.

A trickier version of this averaging objection states that each individual responds to only one cue at a time but to different cues on different trials. This will produce parallelism and significant main effects in the individual analyses even though there is no actual integration. This no-integration hypothesis can be ruled out with a variability analysis. In the example of Figure 4.5, responses to the 7 × 11 rectangle should be more variable than responses to the 9 × 9 rectangle because the effective cue value varies from trial to trial in the former case but not in the latter (see Section 4.2.2).

Such single-cue responding presents a potential problem in studies with young children or animal subjects. Studies to date, however, have shown unexpectedly good integrational capacity in young children (Anderson & Butzin, 1978; Anderson & Cuneo, 1978a).

Specific Comparisons. The test of the Row × Column interaction is a global, omnibus test against any and all possible deviations from the model. However, it is not sensitive to particular patterns of deviation and can therefore be misleading. If such patterns are anticipated, it is often possible to increase power by testing corresponding components of the interaction. In such cases, the omnibus test might well be superfluous.

In practice, deviations from parallelism are often concentrated in the linear × linear or linear × quadratic components of the interaction. These can be tested as shown in Section 2.2.2. It is simpler, however, to adopt any approximate a priori scaling of the stimulus levels and to employ standard orthogonal polynomial analysis. For example, the stimulus levels could be considered to be equally spaced in terms of rank order. This test is valid for its purpose of assessing deviations from parallelism and may actually be more powerful than the tests of Section 2.2.2. This test can lose power to the extent that the stimulus levels are not actually equally spaced, but this loss would ordinarily be small as long as the rank order is correct. At the same time, there is a gain in power because the unreliability in the estimated linear–quadratic coefficients is avoided (Note 2.2.2d).

Prediction from Estimated Parameters. Sometimes it is of interest to compare the observed cell means with the predicted values obtained from the estimated scale values. From Eqs. (1), it follows that

$$R_{ij} = \check{R}_{i.} + \check{R}_{.j} - \check{R}_{..}. \tag{2}$$

This predictive scheme generalizes directly to multifactor designs. In a three-factor design, for example, the corresponding formula is

$$R_{ijk} = \bar{R}_{i..} + \bar{R}_{.j.} + \bar{R}_{..k} - 2\bar{R}_{...}.$$

Triangular Designs. In certain tasks, it may be possible and desirable to pair each stimulus with every other stimulus although not necessarily with itself. Paired-comparison preference judgments is one such task and leads to a triangular type design.

The subtracting model for preference judgments in a triangular design was studied in a pioneering paper by Scheffé (1952), although not much has been done with it since (see Shanteau & Anderson, 1969). An analysis of the adding model for paired combinations was given by Anderson (1962c, 1972b). For triangular designs, the adding and subtracting models are not statistically equivalent as they are for factorial designs. Bechtel (1967a,b) presents a development of this topic.

Triangular designs seem to have limited usefulness in the study of linear models. Preference judgments do not require a triangular, paired-comparison design; a factorial design, with different stimuli in each factor, will ordinarily be simpler, more informative, and require fewer pairings (e.g., Section F1.3.4). Furthermore, order or position effects are treated as an additive constant in triangular designs, whereas the evidence indicates that they should be represented by a multiplicative weight parameter (Section 3.6), or with a more complex representation (Carterette & Anderson, 1979).

Identifiability. When the factorial data matrix exhibits parallelism, it can be expressed in additive form, as shown explicitly in Eqs. (1). The marginal means may be identified as scale values because they add up to reproduce the given data matrix (Eq. [2]). However, the possibility must be considered that some other, quite different set of stimulus values would also add up to reproduce the given data matrix. Both sets of scale values would be equally good, therefore, and the choice between them would be arbitrary. The following elementary argument resolves this question of uniqueness.

Let $\bar{s}_{Ai}$ and $\bar{s}_{Bj}$ denote one set of stimulus parameters, and let $g(S_{Ai})$ and $h(S_{Bj})$, where g and h are arbitrary functions of the physical stimuli, denote another. From Eqs. (1) and by assumption

$$R_{ij} = C_0 + \bar{s}_{Ai} + \bar{s}_{Bj} = g(S_{Ai}) + h(S_{Bj}).$$

Fix i, so $\bar{s}_{Ai}$ and $g(S_{Ai})$ are both constant, and denote their difference by c_1. Then the above equation yields

$$h(S_{Bj}) = \tilde{s}_{Bj} + C_0 + c_1.$$

Thus, $h(S_{Bj})$ actually equals $\tilde{s}_{Bj}$, plus a constant, which shows that any two sets of scale values of $\tilde{s}_{Bj}$ are equivalent. Similarly

$$g(S_{Ai}) = \tilde{s}_{Ai} + C_0 + c_2.$$

Substituting the last two equations into the first and rearranging implies $c_1 + c_2 + C_0 = 0$. Hence

$$g(S_{Ai}) = \tilde{s}_{Ai} - c + C_0/2,$$
$$h(S_{Bj}) = \tilde{s}_{Bj} + c + C_0/2,$$

where $c = c_1 + C_0/2$ is a constant. Thus, the gross stimulus parameters are unique up to an additive constant of equal and opposite value for row and column variables (see also Aczél, 1966).

Estimation of Weights. When the same stimulus values apply to each factor of a multifactor design, the linear model can provide estimates of weights as well as of scale values. Let $X = 1, 2, \cdot \cdot \cdot, N$ index the design factors, and let $t = 1, 2, \cdot \cdot \cdot, T$ index the stimulus levels within each factor. It is assumed that weights are equal within each factor and that scale values are equal across factors: $w_{Xt} = w_X$ for all t, and $s_{Xt} = s_t$ for all X. Then the marginal means for factor X can be written

$$R_{Xt} = C_X + w_X s_t,$$

where C_X depends on the weights of the other factors.

The N sets of these marginal means constitute a two-way, $N \times T$ design. In this two-way design, the means of the T factor provide a linear scale of the common stimulus values that is more reliable than the marginal means of any one design factor. For each X, the values of R_{Xt} are a linear function of these scale values with slope proportional to w_X. These slopes estimate the weight parameters on a ratio scale. This relationship is useful in estimating weights in serial integration tasks, especially with psychophysical stimuli for which the assumption of equal scale values across serial positions is reasonable (Section 3.6; Anderson, 1964c,d).

This case has also been considered by Bogartz (1982), who points out that it allows a test of the assumption of equal weighting within each design factor. The test of additivity on the complete design does not detect unequal weighting because of the confounding of weight and value discussed previously. With unequal weighting, however, the marginal means for two design factors will not in general be linearly related. Bogartz presents a likelihood ratio test of the null hypothesis of equal weighting, and the analysis of Section 3.4 is also applicable. This case is interesting because it shows how weight parameters can be meaningful even within the strict additive model.

A Nondetectable Interaction. The test of goodness of fit is not a simple test of the model per se, but rather a test of a compound hypothesis that the model is correct and that the independence assumption holds. Success in the test of fit is ordinarily taken to support both parts of the compound hypothesis. In particular, therefore, success in the test of fit is ordinarily considered evidence against the presence of stimulus interaction.

However, a linear interaction is not detectable by the parallelism test for a linear model. The model

$$R_{ij} = (s_{Ai} + c_1 s_{Bj}) + (s_{Bj} + c_2 s_{Ai}),$$

where c_1 and c_2 are constants, explicitly contains an interaction in which the scale value of each stimulus shifts as a linear function of the scale value of the other stimulus. This model can be rewritten

$$R_{ij} = (1 + c_2)s_{Ai} + (1 + c_1)s_{Bj}.$$

This is the form of a simple linear model, and therefore the R_{ij} will exhibit parallelism.

A linear interaction can depend only on the scale values, not on further specific relations among the stimuli. Inconsistency and redundancy interactions would not ordinarily be linear, since they depend on specific semantic relations among the stimuli. However, assimilation and contrast effects might give rise to linear interactions. An interesting instance of this problem arose in the change-of-meaning issue in person perception (Sections F3.2 and F4.1).

Cognitive Units. Implicit in the statement of the linear model is the assumption that the row and column variables correspond to operative cognitive units. It is possible, however, that the integration obeys a linear model but with different cognitive units. In this case, the data may not exhibit parallelism.

To illustrate this issue, consider the task of judging motion-time of balls rolling down an inclined plane. These judgments will depend on travel distance down the plane and initial height of the ball above the base level of the plane. An adding rule might be expected with children (see Figure 4.5). Hence a Distance × Height design will yield parallelism—if Distance and Height are the cognitive units.

But the slope, or steepness of the plane may be more salient than height. Subjects may actually obey a Distance + Steepness rule. In that case, a Distance × Steepness design will exhibit parallelism, but the Distance × Height design will not; the response in each cell will be the Distance term plus a Steepness = Height/Distance term that will not be constant for a fixed level of Height.

An adding process is thus not sufficient to produce parallelism. To obtain parallelism, it may also be necessary to match the terms of the model and the factors of the design to the operative cognitive units. Observed parallelism may thus confer a degree of construct validity on the terms of the model that would not otherwise be available. An empirical illustration is given by the Height + Width rule in children's judgments of area (Anderson, 1980a, pp. 14–15, in press-a).

Model analysis can thus be helpful in establishing construct validity for the stimulus and response terms of the model. Of course, distinct cues can act jointly as a molar unit without any further psychological unity (see also Sections F1.1.5, F1.6.5, and F1.8.2).[a]

2.2 Multiplying Models

2.2.1 MODEL AND PARAMETERS

For a two-way factorial design, the multiplying model may be written

$$R_{ijx} = C_0 + s_{Ai}s_{Bj} + e_{ijx}, \tag{3}$$

where the notation is similar to that of the linear model of Eqs. (1). The error term is treated as additive, an assumption that has some support for the kinds of experiments under consideration (e.g., Anderson & Shanteau, 1970).[a]

The multiplying model is harder to work with than the linear model because the parallelism property no longer holds. If the s_{Bj} were known, then each row of data would plot as a straight-line function of the s_{Bj} with slope s_{Ai}; if the s_{Ai} were known, then each column of data would plot as a straight-line function of s_{Ai} with slope s_{Bj}. The data would exhibit the form of a linear fan except for error variability. Unfortunately, neither the s_{Bj} nor the s_{Ai} are ordinarily known a priori. Nevertheless, this linear fan idea can be pursued to a successful conclusion.

The essential idea is that the model itself can provide the scale values needed for the test of fit. Ignoring error and averaging Eq. (3) over rows yields

$$\bar{R}_{.j} = C_0 + \bar{s}_A s_{Bj}. \tag{4}$$

If the model is correct and the observed response is on a linear scale, then Eq. (4) provides estimates of the column stimulus parameters. Thus, the marginal means of the factorial design provide linear scales of the stimuli.

Each row of data will plot as a straight-line function of the column means, error variability being ignored. From Eqs. (3) and (4),

$$R_{ij} = C_0 - (s_{Ai}/\bar{s}_A)C_0 + (s_{Ai}/\bar{s}_A)\bar{R}_{.j}. \tag{5}$$

For row i, Eq. (5) says that R_{ij} is a linear function of $\bar{R}_{.j}$. The intercept and slope depend only on i and so are constant in each row. The set of row curves constitute a linear fan having a common point of intersection. The multiplying model thus implies a simple relationship between two observables, R_{ij} and $\bar{R}_{.j}$. This linear fan relation provides the basis for analysis.

This discussion may be formalized as the following theorem.

Linear Fan Theorem. *Suppose that the multiplying model holds, so that $r_{ij} = s_{Ai}s_{Bj}$, and that the observable response is a linear function of the implicit response, so that $R_{ij} = C_0 + C_1 r_{ij}$. Then the row and column marginal means of the response matrix will constitute linear scales of the subjective values of the stimulus variables, and the appropriate factorial plot of the observable response will exhibit a linear fan pattern.*

An observed linear fan thus supports both premises of the theorem: If either premise is incorrect, the linear fan pattern will not, in general, be obtained. It is logically possible, of course, for violations of the two premises to cancel each other. There is also a uniqueness problem, noted in Section 2.2.3. Subject to these qualifications, however, an observed linear fan accomplishes three simultaneous goals:

1. It supports the multiplying model.
2. It supports response linearity.
3. It provides linear stimulus scales.

2.2.2 STATISTICAL ANALYSIS

Bilinear and Residual Components. If the multiplying model holds, then there is real Row × Column interaction. However, this interaction should be concentrated in the bilinear component, and the residual component should be nonsignificant. To establish the multiplying model, both tests are required.

The statistical details of the test of the multiplying model are somewhat complicated, more so for correlated than for independent responses. These details are considered in the next three subsections. All cases employ the same formula for calculating the algebraic value of the bilinear component, so this is given first.

Suppose that there are n scores in each cell of the design, with T_{ij} the sum of the n scores in cell ij. The algebraic value of the bilinear component is denoted by LL and has the expression

$$LL = \Sigma\Sigma l_i l_j T_{ij} / \sqrt{n\Sigma\Sigma(l_i l_j)^2} \, , \tag{6}$$

where

$$l_i = \bar{R}_{i.} - \bar{R}_{..}, \quad \text{and} \quad l_j = \bar{R}_{.j} - \bar{R}_{..}.$$

The l_i are the row means expressed as deviations from the grand mean. They are the linear polynomial coefficients, relative to the subjective metric for the row stimulus. The same holds for the column deviations, l_j. In each cell of the design, the coefficient for the bilinear component is just the product of the corresponding row and column deviation scores. These product coefficients sum to zero and plot as a linear fan in the stimulus metric. Thus, LL differs from zero to the extent that the cell entries, T_{ij}, correlate with this linear fan defined by the marginal means.

Independent Responses. Statistical analysis of the bilinear and residual components is complicated by the fact that the coefficients for the bilinear component are calculated from the data. Since their sampling error must be taken into account, the statistical theory is more difficult than for ordinary orthogonal polynomial analysis in which the coefficients are known constants. When the responses are statistically independent, however, the F ratios for the bilinear and residual components can still be interpreted in the usual way under the assumptions of homonormality.[a]

The sum of squares for the bilinear component is given by

$$SS_{\text{Bilinear}} = LL^2. \tag{7}$$

This is simply the square of the algebraic value of the bilinear component in the numerator of Eq. (6), divided by the customary normalizing factor that puts it on the same scale as the overall interaction. This bilinear sum of squares has 1 df. The residual sum of squares is obtained by subtracting the bilinear sum of squares from the overall interaction sum of squares. Its degrees of freedom are one less than for the overall interaction. There is a single error term, based on within-cell variability, and it is used in all the statistical tests.

The standard case of independent responses arises when each subject serves under one condition and contributes one score to a single cell of the design. Such tests will not often be useful, however, in part because individual differences limit power, in part because the bilinear test assumes common subjective stimulus metrics across subjects.

Individual Subject Analysis. Individual subject data are often treated as independent responses and analyzed as indicated in the preceding subsection. Most initial tests of the multiplying model were made in this way, with each subject receiving the complete factorial design two or more times (e.g., Anderson & Shanteau, 1970). This approach assumes that responses are equivalent across replications and differ only because of response variability. If there were substantial changes in stimulus parameters across successive replications, then the analysis of the next subsection might be required, with replications treated as subjects.

Correlated Responses. The usual case of correlated responses arises in repeated measurements designs in which each subject serves in all conditions. The responses in any two cells are then correlated across subjects owing to differences in their individual value systems. Similar correlation may apply to several replications from a single subject if there is substantial fluctuation in parameter values across replications. In either case, the correlation among the scores complicates the analysis.

In principle, the analysis should parallel that of ordinary trend tests for repeated measurements designs. Thus, the Row × Column interaction would be broken down into bilinear and residual components, with a corresponding breakdown of the Row × Column × Subjects error term. Unfortunately, the residuals are biased by individual differences in parameter values. There are three ways to handle this problem.

The first way to get a proper test of goodness of fit is to break down the Row × Column interaction into its polynomial components. Two illustrative components will be considered here, the linear × linear and the linear × quadratic.[b]

The linear × linear (or bilinear) component is computed separately from the data for each subject, using the formulas of Eq. (6), with n denoting the number of scores in each design cell for the given subject. The magnitude of the LL score is an index of the amount of linear fanning in each subject's data. If the multiplying model holds, these LL scores are systematically different from zero. Accordingly, a test of the null hypothesis that the true mean LL score is zero constitutes a necessary condition for the model. This null hypothesis is subject to the usual t or F test. The sum of squares for the bilinear component on 1 df is

$$SS_{L \times L} = (\Sigma LL)^2/N, \qquad (8)$$

where the sum is over the N subjects. It has the standard error term on $N - 1$ df

$$SS_{L \times L \times \text{Subjects}} = \Sigma LL^2 - SS_{L \times L}. \qquad (9)$$

The ratio of the two corresponding mean squares may be treated as an F ratio on $(1, N - 1)$ df.

The linear $\times$ quadratic component is treated in an exactly similar way to obtain an LQ score for each subject

$$LQ = \Sigma\Sigma l_i q_j T_{ij} / \sqrt{n\Sigma\Sigma(l_i q_j)^2}. \qquad (10)$$

The l_i are computed as in Eq. (6). The q_j are the quadratic coefficients, computed to be orthogonal to the linear l_j (Keppel, 1973; Weiss, 1980b). If the model is correct, then the true mean LQ score is zero. This null hypothesis is subject to the usual t or F test. The systematic and error sums of squares are

$$SS_{L \times Q} = (\Sigma LQ)^2/N, \qquad (11)$$

and

$$SS_{L \times Q \times \text{Subjects}} = \Sigma LQ^2 - SS_{L \times Q}. \qquad (12)$$

The ratio of the two corresponding mean squares is an F ratio on $(1, N - 1)$ df. The QL, QQ, and other polynomial components may be handled in the same way.

If the multiplying model holds, then the LL component should be significant, whereas all other polynomial components should be nonsignificant. If no components are significant, then the simpler linear model may apply. If the multiplying model is otherwise incorrect, then the deviations would generally be expected to appear in the lower order components, and only these would ordinarily be tested. These calculations may be performed using the POLYLIN program described later.

The second way to test the multiplying model employs the general test for nonlinear models (see Section 4.4). Equation (3), including the C_0 term, would be fitted separately for each subject to obtain a matrix of deviations from the best-fit model for each subject. If the model holds, then the true mean of these deviation scores is zero in every cell of the design. Applying analysis of variance for repeated measurements to these deviation scores should yield all nonsignificant effects. This tests only the residual from the model; a separate test would be needed to establish a significant degree of linear fanning. This could be done by testing the bilinear component or even the overall interaction term in the raw data. No applications of this second procedure seem to have been made.

The third way to test the multiplying model is to use the parallel to ordinary trend tests already noted. Equations (8) and (9) may be used to calculate systematic and error sums of squares for the bilinear component. Systematic and error sums of squares for the residual interaction would then be obtained by subtraction

$$SS_{A \times B: \text{ Residual}} = SS_{A \times B} - SS_{L \times L}, \tag{13}$$

$$SS_{A \times B \times \text{ Subjects: Residual}} = SS_{A \times B \times \text{ Subjects}} - SS_{L \times L \times \text{ Subjects}}. \tag{14}$$

These sums of squares have $(I - 1)(J - 1) - 1$ and $(N - 1)[(I - 1)(J - 1) - 1]$ df, respectively, where I, J, and N are the number of rows, columns, and subjects. The ratio of the corresponding mean squares would then be treated as an F ratio with the listed df.

Unfortunately, due to individual differences in parameter values, this third method has a bias in the test of the residual. In a 2×3 design, for example, the interaction has 2 df and can be broken down into bilinear and residual on 1 df each. This residual, however, will not in general equal the linear $\times$ quadratic component computed separately from Eq. (12).

The initial studies of the multiplying model in this research program used individual subject analysis. A few subsequent tests with group data either relied on the graphical test or used the biased test just outlined. It was thought at the time that the bias would be negligible, but later results have indicated that the bias can be serious, especially in small designs. Nearly all the experiments in question have been reanalyzed using the first method to test the various linear–quadratic components, but only a few minor changes in the conclusions have resulted.[c]

The preceding test procedures deserve one or two additional comments. The writer has shown that the individual LL scores are unbiased estimates, subject only to the assumptions that the error terms, e_{ijx}, have a common symmetric distribution across cells and are independent within each individual subject (or within each replication for an individual subject analysis). Accordingly, the individual LL scores allow a valid test of the bilinear component. Since the LQ score is orthogonal to the LL score, it allows a valid test of the residual. It may be added that the use of these polynomial component scores effectively reduces the repeated measurements design to the more robust case of independent responses.

It is not correct to test the bilinear component against the error term for the overall interaction. Individual differences often concentrate in the bilinear component, causing its proper error term to be markedly larger than the error term for the overall interaction. Using the overall error term will produce too many significant results.

Extraction of the error term for the bilinear component will generally reduce the residual error. Strictly speaking, therefore, it is also incorrect to use the overall error to test the residual interaction, for that would yield F's that are somewhat too small. However, the effect of this bias decreases with the size of the design because it is averaged over the residual df. For larger designs—say, with more than 10 df for residual interaction—this biased test may be adequate, at least for initial investigations.

POLYLIN. An extension of Shanteau's (1977) POLYLIN program provides a convenient method for testing goodness of fit for the multiplying model; indeed, for the general class of multilinear models described in Section 3.3. The program computes linear and quadratic components of the interactions, as illustrated in Eqs. (6) and (10). It assumes a complete repeated measurements design but allows up to four stimulus variables as well as replication within each subject. The multilinear components are obtained for all interactions, as are the linear × quadratic and quadratic × quadratic components of all two-factor interactions. Tests of fit may be performed at the individual or group levels, following the guidelines indicated above (see Note 2.2.2c).

Individual tests rest on the assumption that the responses are independent, as already discussed. POLYLIN provides sums of squares for the indicated polynomial components of the various interactions. A separate analysis of variance for each individual is also required in order to obtain sums of squares for the overall interactions as well as the common error term. This error term may be used to test each polynomial component as well as the interaction residuals.

Group tests employ the algebraic LL and LQ components defined in Eqs. (6) and (10), the analogous QQ component, and the trilinear and quartilinear components. These are obtained for each individual, and a separate statistical test is made on the null hypothesis that the true mean over subjects of each component is zero, as illustrated in Eqs. (8) and (9). These polynomial interaction tests may also be applied to the multilinear models of Section 3.3 for testing goodness of fit for both adding and multiplying operations.[a]

This program has recently been put in general form by Weiss (1980b, 1982). The Weiss–Shanteau POLYLIN allows up to four design factors and can provide a complete breakdown of each interaction into orthogonal polynomial components for each individual. Besides individual subject analyses, general POLYLIN allows specific tests of selected interaction components on a group basis as well as a valid group test of all residual interactions.

2.2.3 OTHER CONSIDERATIONS OF DESIGN AND ANALYSIS

Distribution-Free Tests. Distribution-free tests of the multiplying model follow the rationale indicated in Section 2.1.2. In a repeated measurements design, for example, the LL score would be calculated using Eq. (6). A signed-ranks test could then be applied instead of analysis of variance. The same procedure could be used to test components of the residual interaction, such as the LQ score of Eq. (10). Distribution-free tests may deserve more consideration because results from the present research program have suggested that a few individuals may yield rather deviant LL scores.

Stimulus Selection. The statistical analysis treats the physical stimuli as nominal, so no prior scaling is necessary. As with the linear model, the stimulus values are derivative from the analysis and need not be known beforehand.

Even more than for the linear model, however, the cogency of the experiment depends on judicious choice of stimulus levels, especially for small designs. A 2×3 design is the smallest to allow a complete test of the multiplying model; it breaks down the interaction on 2 df into linear $\times$ linear and linear $\times$ quadratic components. However, if two of the three column levels are nearly equal in effective value, the design effectively reduces almost to a 2×2, and the test of the residual probably has little power. Again, if one row stimulus has zero value in a $2 \times J$ design, that row of data will plot as a horizontal line, and the two rows necessarily follow the linear fan form.

Averaging over subjects can cause problems because the subjective spacing of the stimuli on the horizontal axis that yields the linear fan pattern may vary across subjects. This problem has not seemed serious for experiments such as those illustrated in Figure 4.2, in which the stimuli have approximately the same metric across subjects. However, it could be serious if the subjective values had different rank orders across subjects. Pilot work is nearly always advisable, therefore, and it may be necessary to preselect stimuli on an individual basis (see also Section 1.3.5).

More Efficient Stimulus Estimates. A practical difficulty can arise when the s_{Ai} (or the s_{Bj}) have both positive and negative values. Suppose that the true mean $\bar{s}_A$ is exactly zero in Eq. (4). Then the observed differences among the column means, $\bar{R}_{.j}$, are mere error variability, useless for estimating the scale values. Something of the same problem remains even if the true $\bar{s}_A$ is not exactly zero (see e.g., Figure F1.16).

A complementation method can be applied to this problem. The entries in each downward sloping row may be subtracted from some convenient constant such as the upper end point of the response scale. That makes the slope positive but leaves its magnitude unchanged. The column means are therefore still a linear scale for the s_{Bj}, but with lower relative variance than the original data matrix. Hence the power of the test of the linear fan pattern is increased. The complementation is only used for parameter estimation; the test of fit itself is performed on the original data.

By the preceding argument, any row that has zero slope merely adds variability to the estimates. Similarly, rows with relatively small slope may do more harm than good. Such rows should therefore be omitted when estimating the column means, although an a priori decision would ordinarily be needed to avoid possible selection bias. The question of how large the slope needs to be for its inclusion to be beneficial has not been studied.

Adding–Multiplying Model. In some tasks it is a reasonable hypothesis that the same stimulus may have both adding and multiplying effects. This more general model may be written

$$R_{ij} = w_0 + w_A s_{Ai} + w_B s_{Bj} + s_{Ai} s_{Bj}, \tag{15}$$

where the coefficient w_{AB} of the product term has been set at unity for simplicity. The zero points of the stimulus scales may be changed as follows. Let

$$s'_{Ai} = s_{Ai} + w_B, \tag{16}$$

$$s'_{Bj} = s_{Bj} + w_A, \tag{17}$$

$$C_0 = w_0 - w_A w_B. \tag{18}$$

Substitution into Eq. (15) yields the same multiplying model

$$R_{ij} = C_0 + s'_{Ai} s'_{Bj}. \tag{19}$$

Equations (15) and (19) are thus linearly equivalent and so cannot be distinguished by the given tests of goodness of fit (Anderson, 1970b). This equivalence has the great advantage that the tests do not require knowledge of the stimulus zeros, but it leaves an open substantive question in certain tasks. In the experiment shown in Figure 6.3, for example, dating preference was hypothesized to be the product of attractiveness and probability. It seems reasonable to expect, however, that attractiveness might also have an adding effect. Again, in developmental studies of the general purpose adding rule of Figure 4.5, it is an open question whether the transition to the adult multiplying rule is all-or-none or represents an evolving compromise wherein the two rules act jointly.

To assess this more general model requires collateral information about the stimulus zeros. This information could be combined with the marginal means to obtain ratio scales of the stimuli, and these stimulus variables could be used in a structural regression for R_{ij}. Significant additive components would then imply genuine adding effects. To obtain such collateral information would seem relatively straightforward for the stimulus variables in the cited experiments, although no analyses of this kind seem to have been made. Probabilistic all-or-none transition could presumably be assessed with a variance argument like that of Section 2.1.4.

Logarithmic Transformation. A logarithmic transformation is sometimes suggested as a device to reduce a multiplying model to an adding model. This would allow the simpler parallelism analysis of Section 2.1. However, this device has limited usefulness.

From Eq. (3) it can be seen that the logarithmic transformation produces additivity only when $C_0 = 0$. In other words, the response must be on a ratio scale. Furthermore, the stimulus values must all be positive (or all negative), because the logarithm of negative numbers is not defined. Also, the error term in Eq. (3) must be multiplicative rather than additive, contrary to existing data. Finally, the log transformation has limited generality since it does not apply to the compound multilinear models of Section 3.3.

Uniqueness.[a] A peculiarity of the multiplying model is that the derived stimulus values may be unique only up to a power transformation. To illustrate, suppose that $r_{ij} = s_{Ai}s_{Bj}$ with positive stimulus values. Then $R_{ij} = r_{ij}^n = s_{Ai}^n s_{Bj}^n$ also has the multiplying form and will also obey the linear fan analysis. In other words, the linear fan theorem holds even when the observed response is a power function of the implicit response. The test of the multiplying model still applies, of course. However, the scale value estimates may not be a linear scale but only a power function of the true scale values.

This lack of uniqueness may be remedied in various ways. Since it does not affect linear models, one remedy is to incorporate an adding operation, if feasible, to obtain a multilinear model of the form $AB + C$ (Model 5 of Section 3.3). Perhaps the simplest remedy, however, is an appeal to response generality (Section 3.1). The linearity of the rating response has been established in numerous experiments with other models that disallow the power uniqueness problem. For most judgment tasks considered in this book, therefore, this nonuniqueness would seem to be mainly a mathematical oddity.

Averaging Bias in Stimulus Values. The expression for the marginal means in Eq. (4) may be biased if the data are averaged over a group of subjects with different values of the stimulus parameters. In general, the average value of a product is not equal to the product of the average values

$$\text{Ave}(s_{Ai}s_{Bj}) \neq \text{Ave}(s_{Ai})\text{Ave}(s_{Bj}). \tag{20}$$

If the data are averaged over subjects with different values of the stimulus parameters, the marginal means of the data table will not equal the means of the stimulus parameters. Pooling data across a group of subjects, although desirable for greater reliability, may introduce a bias in the parameter estimation procedure. This problem of averaging bias in group data may not be serious, but it needs to be kept in mind.

Predicting from Estimated Parameters. With error variability ignored, Eq. (3) implies

$$R_{ij} - C_0 = (\bar{R}_{i.} - C_0)(\bar{R}_{.j} - C_0)/(\bar{R}_{..} - C_0). \tag{21}$$

Thus, the cell means are predictable from the marginal means if the constant C_0 is estimated and if $\bar{R}_{..} - C_0$ is not equal to zero. It may be useful, therefore, to try to establish the zero point on the response scale from auxiliary considerations. The statistical properties of this prediction procedure have not been studied, however, and variability in the estimated denominator could be a serious problem. Hence it may be preferable to use the direct approach of Section 4.4.

Ratio Scaling. The multiplying model allows for estimation of the psychological zero points of the stimulus and response scales under certain conditions. The zero level of s_{Ai} is that value that produces a horizontal curve. Prior knowledge about the stimulus metric can be used to select the zero level stimulus or to interpolate between positive and negative values, that is, between upward and downward sloping curves in the linear fan. Possession of these zero points can be helpful for certain questions: comparing two sets of scale values, for example, or testing the adding–multiplying model of Eq. (15).

The zero point in the response scale is defined by C_0 in Eq. (3). This can be determined if some s_{Ai} is zero, as indicated by a horizontal curve, for then $R_{ij} = C_0$, so C_0 is the negative of the true response zero and $R_{ij} - C_0$ is a ratio scale. Or the zero might be determined by extrapolation to the intersection point of the linear fan (e.g., Figure F1.18).

Comparing Two Sets of Scale Values. In some situations, estimated scale values of the same set of stimuli may be obtained in two different ways. In psychophysical judgment, for example, the question arises whether sensation scales obtained from bisection are the same as those obtained from averaging (Figure 3.1 of Section 3.1; see also Note 3.1b). In decision theory and general multiattribute models, a basic question is whether self-estimated scale values are equivalent to the functional scales (Table 6.2 of Section 6.2).

The null hypothesis in each case is that the two sets of estimates are linearly equivalent. Ordinary linear regression is not appropriate, of course, since it ignores variability in whichever estimates are used as the predictor variable. However, the linear fan test is applicable. The row factor corresponds to the two estimation methods, and the column factor corresponds to the common stimuli. Equation (3) is then applicable, with s_{Bj} as the stimulus values and s_{Ai} representing the scale units for the two methods.

Interest would usually center on the linear × quadratic and perhaps the linear × cubic terms. These may be tested according to the type of design (Section 2.2.2). To compare equivalence of more than two sets of scale values simultaneously requires a semilinear model because both zero point and unit will depend on the method (these correspond to A_i and A'_i in Eq. (1) of Section 3.4). With only two sets of estimates, the semilinear model reduces to a multiplying model.

Note on Power. The linear fan analysis provides a provisional set of stimulus values that best fit the multiplying model to the data. This is a solid advantage; failure of the model cannot then be attributed to shortcomings in the stimulus values.

Concern sometimes arises that this analysis may force almost any set

TABLE 2.1
Illustrative Deviations from Linear Fan Pattern

		A			B			C		
										Example
Row 1	2	4	6	2	4	8	2	4	6	(6)
Row 2	4	8	12	4	8	10	4	8	9	(16)
Means	3	6	9	3	6	9	3	6	7.5	(11)

NOTE: Each example represents a 2 × 3 design.

of data into the linear fan pattern. This is clearly not the case because parallel data will remain parallel under the linear fan analysis. Better appreciation of the limits of the linear fan analysis can be gained by considering some numerical examples.

Three examples for a 2 × 3 design are given in Table 2.1 and Figure 2.1. Example A obeys the multiplying model, because the second row is twice the first row. Each row is plotted as a function of the marginal means in Panel A and exhibits the linear fan pattern.

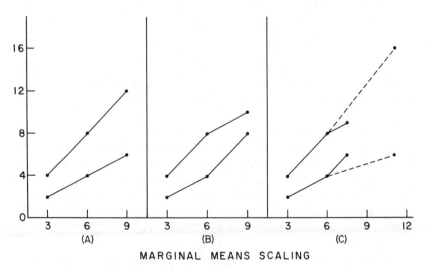

MARGINAL MEANS SCALING

FIGURE 2.1. *Linear fan analysis is sensitive to real deviations from the multiplying model. Panel A presents linear fan analysis of data from a 2 × 3 design that obeys a multiplying model. The third column of data is then altered in three different ways so that the data no longer obey the multiplying model, as shown in Table 2.1. Linear fan analyses of these altered data, presented in Panels B and C, do not exhibit the linear fan pattern, thereby illustrating the power of linear fan analysis to detect incorrect models.*

Example B is the same as Example A except in the third column, in which one entry has been increased by 2, the other decreased by 2. The column means remain the same, but the factorial graph now assumes the barrel shape shown in Panel B of Figure 2.1. This barrel shape is quite distinct from a linear fan, and any change in the horizontal spacing would only accentuate the difference.

Example C embodies just one change from Example A: The lower right entry in Table 2.1 is changed from 12 to 9. This changes the marginal means and produces the stubby barrel shape indicated by the solid curves in Panel C of Figure 2.1. The complementary change, from 12 to 16, is given in parentheses in the table and by dashed lines in the figure. This change, although larger in magnitude, seems less marked. Overall, however, it seems clear that the linear fan analysis does not misrepresent the data even in this small design.

2.3 The Averaging Model

2.3.1 MODEL AND ANALYSES

In the averaging model, the response, R, to a stimulus combination or set is the weighted average

$$R = C_0 + \Sigma ws/\Sigma w. \tag{22}$$

Division by the sum of the absolute weights, Σw, normalizes the relative weights, $w/\Sigma w$, so that they sum to unity within each stimulus set. The independence assumption applies to the absolute weights and to the scale values. However, the relative weight of any one stimulus depends on the other stimuli in the set.

The sum in Eq. (22) is taken over all effective stimuli. These may be discrete stimuli manipulated by the investigator, as in the attitude experiment shown in Figure 4.3, or discriminable attributes of a unitary stimulus, as in the face judgments shown in Figure 6.3. The sum may include stimuli obtained from memory as well as external stimuli presented by the investigator. For many purposes, the internal stimuli can be treated as a molar unit S_0 with molar parameters w_0 and s_0. This is also called the prior belief or initial state, which plays a vital role in averaging theory.

Equal-Weight Case. Equal weighting means that all levels within each design factor have the same weight. In a two-factor design, for example

$$R_{ij} = C_0 + (w_0 s_0 + w_A s_{Ai} + w_B s_{Bj})/(w_0 + w_A + w_B). \tag{23}$$

Here w_A and w_B are the weights for the row and column factors; index subscripts are omitted to indicate constancy. The sum of weights in the denominator has the same value in all cells of the design and can be absorbed into the arbitrary scale unit. Accordingly, the model has a linear form and can be written

$$R_{ij} = C_0 + \bar{s}_0 + \bar{s}_{Ai} + \bar{s}_{Bj}, \tag{24}$$

where $\bar{s}$ denotes gross stimulus value, as in the linear model of Eq. (1b).

Essentially all results for linear models of Section 2.1 apply directly to the equal-weight case of the averaging model. The parallelism property holds, and the statistical analyses remain the same. Thus, the averaging model is easy to work with when the equal-weight condition can be satisfied.

Differential-Weight Case. In general, each stimulus may have its own weight as well as its own scale value. The sum of the absolute weights in the denominator of Eq. (22) is therefore variable across sets and the model becomes inherently nonlinear. The methods for dealing with nonlinear models given in Section 4.4 will be necessary for many analyses. Design considerations for identifiability of parameters are discussed in Section 2.3.2.

Semilinear Case. An interesting special case arises when the equal-weight condition applies to all design factors but one. If the column stimuli are equally weighted, so that $w_{Bj} = w_B$, and the row stimuli are differentially weighted, then the model may be written

$$R_{ij} = C_0 + (w_0 s_0 + w_{Ai} s_{Ai} + w_B s_{Bj})/(w_0 + w_{Ai} + w_B). \tag{25}$$

Several properties of this model deserve notice.

First, the mathematical form of Eq. (25) is that of a compound adding–multiplying model (Section 3.4). It can be rewritten as

$$R_{ij} = C_0 + (w_0 s_0 + w_{Ai} s_{Ai})/(w_0 + w_{Ai} + w_B)$$
$$+ w_B s_{Bj}/(w_0 + w_{Ai} + w_B). \tag{26}$$

With suitable change of notation, this becomes

$$R_{ij} = C_0 + A_i + B_j A_i', \tag{27}$$

in which A_i and A_i' depend only on the row stimulus, and B_j depends only on the column stimulus. The two-parameter role of the row stimulus is brought out more clearly in Eq. (27) than in Eq. (25).

Second, the column means give a linear measure of the scale values of the column stimuli. The average over rows is

$$\hat{R}_{.j} = c_1 + c_2 s_{Bj}, \tag{28}$$

where c_1 and c_2 are complicated constants whose exact expressions are not of present interest. By Eq. (28), s_{Bj} is a linear function of $\hat{R}_{.j}$, which establishes the result.

Third, each row of data should plot as a linear function of the column means. For fixed i, R_{ij} is a linear function of s_{Bj}, by Eq. (26), and hence also of $\hat{R}_{.j}$, by Eq. (28). This simple graphical test can be translated into an analysis of variance test (Section 3.4).

Finally, a linear scale of row weight is available (Anderson, 1971a, p. 184). By subtracting the theoretical responses for columns 1 and 2, for example, it follows that

$$\begin{aligned} w_{Ai} &= -(w_0 + w_B) + w_B(s_{B1} - s_{B2})/(R_{i1} - R_{i2}) \\ &= c_3 + c_4/(R_{i1} - R_{i2}). \end{aligned} \tag{29}$$

In practice, this equation has not been very useful, apparently because of statistical problems produced by the presence of the observed difference, $(R_{i1} - R_{i2})$, in the denominator. In principle, however, Eq. (29) does allow direct estimation of the weight parameters from the raw data. This illustrates a fundamental difference between averaging models and linear models: Weight parameters are identifiable within the averaging model even with a two-factor design.

2.3.2 IDENTIFIABILITY OF PARAMETERS

With suitable design, the averaging model can provide weight estimates of different stimuli that are on ratio scales with a common unit. Also, estimates of scale values can be obtained on linear scales with common zero and common unit. Stimuli of different quality can then be validly compared in importance and value.

However, suitable design is necessary. In the equal-weight case, for example, the averaging model reduces to a linear model, and so the weight parameters are not generally identifiable with data from a regular factorial design (Section 2.1). Since considerations of identifiability or uniqueness are often important in choice of experimental design, this matter requires detailed discussion.[a]

Maximal uniqueness may be obtained by using a family of partial designs, each of which includes only some of the variables. Estimation of w_0 and s_0 requires that set size or design size be varied. However, a suitably chosen family of partial designs of the same size can provide maximal uniqueness for the design variables themselves. A single design can provide linear scales either of weight or of scale value within each design factor.

Two-Factor Example. A simple illustration of the uniqueness problem for scale values with a two-factor design will be given first. For simplicity, w_0 is assumed to be zero, so the model becomes

$$R_{ij} = C_0 + (w_{Ai}s_{Ai} + w_{Bj}s_{Bj})/(w_{Ai} + w_{Bj}). \tag{30}$$

Empirically, the R_{ij} are observables, and the question is whether there exists some set of weights and scale values that will fit the observed data. If no such set exists, then of course the model is invalid. But if one such set exists, there might be others that do equally well. This is in fact the case. To illustrate this lack of uniqueness, let $\{w_{Ai}, s_{Ai}, w_{Bj}, s_{Bj}\}$ be one set of parameters that predicts the R_{ij} and satisfies Eq. (30). Let

$$
\begin{aligned}
w'_{Ai} &= w_{Ai}, \\
w'_{Bj} &= w_{Bj},
\end{aligned} \tag{31}
$$

$$
\begin{aligned}
s'_{Ai} &= s_{Ai} - b/w_{Ai}, \\
s'_{Bj} &= s_{Bj} + b/w_{Bj}.
\end{aligned} \tag{32}
$$

Then $\{w'_{Ai}, s'_{Ai}, w'_{Bj}, s'_{Bj}\}$ is another set of parameters that will also predict the R_{ij}. This may be shown by substituting the primed parameters in place of the unprimed values in Eq. (30). The terms in b cancel out, so the expression reduces back to Eq. (30). Every value of b thus gives a different set of scale values that will fit the data, and there is no way to choose among them on the basis of the given data.[b]

In the equal-weight case, the scale values are on linear scales because b/w_{Ai} and b/w_{Bj} are both constants in Eq. (32). This is necessary, of course, for the equal-weight case corresponds to a linear model. But if the weights are unequal within each design factor, then the scale values lose all uniqueness; the s'_{Ai} and the s_{Ai} may even have different rank orders.

A higher level of uniqueness can be achieved by obtaining judgments of single stimuli as well as of the pairs. Let R_i denote the response to the individual row stimuli alone. Since $w_0 = 0$ by assumption

$$R_i = w_{Ai}s_{Ai}/w_{Ai} = s_{Ai}. \tag{33}$$

However, the R_i are not predicted by the primed parameters of Eqs. (31) and (32) because $s'_{Ai} \neq s_{Ai}$ unless $b = 0$. When judgments of the single stimuli as well as their combinations are obtained, therefore, the nonuniqueness in the scale values is eliminated and the estimates are on a common linear scale. This illustrates the essential idea for obtaining uniqueness.

In practice, unfortunately, the initial state, s_0, cannot generally be neglected. Because of this term, which is required by the general averaging model, the response to a single stimulus does not equal its scale value (see Eq. [53] of Section 2.3.4). This markedly complicates the formal model analysis and the statistical estimation.

Uniqueness Result for Averaging Theory. To consider the general design case, it is convenient to change notation to let $X = 0, 1, 2, \cdots$, index the design factors, and let t index stimulus levels within design factors. The internal state, which is indexed by $X = 0$, is assumed to have only one level, s_0, with $w_0 \neq 0$. In this notation, the model is

$$R = C_0 + \Sigma_X w_{Xt} s_{Xt} / \Sigma_X w_{Xt}. \tag{34}$$

Consider a complete N-factor design in which the data obey this equation exactly. Let $\{w_{Xt}, s_{Xt}\}$ be one solution to this equation. Let

$$w'_{Xt} = w_{Xt} + a_X; \tag{35}$$

$$s'_{Xt} = s_{Xt} - (a_X s_{Xt} + b_X)/(w_{Xt} + a_X). \tag{36}$$

Here the a_X and b_X are constants for each design factor, subject to the condition that

$$\Sigma a_X = \Sigma b_X = 0. \tag{37}$$

Then $\{w'_{Xt}, s'_{Xt}\}$ is also a solution to Eq. (34) and will also account for the data exactly. This follows by substitution, just as illustrated in the two-factor example.

The level of uniqueness allowed by this single design may be adequate for some purposes. Equation (35) means that the weights for variable X involve an arbitrary additive constant, a_X, so the weights are on a linear scale within each design factor. Also, weight differences are comparable across design factors because a_X cancels on subtraction within each design factor.

The uniqueness properties of the scale values in the N-way design are the same as for the two-way design. When the weights within a design factor are unequal, then the scale values lose all uniqueness. When the weights are equal, then the scale values are on a linear scale. The N-way design can thus provide a linear scale of weights or of scale values, but not both.

The maximum level of uniqueness for the weights is a common ratio scale. The unit of this scale is arbitrary because all the weights may be multiplied by a constant without changing the model predictions.

The maximum level of uniqueness of the scale values is ordinarily a common linear scale. Ordinarily, the observable response measure is unique only up to a linear transformation; if it is changed by a linear transformation, the same transformation must be applied to the scale values in order to maintain the model. Moreover, a linear transformation between the observable response, R, and the implicit response, r, must also be allowed. In some situations, zero points may be determinable to yield a ratio scale. For the present discussion, however, the maximal uniqueness of scale values will be taken as a linear scale with common unit and common but unknown zero for all variables.

To eliminate the indeterminacies and attain maximal uniqueness for the parameters, it is necessary to force each a_X and b_X to be zero. That can be done by using a family of partial designs, each of which includes only some of the variables. Each partial design requires $\Sigma a_X = \Sigma b_X = 0$, where the sum is over only those variables included in that design. With suitable choice of partial designs, therefore, each individual a_X and b_X can be forced to be zero. This procedure will be illustrated for the cases of two, three, and four stimulus variables.

Two Stimulus Variables. By virtue of Eq. (37), the two-factor design requires that

$$a_0 + a_1 + a_2 = 0. \tag{38}$$

Similarly, the two one-factor designs impose the conditions

$$a_0 + a_1 = 0,$$
$$a_0 + a_2 = 0. \tag{39}$$

No other conditions are available, but these three are easily seen to imply $a_0 = a_1 = a_2 = 0$. Exactly the same holds for the b_X. The problem of identifiability can be solved, therefore, by judging the single stimuli together with their combinations. When the model is fit to all these data at once, the parameter estimates can attain maximal uniqueness.

In certain situations, as in psychophysical averaging, there is no prior information, and w_0 would naturally be fixed at zero in the model and in the estimation procedure. The model for the one-factor designs then reduces to $R = C_0 + w'_{Ai}s'_{Ai}/w'_{Ai} = C_0 + s'_{Ai}$, regardless of the value of w'_{Ai}. The scale values attain their maximum level of uniqueness in this design family, as indicated in the two-factor example. Moreover, since the scale values may be estimated directly, the model equations may be rewritten as a set of homogeneous linear equations of the form $(w_{Ai} + w_{Bj})R_{ij} = w_{Ai}R_i + w_{Bj}R_j$, and the weights are unique up to a scale unit. A similar approach applies to larger designs (see also Eqs. [48–49]).

Three Stimulus Variables. With three stimulus variables, there are three two-factor designs in addition to the complete three-factor design. These four designs impose the four conditions

$$a_0 + a_1 + a_2 + a_3 = 0, \tag{40}$$

$$a_0 + a_1 + a_2 \qquad = 0, \tag{41}$$

$$a_0 + a_1 \qquad + a_3 = 0, \tag{42}$$

$$a_0 \qquad + a_2 + a_3 = 0. \tag{43}$$

These four equations imply that $a_0 = a_1 = a_2 = a_3 = 0$, and similarly for the b_X. This family of designs thus provides maximal identifiability of the parameters.

Two special cases of smaller design families deserve mention. The first uses just the three two-factor designs. Only Eqs. (41)–(43) are available and they do not suffice to force the a_X to be zero. This case could be handled by arbitrarily setting $w_0 = 0$ in the actual estimation procedure. In effect, that sets $a_0 = -w_0$. Equations (41)–(43) then imply

$$a_1 = a_2 = a_3 = -w_0/2.$$

Thus, the weight estimates are on a linear scale with common unit and common but unknown zero point. A similar argument holds for the scale values.

The other special case uses the three-factor design and just one two-factor design, say with Variables 1 and 2. Equations (40) and (41) imply that $a_3 = 0$ and similarly $b_3 = 0$. These two designs thus provide maximal uniqueness for the parameters of Variable 3. This approach may be efficient when empirical questions about parameter values can be focused onto one variable.

Four Stimulus Variables. With four stimulus variables, there are six two-factor designs, four three-factor designs, the complete four-factor design, and the four one-factor designs. Only five designs are necessary for maximal identifiability, but not every five will suffice. For example, the four-factor design and the four two-factor designs with Variables 1 and 2, 3 and 4, 1 and 3, and 2 and 4 yield

$$\begin{aligned}
a_0 + a_1 + a_2 + a_3 + a_4 &= 0, \\
a_0 + a_1 + a_2 \qquad &= 0, \\
a_0 \qquad + a_3 + a_4 &= 0, \\
a_0 + a_1 \qquad + a_3 \qquad &= 0, \\
a_0 \qquad + a_2 + \qquad a_4 &= 0. \tag{44}
\end{aligned}$$

This family of designs is statistically attractive, since each variable occurs equally often. However, $a_0 = 0$, $a_1 = a_4 = 1$, $a_2 = a_3 = -1$ is a nonzero solution of these equations. Accordingly, these designs do not provide maximal uniqueness.

However, uniqueness can be obtained from the design family corresponding to the following conditions

$$
\begin{aligned}
a_0 + a_1 + a_2 + a_3 + a_4 &= 0, \\
a_0 + a_1 + a_2 &= 0, \\
a_0 + a_1 \phantom{{}+ a_2} + a_3 &= 0, \\
a_0 + a_1 \phantom{{}+ a_2 + a_3} + a_4 &= 0, \\
a_0 \phantom{{}+ a_1} + a_2 + a_3 &= 0.
\end{aligned}
\tag{45}
$$

Subtraction of the middle three equations from the first implies $a_0 + a_1 = 0$. The middle three equations then imply $a_2 = a_3 = a_4 = 0$. The last equation then implies $a_0 = 0$ and hence also $a_1 = 0$. The same results hold for the b_X, so maximal uniqueness can be obtained from this design family. It may not be statistically optimal, however, since Variable 1 occurs in four designs, Variable 4 in only two designs.

Comments. The value of w_0 cannot be estimated when all designs in the family have the same size. With four stimulus variables, for example, the six conditions from the six two-factor designs have the solution

$$
a_1 = a_2 = a_3 = a_4 = -a_0/2.
$$

Hence a_0 is arbitrary and would be set at some arbitrary value in the numerical analysis. It is straightforward to show that an analogous equation holds in general when all designs in the family have the same size. To estimate w_0, therefore, it is necessary to vary set size.

It may be preferable, of course, to use only one set size and to leave w_0 arbitrary. This can be done by setting $w_0 = 0$ in the estimation process, that is, by eliminating the initial state term from the model. The parameters for the manipulated stimulus variables can still attain maximal uniqueness.

The method of partial designs assumes that all responses are comparable. This may not be the case if sets of different size are judged in separate groups. By virtue of the set-size effect, the true range of subjective response will generally be greater for larger sets. However, subjects tend to spread overt ratings over the entire scale (Section 1.1.8). Thus, the observed range for a group of smaller sets would be greater when judged separately than when judged intermixed with larger sets. Although the parameter estimation might be extended to include a scaling constant to adjust for such differences in response range, it would seem generally preferable to present all the sets in intermixed order.

An incidental, general moral from the foregoing discussion is that the level of uniqueness depends critically on the experimental design. Discussions of measurement theory often assume that the scale type, which corresponds to level of uniqueness, resides in the response numbers per se or in their relation to the quantity being measured. The averaging model makes clear that the same data can have quite different scale properties in different designs.

Equal-Weight Case. When the levels within a variable are unequally weighted, a single design can provide linear scales of weights separately within each variable (Eq. [35]). This result is empty in the equal-weight case because it has only a single weight for all levels of each variable. Moreover, these weights are not even comparable across variables. Without auxiliary information, therefore, a single design yields no information about weights in the equal-weight case.

The method of partial designs, however, can provide a ratio scale of weight even in the equal-weight case. This is accomplished by choosing partial designs that will force each a_X in Eq. (35) to be zero in the manner indicated. The several w_X are then on a ratio scale with common unit and thus provide valid comparisons of importance of qualitatively different variables.

An interesting alternative approach to the equal-weight case is presented by Norman (1976a), who demonstrated a relationship between the weight parameters and mean squares from the analysis of variance. Norman considered the three two-factor designs obtainable from three stimulus variables. Variable 1 appears in two of these designs, and the theoretical expressions for the two corresponding mean squares in the analysis of variance are

$$MS_{1(1\times2)} = [w_1/(w_0 + w_1 + w_2)]^2\sigma_1^2,$$

$$MS_{1(1\times3)} = [w_1/(w_0 + w_1 + w_3)]^2\sigma_1^2, \qquad (46)$$

where $MS_{1(1\times X)}$ denotes the mean square for Variable 1 in the $1 \times X$ design ($X = 2, 3$), and σ_1^2 is the variance of the scale values of the levels of Variable 1.

Let c_1^2 denote the ratio of the two mean squares of Eqs. (46). Since σ_1^2 cancels in this ratio, c_1^2 is a function only of the weights and is constant, independent of any linear transformation on the scale values. Variables 2 and 3 may be treated similarly to yield the three equations

$$c_1 = (w_0 + w_1 + w_3)/(w_0 + w_1 + w_2),$$

$$c_2 = (w_0 + w_2 + w_3)/(w_0 + w_1 + w_2),$$

$$c_3 = (w_0 + w_2 + w_3)/(w_0 + w_1 + w_3). \qquad (47)$$

The unit of the weight scale may be set arbitrarily by requiring, say, $w_1 + w_2 + w_3 = 1$. However, only two of the three equations are independent, so one further condition is needed for a solution. Norman obtained this by setting $w_0 = 0$, which allows a linear scale although not a ratio scale for the other three weights. Further results yielded expressions for the scale values on a common linear scale.

This method is interesting because it provides closed expressions for the weights and scale values in terms of quantities from the analysis of variance. However, its practical value may be limited since, among other particulars, it requires equal weighting within each stimulus variable. With unequal weighting, iterative numerical methods are generally required (e.g., Birnbaum & Stegner, 1981; Leon, Oden, & Anderson, 1973; Norman, 1976b, 1979; Zalinski & Anderson, 1977, in press).

Comments. Although parameter estimation for the general averaging model is straightforward in principle, little is yet known about practical statistical problems. Reliability, bias, and robustness of the parameter estimates will depend jointly on the numerical analysis procedure and on the family of experimental designs. More empirical studies are needed, as well as studies with artificial data, for investigation of these statistical problems. The following comments touch on some relevant considerations.

One major problem is that it may be necessary to estimate parameters separately for each individual. It is tempting to use group means for greater stability, and that may be adequate to obtain a rough idea of relative magnitude. Weights estimated from group means, however, have a bias that appears to decrease differences among the weight estimates relative to the true individual means. Regardless of bias, valid significance tests cannot be obtained for weight estimates that are based on group data. Proper allowance for individual differences requires tests using individual estimates. It is desirable, therefore, to obtain enough judgments to ensure adequate reliability of the individual estimates.

Reliability of the estimates will depend on the structure of the design family. When w_0 is to be estimated, set size must be varied, but the optimal mode of variation is not known. When w_0 is not of interest, it can be fixed at zero if all sets have equal size. This eliminates the internal-state term that is common to the theoretical expression in every cell of the design, and may perhaps increase estimation stability.

Implicit Inferences. One possible problem with using partial designs is that subjects may make implicit inferences about "missing" variables. The preceding discussion assumed that the response to any set of information was an average of only the internal state and the stimuli explicitly given in the set. This seems reasonable when the various stimuli are similar in nature and contain no salient dimensional structure. The personality adjective task is of this type, and indeed the constancy of w across set size (Section F2.4) indicates that such implicit inferences did not occur in this task.

However, implicit inferences may occur when the dimensions or attributes are made salient so that lack of information on some attribute may be noticeable. One obvious possibility is that the missing information is inferred to have an average value or, more generally, the value of the expectancy associated with the internal state. A second possibility is that the missing information is inferred to have a value equal to the value of the given information. Both possibilities can be allowed for by taking w_0 as a function of set size.

Evidence for implicit inferences was reported by Zalinski and Anderson (1977, in press), who used four distinct, salient dimensions of job satisfaction. The responses to the most positive and negative two-cue combinations were more extreme than predicted, with a complementary result for four-cue combinations. This pattern is consistent with the hypothesis that missing information is inferred to have a value equal to the value of the given information. The effect was small; estimated weight for the inferred cue was about 5% of the weight of a given cue.

Strong implicit inferences were reported by Leon (1980) for children's judgments of deserved punishment from given information about an actor's intention and the damage caused by the actor. In one class of stimulus stories, implicit inferences were already present at the third-grade level. In another class of stories, the inferences did not develop fully even by seventh grade but were present in adults (see also Hommers & Anderson, in press). Evidence for implicit inferences about missing motivation information in attributional judgments of expected performance by adults is reported by Singh, Gupta, and Dalal (1979). Beyond their bearing on model analysis, these results illustrate how averaging theory can provide novel evidence on inference processes.

2.3.3 OTHER RESULTS ON THE AVERAGING MODEL

Regression Analysis. A potentially valuable regression-type analysis for the averaging model may be obtained with an extension of relations considered by Wyer (1969) and Hodges (1973) (see Section F2.4.4). From Eq. (34), the response to a set of n stimuli may be rewritten as

$$R = C_0 + (w_0 s_0 + \Sigma w_{Xt} s_{Xt})/(w_0 + \Sigma w_{Xt}).$$

Similarly, the response to a single stimulus is

$$R_{Xt} = C_0 + (w_0 s_0 + w_{Xt} s_{Xt})/(w_0 + w_{Xt}).$$

From this last equation, straightforward algebra yields

$$w_{Xt} s_{Xt} = (w_0 + w_{Xt})(R_{Xt} - C_0) - w_0 s_0.$$

Substitution into the first equation and simplification yield

$$R = [(1 - n)w_0(C_0 + s_0) + \Sigma(w_0 + w_{Xt})R_{Xt}]/(w_0 + \Sigma w_{Xt}). \quad (48)$$

The virtue of Eq. (48) is that the unobservable s_{Xt} have been replaced by the observable R_{Xt}. This opens up the possibility of substantial simplification in analysis and even in design. To illustrate, consider the equal-weight case, with $w_{Xt} = w_X$. The sum of the weights in the denominator is a constant and may be set equal to 1. Let

$$\alpha = (1 - n)w_0(C_0 + s_0), \qquad \beta_X = w_0 + w_X.$$

Then Eq. (48) can be written in the form of a standard multiple linear regression

$$R = \alpha + \Sigma \beta_X R_{Xt}. \quad (49)$$

Equation (49) thus provides a basis for testing goodness of fit and for estimating weight parameters without concern for scale values.[a] It should be emphasized that standard regression analysis is not appropriate for Eq. (49). It must be treated as a functional regression in the manner outlined in Section 4.3 to allow for variability in the predictors R_{Xt}.

Equation (49) may prove helpful because it avoids the need to estimate scale values and also introduces additional information into the estimation. Moreover, factorial design is not necessary. Incomplete designs can be used, and applications to natural situations in which the stimulus attributes are not under experimental control may also be possible.

Equation (48) may be even more helpful because it applies to the case of unequal weights, in which each stimulus has its own weight parameter as well as its own scale value. The estimation of so many parameters in a nonlinear model can be problematical. Equation (48) halves their number although, unfortunately, the model remains nonlinear. It is again necessary, of course, to allow for unreliability in the R_{Xt}. Regrettably, there is essentially no information available on the practicability of this regression approach.[b]

Qualitative Weight Estimation. Importance or weight of different kinds of information may be compared using a qualitative estimation scheme.

This scheme estimates comparative weights in a simple way, without the statistical complications of the exact methods previously considered. The principle of this qualitative scheme may be illustrated with a two-factor design in which the A factor is equally weighted and the B factor is unequally weighted. In this case, the averaging model has the form

$$R_{ij} = C_0 + (w_0 s_0 + w_A s_{Ai} + w_{Bj} s_{Bj})/(w_0 + w_A + w_{Bj}).$$

The difference in response between rows 1 and 2 is thus

$$R_{1j} - R_{2j} = [w_A/(w_0 + w_A + w_{Bj})](s_{A1} - s_{A2}).$$

Since the column stimulus appears only as the weight parameter, w_{Bj}, in the denominator, this equation implies that the greater the weight of the column stimulus, the less the difference between the two responses. In other words, the difference between the two responses in any column indexes the weight of the column stimulus.

This qualitative scheme led to the discovery of a negativity effect: Information that is more negative has greater weight (Anderson, 1965a). Because this experiment used only a 2 × 2 design, however, the negativity interpretation depended heavily on the assumption of linearity in the response scale (see Section F4.4.2).

A robust version of this qualitative estimation scheme is obtainable by adding a third factor, C. In graphical terms, an $A \times C$ factorial plot would be made for each level of B. Straightforward extension of the foregoing equation shows that the curves in these factorial plots will lie closer together for levels of B with greater weight. The vertical spread is thus an index of importance for levels of B. The C factor may be treated similarly.

A variant of this three-factor design, in which the B factor is a manipulation of the weight for the C factor, appears in a study of group centrality by Anderson, Lindner, and Lopes (1973), in a study of informational content in attribution theory by Himmelfarb and Anderson (1975), and in a study of information relevance in person perception by Anderson and Lopes (1974). This last application is shown in Figure F4.17: The two curves of each pair are closer together for the more relevant information.

This three-factor estimation scheme is robust in two ways. First, it is not sensitive to unequal weighting of the A factor and, of course, allows unequal weighting on both other factors. Second, it is not sensitive to response nonlinearity so long as the several $A \times C$ graphs cover a common response range. This advantage is also illustrated in Figure F4.17.

This qualitative estimation scheme can provide importance comparisons that avoid the shortcomings of the studies discussed in Section 6.1.4. In moral judgment, for example, the hypothesis is that personal injury is more important than property damage. Since intent and outcome are integrated by an averaging rule (Leon, 1980; Surber, 1977), the effect of intent should be less for personal injury than for property damage. In principle, this prediction is testable in a 2 × 2 design, with two levels of intent and the given two levels of outcome. However, a three-factor design seems desirable for robustness. A similar approach applies to the hypothesis that causal cues are more informative and important than noncausal cues. This qualitative estimation scheme bypasses the difficulties of attempting to equate scale values and provides simple comparisons of importance.

Other Estimation Procedures. A few other estimation procedures have also been considered. One useful device is to define each stimulus variable with a single stimulus and to attach quantifiers to control the levels of the variable. In an application to psycholinguistics (Anderson & Lopes, 1974), each design factor was defined by a single trait adjective, and adverbial quantifiers were used to vary levels within factors. The rationale was that the adjective would control the relevance of the stimulus information to the dimension of judgment, and hence the weight parameter, while the quantifiers would control the scale value. Equal weighting and parallelism were expected, therefore, although this expectation was not completely realized (Section F4.4.4).

In some tasks it may be reasonable to take the weight parameter as a function of scale value. With all positive stimuli, the linear function $w = 1 + as$, would allow for an extremity weighting effect. With both positive and negative stimuli, the same goal could be obtained in various ways, for example, with the quadratic function $w = 1 + as + bs^2$.

One advantage of this device is that it reduces the number of parameters. In an application to clinical judgment (Anderson, 1972b), an evaluation of nine weight parameters was reduced to one or two constants in the specified w–s relation. A second advantage is that it can eliminate the indeterminacy of Eqs. (35)–(37) and allow complete identification of the parameters. It may also perhaps improve stability in the numerical analysis, although on this there is no evidence.

Use of a w–s relation in parameter estimation assumes that weight can be expressed as a simple function of scale value. This seems appropriate for the quantified stimulus variables already mentioned or for psychophysical stimuli. It would not be appropriate when two stimuli of equal value can have unequal weight. Even in that case, however, an approximate solution may be adequate for some purposes.

Another possibility of eliminating the nonuniqueness of Eqs. (35)–(37) arises in tasks in which the same or equivalent stimuli can be used in two factors of the design. Consider a two-way design, and let $X = A, B$ in Eq. (36). If the stimulus in row 1 has the same scale value as the stimulus in column 1, then $s'_{A1} = s'_{B1}$, and also $s_{A1} = s_{B1}$. It is not hard to show that that requires $b_A = - a_A s_{A1}$ in Eq. (36). If other stimuli of equivalent value can be used similarly in, say, row 2, column 2, then similarly, $b_A = - a_A s_{A2}$. If $s_{A1} \neq s_{A2}$, then $a_A = b_A = 0 = - a_B = - b_B$. Accordingly, this device can provide complete identification of the parameters in a two-way design, even with row–column asymmetry in the weight parameter. This approach is potentially applicable to decision tasks in which the row and column stimuli are the same except for differences in reliability or salience across the two factors.

A related case has been considered by Blankenship (1974), who obtained a closed algebraic expression for the weights. A square, two-factor design is assumed with corresponding row and column stimuli having equal scale values but unequal weights. The internal state is assumed to have zero weight so that the model becomes

$$R_{ij} = C_0 + (w_{Ai}s_{Ai} + w_{Bj}s_{Bj})/(w_{Ai} + w_{Bj}).$$

By assumption, $s_{Ai} = s_{Bj}$, so the response in the diagonal cells can be written as,

$$R_{jj} = C_0 + s_{Bj}.$$

Define a new data matrix

$$Q_{ij} = (R_{jj} - R_{ij})/(R_{ij} - R_{ii}). \qquad (i \neq j)$$

Then

$$Q_{ij} = (C_0 + s_{Bj} - R_{ij})/(R_{ij} - C_0 - s_{Bi}).$$

Substituting the expression for R_{ij} into this last equation and simplifying yields

$$Q_{ij} = w_{Ai}/w_{Bj}. \qquad (i \neq j)$$

Thus, the ratio of the weights is equal to a ratio of observables.

This result is interesting because it provides a closed algebraic expression for the averaging model with differential weighting. In practice, due to instability resulting from the difference of observed values in the denominator of the Q_{ij}, it may not be too useful. However, it bears on the issue of whether order effects in psychophysical judgment are to be interpreted in terms of weight or of scale value (Anderson, 1971b; Carterette & Anderson, 1979).

Set-Size Equation. The set-size effect refers to systematic changes in response as more information of equal value is added. A special case of the averaging model for this basic effect is considered here. This special case assumes that all pieces of information have the same weight, w, and the same known value, s. The response to a set of n such stimuli is the average

$$R(n) = C_0 + (nws + w_0 s_0)/(nw + w_0). \tag{50}$$

Thus, $R(n)$ is a growth function of n with asymptote s.

It is no restriction to set $w + w_0 = 1$. If the values of C_0 and s_0 can be assumed, then w is the only remaining unknown in Eq. (50). Accordingly, w could be estimated for one set size and used to predict the response to the other set sizes. This would be unsatisfactory, however, because the outcome would depend on which set size was chosen for estimation.

A satisfactory test can be obtained by solving Eq. (50) for w. For simplicity, suppose that $C_0 = s_0 = 0$, as might be reasonable if the response scale is centered at zero. Then

$$w = R(n)/[ns - (n - 1)R(n)]. \tag{51}$$

An estimate of w is then available for each n. The test of the model hinges on the constancy of w, which is theoretically independent of set size.

The presence of the observed value, R_n, in the denominator of Eq. (51) causes a ratio bias that can, due to individual differences, be serious for group data. For single subject data, however, this ratio bias may not be serious, and in any case would probably be roughly constant as a function of n. By estimating w for each subject for each set size, therefore, a simple and statistically powerful test can be obtained. An experimental illustration is given in Anderson (1967b; see also Section F2.4).

Results obtained by Alf (1971) allow different scale values for different stimuli. The values of C_0 and s_0 are assumed to be zero. The relative weight of a single stimulus is denoted by w, so that $w + w_0 = 1$. The response to a single stimulus of value s_i is

$$R_i = (w_0 s_0 + w s_i)/(w_0 + w) = w s_i.$$

The response to a pair of stimuli with values s_i and s_j is

$$\begin{aligned} R_{ij} &= (w s_i + w s_j)/(1 + w) \\ &= (R_i + R_j)/(1 + w). \end{aligned}$$

This last equation provides an estimate of w in terms of observed responses

$$1 + w = (R_i + R_j)/R_{ij}. \tag{52}$$

With three stimuli, there are three such estimates, and all should be equal if the model is correct. The estimates are not independent but should be equally intercorrelated and thus testable in a repeated measurements design. Once w has been estimated, the s_i may be obtained directly. Alf (1971) gives a more sophisticated treatment using least squares. Analogous results hold for larger sets. If C_0 or s_0 are not zero, of course, then the analysis becomes more complicated.

An interesting analysis for the set-size effect was developed by Ostrom, Werner, and Saks (1978), who applied averaging theory to study jurors' predispositions. Predisposition was defined in terms of the w_0–s_0 representation of prior attitude. The essential design requirement was a two-way factorial, with variation in set size and in evidence scale value. The leverage provided by the set-size variation allowed the derivation of closed formulas for all parameters, even in a 2 × 2 design. These formulas are given in an appendix to that paper and will not be considered here. Substantive implications of this study are discussed in Section F4.3.2.

Nondetectable Interactions. Averaging processes may embody certain interactions that can escape detection in the model analysis. In the discussion of linear models, it was noted that a linear interaction among the scale values will not be detectable (Section 2.1.4). This also holds for the equal-weight case of the averaging model because it has the linear form.

In addition, a certain type of interaction can be masked by conservation of weight. This would require an interchange interaction, in which weight lost by one stimulus is gained by another stimulus in the set. Since the sum of the weights would remain constant, parallelism would be obtained. Conservation of weight would not be expected with redundancy interactions, for example, but might be found in decision tasks with inconsistent stimuli of which one is specified to be correct. No empirical examples are known, but a related case of symmetrical–proportional discounting in a 2 × 2 design is discussed by Anderson, Lindner, and Lopes (1973, p. 405).

2.3.4 AVERAGING THEORY AND PSYCHOLOGICAL MEASUREMENT

In the functional measurement view, the foundation of psychological measurement lies in the investigations that establish the empirical validity of algebraic models. These experimental investigations indicate considerable generality of the averaging model. The averaging model puts certain traditional problems in a new light and suggests the need for some conceptual reorientation in measurement theory. Four aspects of this matter are noted here.

Concept of Weight. A concept of weight or importance, as distinct from scale value, seems intuitively reasonable and has been widely used. Under scrutiny, however, the concept of weight begins to blend into that of scale value and becomes slippery to pin down. Thus, the linear model of Section 2.1 confounds weight with scale value except under special conditions.

Traditional approaches to psychological measurement have relied on linear or additive models. Because weights are not generally determinate in linear models, measurement theory has largely ignored the problem of measuring weight. The very term *scaling* reflects this overriding concern with scale values. Even when weights are considered, they are virtually always required to be constant for each stimulus dimension.

Averaging theory leads to a different perspective, in which weights are generally determinate. Indeed, weights are more interesting than scale values because of their dependence on diverse contextual factors (Section F4.4). From this psychological standpoint, moreover, it becomes clear that weights cannot normally be required to remain constant along a given stimulus dimension. Subtle difficulties arise in attempting to measure weights, as was seen in the preceding discussion of uniqueness and as will be seen again in Chapter 6. Nevertheless, the averaging model has provided a theoretical foundation for the concept of weight, in principle and in fact.

Initial-State Variable. The weight parameter can intrude on the measurement of scale values proper as a result of the operation of the initial state, S_0. The response to a single stimulus, S_{Ai}, is

$$R_i = C_0 + (w_0 s_0 + w_{Ai} s_{Ai})/(w_0 + w_{Ai}). \tag{53}$$

In the equal-weight case, with $w_{Ai} = w_A$, the denominator is constant, and so R_i is a linear function or linear scale of s_{Ai}. In the differential-weight case, however, R_i need not even be a monotone function of s_{Ai}. This is an unpleasant property of the averaging model, for it can markedly complicate analysis and interpretation.

In principle, the problem may be bypassed by asking subjects to judge the value of the stimulus per se, but that may be difficult to implement. In the personality adjective task, for example, it is unclear how the task could call for the likableness value of the adjective without triggering judgments about likableness of a person described by that adjective. The person judgments would involve the initial state and

TABLE 2.2
Disordinality of Averaging Model

Row	Column stimulus parameters	
	$s_{B1} = 1, \quad w_{B1} = 1$	$s_{B2} = 5, \quad w_{B2} = 1$
$s_{A1} = 5$ $w_{A1} = 1$	3.0	5.0
$s_{A2} = 4$ $w_{A2} = 9$	3.7	4.1

NOTE: Entries are theoretical values calculated from the averaging model ($w_0 = 0$).

hence the weight parameters. Other tasks may not suffer from this problem, but the matter has not received systematic study although it is important for self-estimation methods (Section 6.2).

To the extent that the averaging model holds, therefore, measurement of scale values is intimately related to measurement of weight. Moreover, this value–weight relation raises a question about scaling methods based on traditional conceptualizations, which do not provide for scaling of weight.

Disordinality. In general the response in the averaging model cannot be represented as a monotone function of the physical stimulus variables. A given level of one variable can increase or decrease the response, depending on the level of the other variable. This disordinality is illustrated in Table 2.2, in which the response shows an increase down the first column but a decrease down the second column. Graphically, these data correspond to a crossover interaction. The disordinality of the averaging model, together with the empirical prevalence of averaging processes, show that measurement theory cannot be constructed on an ordinal basis.

Measurement and Substantive Theory. Averaging theory embodies a different way of thinking about psychological measurement from that which prevails in traditional approaches. In the Thurstonian approach, for example, there is just one basic scaling model, which rests on the method of paired comparisons. The comparison process is not of main interest, however, but a device for scaling. Paired comparisons is intended as a general scaling method that can provide stimulus values in diverse areas. The Thurstonian system thus treats measurement as a methodological preliminary for substantive work in diverse areas. This approach looks reasonable, seemingly much like the approach of physics. However, it has not worked too well.

Three main differences appear in averaging theory. First, primary concern is substantive, focused on problems of stimulus integration. Measurement is necessary for, but derivative from rather than prior to, model analysis. It is the substantive model itself, not a general scaling model, that provides the base and frame for measurement.

Second, the main measurement problem in averaging theory, and more generally in functional measurement, concerns the response. The paired comparisons approach, by contrast, is concerned with stimulus scaling and largely ignores the response. This shift from stimulus to response measurement is fundamental for psychological measurement.

The third difference lies in the constructivist principle, according to which values are not inherent properties of the stimuli but result from a constructive valuation process. The conception of measurement transferred from physics that sees values as constant, general properties of objects is inadequate for psychology. In psychology, values depend on the immediate goal of the organism and on a complex of background knowledge, both of which are basic in the valuation operation. Values are not fixed but variable. Although this conceptualization may not seem amenable to exact theory, averaging theory provides a practicable way to proceed by virtue of the principle of molar unitization. Related discussions are given in Sections 7.14–7.17 and in Chapter 5 of *Foundations*.

NOTES

2.1.1a. Linear models will also be called *additive* or *adding-type models*. Unhappily, no terminology seems to be without objection or easy to adhere to. The term *linear model* has traditionally been used in psychology to refer to regression analysis with prespecified values of the stimulus variables; this yields a prediction equation, which is conceptually different from the structural equation that is desired for process analysis (Section 4.3.1).

The term *additive* can be misleading because most empirical instances stem from the averaging model, which is inherently nonadditive and exhibits an additive form only under an equal-weighting condition (Section 2.3). From a substantive standpoint, therefore, the averaging model provides a theoretical foundation from which the linear model can be seen as a good approximation in some applications and a poor approximation in others.

In certain situations, of course, it will not be known whether an observed pattern of additivity in the data reflects an averaging process or an adding process. The term *adding-type model* is used to include both strict adding (and subtracting) models, adding models with subadditivity, and averaging models. The term *adding-type* will generally be used for substantive reference. The term *linear* is used here, since the main concern is formal.

2.1.1b. The response may be conceptualized as a distribution by virtue of the error term of Eqs. (1). Beyond this response variability, the implicit response on any trial may be considered a confidence function over the response scale, with the overt response at the center of this distribution, except for response variability. Confidence seems to be an important aspect of judgment and has been widely discussed, although not much is known about it (see also Section F2.4.4).

The concept of stimulus or stimulus value is also more complex than the point representation ordinarily employed in the integration models. One standard conception treats the stimulus as a random variable that, as in Thurstonian theory, is analogous to the concept of response variability just discussed. Similarly, a conception of stimulus value as a distribution of stimulus uncertainty could also be considered, in direct analogy to response uncertainty. Indeed, the psychological stimulus value is a response at the valuation stage (Section 7.15). Finally, the stimulus may also be represented as a set of features with weight and scale value as summary molar statistics. These questions about structure in stimulus and response deserve study but may largely be bypassed here by considering the point concepts to be means of distributions, a treatment that has some mathematical justification (Sections 5.7 and F1.6.5; Anderson, 1961c, 1964b).

2.1.1c. With a finite set of stimulus levels, it is also possible that a nonlinear integration rule can appear linear for the specific stimuli that happen to be used. Suppose that a linear rule did hold for a given design and that the design is extended to add one level of one variable. Over this extended stimulus domain, the linear rule could become nonlinear in infinitely many ways by assigning arbitrary values to the response in the added cells. This is not entirely a mathematical curiosity. In a 2×2 design with the same stimulus values for rows and columns, the nonlinear ratio model $A/(A + B)$ produces parallelism.

2.1.1d. Marginal means scaling is also possible with unequal numbers of observations in different cells, as long as there are no empty cells. In this case, the data matrix is replaced by the matrix of cell means and (unweighted) marginal means are obtained from this latter matrix. This does not give a minimum variance solution, although presumably not much would be lost for moderate variations in cell numbers.

2.1.2a. The term *distribution-free* is not strictly accurate because all such tests require some distributional assumption. The signed-ranks test, for example, uses the assumption that the sampling distribution of each individual I_x is symmetrical (see, e.g., Hollander & Wolfe, 1973; Lehman, 1975). With symmetry, the binomial sign test could also be used.

2.1.2b. Quite different considerations arise when the distributional assumptions are an essential part of the model. In such cases, it may be possible to increase both generality and power by developing alternative approaches that bypass the distributional assumptions (e.g., Sections 3.10 and F1.5.7; Anderson, 1969b).

2.1.2c. The sphericity condition is discussed by Huyhn and Mandeville (1979), who point out that it is more general than the condition of equality of variances and covariances (intercorrelations) usually cited in textbooks. The latter condition is sufficient, but the F tests are valid under the more general sphericity condition, which is both necessary and sufficient. The sphericity condition requires equal variances and zero covariances (in terms of a set of orthogonal variables instead of the original raw scores) associated with each error term in a repeated measurements design, which allows for unequal variances to be associated with main effects and interactions. Huyhn (1978) shows that two approximate tests behave well under representative deviations from sphericity and also discusses some alternative test procedures.

2.1.2d. In single trimming, the smallest and largest observations are omitted. In single Winsorization, they are given the values of their nearest neighbors (Dixon & Massey, 1969). Either technique can reduce the variance produced by outliers, although at the expense of reducing generality. These techniques can be useful when sample sizes are necessarily small, as with clinical populations. Both techniques are treacherous because they tempt the investigator to take advantage of chance fluctuations in the data. Either technique requires explicit justification, therefore, and it does not seem extreme to say that any decision to use them should be put in writing before the data are collected.

2.1.3a. Accordingly, significant Row × Subject interaction is not adequate evidence for genuine individual differences in values of the row stimuli. If all subjects had identical values but different response units, then their row means would be linearly related but unequal and hence yield nonparallelism in the Row × Subject factorial graph. As a consequence, it is often difficult to establish or assess individual differences in value, even though their reality cannot be questioned. The example of Figure 1.4 depends on the nonlinear relation between the elevations of the row curves for the two subjects. More generally, the hypothesis of genuine individual differences in value could be assessed by analyzing the Row × Subject data table in terms of a semilinear model or, for two subjects, in terms of a multiplying model. See "Comparing Two Sets of Scale Values" in Section 2.2.3.

2.1.4a. By similar reasoning, the success of any model supports the hypothesis that the factors of the design, the response variable, or both correspond to cognitive units; this provides construct validity for the terms of the model. It should be recognized, however, that several distinct cues can act jointly as a unit stimulus without any further psychological unity (see also Sections F1.1.5, F1.6.5, and F1.8.2). For an interesting failure of cognitive unitization, see Farkas and Anderson (1979).

2.2.1a. An analog process for multiplication (Graesser & Anderson, 1974) can yield additive error. Each level of one factor can be represented as a distance along a graphic response scale. This distance can be considered the upper end of a new response scale, along which each level of the second factor can be represented in the same way as the first. Because of this serial processing, response errors of the two factors add rather than multiply. Response variability can thus provide clues about processing.

2.2.2a. The bilinear component corresponds to Tukey's (1949) "one degree of freedom for non-additivity." In effect, Tukey proved that $SS_{Bilinear}/\sigma^2$ and $SS_{Residual}/\sigma^2$ have statistically independent chi-square distributions (see Scheffé, 1959, pp. 129ff), thereby justifying the use of the residual as an error term for the nonadditive component when there is only one score in each cell of the design and no regular error term is available. Tukey was not concerned with model analysis, but rather advocated transformation to remove the nonadditivity and thereby increase power for tests of main effects (Section F5.6.1).

The potential significance of the bilinear test for scaling was noted by Mandel (1964), who also developed the test for the semilinear model of Section 3.4. The bilinear analysis was developed independently in the present research program to solve the problem of joint simultaneous measurement of subjective probability and utility (Anderson & Shanteau, 1970; Section F1.5.1). Only the case of independent responses was considered by Tukey and Mandel, whereas the present analysis applies also to correlated responses.

2.2.2b. These computational formulas follow Grant's (1956) trend test for repeated measurements designs. They concur with the standard rule that the proper error term for any systematic source is its interaction with subjects. Some writers (e.g., Kirk, 1968; Winer, 1971, pp. 296ff) have suggested that polynomial components of the interaction can be tested against the error term for overall interaction. This assumes that the different components have equal variance, which would seem to be seriously incorrect unless all components had zero true mean. If the true linear × linear component is nonzero, its variability will include the real individual differences in this component. This variance would therefore be larger than a higher order polynomial component that included little or no individual differences.

The seriousness of this problem may be illustrated with analyses of the experiment on Performance = Motivation × Ability shown in Figure 4.2. These analyses compare error mean squares for the linear × linear component with error mean squares for the three linear–quadratic components. For the college track scenario, which is plotted in Figure 4.2, the linear × linear error mean square was 24.97; mean squares for the linear × quadratic, quadratic × linear, and quadratic × quadratic components were 3.41, 4.22, and 3.49, respectively, with a mean of 3.71. For the school grades scenario, which yielded a similar pattern of data, the corresponding values were 11.85 for linear × linear, and 2.93, 2.61, and 2.54 for the respective linear–quadratic components, whose mean was 2.69. Thus, the linear × linear variance was 6.7 times larger than the linear–quadratic variance for the college track judgments and 4.4 times larger for the school grades judgments.

2.2.2c. In an initial test of the multiplying model using group data, it was incorrectly stated that the bias should be negligible (Graesser & Anderson, 1974). Correction notes were given in Anderson (1976b, p. 689; 1977b, p. 214) and in Anderson and Shanteau (1977, p. 1161).

These reanalyses were performed using a modified version of Shanteau's (1977) POLYLIN, with subroutines added by James Zalinski and the writer for computing the indicated linear and quadratic interaction components for each individual. The recent version by Weiss (1982) provides proper group tests of all interaction residuals.

For the study of Performance = Motivation × Ability cited in the previous note, the original analysis showed a significant interaction, and inspection of the graph showed this to be concentrated in the linear × linear component. The reanalyses provide a more appropriate test of goodness of fit. The linear × linear components were significant, $F(1, 19) = 12.14$ and 11.67, for the track and grades scenarios, respectively. The F's for the linear–quadratic components, listed in the order of the previous note, were 1.61, 1.72, .01, .27, 2.06, and 4.26, of which only the last approached significance. This test of goodness of fit thus agrees with the original analysis of the multiplying rule.

2.2.2d. Power can be increased, often substantially, if a priori estimates of the stimulus values are available; this is because the sampling variability in the estimated marginal means in Eqs. (6) and (10) is avoided. Approximate a priori values may be obtainable with certain psychophysical dimensions, such as length, for which subjective and objective values appear to be proportional (e.g., Anderson & Cuneo, 1978a, p. 345; see also Note 4.3.3a), and with quantified stimuli, for which the levels are specified by nominal quantifiers (e.g., Anderson & Butzin, 1974, p. 600). This approach implicitly allows individual zero and unit parameters for each subject.

2.2.3a. Uniqueness properties of the stimulus scales follow from Pexider's equations (Aczél, 1966). Suppose that the implicit response obeys the multiplying model, $r_{ij} = s_{Ai}s_{Bj}$, and that the observed response, R_{ij}, exhibits the linear fan pattern, thereby being representable as a product of the two stimulus factors. Let $R_{ij} = C_0 + C_1 r_{ij} = C_0 + C_1 s_{Ai}s_{Bj}$ be one such product representation. Let $R_{ij} = C_0 + C_1 f(r_{ij})$ be any other representation where f is an arbitrary continuous function, subject to the requirement that $f(r_{ij}) = f(s_{Ai}s_{Bj})$ be representable as a product, $g(s_{Ai})h(s_{Bj})$, where g and h are arbitrary functions. Then for s_{Ai} and s_{Bj} positive (Aczél, p. 144, Theorem 4), all nontrivial functions satisfying the given requirement must be power functions with a common exponent: $f(r_{ij}) = abr_{ij}^n$, $g(s_{Ai}) = as_{Ai}^n$, and $h(s_{Bj}) = bs_{Bj}^n$, where a and b are arbitrary constants. The case of negative and zero stimulus values may be treated analogously (Aczél, p. 41, Theorem 3).

2.3.2a. Since it has sometimes been argued that the indeterminacy of weight estimates found in the additive model applies also to the averaging model, it may be helpful to illustrate the basic structural difference between these two models. Consider three items of information, with scale values, s_i, and weights, w_i, and assume $w_0 = 0$. The three items are to be judged singly and in pairs within the same experimental session (Section 1.1.8). The theoretical values of the responses are

$$R_1 = w_1 s_1 / w_1 = s_1;$$
$$R_2 = w_2 s_2 / w_2 = s_2;$$
$$R_3 = w_3 s_3 / w_3 = s_3;$$
$$R_{12} = (w_1 s_1 + w_2 s_2)/(w_1 + w_2);$$
$$R_{13} = (w_1 s_1 + w_3 s_3)/(w_1 + w_3);$$
$$R_{23} = (w_2 s_2 + w_3 s_3)/(w_2 + w_3).$$

The first three equations provide the scale values. The unit of the weight scale is arbitrary and may be fixed in any convenient way, for example, by setting $w_1 = 1$. The fourth and fifth equations may then be solved for w_2 and w_3. These values must then also satisfy the last equation, which can thus provide a test of goodness of fit. If the model is correct, the three weights are comparable on the same ratio scale. As this example shows, the structure of the averaging model does allow separation of scale value and weight.

Two comments should be added. First, the assumption that $w_0 = 0$ is not generally applicable; that complicates the estimation procedures. Nevertheless, the principle of this illustration remains the same. Second, it is not necessary to vary set size, for a linear scale of weight can be obtained within each factor of a single design. One simple case arises in the semilinear model, as shown in Eq. (29) (Anderson, 1971a, p. 184, Eq. [12]).

2.3.2b. I am indebted to Burton Rodin for pointing out this lack of uniqueness.

2.3.3a. Practical applications of this regression approach may more conveniently set one weight equal to 1, especially w_0, if it was known to be nonzero. Then the β_X in Eq. (49) would estimate the relative weights of the stimulus variables.

This regression technique requires that responses to sets of different sizes be comparable, with the same scale zeros and units. This could not be expected if sets of different size were judged in separate sessions (Section 1.1.8). Of course, the regression analysis could be extended to include such scaling constants.

2.3.3b. In Eqs. (48) and (49), the overall response, R, and the responses to the individual stimuli, R_{Xt}, are observables, subject to error. An obvious, but incorrect approach is to substitute the R_{Xt} in the right side of either equation and apply standard least squares regression to estimate the weight parameters. This is incorrect because it does not take account of the error variability in the R_{Xt}. The anomalously high estimate of s_0 reported by Wyer (1969) may reflect his use of standard regression analysis rather than functional regression. An additional complication in this study is that the single and paired adjectives were presented in sequential blocks and so the responses may not have been comparable (see previous note).

For a functional regression, it is desired to perform a least squares fit in which the R_{Xt} are estimated in the same manner as R. This entails minimization of the weighted sum of squares,

$$w\Sigma(R - \hat{R})^2 + (1 - w)\Sigma(R_{Xt} - \hat{R}_{Xt})^2.$$

Here w is a relative weight that allows for possible unequal variance in R and the R_{Xt}; the two sums are normalized to represent mean deviation for a single observation. With assistance of Chris Dickey and Jim Zalinski, I have developed a computer program for this regression that is not ready for export but may be helpful to others who wish to pursue this problem.

3

Special Models and Applications

This chapter presents a number of other models that have been studied in this research program. These are not new models for the most part, but rather applications of the three basic models in particular areas. They have some substantive interest, therefore, and they also illustrate various problems in practical model analysis.

3.1 Generality in Model Analysis

The problem of generality pervades scientific inquiry. Any one investigation is confined to a little sample of behavior obtained under a more or less ill-defined aggregate of experimental conditions. With such uncertain signs, investigators pursue their hopeful searches for underlying order and generality. Of the many ramifications of the problem of generality, this section takes up several that occur within the domain of model analysis.[a]

Empirical Generality. Within any one experiment, the test of goodness of fit assesses the internal structure of the data; that is, the test asks whether the pattern in the data is consistent with the algebraic structure of the model. The parallelism and linear fan tests are simple examples, but the same holds for any algebraic model. Such tests of internal structure can provide powerful assessments of the model.

But no one experiment goes very far by itself. When the outcome of some experiment disagrees with background knowledge, it naturally comes under suspicion as being a statistical fluke or a consequence of some peculiarity of procedure (e.g., the Height + Width rule of Figure 4.5). Some degree of plain empirical generality and replicability is required to establish any result.

However, the problem of generality is not merely empirical. It is an accepted principle that only an interlocking body of concepts and experiments can provide the generality needed in science. Three aspects of this problem of theoretical generality will be noted here. These relate to the three stages of the functional measurement diagram of Figure 1.2.

Stimulus Generality. Stimulus generality refers to invariance of stimulus values across different tasks. Functional measurement can provide scale values of the same stimuli in different tasks, and these can be compared to see if they are linearly equivalent. One example from psychophysics may be noted.

In judgments of grayness, Figure 3.1 shows that the bisection task of Section F1.3.8 yielded essentially the same scale as was obtained from

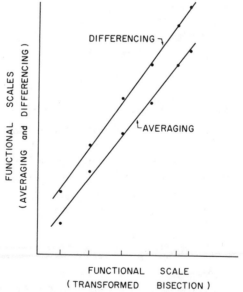

FIGURE 3.1. *Cross-task generality of functional scales of grayness. Points on horizontal axis denote scale values obtained from transformed bisection data of right panel of Figure F1.11. The two curves represent functional scales obtained from untransformed judgments of average grayness and of difference in grayness for the same Left chip × Right chip design used in the bisection task. Linearity of each set of data points and near equality of curve slopes implies that all three tasks yield equivalent scales of grayness. (After Anderson, 1976c.)*

tasks of averaging and differencing (Anderson, 1976c; Weiss 1972, 1973a, 1975). This cross-task stimulus invariance is important because the perceptual–cognitive requirements are different in the three tasks. In bisection, the response is a physical stimulus that is supposed to equalize two sensory differences. In differencing, the response is verbal and is supposed to represent the magnitude of one sensory difference. Averaging also asks for a verbal magnitude response, but the integration operation is different. Stimulus invariance across these three tasks is not unexpected, of course, but it does need proof. Similar evidence for invariance of subjective length and heaviness is given in Note 3.1b. [c]

The idea that stimulus scales are invariant across different tasks is often taken as self-evident. In the integration-theoretical view, however, stimulus values depend on the valuation operation as defined by task, instructions, and context. The same stimulus may have many values, therefore, depending on the task (Section F1.1.3). This becomes obvious in social judgment, in which different tasks set up quite different dimensions of judgment.

In psychophysics, it is true, sensations such as grayness and heaviness have traditionally been treated as unitary, conscious qualities. This view seems reasonable on introspective grounds, but it is not necessarily correct. There are many stages between the observable stimulus and the observable response. Different tasks may tap different stages that yield different quantitative measures. For example, various writers have suggested that judgments of magnitude of single stimuli yield measures different from comparative judgments of differences between two stimuli (see, e.g., Sections 7.15 and F5.6.2).

The evidence of introspection has heuristic value, but cross-task generality of stimulus scales cannot be taken for granted. Rather, it must be shown how far it holds empirically. The cited work on grayness and similar work on heaviness and length (Anderson, 1972a, 1974c) provide evidence for invariance of psychophysical scales (see Note 3.1b, Figures 3.5 and 3.6). To the extent that stimulus invariance can be established, it provides a useful tool for other analyses (e.g., Section 5.6), as well as interesting information on cognitive processing.

Response Generality. In the present context, response generality refers to linearity of the same response method across a range of tasks. The main point to be made here is that the rating method, with suitable precautions, has been shown to provide linear scales in many different tasks. This response generality has been illustrated in the experimental studies of the *Foundations* volume.

Response generality is broader than stimulus generality since it bridges stimulus domains. Thus, the success of the rating method in the initial studies of person perception conferred confidence for its use in other areas. This provided reassurance when the results of the rating method disagreed with prevailing views in psychophysics (Section 1.1.1).

Model Generality. Model generality refers to the operation of the same integration function across different tasks. Many tasks do not follow a simple model, of course, but the cumulative evidence indicates the operation of a fairly general cognitive algebra.

Compound Generality. Stimulus, response, and model generality are not independent, for they interrelate as indicated in the functional measurement diagram (Figure 1.2). Thus, the cross-task invariance of the three grayness scales in Figure 3.1 provides increased support for each of them. It also adds support to the linearity of the rating response and to the validity of the three models. Such compound generality provides interlocking support that is stronger than could be obtained with any one type of generality alone (Anderson, 1972a, p. 394).

3.2 Two-Operation Models

Models with two or more integration operations can provide a higher level of theoretical constraint than is possible with one-operation models. The multilinear models of Section 3.3 are the best examples, but the two-operation logic is more general and more useful. This logic deserves preliminary discussion, therefore, with particular reference to questions of response and model validation.[a]

Two-Phase Method for Monotone Analysis. Two-operation models have special usefulness for providing a base and frame for transforming monotone response scales to true linear scales. The procedure is straightforward and practicable. To illustrate, suppose that some behavior is hypothesized to follow a three-factor model with two adding operations

$$R = A + B + C,$$

but that the data do not exhibit parallelism. A monotone transformation could be applied to minimize the $A \times B$ interaction and to make the $A \times B$ factorial graph as parallel as possible. If the model is correct, then this transformation rectifies the observed response measure and produces a true linear scale.

The shortcoming of this transformation procedure is that the $A \times B$ design may not be large enough to impose adequate constraint. Monotone transformation is so flexible that it can readily eliminate the $A \times B$ interaction even though the model is not true. Lack of power to detect discrepancies from model prediction under monotone transformation is a serious practical problem.

This problem can be effectively attacked with a two-phase approach, using one operation to transform the response and the other to test goodness of fit. If the given model is not true, then the transformation that eliminates the $A \times B$ interaction will not in general yield a linear response scale. The $B \times C$ interaction would be expected to be significant, therefore, because it is not constrained to be minimal by the response transformation. It thus provides a test that has a normal level of power. Numerical examples are given in Section 5.6.

Because the procedures of Section 1.1 appear to yield linear rating scales, monotone response transformation has had only occasional use in this research program. The same principle applies, however, even when the response scale is linear. In this case, one operation may still be used to validate the model as though an identity transformation had been used. This logic has been employed frequently, and a few aspects will be noted next.

Cross-Validation. When both integration operations obey a simple model, that adds solidity to both of them. An example is provided by the probability averaging model of Section F1.7.1, in which both averaging and multiplying operations are involved. These two operations are independent, so one could fail while the other succeeded. The success of each buttressed the other. A striking example of the same logic appears in the inequity model of Anderson and Farkas (1975), presented in Figure F1.25.

Response Validation. In some two-operation tasks, one operation will obey a simple model but the other will not. If only the latter operation had been studied, the discrepancies might be attributable to nonlinearity in the response scale. Success of the one model provides in-context support for response linearity and hence eases the problem of localizing the failure of the other model. A notable example of this rationale was given by Shanteau's (1970b, 1974) study of subadditivity in a utility model of the form $AB + CD$. The success of the multiplying model supported the linearity of the response scale, so that the subadditivity was more securely interpreted as being psychologically real. Two-operation averaging models have been used similarly in studies of inconsistency discounting (Anderson & Jacobson, 1965) and differential weighting (Lampel & Anderson, 1968). The methodological value of a second operation for response validation is illustrated in a study of information seeking by Shanteau and Anderson (1972, p. 275).

Configural Integration. The theme of response validation may be pursued systematically by adding a second operation specifically to provide a validational base for the response scale. This approach could be useful in the study of stimulus interaction and configural integration.

In a study of adults' judgments of rectangle area, for example, Anderson and Weiss (1971) found a small discrepancy from the physicalistic Height × Width rule. This discrepancy was attributed to a height–width illusion, although not without some uncertainty about response linearity. To help resolve this uncertainty, the task could be extended to obtain judgments of combined area of two rectangles. An initial integration is required to obtain subjective area of each rectangle. A second integration is needed to combine these two areas. The second operation would be expected to follow an adding rule, of course, and this could provide a validational base for the response scale. The deviations from the true Height × Width rule could then be more confidently interpreted as a height–width interaction (see also Anderson, 1980b; Anderson & Cuneo, 1978a, Experiment 6; Klitzner, 1975).

Moreover, functional scales from the adding operation could provide direct information on configural integration. Regardless of the nature of the integration operation for determining the area of the separate rectangles, functional scaling from the two-rectangle design could provide linear scales of their effective values. Figures of arbitrary shape could also be used instead of rectangles. As noted in Anderson and Weiss (1971), "This would be an important result, since it would give a theoretically valid measure of the effective phenomenal size of the components. Such measures would provide a solid base for the study of the processes underlying the valuation of the components [p. 548]." This same principle applies generally to the study of configural processing.

Adding–Subtracting Models. The task of judging the difference between two objects, each of which requires a prior integration, can be represented by the following schematic two-operation model

$$R_{ijkl} = [A_i \circledast B_j] - [C_k \circledast D_l].$$

It is assumed that the differencing operation is valid. It is desired to test the hypothesis that the generalized integration operation, $\circledast$, is addition or subtraction. To do this, choose A_i and C_k to have equal value. Under the given hypothesis, the equation then reduces to

$$R_{ijkl} = [A_i \pm B_j] - [C_k \pm D_l]$$
$$= (A_i - C_k) \pm (B_j - D_l)$$
$$= (B_j \pm D_l),$$

independent of A_i and C_k. For fixed j and l, therefore, there are ik responses; all should be equal if ⊛ is an adding or subtracting operation.

The first applications of this idea appear to be those of Schmidt and Levin (1972) and Birnbaum (1974a), who obtained judgments of difference in likableness of two persons, each described by two adjectives. Although their results left some doubt about the validity of the differencing operation, they did suggest that ⊛ was nonadditive, possibly an averaging operation. The test has the advantage, pointed out by Birnbaum, that it is valid even when the response scale is only monotone (see Section F2.3.5).

Hybrid Models. A somewhat different problem can arise if the integration involves two operations on the same stimuli. Two-factor design with monotone transformation seems unlikely to have enough power to detect that neither operation is sufficient (see, e.g., Figure 5.2). Three-factor design may be able to handle such situations by using three-factor transformation or the two-phase logic already mentioned.

Hybrid models deserve more serious consideration than they have received. There is an either–or tendency in model analysis that is quite natural but that has little a priori justification. One example from psychophysics concerns the question of whether subjects make difference or ratio judgments, a question that goes back to the time of Galileo (Drake, 1978, p. 307). The plausible hypothesis that the overt response may be a compound of both difference and ratio judgments has been neglected. This hybrid hypothesis would lead to a model of the form

$$(A - B) + w(A \div B),$$

where w is a relative weight. The results of Section 5.6 indicate that two-factor design is unable to discriminate this hybrid model from a pure difference model or a pure ratio model when monotone transformation is allowed.

If the weight parameter in this ratio–difference model is constant, then the model has a semilinear form. If the response measure is linear, therefore, then the analysis of Section 3.4 applies. If monotone transformation is allowed, then some form of two-operation model could provide a basis for evaluating the simple ratio and difference models. A related approach, in terms of stimulus generality, has been pursued by Birnbaum (e.g., 1978).

The problem of hybrid models also arose in the adding–averaging question. Although this question was also approached with either–or thinking, the hybrid model is not unattractive (Section F2.4.3). In person perception, the evidence points to a pure averaging process. However, Shanteau's (1974, 1975a) subadditivity effect for commodity bundles might perhaps result from an averaging process overlaid on an adding process.

Distinct Tasks. In the preceding discussion, both operations were assumed to be part of the same task. A related method would employ two distinct tasks with the same stimuli, with the expectation that both tasks would yield equivalent stimulus scales (e.g., Anderson, 1972a, Figure 2). This method can also provide constraint on response transformation (Birnbaum & Veit, 1974). This approach, however, falls more properly under the concept of cross-task stimulus generality already discussed in Section 3.1.

Interlaced Designs. A final method following a rather different rationale also deserves mention. It employs two distinct, interlaced designs, that both require similar judgments. Only one design, however, is expected to follow a simple model. For example, one design would present stimulus combinations selected to avoid interaction or configural integration. The other design, perhaps of greater interest, would be constructed to include interactive combinations. If the response range of the first design interlaces that of the second, then it can validate the response for the second design, thereby facilitating interpretation in terms of true interaction.

3.3 Multilinear Models

Multilinear models rest on linear and multiplying models as building blocks. A multilinear model can be defined as a sum of products of several stimulus factors such that each factor occurs in each product in all-or-none fashion, that is, with exponent 0 or 1. The more common multilinear models are listed in schematic notation in Table 3.1 (Anderson, 1974f).

With three stimulus variables, there are just five linearly distinct multilinear models. These are Models 2, 4, 5, 7, and 9 in Table 3.1. The first and second are simple adding and multiplying models. The other three represent compound adding–multiplying operations. Models 3 and 3a, AB and $AB + A + B$, are linearly equivalent, as shown in Eqs. (15)–(19) of Section 2.2. Similarly, $AB + A + B + C$ is equivalent to $AB + C$.

TABLE 3.1
Summary Analysis for Illustrative Multilinear Models

Model	Bilinear interactions	Trilinear interactions	Zero interactions
1. $A + B$			AB
2. $A + B + C$			AB, AC, BC, ABC
3. AB	AB		
3a. $AB + A + B$	AB		
4. ABC	AB, AC, BC	ABC	
5. $AB + C$	AB		AC, BC, ABC
6. $AB + C + D$	AB		$AC, AD, BC, BD, CD, ABC,$ $ABD, ACD, BCD, ABCD$
7. $AB + AC$	AB, AC		BC, ABC
8. $ABC + D$	AB, AC, BC	ABC	$AD, BD, CD, ABD, ACD,$ $BCD, ABCD$
9. $AB + BC + AC$	AB, BC, AC		ABC
10. $AB + CD$	AB, CD		$AC, AD, BC, BD, ABC,$ $ABD, ACD, BCD, ABCD$

SOURCE: After Anderson (1974f).

Each model has a unique pattern of linear interaction that is listed in Table 3.1. This interaction pattern mirrors the algebraic structure of the model. In practice, therefore, the observed pattern of interaction provides a diagnostic device to determine which, if any, of these models is operative. Two experimental illustrations are given in Section F1.7.1.[a]

Another illustration of model diagnostics appeared in a study of information purchase by Shanteau and Anderson (1972). Individual analyses showed that the majority of subjects followed the hypothesized three-factor multiplying model. A substantial minority, however, followed alternative rules of the form $AB + C$, for example, or even $A + B + C$. This suggests that they may have been simplifying the task by shifting from multiplying to adding.

The most common four-factor model is $AB + CD$, which appears frequently as a weighted sum. In the model for subjective expected value studied in Section F1.7.1, for example, A and C correspond to probability weighting factors, whereas B and D correspond to the values of the objects that may be won. A methodological point from that experiment is that the failure of the adding operation did not appear in the two-way interactions but was only revealed in the three-way interactions (Anderson & Shanteau, 1970). It may not be adequate, therefore, to study multistimulus integration just two factors at a time.

If $AB + CD$ actually represents an average rather than a sum, then differential weighting will cause specific patterns of deviation from parallelism and may cause deviations from the two linear fan predictions. An illustration from a study of source reliability is given in Section F4.4.3. This possibility needs to be kept in mind because of the ubiquity of averaging processes.

The diagnostic value of these functional measurement tests also appeared in a study of fairness judgments (Section F1.7.4) and in an experiment on the Height + Width rule for children's judgments of rectangle area (Section F1.3.6). In the former experiment, the interaction pattern pointed directly to the operative model. In the latter experiment, the pattern of judgments of total area of two rectangles provided helpful support for the linearity of the response scale.

One experiment has even studied a six-factor integration task with good success. Subjects judged total value of two gambles, one to win a food item, the other to win a beverage, each with independent probabilities and independent motivational states. Individual analyses provided reasonably good support for the MEV model

$$R = \text{Motivation}_1 \times \text{Expectancy}_1 \times \text{Valence}_1$$
$$+ \text{Motivation}_2 \times \text{Expectancy}_2 \times \text{Valence}_2,$$

where subscripts 1 and 2 represent food and drink, respectively. The success of so complex a model is a good argument that cognitive algebra reflects natural mental operations (Klitzner & Anderson, 1977).

As a practical matter, six factors may be too many. The main effect of an average factor can only claim one-sixth of the total range of response. Two-way interactions are typically only a fraction the size of the main effects; three-way interactions, in turn, are typically only a fraction the size of the two-way interactions. Accordingly, these interaction tests can suffer from lack of power. In the cited study, the two-way multiplying interactions were highly significant, although uncomfortably small in magnitude. Power did not appear to be a problem for the two-way interactions, therefore, but the three-way interactions did not appear to be informative. An obvious remedy is to hold one or more factors constant at some fixed value, thereby increasing the effective magnitudes of the other factors (Section 1.3.7).

Statistical analysis of multilinear models rests on the parallelism and linear fan theorems. The interaction test for parallelism applies to each two-factor subdesign, and related tests apply to higher order subdesigns. Much the same holds for linear fan tests. The guidelines of Sections 2.1 and 2.2 apply also to these more complex models. In addition, the marginal means of the data tables can provide linear scales of stimulus values. This property, which is common to the two-factor adding and multiplying models, continues to hold even though the marginal means are averages over multiple factors in the multilinear models.

Marginal means scaling holds for any operation that is correct, even though the independence assumption may fail for other operations in the model.[b]

3.4 Semilinear Models

In the multilinear models of Section 3.3, each stimulus variable is assumed to correspond to a single term in the model although this term may appear in more than one place (e.g., Model 9 of Table 3.1). In some models, however, a single stimulus may have two distinct effects. The w–s representation of averaging theory is one example, and another appears in the multiattribute model of Figure 6.3. Another class of such models, the semilinear models, has a straightforward analysis that will be discussed here.

Statistical Analysis. For a two-factor design the semilinear model can be written in symbolic form as

$$R_{ij} = A_i + A_i'B_j. \tag{1}$$

where A_i and A_i' are the two distinct effects of the row stimulus. The column means are a linear function of the values of the column stimuli:

$$\bar{R}_{.j} = \bar{A}_. + \bar{A}'B_j.$$

For row i, R_{ij} is a linear function of B_j and hence of $\bar{R}_{.j}$. This model allows a graphical test, therefore, because each row of data must plot as a straight-line function of the mean row, that is, the row of column means. These straight lines will not in general intersect at a common point, however, a feature that distinguishes the semilinear model from the multiplying model.

For the case of independent scores, an analysis of variance test has been given by Mandel (1964, Sections 9.4 and 9.5). Sums of squares for rows, columns, and interaction are calculated as usual. The sum of squares for interaction is broken down into two parts, one part for the slope factor, A_i', the other for the residual from the model fit. The computing formulas are

$$SS_{Residual} = SS_{Rows \times Columns} - SS_{Slopes}, \tag{2}$$

$$SS_{Slopes} = (1/I)[\Sigma(b_i - 1)^2] \, SS_{Columns}, \tag{3}$$

$$b_i = \Sigma_j l_j T_{ij} / n\Sigma_j l_j^2,$$

$$l_j := \bar{R}_{.j} - \bar{R}_{..}.$$

Here the row deviations, l_j, are the linear coefficients for the column variable, as in Eq. (6) of Section 2.2, and T_{ij} is the total of the n scores in cell ij. The term b_i is the slope of the data in row i considered as a function of the l_j.

Slopes and residual have $(I - 1)$ and $(I - 1)(J - 2)$ df, respectively, where I and J denote the total number of rows and columns. The semilinear model requires a significant slopes term and nonsignificant residual. The multiplying model is a special case in which the sum of squares for slopes is concentrated in the bilinear component. To rule out this special case would require a significant slopes residual, $SS_{Slopes} -$ $SS_{Bilinear}$, on $(I - 2)$ df.

Experimental Applications. Semilinear models have arisen in several areas. The averaging model assumes a semilinear form when one factor is equally weighted, the other unequally weighted (Section 2.3.1). Sjöberg (1968) has suggested that the nominal Subjective probability × Subjective value model may include an additive probability component. Other experimental instances appear in comparative judgment (Section 3.5) and in the shape function model (Section 3.9). The problem of comparing estimated scale values for the same set of stimuli obtained from several different tasks can also be put into the form of a semilinear model (Sections 2.1.4 and 2.2.3; see also Mandel, 1964, Chapters 13 and 14). However, all published work on stimulus invariance in integration studies has used other methods of analysis.

For statistical testing, the assumption of independent scores required in Mandel's (1964) procedure would usually be practicable only in individual subject designs (Section 2.1.3). Statistical analysis for repeated measurements designs faces the problems discussed in Section 2.2.2 and has not been considered in detail. It would seem, however, that the interaction components involving nonlinear column effects would be appropriate tests for deviations from the model. Theoretically, each row curve is a linear function of the column means, so that Row : Linear × Column : Quadratic and Row : Linear × Column : Cubic, in particular, should be zero except for error variability. These components may be obtained as indicated in Section 2.2.2. Alternatively, the general method of Section 4.4 for nonlinear models could be employed.

3.5 Ratio Models and Comparison Processes

Comparison processes are involved in many situations, with the response to a given stimulus determined partly or wholly by its relation to contextual stimuli. Judgments of relative sensory magnitude in psychophysics are of this type, as are fair share judgments in equity theory. Comparative processes also appear to be a causal factor in geometrical illusions.

Single Comparison. Comparative judgment naturally gives rise to ratio-type models, and they have been considered by numerous investigators.[a] The simplest ratio model for comparison of two stimuli, S_{Ai} and S_{Bj}, can be written as

$$R_{ij} = C_0 + s_{Ai}/s_{Bj}. \tag{4}$$

This is a dividing model and may be tested by the linear fan analysis. A successful graphical application is illustrated in a reanalysis of data on adaptation-level theory of anchor effects (Anderson, 1974a, Figure 10).

On the whole, however, this particular ratio model has done poorly. Evidence from psychophysical judgment is reviewed in Anderson (1974a, pp. 266–271). A striking failure in fair share judgments is given in Anderson (1976a, Figure 1). There is some evidence that subjects may follow a subtracting rule rather than the dividing rule, both in psychophysical judgment (Birnbaum & Elmasian, 1977; Torgerson, 1961) and in social judgment (Anderson, 1976a; Anderson & Butzin, 1974; Graesser & Anderson, 1974; see Section F1.5.6).

A more successful ratio model has the relative ratio form

$$R_{ij} = C_0 + s_{Ai}/(s_{Ai} + s_{Bj}). \tag{5}$$

Models of this form have been applied in psycholinguistics, equity theory, and decision theory (see Section F1.7.4). Why the relative ratio of Eq. (5) should do well and the simpler ratio of Eq. (4) do poorly is not clear. The two models have been applied in different experimental situations, so the evidence sheds little light on their relative merit. It may be noted, however, that the relative ratio model can be derived from averaging theory (Section F1.6.4).

The relative ratio model of Eq. (5) has the same form as a choice model used by Bradley and Terry (1952) and by Luce (1959), but there is a fundamental difference between them. The choice model applies only to choice probabilities, and hence only to stimulus alternatives that are imperfectly discriminable. The relative ratio model can do the same, but it also applies more generally to suprathreshold, nonprobabilistic discrimination. It thus becomes practicable to cover a substantial range of stimuli with individual subject design and analysis. The characteristic pattern of the factorial plot from this model is a barrel shape (see Figure 5.2). Illustrative analyses are given in Oden (1977a, 1978), Leon and Anderson (1974), and Farkas and Anderson (1979).[b]

Multiple Comparison. An interesting problem arises when two comparison stimuli, S_{Bj} and S_{Ck}, are present. Under one generalization of Eq. (5), the two comparison stimuli are first integrated and then S_{Ai} is compared to their resultant

$$R_{ijk} = C_0 + s_{Ai}/(s_{Ai} + s_{Bj} + s_{Ck}). \tag{6}$$

Under an alternative generalization, S_{Ai} is compared separately to each comparison stimulus and then these two comparative judgments are integrated

$$R_{ijk} = C_0 + s_{Ai}/(s_{Ai} + s_{Bj}) + s_{Ai}/(s_{Ai} + s_{Ck}). \tag{7}$$

These two equations can be distinguished in terms of their interaction structure. The $B \times C$ interaction, for example, is nonzero in the first equation and zero in the second. This implication also holds when the stimuli in parentheses are integrated by an arbitrary, nonadditive rule.

Although the problem of comparison structure seems to have fundamental interest, not much data are available. Adaptation-level theory (Helson, 1964; Restle, 1971) is based on a pooling assumption analogous to that of Eq. (6), but none of the associated experimental studies seem to provide an adequate test of fit. However, a comparison of adaptation-level theory and information integration theory in a study of geometrical illusions has favored the second equation (Clavadetscher & Anderson, 1977). Support for a similar model of comparison structure has been obtained by Farkas and Anderson (1979) and Anderson (1976d). Such structural studies may be useful in cognitive analysis.

3.6 Serial Integration

The problem of serial integration has received considerable attention in integration theory. Stimuli must be presented in some serial order in time and space, and this serial order may need to be taken explicitly into account. A novel property of the model presented here is that it can determine the effect of each serial position on the final response. It is possible, in other words, to dissect the final response to obtain a complete serial position curve.

Model and Assumptions. The notation of Eq. (34) of Section 2.3.2 will be used as a convenient way to allow for multiple factors corresponding to multiple serial positions. Value and weight of the tth stimulus at the Xth serial position will be denoted by s_{Xt} and w_X, respectively. The stimuli that can be presented at any given serial position are assumed to have equal weight among themselves, so w_X does not depend on particular stimuli. The response, R_n, is measured after the last of a sequence of n stimuli has been presented.

The model is just a weighted sum or average of the effects of the stimuli at the successive serial positions

$$R_n = \sum_{X=0}^{n} w_X s_{Xt}. \tag{8}$$

The sum is over all serial positions in some specific sequence of n particular stimuli. There is nothing new about this model except its application to serial presentation.

Goodness of Fit. The essential idea in the analysis of the serial integration model is to make each serial position correspond to a factor of a factorial design. Then the graphical test of parallelism applies directly, as do the statistical tests of interaction.

This method of testing begins to be cumbersome when more than a few serial positions are tested. With only two stimulus levels at each of six serial positions, the complete factorial design generates $2^6 = 64$ different sequences. To study larger numbers of serial positions may require fractional replication, skipping, ganging, or incomplete design. In an experimental application to intuitive statistics, a 2^6 design was reduced by fractional replication to 2^3 conditions that allowed a test of goodness of fit and an orthogonal estimation of the six weight parameters for the six serial positions (Anderson, 1964d).

Estimation and Scaling. In the serial integration model, linear scales of the stimuli are obtained from the marginal means, exactly as in Section 2.1. The serial weight parameter, of course, is confounded with the scale unit and can only be estimated under special conditions.

In certain tasks, these serial weights could be of primary interest. The following method for obtaining serial weights has proved useful in several experiments. Suppose that just two stimuli are used at each serial position and that the difference between their scale values is constant across serial position. From Eq. (8), it follows that the difference, D_X, between the two marginal means at serial position X is

$$D_X = w_X(s_{X1} - s_{X2}). \tag{9}$$

Since the difference in parentheses is constant across serial position by assumption, w_X is proportional to the observable D_X. These differences in marginal means are thus estimates of the serial weights on a ratio scale. Experimental applications have been made in person perception (Section F2.5), as well as in attitude theory, psychophysics, decision theory, and learning theory.[a]

A straightforward extension allows for more than two stimuli at each serial position. As before, it is assumed that the stimuli have the same effective values, up to an additive constant, at each serial position. The marginal means at serial position X then can be written in the multiplicative form $C_X + w_X s_{Xt}$, where C_X equals C_0 plus the average of $w_X s_{Xt}$ taken over the levels of all other factors in the design. The given expression has the form of a semilinear model. In form, the set of marginal means may be considered a Row $\times$ Column, Stimulus value $\times$ Serial position design. In this design, the row means provide a linear scale of the common stimulus values. The entries in column X of this design will plot as a straight-line function of these row means, and their slopes will provide estimates of the w_X on a ratio scale.

Serial Position Curve. Under the given assumptions, Eq. (9) provides estimates of the weight at each serial position. These weights, however, may depend not only on serial position per se, but also on the free or natural weight of the stimuli presented in that serial position. To obtain a pure serial position curve, these two determinants of the weight must be separated.

Perhaps the simplest approach is to use only stimuli that have the same natural weight. This weighting condition would presumably be satisfied in psychophysical averaging, for example, if the same actual stimuli were presented at each serial position. Under this condition, the observed differences among the weight estimates would mirror the effects of position per se, thereby yielding a pure serial position curve (e.g., Weiss & Anderson, 1969; Section F2.5.4).

Serial Averaging. In one view, serial averaging is a successive integration procedure in which the response at each position, explicit or implicit, is a compromise or average of the previous response and the present stimulus. The change in response is then a proportion of the possible change, that is, of the distance between the previous response and the present stimulus. In this proportional change form,

$$R_n = R_{n-1} + w_n(s_n - R_{n-1}), \tag{10}$$

which can be written explicitly as a weighted average

$$R_n = w_n s_n + (1 - w_n)R_{n-1}. \tag{11}$$

By recursion, $R_{n-1}, R_{n-2}, \ldots$, may be successively eliminated so that Eq.

(11) can be expressed in the same form as Eq. (8). Because Eq. (11) represents a strict step-by-step integration, the resultant weight for each serial stimulus is a prescribed function of the serial position weights. Equation (8), in contrast, does not impose such a restriction. It could thus apply to situations in which the serial stimuli are stored separately in memory and integration occurs at the end of the sequence.

Learning Curves and Sequential Dependencies. Learning may be considered serial integration, with the reinforcing stimulus on each trial integrated into the underlying response on that trial. This integration view has special interest for partial and varied reinforcement because the reinforcing stimuli may differ from one trial to the next. The plot of the response as a function of the pattern of reinforcement over short blocks of trials can then provide a revealing picture of the learning process. Such plots are called *subsequence curves* and *sequential dependencies.*

Sequential dependencies are important because they provide more detailed process information than does the mean learning curve. In principle, sequential dependencies provide a sufficient set of statistics for the learning process. Interpretation of sequential dependencies is sometimes tricky, however, due to the operation of stochastic components in the learning process. Although special cases of sequential dependencies had been considered by a number of writers, the first general analysis for learning models was developed by Anderson (1959a).[b] This analysis, formulated within the framework of the linear operator models of Bush and Mosteller (1955), emphasized the theoretical and empirical primacy of sequential dependencies.

> The fundamental quantities in the empirical study of discrete-trial learning are the trial-to-trial increments and decrements in the observable properties of the response system. Similarly, in the theory of learning, the basic quantities are the trial-to-trial increments and decrements in the relevant constructs or intervening variables of the theory. Thus it would seem that these sequential dependencies within the sequence of stimuli and responses should be more useful, both for descriptive and theoretical purposes, than the curve of performance versus trials. Since these dependencies directly reflect the action of the reinforcing events, they are more immediately interpretable and contain considerably more information than the mean learning curve.
>
> To illustrate this last point more clearly, consider an avoidance-conditioning situation and suppose that response strength is decreased on avoidance trials and increased on non-avoidance trials. Then, even when the learning curve has reached asymptote, the true response strength of a subject will still rise and fall in a lawful, though probabilistic, way about his constant mean response level, and the evaluation of these increments and decrements will provide information about the learning process even

after the learning curve has lost its usefulness. Similar considerations apply, of course, when the increments and decrements are controlled by variation of the reinforcing stimuli applied by the experimenter.

Although many situations exist in which the learning curve is the sufficient object of interest, even in the above simple situation it can be misleading since it represents an average or resultant of the incremental and the decremental process. The same resultant may arise from a weak incremental and weak decremental process as from a strong incremental and strong decremental process. Moreover, differences in the mean performance level for different experimental conditions cannot be unambiguously attributed to differences in either process, since they may be due to differences in the strength of one, or the other, or both [Anderson, 1959a, p. 248].

Sequential dependencies were important in the study of probability learning, in which they were instrumental in the shift from an S–R conditioning orientation to a cognitive approach.[c]

3.7 Conjunctive and Disjunctive Models

A conjunctive decision rule sets up a passing criterion on each of several dimensions, all of which must be satisfied simultaneously. For example, success in graduate school depends on being above certain minima in intelligence and motivation. Use of a point criterion has been customary in model analysis, with the consequence that no amount of motivation could compensate for an intelligence level below the cut point. Because it disallows any compensation between motivation and intelligence, the use of point criteria is not realistic.

Averaging theory provides a more flexible analysis of the conjunctive integration rule. Each dimension would have a weighting function with high values below some threshold band, decreasing toward a low asymptote at very high values. Any stimulus value that fell below the threshold band could dominate the response by virtue of its high absolute weight because the effective, relative weights must sum to one. In effect, the point threshold is replaced by a region, and limited compensation of one factor by another is permitted.

A special case of the conjunctive model has a differential weighting function on only one dimension; each other dimension is equally weighted within itself. The model is then a semilinear averaging model of the kind considered in Section 3.4. An experimental illustration from Lampel and Anderson (1968) is discussed in Section F2.3.4.[a]

Disjunctive rules require passable performance on only one dimension. For example, success in research might result from achievement as a theoretician, or as an experimentalist. Much the same averaging-theoretical analysis applies, except that the weighting function for dis-junctive models would be complementary to that for conjunctive models. Thus, any one stimulus that was above the threshold band could dominate the average and so produce a passing judgment.

3.8 Probability Models

Mathematical probability theory gives rise to simple algebraic models that have been considered by a number of writers. In the present theory, a major question is whether the cognitive algebra of probability is isomorphic to the mathematical algebra. The multiplication rule for joint probability will be considered briefly, for illustration.

The joint probability of two events, A and B, can be written,

$$\text{Prob}(A \text{ and } B) = \text{Prob}(A)\text{Prob}(B|A),$$

where Prob(B|A) is the conditional probability of B, given A. This is a simple multiplying model that can be analyzed as shown in Section 2.2.

The success of this multiplying rule will no doubt depend on how the task is operationalized for the subject. An attractive possibility is suggested by the urn task that has become standard through the pioneering work of Edwards (1968, 1971) on Bayesian decision theory. The A factor in the design could correspond to a group of urns, each filled with dice, and the B factor could correspond to the colors of these dice. The subject would estimate the probability that one die chosen at random would come from Urn A_i and have Color B_j. Equation (12) can be extended to three events, the third of which could be represented by the face turned up in a throw of the selected die.

Equation (12) can also be viewed as a useful prescription for breaking the judgment into stages. The urn example seems likely to work well, in part because its physical structure is conducive to the prescribed rule. The events of daily life are ordinarily less well defined and may not follow so simple a rule. However, the model did remarkably well in Lopes's (1976b) study of poker (Section F1.5.2).[a]

3.9 Shape Function Model

Some questions require comparison of shapes of different functions. One example from learning theory appears in the question whether level of original learning affects rate of forgetting. To answer this question, some way of comparing retention performance independent of level of original learning is required. It seems safe to say that such comparisons can only be done within the framework of some theoretical model. A *shape function method* that has some degree of generality will be outlined here (see Anderson, 1963).

It is assumed that observations $R_i(n)$ are obtained for individuals i over a sequence of trials or time points, $n = 1, 2, \ldots , N$. The shape function model can then be written

$$R_i(n) = R_i(N) + [R_i(1) - R_i(N)]f_i(n). \tag{13}$$

Here $R_i(1)$ and $R_i(N)$ are the initial and final levels of response, and $f_i(n)$ is the shape function. The essential property of this model is that the shape function is algebraically separated from the initial and final levels of response.

A well-known special case of the shape function model is the linear operator model of mathematical learning theory (Anderson, 1959a, 1964b; Atkinson & Estes, 1963; Bush & Mosteller, 1955; Sternberg, 1963). The shape function for the linear operator model is

$$f_i(n) = (1 - \theta_i)^{n-1},$$

where θ_i is the learning rate parameter. The shape function model is more general in that it does not require the learning rate to be constant over trials.

To test whether the mean shape functions are the same under two different experimental conditions, Eq. (13) would be fitted to estimate the shape function for each individual. These shape functions would represent the trials factor in a Conditions $\times$ Trials design. The null hypotheses of no main effect and no interaction of conditions could be tested with the usual repeated measurements analysis of variance.

The essential idea of the shape function method was suggested by Beier (1958), and one application is given in Logan, Beier, and Kincaid (1956). Statistical problems and other applications are discussed in Anderson (1963), and an application to approach–avoidance gradients is given in Anderson (1962b). A generalization to include an all-or-none component was presented by Warburton and Greeno (1970).[a]

As it stands, Eq. (13) will fit the data exactly and so is not testable without further assumptions. This problem will not be pursued here except to note, again, that the shape function model does include various standard learning models as special cases and would be testable in those cases.

Any comparison of curve shape among conditions that have different initial or final levels rests on some assumption about the underlying theoretical model. This point may be emphasized by comparing the shape function method with the analysis of covariance, which is sometimes employed in the belief that it "equates" for systematic differences. To illustrate, let $R_i(N) = 0$ and take the dependent variable to be the mean response over the N trials. Then Eq. (14) expresses the regression of the dependent variable $\bar{R}_i(n)$ on the covariate $R_i(1)$

$$\bar{R}_i(n) = \bar{f}_i|(n)R_i(1). \tag{14}$$

The standard application of covariance assumes an adding model, whereas Eq. (14) embodies a multiplying relationship. As a consequence, the standard covariance test for differences in elevations between conditions would, in general, give a result different from shape function analysis.

The shape function method is generally applicable to any comparison among curves that embody the given form. This may be emphasized by rewriting Eq. (13) in different notation

$$R_i(n) = a_i + (b_i - a_i)f_i(n). \tag{15}$$

If all shape functions are the same, $f_i(n) = f(n)$, then Eq. (15) has the form of a semilinear model. If, also, either a_i or b_i is constant, then the semilinear model reduces to a multiplying model, and linear fan analysis would be applicable.

3.10 Integration Decision Model for Choice Response

The present model applies an integration-theoretical approach to problems of choice response. The model employs concepts from signal detection theory and Thurstonian scaling theory and shows how these relate to functional measurement. Most applications of signal detection theory and Thurstonian scaling have considered choices among unitary stimuli, whereas the present emphasis is on stimulus integration in compound stimuli. A major goal of the present approach is to bypass the distributional assumptions that are central in signal detection theory and Thurstonian scaling.

Integration Decision Model. Consider a stimulus field of N sources, each of which can be in various states. Each source–state combination is assumed to correspond to an independent distribution of information values, u_{Xt}, for Source X in State t. On any trial, the total accumulated information is taken to be a weighted sum

$$I(A) = \sum_A w_X u_{Xt}, \tag{16}$$

where w_X is the relative importance of Source X, u_{Xt} is the random value of Source X in State t, and the sum is over all sources in some given array, A, of states.

Let s_{Xt} and σ_X^2 denote the mean and variance of u_{Xt}, and let $s_{I(A)}$ and σ_I^2 denote the mean and variance of $I(A)$. Then

$$s_{I(A)} = \sum w_X s_{Xt}, \tag{17}$$

and, since the u_{Xt} are independent by assumption,

$$\sigma_I^2 = \sum w_X^2 \sigma_X^2.$$

As the notation indicates, the variance is assumed constant over states within a source, so that the variance of $I(A)$ is constant, independent of the particular array, A, on any trial. For simplicity, σ_I^2 is set equal to unity, which may be done without loss of generality for fixed N.

The subject is assumed to make categorical responses using some criterion. In a yes–no task, for example, the response will be *yes* or *no* according to whether the value of $I(A)$ is above or below the criterion, k. The observed data, therefore, are choice proportions.

To obtain a theoretical relation between these observable choice proportions and the structural model of Eq. (16), some assumption must be made about the distribution of the underlying u_{Xt}. The usual assumption that the u_{Xt} are normal implies that $I(A)$ is also normal. Hence the observed proportion of *yes* responses, conditional on a given array of source states, corresponds to the unit normal deviate

$$z_{\text{yes}}(A) = s_{I(A)} - k = -k + \sum_A w_X s_{Xt}. \tag{18}$$

Thus, $s_{I(A)}$ is a linear function of the observable $z_{\text{yes}}(A)$, which is itself a linear function of the source values and of the criterion. Equation (18) is the basic result for the distributional model. Several possible applications may be noted.

Stimulus Integration. Suppose that the stimulus arrays are constructed from factorial designs in which the sources are the factors, each with several states or levels of equal weight and variance. If z_{yes} is used as the dependent variable, Eq. (18) implies that all interactions are zero. If the model passes this test of fit, it may be used to measure parameters. For a complete design, the marginal means estimate the values of the information states, s_{Xt}, on linear scales. In practice, of course, modifications may be needed to allow for empty cells that would result from choice proportions near 0 or 1. This application could be employed to study integration across two or more sensory modalities.

Criterion Scaling. Criterion scaling represents an important application of the model that could be accomplished by manipulating the criterion as a factor in the design. Two standard methods for controlling the criterion are instruction and variation of stimulus probabilities. In addition, several criteria could be maintained simultaneously by requiring a rating response. Since Eq. (18) is linear in k, the marginal means of the criterion factor will provide linear scales of the criterion values.

This treatment of the criterion brings out an important difference between the present approach and that used in signal detection theory. In signal detection theory, the criterion lies on a statistical likelihood axis and does not have a simple algebraic form. In the present model, the criterion lies on the information axis itself and has a simple theoretical expression.

Serial Integration. Serial presentation of the stimulus sources would be expected to introduce memory effects. The present approach allows weight to depend on serial position, and a complete serial curve can be obtained (Section 3.6). Such curves could be useful in studying memory factors. Previous models for serial integration in signal detection have required perfect memory for past stimulus information, in line with the Bayesian origin of signal detection theory (Green & Swets, 1966, p. 238; Ulehla, Canges, & Wackwitz, 1967).

Recognition Memory. Signal detection theory has often been applied to recognition memory, with familiarity or memory strength as the information variables u_{Xt}. The present model would allow contextual cues to recognition as a factor in the design. Of course, such cues might operate as multiplicative weights rather than as additive information values.

It would also be possible to study the response to sets of several memory items. For example, subjects can be required to categorize as "familiar" or "unfamiliar" sets with both old and new items in varied proportion. All items in the set will then represent sources having, in the simplest case, equal weight and the same two mean states. For fixed set size, z_{yes} would be a linear function of the number of old items.

The d' Statistic. Finally, the special case of one source with two states has special interest. It is the case usually considered in signal detection theory. The two states are called *signal* and *noise*, with scale values s_S

and s_N. These may be considered the rows in a two-way factorial design in which the column stimuli represent the criterion value, k_j. Equation (18) then becomes

$$z_{yes,j}(S) = -k_j + ws_S,$$
$$z_{yes,j}(N) = -k_j + ws_N. \tag{19}$$

The difference between these two expressions is the well-known d'

$$d' = z_{yes}(S) - z_{yes}(N) = w(s_S - s_N). \tag{20}$$

Thus, d' is theoretically constant, independent of the criterion, k_j.

The constancy of d' corresponds to the parallelism property of functional measurement. In signal detection theory, the standard test of the model is in terms of the ROC curve: From Eq. (19), $z_{yes,j}(S)$, when plotted as a function of $z_{yes,j}(N)$, should have unit slope. This ROC test is equivalent to the test of parallelism in a two-way design: One factor is the criterion, the other factor is the two-state source. The factorial plot should be two parallel curves.[a]

Comments. The present integration-decision model was originally developed in a signal detection framework (Anderson, 1972c, 1974a), but it differs in two basic respects, both of which relate to the origin of signal detection theory in normative statistical decision theory. First, the criterion is here considered to lie on the raw information axis itself, not on the likelihood axis of statistical theory. Second, the present model is descriptive rather than normative. It can allow, in particular, for memory effects in serial integration that are disallowed in the normative, Bayesian approach to signal detection theory.[b]

Because of these two differences, the present model seems conceptually closer to the Thurstonian framework. That framework has been largely limited to scaling, but Lee (1971) has emphasized its decision-theoretical aspects. Some applications to integration problems have also been made (Bock & Jones, 1968, Sections 7.3.3, 8.5). An approach similar to the present formulation was independently developed by Kinchla (Kinchla & Collyer, 1974; see also Collyer, 1977).

A major problem in the analysis of choice data, particularly for integration tasks, is the lack of sensitivity. Green and Swets (1966, Chapter 9) compare two integration models, one based on signal detection theory, the other based on assumptions similar to those of high threshold theory, in which no integration occurs. Despite the radical difference between these two models, data from the integration tasks did little to distinguish between them. Some more sensitive approach would be desirable, and that possibility is considered next.

Distribution-Free Model. The integration-theoretical approach potentiates a fundamental shift away from the conceptual structure of signal detection theory and Thurstonian theory. This shift is from distributions, normal or otherwise, to the algebraic structure of the integration model.

Algebraic structure and normal distributions were both employed in the preceding analysis. Their roles can be brought out by comparing Eqs. (17) and (18). In Eq. (17), the informational state of the subject is a numerical variable, but this is mapped into a dichotomous yes–no response by the decision output system. The z-transformation of the observed proportions allows reconstruction of the structure of the original informational state, as it depended on the stimulus design. The z-transformation inverts the choice dichotomization, allowing a recovery of the basic numerical information represented by $s_{I(A)}$ in Eq. (18).

Numerical observations of $I(A)$ or of $s_{I(A)}$ would be more useful and more efficient than having to accumulate enough trials to estimate a choice proportion. More important, numerical response measures would bypass the need for distributional assumptions altogether. The structure of the integration model provides a sufficient base and frame for theoretical analysis.

In this approach, therefore, main attention would shift to the study of integration tasks and the use of numerical response measures. Work on signal detection theory has shown that ratings and reaction times, for example, carry more information than does choice response (e.g., Carterette, Friedman, & Cosmides, 1965; Egan, Schulman, & Greenberg, 1959; Watson, Rilling, & Bourbon, 1964) and thus are proper numerical responses for threshold stimuli. Suprathreshold stimuli could also be studied; a shift to the algebraic approach would eliminate the restriction to threshold stimuli that is inherent in the distributional approach (see also Section F1.5.7).

Monotone analysis of the response measure would presumably be needed, but, with the methods described in Section 5.6 this seems to be practicable. Monotone transformation serves the same purpose as the z-transformation (Anderson, 1970b, p. 163), but monotonicity is less demanding than normality.

The preceding analysis provides another illustration of the shift in thinking that accompanies an integration-theoretical approach. Signal detection theory has been concerned largely with judgments of single stimuli, which did not exhibit an algebraic model that could be used as a structural frame to replace the distributional assumptions. Thurstonian paired comparisons did entail an explicit subtracting model, but that was an as-if formalism derivative from the distributional assumptions. The shift from distributional assumptions to algebraic structure reflects a corresponding shift in theoretical orientation.

This integration approach may be generally useful in decision tasks in which the overt response is not numerical but categorical or a yes–no decision. Many judgments have this character, from recognition memory and consumer purchases to decisions for or against hiring and promotion. The concept of a criterion from decision theory allows analysis of categorical response within the framework of the standard integration models. These models provide a conceptual framework for valuation and weighing of evidence. They can also be used for criterion analysis, either by considering the criterion as one factor in the decision model or by treating the criterion itself as an integrated resultant of operative stimulus factors. This approach allows use of suprathreshold stimuli that are typical of many actual decisions.

3.11 Rating as an Averaging Process

The ability of subjects to give numerical rating responses is remarkable but it has not received much theoretical attention. The rating method has generally been treated as a tool that is subject to various undesirable biases, whereas it and its biases reflect interesting and presumably important cognitive processes. This section and the two that follow deal with three treatments of some of these rating processes.[a]

Rating is assumed to involve locating the given stimulus relative to the end points (Section 1.1.3). This may be conceptualized in terms of similarity judgments. Let S be a given stimulus, let S_L and S_U be the lower and upper end anchors, respectively, and let R_L and R_U be the corresponding responses on the rating scale, ordinarily the rating end points. It is assumed that the subject judges the similarity between S and each end anchor and selects a response, R, proportionately located between the two end responses. This assumption may be written

$$(R - R_L)\text{Sim}_L = (R_U - R)\text{Sim}_U,$$

where Sim_L and Sim_U denote the similarities of S to S_L and S_U. Hence

$$R = (\text{Sim}_L R_L + \text{Sim}_U R_U)/(\text{Sim}_L + \text{Sim}_U). \tag{21}$$

Equation (21) represents the response to a given stimulus as an average of the two end responses, with weights equal to the similarities of the given stimulus to the end stimuli.[b]

This formulation brings out three aspects of the response process that need theoretical consideration. First and most prominent is the similarity judgment, on which some comments have been given in Section F5.6.5. It may also be possible to employ Eq. (21) as a similarity scaling technique to provide molar constraints on molecular similarity models.

The second aspect of the response is its quality or dimension. Stimulus values are not simply properties of the stimulus, but depend on the dimension of response (Section 7.15). This aspect is intimately related to the first, for the similarity judgment is made with respect to the operative response quality. The similarity judgment is thus related to the valuation operation that defines the response dimension. This relation, however, has not received much attention.

Third is the numerical character of the response. People can make continuous responses, most notably in motor skills to which the rating skill may be related. Work with children, as well as considerations of cognitive economy, have suggested the existence of a general purpose metric sense (Sections 1.1.3 and F1.1.6). A single response capability may underlie rating on response dimensions of diverse quality. To treat these response numbers as a true linear scale is a more complex issue, of course, as has been discussed in Section 1.1.

3.12 Range–Frequency Theory

In Parducci's (1965, 1974) range–frequency formulation, the overt response is an integration of two covert response tendencies. The range tendency operates to yield a response that is proportional to the subjective magnitude of the stimuli. The frequency tendency reflects a tendency to use the steps on the rating scale equally often. These two tendencies generally imply different responses to the same stimulus. If only the range tendency is operative, the distribution of overt responses will have the same shape as the underlying set or distribution of stimuli that are to be rated. If only the frequency tendency is operative, the distribution of overt responses will be uniform or flat across the rating scale, regardless of the actual distribution of subjective values.

Qualitative Tests. One main concern in the experimental work on range–frequency theory has been to compare it with Helson's (1964) theory of adaptation level as applied to rating judgments. Parducci has found a critical test that provides a qualitative demonstration of the superiority of range–frequency theory.

In one such test, subjects rated apparent size of squares on a 9-category scale. Figure 3.2 shows the mean ratings plotted as a function of square size. The critical aspect is the crossover of the curves for the

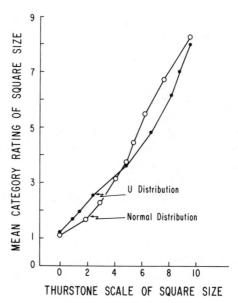

FIGURE 3.2. *Crossover supports range–frequency theory, infirms adaptation-level theory of rating judgments. Curves plot mean rating of squares from U-shaped and normal distributions. (After Parducci & Perrett, 1971.)*

U-shaped and normal distributions. This crossover is predicted by range–frequency theory because the frequency tendency shifts responses from the center toward both ends in the normal distribution and from both ends toward the center in the U-shaped distribution.

Adaptation-level theory claims that the rating of any stimulus is a linear function of the distance between the value of that stimulus and the adaptation level, which is a function of the distribution of stimuli. If the two distributions have the same adaptation level, then the two response curves should be identical; if they have different adaptation levels, then one curve should lie entirely on one side of the other with no crossover. The crossover seen in Figure 3.2 thus provides a strong, qualitative test that infirms adaptation-level theory.

Even more striking is Birnbaum's (1974b) test, shown in Figure 3.3. Subjects rated three-digit numerals on a 9-category scale ranging from "very very small" to "very very large." The two distributions of numerals had a W or inverted-W shape, as indicated by the density of circles on the two lines at the foot of the graph. The critical feature is the double crossover of the response curves for the two distributions. The double crossover is qualitatively inconsistent with Helson's adaptation-level theory; it is predicted by Parducci's range–frequency theory.

Quantitative Tests. This section illustrates a functional measurement approach to range-frequency theory (Anderson, 1972c, 1974a, 1975a). It is assumed that the rank order of the stimuli is known and that the stimulus distributions and the response measure are effectively continuous. Each stimulus is assumed to have two values, both expressed in percentile form: *f* is the ordinary frequency percentile of the stimulus distribution, calculable in the usual way; *s* is the range percentile, that is, 100 times the subjective distance between the given stimulus and the lower end of the stimulus range, divided by the subjective distance between the upper and lower ends of the stimulus range. The actual response to any stimulus is a compromise between the range and frequency tendencies, represented as an average of the two corresponding values

$$R = C_1[ws + (1 - w)f]. \qquad (22)$$

The constant, C_1, is a unit parameter that may here be set equal to unity. Three methods have been suggested for testing this model.

The constant-range method compares the response to common

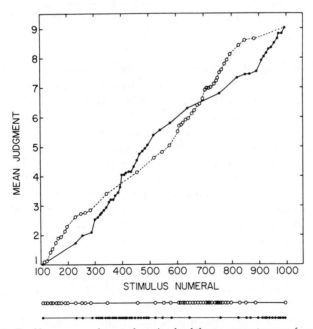

FIGURE 3.3. *Double crossover rules out adaptation-level theory, supports range-frequency theory. Curves plot mean category rating of magnitude of three-digit numerals for two distributions, one with a W shape, the other with an inverted-W shape, as indicated by the density of circles on the two lines at the foot of the graph. (After Birnbaum, 1974b.)*

stimuli from distributions that have the same range. Let f_1 and f_2 denote the frequency percentile functions from two distributions, 1 and 2, that have the same end stimuli. Any stimulus common to both distributions has the same range value (on the range percentile scale). Hence Eq. (22) yields

$$R_1 = ws + (1 - w)f_1, \qquad R_2 = ws + (1 - w)f_2,$$

so that

$$R_1 - R_2 = (1 - w)(f_1 - f_2). \tag{23}$$

This result provides a strong test because w is the one unknown. The response term, $R_1 - R_2$, is observable, and the frequency term, $f_1 - f_2$, is known from the stimulus distributions. Hence w may be calculated for each common stimulus; all should yield the same value of w. Once w has been obtained, it may be used to estimate the range value of each stimulus.

The range-extension method compares across stimulus distributions that have different ranges. For illustration, consider several distributions that are identical over their lower domain up to some medium stimulus but differ for higher stimuli, in particular by having different upper end stimuli. Any stimulus in the lower domain has the same f value in all distributions because the distributions are identical over the lower domain. Furthermore, the range values of the stimuli in the lower domain are proportional across distributions by virtue of their percentile representation. For stimuli in the lower domain, therefore, the response for distribution i may be written

$$R_i = w(c_i s) + (1 - w)f, \tag{24}$$

where c_i is the range proportionality constant for distribution i.

This equation has the semilinear form, and the test of Section 3.4 may be applied, with the common stimuli constituting one factor in the design and the several distributions constituting the other factor. A simple visual test may also be obtained by pairwise subtraction among three or more distributions. For example

$$R_1 - R_2 = (c_1 - c_2)ws \quad \text{and} \quad R_1 - R_3 = (c_1 - c_3)ws.$$

The two response differences should plot as straight-line functions of each other.

The range-extension method may provide more power than the constant-range method, which only allows manipulation of distribution shape within a fixed range. The range-extension method has the added advantage that it holds even if the rating categories tend to be used with unequal frequency.

An application of functional measurement to range–frequency theory has also been made by Birnbaum (1974b), who provided a third method of analysis. This method applies when the stimulus variable has a physical metric, as with psychophysical dimensions. In terms of Figure 1.2, $s = V(S)$, and $V(S)$ may be expanded as a power series. Thus, Eq. (22) may be written

$$R = w[c_0 + c_1 S + c_2 S^2 + \cdots] + (1 - w)f.$$

The power series is merely a curve-fitting device, and other curves might be more useful. Because the stimuli typically are spaced fairly densely on the physical metric, this approach can be expected to provide a reasonable approximation to the valuation function for the price of estimating a few coefficients. Data from a single distribution could thus provide an approximate test of goodness of fit as well as an estimate of the valuation function, that is, the psychophysical function.

Generalized Range–Frequency Model. The foregoing analyses, except for the range-extension method, rest on the equal-frequency assumption that subjects tend to use each response category equally often. This allows the frequency value, f, to be treated as known, which provides the basis for a simple analysis. This assumption may not always be true, and in principle Parducci allows the possibility of unequal tendencies to use each response category. This complicates the analysis because f is no longer known.

A more general range–frequency model may be obtained by relaxing the equal-frequency assumption and the analogous assumption that the range values are independent of the response scale. Let s^* and f^* denote these generalized range and frequency values, with s^* independent of the distribution of stimuli and f^* independent of the stimulus magnitudes. Choose several distributions with the same end stimuli. Choose a larger upper end stimulus and stretch the original distributions to cover this larger range while leaving them unchanged below some intermediate stimulus. Any common stimulus in the lower range will then have the same generalized frequency value, f^*, in each distribution and in its extension; it will also have the same generalized range value in all distributions with the same end stimuli. For each such stimulus, therefore, the generalized model implies

$$R_{ij} = ws_i^* + (1 - w)f_j^*, \tag{25}$$

where i indexes the ranges and j indexes the original distributions. The key model properties of additivity and independence then imply that the interaction in this factorial array is zero. In this manner, therefore, the generalized range–frequency model can be tested exactly in terms of the raw data without estimating any parameters.

Despite the impressive qualitative success of the range–frequency model, quantitative studies have been notably lacking. The methods of the earlier studies rest on Thurstonian scaling and do not allow a satisfactory test. The essential idea of the constant-range method was used by Parducci and Perrett (1971, pp. 445–447) on a post hoc basis with the arbitrary assumption that $w = \frac{1}{2}$. The model did not do well in these tests, but the matter seems not to have been followed up. Birnbaum's (1974b) analysis provided a more satisfactory test, although its generality is limited by the use of numeral stimuli. Further work would be desirable because of its bearing on the response process.

Measurement Problems. Because it deals with numerical judgments of single stimuli, the range–frequency model is attractive as a scaling procedure. The structural basis resides in the integration rule for the range and frequency tendencies that underlie the overt rating. As Birnbaum (1974b) has also emphasized, the properties of additivity and independence provide the constraint needed to test and validate the range–frequency model. A few questions regarding measurement deserve comment.

The first question concerns a hidden assumption of response linearity in range–frequency theory. The assumption that the range tendency will produce a response distribution that mirrors the distribution of subjective values entails some assumption about the linear character of the rating response. On this question, however, range–frequency theory remains obscure.[a]

An associated question concerns the interpretation of the distribution effect. Thurstone (1929) considered it to be a bias that he saw no way to eliminate, and Stevens adopted a similar view, which he used as one of his main criticisms of the rating method. However, Helson (1964) asserted that the distribution effect represented a "profound change in sensory character. . . . with change in *sensory character* of the stimuli there must be a difference in physiological process [p. 136]." Helson's view was adopted in social judgment theory, as noted in Sections 1.1.5 and 1.1.6, and gave rise to the continuing belief that stimulus distributions produce genuine contrast.

Along with its theoretical interest, the two interpretations of the distribution effect lead to different scaling practices. Under the bias interpretation, the effect should either be eliminated, as indicated in Section 1.1, or employed as a base for measurement, as in the range–frequency model. It would hardly be proper to eliminate the effect, however, if it represented genuine contrast or change in affective value.

The range–frequency model itself bypasses the problem of interpreting the distribution effect because the affective zero is lost in the percentile representation. There is, however, a further question concerning the range value. A natural interpretation is that the range value is the subjective value of the stimulus, in particular, the sensation value in psychophysical tasks. Although Parducci often treats the distribution effect as genuine, he prefers a nominal interpretation of the range value as a model parameter, in part because of proper concern that cross-task generality of range values has yet to be demonstrated. This interpretation would perhaps be consistent with other views that allow the possibility of a family of stimulus values across successive processing stages of a given stimulus (Anderson, 1975a; Marks, 1982). It would be desirable, therefore, to compare functional scales from single stimulus ratings to those obtained from the more usual kind of integration task.

3.13 An Iterative Technique

A procedure intended to neutralize the distribution effect was proposed by Stevens (1957; Stevens & Galanter, 1957, pp. 381–382). If subjects tend to use each rating category equally often, their responses to an arbitrary distribution of stimuli will be biased. This bias would presumably be neutralized, however, if the distribution could be chosen so that each response category in fact was used equally often.

The iterative technique has been presented as an algorithm, but its rationale and justification have remained obscure. Stevens and Galanter (1957) claim that the iteration converges to the "pure form of the category scale, which is not in general an equal-interval scale of the psychological magnitude [p. 382]." However, Pollack (1965) speaks of the potential of the iterative technique for producing "unbiased psychophysical functions [p. 565]," and Montgomery and Eisler (1974) treat the result as an "equal interval scale [p. 441]."

The disagreement among these writers reflects the lack of any theoretical basis for understanding what assumptions are implicit in the iterative technique or for ascertaining what it does. The following discussion presents one approach, based on a mixture of ideas from information integration theory and range–frequency theory.

The iterative technique illustrated in Figure 3.4 is patterned after Pol-

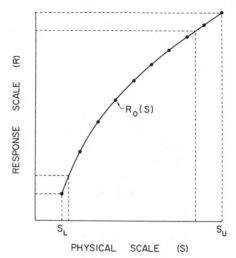

FIGURE 3.4. *Graphical illustration of iterative technique for rating response; see text. (From N. H. Anderson, On the role of context effects in psychophysical judgment. Psychological Review, 1975, 82, 462–482. Copyright © 1975 by the American Psychological Association. Reprinted by permission of the publisher and author.)*

lack (1965). For present purposes, the stimulus variable is assumed to have a physical metric, denoted by S. The curve $R_0(S)$ represents the response to a distribution of stimuli that are equally spaced on the physical scale and presented with equal frequency. This curve is bowed downward, with high responses being more frequent than low. To equalize response frequencies, it is necessary to increase the density of stimuli in the lower range where the response curve rises faster.

To accomplish this response equalization, divide the response range on the vertical axis into k equal parts, the first and last of which are shown in Figure 3.4. From each dividing point, project a horizontal to the curve $R_0(S)$ and drop a vertical to the stimulus axis. As Figure 3.4 shows, the original equal spacing on the horizontal axis has been changed: The first two stimuli are closer in the new distribution than in the old; the last two stimuli are farther apart.

The $k + 1$ stimuli obtained in this way constitute the new distribution. Each is presented equally often, but their unequal spacing on the physical scale tends to equalize the response frequencies. This new response distribution, $R_1(S)$, is treated similarly as the basis for the next iteration.

To formalize this iterative procedure, let $F(S)$ denote the cumulative frequency function of the stimulus distribution and let V be the psychophysical function so that $V(S)$ represents subjective value. These two functions, together with the response function, $R(S)$, will be treated as continuous, rather than discrete, and normalized to the percentile form. The foregoing description of the iterative technique can then be restated to say that the frequency of stimuli between S_1 and S_2 on iteration n is set equal to the difference in their response values on the preceding iteration: $F_n(S_2) - F_n(S_1) = R_{n-1}(S_2) - R_{n-1}(S_1)$. The essential content of the iterative technique, in other words, is that the response function on one iteration defines the frequency function on the next iteration

$$F_n(S) = R_{n-1}(S).$$

If the iteration converges, rather than oscillating, then the frequency and response functions become identical

$$F_\infty(S) = R_\infty(S).$$

This does not define the shape of the response function, however, for that depends on the physical metric of S.

The main conceptual problem for the iterative technique is the lack of any basis for interpreting this last equation. As already noted, Pollack assumed $F_\infty(S) = V(S)$, whereas Stevens assumed otherwise. Some theory of the response process is required to address this question.

Range–frequency theory provides a straightforward analysis. In the present notation, Eq. (22) may be written

$$R_n(S) = wV(S) + (1 - w)F_n(S) = wV(S) + (1 - w)R_{n-1}(S). \quad (26)$$

This difference equation converges under very general mathematical conditions to yield

$$R_\infty(S) = V(S). \quad (27)$$

If the range–frequency model is correct, therefore, the limiting response function is equivalent to the psychophysical function. But this conclusion depends on the equal-frequency assumption; unless that holds, the limit response function is not in general interpretable.

The iterative technique will converge under more general conditions than assumed in the range–frequency model. For example, the weight parameter in Eq. (26) could be allowed to depend on stimulus value. Equation (27), however, depends on the implicit assumption of range–frequency theory that the response scale is linear. Under the assumption that the response scale is monotone, the iterative technique of itself allows no interpretation of the limit function it produces. Even with a linear response scale, moreover, the meaning of the limit function depends on the equal-frequency assumption. Unless that holds, the iterative technique does not neutralize the distribution effect (Anderson, 1975a).

3.14 Tradeoff Analysis

Judgments and decisions often require compromises in which benefits along one attribute dimension are traded off against losses along another attribute dimension. Two common trading dimensions are time and money. Desired conditions may be omitted from a thesis experiment, for example, in order to finish in reasonable time. Similarly, a less flexible apparatus may be purchased to keep down costs. Rarely will one choice alternative be optimal on every attribute dimension, so tradeoffs are pervasive in judgment and decision making.

Tradeoff Models. The central problem in tradeoff analysis concerns subjective values, for it is these that are traded off. A simple tradeoff model will be considered to illustrate how functional measurement may be used for this purpose.

Suppose that two stimuli, S and T, are each varied along two attribute dimensions, A and B. Thus, S and T may be represented as (S_{Ai}, S_{Bj}) and (T_{Ak}, T_{Bl}), respectively. The subject's task is to adjust one attribute, say S_A, so that S and T are equal in overall value. Symbolically,

$$\mathbf{V}(S_{Ai}^*, S_{Bj}) = \mathbf{V}(T_{Ak}, T_{Bl}),$$

where S_{Ai}^* denotes the physical value of the adjusted attribute and $\mathbf{V}$ is the overall stimulus value function. If the value function is additive, the equality may be written

$$\mathbf{V}_A(S_{Ai}^*) = \mathbf{V}_A(T_{Ak}) + \mathbf{V}_B(T_{Bl}) - \mathbf{V}_B(S_{Bj}), \qquad (28)$$

where $\mathbf{V}_A$ and $\mathbf{V}_B$ are the value functions for the corresponding attribute dimensions.

The key to tradeoff analysis lies in the subjective values. If these were known, Eq. (28) would be easy to test. But what the investigator observes are the physical values of the response, S_{Ai}^*, not the subjective values, $\mathbf{V}_A(S_{Ai}^*)$. For the stimuli, similarly, it is the physical, not the psychological values that are manipulated. In some applications, it may be reasonable to assume some convenient form for the value functions. The value of money, for example, might be taken as a function of diminishing returns with one or two parameters that allow for individual differences. Such working approximations can be practical, but a theoretical foundation for them is desirable.

Functional measurement provides an analysis of the tradeoff model that is essentially assumption-free. In general, this requires the response transformation procedures of Chapter 5. The idea is to vary the three stimulus variables on the right of Eq. (28) in a three-factor design. The observable response variable, S_{Ai}^*, is transformed so as to maximize the additivity in the data. No assumptions about the stimulus values are needed. The response itself may be only on a nominal scale (Note 5.2c). All that is at issue is the additive structure of the model, and this may be tested with the methods of Chapter 5. When the response scale is linear, of course, transformation is not needed, and the methods of Chapter 2 may be applied directly.

A variant tradeoff model arises when subjects make a numerical assessment of the sum or difference of S and T:

$$R = \mathbf{V}(S_{Ai}, S_{Bj}) \pm \mathbf{V}(T_{Ak}, T_{Bl}).$$

If R is linear, then the two-way $S \times T$ design will exhibit parallelism. Or, if the sum or difference operation is assumed to hold, then transformation to additivity will yield a linear response. This approach may be useful as a separate check on the additivity assumption of Eq. (28) or as a means to analyze nonadditive and configural rules. This approach may be feasible with a rating response or perhaps with a money response. An empirical illustration is given in Shanteau and Anderson (1969).

Psychophysics. Tradeoff is involved in the classical problem of bisection, in which subjects adjust one stimulus so it lies midway in value between two other stimuli. In this task, subjects equate two subjective differences by trading off one to the other. This task has seemed attractive for sensation measurement because it relies on a nonverbal perceptual matching. Since the response is measured on the physical scale, however, the model analysis requires transformation as discussed in Section F1.3.8.

A second example appears in perceptual trading relations. In binaural localization, for example, a sound appears to be located toward the ear at which loudness is greater or arrival time is earlier, a perceptual capability that has survival value. Apparent location of the sound depends on integration of both cues, namely, the loudness difference and the time difference between the stimuli delivered to the two ears. The standard approach with trading relations involves measuring what physical magnitude of one cue is needed to just offset a given magnitude of the other cue (Durlach & Colburn, 1978). This information is not sufficient to determine either the sensation values or the integration rule.

A potentially more informative approach is to vary the stimuli at the two ears independently in a factorial design. The foregoing tradeoff analysis could then be applied to determine whether the binaural integration followed an algebraic rule (Anderson, 1977a, p. 214).

Intuitive Physics. The development of knowledge structures in intuitive physics provides an instructive example of tradeoff analysis (Wilkening & Anderson, 1982). On the left arm of a center-pivoted rod, the number and location of a group of unit weights was varied experimentally. On the right arm of the rod, another group of unit weights was given, and subjects moved this group to the location where they thought the two sides would balance. In order to study preexperimental knowledge, the rod was fixed so no actual balancing occurred.

In this task, younger children are expected to apply a general-purpose adding rule, whereas older children may apply a multiplying rule similar to the physical torque rule. These two rules may be written

$$\mathbf{V}(D_R^*) = \mathbf{V}(D_L) + \mathbf{V}(W_L) - \mathbf{V}(W_R),$$
$$\mathbf{V}(D_R^*) = \mathbf{V}(D_L)\mathbf{V}(W_L)/\mathbf{V}(W_R),$$

where D and W denote the physical values of distance and weight, R and L denote the right and left arms of the rod, and the asterisk denotes the adjusted distance response. For simplicity, subscripts are omitted in the valuation functions. Even though the $\mathbf{V}$ functions may be unknown, the analysis automatically allows for subjective values.

These two rules are monotonically equivalent, so the foregoing method of analysis would provide a joint test of both rules but would not distinguish between them. This ambiguity might be resolvable by using two groups of weights on the left arm, with the expectation that this integration will obey an adding rule. This would allow use of the two-phase method of Section 3.2. A simpler and more useful way is to appeal to the evidence that the subjective and objective values of distance are proportional in this task (see, e.g., Figure 3.6). In that case, the physical value of the observed response, D_R^*, is a linear scale, and the factorial graph may be interpreted even if the integration does not obey any simple rule.

Utility Theory. Most work on tradeoff analysis has been in utility theory, especially in connection with mathematical analyses of the additive model (see Keeney & Raiffa, 1976, Chapter 3). Not much experimental evidence is available, but what there is raises questions about this approach.

One line of evidence suggests that different values may be obtained when subjects judge values of single bets from when they choose between two bets (Lichtenstein & Slovic, 1971, 1973; Lindman, 1971; Slovic, 1975). These two response modes may even yield opposite preferences, which would limit the generality of stimulus values obtained from a tradeoff task.

These results have been interpreted in terms of a serial weighted integration, in which amount to be won or lost is weighted more heavily in the single bets. This interpretation is plausible, but more detailed model analysis is desirable. Indeed, this interpretation seems to rest in part on a claim that probability and value are added (Slovic & Lichtenstein, 1968), whereas reanalysis and new data by Shanteau (1970b, 1974, 1975a) both supported the multiplying rule.

A second line of evidence is the subadditivity effect for commodity bundles discovered by Shanteau (1970b, 1974, 1975a). Subadditivity is clearly contrary to the additivity assumption on which utility theory is founded. Unfortunately, little effort has been made to replicate and study subadditivity.

A rather different aspect of tradeoff analysis has been stressed by Keeney and Raiffa (1976). Many decisions require choosing between courses of action whose consequences are unclear. Valuation of each course of action requires envisaging some spectrum of consequences and trying to forecast how one would feel about each consequence if it were actualized. This is hard to do and liable to error. It is also hard to study, but it may be more important than the tradeoff analysis itself.

Response Scaling in Tradeoff Analysis. Two different approaches to response scaling may be used in tradeoff analysis. One approach, already considered, relies on the structure of the integration rule to induce a scaling of the dependent variable. This approach works well when the integration rule has some simple form, and it may be adequate even when the integration rule is only approximate. However, there is enough evidence on deviations from the adding model, either in the form of subadditivity or differential weighted averaging, to indicate the need for caution in analysis of tradeoff tasks.

The second approach to response scaling relies on response generality. Existing evidence indicates that ratings can yield linear scales under certain conditions. Similarly, subjective and objective values appear to be linearly related for length, angle, and time, at least within certain ranges. Such physical scales may be used directly in tradeoff analysis, as suggested in the discussion of intuitive physics. Possession of a linear response greatly facilitates interpretation of the data, especially when the integration does not follow a simple algebraic rule.

NOTES

3.1a. A more complete discussion of generality would need to take up the central issue of process generality (Section F1.8.2).

3.1b. Because stimulus invariance has both methodological and substantive significance, two additional studies will be noted. Anderson (1972a) used both the weight–size

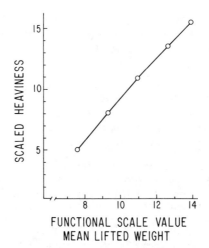

FUNCTIONAL SCALE VALUE
MEAN LIFTED WEIGHT

FIGURE 3.5. *Stimulus invariance of subjective heaviness. Functional scale of heaviness obtained from weight-size task is plotted as a function of functional scale of heaviness obtained from weight-averaging task. The near-linearity of the curve means that the two subjective scales are equivalent. (After Anderson, 1972a.)*

illusion (illustrated in Figure 4.7) and a weight-averaging task in which subjects judged average heaviness of two unseen weights lifted in succession with the same hand. Both tasks obeyed an adding-type model, thereby providing two functional scales of the stimulus weights.

The question is whether these two functional scales are equivalent. This may seem unlikely. The integration operation comes before the conscious sensation of heaviness in the weight–size task but after the conscious heaviness sensations in the averaging task. Presumably, therefore, the sensory representations of the stimulus weights have different cognitive loci and so need not be equivalent.

Empirically, however, the two functional scales appear to be equivalent. One is plotted as a function of the other in Figure 3.5, and the observed linearity implies equivalence. The generality of this outcome is limited by the small range of gram weight, but it illustrates the utility of contextual effects as a tool for stimulus scaling (Anderson, 1970a, 1975a) and, more generally, the potential of integration tasks for analysis of processing. It also supports the use of stimulus invariance as a heuristic in monotone analysis.

A second illustration of stimulus invariance is shown in Figure 3.6, which plots functional scales of length obtained from three different tasks as a function of physical length. The three curves are parallel, which means that all three yielded equivalent scales; and linear, which means that subjective length is proportional to objective length over this stimulus range. Similar graphs for functional scales of heaviness and apparent area are given in the original report (Anderson, 1974c, Figure 3).

In the given task, subjects made intuitive judgments of "total magnitude" of stimulus pairs, including two lengths, one length and one lifted weight, and one length and one area. The three respective factorial graphs exhibited parallelism, which supports the hypothesized adding model. Parallelism also supports the rating response as a linear scale and provides linear scales of subjective stimulus value. These results, shown in Figure 3.6, demonstrate cross-task stimulus invariance.

(The length–length curve in Figure 3.6 has a slope of one-half, allowing for the different scale factors for horizontal and vertical. This slope value results from averaging the marginal means over the second design factor. Cross-task generality requires only that the other two curves be linear functions of the length–length curve, or that the three curves exhibit a semilinear fan pattern (Section 3.4). That all three are parallel means that all three stimulus dimensions had equal effective range.)

Magnitude estimation does not obey the adding model in tasks of this kind; that shows the task is not trivial. Subjects are not simply assigning a number to each stimulus and adding the numbers, for that would yield parallelism even more easily with magnitude estimation than with rating. The adding model is an obvious hypothesis, and its verification may not seem surprising—but it would not be verified unless the response measure was a true linear scale. The observed parallelism thus supports the rating method over magnitude estimation. It validates the verbal reports as true measures of sensation.

3.1c. Two statistical problems concerning stimulus generality should be kept in mind. First, estimated stimulus values contain unreliability; this must be allowed for in any use of these values. It is not generally appropriate, therefore, to use stimulus values in another task as though they were error-free. This is a well known problem in linear regression (Sections 4.2.4 and 4.3.3), and it applies generally to model analysis.

The second problem arises when it is desired to reject the null hypothesis that one common set of stimulus values operates in two tasks. The direct, usually difficult way is to make a joint, simultaneous test of both models based on a common set of estimates. An attractive alternative is to make separate estimates for each model and show a nonlinear relation between them. With this alternative, however, it is important that the estimation procedure be unbiased. Moreover, the comparison of the two sets of stimulus estimates must allow for the unreliability in both sets (Section 2.2.3).

3.2a. The term *two-operation model* is used instead of the previous term *two-stage*

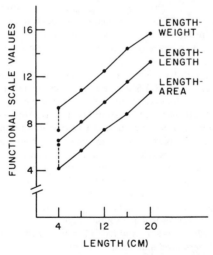

FIGURE 3.6. *Stimulus invariance of subjective length. Each curve plots functional scale of length as a function of physical length from one task of judging total magnitude. Parallelism of the three curves means that the three tasks yield equivalent length scales. Linearity of the curves means that physical length provides a linear measure of subjective length. Top and bottom curves are displaced two units upward and downward, respectively. (After Anderson, 1974c.)*

model (e.g., Anderson, 1974a) to avoid confusion with a two-stage formulation used by Curtis (1970; see Section F5.6.3) and to avoid the implication that the two integration operations necessarily proceed in successive stages.

3.3a. The potential power of multilinear models has also been stressed in a series of ingenious papers by Birnbaum (e.g., 1974a, 1976, 1978; Birnbaum & Mellers, 1978; Birnbaum & Veit, 1974). These papers have applied a functional measurement approach to various substantive problems, most notably the vexing and difficult problem of distinguishing ratio from difference judgments in certain psychophysical tasks. These papers provide leverage on substantive problems that are outside the scope of the present discussion (see e.g., Birnbaum, 1979; Eisler, 1978).

3.3b. To illustrate, consider the model $(A + B) ⊛ C$, in which the operation $⊛$ is addition or multiplication although the values of C are not independent of the values of A and B. For each separate level of C, therefore, the C effect can be represented as a linear transformation on the basic $A \times B$ parallelism pattern. Hence the marginal means of the $A \times B$ table are linearly equivalent across levels of C. Each such set of marginal means thus provides a linear scale, and so does their average. This result allows for subadditivity in C, for example, but not for nonlinear transformations such as $(A + B)^C$.

3.5a. Ratio models are not restricted to comparison processes. Perhaps the best-known example is Herrnstein's (1970) "matching law," which states that organisms distribute their responses between two alternatives in proportion to the two corresponding rates of reinforcement. A measurement-theoretical view of this ratio model is given in Section F5.6.7, and an experimental application of functional measurement is given by Farley and Fantino (1978).

3.5b. Oden (1979; Oden & Massaro, 1978) has shown that various generalizations of the relative ratio model can be reduced to the same form. For example, weights may be included to obtain the four-variable model

$$w_{Ai} s_{Ai}/(w_{Ai} s_{Ai} + w_{Bj} s_{Bj}),$$

which can be written in the relative ratio form

$$s/(s + w),$$

where $s = s_{Ai}/s_{Bj}$ and $w = w_{Bj}/w_{Ai}$. Variation of one s variable and one w variable would provide a two-factor test of the model. Applications in which weights represent adaptation or attention factors can be expected.

A second generalization arises when s_{Ai} and s_{Bj} may be considered to be redundant or to possess common elements. If the redundancy or common part is subtracted from each term in proportion to its relative magnitude, the value of the ratio remains unchanged. The ratio model thus has a simple way of handling redundancy.

3.6a. Two interesting studies of rule learning in serial integration tasks were made by Norman (1974a,b).

3.6b. This analysis of sequential dependencies was presented at the workshop on mathematical learning models, directed by R. R. Bush and W. K. Estes at Stanford University, summer 1957. P. Suppes subsequently presented some related results at this workshop, on which he and Estes had been working independently (see Estes & Suppes, 1959, p. 163). Their development used a more explicit representation of the sample space of the random variables employed by Anderson (1959a). Estes and Suppes feel that their approach is more direct and simple, whereas Anderson feels that the random variable approach is more direct and simple.

3.6c. The role of sequential dependencies is nicely illustrated in the case history of mathematical models of probability learning. Early investigators (e.g., Hake & Hyman,

1953) suggested that subjects responded to stimulus patterns over short subsequences of trials, and this view is generally accepted today (see Jones, 1971; Myers, 1976). Initially, however, a simple class of mathematical models prevailed that did not allow for memory of events in the preceding subsequence. It is interesting to consider some of the reasons why this area developed as it did.

One reason was the difficulties with the subsequence view. Interpretation of sequential dependencies is tricky, a fact that only became clear in the model analyses. For example, the response pattern, "win–stay, lose–shift," which was popularly interpreted as a "strategy," could be produced by the simplest conditioning processes. Such conditioning processes could also be shown to simulate memory for past events. These interpretational problems stem from the probabilistic nature of the process; they are only more complex if the simple models do not hold. Popular interpretations of subsequence effects did not take these difficulties into account and so were not generally justified or correct.

The second main reason for the slow acceptance of the sequential dependency approach was the success of the simple models in predicting mean learning curves. Most striking was Estes's and Burke's (1953) derivation from stimulus sampling–conditioning theory of the "matching behavior" discovered by Grant and Hake (1949), in which subjects' frequencies of predicting random binary events matched the actual event frequencies. In light of such successes with mean learning curves, it was easy to believe that discrepancies in sequential dependencies were nuisance complications rather than basic flaws.

At this time, moreover, stimulus sampling theory was intellectually congenial because it embodied the then-dominant learning-as-conditioning views of Hull, Skinner, and Pavlov. Furthermore, this work, together with the more mathematical approach developed by Bush and Mosteller (1955), brought a respectable level of precision to learning theory. It exerted great influence on the graduate students of that era.

In the realm of probability learning, however, study of sequential dependencies cast increasing doubt on the mathematical models. The first systematic empirical study (Anderson, 1956, 1960) concluded that the success of the conditioning models in predicting matching behavior was a fortuitous consequence of averaging out sequential dependencies that disagreed with the models.

> Thus, although the conditioning process assumed in current mathematical models for the two-choice task may well occur, it would appear that the models neglect much of the underlying processes. Furthermore, since the mean learning curve comprises an average of the sequential increments and decrements in response probability, the agreement between obtained and predicted "matching solution" behavior must be considered fortuitous [Anderson, 1960, p. 90].

This study was designed to test a simple generalization of the conditioning formulation to include two response tendencies, alternation and repetition, both defined with respect to the previous event. In the initial experiment, this model gave a good account of the mean learning curve for the acquisition phase, but a long-term transfer effect was obtained that seemed contrary to all current formulations. Accordingly, the strategy of testing models was abandoned in favor of a parametric, empirical study of sequential dependencies. The sequential dependencies indicated, however, that it would be necessary to allow for memory of more than one previous event. Collateral results by Anderson and Whalen (1960), who explored the use of a numerical response measure for construction of subsequence curves, showed similarly that predictions from the current mathematical learning models disagreed with the observed subsequence curves.

But Estes (1964) argued that these discrepancies from the models were not serious. They could reflect interfering tendencies from preexperimental experience that were not completely adapted out even in the several hundred trials that had become common in probability learning. In Estes's view, therefore, the observed discrepancies were nuisance complications superposed upon the basic conditioning process assumed in the S–R conditioning formulation.

Such an interpretation of theoretical discrepancies is not unreasonable (see Section 4.2.1). This particular interpretation was readily testable, moreover, since it implied that more extended training would eliminate the discrepancies and reveal the pure form of the S–R conditioning process envisaged in Estes's theory. Indeed, seemingly strong support for Estes's (1964) view was provided by data from the last session of a three-session experiment by Friedman, Burke, Cole, Keller, Millward, and Estes (1964). The conditioning model gave an impressive account of sequential dependencies, presumably because the first two sessions had eliminated the interfering response tendencies and laid bare the S–R conditioning process. Estes (1964) concluded

> There seems to be little room for doubt that it is possible to abstract from the phenomena of probability learning evidence for the pervasive operation of a relatively simple form of conditioning.... The structure of the choice data can be accounted for quite well on the basis of an elementary learning process [pp. 121–122].

Unfortunately, Estes's interpretation was undercut by a peculiarity of the stimulus sequences, in which event frequency shifted every 48 trials over the first two sessions of the experiment. This shifting introduces nonrandom components into the sequence as a whole so there are more long event runs than are expected by chance. Since an 80:20 frequency schedule was used in the third session, the first two sessions may have trained in the specific behavior that the conditioning model could handle. This interpretation agrees with the long-term transfer effects previously mentioned. This alternative interpretation was pointed out by Anderson (1964a): "Instead of assuming that practice trains out the interfering response tendencies, it may be suggested that practice trains in the very behavior described by the models; that different practice regimes will train in different sorts of behavior; and that each will require a different model [p. 138]."

To test these two interpretations, Friedman, Carterette, and Anderson (1968) used properly random sequences and ran each subject 25 sessions. This eliminated the artifact just mentioned and also gave more than ample time for preexperimental response tendencies to adapt out. However, the sequential dependencies in the data did not agree with Estes's theoretical prediction (see also Jones, 1971, p. 153). Friedman et al. (1968) concluded, "These models disagree with the data in almost every respect [p. 453]."

Sequential dependencies were also important in a related experiment that made a direct test of the element conditioning process basic to stimulus sampling theory (Anderson, 1966b). The essential idea derived from Burke, Estes, and Hellyer (1954), who presented evidence for concrete identification of the stimulus elements postulated in stimulus sampling theory. By incorporating a sequential dependency analysis, Anderson's (1966b) experiment obtained much greater sensitivity. Across six experiments, however, the data failed to support the stimulus conditioning model. This experiment has special significance because the sequential dependency test of the stimulus conditioning assumption is theoretically valid even though interfering response tendencies are present.

These two sequential dependency studies confirmed the concern expressed by Anderson (1964a), who noted that despite many attractive features of stimulus sampling–conditioning theory, two negative aspects stood out. The first was that interest in the theory led to neglect of the behavior:

> As has been noted, the existing data indicate that there is much in the behavior which is neglected by the stimulus sampling models. Indeed, it would almost seem that what is neglected is just what is most of interest, and in this respect one must question the net usefulness of the theory [p. 141].

The second was that the model analyses did not really seem to support the basic conceptualizations of the theory.

> It is in this latter respect that I feel uneasy about the present state of affairs. The failure to account for the sequential dependencies shows that the model assumptions about the action of the reinforcing stimuli are inadequate. More generally, the present models do not allow for any memory effect and yet the existing evidence gives every indication that memory, in one role or another, plays an important part. In addition, there is also some evidence of a transfer effect which is outside the scope of the models and perhaps of the theory itself [p. 141].

It may be true that available evidence does not compel the conditioning models to be given up (see Myers, 1976, p. 184). The study of sequential dependencies has suggested, however, that probability learning may be more fruitfully conceptualized as cognitive or informational learning.

Probability learning makes an interesting case history of scientific inquiry. Only one facet has been touched on here. Contributions have been made by numerous workers and these, together with more recent approaches, especially on sequence learning, are discussed in careful reviews by Jones (1971) and Myers (1976). In its initial decade-and-a-half, probability learning was a major focus of mathematical psychology and absorbed concentrated efforts of numerous highly capable investigators. On the positive side, it was a main path to notable improvements in understanding of and capability with mathematical approaches to learning. Although these models have not been very successful, they had an important developmental role. They provided a new standard of theoretical clarity. They showed that various popular interpretations did not take into account technical problems that cast doubt on their justification and validity. And they provided an efficient, if negative, analysis of the qualitative conceptions on which the models were based.

The realm of probability learning, however, has not yielded very many substantive results. The concentration on theory led to neglect of what was most of interest in the behavior. On the negative side, therefore, disappointingly little substance remains from all this work.

3.7a. Conjunctive averaging can produce a pattern of data that looks very much like a multiplying rule (Section F2.3.4). An observed linear fan pattern is thus not sufficient evidence of multiplying, even if the response scale is known to be linear (Levin, 1977).

3.8a. Other algebraic probability models can also be tested using functional measurement because it allows for personal values of the probability terms. These models have done well in the tests that have so far been made (Leon & Anderson, 1974; Shanteau, 1970a, 1972; Wyer, 1975a; Sections F1.3.3, F1.5.1, F1.5.2, and F1.7.1). In the present view, the success of these probability models results from the operation of a general cognitive algebra, not from the normative status of the models. Support for this view is found in studies in which the behavior continues to follow an algebraic model even though the normative standard does not (e.g., Lopes, 1976b; Shanteau & Anderson, 1972, Figure 2).

3.9a. The shape function method has been applied by Kirk (1964) to show that differences between reversal and nonreversal shifts in concept formation depend on two factors: difficulty in mediator learning and resistance to extinction of the overt response. Virtually all previous studies of reversal–nonreversal shifts had used dubious response measures obtained by training to a criterion, shifting, and retraining to a criterion. Since reversal and nonreversal groups begin retraining at different levels, typically 0% and 50% correct, respectively, the number of trials or errors to the retraining criterion are not comparable across groups. These problems can sometimes be avoided by running fixed numbers of trials and using a simple statistic derived from the shape function.

Although the substantive results of Kirk's (1964) study are not of present interest, they may be summarized briefly:

> Increasing mediator learning difficulty produces slower learning during shift in the nonreversal groups but does not affect the reversal groups. This is because the nonreversal groups must learn a new mediator; a task made increasingly difficult by increasing the mediator difficulty. The reversal groups do not learn a new mediator.
>
> Reducing the overt response extinction rate produces a slower shift learning in the reversal groups. These groups must first extinguish the old incorrect overt response during reversal before they can learn the new correct response. Extinction of the overt response is not part of the nonreversal shift [pp. viii–ix].

Kirk's thesis thus raised two important questions for mediational theory. One concerned the problem of comparing groups that were systematically different, which is central to the reversal–nonreversal paradigm. The other concerned the role of the extinction process in the reversal shift learning, which had been neglected in previous treatments (e.g., Kendler & Kendler, 1962).

3.10a. The factorial plot may have certain advantages over the ROC curve, the shape of which depends on sampling variability in both variables. Factorial plots also generalize directly to multistate sources, corresponding to several signal intensities, for example, which would yield as many curves of z scores. If desired, the spacing on the horizontal axis can be defined by the overall mean curve, as in the linear fan analysis of Section 2.2.

Empirically, d' is often not constant (Green & Swets, 1966, pp. 94ff). Instead, the ROC curve in z-score form often has slope less than unity. In present terms, the two curves of Eq. (19) diverge as the criterion increases. Various explanations have been suggested for this discrepancy, but careful analysis by Krantz (1969) and Luce and Green (1974, p. 300) has shown that they are hard to discriminate empirically. Green and Swets favor the interpretation that the signal distribution has greater variance than the noise distribution. A low-threshold theory might seem more attractive, on the argument that substantial variance differences are not expected with hardly discriminable stimuli. The integration model in the text may be helpful on this question, for variance effects would be expected to increase with signal strength, whereas low-threshold effects would be expected to decrease.

3.10b. The normative–descriptive difference also appears in the concept of weight. Signal detection theory, reflecting its origins in statistical decision theory, has only a single stimulus parameter, representing the amount of statistical information in the stimulus relative to the decision task. The two-parameter, w–s representation of integration theory is conceptually different. It may seem straightforward to generalize the signal detection model to include weight parameters that represent memory and analogous effects. However, signal detection theory is a complex structure built on the central assumption of an ideal observer. Giving up the normative assumption about weighting would require reconsideration of the entire theoretical structure.

A qualitative difference between the two theories may be obtainable with uninformative stimuli. Integration theory predicts that adding uninformative or nondiagnostic stimuli can decrease detectability; signal detection theory predicts no effect. This issue seems pertinent to nonsensory tasks, such as recognition memory. Similarly, discrepancies from signal detection theory observed in the text identification task of Ulehla, Canges, and Wackwitz (1967) may also point to a need to reconsider how the stimulus representation and the integration operation should be conceptualized (see also Section F2.3.6).

3.11a. Two interesting papers on bias in numerical responses (Poulton, 1968, 1979) are also relevant to rating theory. Poulton (1979, pp. 782, 796) carefully points out that certain biases relate only to the zero and unit of the response scale and so would not be considered biases when only a linear response scale is needed. This difference partly, although not fully, resolves the contrast between Poulton's ideal procedure of obtaining only a single judgment from each subject and the procedure of within-subject design advocated in Section 1.3.1.

Despite the interest of Poulton's discussion, some of his assertions seem arbitrary. For example, he states that the stimulus spacing effect, which corresponds to the distribution effect of Section 1.1.6, can be avoided by using geometric spacing and presenting the stimuli equally often. However, this rests on the arbitrary assumption that the psychophysical function is logarithmic. It also rests on certain other assumptions that become explicit in the discussions of range–frequency theory of Section 3.12 and the iterative technique of Section 3.13.

Poulton writes from a traditional perspective (e.g., Stevens, 1971, p. 448), in which the only way to measure sensory magnitude is to eliminate the biasing influence of all contextual factors. In the functional measurement approach, context effects need not be undesirable biases: They can be put to good use to provide a base for psychological measurement (Anderson, 1970a, 1975a, pp. 477–478). This approach has the capability, which is lacking in Poulton's formulation, of providing a validated measurement scale against which to assess the presence of bias. Poulton's models for bias might thus be treated as integration models and studied in their own right (see also Sections 3.12 and 3.13).

3.11b. A more complete theory of rating would need to allow for other factors, including imposed tendencies to use the responses with unequal frequency and additional reference anchors besides the two end stimuli. Both factors could be incorporated within an averaging rule, the response factor in terms of the frequency tendency discussed in Section 3.12, the stimulus anchor factor by including additional terms in Eq. (21) for which the weights are determined by salience factors as well as by similarity. The sequential dependencies discussed in Section 1.1.5 may reflect such anchoring effects produced by the preceding stimulus presentations.

3.12a. This question may be pointed up by assuming that the distribution effect represents a real change in affective value. The integrated resultant of the range and frequency tendencies in Eq. (22) would then properly be considered as the implicit response, r. In this case, range–frequency theory employs an unstated assumption that the implicit affective response is mapped linearly onto the overt response scale.

If the distribution effect is not real, then the matter becomes more complicated. One interpretation would incorporate a final integration stage in which the frequency value is integrated with the effective response from the prior stage to produce an implicit output that leads directly to the observed response. An alternative interpretation is that the stimulus distribution affects the response operation itself. For example, the distribution effect might not be mediated by tendencies to use each category equally often, but instead by weighting parameters in a response model similar to that of Eq. (21).

4

Problems in Model Analysis

Although this chapter is primarily concerned with testing models, the orientation is conceptual rather than statistical. Section 4.1, for example, takes up the subject of weak inference methods, methods that seem to test the models but do not really do so. The statistical aspects are elementary, requiring little more than visual inspection. The issue is conceptually important, however, because it makes clear an essential feature of model analysis. Also, it illustrates how methods developed for prediction may be inadequate for understanding.

Section 4.2 discusses certain problems that arise in accepting and rejecting models. This requires a shift away from the customary thinking about statistics that is appropriate to most experiments. Also of interest is the problem of model tests based on separate estimates of the parameters. Simple statistical considerations show that, contrary to frequent belief and practice, reliance on separate estimates can decrease reliability and lose validity.

The prediction-versus-understanding distinction arises again in Section 4.3, this time in a corresponding statistical distinction between predictive and structural regression. This is a subtle but basic distinction, one that severely handicaps traditional regression methods when applied to process models. Regrettably, only a little progress has been made toward adapting the statistical theory of structural regression to problems of information integration.

Finally, Section 4.4 presents an interesting method for testing goodness of fit for nonlinear models. This replications method capitalizes on a typical characteristic of psychological experiments to obtain what appears to be a general method for nonlinear analysis.

4.1 Weak Inference

Much work on judgment and decision has relied on "weak inference"—methods that seem to test the theory but do not really do so. The most frequent form of weak inference has been the use of correlations to assess linear models: Correlations of .95 and up between predicted and observed values have been common and have been commonly taken to support the model. But near-perfect correlations can readily be obtained from models that are seriously incorrect. Such correlation analyses are therefore fundamentally inadequate and misleading.

This problem of weak inference is not new, but only recently has its severity begun to be appreciated. Accordingly, it is desirable to illustrate the problem with some empirical examples.

4.1.1 INITIAL WARNING

An indication of the shortcomings of correlation–scatterplot statistics came in one of the first experiments in this research program, an initial test of the integration model for person perception that was presented in Figure 1.4 of Section 1.2. The original report followed customary procedure by presenting correlation–scatterplots of predicted versus observed values. Of the 12 subjects in the experiment, the 2 with the largest discrepancies and the 1 with the smallest discrepancies are replotted in Figure 4.1. The lowest correlation is .95, and the mean correlation for the 12 subjects was .967 (see Table F2.1). In each panel of Figure 4.1, the points cluster closely around the diagonal line of perfect, error-free fit.

These correlation–scatterplot statistics might seem to provide strong support for the model. The model did fairly well, actually, but the evidence came from the analysis of variance. On both empirical and ra-

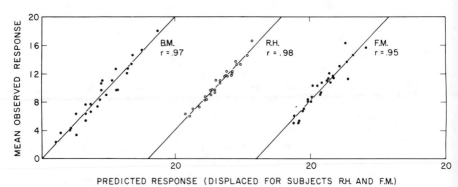

FIGURE 4.1. *Correlation–scatterplot analyses of observed person impressions as a function of values predicted by adding model. (After Anderson, 1962a.)*

tional grounds, it became clear that correlation–scatterplot statistics are often meaningless in model analysis.

Some sign of this conclusion can be seen in Figure 4.1. Subject F. M. showed significant discrepancies in the parallelism test despite the high correlation of .95. Subject B. M. shows larger discrepancies, but these were not significant because B. M. was more variable in responding. As this comparison shows, the scatterplot is inadequate because it confounds systematic and error variabilities. The higher correlation for B. M. merely reflects the larger range covered by his responses (see Section 7.9). Without the analysis of variance test, no conclusion about the model would have been warranted.

4.1.2 WEAK INFERENCE WITH CORRELATION AND SCATTERPLOT

The correlation coefficient is not a valid model test because it measures the wrong quantity, namely, the degree of agreement between predicted and observed values. A valid test must assess the deviations from prediction (Anderson, 1962a, p. 818). It may seem odd that a model with a high predictive correlation can be wrong, but that is typical in many research areas. This fact may be illustrated with some typical examples that show high correlations together with substantial deviations from the model.

Correlations. All the following examples embody the same logic. In each case, there are two stimulus variables that determine the response. An additive or linear model is used to obtain predicted values, and these are correlated with the observed values. In each case, these correlations are higher than .95, an outcome that might be taken as strong support for the model. In each case, however, the deviations from the model are highly significant. The linear model implies no interaction term in the analysis of variance; in graphical terms, this corresponds to parallelism in the factorial plot. Both tests show clear discrepancies from the linear model. In each case, therefore, the correlation is misleading because it gives no hint about the real discrepancies from the model.

One example from decision theory was cited in Anderson (1969c, p. 64). Subjects judged desirability of working at certain occupations in certain cities (Sidowski & Anderson, 1967). The linear model yielded correlations of .986 and .987 in two experiments despite the presence of a sizable and meaningful interaction (see also Section 5.5). Two examples from social judgment were cited in Anderson (1971a, p. 193). In a study of date ratings, the linear model yielded a correlation of .985 despite a strong, meaningful interaction between personality trait and photograph (Lampel & Anderson, 1968; see Table 5.2 and Figure F2.5). Even in an experiment that was designed specifically to obtain a large configural effect, the correlation was .977 (Anderson & Jacobson, 1965; see Figure F3.6). Similar results have been common in perception and psychophysics. In the right panel of Figure 1.3, for example, the curves are markedly nonparallel, yet the linear, additive model yielded a correlation of .983.

Each example tells the same story. The model analysis yields high correlations, yet the analysis of variance reveals significant discrepancies. Furthermore, the factorial graphs show clear deviations from parallelism. In short, the correlation conceals and obscures what the factorial analysis reveals and makes clear.

Scatterplots. More dramatic than the correlations are the scatterplots themselves. The left panel of Figure 4.2 plots subjects' predictions of performance as a function of given information about motivation and ability. The curves are not parallel but exhibit the linear fan form implied by the model, Performance = Motivation × Ability (Section F1.5.6). The nonparallelism is reliable, as shown by the significant interaction term, $F(9,171) = 7.98$, $p < 10^{-6}$. Clearly, an additive or linear model is not appropriate for these data.

Nevertheless, the additive model was fitted to the data using a least squares criterion. As in the other examples cited here, the scale values of

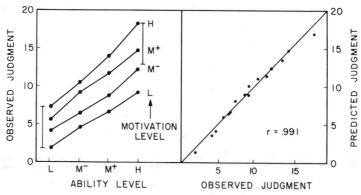

FIGURE 4.2. *Judged Performance = Motivation × Ability. Left panel shows factorial plot for judgments of expected performance as a function of given information about ability (horizontal axis) and motivation (curve parameter). Linear fan pattern, emphasized by two equal-length vertical bars, supports multiplying model, infirms adding or linear model. Right panel plots judgments predicted by linear model as a function of observed judgments from left panel. Tight scatterplot and high correlation of .991 in the right panel obscure and conceal the marked deviations from parallelism in the left panel. (Data reanalyzed after Anderson & Butzin, 1974.)*

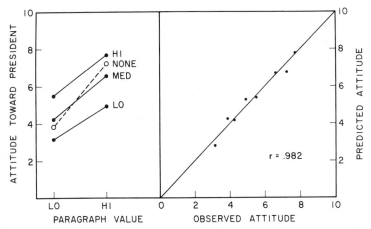

FIGURE 4.3. *President attitudes obey averaging model. Left panel shows factorial plot for judgments about statesmanship of United States presidents as a function of given biographical paragraphs. Parallelism of the solid curves supports adding-type model. Crossover of the dashed curve supports averaging model, rules out additive or linear model. Right panel plots judgments predicted by additive model as a function of observed judgments from the left panel. Tight scatterplot and high correlation of .982 obscure and conceal real nonadditivity visible in the factorial plot. (Data reanalyzed after Anderson, 1973b.)*

the stimuli were estimated from the data. That is statistically optimal; had ordinary regression analysis been used, the model could have failed merely due to invalidity in the scale values (Section 4.3.3). The present procedure avoids this ambiguity.

Of course, the additive model cannot fit this linear fan pattern very well because it necessarily predicts four parallel curves. What is surprising is how well the additive model seems to do. Its predictions are plotted against the observed values in the right panel of Figure 4.2. All the points would fall on the diagonal line in this scatterplot if there was no response variability and if the model was correct. In fact, the points cluster very closely around the diagonal, and the correlation between predicted and observed is .991. Had only these correlation–scatterplot statistics been presented, it would have seemed that the additive model had done very well.

A more striking example appears in the experiment on attitudes toward United States presidents, summarized in the left panel of Figure 4.3. The crossover of the dashed curve has substantive interest because it agrees with the averaging model (Section 5.4). The additive model cannot account for this crossover because it predicts four parallel curves. But when the additive model was fitted to the data, it seemed to do quite well, as shown in the right panel. The correlation between predicted and

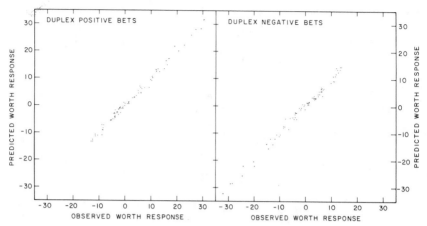

FIGURE 4.4. *Weak inference test of additive utility model. Each panel shows scatterplot of predictions from additive model as a function of observed judgments of subjective expected value, or worth. These tight scatterplots yielded exceptionally high correlations of .996 and .995 for the two respective panels, thereby obscuring real deviations from additivity that were revealed by analysis of variance. (After Anderson & Shanteau, 1970.)*

observed is .982, and the points cluster closely around the diagonal line of errorless, perfect fit.

Crossover interaction together with a high correlation from an additive model is not peculiar to one set of data. Other examples have been given elsewhere (e.g., Figures 2 and 3 of Anderson and Shanteau, 1977). It is not surprising that investigators who looked only at correlation-scatterplot statistics concluded that the additive or linear model was basically correct. In the cited experiments, however, the crossover shows that the data are inherently nonadditive. What is clear in the factorial plot is concealed by the scatterplot.

An example from decision theory was reported by Anderson and Shanteau (1970, Figure 2) and is reproduced here as Figure 4.4. Subjects judged the value of combinations of two independent chances to win or lose small sums of money. Utility theory implies that the value of the sum is the sum of the values, and Figure 4.4 plots the values predicted from this additive model against the observed judgments. The correlations are exceptionally high, .996 and .995 for the two respective panels. The predicted points cluster closely around the diagonal line of perfect fit. Reliance on this standard form of analysis would undoubtedly have led to the conclusion that the additive model had done very well. The analysis of variance, however, showed significant interactions that were the first indication of a pervasive subadditivity effect (Shanteau, 1970b, 1974).

An interesting note to the preceding experiment is that predictions could also be made using objective expected values calculated from the objective values of probability and money. These correlations were just a bit smaller, .990 for both conditions. Yet the subjective values of probability and money were nonlinearly related to the objective values. Here again, correlational analysis would have been misleading.

The problem of weak inference is not limited to the linear model, as shown in the following application of a nonlinear model to linear data. In the left panel of Figure 4.5, the data points show how 5-year-old children judged area of rectangles. The parallelism of the dotted curves points to an additive rule, Height + Width. This parallelism pattern was the first sign of a general purpose adding rule in children's judgments (Anderson, 1980a; Cuneo, 1980, 1982; Wilkening, 1980, 1981).

The Height + Width rule is naturally suspect. A primitive perception of global area would mimic the correct physical Height × Width rule; the child need only look to see how large the rectangle is. Some semblance of this Height × Width rule should appear even if the child did not perceive area very accurately or use the response scale very well. Perhaps, therefore, the multiplying rule was truly operative but the experiment lacked power to detect it (Bogartz, 1978). Support for this view might be seen in the right panel, which shows a very high correlation of .977 between the actual data and predictions from the multiplying model.[a] The points cluster closely around the diagonal line of per-

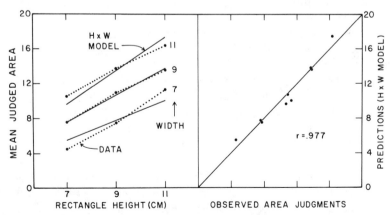

FIGURE 4.5. *Children judge area of rectangles by Height + Width rule, as shown by parallelism of dotted data curves in left panel. Factorial plot of predictions from Height × Width rule, given by the three solid lines, exhibits systematic pattern of discrepancies from the data. This pattern of discrepancies is obscured in right panel, which scatterplots the Height × Width predictions as a function of the actual judgments. (After Anderson & Cuneo, 1978a.)*

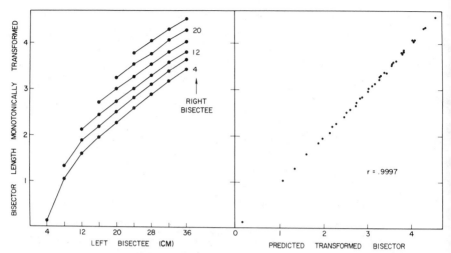

FIGURE 4.6. *Length bisection is monotonically nonadditive. Left panel shows factorial plot of mean length of bisector response as function of lengths of left and right bisectees, monotonically transformed to be as additive as possible. Moderate nonadditivity still remains as shown by the nonparallelism, which is best appreciated by measuring vertical spreads. Right panel shows observed values from left panel as a function of values predicted by adding model. Tight scatterplot and extraordinarily high correlation of .9997 obscure and conceal real deviations from adding model. (From Anderson, 1977a. [Copyright © 1977 by the Psychonomic Society. Reprinted by permission.])*

fect data, although in this case some sign of systematic discrepancies can be seen, at least in hindsight.

The factorial plot of predictions from the multiplying model is shown as the linear fan of solid lines in the left panel of Figure 4.5. The discrepancies between these solid curves and the data points exhibit a systematic and meaningful pattern. Here again, the factorial plot is more revealing than the correlation and scatterplot.

One final example, taken from psychophysics, is presented in Figure 4.6. The left panel plots the data from a length bisection task, monotonically transformed to be as additive as possible. The right panel plots these transformed data as a function of the values predicted by the additive model for bisection. The correlation of .9997 is surpassingly high. Deviations from the line of perfect fit are miniscule. It might seem that the bisection model held for length—but it does not: The factorial graph in the left panel shows substantial convergence to the right that is appreciated better by measuring the vertical spread.

Related Indexes. Various other statistical measures have been employed to evaluate models that suffer the same shortcomings as correlation and scatterplot. For example, percentage of variance accounted for is functionally equivalent to a correlation coefficient. To illustrate, consider length bisection in Figure 4.6. The additive bisection model accounted for 99.9% of the systematic variance, yet there was a highly significant and apparently important nonadditive component. In Figure 4.3, similarly, the linear model accounted for 96.4% of the systematic variance despite the crossover interaction.

Two other indexes, mean magnitude deviation and root mean square deviation, are condensed summaries of the scatterplot. They are less informative, therefore, and suffer the same basic shortcoming of confounding systematic and random effects. The same holds for the stress measures used in multidimensional scaling. Without a measure of random effects, tests of fit are not generally possible.

4.1.3 COMMENTS ON WEAK INFERENCE

How can models that are so bad look so good? How can correlation-scatterplot analyses seem to support a linear model when the factorial data show crossover interactions? One reason is that the correlation is a global statistic, insensitive to the local discrepancies associated with the crossover. And although the scatterplot is more informative, it too can be misleading, as illustrated in Figures 4.1–4.6.

Another reason is that high correlations are typically guaranteed whenever the stimulus variables cover a substantial range. In a factorial design, in particular, the linear or additive model is equivalent to the analysis of variance model with the interaction term deleted. The square of the correlation between predicted and observed equals the proportion of systematic variance accounted for by the main effects. But the main effects in the foregoing experiments are trivial, and the same holds for many experiments on judgment and decision theory. The proper test of the additive model comes from the statistical interaction term. Similar comments hold for nonlinear models.

A surprising proportion of recent work on judgment and decision rests on such weak inference methods, in areas as different as clinical judgment, social attitudes, decision theory, and psychophysics. In clinical judgment, for example, it was repeatedly found that traditional linear regression failed to reveal suspected configural processes. One suggestion was that the linear model had such great power that it obscured real configural processes. In fact, the failure was caused by the lack of power in the weak inference methods used to analyze the data. A related suggestion was that the linear model was robust, that is, insensitive to deviations from assumptions. Here again, the insensitivity was not in the model, but in the methods of analysis. Standard techniques from analysis of variance were readily able to demonstrate configural processes (e.g., Anderson, 1969c, 1972b). What has been taken to show the value of the linear model often shows instead the inadequacies of weak inference methodology.

A review of weak inference by Anderson and Shanteau (1977), which included reanalyses of three cases from popular areas of decision theory, commented:

> In each of these examples from decision theory, high correlations provided initially compelling support for the model in question. This led to further, often intensive, research on the psychological processes that were presumed to lie behind these models. Reanalysis and later evidence have shown that these correlations were deceiving. They did more to obscure than to reveal the underlying processes. As a consequence, much labor came to nothing [p. 1163].[1]

The extreme persistence of weak inference methods is not easy to understand. However, one cause seems to be a failure to distinguish the goal of prediction and the goal of understanding. Anderson and Shanteau (1977) note that these two goals require different methods:

> It should be reemphasized that no criticism is intended here of practical prediction with linear models. Indeed, the present examples extend previous work in a significant respect: They demonstrate that good predictive ability can often be obtained even when the linear model severely misrepresents the psychological processes.
>
> It follows directly, of course, that the linear model is not too useful for the goal of understanding, at least as usually applied. The linear model is good for prediction because it is simple, easy to use, and because it glosses over discrepancies in part of the data. But, as has been shown above, such discrepancies can provide important clues to psychological process.
>
> Unfortunately, there seems to be an overwhelming tendency to slip from the predictive mode into the interpretive mode. The practical usefulness of the linear model has tended to blind investigators to its severe limitations for theoretical analysis. When the linear model seems to do so well at prediction, it is hard to avoid thinking and implying that in some way it has deeper psychological truth. This idea, often largely implicit, colors the overall conception and has exerted important constraints on choice of problem and method.
>
> Although it could be wished otherwise, the goals of prediction and understanding are often incompatible. The above examples show that the methods that work so well for practical prediction can be extremely misleading in the search for understanding. Attempts to pursue one goal with tools appropriate to the other are risking the entire investigation [p. 1168].[2]

[1,2]From N. H. Anderson & J. Shanteau, Weak inference with linear models. *Psychological Bulletin*, 1977, *84*, 1155–1170. Copyright © 1977 by the American Psychological Association. Reprinted by permission of the publisher and authors.

4.2 Goodness of Fit and Power

The necessity for testing goodness of fit is well illustrated by the examples of the previous section. However, the evidence value of a test of fit depends entirely on its power to detect discrepancies from the model. The problem of power has basic importance, therefore, and requires more detailed discussion.

4.2.1 ACCEPTING AND REJECTING MODELS

Null Hypothesis Logic.[a] Attempts to establish algebraic models face the problem that accepting the model corresponds to accepting a statistical null hypothesis. The linear model, for example, implies zero interaction, and this test provides an assessment of the model. Unfortunately, the null hypothesis logic, which is so useful in ordinary experimental work, is awkward in testing models. In ordinary experiments, the investigator usually desires to reject the null hypothesis. Since failure to reject is ordinarily failure pure and simple, it is advantageous to avoid weak experiments.

In model tests, however, failure to reject can seem like success. This sets up a selection tendency toward weaker experiments or toward weaker statistical analyses. Such selection tendencies may be one reason for the popularity of the correlation–scatterplot analyses discussed in the previous section.

Only to the degree that an analysis has power to detect discrepancies from a model can it be taken as support for the model. Some aspects of statistical power calculations are given in Section 4.2.2. However, the following empirical guide may sometimes be more convenient and useful.

Empirical Guide on Power. As a working guide, the following rule about power is suggested: *Power is adequate when the discrepancies are significant statistically but unimportant substantively.* This rule seems paradoxical, for it means that the null hypothesis implied by the model must be rejected before the model can be accepted. Nevertheless, this rule seems to represent common sense and common practice. If the discrepancies are statistically significant, that is prima facie evidence for adequate power. But if they are not substantively important, then it seems reasonable to accept the model.

An essential element in this reasoning is that tests of models always rest on certain simplifying assumptions that will seldom hold exactly. Significant discrepancies may reflect unimportant failures to meet the simplifying assumptions rather than important failures in the theoretical

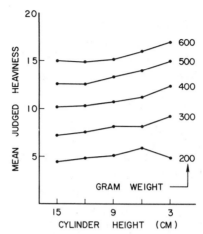

FIGURE 4.7. *Integration rule for weight–size illusion. Judgments of felt heaviness of lifted cylinders plotted as a function of cylinder height (horizontal axis) and gram weight (curve parameter). Parallelism supports adding rule, Heaviness = Weight + Size, except for deviant point at lower right. (After Anderson, 1972a.)*

structure. In rating scales, for example, number or position preferences cannot be eliminated completely, hence ratings will never provide perfect linear scales. In the person perception experiments, some slight redundancy or inconsistency effects must always be expected, and they will produce deviations from parallelism. Similarly, the equal weighting condition of averaging theory will rarely be satisfied exactly. Minor failures of such simplifying assumptions will tend to produce significant discrepancies in the test of fit without necessarily causing any theoretical concern.

It may seem untidy logic to think that the best support for a model will come from experiments that find significant discrepancies. It can certainly be uncomfortable to make this argument in a report for publication. This viewpoint seems to have a reasonable basis, however, and it does seem to represent actual decision making in science.

An experimental example may help make this point. In a study of the weight–size illusion, subjects judged felt heaviness of lifted cylinders that varied in height and gram weight. The overall parallelism of the factorial plot in the left panel of Figure 4.7 supports the hypothesis that the weight and size cues are integrated by an adding-type rule, Heaviness = Weight + Size. But there is one deviant point, at the lower right, and this one-point discrepancy produced a significant interaction. When this deviant point was omitted from the analysis, the interaction did not approach significance (Anderson, 1972a, p. 390). It seems reasonable, therefore, to discount the deviant point and interpret the data as strong support for the Weight + Size rule. Indeed, the significant discrepancy itself helps support the model by demonstrating the great power of the analysis of variance test.

At an abstract level, this empirical rule about power lacks force because it lacks a criterion for importance of discrepancies. In practice, it seems to work moderately well. Perhaps it would be better to say that the rule reflects practice, that it describes how investigators do and should behave. It provides no routine recipe but recognizes that research focuses on the uncertain, the provisional, and the partially known. No fixed rule seems possible, therefore, but the following experimental examples bring out some of the relevant considerations (see also Anderson, 1977b).

Interpretation of Significant Discrepancies. The first example comes from the weight–size experiment of Figure 4.7 just considered. It seems plausible to discount the one deviant point since the rest of the data do exhibit parallelism. In fact, the deviant point would seem to represent an end effect associated with the stimulus end anchors. The low end anchor, which the subject was instructed to rate "1," weighed 100 grams but had the same 3-cm height as the deviant stimulus. This height cue could have facilitated a few extra "1" responses to the given stimulus, thereby producing the deviant response. This deviant point has considerable methodological interest, therefore, because it illustrates the importance of end anchors as well as the statistical power of the analysis of variance test.

A second example appears in the right panel of Figure 1.3. Subjects were instructed to judge average grayness of two Munsell chips using a magnitude estimation response. The natural model implied by these instructions is an arithmetic average, so the data should exhibit parallelism. However, the data are far from parallel. In this experiment the model was considered to be correct, so the nonparallelism was attributed to bias in the method of magnitude estimation. By itself, of course, this one graph hardly allows so definite an interpretation. However, the left panel of this same figure shows that parallelism was obtained when a rating response was used, which helps solidify the conclusion that magnitude estimation suffers from nonlinear response bias.

A different outcome is illustrated by the crossover interaction of Figure 4.3, which shows attitudes toward presidents. The crossover cannot be accounted for by monotone response bias. An interpretation in terms of stimulus interaction also seems to be inapplicable (Section F4.1). In this case, therefore, the adding model itself is rejected.

In many cases, however, interpretation of significant discrepancy will remain more or less doubtful. In the experiment on subjective expected value of Figure 4.4, the discrepancies from the adding model were small. In this initial experiment, it was possible to hope that they might not reflect adversely on the model itself, but later work revealed pervasive subadditivity. Again, in the study of length bisection of Figure 4.6, the nonadditivity has tentatively been interpreted as a basic shortcoming in the bisection model itself.

4.2.2 POWER CONSIDERATIONS

Determinants of Power. Statistical power is defined as the probability of rejecting the null hypothesis. The power of tests of main effects and interactions in factorial designs can be calculated by using a general formula together with tables presented in Cohen (1969) or in various statistical texts (e.g., Keppel, 1973; Winer, 1971). For present purposes, it is enough to consider the special case of testing the null hypothesis, that some true mean, μ, has the value 0. Let n be the number of observations, and let σ be their standard deviation. Then power depends on the ϕ statistic

$$\phi = \sqrt{n}(\mu/\sigma).$$

This formula indicates that power may be increased by increasing n or μ or by decreasing σ. The effect of n follows a square root law of diminishing returns, so it may not be worthwhile to increase n beyond some moderate value. To get substantial increases in power, therefore, it is desirable to increase the size of the effect, or to decrease the variability.

Variability may be decreased by various experimental procedures, such as those discussed in Chapter 1. Of course, the greatest decreases in variability are obtained by shifting from between-subject to within-subject design, or from within-subject to individual subject design. Strictly speaking, the component of variability that constitutes the error term decreases as the between-subject variability, for example, could itself remain constant.

Individual variability is interesting because it appears to vary markedly, even in careful experiments (e.g., Shanteau, 1974, Table 2; Table F2.1). Why some subjects are highly variable and others are not is an unexplored problem that deserves investigation. There is a potential practical benefit, either from discovery of better procedures to reduce within-subject variability or from development of a screening test to stratify or screen out the highly variable subjects. There is also theoretical interest in the possibility that individual differences in variability may shed light on the role of response processes.

Increasing power by increasing the size of the effect is not ordinarily sought after in model analysis because the effect is usually a discrepancy from the model. Nevertheless, it is still important to maximize the opportunity for detection of any such discrepancies. It is generally necessary to have substantial main effects, therefore, to allow possible interactions to manifest themselves. It is also usually desirable to have the stimuli more or less equally spaced.[a] Finally, the use of specific comparisons (Section 2.1.4) deserves re-emphasis, as they can markedly increase power by concentrating the effect or potential effect in a single index.

Illustrative Power Calculations. A power calculation may be used to compare efficiency for between- and within-subject designs. The solid curves in Figure 4.3 test a parallelism prediction in a study of attitudes toward United States presidents. Each of 48 subjects made judgments in all six conditions, and the repeated measurements error mean square was 1.48. Between-subject variability, calculated from these same data, was 2.64, only 1.78 times larger. To get equal power would thus require only 1.78 times as many scores per condition, or a total of 85 subjects per condition. But there were six conditions, so the total need would be 6 × 85 = 510 subjects. Even in this very small 2 × 3 design, therefore, a between-subject test of the model is almost prohibitively expensive.

Under these conditions, a between-subject design with, say, 24 subjects per cell would be pointless because of low power. A nonsignificant result would provide no particular support for the null hypothesis; a significant result would come under suspicion of being a false alarm.

The power advantage of the within-subject design in this example is not especially marked. The ratio of between- to within-subject variability can go substantially higher than the cited value of 1.78 (e.g., Anderson, 1965b, Table 2). Also, the 2 × 3 design is quite small. Typical experiments contain from 20 to 200 conditions for which between-subject design is generally infeasible. It should be added that these power considerations do not rule out between-subject variables, for they can sometimes be included in mixed designs where their interactions have a within-subject error term (Section 2.1).

One problem in calculating power is that it depends on the magnitude of the discrepancy from the model prediction, namely, μ in the cited ϕ formula. Not only is this discrepancy generally unknown, but it is typically hypothesized to be zero. Thus, a clear basis for calculating power may not be available. One standard device is to assume some magnitude of discrepancy that would be important to know about if it in fact obtained. Power may then be calculated as the probability of detecting that large a discrepancy. In some cases, however, there is an alternative hypothesis that predicts a value for μ. A case of general interest concerning an all-or-none, no-integration interpretation of parallelism will be used for illustration.

Evidence for a Height + Width rule in children's judgments of rectangle area was given by the parallelism of Figure 4.5. However, an alternative interpretation was possible within Piagetian theory, which asserts that children of this age are incapable of integrating two stimulus dimensions but instead "center" on one or another dimension and use it as the sole basis for judgment. Any individual child would thus judge on the basis of height in some trials and on the basis of width in other trials. This all-or-none, one-dimensional hypothesis also predicts parallelism, but as an artifact of averaging over trials (Section 2.1.4).

A variability test may be used to discriminate between these two interpretations. The integration hypothesis implies that response variability should be equal for the 9 × 9 and the 7 × 11 rectangles because these have the same value of height + width. In contrast, the one-dimensional hypothesis implies that response variability should be markedly less for the 9 × 9 than for the 7 × 11 rectangle: For the 9 × 9 rectangle, response based on height will equal response based on width; for the 7 × 11 rectangle, response based on a height of 7 will be systematically and substantially less than response based on a width of 11. Hence response variability across successive trials for an individual subject will be greater for the 7 × 11 rectangle.

To make this test, two variability scores were obtained for each of 33 children. One score was the standard deviation of the responses from the two presentations of the 9 × 9 rectangle; the other score was the standard deviation of the two corresponding responses to the 7 × 11 rectangle. The means of these two variability scores were 2.54 and 2.10, respectively. The difference was not significant, $F(1,32) = .96$, and was actually opposite to the prediction from the one-dimensional, no-integration hypothesis.

To take the null outcome of this significance test as serious evidence against the one-dimensional hypothesis, it must be shown that the test had adequate power to detect the effect actually predicted by that hypothesis. Fortunately, the one-dimensional hypothesis led to a numerical prediction of the expected effect, and a straightforward power calculation showed that an effect of this predicted size would have been detected with a probability of .99 with only six subjects. The actual n of 33 thus provides more than ample power and thereby justifies rejection of the one-dimensional hypothesis (Anderson & Cuneo, 1978a, p. 363).[b]

One final power calculation has general interest for interpretation of marginally significant results. Given that an F ratio is just significant at the .05 level, what is the probability of obtaining a significant result in an exact replication? A best guess would be obtained by using the observed means and variance in the ϕ formula. However, the following simple argument shows that the power is about one-half. The observed F ratio is a random sample of size 1 from the operative sampling distribution of F ratios. It is an unbiased estimate of the mean of that distribution and an approximate estimate of the median. The replication experiment will yield a new sample of size 1 from this same distribution; it has one-half chance of being above the median, hence approximately one-half chance of being above the mean. Since this mean is estimated by the observed F, which is just significant, the best guess is that power is only about one-half. Use of the ϕ formula corroborates this reasoning. As this example suggests, marginally significant results cannot be taken very seriously without collateral support.

Confidence Intervals. A sample value is an estimate and so is meaningful only in relation to its variability; that indicates the range of true values that might reasonably underlie the observed sample value. The same sample mean could have quite different implications, depending on the size of its confidence interval.

In a study of primacy–recency, for example, the mean primacy in a two-adjective condition was only .04, much less than the average value of .69 for various six-adjective conditions (Anderson & Barrios, 1961, Experiment 2). At face value, the sample mean of .04 suggests that any true primacy effect is near zero in the two-adjective condition. It could be argued, however, that the true effect is substantial and that the observed effect is small by chance. To claim that the true effect is negligible, therefore, requires showing that the observed effect is not expected to be greatly different in repeated samples. This was done by setting up the 95% confidence interval around the sample mean, which had the value of .04 ± .12. On this basis, it seems reasonable to believe that the two-adjective condition produces little or no primacy. A more extensive application of confidence interval technique appears in studies of the dilution effect in decision theory discovered by Shanteau (1975b; Troutman & Shanteau, 1977; see Section F2.3.6).

Unfortunately, confidence intervals have limited usefulness for testing algebraic models. Consider the common case of a two-way factorial graph for a linear or a multiplying model, with data averaged over a group of subjects. Confidence intervals around single points, based on between-subject variability, are clearly irrelevant because the model test employs within-subject variability. Confidence intervals could be calculated for the difference between two points, but even that would not be very satisfactory. The parallelism and linear fan tests both rest on the overall pattern of the factorial graph, not on the difference between any two points. The linear fan test, moreover, is primarily concerned with the residual interaction, not with the graph itself.

Visual inspection can provide a fairly good assessment of point variability in terms of pattern roughness. In Figure 4.7, for example, the lowest right point is suspect because it disagrees with the visual pattern of the rest of the graph. However, visual inspection is less useful for assessing the reliability of pattern variability, especially in group data.

Confidence intervals may be more useful when the test of fit employs a specific comparison, such as the LL or LQ interaction components of Section 2.2.2. Confidence intervals around such algebraic values provide a test of significance; they also carry information about power as reflected in the width of the interval.

For parameter estimation, of course, confidence intervals are appropriate and in some sense necessary. The same parameter estimate would have rather different meaning depending on whether its confidence interval was wide or narrow. Intuitive estimates of variability underlie almost any interpretation of observed results. They can be useful and efficient, but they can also be misleading. Explicit calculation of confidence intervals seems desirable when primary interest is on the parameter values themselves. It should be noted that within- and between-subject confidence intervals may involve different design considerations.

4.2.3 COMPARING MODELS

More than one model may be proposed for some situation, but it is often difficult to discriminate among them. Qualitative tests are ideal (Section 5.4) but cannot always be found. Quantitative analysis may seem well suited to this purpose, and it is—to a certain extent. After a problem has been under study for a time, however, most bad models have been weeded out and it may not be easy to find ways to discriminate among those that remain.

The weak inference methods of Section 4.1 are even less suited for comparing two models than for assessing a single model. The correlation statistic is subject to the additional problems noted in Section 7.9 and need not be considered further. The mean magnitude discrepancy may sometimes provide rough guidance, but it is subject to the problems considered next.

Valid significance tests for each of two models can be obtained by applying the method of Section 4.4 separately to each model. These tests could be supplemented with a similar test on the matrix of differences between the predictions of the two models. The problem comes in attempting to use these tests for comparing the models. To illustrate, suppose that the separate tests yield significant discrepancies for one model but not for the other. It does not follow that one model is better than the other: The one test might be just significant and the other just not significant. But suppose that the discrepancies from prediction are smaller for one model than for the other in every cell of the design and that the test on the matrix of differences shows this superiority to be significant. It still does not follow that one model is essentially superior to the other.

An obvious problem is that one model may have more parameters than another. The model with more parameters will generally fit better, of course, so a fair comparison must make due allowance for number of parameters. Such allowance may be possible when one model is a special case of another. Thus, the linear model can be represented as a special case of the compound adding–multiplying model (Eq. [15] of Chapter 2), and analysis of variance provides a valid test of the hypothesis that addition of the bilinear component adds real predictive power. In general, however, comparisons among models with different numbers of parameters can be difficult to interpret.

Even when two models have the same number of parameters, fair comparison may not be possible. The parameters may have different structural roles in the two models, and the statistical properties of the estimates may be different. This problem has been discussed for discrete-choice learning models by Sternberg (1963, p. 95), who notes that it casts doubt on various comparative studies of stochastic learning models. The same problem applies to the algebraic models considered here.

A related aspect of this last problem is that different models may be sensitive to different aspects of the data. One model may predict a linear fan, for example, another a barrel-shaped set of curves. A global test of fit may not be appropriate in either case. Instead, each model deserves a specific test based on a different aspect of the data.

Finally, and most important, comparative tests cannot establish models. They may show that the poorer model is inadequate; they do not show that the better model is any good. To establish the better model still requires absolute tests of that model alone (Section 4.1).[a] This point deserves emphasis because comparative analysis can easily give the illusion of progress by demolishing straw models.

The need for comparative evaluation of different models and different theoretical formulations goes without saying. Such comparisons deserve more emphasis than they currently receive. However, evaluating goodness of fit for a single model does not follow any cut-and-dried routine, and comparing two models does so even less. These brief comments are intended to call attention to some of the problems with the hope that such comparisons can be made more effective.

4.2.4 GOODNESS OF FIT WITH SEPARATE PARAMETER ESTIMATES

A not infrequent concern about the tests of goodness of fit of Chapter 2 is that they typically estimate the model parameters from the very data to be predicted. This raises a natural suspicion that the model is somehow taking unfair advantage of the data. It is sometimes suggested, therefore, that tests of fit should be made with parameters that have been estimated separately and independently from some other set of data.

This approach seems reasonable and indeed reflects the orientation of traditional scaling theory, which sees scaling as a methodological preliminary to substantive inquiry. Curiously enough, reliance on separate parameter estimates turns out to be generally inferior, at least with the methods in common use. This matter is interesting because it illustrates how elementary statistical considerations can reveal pitfalls in what seems to be an obvious and natural method of analysis. For simplicity, the following discussion is restricted to the linear model, although most of it holds in general.

Bias and Reliability. The first difficulty with separate parameter estimates is that they may be biased or systematically different from the true parameters. Then the model predictions using these parameter estimates will also be incorrect. That will cause the model to fail the test of goodness of fit even though the model itself may be correct.

Unfortunately, the investigator will know only that the model failed the test, with no way to decide whether the parameters or the model itself was at fault. This uncertainty can be avoided by using the methods outlined in Chapter 2. By using the given data, best possible estimates of the parameters can be obtained, together with a valid test of fit. If the model fails using these parameter estimates, then the fault is definitely elsewhere.

The second difficulty with separate parameter estimates is that their reliability must be taken into account in order to obtain a valid test. This is seldom done. Instead, the estimates are treated as though they were true, errorless values. But that means that the nominal error term in the test of fit is smaller than it should be. At the same time, the actual errors in the parameter estimates do not appear as random variability in the test, but as bias. Accordingly, the test of goodness of fit is not valid.

A valid test can be obtained if the parameter estimates are unbiased and if their variability is taken into account in an appropriate way. Unless due care is used, however, this variability will artificially inflate the error term for the model test.

Interaction Illustration. An example may help illustrate some of the statistical considerations. Suppose that each of a number of subjects responds once in each cell of a 2 × 2 design, and let R_{ijn} be the response of subject n in cell ij. Consider the hypothesis that a linear model can account for the data. This model is equivalent to zero interaction. To test this null hypothesis using the methods of Chapter 2, each subject would be given an algebraic interaction score,

$$I_n = (R_{11n} - R_{12n}) - (R_{21n} - R_{22n}).$$

This score is nonzero to the extent that this subject's data depart from parallelism. The null hypothesis to be tested, therefore, is that the mean value of I_n is zero. This test may be done in various ways. A direct t test on the I_n scores is equivalent to the interaction test in the analysis of variance. Of course, a signed-ranks test or other distribution-free test could also be used (Note 2.1.2a).

The alternative method assumes that separate estimates of the stimulus values are available. For example, the subject might rate each single stimulus. These independent parameter estimates would then be substituted into the linear model to obtain predicted responses for each subject in each cell of the design. The test of fit then requires that these predicted values be compared to the observed R_{ijn}.

However, any attempt to compare these predicted and observed values faces three difficulties. Bias and unreliability have already been mentioned. Bias in the estimates confounds the test of the model. The effect of unreliability in the estimates depends on how it is handled. The most common procedures either convert unreliability into bias or inflate the error term in the test of fit.

The third difficulty is that the global nature of the comparison between predicted and observed reduces power. In the given example, the test would have 4 df since there are four cells to be compared. In terms of analysis of variance, these 4 df correspond to the Mean, Row, Column, and Row × Column terms. However, all real deviations from the model will be concentrated in the Row × Column term. If the parameter estimates are unbiased, then the first three terms are zero in principle; including them in the test decreases power to detect real interaction.

At this point, it might seem that the matter could be solved by going directly to a test of the interaction. Thus, each subject could be given a deviation score between the predicted and observed values in each cell of the design. The interaction component would then be calculated using the preceding equation for I_n, but with R_{ijn} representing the deviation score. But this calculation will yield exactly the same value of I_n as was obtained with the raw data; the interaction component of the predicted values cancels to zero because the predictions were made from a linear model. The separate estimates of the parameters are unnecessary and irrelevant.

Comments. Inappropriate methods are sometimes adopted without realization of their shortcomings. Standard regression analysis is a prime example. It typically rests on the use of separate estimates of scale values and does not provide proper tests of the linear model (Section 4.3). The suspicion about estimating parameters from the data at hand seems to originate in part from work with correlation–regression analysis. The mean discrepancy from prediction will be smaller, and the correlation between predicted and observed will be higher, when parameters are estimated from the given data. This is a legitimate concern in prediction studies because the correlation will typically shrink when the same parameters are applied to a new sample of data. However, testing models involves other considerations than prediction (Section 4.3.1).

A variant argument is that the true test of the model rests on whether the parameter estimates are generalizable from one situation to another. This argument represents an attractive half-truth; model generality is more basic than, and independent of, parameter generality (Section 3.1).[a]

As a concluding comment, it should be emphasized that there are situations in which separate parameter estimates are useful and even necessary. This important issue is discussed further in the next section and in Chapter 6.

4.3 Regression Analysis

An important frontier of information integration studies concerns situations in which stimulus attributes are under limited experimental control. In face perception, for example, controllable factors such as pose, gesture, and makeup can only modify facial attributes already possessed by the subject. Similar problems affect the study of most natural situations, such as marital decision making.

This kind of situation has usually been studied with standard regression analysis, relying on separate estimates for scaling the predictor variables. It would be desirable, accordingly, to employ regression techniques to study problems of information integration. Doing so might seem straightforward at first glance, but it turns out otherwise.

Some of the problems involved in adapting regression-type techniques to the study of integration processes are discussed in this section. Other relevant considerations are given in Sections 1.3.8, 1.3.9, 2.3.3, 4.1, 6.1, 6.2, 7.2, and 7.3. These sections are far from complete but they should help point up some of the many problems that require further study. Unless otherwise stated, only linear regression will be considered, although much of the discussion also applies to nonlinear regression.

4.3.1 UNDERSTANDING VERSUS PREDICTION

The usual regression methods are oriented to prediction and are often inappropriate for the study of process. This matter is sufficiently common and troublesome that the prediction–understanding polarity requires preliminary discussion in the regression context.

Functional Equation versus Predictive Equation. The distinction between prediction and understanding made in Section 4.1.3 has a statistical parallel corresponding to a distinction between prediction equation and functional or structural equation. Standard regression analysis yields a prediction equation. In a structural equation, on the other hand, the variables are treated as substantive factors connected by some functional law (see, e.g., Goldberger, 1973; Graybill, 1961). Both methods of analysis have appropriate applications, but they yield different results. In general, structural equation analysis is in order when there is any interest beyond bare prediction.

To illustrate the distinction, consider consumer decisions by married couples as a function of the separate preferences of husband and wife. Separate measures of husband and wife preferences would be obtained for use as predictors in a two-variable linear regression. Although errors of unreliability in the predictors are ignored in the regression, that is appropriate for prediction (Malinvaud, 1966, p. 335). Furthermore, the implicit assumption of linearity in the measured preference scale is usually an adequate approximation. To a marketing analyst or an economic forecaster, therefore, the standard linear regression equation provides a handy tool.

Standard regression analysis may not, however, be relevant to the person who wishes to study marital adjustment processes. Process analysis might be interested, for example, in the relative weight or marital power of husband and wife as they depend on the type of consumer decision, on the two personalities, on the duration and harmoniousness of the marriage, and so forth. The regression weights are the wrong weights for such process analysis. Even if all desired assumptions are correct, the mere fact that the preferences are not perfectly reliable causes bias in the weight estimates (Section 4.3.3; see also Section 6.1).[a] Although this bias is no problem for prediction per se, it becomes a problem as soon as any attempt is made to attach meaning to the weights.

Redundancy versus Correlation. A more qualitative aspect of the difference between understanding and prediction is mirrored in the distinction between causal redundancy and correlation. In many investigations, the relevant attributes are not orthogonal or independent. For example, convenience and cost are positively correlated for most consumer goods. Analysis of situations with correlated attributes presents serious difficulties.

Environmental correlation has a basic role in certain approaches. In the usual regression analysis, in particular, environmental correlation is an integral component of the model. The same applies to theoretical formulations that attempt to build on the statistical structure of the environment. But the environmental correlation is a statistical property of an aggregate of situations; it is conceptually distinct from the causal structure of the environment that operates in each individual situation. The correlation would be viewed rather differently depending on whether the investigator is interested in prediction or in understanding.

This basic distinction between causal structure and environmental correlation can be illustrated in typical stimulus integration tasks. Suppose, for example, that the subject judges likableness of persons described by a photograph and a personality trait adjective. If the photographs and traits are combined in a complete factorial design, then they are statistically uncorrelated and independent within the experimental environment. The omission of just one combination, so that one corner cell of the design is empty, say, will induce a correlation between the two attributes. More generally, the investigator might omit combinations in which one attribute was very positive, the other very negative, thereby producing a positive correlation between the two attributes.

But this correlation has no necessary or likely relation to the integration rule. The correlation is a statistical property of the aggregate of stimulus combinations. The integration rule refers to processes that operate in the judgment of each individual combination. There is neither logical nor psychological necessity that the operative integration processes depend on the aggregate of combinations that the experimenter happens to present. After all, the likableness of each person depends on his or her attributes, not on the attributes of some entirely different person.

The subject may, of course, view two attributes as being information-ally redundant, a kind of subjective correlation. For person perception, substantial subjective correlations appear in the form of halo effects (Section 6.2.4). However, the very concept of halo implies that subjec-tive correlation is essentially different from statistical correlation in the environment at large. And neither of these correlations has any definite relation to the correlation over the particular aggregate of stimulus com-binations selected by the experimenter.

It should be emphasized that subjective correlations, whether in the form of redundancy or inconsistency, are important for the study of stimulus integration. As already indicated, however, subjective correla-tion is an essentially different concept from statistical correlation, either in the experimental environment or in the environment at large.[b]

Measurement Problems in Regression Analysis. An occasional misuse of regression analysis is related to the two basic problems of measurement (Anderson, 1972b, pp. 98–99). In some applications, a linear regression model is augmented by adding, say, squares of the predictor variables. Significance of a square term is often interpreted as nonlinearity in the regression equation. But a significant square term is ambiguous. It can come from nonlinearity in the true process model; this has been the customary interpretation. It can also come from nonlinearity or bias in the measurement scales of the predictor variables. The theoretical mean-ing is quite different in these two cases.

A similar problem arises with respect to response measurement. In some applications, a linear regression model is augmented by adding cross-products of the predictor variables. The significance of the cross-product terms has commonly been interpreted as evidence of configural-ity or interaction in the psychological processing. However, cross-product terms can be obtained from the simplest linear model if the response scale is not linear. The theoretical meaning of the cross-product term is quite different in the two cases.

For predictive purposes, of course, nonlinearity in the measurement scales of the predictors, or of the response, is often of minor importance. It is much easier and almost equally effective to add squares, cross products, or other such terms than to try solving the measurement prob-lems. But that very fact re-emphasizes the difference between prediction and understanding.[c]

4.3.2 NONORTHOGONAL ANALYSIS OF VARIANCE

Standard analysis of variance is based on a linear structural model that may be applied to arbitrary designs with variable numbers of observations per cell, including the important case of empty cells with no observations. This problem has been treated extensively by Searle (1971, especially Chapter 7). One important result is that the interaction test in a nonorthogonal design has the same interpretation as in a complete factorial design.[a] Hence a valid test is available for adding-type models. If the additive model can be accepted, functional scales of stimulus value can be obtained. In the case of no empty cells, stimulus values may be estimated from the marginal means of the matrix of cell means, although these estimates will not have minimum variance unless all cell n's are equal. If some cells are empty, then a least squares solution is ordinarily required to obtain the stimulus values. These results require only that the design be connected. For a two-way design, *connectedness* means that all nonempty cells can be connected by a single line that turns only by 90 or 180° at nonempty cells. Designs that are not connected may be partitioned into connected subdesigns that may be treated as indicated. Although these nonorthogonal analyses are limited to linear models with interaction terms included, the significance tests may also be applied to the discrepancy matrix of Section 4.4 for nonlinear models.

The problem of testing main effects in nonorthogonal analysis of variance has occasioned considerable argument in both statistical and psychological journals. Various procedures have been advocated, some of which test hypotheses that depend on the number of observations in each design cell. However, it now seems generally agreed, following Searle (1971), that proper tests for main effects should not ordinarily depend on the numbers of observations in different cells. Clear discussions are given by Speed, Hocking, and Hackney (1978) and Herr and Gaebelin (1978), who also list which hypotheses are tested by standard computer programs.

Nonorthogonal analysis still presents many statistical problems. Correlated scores, which appear in repeated measurements designs, have received little attention. The standard assumption of independent scores does, however, allow nonorthogonal analysis for individual subject designs in which replications are equivalent (Section 2.1.3). Except for Searle (1971) and a short section in Speed *et al.*, the important case of empty cells is generally disallowed, sometimes without explicit statement.[b] Not much information is available on estimation or approximate methods, and nonlinear models have not been much considered.[c] These problems are also present in structural, or functional, regression.

4.3.3 USE OF SEPARATE PARAMETER ESTIMATES

Model analysis can be simpler when parameter values, including scale values or predictor values in particular, are known beforehand. For many tasks of judgment and decision, self-estimates of the parameters are obtainable (Section 6.2). In some tasks, physical metrics of stimulus attributes can be used.[a] Capitalizing on the information in such parameter estimates can simplify the analysis and allow simpler experimental designs. However, separate parameter estimates will generally also contain misinformation in the twin forms of unreliability and invalidity. Attempts to exploit the information may fall victim to the misinformation.

Parameter Values Known without Error. When the parameter values are known without error, the analysis is reasonably straightforward. These known parameters are substituted into the model, thereby reducing the number of parameters that must be estimated from the data at hand. In principle, this is direct and simple.

Even in this ideal case, however, there are two problems. First, the parameter estimates may not be on an absolute scale but only on a linear or ratio scale. Zero and unit parameters may therefore need to be estimated in the analysis (Sections 4.3.5 and 4.3.6). Second, objective values are not infrequently used in place of subjective values. That the objective values are known exactly is irrelevant if the interpretation implicitly rests on subjective values. This problem sometimes causes misconceptions in theoretical interpretation (e.g., Anderson & Butzin, 1978).

Valid but Unreliable Parameter Values. Standard regression analysis assumes that the predictor values are known exactly. In psychological research, however, these values are usually estimates that include error of measurement. This subsection considers the case in which the predictor estimates are on valid linear scales, subject only to unreliability. Unreliability affects the test of goodness of fit, a problem that is discussed in Section 4.4. Unreliability also biases the estimates of operative weight parameters. The bias problem, already noted in the discussion of functional equations in Section 4.3.1, will be taken up here (see chapters in Goldberger & Duncan, 1973; Graybill, 1961).

Within the context of marital decision making, consider a one-variable analysis of the husband's consumer decisions before marriage. Suppose that these obey an exact linear model

$$R = ws + e,$$

where R is his observed decision, w and s are his true weights and preference values, and e is a random variable with zero mean that represents the combined effect of all other causes of the decision.

The separate predictor value of preference, denoted here by s', is assumed to be an exact measure of true preference, except for unreliability, denoted by e'. Hence

$$s' = s + e', \quad \text{or} \quad s = s' - e'.$$

The seemingly obvious step is to substitute this expression for s into the preceding expression for R to obtain

$$R = ws' + e'',$$

where $e'' = e - we'$. Since both R and s' are observables, this last equation looks like a standard linear regression of R on s'. Hence standard regression technique would seemingly estimate the weight parameter w. However, e'' depends on w, with the consequence that the regression weight b is systematically different from w

$$\begin{aligned} b &= \text{Cov}(R,s')/\text{Var } s' \\ &= [\text{Var } s/(\text{Var } s + \text{Var } e')]w. \end{aligned}$$

Thus, b is smaller than w by the variance ratio in brackets (see, e.g., Goldberger, 1973). This bias can be substantial. Isaac (1970) presents a case from signal detection for which standard regression yielded a slope coefficient of .77, whereas functional regression yielded a value of 1.04.

In some cases, however, it would seem that the bias could be neglected. For self-estimation of scale values on a 10-point rating scale, Var s would be of the order of 25. Empirically, Var e' would be of the order of 1 for most adults. Thus, the bias would only be about 4%, at least when the true values cover the full range.

Invalid Parameter Values. For present purposes, invalidity in parameter values will be limited to the case of a nonlinear relation between the given and the true values. The correct model in general cannot then fit the data because of discrepancies stemming from the incorrect parameters. The model will tend to fail, therefore, regardless of whether it is correct or incorrect. The investigator, however, sees only the failure and will be uncertain about its cause.

This ambiguity can be avoided if the parameters can be estimated from the data (Section 4.2.4). In the initial stages of investigation, therefore, analysis of variance procedures have an important advantage. At this stage, the primary need is to establish the integration model, and even mild bias in the parameters can markedly affect the theoretical interpretation. When it is not necessary to use separate estimates of the parameters, therefore, it may be poor policy to do so. Once some confidence has been gained about the operative models and about methods for obtaining valid parameter estimates, then traditional regression methods become more useful.

4.3.4 GOODNESS OF FIT IN REGRESSION ANALYSIS

Experimental analysis in judgment-decision theory typically uses repeated measurements design, in which each individual responds under a number of different stimulus conditions. Such design leads to statistical analysis rather different from traditional regression analysis. Accordingly, repeated measurements regression and the closely related individual regression are considered first; some comments on traditional between-individual regression follow.

One basic problem in testing goodness of fit is to allow for unreliability in the predictor estimates. Methods for doing this in functional linear regression are discussed in Graybill (1961); Searle (1971); Warren, White, and Fuller (1974); Rock, Werts, Linn, and Jöreskog (1977); as well as in various chapters in Goldberger and Duncan (1973). This problem will not be considered here, but the following replications method seems to provide a proper test of goodness of fit even when a traditional linear prediction equation is used. Although the regression parameters may be biased, systematically different from the structural parameters, the deviations from prediction are unsystematic under the operative assumptions that the linear model holds and that the predictor values are valid although unreliable. This property of the replications method may be important if, as may be conjectured, it holds also for nonlinear models involving products, such as the averaging model and the multiattribute model of Section 4.3.6.

Repeated Measurements Regression. Goodness of fit may be tested in repeated measurements regression by using the replications method of Section 4.4.1. The procedure is straightforward. Since each individual serves under a number of stimulus conditions, the regression model may be fitted separately for each individual. The values predicted by the regression equation are subtracted from the observed values to obtain a set of deviations from prediction for each individual, one for each stimulus condition. These deviation scores form a Conditions × Subjects design and the model-implied null hypothesis states that the true mean discrepancy is zero in each condition. A significant F for the mean square between conditions, tested against the Conditions × Subjects interaction, would imply real discrepancies from the model predictions.

To illustrate, consider the dating judgments of Shanteau and Nagy in which the stimulus conditions were seven photographs (Figure 6.3). Each subject made three judgments of each photograph, one of overall date preference, and two of the predictor variables of physical attractiveness and probability of acceptance. In this case, the regression model included a multiplicative component as well as possible additive components for the separate predictors (Section 4.3.5). This regression equation was fitted separately for each subject to yield a matrix of seven deviations from prediction, one for each stimulus condition for each subject. Although the actual analyses were performed at the individual level, a group test could be obtained by treating this Conditions × Subjects design as indicated.

As this example indicates, repeated measurements regression has a different structure from traditional, between-individual regression. In the traditional usage, the model is fitted across individuals, each of whom is effectively under a single stimulus condition. In the repeated measurements case, the model is fitted across stimulus conditions for a fixed individual. As one consequence, stronger tests of the model can be obtained by choosing stimulus conditions to test specific hypotheses or to cover a greater range than may be obtained from individual differences.

An advantage of repeated measurements regression is that unreliability in the parameter estimates, because it is independent across individuals, is included in the error term in a valid way.[a] It is this property that allows a proper test of fit based on prediction equations. A common problem with traditional regression analysis, in which unreliability in predictor values may invalidate the test of fit (Section 4.2.4), is thereby avoided.

Repeated measurements regression has often been done incorrectly, that is, without separation of between- and within-individual variability. Examples appear in psychophysics in which judged magnitude is analyzed as a power function of the physical value of the stimulus variable considered as a predictor. It is incorrect to fit a single function to the group data because there is then no way to break down the discrepancies from the model into the appropriate error terms. This procedure does not provide a proper test of the model and can be expected to suffer serious bias.

Individual Regression. In individual regression, each individual serves under a number of different stimulus conditions, just as with repeated measurements regression, but the model test is also made at the individual level. Statistical analysis begins the same way as for repeated measurements regression. The model is fitted separately for each rep-lication (or blocks of replications for greater stability) to yield a matrix of deviation scores, one for each condition. These deviation scores consti-tute a Conditions × Replications design that forms the data base for testing the model-implied null hypothesis that the true mean discrep-ancy is zero in each condition. Further details depend on whether replications are considered equivalent or as a systematic factor. This problem is discussed under individual subject design in section 2.1.3, and the same considerations and tests apply here.

An alternative approach would begin by fitting the model to the con-dition means, averaged across replications, and would use within-condition variability as the error term. This error term is proper when replications are equivalent, but the test itself is not strictly correct be-cause unreliability in the separate estimates of the predictors may appear as systematic deviations from the model (Section 4.2.4). A correct model may therefore tend to fail. This approach may nevertheless be useful, in part because the biasing effects of the unreliability may be small, in part because fitting the model to the condition means may increase accuracy.

Replication is essential: The individual must respond to the stimulus conditions on more than one separate occasion, and these replications must be independent. This includes not only the main response dimen-sion but also any predictor variables that are not constant across rep-lications. Individual fitting of regression equations is not uncommon in judgment and decision theory. Owing to reliance on traditional regres-sion techniques, however, the necessity of replication as a basis for a proper error term has generally gone unrecognized.

Between-Individual Regression. In most applications of regression analysis in psychology, each individual or case contributes one re-sponse. A single regression is fitted to the responses of a group of individuals, and the model-implied null hypothesis is that the dis-crepancies between the observed responses and those predicted from the regression equation are no larger than would be expected from chance. Accordingly, the test of fit requires some measure of the mag-nitude of the chance factors or, in other words, of the error variability.

In true experiments, where individuals are randomly assigned to ex-perimental conditions, the appropriate error term is the variability among individuals who receive the same experimental treatment. In most regression analyses, however, there are no experimental condi-tions. In their place are the values of various predictor variables, scores on psychological tests, for example, or demographic variables. If two individuals chanced to have the same values on the predictors, then the variability between them could be used as an error term. In general, however, no two individuals need have the same predictor values. It may be a problem, therefore, to obtain an appropriate error term.

A common solution to this problem is to reduce each predictor variable to a limited number of discrete levels. With each predictor considered as a design factor, some cells of the resulting design may be expected to contain a number of individuals. These cells provide a within-cell response variance that is used as an error term. Numerical predictors have the advantage of factoring out much of the individual differences in the predictor variables, although other factors act to inflate the error term.

For the kinds of studies considered in this book, it seems unlikely that between-individual regression will be very useful. Even where applicable, it will have relatively low power (Sections 1.3.1, 4.2.2, and 1.1.8). This limitation may be appreciated by imagining a between-individual regression for the study by Shanteau and Nagy previously cited, which would require a different group of subjects for each photograph. Of course, there may be no alternative to between-individual regression in many social or medical situations.

Traditional Significance Tests. The dominating concern with prediction in traditional regression analysis has led to significance tests that are often severely inappropriate for process analysis. The most common significance test in regression analysis asks whether some predictor variable is significantly correlated with the criterion to be predicted, or more generally, whether it adds a significant increment in predictability to some other set of predictors. Although such tests are obviously useful in practical prediction, they may not be helpful for understanding.

One problem may be illustrated by considering a two-variable regression in which addition of the second predictor produces a significant decrease in unexplained variance. That might seem to rule out a one-dimensional causal explanation and to imply that more than one causal factor underlies the response. This implication is false (e.g., Brewer, Campbell, & Crano, 1970). To see this, consider the case in which the two predictors are parallel forms of the same test and hence substantively equivalent. The second predictor should increase reliability and hence decrease unexplained variance. This case may seem extreme, but it is not ruled out merely because the two predictors do not appear equivalent. Moreover, the very same problem arises if the second predictor contains two components, one equivalent to the first predictor, the other uncorrelated with the criterion. This illustrates a general difficulty in causal interpretation of correlated variables; significant increases in predictive power may have no bearing on the validity of the explanatory model. In particular, therefore, partial correlations are seldom causally interpretable (Section 7.9).

A second problem arises if an added predictor does not produce a significant decrease in unexplained variance. This may only reflect a poor choice of predictor, one that is either irrelevant or one that is already taken into account through its intercorrelations with the other predictors. It says little or nothing about the central question of whether the unexplained variance contains a systematic component. Nor does it speak to the structure of the causal process (Section 4.3.1).

Variance–Covariance Matrix. In standard regression analysis, the inverse of the variance–covariance matrix purports to give various information about statistical reliability, including standard errors of the regression weights and goodness of fit of the model. However, these statistics depend sensitively on the joint assumptions that the regression equation is correct and that the true values of the predictors are used. In model analysis, just these assumptions are usually at issue, and it seems advisable to avoid analyses predicated on their truth. Deviations from the regression equation, in particular, tend to hide themselves by inflating the error term.

4.3.5 REGRESSION ANALYSIS FOR MULTIPLYING MODELS

Multiplying operations occur frequently, in various integration tasks as well as in the form of a weighting operation in averaging and adding models. The linear fan property of Section 2.2 provides the basis for analysis, but it must be adapted to the use of separate estimates of the parameters. This section shows that a linearity test in common use is invalid, but that a standard regression analysis can be applied.

The strong assumptions are made throughout that the parameter estimates are measured on true linear scales without error. These assumptions are standard in regression analysis and are presumably even more important for the multiplying model and other nonlinear models than for the linear models already considered. Unfortunately, very little seems to be known about this problem.

From Section 2.2, the basic model can be written

$$R_{ij} = s_{Ai}s_{Bj} + C_0. \tag{1}$$

Subscripts A and B are included for notational consistency, but factorial design is not assumed. The separate estimates of the parameters are denoted by $\hat{s}_{Ai}$ and $\hat{s}_{Bj}$, where the "hats" distinguish them from the true values in Eq. (1). The problem at issue is to test the multiplying model using these separate parameter estimates.

Linearity Test. An obvious first step is to substitute the parameter estimates in the right side of Eq. (1) to obtain predicted values

$$\hat{R}_{ij} = \hat{s}_{Ai}\hat{s}_{Bj}. \tag{2}$$

Of course, these predicted responses will not in general equal the observed, even with response variability and the additive constant C_0 disregarded. This direct comparison would be unfair to the model because it rests on the unrealistic assumption that the parameter estimates are identical to the true values.

However, on the given assumption that the parameters in Eq. (2) are linear functions of the true values, it might seem that predicted and observed responses will be connected by a linear relation

$$R_{ij} = c_1\hat{R}_{ij} + c_0 = c_1\hat{s}_{Ai}\hat{s}_{Bj} + c_0, \tag{3}$$

where c_1 and c_0 are regression constants. This linearity test is implicit in the practice of reporting the correlation between R_{ij} and $\hat{s}_{Ai}\hat{s}_{Bj}$ as support for the multiplying model.

This linearity test rests on the implicit assumption that the parameter estimates are actually on ratio scales. Unless these estimates are measured from the true zero, the linear relation will fail even though all other assumptions and the basic model are correct.

To illustrate this flaw in the linearity test, suppose that the $\hat{s}_{Bj}$ are on a ratio scale, but that the $\hat{s}_{Ai}$ are on a linear scale with unknown zero. If the linearity test is to be valid, it must yield the same result under arbitrary choices of the zero point. However, the zero point can be chosen so that $\hat{s}_{Ai}$ is either positive or negative for some given i. But then R_{ij} will be an increasing or decreasing function of $\hat{s}_{Bj}$, depending on this arbitrary choice. That is clearly unacceptable.

The requirement of ratio scales for the linearity test has been noted by Schmidt (1973) and Birnbaum (1973). Schmidt pointed out that in virtually every previous study of the expectancy–valence model of work motivation the investigator was unaware of the problem and had used inappropriate analyses. This is also true of similar models that have been used in attitude theory. Birnbaum pointed out the striking fact that the linearity test can actually produce higher correlations from an incorrect adding model than from the true multiplying model. Schmidt also claimed that the multiplying model cannot be tested using linear stimulus scales, but as Birnbaum pointed out, and as is shown by the linear fan theorem of Section 2.2, functional measurement provides a correct test for factorial design. This approach can be applied directly to regression analysis based on separate parameters as follows.

Regression Test. A correct test of the multiplying model can be obtained by allowing for the zero points of the estimates in the regression analysis. By assumption, the parameters are on linear scales, so the estimates are linear functions of the true values, and conversely

$$s_{Ai} = a_1 \hat{s}_{Ai} + a_0,$$
$$s_{Bj} = b_1 \hat{s}_{Bj} + b_0.$$

Here a_1 and b_1 represent the units, and a_0 and b_0 represent the zeros of the scales of the estimates. To bring out the importance of the zero points, the unit parameters will be set equal to unity. Substitution of the above expressions in Eq. (1) and simplification yield the regression equation

$$R_{ij} = c_1(\hat{s}_{Ai}\hat{s}_{Bj} + b_0\hat{s}_{Ai} + a_0\hat{s}_{Bj} + a_0 b_0) + c_0. \tag{4}$$

If the multiplying model holds, therefore, ordinary regression analysis using the three predictors, $\hat{s}_{Ai}$, $\hat{s}_{Bj}$, and $\hat{s}_{Ai}\hat{s}_{Bj}$, will fit the data. Equation (4) thus provides a basis for a proper test of goodness of fit. This test has two parts, just as in Section 2.2. Stepwise regression is used to test that the product term contributes significantly over and above the additive terms in the two predictors. This corresponds to testing for a significant linear × linear component of the interaction after the main effects have been allowed for. Of course, the design must also provide a test of the discrepancies from the complete model of Eq. (4), which is analogous to the test of residual interaction. Similar procedures could presumably be applied to more complex multilinear models of the kind listed in Table 3.1.

This analysis, it should be noted, does not distinguish between the simple multiplying model of Eq. (1) and compound models that include additive terms. This problem has been explained in the discussion of Eq. (15) of Section 2.2, and the same considerations apply here. To distinguish between simple and compound models requires auxiliary information on the zero points of the predictors. Equation (4) shows that, oddly enough, knowledge of the zero point of one predictor allows a test for an additive contribution by the other predictor. If the zero point of s_{Ai} is known, so that $a_0 = 0$, then the term in s_{Bj} drops out of Eq. (4). Hence a significant effect of s_{Bj}, after fitting the product term, would indicate a real additive effect.

A corollary is that regression analysis based on Eq. (4) will yield invalid estimates of the regression constants unless the zero points of the stimulus scales are known. Analysis of variance is subject to the same difficulty (e.g., Anderson, 1977c, pp. 144–145). This can be important in any attempt to go beyond bare prediction to consider the meaning of the results.

4.3.6 REGRESSION ANALYSIS FOR MULTIATTRIBUTE MODELS

The discussion of the preceding section may be extended to multiattribute models that contain two multiplying operations. In the usual formulation, each attribute is assumed to have two parameters, a scale value, and a weight. For the case of two attributes, the model can be written

$$R_{ij} = w_{Ai}s_{Ai} + w_{Bj}s_{Bj} + C_0. \tag{5}$$

All the conditions for Eq. (1) will be assumed to hold here as well. It is first shown that the commonly used linearity test is valid only under very special conditions. A less restrictive regression analysis is also considered.

Linearity Test. In the standard application of multiattribute models, the separate estimates of the weights and scale values are multiplied for each attribute, and these products are summed to yield a single predictor. When a criterion is available, high correlations with this predictor are taken to support the basic model. Implicit in this approach is the assumption that the criterion is linearly related to the multiattribute predictor because the correlation is based on a linear regression.

For the two-attribute case, the predicted values would be

$$\hat{R}_{ij} = \hat{w}_{Ai}\hat{s}_{Ai} + \hat{w}_{Bj}\hat{s}_{Bj},$$

where hats denote estimated parameters, as in the previous section. To test goodness of fit requires a test of the linear relation

$$R_{ij} = c_1\hat{R}_{ij} + c_0,$$

where c_1 and c_0 are regression constants. It is assumed that the basic model of Eq. (5) is correct and that the estimates of the weights and scale values are on linear scales.

However, the linearity test demands three further conditions on the parameter estimates. First, the w-estimates must be on ratio scales that have the same unit for all attributes. Second, the s-estimates must be on linear scales that have the same unit for all attributes. Third, either these linear scales must actually be ratio scales or the w_{Ai} must all be equal and so also the w_{Bj}. Unless these three conditions are satisfied, the model will fail the linearity test even though it is really correct (Anderson & Graesser, 1976, n.1).[a]

These are stringent conditions. They can be satisfied when the attributes are similar, as in Anderson and Graesser (1976). When the attributes are qualitatively different, however, the requirements of common units may not be possible even in principle. The problems of obtaining a valid test of the basic multiattribute model have gone largely unrecognized in previous work, presumably because of the prevalence of weak inference methods that did not actually test the model.

Regression Test. A less demanding test can be made by asking whether or not the observed R_{ij} can be expressed as the two-variable regression

$$R_{ij} = c_1 \hat{w}_{Ai} \hat{s}_{Ai} + c_2 \hat{w}_{Bj} \hat{s}_{Bj} + c_0.$$

This test has the advantage that it does not require common units, but it does require further conditions. Specifically, the estimates of s_{Ai} must be on a ratio scale or else the w_{Ai} must all be equal, and similarly for the B attribute. If the w_{Ai} are not all equal, then their estimates must be on a ratio scale.[b]

Applications of multiattribute models have nearly always assumed equal weighting across the levels of each attribute. In this case, the preceding regression test requires only that the s-estimates be on linear scales. The equal weighting assumption is uncertain, but no evidence appears to be available, due in part to lack of tests of goodness of fit in studies with multiattribute models. There is, of course, ample evidence for differential weighting in the averaging model, which suggests that differential weighting must generally be expected in multiattribute models.

The question of differential weighting is testable when the $\hat{s}_{Ai}$ and $\hat{s}_{Bj}$ are on valid linear scales. For example, an adding model could be fitted to the data using least squares estimation of the gross stimulus parameters, $\bar{s}_{Ai} = w_{Ai} s_{Ai}$ and $\bar{s}_{Bj} = w_{Bj} s_{Bj}$, in a (nonorthogonal) analysis of variance. The $\bar{s}_{Ai}$ would then be a linear function of the $\hat{s}_{Ai}$ if and only if the w_{Ai} were all equal, and similarly for the B variable. The confounding of weight and scale value in the linear model (Section 2.1) can thus be resolved using separate parameter estimates. This is an interesting substantive question that deserves further study.

4.4 Statistical Analysis of Nonlinear Models

Many models do not have simple analyses in terms of the parallelism and linear fan properties. This section presents an approach to the analysis of nonlinear models. The two basic statistical problems in model analysis are estimating parameters and testing goodness of fit. Both problems can be troublesome for nonlinear models, especially for integration models in which the number of parameters tends to be fairly large. Recent developments have made both problems tractable. Although serious practical difficulties remain, the analysis of nonlinear models in typical psychological research is in principle straightforward.

Parameter estimation has become feasible with computer programs developed in numerical analysis; these can estimate a few dozen parameters in a minute or less. The present research program has used Chandler's (1969) STEPIT routine, which has been widely employed in psychology. The University of California, Los Angeles Biomedical Series contains two more-recent programs (Dixon & Brown, 1977). Two practical difficulties with such programs are noted later.

Goodness of fit can be tested with a simple application of analysis of variance that was discovered in the present research program. This *replications method* capitalizes on a characteristic feature of psychological research: that it is usually possible to run a number of replications of the same basic design. Exact tests are thus possible at either group or individual level for general nonlinear models. One practical difficulty is discussed later.

4.4.1 GOODNESS OF FIT

Testing goodness of fit for nonlinear models has always been a problem. The linear model provides an orthogonal decomposition of variance in which 1 df is used up for each estimated parameter. For nonlinear models, however, the parameter estimates are in general not independent, and so the degrees of freedom associated with any systematic effect are not known. When only two or three parameters are estimated from a design of any size, the rule of 1 df per parameter may be adequate. When many parameters must be estimated, as in typical integration models, uncertainty becomes acute.

Replications Method. The present method for testing goodness of fit requires a number of replications of the design. To illustrate, suppose that each of N subjects has been run through a two-factor design. The model is fitted to the data separately for each subject using STEPIT, say, and predicted values are then computed for each subject. In each cell of the design, the predicted value is subtracted from the observed value to yield a separate matrix of deviations from prediction for each individual subject. The test of fit is based on these matrices of deviation scores.

The deviation scores for each subject are correlated through their dependence on a common set of parameter estimates. However, the deviation scores for different subjects are independent, since the model was fitted separately for each subject. Accordingly, repeated measurements analysis of variance may be applied to these deviation matrices. These matrices form a Row × Column × Subject design and may be analyzed in the usual way. Sums of squares are calculated as in any three-way design, and each systematic source is tested against its interaction with subjects.[a]

Nothing should be significant in this analysis. If the model is correct, then the deviation scores represent random variability and should show no systematic trend over subjects. The row means, for example, should all be equal except for random variability, and the main effect of Rows should be nonsignificant when tested against Row × Subject interaction. Most important, the Row × Column interaction should be nonsignificant when tested against the Row × Column × Subject interaction.

This replications method may be applied to individual analysis when each individual serves in a number of replications of the design. Each replication or block of replications may then be treated in the same way as each subject in the foregoing group analysis. The deviation scores are correlated within any one matrix but are independent across matrices. Accordingly, the repeated measurements analysis is again applicable and the model implies that all systematic sources should be nonsignificant when tested against their interaction with Replications.

This replications method may be applied in a similar manner to designs with more than two factors. Nonorthogonal designs may be handled by testing Cells against the Cell × Subject interaction or with specific comparisons (Section 2.1).

Comments. This test of goodness of fit often seems suspect when first encountered, and a few comments may make it more reasonable. The main intuitive objection is that close fits can be expected when many parameters are estimated. But the error terms consist, in effect, of the small deviations from that close fit. The test is thus sensitive to systematic deviations, even when these are small.

Furthermore, when the replications method is applied to a linear model using a least squares criterion, it is equivalent to the ordinary analysis of variance. The linear model will fit the row and column means exactly, so that these sources will have zero sums of squares in the deviations analysis. The test of interaction on the deviation scores is equivalent to the test of interaction from the ordinary analysis of variance.

Finally, any specific comparison on the deviation scores can be tested directly. The comparison can be computed separately to yield a single score for each matrix of deviations. If the model is correct, then the true mean of these comparison scores is zero. This null hypothesis may be tested in any convenient way, by F test or by some distribution-free test in the manner of Section 2.1.2.

Two cautions about the replications method should be added. Neither its formal statistical properties nor its practical experimental properties have been adequately studied. It is possible, for example, that the test is overly sensitive to small deviations from prediction that have no practical significance. In particular, systematic deviations may arise merely from biases associated with nonlinear estimation and prediction (see Note 4.4.2a). Although the bias problems may not be serious, it would be desirable to study them using artificial data with representative nonlinear models.

The second caution is that group tests, although sensitive to model deviations that are systematic across subjects, may overlook real, idiosyncratic deviations at the individual level. A warning on this point appears in the first published application of the replications method (Leon & Anderson, 1974, Table 1), in which the error terms for two interactions were much larger than for the other sources. Since these error terms were interactions with subjects, their relatively large size suggests possible real discrepancies of different form for different subjects.

These cautions aside, the test has so far given satisfactory performance. Oden (1974, 1977a,b, 1978) has used it extensively to study cognitive algebra in psycholinguistics. The test plays a key role in monotone analysis (Chapter 5). It could also be used in multidimensional scaling, which has lacked a test of goodness of fit (Anderson, 1975a, 1975b).

4.4.2 PARAMETER ESTIMATION

In principle, existing computerized programs for numerical analysis provide straightforward solutions to the problem of estimating parameters in general integration models. However, three practical problems should be kept in mind. The first problem is that these programs can converge on, and be trapped at, a local minimum, thereby missing the optimal solution. Local minima solutions can be sometimes ruled out because the parameter values are unreasonable for the situation in question or avoided by using collateral information to obtain a good approximate set of initial values.

Seriousness of the local minimum problem depends on the form of the model and on the structure of the experimental design. The problem is said to be serious in nonmetric multidimensional scaling. As yet, however, no instance of this problem has appeared in this research program, perhaps because the applications have been to numerical response data, perhaps because good initial values have typically been available.

The second problem involves bias and variability in the parameter estimates. The linear model for a complete factorial design provides a useful reference point. In this case, hardly more than some form of statistical independence is required to ensure that the marginal means are unbiased estimates of the scale values (Section 2.1.1). Moreover, these estimates are robust in the sense that they are relatively insensitive to deviations from the linear model. For nonlinear models, however, parameter estimates may be biased and not robust. These problems may not often be serious, but not much is known about them.[a]

The third problem, perhaps the most serious, is that the parameter estimates may be unstable. This problem arose in two applications of the differential weighted averaging model (Leon, Oden, & Anderson, 1973; Zalinski & Anderson, 1977, in press). For a few individual subjects, estimates of scale value diverged toward impossibly large values in return for miniscule improvements in the least squares index of discrepancies. In the former study, the estimation accordingly was performed on a subgroup basis. In the latter study, the weight estimates, which were of primary interest, were relatively unaffected and the problem was handled by constraining the scale values to lie within reasonable bounds. The pooled group data did not present any stability problems in either study. Unfortunately, pooled group data typically produce biased parameter estimates for nonlinear models. These biases appeared to be substantial for the weight parameter in the second study mentioned, due to substantial individual differences.[b]

Similar instabilities for quite different models have been reported by other users of the STEPIT program, but their cause is unknown. That they did not occur in the group data for the two cited applications suggests that they might be merely a matter of variability, resolvable by collecting more data for each individual. In both these applications, however, the amount of individual data was considerable. It is possible, therefore, that the instability reflected a lack of robustness. In other words, the estimation procedure may be overly sensitive to minor violations of the assumptions of response linearity, of no stimulus interaction, or to minor deviations from the model itself in the individual data.

There is a need, therefore, for statistical studies using artificial data to assess the possible causes of instability. Such studies may also suggest kinds of designs that could help avoid the problem. For the averaging model, in particular, appropriate variation of set size might reduce instability and increase efficiency. Again, it may be possible to include the same stimuli within two designs, one with equal weighting and one with unequal weighting, and to use the scale value estimates from the former for estimating the weight parameters in the latter. The regression analysis of Section 2.3.3 also deserves consideration.

Other devices are possible when primary interest is the parameter estimates rather than goodness of fit, for approximate methods are then often appropriate. Weight can be specified as a function of scale value, for example, as in the application cited in Section 2.3.3. Analogously, if the stimulus has a physical metric, scale value may be taken to be some simple function of that metric (e.g., Anderson, 1968c; Birnbaum, 1974b; Cuneo, 1982). Finally, it may be possible to employ self-estimates of the scale values to help estimate the weights (Section 6.2).

4.4.3 PARAMETER ESTIMATION VERSUS GOODNESS OF FIT

The relative importance of the two goals of estimating parameters and testing goodness of fit depends on the state of knowledge. During initial stages of investigation, goodness of fit is typically primary, for even small deviations from model prediction may signal basic flaws in conceptual structure. Parameter estimation is vital for the purpose of testing goodness of fit, of course, but the parameter values need not have any great interest in themselves. This orientation has been characteristic of much work in this research program. Primary concern has been with integration processes, and measurement has been largely incidental to that end.

In later stages, after an integration model has been fairly well established, measurement may become more important. The model becomes a tool for evaluating effects of various stimulus manipulations on parameter values. For these purposes, some inaccuracy in the parameter estimates may be acceptable, and simpler approximate methods may be desirable. In general, some degree of approximation may easily be tolerable when the basic conceptual representation is known to be adequate.

Various kinds of simplification are considered throughout this book. Most important is the use of prior scale values, which may be obtained in various ways: from self-estimates (Sections 4.3 and 6.2); from a physical metric (Note 4.3.3a); or from functional scales obtained in other integration tasks with the same stimuli (see Figures 3.1, 3.5, and 3.6).

The use of numerical rating responses under suboptimal conditions also deserves mention. In certain situations, it may be awkward or impossible to use procedures such as those of Section 1.1 to eliminate rating biases and obtain a linear response scale. Although the rating biases have been a serious matter in establishing models, they may be less serious for some estimation applications. Indeed, when the model is known to be correct, it may be employed as a frame for transforming the observed response into a true linear scale (Chapter 5).

Also important is the use of simpler designs. Factorial design seems close to essential for establishing models, but it may be unduly demanding when the model is known to be applicable. Among the simplifications are fractional replication, nonorthogonal design, and regression analysis (Sections 1.3.7 and 4.3).[a]

Cognitive algebra can provide a standard against which approximate methods can be assessed, as well as guidance in using them. For example, self-estimated parameters may be evaluated by comparing them with functional scales, and this provides a way to develop self-estimation procedures (Section 6.2). Similarly, the empirical work on averaging theory may justify using a linear model when set size is constant and the equal weighting condition holds (Section 2.3). Indeed, the additive and linear models, although they fail to handle averaging processes and subadditivity, may nevertheless be approximately correct in certain situations. The loss of accuracy may be more than compensated by the gain in simplicity and practicability. What is already known about cognitive algebra, although modest in itself, may still provide an effective foothold for further study of approximate methods.

NOTES

4.1.2a. Bogartz's (1978) criticism of the Height + Width rule found by Anderson and Cuneo (1978a,b) used mean magnitude discrepancy rather than either correlation or scatterplot. Mean magnitude discrepancy may be viewed as a one-number summary of the scatterplot, since it is the mean deviation of the points from the diagonal line. Hence it also tends to be misleading, as noted later in the text.

The data in Figure 4.5 are from Experiments 1, 2, 3, and 5 of Anderson and Cuneo (1978a), the same data considered by Bogartz. The multiplying model was fitted using the marginal means in Eq. (21) of Section 2.2, with C_0 set equal to zero. Predictions from Bogartz's Table 5 yielded a slightly higher correlation but the same patterns as in Figure 4.5.

4.2.1a. A related discussion of null hypothesis logic is given in the exchange among Grant (1962), Binder (1963), Edwards (1965), and Wilson, Miller, and Lower (1967).

4.2.2a. For example, Klitzner's (1977) study of snake phobia, presented in Figure F1.17, would have provided a stronger test of the Motivation × Incentive model had the three fear stimuli been equally spaced. This problem had been given considerable attention in the pilot work, but the pilot results did not hold up in this respect. As a consequence, the 3 × 3 design was effectively reduced almost to a 2 × 3 design, which is the smallest that will allow a test of the multiplying model. Insurance against such outcomes can be obtained in some situations by using more than three levels of the stimulus variable.

4.2.2b. This power calculation was performed as follows: The data showed that mean responses to the 7 × 7, 9 × 9, and 11 × 11 rectangles were approximately 5, 10, and 15, respectively. Accordingly, the one-dimensional hypothesis implies that the distribution of responses to the 7 × 11 rectangle is bimodal, with modes at 5 and 15 and a mean of 10. The variance around each mode was taken equal to 2.54^2, the variance of the responses to the 9 × 9 rectangle, because response variability was approximately constant along the response scale. Hence the variance of the bimodal distribution is estimated as $2.54^2 + (10 - 5)^2 = 31.45$. The one-dimensional hypothesis thus implies a standard deviation of approximately 5.61, substantially larger than the comparison value of 2.54.

The actual power calculation may be made by using the cited ϕ formula. The value of μ is taken as the difference between the standard deviation of 5.61 predicted by the one-dimensional hypothesis and the standard deviation of 2.54 predicted by the integration hypothesis, which equals 3.07. The value of σ is estimated as the square root of the error mean square from the cited F test on the actual difference scores. This value was 1.38. Hence the ϕ formula yields

$$\phi = (3.07/1.38)\sqrt{n} = 2.22\sqrt{n}.$$

This result may be used to calculate the power for a given n or to determine the n needed to obtain any desired power. For the latter purpose, Table A-12c of Dixon and Massey (1969) may be consulted (with $\phi = d'$), with a one-sided significance level of .025 (corresponding to a two-sided significance level of .05). The table shows that five subjects would provide power of .95 and six subjects would provide power of .99. The actual n of 33 thus provides more than ample power.

All-or-none hypotheses in other areas may perhaps be tested in a similar manner. As this example indicates, numerical response measures and variability information can provide powerful tests of differences that would not be detectable in mean responses. An added virtue of this test is that the response measure need not be linear, but only monotone.

4.2.3a. In a strictly statistical sense, it can be argued that any test of goodness of fit involves a comparison between two models. For example, the test of parallelism can be considered a comparative test of two models, one with, the other without a statistical interaction term. However, the discussion in the text is concerned with comparing two bona fide psychological models.

A distinction is sometimes made between statistical power, as discussed in the text, and inferential or discriminative power, which is measured by the degree to which the data will discriminate among different theoretical interpretations. For example, a statistically powerful test of the parallelism prediction does not discriminate between the adding model and the averaging model with equal weighting. However, it does discriminate between linear and nonlinear models, even if the latter are not given explicit a priori form.

4.2.4a. Examples of cross-task invariance of stimulus values are given in Figures 3.1, 3.5, and 3.6. This issue has also been pursued by Birnbaum (e.g., 1978), but such demonstrations remain infrequent, even for psychophysical quantities for which stimulus invariance is plausible and theoretically important (Section F1.3.7). In decision theory and social judgment, strict parameter generality cannot often be expected because parameters typically refer to molar units whose constitution depends on context (Section 7.15).

4.3.1a. As another illustration of the distinction between prediction equations and structural relations (Anderson, 1974f, p. 79), consider a judge who wishes to diagnose clinical condition from a set of MMPI variables. Three aspects of this problem may be of interest. First, actuarial data may be obtained and used to develop a regression equation. In this approach, each variable is considered a random variable defined over some population of patients. The regression has only a predictive function and says nothing about causation or structural relation.

Next, suppose that judges themselves wish to make the diagnoses, combining the MMPI scores according to their clinical intuition. This case may be treated exactly as the first, developing regression equations that will predict the judges' predictions. In this case, it would be of concern how well the judges' regression equations agreed with, and could be used instead of, the actuarial equation.

Finally, suppose that it is desired to test whether judges actually combine the MMPI scores in an additive manner. Interest now shifts from actuarial prediction of the judges' behavior to understanding their thought processes. The usual regression equation is no longer conceptually appropriate. Instead, it is necessary to look for the functional relation, in which the predictors are considered stimulus cues or mathematical variables.

The usual regression equation will generally be different from the functional relation. The one cannot substitute for the other, so it is important to keep in mind what goal is sought. Nearly all applications of regression analysis in judgment theory have actually given prediction equations rather than functional relations and they need to be interpreted in that light.

4.3.1b. Some approaches take the statistical structure of the environment as the foundation for psychological analysis. For example, Garner (1962) and Garner and Morton (1969) have attempted to formulate problems of perception in terms of Shannon's (1948) statistical theory of information. These approaches have the attraction of dealing with physical observables and avoiding subjective concepts. In the present view, however, objective correlation is no substitute for subjective correlation.

4.3.1c. An instructive conjunction of difficulties in using regression-correlation analysis is provided by Brunswik's (1956) probabilistic functionalism, especially as developed by Hammond and his followers (e.g., Hammond, McClelland, & Mumpower, 1978, 1980; Hammond, Stewart, Brehmer, & Steinmann, 1975). The basic model employed in this theory is an ordinary regression equation. It is distinguished from other regression formulations mainly by its use of such terms as *function form, judgment policy,* and *cognitive system* in referring to the regression equation. The trouble is that these terms cannot have the psychological significance that is implied by their common language meanings because their theoretical definitions are arbitrary, if not indeterminate. Unfortunately, much of the theory seems to subsist in the common language meanings of these terms.

Weight values, which are considered central to the individual's cognitive system, are theoretically indeterminate. One problem arises from stimulus intercorrelations, which render regression weights ambiguous as measures of importance (Section 6.1.1). Hammond *et al.* (1975, pp. 286ff) recognize this ambiguity and suggest two ways to obtain nonambiguous weights, but neither way is valid. Even for uncorrelated stimuli, weights are indeterminate due to the unit-confounding problem illustrated in the temperature–humidity example of Section 6.1.1. Since the units are arbitrary, even for physical scales, so too are the weights. This can be an advantage for practical regression—but not for describing a cognitive system.

Moreover, weights are confounded with function form, and both depend on the particular sample of cue values. Hammond *et al.* (1975, p. 282) recognize that this confounding is undesirable and present a rescaling of the weight parameter that they claim will solve the problem. This rescaling does not solve the problem, however, because the rescaled weight depends on the original regression weights for the linear and quadratic components. Accordingly, the rescaled weight depends on the particular sample of cue values and is also confounded with function form.

Function form is also considered part of an individual's cognitive system. But function form is defined arbitrarily, typically in terms of the linear and quadratic components of a given stimulus variable in the regression equation. This is a curve-fitting procedure with little cognitive significance.

Function form also depends on the response metric, as indicated in the text. Apparently the response is supposed to be a linear (interval) scale (Hammond *et al.*, 1980, p. 210), but the theory never addresses this measurement problem. Response scales of desirability and preference therefore cannot be considered more than monotone, so the function forms are arbitrary (see also Section 7.10). Without a solution to the measurement problem, analyses that purport to determine "cognitive dependence on linear and nonlinear cues" (Hammond & Summers, 1965, p. 215) lack cognitive meaning.

Social judgment seems generally outside the province of this theory because objective physical metrics are required for the stimulus variables (e.g., Hammond *et al.*, 1980, p. 210). Likableness, deservingness, blame, and other social concepts must be handled arbitrarily because they have no objective physical metric.

These problems are acute because of systemic ambiguity in the theory. On the one hand, explicit disclaimers are made that the formulation is not intended to apply to analysis of cognitive process. On the other hand, the regression analyses are continually interpreted in cognitive terms.

On the one hand, Hammond *et al.* (1975) emphasize that their formulation "is not a law-seeking theory. It is not aimed at finding the laws of human judgment [p. 276]," and that it is a misconception to say that they "offer their models as psychological laws—that is, as isomorphic representations of the process underlying judgment [p. 290]." On the other hand, Hammond *et al.* (1975, 1980) continually present these regression analyses as analyses of the "cognitive system" and as "descriptions of the *judgment policies* which individuals bring to particular judgment or decision problems [p. 223]." *Cognitive system* and *judgment policy* seem to refer to processes underlying the judgment—but they do not within the theory. Even within the theory, these policy descriptions depend on arbitrary and indeterminate choices in fitting a regression curve.

It should be emphasized that many investigators have employed regression analysis to good effect in many problems, including that of helping people improve their judgments and decisions. The same may be true of various studies using the Brunswik–Hammond formulation. For such purposes, arbitrary but sensible curve-fitting can be useful and efficient; no objection is being raised to that (Section 6.1.4). What is of concern is the conceptual ambiguity, in which arbitrary descriptions are couched in cognitive terms.

This conceptual ambiguity may be illustrated with the concept of weight. The statement that "the concept of *weight* refers to the relative importance judges place on cues in making judgments of preference or inference [Hammond *et al.*, 1980, p. 217]" seems to define weight as the relative importance that judges place on cues in making judgments of preference or inference. But when the theory is examined, as already pointed out, the actual definition of weight is found to be mathematically indeterminate. Because of the unit confounding, in particular, the theory cannot provide even an ordinal index of weight.

Much of what has been claimed for the theory rests on common language implications of terms such as *weight, function form,* and *judgment policy.* But since the mathematical expressions for these terms within the theory are arbitrary or indeterminate, the data analyses can hardly have the significance implied by the common language meanings of these terms. These problems are known (e.g., Hammond *et al.*, 1978), but they have been largely ignored and left unresolved. Until they can be resolved, they cast doubt on the theory and the associated research.

4.3.2a. In nonorthogonal design with empty cells, it is mathematically possible that equal and opposite interaction components are present but cancel to leave zero net effect (Searle, 1971).

4.3.2b. The principle is often stated that nonorthogonal analysis should estimate the same parameters and test the same hypotheses as when all cell n's are equal. That is not possible when any cell is empty; in particular, the interaction parameter for that cell cannot be estimated.

4.3.2c. The STEPIT program (Chandler, 1969) provides least squares estimation for general nonlinear models and can allow empty cells. The ADDALS program (Young, de Leeuw, & Takane, 1976) can perform least squares analysis for linear models with empty cells, with or without monotone response transformation. Statistical properties of these estimation procedures do not seem to have received much attention.

4.3.3a. In an initial application of the serial integration model to intuitive statistics, subjects estimated the cumulative average of a sequence of two-digit numbers (Anderson, 1964c,d). It seemed reasonable to expect that subjective and objective numbers would be equal, and the design provided a test that supported this expectation. With scale values known, weight estimation is of course much easier. In a later experiment on outlier discounting, therefore, the objective numbers were used as scale values to estimate the effective weight parameter in each separate condition (Anderson, 1968c). A similar approach has been employed by Birnbaum (1976), Levin (1975), Levin, Kim, and Corry (1976), and Lichtenstein, Earle, and Slovic (1975).

Two physical dimensions for which objective value gives an approximately linear scale of subjective value are position or length (Figure 3.6; Bogartz, 1979; Cuneo, 1978, 1982 Weiss & Anderson, 1969, 1972), and temporal duration (Blankenship & Anderson, 1976).

This linearity property also underlies the interpretation of Wilkening's (1979, p. 31) interesting demonstration that children who judged rectangle area by the Height + Width rule also judged rectangles of equal area and unequal height + width to be unequal in area, but rectangles of unequal area and equal height + width to be equal in area. Children who followed the Height × Width rule did just the opposite.

These dimensions are also potentially useful as quantifiers in other tasks. For example, numbers could be used to represent prices in utility theory or amount of honesty in psycholinguistic judgment (Figure F1.16). Similarly, a bar graph could be used to quantify the scale value of a message in attitude studies. The linearity assumption would need to be established initially, of course, in terms of the actual dimensions of judgment (see also Note 1.3.5a).

4.3.4a. Invalidity in the predictor estimates also goes into the error to the extent that it is unsystematic across subjects.

4.3.6a. The algebraic analysis is straightforward. It is assumed that the multiattribute model holds with the true parameter values given by the equation

$$R_{ij} = w_{Ai}s_{Ai} + w_{Bj}s_{Bj} + C_0 .$$

The corresponding expression with the separate parameter estimates, denoted by hats, yields the predicted response

$$\hat{R}_{ij} = \hat{w}_{Ai}\hat{s}_{Ai} + \hat{w}_{Bj}\hat{s}_{Bj} .$$

It is also assumed that the estimates are on linear scales so that each estimate is a linear function of the true values. Thus

$$\hat{s}_{Ai} = a_1 s_{Ai} + a_0 , \qquad \hat{w}_{Ai} = d_1 w_{Ai} + d_0 ,$$
$$\hat{s}_{Bj} = b_1 s_{Bj} + b_0 , \qquad \hat{w}_{Bj} = e_1 w_{Bj} + e_0 .$$

The constants in these four linear relations represent the units and zeros of the measurement scales of the estimates.

The linearity test requires that

$$R_{ij} = c_1 \hat{R}_{ij} + c_0 = c_1(\hat{w}_{Ai}\hat{s}_{Ai} + \hat{w}_{Bj}\hat{s}_{Bj}) + c_0$$

where c_1 and c_0 are constants. Substitution yields

$$R_{ij} = c_1(d_1 a_1 w_{Ai}s_{Ai} + e_1 b_1 w_{Bj}s_{Bj}) + c_1(d_1 a_0 w_{Ai} + e_1 b_0 w_{Bj})$$
$$+ c_1(d_0 a_1 s_{Ai} + e_0 b_1 s_{Bj}) + c_1(d_0 a_0 + e_0 b_0) + c_0.$$

This equation imposes certain conditions on the units and zeros that can be most easily understood by considering the graph of the observed responses as a function of the predicted responses. Since the model is true by assumption, this graph will be a straight line if the parameter estimates are appropriate. Suppose then, that a given set of estimates was used to generate predicted values and that the resultant graph of observed versus predicted values was a straight line. If the zero of the scale of w_{Ai} was arbitrary, then the straight-line relation would have to remain invariant if d_0 was increased by some constant h. But increasing d_0 by h means adding the term $h(a_1 s_{Ai} + a_0)$ to each predicted $\hat{R}_{ij}$ on the horizontal axis of the graph, whereas the observed values remain the same. This added term is not constant, since it depends on s_{Ai}, so the straight line would be fractured. It follows, therefore, that d_0 is not arbitrary. Since s_{Ai} is a continuous variable, d_0 can have a unique value. Since $d_0 = 0$ is an acceptable value, it must be the unique value.

By this reasoning, therefore, the linearity test requires that the w_{Ai} be on a ratio scale, and also the w_{Bj}. Similar reasoning shows that the sum in the second parenthesis in the equation must be constant, which requires $a_0 = 0$ or $w_{Ai} = w_A$ and $b_0 = 0$ or $w_{Bj} = w_B$. Finally, it is also necessary that the weight estimates have a common unit, $d_1 = e_1$, and similarly for the scale value estimates, $a_1 = b_1$. These are the three necessary conditions for the linearity test mentioned in the text.

The regression test is less demanding, for it employs three parameters in the relation

$$R_{ij} = c_1 \hat{w}_{Ai}\hat{s}_{Ai} + c_2 \hat{w}_{Bj}\hat{s}_{Bj} + c_0$$
$$= c_1(d_1 a_1 w_{Ai}s_{Ai} + d_1 a_0 w_{Ai} + d_0 a_1 s_{Ai} + d_0 a_0)$$
$$+ c_2(e_1 b_1 w_{Bj}s_{Bj} + e_1 b_0 w_{Bj} + e_0 b_1 s_{Bj} + e_0 b_0) + c_0.$$

Here again, d_0 and e_0 must be zero, by essentially the reasoning already used. Similarly, $a_0 = 0$ or $w_{Ai} = w_A$ and $b_0 = 0$ or $w_{Bj} = w_B$ must hold. There is no restriction on units, however, because any arbitrary change in d_1, say, can be compensated by a change in c_1 and a complementary change in c_0.

4.3.6b. These conditions can be relaxed still farther, of course, by allowing zero and unit constants for each of the four predictors, following the analysis of Section 4.3.5.

4.4.1a. The grand mean $\hat{R}_{..}$ has sum of squares $N\hat{R}_{..}^2$, where N is the total number of deviation scores. It may be tested against $MS_{Subjects}$. Often, however, this source will automatically be zero in the model fit.

4.4.2a. Least squares estimators of parameters in nonlinear models will be *consistent*, approaching the true values as sample size becomes large, if certain regularity conditions are met. In contrast to linear regression, however, parameter estimates would generally be biased for finite samples. An expository overview of nonlinear regression is given by Gallant (1975); other relevant papers are Jennrich (1969) and Malinvaud (1966, Chapter 9, 1970). These treatments assume that the predictor variables are known without error. Additional bias problems would arise if the predictors are themselves subject to error. The case of a product of two random variables is discussed by Bohrnstedt and Marwell (1977), who cite previous work. Statistical work on the nonlinear models that arise in information integration is desirable to provide guidance about the conditions under which bias would and would not be a serious practical problem.

4.4.2b. Work in progress with James Zalinski suggests that the procedure of bounding the scale values controls the instability without introducing noticeable bias in the parameter estimates.

4.4.3a. The different ramifications of the two purposes of testing models and of estimating parameters appear even in choice of design shape. For testing models, square designs would seem to be most effective. For estimating parameters, however, long, thin designs may be most efficient (Anderson, 1973a; Section F2.2.2).

5

Monotone Analysis

This chapter discusses the problem of monotone analysis. Linear response scales, which have played a major role in previous chapters, will not always be available. Many behavioral and physiological response measures, in particular, seem unlikely to be linear scales. In many cases, however, the observed response will be a monotone function of the underlying response measure. The general study of stimulus integration thus requires a capability for analysis based on monotone response measures.

The idea in monotone analysis is to use the postulated model to induce a metric on the response variable. The algebraic structure of the model provides a base and frame for measurement of the response variable and also the stimulus variables. With two or more stimulus variables in factorial-type design, sufficient constraint is potentially available to solve both measurement problems and to provide the necessary test of goodness of fit. No auxiliary assumptions are needed. No prior scales are required. All that is at issue is the algebraic structure of the model. That provides the base and frame for measurement in a way that is scale-free, or fundamental, not dependent on prior measurements.

The idea of monotone analysis has long been known in the area of optimal scaling in statistics. Indeed, Fisher (1938, 1958) presented a method for categorical or nominal scaling that does not even require a monotone response. For various reasons, however, optimal scaling has had little contact with measurement theory. Functional measurement brings these statistical procedures to bear on problems of measurement theory.

Model analysis is markedly more difficult when the response scale is not linear but only monotone. Indeed, this section shows that monotone analysis is even more demanding than has generally been recognized. Nevertheless, the problems of monotone analysis seem generally tractable due, in large part, to techniques developed by workers on statistical problems. By employing these techniques within the functional measurement framework, a rigorous error theory for testing goodness of fit has been obtained, together with practicable methods for securing adequate power. Although many difficulties and problems still remain, the procedures that now exist seem sufficient to allow effective empirical investigation in many areas with monotone analysis."

5.1 Monotone Transformation Principle

The principle of monotone response transformation is central to functional measurement. The observed response will often be a monotone scale, but often not a linear scale. Measurement theory must therefore be able to handle monotone response scales. In principle, this is simple. If the observed response is indeed a monotone scale, then some monotone transformation will make it into a proper linear scale. In practice, of course, this is not simple. Two problems must be solved. The first problem is theoretical: that of providing a criterion to select the appropriate monotone transformation. The second problem is technical, comprising several aspects of statistical procedure.

Theoretical Foundation. In the functional measurement approach, the criterion for monotone transformation is the algebraic model:

> The logic of the present scaling technique consists in using the postulated behavior laws to induce a scaling on the dependent variable [Anderson, 1962b, p. 410].

If the model is correct, it constitutes a scaling frame on which a monotone response can be transformed into a true linear scale.

The force of this criterion, it should be recognized, rests entirely on substantive foundations. The algebraic model must hold empirically. Unless the model is substantively correct, it cannot provide valid measurement. The foundations of measurement theory reside in empirical investigations of the kind illustrated in the *Foundations* volume.

An alternative view is often taken. This view focuses on mathematical or statistical problems, especially problems in monotone analysis. These technical problems are important, and most of this chapter is devoted to them. In the present view, however, the foundation of measurement resides in empirical theory, not in mathematical–statistical developments. This view is discussed in the *Foundations* volume and is repeated here to put the following discussion of technical problems in perspective.

Technical Problems. Although monotone analysis is not difficult in principle, it has been extremely difficult in practice. Three main technical problems arise. First is the problem of computing the response transformation. This has become practicable with modern developments in numerical analysis and optimal scaling. Second is the problem of testing goodness of fit. Fairly general solutions to this problem have been developed as part of the work on integration theory. Third is the problem of power, a problem that is especially troublesome with monotone analysis.

Because of practical difficulties involved in these problems, satisfactory applications of monotone analysis have been rare. Various investigators have employed monotone transformation or ordinal tests, but few have provided valid tests of goodness of fit. And on the critical problem of power, little is yet known. The next three sections take up these three problems. Unless otherwise stated, the discussion will be restricted to adding models, although much of it applies more generally.

5.2 Response Transformation Procedures

This section gives a brief overview of various procedures that have been used for response transformation. The main interest is the use of these procedures in measurement theory.[a]

FUNPOT. An obvious approach to response transformation is to expand the observed response measure in a polynomial power series (Anderson, 1962b). The coefficients of successive powers would be chosen so as to minimize the deviations between the transformed data and the hypothesized model. In principle, this procedure will find the desired transformation if one exists. It may be applied to models of any algebraic form.

For linear models, a statistical treatment of polynomial response scaling was developed by Bogartz and Wackwitz (1971). Their procedure consists of a stepwise regression based on an orthogonal decomposition of the interaction.[b] The usual analysis of variance test can be applied at each step to assess significance of the residual interaction in the transformed data. A computer program, FUNPOT, that implements this procedure was developed by Weiss (1973b, 1975) in his work on the bisection problem in psychophysics.

The FUNPOT method transforms the entire response distribution within each cell, not just a measure of central tendency. As a consequence, even a relatively small design may provide sufficient constraint on the transformation. Specified two-factor interactions can be eliminated, thus allowing an analysis of multilinear models that contain at least one adding operation. Most important, the method provides an apparently valid test of significance.

In practice, unfortunately, FUNPOT has not been too useful. The transformation is not constrained to be monotone, but there is no routine way to test whether observed nonmonotonicity is statistically significant. Also, power series do not seem generally useful for interpolation or extrapolation. Although these and other technical problems may be overcome (e.g., Winsberg & Ramsay, 1980), later work in this research program has employed the monotone regression programs discussed next.

MONANOVA. This method, developed by Kruskal (1965), computes a monotone transformation chosen to minimize the interaction term in factorial analysis of variance. In other words, the data are monotonically transformed to fit a linear or adding model as closely as possible.

Kruskal's method is a powerful tool for analysis of algebraic models. It provides a practicable way to employ the principle of monotone transformation. Although Kruskal's computer program is not as flexible as later programs, his statistical work forms the basis of most later work on monotone transformation.

ADDALS. The ADDALS method (de Leeuw, Young, & Takane, 1976; Young, de Leeuw, & Takane, 1976) is similar to MONANOVA in that it computes a monotone regression to fit a linear model. For this purpose, ADDALS is basically equivalent to MONANOVA but has the advantage that the transformation can operate on the individual data, not merely on the cell means. Unless otherwise stated, all response transformations reported in this book were done with the ADDALS program.

The ADDALS program has other features, including a capability for handling missing data or empty cells both in monotone regression and in ordinary analysis of variance. It can also be applied to categorical response data on a purely nominal scale. The response function itself must be single-valued, of course, and hence monotone, but the rank order need not be known a priori.[c]

Two Uses of Monotone Transformation. Two different goals may be sought with monotone response transformation. One goal is statistical, to increase power. The other goal is substantive, to establish empirical validity of an algebraic model. These goals are distinct and not necessarily compatible. A few comments on this distinction will help clarify the role of response transformation in psychological theory.

Transformation to increase additivity reduces interactions and hence increases power on main effects. Most experiments are primarily concerned with establishing main effects, and transformations to additivity have long been a standard tool in statistical analysis. This represents the optimal scaling tradition to which MONANOVA and ADDALS make basic contributions (see also Section F5.6.1). "In the optimal scaling tradition, the basic goal is to obtain a transformation of the dependent (and independent) variables so that the additive model fits as well as possible [Young *et al.*, 1976, p. 527]." The additive model is thus imposed arbitrarily, with only peripheral concern for its theoretical validity, in order to optimize statistical properties such as normality and power.

From the standpoint of psychological theory, of course, the term *optimal scaling* is not entirely appropriate. If some nonadditive model is correct, then optimal scaling will systematically misrepresent the functional psychological scales.

Use of monotone regression in psychological measurement faces two serious statistical problems. This point was brought home in an early attempt to use MONANOVA for psychological measurement (Weiss & Anderson, 1972). In this study, numerical ratings from a psychophysical averaging task obeyed the parallelism theorem and so supported an additive integration model. These ratings were reduced to rank orders, and MONANOVA was able to reconstruct the original metric information from these rank orders. This outcome is shown in Figure 5.1, which plots the marginal means of the transformed data as a function of the marginal means of the raw data. The essential feature of these data is that the curve for each subject is linear, showing that the reconstructed metric is equivalent to the original metric. This was a striking accomplishment for this relatively small 5×5 design. It showed that monotone regression can be a powerful tool for scaling—if the additive model is known to be correct.

For psychological theory, however, transformation to additivity is only appropriate if the additive model holds empirically. Because

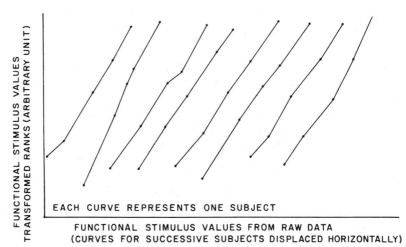

FIGURE 5.1. *Monotone regression reconstructs original response metric from ranks using averaging model as scaling frame. Subjects made graphic ratings of average inclination of two angles in a 5 × 5 design; these data showed the expected pattern of parallelism. Data for each replication for each subject were reduced to rank orders and transformed to additivity using MONANOVA. These transformed data are also parallel, so their marginal means will estimate the functional stimulus values—if the response transformation has been able to reconstruct the original response metric. To test this, the marginal means from the transformed data are plotted as a function of the marginal means of the original data, with a separate curve for each subject. Each curve is essentially linear, showing that the two sets of marginal means are linearly equivalent, and hence that the transformation did reconstruct the original response metric. (After Weiss & Anderson, 1972.)*

nonadditive models are prevalent, it is necessary to test goodness of fit. In the cited experiment, the test of fit was performed on the original metric data, but this would not generally be possible. Unfortunately, although the stress values used in the monotone transformation are useful for guiding the computation, they have little value for testing goodness of fit.[d]

No less important is the question of power. As may be expected, and as will be shown later, monotone transformation has so much flexibility that it can make many nonadditive models look additive. For substantive purposes, therefore, appropriate use of monotone transformation requires primary attention to the twin questions of goodness of fit and of power.

5.3 Goodness of Fit and Power

From a statistical standpoint, any model test is characterized by two general parameters, namely, its significance level and its power. The first problem in testing goodness of fit is obtaining a test that has a valid significance level. This is not enough, however, for a valid test is useless unless it has reasonable power. Both aspects of testing goodness of fit present serious difficulties when the response scale is only monotone.[a]

Goodness of Fit. Two difficulties are involved in testing goodness of fit with monotonically transformed data. First, the transformation uses up an unknown number of degrees of freedom. Second, the deviation scores are intercorrelated through their dependence on the monotone transformation. Consequently, standard analysis of variance does not provide a valid test.[b]

Fortunately, the replications method of Section 4.4.1 provides a simple way to test goodness of fit. The idea is to transform separately for each of a number of independent replications. Although the deviations are intercorrelated within each replication, they are independent across replications, so repeated measurements analysis is applicable. With monotone analysis, the main effects may not be zero, but the interaction test itself provides a proper test of the model. This method resolves both difficulties and provides a valid test of significance.

This test of fit depends on availability of procedures for response transformation. As yet, such procedures are not generally available for nonlinear models. However, some models that have a nonlinear form, as in Figure 5.2, are monotonically linear and so perhaps may be analyzed in this way. In addition, the two-phase method of Section 5.6 can sometimes be used for nonlinear operations.

Power. Ordinary model analysis is sometimes criticized on the ground that the flexibility provided by estimating a few parameters can make it too easy to fit the model to the data. Monotone analysis adds a new dimension of flexibility: It transforms the data to fit the model. It is a clear danger, therefore, that monotone transformation will too readily produce a good fit to an incorrect model (Anderson, 1962b, p. 410).

This points up the problem of power in monotone analysis, which is a direct extension of the ordinary statistical concept of power. In the test of goodness of fit, the null hypothesis is that deviations from the model in the transformed data result only from response variability. The power of this test is the probability that a significant discrepancy will be obtained, given that the true model is monotonically different from the tested model. Unless this test has adequate power to detect such differences, its failure to do so can hardly be taken as support for the model.

Four determinants of power are stimulus levels, size of design, number of replications, and number of factors in the design. The choice of stimulus levels within each factor of the design can be crucial for power. This point is illustrated by the crossover interaction of the adding–averaging test of Table 5.2 in Section 5.4. With no more than a 2 × 2 design, very high power can be obtained in the test of the adding rule—if the stimulus levels are chosen so as to yield the crossover. This point is not peculiar to qualitative tests of incorrect models, but applies equally well, although in a different way, to accepting models, as noted in the later discussion of ordinal tests. Choice of stimulus levels depends heavily on prior knowledge, so this point also illustrates the pervasive, often silent, role of background knowledge in scientific research.

The 2 × 2 design also illustrates the importance of design size. Unless there is a crossover, the data can always be transformed to parallelism or virtual parallelism. Unless there is a crossover, therefore, the 2 × 2 design has zero power for monotone analysis. More generally, a 2 × n data table without intersection points can always be transformed to parallelism (Levine, 1970). Not much information about appropriate design size is available. However, the evidence presented in this chapter suggests that two-way designs of ordinary size with a single score per cell are not generally adequate.

An increase in number of replications can increase power in two ways. More data naturally reduces the relative effect of response variability. If the medians were transformed in each cell of the design, for example, they would be more reliable when based on more replications. In addition, multiple replications yield a little distribution of data in each cell of the design. These distributions overlap across cells, and this overlap provides additional constraint beyond that provided by any measure of central tendency.

The fourth way to increase power is to use more than two factors in the design. Intuitively, it would seem that adding a third factor would markedly increase design constraint and hence also power. The results of Section 5.6 indicate that this method can be very effective.

5.4 Ordinal Tests

Model analysis can aim at rejecting a model or at establishing it. These two goals have unequal difficulty, for it is often easy to reject a model and always difficult to establish one. Nowhere is this asymmetry sharper than in ordinal analyses that utilize only rank-order properties of the data. Accordingly, these two goals will be discussed separately. The present discussion will be limited to one ordinal test, the well-known crossover test. However, many of the same considerations apply

TABLE 5.1
Ordinal Test of Adding versus Averaging

Adjectives	Liking	Adjectives	Liking
3H	16.41	3L	1.44
3H3M$^+$	14.77	3L3M$^-$	3.08

SOURCE: After Anderson (1968a).

to the cancellation tests of conjoint measurement that are taken up in Section 5.5. It will also be pointed out that standard multiple comparison procedures can be employed for all these ordinal tests.[a]

Model Rejection with Ordinal Tests. The most useful ordinal test is the crossover test, which has been widely used for rejecting additive models. It has been a standard tool in the adding–averaging issue. This crossover test has advantages of efficiency and of eliminating a whole class of models at once (Section F2.3.1). The following two experimental examples illustrate some relevant statistical considerations.

In the first example, subjects judged likableness of persons described by three or six trait adjectives. Table 5.1 shows that a person described by three favorable adjectives (3H) has mean likableness of 16.41. If three mildly favorable adjectives (3M$^+$) are added, then likableness should increase—if an adding rule holds. In fact, likableness decreases to 14.77, contrary to the adding rule.

To assess the statistical reliability of this decrease, subjects were given scores equal to the difference between their responses to the 3H and the 3H3M$^+$ descriptions. The model-implied null hypothesis that these difference scores have true mean zero was tested by analysis of variance, which yielded $F(1, 82) = 36.86$. Since the critical F ratios are 3.97 and 7.00 at the .05 and .01 significance levels, respectively, the observed difference is evidently reliable. The corresponding test with the negative descriptions in Table 5.1 was also contrary to the adding hypothesis, $F(1, 82) = 75.06$.

It deserves emphasis that these analyses of variance provide true ordinal tests: A linear (equal-interval) scale is not necessary. Normality could be a problem in certain experimental situations, but the response measure itself need only be monotone (Section 1.1.9). These tests are thus scale-free.

The comparisons in Table 5.1 are not actually crossover tests. Indeed, each comparison provides a separate test of the additive hypothesis. However, these tests do depend on the condition that the M$^+$ traits are truly positive and the M^- traits truly negative. Collateral evidence was thus required to ensure that this condition held (Note F2.3.2a).

True crossovers are shown in the second experimental example, in which females judged "dateableness" of males described by a photograph and zero or two personality trait adjectives (Lampel & Anderson, 1968). The relevant data are shown in Table 5.2, and one crossover is exhibited in the 2 × 2 subdesign indicated in boldface type. The HM adjectives raise the response to the low photograph alone from 2.35 to 4.46; they lower the response to the high photograph alone from 16.71 to 13.49. In graphical terms, the two row curves of this 2 × 2 subdesign cross over, contrary to an adding model.

To demonstrate the reliability of the crossover requires two separate tests, one on the increase for the low photograph, the other on the decrease for the high photo. Both differences must be significantly different from zero if the adding hypothesis is to be ruled out. The simplest test, of course, would be an analysis of variance of each difference score. However, that requires an explicit a priori hypothesis that these two differences are the critical ones. Such an a priori hypothesis was not entirely justified in this experiment due to uncertainty about the values of the nominal H, M, and L adjectives; theoretically, the HM adjectives could increase the response to the high photograph even under the averaging rule.

Accordingly, Lampel and Anderson (1968) employed a multiple comparisons procedure that took account of the theoretical hypothesis. This was Dunnett's test, which compares each of several means against a single (control) mean while maintaining a specified significance level on the aggregate of tests (e.g., Winer, 1971). This test was applied to each column of the design to compare each of the four photograph–adjective

TABLE 5.2
Ordinal Test of Adding versus Averaging

| | Photograph value | | | |
| | Low | High | Low | High |
Adjectives	Mean likableness		Critical difference	
HH	5.79	17.15		
HM	**4.46**	**13.49**	2.11	−3.22
None	**2.35**	**16.71**	—	—
LH	3.81	11.83	1.46	−4.88
LM	2.51	9.24		

SOURCE: After Lampel and Anderson (1968).

means with the photograph-alone mean, which was treated as the control. A preliminary analysis of variance was applied to the five conditions in each column to get estimates of error variance (2.39 for the Low photograph, and 4.23 for the High photograph). Dunnett's test yields critical values that must be exceeded for any difference between two means to be significant. For the Low photograph, these critical values were .86 and 1.06 at the .05 and .01 levels, respectively. The observed difference of 4.46 − 2.35 = 2.11 is thus clearly reliable. For the High photograph, the corresponding critical values were 1.14 and 1.41, so the observed difference of 13.49 − 16.71 = −3.22 is also reliable. Because both differences are reliable, so is the crossover. A second crossover, also reliable, is provided from the 2 × 2 subdesign of the "none" and LH rows of Table 5.2. The advantage of multiple comparisons procedure is that it controls the significance level for the aggregate of tests. Thus, the probability of even one false alarm among each aggregate of mean comparisons is no greater than the assigned level of significance.[b]

Distribution-free tests could also be employed, at least if a priori hypotheses about specific pairs of means were available. Of the 40 difference scores for the 40 subjects between the Low photograph with HL adjectives and with no adjectives, 34 were positive, 3 zero, and 3 negative, which is clearly different from 50:50 by binomial sign test (see Note 2.1.2a). The other three comparisons yielded even stronger binomial results. For smaller numbers of subjects binomial-type tests would lack power, but rank-type tests could be used.

Although the early work in this research program typically used ordinal tests of the kind indicated, later work has tended to rely on visual inspection, often with some analysis of variance test of interactions. In Figure 6.1, the five points show a clear crossover pattern and no statistical test was reported. In Figure F1.22, similarly, the crossover seemed clear by inspection and no statistical test was reported. The most pertinent interaction test would involve a comparison between two rows of the design, although various related procedures have also been used. Such interaction tests are more or less dependent on the linearity of the response scale and so are not true ordinal tests. If the response scale is linear, of course, then significant interaction in the analysis of variance rules out the additive model. A common procedure, therefore, has been to use one design with equal weighting to demonstrate parallelism and hence response linearity, and an auxiliary design to demonstrate the crossover, as in the experiments of Figures 6.1 and F1.22.

Goodness of Fit for Ordinal Tests with Multiple Comparisons. A statistical basis for ordinal tests is available with multiple comparisons procedures.

This has already been illustrated in the analysis of Table 5.2, which seems to be the first such application of parametric procedures. Surprisingly, distribution-free multiple comparisons do not seem to have been considered for ordinal tests. Person and Barron (1978) performed a rank-sum test between every pair of conditions but did not allow for the number of tests. Because these model analyses involve large numbers of tests, such pairwise testing severely inflates the significance level, as illustrated later. Parametric multiple comparisons procedures, independently suggested by Busemeyer (1980), have also been overlooked, perhaps because of the popular belief that parametric statistics are not valid when the response scale is merely monotone. For the purpose at hand, however, only a monotone scale is needed, so the parametric procedures are proper ordinal tests of the model per se (Section 1.1.9).[c]

For general model analysis, a multiple comparisons procedure must be able to assess the difference between each and every pair of conditions while maintaining an experimentwise significance level at some assigned alpha value. That is, the probability that the aggregate of all possible two-condition comparisons from a given experiment will contain even one false alarm (Type I error) must be at most α.

The most generally suitable parametric procedure would thus seem to be Tukey's HSD test (e.g., Kirk, 1968, Chapter 3). Similarly, the most generally suitable distribution-free procedures would seem to be the Steel–Dwass rank-sum test for independent scores and the Nemenyi signed-ranks test for repeated measurements (Hollander & Wolfe, 1973; Miller, 1966).[d] In each case, the factorial design is treated as a one-way design. Tukey's test provides a single critical value against which to compare the difference between every pair of condition means. The rank tests provide a single critical value against which to compare two-sample rank-sum statistics between every pair of conditions. These critical values are chosen to maintain the assigned significance level for the largest obtained difference, that is, for the comparison of the two extreme conditions.

To implement crossover analysis, the investigator would inspect all possible 2 × 2 designs. If even one showed a crossover with both differences significant, as in Table 5.2, then the additive model could be rejected at the alpha level of significance. This same approach can be used to implement the double cancellation test of conjoint measurement (Section 5.5).

Inasmuch as no multiple comparisons rank test of crossover has been reported for repeated measurements design, an example is given here. For this purpose, the signed-ranks test presented by Hollander and Wolfe (1973, Section 7.7A) was applied to the original data of the experiment already analyzed in Table 5.2. The test statistic $t(\alpha, 15, 40)$ was chosen to maintain an experimentwise significance level for the complete set of 15 conditions in the original experiment. With 40 subjects, the significance points of the test statistic were 662.3 and 696.6 for α = .05 and .01, respectively. The four critical comparisons yielded rank sums of 777, 751, 700.5, and 817.5, which are all larger than the significance point. This implies that both crossovers are real, so the additive model may be rejected.[e]

Multiple comparisons procedures present two serious problems for model analysis that need more detailed study. The first concerns the sacrifice of power required to maintain an experimentwise significance level. The larger the design, the larger the critical difference and the lower the power on any given two-condition comparison. A 4 × 5 design is pretty small for ordinal analysis, yet it yields 20 conditions. If the usual critical difference for a t test between two means was applied to test the difference between the largest and smallest obtained means, the false-alarm rate would increase from .05 to greater than .90 (Kirk, 1968, p. 78). Looked at in the other direction, maintaining the .05 level experimentwise with the Tukey HSD test entails a t value greater than $5.00/\sqrt{2}$ and hence a significance level less than .0003 for a single comparison of two means. Similar figures would presumably hold for distribution-free tests. The corresponding loss of power is potentially severe, which limits the usefulness of multiple comparisons procedures.

It could be a useful tactic, therefore, at least for rejecting models, to plan two experiments, the first being exploratory and the second confirmatory. The first would employ a large design, a weak significance level, and perhaps a per-comparison significance level instead of an experimentwise significance level in order to pick up prospective deviations from the model. A small second design would then focus on these deviations using a normal significance level to assess their reliability.

The other problem with multiple comparison procedures concerns the statistical assumptions. The assumption of normality, which is usually of least concern in traditional experiments, may be most serious for model analysis with parametric multiple comparisons. The theoretical sampling distribution of the difference between the largest and smallest means, which is the basis for the multiple comparisons test, is calculated on the assumption of normality. The larger the number of conditions to be compared, the more the largest and smallest means depend on the tails of the distribution. If the actual distributions are not normal, therefore, the actual sampling distribution of the difference between the largest and smallest means may be quite different from the theoretical distribution, so the operative significance level may be quite different from the nominal value used by the investigator.

Distribution-free tests are presumably more robust. Although rank tests typically assume that all conditions have the same shape distribution, heterogeneous shapes would presumably not unduly perturb the significance level. For certain nonnormal distributions, moreover, rank tests have more power than parametric tests.

Accepting Models with Ordinal Tests. The sharp asymmetry between rejecting and accepting models is nicely illustrated by the 2 × 2 design. It is large enough to disprove the adding model, as shown by the crossover interactions of Table 5.2. However, it is far too small to provide much support for the model. Indeed, if the data do not cross over, then they can be made parallel by monotone transformation and are ordinally consistent with the model. To provide serious support for a model with ordinal tests, a design that can impose adequate constraints on the data is needed.[f] Unfortunately, little information about minimum acceptable design size is available.

To complicate the problem, any increase in design size simultaneously operates to decrease the power of whatever multiple comparisons procedure may be used. This loss of power cannot be avoided by the use of a priori hypotheses; they can be useful for rejecting models, but an ordinal test aimed at accepting a model must test all possible pairs of conditions. As a further complication, power depends also on the effective ranges of the stimulus variables and on the spacing of the stimulus levels within those ranges. A 10 × 10 design may seem relatively large, yet it would be almost as useless as a 2 × 2 design if each set of 10 stimulus levels consisted of two subsets of nearly equal value.[g]

A pessimistic view of the usefulness of ordinal tests for establishing models is indicated by the results of Section 5.6.[h] Psychologically reasonable nonadditive models readily fail to yield violations of ordinal tests, even in relatively large designs and even with errorless data. These results indicate that ordinal tests and monotone analysis are far more demanding than has generally been recognized. It may be doubted that even one existing empirical ordinal test would meet minimum standards with respect to accepting a model. Strict ordinal analysis is still statistically primitive. Perhaps future work will improve the situation, but at present it seems reasonable to rely on numerical methods for establishing models.

5.5 Conjoint Measurement

A central feature of conjoint measurement is its proposal to base measurement theory on axioms that refer to comparisons of certain response pairs. The independence "axiom," which asserts that there are no crossovers in the data, involves comparing two response pairs, as illustrated in the discussion of Table 5.2. In addition to this long known crossover test, conjoint measurement has introduced some essentially new tests, known as *cancellation axioms*.

These axioms are interesting because, in principle, they allow model tests that rest on the simplest possible data properties, namely, comparison of response pairs. As is well known, however, these axioms assume error-free data. What applications have been made to real data have virtually all rested on some arbitrary criterion because of lack of statistical methods for handling response variability.

The need for adequate statistical methods is illustrated in the next subsection by an inappropriate application of the axiom of double cancellation. The use of multiple comparisons procedures to obtain rigorous axiom tests will then be discussed, together with the associated question of power. Finally, it will be suggested that axiom tests have limited usefulness and that procedures based on monotone transformation are generally superior (see also Section F5.5).

Double Cancellation.[a] The most important of the cancellation tests is double cancellation, which is an essential property for conjoint measurement analysis of two-way designs. Double cancellation may be viewed as an ordinal implication of parallelism in two linked 2×2 designs (Krantz, Luce, Suppes, & Tversky, 1971, p. 250). In a 3×3 design, with R_{ij} the entry in cell ij, double cancellation may be represented by the statement

$$\text{If} \quad R_{21} > R_{12}, \quad \text{and} \quad R_{32} > R_{23}, \quad \text{then} \quad R_{31} > R_{13}.$$

A pertinent example will illustrate the problems that arise in attempting to apply this test to real data.

Krantz, Luce, Suppes, and Tversky (1971, pp. 445ff) attempted to demonstrate the advantages of conjoint measurement by reanalysis of data from a study by Sidowski and Anderson (1967) in which subjects judged the attractiveness of working at certain occupations in various cities. The first experiment yielded an unexpected interaction for the occupation of teacher. In a desirable city, it was as attractive to be a teacher as a lawyer or doctor; in an undesirable city, it was as unattractive to be a teacher as an accountant. The suggested interpretation was that teaching, unlike the other occupations, immersed the person in the socioeconomic milieu of the city. Since the interaction was unexpected, a second, nearly identical, experiment was run for verification. Similar results were obtained.

The data from both experiments were given in Figure 1 of the original report and are reproduced in the upper part of Table 5.3. Since the

TABLE 5.3
Mean Rating of Job Attractiveness for City–Occupation Combinations

Occupation	Desirability of city			
	H	M+	M−	L
Experiment 1				
Lawyer–doctor	7.35	6.82	5.68	4.30
Teacher	7.35	6.78	5.30	3.18
Accountant	5.90	5.48	4.35	3.18
Experiment 2				
Lawyer–doctor	7.08	6.88	6.20	5.14
Teacher	6.95	6.62	5.80	4.10
Accountant	5.25	5.05	4.42	3.22
Experiment 1				
(Lawyer)	7.55	7.05	5.72	4.31
(Doctor)	7.15	6.60	5.65	4.30
Experiment 2				
(Lawyer)	7.00	6.90	5.92	5.27
(Doctor)	7.15	6.85	6.48	5.02

SOURCE: Data after Sidowski and Anderson (1967, Figure 1).

occupations of lawyer and doctor yielded nearly equal judgments, the corresponding data were pooled in the original graph and also here. The curves are clearly nonparallel, and the interaction term was significant by analysis of variance.

Krantz, Luce, Suppes, and Tversky claimed that this interaction was not genuine. By this they meant that the nonparallelism resulted from nonlinearity in the rating response and that the integration process was truly additive. Their analysis deserves attention because it was presented as a general procedure that could apply to any experiment.

Their claim was based on application of double cancellation to the data of Experiment 1. Since double cancellation is ambiguous about tied data, Krantz, Luce, Suppes, and Tversky broke the two ties in the data of Experiment 1 by using the corresponding data of Experiment 2. The means of Experiment 1 showed no violations of double cancellation and, indeed, a monotone transformation was found that made these means parallel. They concluded that the interaction was not genuine and that the data were truly additive: "The interaction between city and occupation, therefore, is attributable to the nature of the rating scale, because it can be eliminated by appropriate rescaling [p. 446]."

This reasoning is not valid. This can be seen by applying the very same test of double cancellation to the data of the replication experiment. Although Krantz, Luce, Suppes, and Tversky did not report such a test, double cancellation is in fact violated in Experiment 2. Specifically, double cancellation requires that

$$6.62 > 6.20 \text{ and } 4.42 > 4.10 \Rightarrow 5.05 > 5.14,$$

which is untrue.

Of course, this failure of double cancellation does not imply that the interaction is genuine. Double cancellation could fail because of response variability. Without an error theory, double cancellation is inconclusive. Hence the violation in Experiment 2 makes clear that the lack of violation in Experiment 1 was also inconclusive.[b]

Goodness of Fit in Conjoint Measurement. Virtually all attempts to apply the conjoint measurement axiom tests have involved some arbitrary, ad hoc criterion (Person & Barron, 1978). Some failures of the axioms must be expected merely from chance, but the expected number of chance failures is not generally determinable. The most common approach has been to select some plausible, arbitrary criterion and to reject the model if the actual number of axiom failures exceeds this criterion. This arbitrary approach can sometimes be effective for rejecting models because it requires no more than a rank-order response. However, a rejected model allows no measurement.

For establishing a measurement model, the arbitrary approach does not provide a satisfactory test of fit. The seriousness of this problem can be illustrated with the axiom of independence or no crossovers. To obtain adequate power, it is desirable to use fairly large designs with the stimulus levels fairly closely spaced.[c] If two stimulus levels are close together, however, then chance crossovers will be numerous, as with lawyer and doctor in the two bottom rows of Table 5.3. The expected number of chance occurrences will depend sensitively on how close together the stimulus levels are and on the response variabilities in the various cells of the design, both of which involve supraordinal, metric properties. It is hard to see how the arbitrary methods that have so far been used in attempts to apply conjoint measurement could determine whether or not the cited lawyer–doctor crossovers are real.

An attempt to resolve the arbitrary nature of previous conjoint tests was made by Person and Barron (1978), who used a procedure somewhat like that illustrated in the analysis of Table 5.2. Thus, a test of the independence axiom of no crossover would require two separate tests, one for each pair of conditions in a 2 × 2 design. But instead of a multiple comparisons test as was used in Table 5.2, Person and Barron applied the two-sample Mann–Whitney U test to all possible 2 × 2 subdesigns without allowance for the inflation of significance level that results from multiple tests. Their effective significance level was thus much higher than their nominal level, but its actual value does not seem to be determinable. Although their procedure seems to have certain advantages over previous approaches, it also is arbitrary and ad hoc.

Valid tests of the conjoint measurement axioms are available with the multiple comparisons procedures of Section 5.4. Thus, double cancellation would be violated by a specific pattern of significant differences among three response pairs. In the preceding notation for a 3×3 design, a significant violation will occur if R_{21} is significantly greater than R_{12}, and R_{32} is significantly greater than R_{23}, but R_{31} is significantly less than R_{13}. All possible 3×3 subdesigns may be scrutinized in this way because the multiple comparisons procedure maintains an experimentwise significance level. Higher order cancellation conditions may be tested in similar manner.

Insufficiency of Axiom Tests. A perplexing problem with the conjoint measurement approach is that tests of the axioms for a finite design are not logically sufficient to guarantee, say, an additive representation. This insufficiency of the axioms has been pointed out by Krantz, Luce, Suppes, and Tversky (1971, pp. 425ff), who present a numerical counterexample with error-free data. Even if all the axioms of a conjoint representation theorem are satisfied, the representation may not exist. Even with error-free data, verification of the axioms of the theorem does not guarantee the additive model nor imply the existence of the measurement scales. This is a definite limitation, because all designs must be finite in practice.

This does not mean that the theorems are in error, of course, only that they are not in general logically sufficient to handle designs with a finite number of levels. Besides verifying the axioms, it is also in general necessary to demonstrate that a corresponding set of inequalities has a solution. Even if the tests of the axioms seem to support some model, further analyses are required for the system of inequalities. These analyses are also complicated by response variability, and their statistical properties may be difficult to determine. Until this problem is resolved, conjoint measurement would seem to be logically incomplete.

Power. The problem of power is acute for conjoint measurement. The difficulties with double cancellation in the analysis of Table 5.3 arose because a 3×4 design is too small and provides too little power for ordinal analysis aimed at establishing models. Moreover, the methods for increasing power used in monotone functional analysis do not seem too useful in conjoint measurement. The addition of a third variable increases potential power but may decrease actual power for conjoint measurement.

The conjoint measurement analyses of the distributive model, $A(B + C)$, and the dual-distributive model, $A + BC$, rest on two corresponding cancellation axioms. Distributive cancellation refers to a specified pattern of inequalities among four pairs of responses, and dual-distributive cancellation refers, similarly, to six pairs of responses (Krantz & Tversky, 1971, p. 158). Multiple comparisons procedures may be applied to test these two cancellation axioms in the manner already indicated for double cancellation. Every one of these four or six pairs must exhibit a significant difference in a specified direction to obtain a significant violation of the model. Even if power is fairly high for the test of each separate pair, power for the simultaneous aggregate of tests will be considerably lower. Thus, the diagnostic methods proposed by Krantz and Tversky to distinguish among the simple polynomials may not be very effective. In contrast, functional measurement makes good use of the additional constraints imposed by a third variable, especially with the two-phase method of Section 5.6.

Axioms versus Monotone Transformation. Krantz and Tversky (1971) emphasize the distinction between ordinal tests of axioms and alternative approaches based on monotone transformation as follows:

> The key feature of the conjoint-measurement approach is that only the ordinal aspects of the data are required to be compatible with the proposed composition principle [p. 152].

> An alternative to testing ordinal properties is to search for an appropriate monotonic transformation of the dependent variable that best satisfies the proposed rule [p. 167].

Krantz and Tversky criticize the frequent use of monotone transformation, as in optimal scaling (Section F5.6.1), without providing for a test of the model in question. Their criticism is correct, for the validity of the scales depends on the validity of the model. Without an appropriate test of goodness of fit, monotone transformation procedures merely assume the validity of the model and hence also of the scales (Krantz *et al.*, 1971, pp. 33, 259; Krantz & Tversky, 1971, p. 167; Luce, 1967, p. 37).

As is well known, however, conjoint measurement has not provided appropriate tests of the models. Even the use of multiple comparisons procedure to test the axioms, in the manner suggested earlier, is not sufficient because the axiom tests are not sufficient. Ironically, the criticism levelled at optimal scaling applies no less to the axiomatic approach of conjoint measurement.

Appropriate tests of goodness of fit have been developed in functional measurement in conjunction with monotone transformation procedures from optimal scaling. Although these methods are numerical, they apply to rank-order or ordinal data. These methods provide a complete solution to the formal measurement problem.

Moreover, these numerical methods have marked advantages over the conjoint axiom approach. This advantage applies especially to the polynomial models considered by Krantz and Tversky.[a] They say:

> The major practical advantage of the direct test of axioms over the general evaluation of numerical correspondence is that, in general, it provides a more powerful diagnostic test between alternative composition rules. The multiplicative and the distributive rules, for example, are so close to each other, in the positive case, that with fallible data it is extremely difficult to distinguish between them on the basis of any overall measure of goodness of fit [pp. 167–168].

However, both models can be analyzed using the two-phase technique of Section 5.6. To assess the multiplicative rule, ABC, and the distributive rule, $A(B + C)$, in the positive case, the data could be monotonically transformed to minimize the $B \times C$ interaction. If the multiplicative rule holds, then all other interactions will also be eliminated and the data will obey the parallelism analysis. If the distributive rule holds, then the $A \times B$ and $A \times C$ interactions in the transformed data will both obey the linear fan analysis (see Figure 5.6).

These numerical methods seem preferable to the direct tests of axioms on every count. These numerical methods provide appropriate tests of significance. These numerical methods are constructive: They provide the desired representation, if it exists, so they are sufficient in finite designs. Moreover, these numerical methods have adequate power for establishing models.

5.6 Monotone Analysis Procedure

A primary problem in monotone analysis is obtaining sufficient design constraint to prevent data generated by an inherently nonadditive process from appearing additive. This is the problem of power already noted in Section 5.3. The purpose of this section is to discuss some practical aspects of this problem and some solutions, including the two-phase method and the distribution method, both of which have shown promise for model diagnosis.[a]

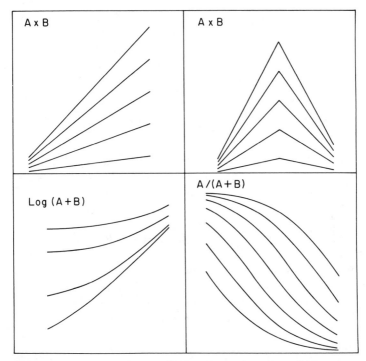

FIGURE 5.2. *Four illustrations of nonparallel data that can be made parallel by monotone transformation of the response scale. Each panel presents a factorial graph for the listed model, with levels of A as curve parameter and values of B on the horizontal axis.*

Power in Two-Factor Designs. Two-factor designs may be generally unable to provide adequate power for monotone analysis, at least when there is only a single score in each design cell. The reason is suggested in Figure 5.2, which presents four panels of data that are monotonically additive. Both upper panels represent a multiplying model, which can be made parallel by a log transformation on the response. The triangular shape of the upper right panel merely represents a nonmonotone relation between the subjective stimulus metric and the objective metric used for the stimulus variable on the horizontal axis. The lower left panel presents a log sum model that can be made parallel by an exponential transformation. Finally, the ratio model $A/(A + B)$ in the lower right panel can be made parallel by inverting, subtracting unity, and taking logs.

Any data pattern that comes close to any one of the patterns in Figure 5.2 can be made at least almost additive. Barring crossovers, most observed data seem likely to come fairly close to one of the patterns exemplified in Figure 5.2. With an infinite number of levels for each stimulus factor, of course, an inherently nonadditive model could not be made parallel. In practice, it is rare to find as many as 10 levels of a stimulus variable. Unless within-cell distributional information can be utilized, two-factor designs seem unlikely to provide sufficient power for establishing models.

The lack of power in two-factor designs is illustrated in Figure 5.3. The left panel presents data from a difference-plus-ratio model, that is inherently nonadditive (Section 5.8). Since the graph has an approximate fan shape, however, a loglike transformation can be expected to make the data approximately parallel. Indeed, application of the ADDALS transformation made the data perfectly parallel, as shown in the right panel. This example has substantive relevance since it indicates that simple two-factor design is unable to resolve the longstanding question whether psychophysical difference judgments obey a subtracting rule, a ratio rule, or some mixture of the two rules.

A similar result holds for the averaging model in the left panel of Figure 5.4. These theoretical data exhibit nonparallelism because of the unequal weighting of the row stimuli. Although this model is inherently nonadditive, the 6 × 5 design does not prevent transformation to additivity. The transformed data, shown in the right panel, are parallel

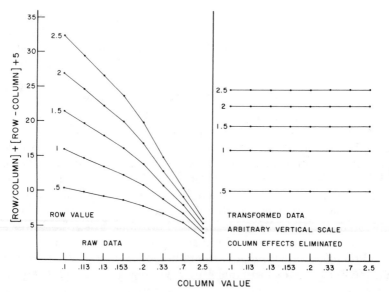

FIGURE 5.3. *Nonadditive ratio-plus-difference model made to appear additive by monotone transformation. Left panel plots original data for model A/B + (A − B) + 5, for listed values of row and column variables. Right panel plots transformed data with column effects eliminated to exhibit the parallelism.*

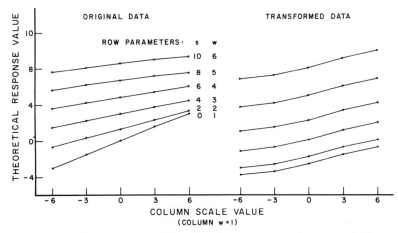

FIGURE 5.4. *Nonadditive averaging model made to appear additive by response transformation. Weight and scale value parameters are listed in the graph for the original data in the left panel. Right panel shows that the same data are parallel after monotone transformation.*

up to one unit in the fifth digit. This example has substantive importance because of the ubiquity of averaging rules. That such data may be transformable to additivity does not justify doing so. Similar examples are given in Figure 5.7 and in Table 5.5.

The import of these examples is clear. The sizes of these designs are on the large side for most practical applications, and their power has been optimized by choosing the stimulus levels at roughly equal spacing. In every case, however, inherently nonadditive data are made to appear additive when monotone transformation is applied.[b]

For certain models, suitable choice of stimulus levels will yield crossovers that may be used to rule out monotone transformation to additivity. The averaging model of Figure 5.4 will yield crossovers if the column stimuli are extended to larger values. The sum-plus-ratio model of Figure 5.7 will also yield crossovers, although not the difference-plus-ratio model of Figure 5.3. But although crossovers may disprove an adding model, they do not prove any other model. It is necessary, therefore, to seek ways to allow valid use of monotone transformation.

Two-Operation Models. There seems to be an almost qualitative difference between the constraints obtainable from models with one and two algebraic operations. The following examples illustrate the ability of two-operation models to resist transformation to additivity.

Results for the model $A + BC$ are presented in Figure 5.5. The three two-factor graphs in the top layer represent model predictions from

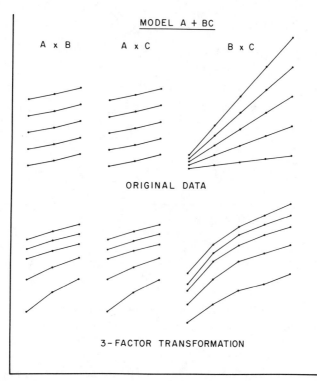

FIGURE 5.5. *Three-factor model* A + BC *resists transformation to additivity. Stimulus levels were 0, 3, and 7 for* A; *1, 3, 5, 7, and 9 for both* B *and* C. *Top panel shows two-factor graphs of original data. Bottom panel shows same data after monotone transformation of the ranks to fit a three-factor adding model. The nonparallelism visible in all three graphs shows that three-factor design can provide substantial protection against inappropriate transformation to additivity.*

stimulus values for a $3 \times 5 \times 5$ design specified in the legend. The parallelism in the two left panels and the linear fan in the right panel mirror the algebraic structure of the model.

These data were reduced to ranks and transformed to fit the three-factor adding model, $A + B + C$, as closely as possible. The resulting two-factor graphs are shown in the bottom layer of Figure 5.5. All three graphs show substantial deviations from parallelism. Although the model $A + BC$ includes one additive operation and one monotonically additive operation, the two together resist transformation to additivity in a design of practicable size.

The model $A(B + C)$ is illustrated in a $2 \times 5 \times 5$ design in Figure 5.6. The upper layer presents the two-factor graphs for the original data, using the stimulus values specified in the legend. The linear fans in the two left panels and the parallelism in the right panel correspond to the algebraic structure of the model.

These data were reduced to ranks and transformed to fit a three-factor adding model. The resulting two-factor graphs are shown in the middle layer of Figure 5.6. All three graphs show substantial deviations from parallelism. With the given stimulus values, therefore, the model $A(B + C)$ also resists transformation to additivity.

A slightly different look at the power obtainable by going from a one-operation to a two-operation model is provided by Figure 5.7. The upper left panel plots data from the two-factor, sum-plus-ratio model, $A + B + A/B$. This model is inherently nonadditive, and even the data from this small, 3 × 4 design are nonadditive. The 2 × 2 subdesign at the

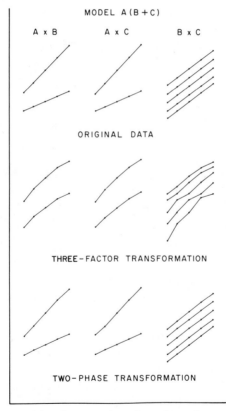

FIGURE 5.6. *Illustration of three-factor transformation and two-phase methods for model* A(B + C). *Stimulus levels were 2 and 5 for* A; *1, 5, 10, 15, and 20 for* B; *and 1.0, 5.2, 10.4, 15.6, and 20.8 for* C. *Top panel shows two-factor graphs for original data. Center panel shows two-factor graphs after monotone transformation of the ranks to fit a three-factor adding model; nonparallelism shows that this three-factor model resists transformation to additivity. Bottom panel shows two-factor graphs after monotone transformation to fit the two-factor adding model* (A ⊛ B) + (A ⊛ C) *in the manner indicated in Note 5.6a.*

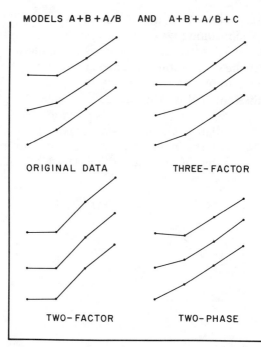

FIGURE 5.7. *Illustration of three-factor transformation and two-phase methods for model (A + B + A/B). Upper left panel shows original data for stimulus values of 4.1, 8.2, and 12.3 for A; 2, 6, 10, and 14 for B. These data are nonadditive, as demonstrated by the crossover interaction in the upper left 2 × 2 subgraph. However, monotone transformation makes this 3 × 4 design virtually parallel, as shown in the lower left panel. This two-factor model was extended to include a third, additive factor, C, to form the model (A + B + A/B) + C, with values of C equal to 1.01, 3.03, 5.05, 7.07, 9.09, 11.11, 13.13, and 15.15. Upper right panel shows the A × B data table after monotone transformation of the ranks to fit a three-factor adding model. The nonparallelism shows that the three-factor model resists transformation to additivity. Lower right panel shows A × B data table after two-phase transformation of the ranks to fit two-factor adding model (A ⊛ B) + C. This model allows reconstruction of the original response metric and thereby also the shape of the original A × B data table.*

upper left of the graph represents a crossover, as shown by the slight downturn in the upper curve and the upturn in the lower curve. Under monotone transformation, the nonadditivity in this two-factor model effectively disappears, as shown by the parallelism in the lower left panel.

This nonadditivity need not disappear, however, if a third factor is included to obtain the model $(A + B + A/B) + C$. Data from this model were reduced to ranks and transformed to fit a three-factor adding model. The resulting $A \times B$ graph is given in the upper right panel and retains the main nonparallelism of the original data.

These three examples illustrate the potential power of multioperation models in preventing misdiagnoses of additivity. When additivity is obtained, therefore, it can provide substantially more support for a true adding model than is possible with the corresponding one-operation model.

Certain limitations of the foregoing three-factor approach require consideration. First, the examples have only considered transformation to fit a three-factor adding model. Similar conclusions would presumably hold, however, for transformations to fit other three-factor models if corresponding computer programs were available. Second, the number and spacing of the stimulus values will strongly affect the outcome. Finally, the three-factor approach is more useful in preventing misdiagnosis than in providing correct diagnosis. For finding the correct model, the following two-phase method has advantages.

Two-Phase Method. In the two-phase method, one operation is used as the frame for the response transformation and another is used for testing goodness of fit. This approach is especially useful when the operation used for transformation is known to have some algebraic form, here taken to be adding.

An example with the model $A + BC$ is shown in Figure 5.8. The upper layer shows the two-factor graphs for the original data in a $5 \times 2 \times 5$ design with stimulus values given in the legend. The parallelism in the two left panels and the linear fan in the right panel mirror the algebraic structure of the model. Corresponding graphs after transformation to a three-factor adding model are shown in the middle layer. As in Figure 5.5, the nonparallelism shows that these data cannot be made additive. The substantial nonparallelism in the center panel shows that the correct model has not been diagnosed.

Results from the two-phase method are shown in the bottom panel. To apply this method, the data were reduced to ranks and treated as a 5×10 design, with the 5 rows representing the levels of A, and the 10 columns representing the 10 levels of the compound variable $B \circledast C$. The ranks were then transformed to fit the two-factor adding model. This fit is practically perfect, of course, because this two-factor model is additive. Hence the two left graphs are practically parallel.

The critical question for the two-phase method concerns the shape of the $B \times C$ graph in the right panel. The two-factor transformation should recover the original response metric, so this graph should have the linear fan form of the original data—as indeed it does. The slight deviations from a linear fan result from the discreteness of the design. Thus, the two-phase method uncovers the correct model.

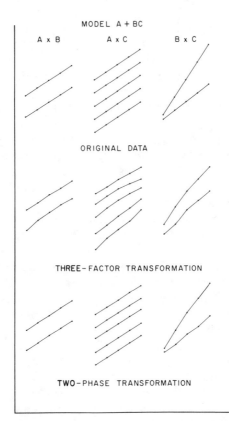

FIGURE 5.8. *Illustration of three-factor transformation and two-phase methods for model* A + BC. *Top panel shows two-factor graphs for values of 0, 5, 10, 15.5, and 20.5 for* A; *1 and 6 for* B; *1, 3, 5, 7, and 9 for* C. *Middle panel shows two-factor graphs after monotone transformation of the ranks to fit a three-factor adding model. Bottom panel shows two-factor graphs after monotone transformation of the ranks to fit a two-factor adding model,* A + B ⊛ C. *This adding operation allows approximate reconstruction of the original response metric and hence recovery of the linear fan shape for the* B × C *integration.*

Two-phase analysis of the model $A(B + C)$ is illustrated in the bottom layer of Figure 5.6. These three graphs show essentially the same pattern as the original data in the top layer. Although the monotone transformation used only the adding operation, $(B + C)$, it was successful in uncovering the multiplying operation (see Note 5.6a).

Two-phase analysis for the model $(A + B + A/B) + C$ is shown in the lower right panel of Figure 5.7. Monotone transformation of the ranked data was applied to minimize nonadditivity in the two-factor model with the compound variable $A \circledast B$ and C. No assumption is made about the integration rule for A and B. The success of this method is apparent in the similarity between the pattern in the $A \times B$ graph from the two-phase analysis and the original data in the upper left panel. Even the slight crossover has been recovered.

The advantage of the two-phase approach is that the transformation employs only one operation and makes no assumption about the other operation. Accordingly, the factorial graph for the other operation provides a way to test the model that avoids the severe loss of power associated with monotone transformation.

This two-phase approach is most effective, of course, when the transforming operation is known to be correct, for the transformation can then construct the true response metric even in relatively small designs (Figure 5.1). Possession of a linear response scale removes a major ambiguity in interpreting the patterns in the factorial graphs involving the other operation. Otherwise prosaic models can thus provide a base and frame for measurement.

When the transforming operation is not correct, the two-phase approach still provides an appropriate test of the complete three-factor model. Because the transformation is performed within a two-factor framework, the previous results indicate that the transforming operation will typically force the data into the prescribed two-factor form. However, the other operation is not so constrained, and the corresponding factorial graphs provide appropriate and effective tests of goodness of fit.

In addition, the two-phase approach can be useful when both operations have the same form. In value judgments of bundles of three or more comparable commodities, for example, it may be assumed that the same process is involved in each integration, and indeed the natural normative model is the multifactor adding model. Empirically, however, the adding model is not generally correct, as shown by Shanteau's (1974) subadditivity effect. Two-phase analysis based on the adding model can demonstrate the presence of subadditivity because the transformation is expected to induce additivity for the transforming operation and to accentuate deviations from additivity for the other operation. Although this technique is not as informative as Shanteau's use of a correct multiplying operation (Section 3.2), it has the advantage of applying more generally to situations in which a qualitative test would seem difficult to obtain.

TABLE 5.4
Monotone Transformation of Crossover Interaction in 2 × 2 Design with Replications

1	2		1.13	1.13		1.41	1.59		1.23	1.27		1.30	1.30
4	3		2.87	2.87		2.80	2.20		2.86	2.63		2.82	2.57
1.10	1.75		1.23	1.80		1.39	1.51		1.14	1.68		1.50	1.69
2.56	2.59		2.62	2.35		2.86	2.25		2.89	2.30		2.76	2.06

NOTE: Upper left 2 × 2 subtable presents original data that exhibit crossover interaction. Monotone transformation reduces the crossover to essentially zero, as shown by the parallelism in the adjacent 2 × 2 subtable. The eight remaining 2 × 2 subtables show means of simultaneous monotone transformation of eight replications of the original data with added response variability, normal (0,1). Six of these eight subtables exhibit the crossover, illustrating the capability of the distribution method to resist transformation to additivity.

Distribution Method. In the distribution method, a single subject is run through the design a number of times, and the data are transformed as a total aggregate. The responses in each cell of the design form a little distribution, and these distributions interlock across cells. This interlocking constraint can provide adequate power to detect real nonadditivity in two-factor designs. Empirical applications in psychophysics are presented in Anderson (1977a,b) and in Carterette and Anderson (1979). Two artificial examples will be presented here to illustrate the principle.

The power of the distribution method is nicely illustrated by applying it to the crossover in the upper left, 2 × 2 subtable of Table 5.4. Although these data are obviously nonadditive, monotone transformation reduces the crossover to arbitrarily small size, as indicated in the 2 × 2 subtable second from top left.

To simulate real data, a random normal number with mean 0 and standard deviation 1 was added to the number in each cell of the original 2 × 2 design. This was done eight times to yield a sample of eight separate responses in each cell, and the transformation program was applied to this aggregate of data. The first application is shown in the top center 2 × 2 subtable. These mean transformed scores maintain the same ordinal relation as in the original data. In the first row, the left entry is smaller than the right; in the second row, the left entry is larger than the right. Thus, the interlocking of the four distributions of eight responses provided sufficient constraint to maintain the crossovers.

The remaining seven 2 × 2 subtables were obtained in the same way. Of the eight, six exhibit the crossover, two do not (top right, bottom left). Across the eight subtables, both relevant differences are highly significant. Even in this small design, therefore, the distribution method justifies the use of monotone transformation.

An extended illustration of the distribution method is shown in Table 5.5, which reports results on the line-segment model given in Subtable (a). In this line-segment model, the two middle curves form parallel straight lines; the top and bottom rows each contain two line-segments that are bowed around the parallel lines. The data have a barrel shape,

TABLE 5.5
Distribution Method Illustrated with Line-Segment Model

			(a) Line-segment model: Original data			
42	51	60	69	74	79	84
40	47	54	61	68	75	82
35	42	49	56	63	70	77
33	38	43	48	57	66	75
Range 9	13	17	21	17	13	9

			(b) Original data in normalized form (rounded range values)			
−1.08	− .49	.10	.69	1.01	1.34	1.66
−1.21	− .75	− .29	.16	.62	1.08	1.53
−1.53	−1.08	− .62	−.16	.29	.75	1.21
−1.66	−1.34	−1.01	−.69	−.10	.49	1.08
Range .59	.85	1.11	1.37	1.11	.85	.59

			(c) Monotone transformation: Error-free data			
− .88	− .42	.12	.50	.88	1.42	1.88
−1.26	− .80	− .26	.12	.50	1.04	1.51
−1.51	−1.04	− .50	−.12	.26	.80	1.26
−1.88	−1.42	− .88	−.50	−.12	.42	.88
Range 1.00	1.00	1.00	1.00	1.00	1.00	1.00

			(d) Monotone transformation: Four runs, two replications per run			
− .98	− .45	.09	.54	.97	1.31	1.84
−1.23	− .61	− .22	.10	.55	1.00	1.59
−1.71	−1.00	− .57	−.15	.30	.75	1.20
−1.85	−1.26	− .91	−.58	−.07	.37	.96
Range .87	.81	1.00	1.12	1.04	.94	.88

(*continued*)

TABLE 5.5 (*Continued*)

(e) Monotone transformation: Thirty-two runs, two replications per run

	− .98	− .38	.12	.54	.92	1.32	1.86
	−1.19	− .67	− .18	.10	.52	.98	1.58
	−1.64	−1.03	− .57	−.15	.23	.68	1.20
	−1.84	−1.33	− .91	−.51	−.06	.39	1.00
Range	.86	.95	1.03	1.05	.98	.93	.86

(f) Monotone transformation: Sixteen runs, four replications per run

	−1.02	− .43	.08	.54	.95	1.32	1.85
	−1.17	− .67	− .24	.13	.54	1.04	1.66
	−1.64	−1.04	− .57	−.15	.22	.68	1.20
	−1.81	−1.33	− .94	−.55	−.07	.41	1.02
Range	.79	.90	1.02	1.09	1.02	.91	.83

(g) Monotone transformation: Eight runs, eight replications per run

	−1.03	− .43	.08	.56	.96	1.31	1.84
	−1.17	− .67	− .24	.12	.54	1.03	1.67
	−1.64	−1.03	− .58	−.15	.22	.67	1.19
	−1.78	−1.33	− .96	−.57	−.07	.42	1.03
Range	.75	.90	1.04	1.13	1.03	.89	.81

as indicated in the row labeled *range,* which lists the difference between the top and bottom rows. For convenience, Subtable (b) presents the same data linearly transformed to the scale range employed in the monotone analysis.

This line-segment model is clearly nonadditive in principle. To make the bowed curves parallel would require nonlinear transformation on the response, but the parallelism of the two middle curves forbids nonlinear transformation over their common response range. With only seven levels of the column variable, however, the data can be transformed to additivity. The results of the ADDALS program are given in Subtable (c): The constancy of the range values in the fifth row testifies to the parallelism of the transformed data.

For this model, even two observations per cell suffice to prevent transformation to additivity. To assess the efficacy of the distribution method, a random normal number with mean 0 and standard deviation 4 was added to each entry in Subtable (a). This process was repeated eight times to yield eight separate replications. The data were transformed two replications at a time so that four independent sets of transformed data were available. The means across these four sets of data are given in Subtable (d), and the range entries in the fifth row show that the barrel shape of the original data has been retained. The interaction term in the analysis was statistically significant, $F(18, 54) = 5.25$. As a further check, this process was repeated three more times. The same barrel shape was obtained, and it was statistically significant in each case. Accordingly, these results show that as few as two replications of the 4×7 design suffice to prevent inappropriate transformation to additivity.

If more than two replications are transformed at a time, more of the original nonparallelism is retained. This can be seen by comparing Subtables (e), (f), and (g), which represent the same 64 replications, transformed 2, 4, or 8 at a time. The range values in the two end columns decrease and the range value in the center column increases with number of simultaneous replications. Although this pattern of results cannot readily be generalized beyond this particular case, it provides some suggestions about apportioning available replications between simultaneous and independent transformations so as to maximize the power.[c]

An alternative way to utilize the distributional information is to employ replications itself as an additive factor. This has the advantage of allowing a main effect of replications, but seems otherwise equivalent. Since this disallows interactions between replications and rows or columns, it is restricted to individual subject analysis. A test of fit may be obtained by splitting the replications into two or more independent subsets with an independent monotone transformation for each subset (Carterette & Anderson, 1979, p. 275).

The distribution method should be used with caution, for its statistical properties have not been studied. However, the foregoing examples emphasize the importance of obtaining and using distributional information. The practice of reducing the data in each cell to a mean or median may conceal real deviations from the model.

Goodness of Fit. The replications method of Section 4.4.1 may be applied to test goodness of fit for all the foregoing procedures. The essential requirement is that separate, independent transformations be performed for each of a number of subjects or for each of a number of replications on a within-subject basis. In either case, replications may be grouped on a within-subject basis for greater reliability.

With monotone transformation, the critical test statistics are the interactions. These should reflect the form of the model, as with the multilinear models of Table 3.1. Specific interaction components may also be tested to increase power or to allow distribution-free tests.

Comment. The foregoing discussion indicates that monotone analysis is practicable but demanding. Many statistical problems have barely been touched on, including the need for monotone regression programs for nonadditive operations and a variety of questions relating to power. These problems will not be elaborated here, but one or two general points deserve comment.

The choice of stimulus levels is important, even critical, for effective monotone analysis. The examples of the Figures 5.5–5.8 demonstrate that appropriate choice is feasible, at least in multifactor designs. It is clear, however, that both the spacing of stimulus levels within each factor and the interrelations of these levels across factors are important for obtaining adequate constraint. Failure to obtain adequate constraint is readily apparent in artificial examples because the program will not reconstruct the original data patterns. In practice, however, deviations from some hypothesized model form would be hard to interpret. More information from artificial examples is desirable as a guide to experimental analysis.

A related problem is that the actual choice is of physical stimuli. These may not be freely variable, and their effective values may not be known definitely. It may often be necessary, therefore, to view monotone analysis as an iterative experimental procedure, in which the choice of stimulus values is improved by successive approximation.

Finally, the importance of background knowledge deserves reemphasis. One form of background knowledge is embodied in expectations that certain algebraic operations will be appropriate for specific tasks, as suggested, for example, by previous work on cognitive algebra. Another form of background knowledge is the metric information that goes into the choice of stimuli, for example, in attempting to choose factor levels to cover some desired range with roughly equal subjective spacing. This metric information may be vague and more or less untrustworthy, but is not less precious for that (Note 5.4g).

5.7 The Nature of Response Variability

Response variability has heretofore been treated casually as an additive term in each integration model. However, an important paper by Busemeyer (1980) pointed out that the place at which variability enters the process affects the data analysis. This section is based largely on Busemeyer's analysis but makes the straightforward extension from an additive model to an arbitrary response measure.

Variability can enter the process before or after the response output function, which corresponds to $\mathbf{M}$ in the functional measurement diagram of Figure 1.2. These two cases may mnemonically be called *pre* and *post*. The observable response for replication x in cell ij may then be written as follows for the two cases

$$\text{pre: } R_{ijx} = \mathbf{M}(r_{ij} + e_{ijx}).$$
$$\text{post: } R_{ijx} = \mathbf{M}(r_{ij}) + e_{ijx}.$$

Here r_{ij} denotes the true or mean implicit response in cell ij, and the error terms have expected value zero. Factorial design notation is employed for consistency, although the results require no assumption about design or integration function.

The main concern is with possible bias arising from the error terms. There is no bias if $\mathbf{M}$ is linear, for then the expected value of R_{ijx} equals r_{ij} in both equations. However, bias may be present if $\mathbf{M}$ is nonlinear, as is assumed in the following. Different considerations are involved in analyses of transformed and untransformed data, so these two cases are considered separately.

Monotone Transformation. To bring out the bias problem for monotone transformation, suppose that $\mathbf{M}$ is strictly monotone and that $\mathbf{M}^{-1}$ is known exactly. It accordingly is applied to the observed responses, but the outcome will be different in the pre and post cases.

In the pre case, the transformed data, denoted by primes, are

$$\begin{aligned} R'_{ijx} &= \mathbf{M}^{-1}(R_{ijx}) \\ &= \mathbf{M}^{-1}[\mathbf{M}(r_{ij} + e_{ijx})] \\ &= r_{ij} + e_{ijx}. \end{aligned}$$

Thus R'_{ijx}, which constitutes the data to be analyzed, has expected value equal to r_{ij} and so is unbiased. The error has the additive form that is typically assumed in both parametric and distribution-free analysis.

In the post case, however, the transformation induces a bias because

$$R'_{ijx} = \mathbf{M}^{-1}[\mathbf{M}(r_{ij}) + e_{ijx}].$$

Unless $\mathbf{M}$ is linear, the expression on the right is not equal to $r_{ij} + e_{ijx}$, and its expected value is not equal to r_{ij}. In principle, however, this bias may be made arbitrarily small by taking R_{ijx} as an average over a number of replications. From the post equation, this average will equal $\mathbf{M}(r_{ij})$ plus an error term that is the average of the error terms for the several replications. The variance of this average error term tends to zero as the number of replications increases.

In practice, of course, $\mathbf{M}^{-1}$ is not ordinarily known but must be estimated from the data. The estimation introduces two different sources of bias that are unrelated to response variability. The first depends on the number and spacing of the levels of each stimulus factor. This bias would seem potentially more serious than the bias of the previous paragraph, although the example of Figure 5.1 suggests that it need not be serious even in a relatively small 5×5 design. The second source of bias arises because estimation of the monotone transformation rests on some assumption, ordinarily about the form of an integration rule. Transformation based on an additive rule, for example, can severely bias nonadditive data, as illustrated in Figures 5.3 and 5.4. These two biases are unrelated to response variability, however, and arise even with error-free data.

Pairwise Tests. The nature of the response variability also affects tests between two conditions in the untransformed data, as in the crossover tests of Section 5.4. To illustrate, consider the null hypothesis that the true means in row 1 and columns 1 and 2 of a two-factor design are equal, that is, that $r_{11} = r_{12}$. This is done by testing for significant difference between the two corresponding observed means, $\bar{R}_{11.}$ and $\bar{R}_{12.}$.

For the post case, there is no bias. Responses in the two cells have the theoretical expressions

$$R_{11x} = \mathbf{M}(r_{11}) + e_{11x}, \qquad R_{12x} = \mathbf{M}(r_{12}) + e_{12x}.$$

Since the error terms are additive, with zero expected value, the test for significant differences is an unbiased test of the hypothesis that $\mathbf{M}(r_{11}) = \mathbf{M}(r_{12})$, which is equivalent to the null hypothesis that $r_{11} = r_{12}$. Standard parametric or distribution-free tests may be applied for this purpose, as discussed in Section 5.4.

In the pre case, bias can arise when the error terms have different distributions. Responses in the two cells have the theoretical expressions

$$R_{11x} = \mathbf{M}(r_{11} + e_{11x}), \qquad R_{12x} = \mathbf{M}(r_{12} + e_{12x}).$$

If e_{11x} and e_{12x} have identical distributions, then the null hypothesis that $r_{11} = r_{12}$ implies that $\mathbf{M}(r_{11} + e_{11x})$ and $\mathbf{M}(r_{12} + e_{12x})$ are also identically distributed. Hence the significance test of $\bar{R}_{11.}$ and $\bar{R}_{12.}$ is a valid test of the null hypothesis even though the expected values of R_{11x} and R_{12x} are biased estimates of r_{11} and r_{12}, respectively. This result implies that the crossover and other ordinal tests are more generally valid than Busemeyer indicated. The significance test itself will be biased, however, if e_{11x} and e_{12x} have different shape distributions. This could happen if the two column stimuli affected response variability without affecting the mean.

Comment. Busemeyer's paper makes clear that the psychological structure of the response variability has direct bearing on practical problems of data analysis. It may be doubted that these biases are often serious, but they deserve detailed study. It is worth adding that the amount of bias depends on the amount of nonlinearity in $\mathbf{M}$, so bias can be reduced by experimental procedures that make the response function more linear (Section 1.1).

The psychological nature of response variability has not received much attention, but some of the factors that produce pre and post variability deserve consideration. A prominent source of pre variability resides in stimulus variability, discussed in Note 2.1.1b, such as is incorporated within Thurstonian theory and signal detection theory. Random variability in the stimulus values produces corresponding variability in the response. Accordingly, the implicit response is treated as a random variable, r_{ijx}, with expected value r_{ij}. The pre equation then applies.

Post variability is to be expected in situations in which extraneous stimuli act directly on the response independent of and subsequent to the integration operation under study. Extraneous stimulus action seems likely with, say, physiological responses such as skin conductance. However, extraneous stimuli may also contribute to pre variability by entering into the integration, as with uncontrolled visual cues in judgments of lifted weight. On the other hand, response uncertainty

(Note 2.1.1b) would presumably operate at the post stage if the actual response was chosen from the prevailing response distribution by some process independent of the immediate stimulus field, for example, by reference to residual stimulation from previous trials. In general, therefore, it seems safest to allow that both kinds of variability will be operative.

5.8 Two Theorems on Uniqueness and Existence

Monotone Additivity Uniqueness Theorem. If the data can be made parallel by one monotone transformation, perhaps another transformation can do the same. If all such transformations are linearly related, any one would be appropriate. However, if any two are nonlinearly related, it would be uncertain which, if either, provided the true linear scale. The following theorem from Aczél (1966, p. 148) resolves this problem by showing that if any additivity-inducing monotone transformation exists, it is unique up to a linear transformation.

Monotone Additivity Uniqueness Theorem. Let $R(x,y)$ be monotonically additive so that

$$\mathbf{M}_0[R(x,y)] = g_0(x) + h_0(y),$$

with $\mathbf{M}_0$ strictly monotone and continuous. Let $\mathbf{M}$ be any other strictly monotone, continuous function that also makes $R(x,y)$ additive

$$\mathbf{M}[R(x,y)] = g(x) + h(y).$$

Then, under quite general conditions, the two solutions are linearly equivalent: $\mathbf{M}(t) = c\mathbf{M}_0(t) + a + b$, $g(t) = c\mathbf{M}_0(t) + a$, and $h(t) = c\mathbf{M}_0(t) + b$, where a, b, and c are constants.[a]

To relate this result to the integration model, take x and y as the scale values s_A and s_B of the row and column stimuli and take $R(x,y)$ as the observable response. The working assumption is that $R(x,y)$ is monotonically additive, and thus

$$\mathbf{M}_0[R(s_A, s_B] = g_0(s_A) + h_0(s_B).$$

Let $g_0(s_A) = \bar{s}_A$ be the gross effect of the row stimulus (Section 2.1) and similarly let $h_0(s_B) = \bar{s}_B$. Then

$$\mathbf{M}_0[R(s_A, s_B)] = \bar{s}_A + \bar{s}_B.$$

Let

$$\mathbf{M}[R(s_A,s_B)] = g(s_A) + h(s_B)$$

be any other monotone additive representation of the data. Then the theorem implies that

$$g(s_A) = c\tilde{s}_A + a;$$
$$h(s_B) = c\tilde{s}_B + b.$$

Thus, the derived stimulus values are on a linear scale, since they are unique up to a linear transformation. Moreover, the gross effects of the row and column factors have a common unit.

Scheffé's Monotone Additivity Existence Theorem. It is sometimes of interest to determine whether some theoretical function of known form can be transformed to additivity. A theorem by Scheffé (1959, pp. 95ff) provides necessary and sufficient conditions for the case in which the two stimulus factors are quantitative variables, as in psychophysical integration. Let $R(x,y)$ be the given function with partial derivatives denoted by subscripts, so that $R_x = \partial R(x,y)/\partial x$, etc. Then there exists a differentiable, strictly monotone function $\mathbf{M}$ that transforms $R(x,y)$ to additivity

$$\mathbf{M}[R(x,y)] = g(x) + h(y),$$

if and only if the following condition is satisfied

$$R_{xy}/R_x R_y = F(R),$$

where F is some function of R.

Scheffé's proof, omitted here, is constructive in that it provides closed expressions for $\mathbf{M}$, g, and h, if they exist. Thus, $\mathbf{M}$ is given by

$$\mathbf{M}(R) = c_1 \int \exp[-\int F(R)dR]dR + c_2,$$

where $c_1 > 0$ and c_2 are constants. To determine $g(x)$, let $\phi(x) = R_x d\mathbf{M}(R)/dR$. Then

$$g(x) = \int \phi(x)dx + c_3.$$

Finally, $h(y) = \mathbf{M}(R) - g(x)$.

To illustrate the application of Scheffé's theorem, consider a model in which the response is the weighted sum of the arithmetic and geometric means

$$R(x,y) = w(x + y) + \sqrt{xy}.$$

Differentiation yields

$$R_x = w + \sqrt{y/x} \ /2, \qquad R_y = w + \sqrt{x/y} \ /2, \qquad R_{xy} = \sqrt{1/xy} \ /4.$$

Straightforward algebra shows that

$$R_{xy}/R_x R_y = 1/[2w(x + y) + 2\sqrt{xy} + (4w^2 - 1)\sqrt{xy}]$$
$$= 1/[2R(x,y) + (4w^2 - 1)\sqrt{xy}].$$

For an equally weighted sum of arithmetic and geometric means, $w = \frac{1}{2}$, and the term in $\sqrt{xy}$ in the last expression vanishes. For the equally weighted case, therefore, the ratio of derivatives is expressible as a function of $R(x,y)$, so $R(x,y)$ is monotonically additive.

As a second example, a weighted sum of a difference and a ratio

$$R(x,y) = w(x - y) + x/y,$$

is inherently nonadditive. Differentiation yields

$$R_x = w + 1/y, \qquad R_y = -w - x/y^2, \qquad R_{xy} = -1/y^2.$$

Substitution and simplification yield

$$R_{xy}/R_x R_y = [(wy + 1)(wy + x/y)]^{-1}$$

Consider the restricted domain $x = y$. On this domain, $R(x,y) = 1$ is constant, but $R_{xy}/R_x R_y = (wy + 1)^2$ is not constant. Hence $R_{xy}/R_x R_y$ cannot be expressed as a function of $R(x,y)$ and so $R(x,y)$ is nonadditive.[b]

5.9 Monotonic Indeterminacy

The problem of monotonic indeterminacy refers to the tradeoff relation between the response scale and the integration rule. Mathematically, a strictly monotone transformation on the response scale can always be compensated for by the inverse operation on the integration rule. Since model and scale must be established jointly, they rest on a monotonic indeterminacy. This is a well-known problem in model analysis that appears in the study of functional equations (Aczél, 1966; Ellis, 1966).

The problem of monotonic indeterminacy has two entirely different levels that should be kept separate. One level is philosophical and applies equally to the laws of physics. At this level, the problem appears to be resolvable only by arbitrary conventions (Ellis, 1966). At the practical level of everyday science, however, the problem appears generally tractable by appeal to considerations of generality. Two empirical examples will be used to illustrate how monotonic indeterminacy can be resolved by various practical considerations.

The essential idea rests on appeal to generality and uniformity across a network of evidence. Three kinds of generality are relevant: stimulus generality, or invariance of stimulus values across tasks; model generality, or reappearance of similar algebraic rules across tasks; and response generality, or linearity of response measures across tasks. Of these, the most important for present purposes is response generality (Section 3.1; Anderson, 1972a, p. 394).

The Height + Width Rule. Certain constraints on integration rules are exerted by the physical environment. Higher organisms depend for survival on highly developed perceptual–motor abilities that include the ability to perceive and act in local space in a more or less veridical way. Accordingly, the finding that adults' judgment of area of rectangles exhibits a linear fan pattern, which points to the physicalistic Height × Width rule, seems hardly more than trivial. But acceptance of this rule suggests that the response measure is a linear scale. This prosaic integration task thus has a useful substantive function.

It is puzzling, however, when children's judgments of rectangle area are found to exhibit parallelism. If children also used the response scale in a linear way, then the observed parallelism (Figure 4.5) would of course imply the Height + Width rule. On the other hand, it seems odd that they should not follow the physicalistic rule. No actual multiplication is necessary; direct perception of area will yield the linear fan pattern.

Perhaps, therefore, the observed parallelism is not genuine but an artifact, reflecting children's inability to use the response scale in a true linear way. For example, suppose that the implicit perceptual response of the children is veridical and follows the Height × Width rule but that they use the response scale in a logarithmic manner. Then, since log Height × Width = log Height + log Width, the factorial graph of the data will exhibit parallelism. The observed response points to an adding rule, whereas the multiplying rule is actually correct.

Three lines of evidence to support the Height + Width rule may be noted briefly. The first relies on two-operation models (Section 3.2). In this task, the children were asked to judge the total area of two rectangles for which the physical rule is $Height_1 \times Width_1 + Height_2 \times Width_2$. If the implicit response obeys this rule but the response scale is logarithmic, then the data will not exhibit parallelism. On the other hand, if the Height + Width rule is genuine and the response scale is linear, then the observed data will exhibit parallelism for every pair of factors. Uniform parallelism was in fact obtained (Anderson & Cuneo, 1978a), which supports both the Height + Width rule and response linearity.

The second line of evidence comes from social judgment. In a variety of tasks with social stimuli, children and adults exhibit similar patterns of data. This suggests, in particular, that both use the response scale in a linear manner.

The third line of evidence is associated with the theoretical interpretation of the Height + Width rule. This was hypothesized to reflect a general purpose adding rule applied by children to handle tasks for which they have not yet developed adult concepts of quantity. If this hypothesis is correct, adding rules should be obtained in other tasks for which the physical rule is also one of multiplying.

One test of this implication studied judgments of numerosity of rows of beads varied in length and density. Although the physical rule is Length × Density, the children obeyed a Length + Density rule when the quantity of beads was beyond their number ability (Cuneo, 1978, 1982). This result agrees with the hypothesis of a general purpose adding rule. Moreover, for smaller numbers of beads that could be counted, these same children exhibited the physicalistic Length × Density rule. Cuneo's elegant result verifies the linearity of the response scale and thereby validates the adding rule as well.

The Weight + Size Rule. Another illustration of the problem of monotonic indeterminacy appeared in a study of the weight–size illusion. Judged heaviness of lifted objects that varied in gram-weight and size exhibited parallelism, as though these two cues had been integrated by an adding rule, Weight + Size (Anderson, 1970a; Figure 4.7). This interpretation disagreed with the popular and plausible hypothesis that subjects really judge density, because the density hypothesis leads to a dividing rule, Weight/Size.

The density hypothesis could still be correct if the response scale was nonlinear. If the implicit perception of heaviness obeyed the Weight/Size rule but subjects used the response scale in a logarithmic way, then the observed data would exhibit parallelism. On this basis, it could be argued that the adding rule implied by the observed data was not genuine. However, there are several lines of evidence to support the adding rule.

The most relevant evidence comes from a study of cross-task validity (Anderson, 1972a) that replicated the weight–size experiment and added a second task in which subjects were instructed to judge the average heaviness of two lifted objects. These averaging instructions obviously call for an averaging rule, and that rule was supported by the observed parallelism. This outcome is barely more than trivial, of course, but it carries the nontrivial implication that the response scale was used in a linear manner in this averaging task. Since the same response scale was used in the weight–size task, it seems reasonable to conclude that it was also used in a linear manner there. This, in turn, supports the Weight + Size rule. Cross-task consistency thus provides a stronger basis for the interpretation than could be obtained by either task alone.

Cross-task validity has a second aspect relating to stimulus invariance. Both experiments yielded functional scales of heaviness, and these were linearly related (see Figure 3.5). This invariance of stimulus values across the two tasks provided further validational support for both adding rules and for the linearity of the response scale (see also Figures 3.1 and 3.6).

Ineluctable Monotonic Indeterminacy. The two preceding empirical examples have illustrated how considerations of stimulus, model, and response generality can provide practical ways of dealing with monotonic indeterminacy. Particular experimental situations may present serious uncertainties, of course, and there is no routine way to handle them. For the most part, however, monotonic indeterminacy no longer seems to be a serious problem at the practical level in judgment theory.

At another level, however, the problem of monotonic indeterminacy appears to have no solution because there is no certain way to fix the model–scale tradeoff. This ineluctable monotonic indeterminacy will be illustrated for the empirical example of heaviness judgments.

In the weight-averaging task, the parallelism in the observed data was taken as joint support for an arithmetic averaging rule for the implicit response

$$r_{ij} = w_1 s_i + w_2 s_j , \qquad (w_1 + w_2 = 1)$$

and a linear response function relating the implied and observed response

$$R_{ij} = C_0 + C_1 r_{ij}.$$

However, parallelism can be obtained in an infinite number of other ways by coupling a nonlinear integration function

$$r_{ij} = \mathbf{M}(w_1 s_i + w_2 s_j)$$

to the nonlinear response scale

$$R_{ij} = \mathbf{M}^{-1}(r_{ij}).$$

If $\mathbf{M}$ is any strictly monotonic transformation, this also will yield parallelism because

$$R_{ij} = \mathbf{M}^{-1}\mathbf{M}(w_1 s_i + w_2 s_j) = w_1 s_i + w_2 s_j.$$

One monotone transformation has special interest for the heaviness judgments. This is the exponential transformation

$$r_{ij} = e^{w_1 s_i + w_2 s_j}$$
$$= e^{w_1 s_i} e^{w_2 s_j}$$

By setting $t_i = e^{s_i}$ and $t_j = e^{s_j}$, this integration rule becomes the geometric mean

$$r_{ij} = t_i^{w_1} t_j^{w_2}, \qquad (w_1 + w_2 = 1)$$

in which the t's act as scale values. If the response follows the inverse monotone transformation, namely, the logarithm, then

$$R_{ij} = \log r_{ij}$$
$$= w_1 \log t_i + w_2 \log t_j$$
$$= w_1 s_i + w_2 s_j.$$

In other words, this geometric averaging rule is monotonically equivalent to the arithmetic averaging rule and both can account for the same data (Anderson, 1972a, p. 394).

The attraction of the geometric averaging rule is that it would be consistent with the density rule for the weight–size illusion. The integration rule for both tasks would then have a multiplying form, and the data would appear parallel because the response scale was used logarithmically in both tasks. The apparent scale values would actually be the logarithms of the t's, but they would still be linearly related across the two tasks.

Various practical arguments against the geometric mean may be given, but none are logically conclusive. For example, the geometric mean disallows both positive and negative values that are found in many tasks of social judgment. This objection could be handled by treating social judgment as different from psychophysical judgment or by disallowing negative values through use of e^s transformation. Again, tasks of judging area or expected value of two objects have been found to obey two-operation models of the form $AB + CD$. Under the logarithmic response hypothesis, this model would take the power product form $e^{AB} e^{CD}$, which is not consistent with expectations from environmental constraints. But neither desire for simplicity nor the environmental constraints can logically compel the form of the model. Similarly, the argument that the graphic rating scale must be psychologically symmetrical and hence could not be logarithmic is also only a plausibility argument.

Indeed, the arithmetic and geometric means represent only two of an infinite number of possible integration rules, all of which have equal logical claim. Choice among these rules may reflect considerations of simplicity and unity, but that is a matter of convention, not of empirical fact (see, e.g., Ellis, 1966).

At the same time, it should be recognized that the many-variable approach of stimulus integration does constrain the form of the models. With two or more stimulus variables, integration rules can be disproved even with monotone analysis. The adding rule is a good example because it has frequently failed. Simple structure cannot arbitrarily be imposed on the data.

Monotonic indeterminacy is as much a problem in physics as in psychology. A lucid discussion has been given by Ellis (1966), who concludes that monotonic indeterminacy in the laws and measurement scales of physics is indeed ineluctable. Psychology is better off because it can operate within the traditional framework of physics, as in the discussion of judging area of rectangles. In any case, this inherent indeterminacy is seldom of concern to the empirical scientist who seeks to establish laws within a coherent framework. That such laws, together with the whole framework, can be transformed to a different formal notation has little relevance before the laws have been established. Classical physics established a coherent framework, and it may now be interesting to speculate whether this is the "true" form or whether some equivalent form would do as well. The real accomplishment, however, is to establish that one coherent system. This is the job that faces psychology today(Anderson, 1974a, p. 231).

5.10 Summary Comments on Monotone Analysis

The concern of this chapter has been with monotone analysis as a tool for the study of algebraic models. This section summarizes the main conclusions.

Goodness of Fit. Proper tests of goodness of fit are essential for establishing a measurement model. The developments in functional measurement appear to provide a reasonably satisfactory solution to the problem of testing goodness of fit. Most important is the replications method, which allows valid tests of fit for arbitrary models, even with monotone transformation (Sections 4.4 and 5.3). Also useful is the two-phase method of Section 5.5, which provides scale-free tests of fit.

It has also been pointed out that existing multiple comparisons procedures allow proper ordinal tests of the crossover interaction and of the cancellation axioms used in conjoint measurement. The first application appears to be the crossover test of Lampel and Anderson (1968), which is discussed in connection with Table 5.2. A similar approach may be applied to the cancellation axioms, as has been independently noted by Busemeyer (1980). These ordinal tests can be effective for rejecting models—but they have serious limitations for establishing models.

Often, analyses are presented as tests of fit that do not really test the model. For example, the correlation between the model predictions and the data is not a proper test of fit. This correlation can be very misleading, as is now generally realized. However, the percentage of variance accounted for, which is still frequently used, is functionally equivalent to a correlation. This and related statistics, such as mean magnitude deviation and root mean square deviation, have limited value for model analysis, even when the response scale is linear (Section 4.1). Their value is even less when monotone transformation is allowed (see, e.g., Figure 4.6). Unfortunately, most attempts to use ordinal or monotone analysis have relied on such inappropriate methods. Few studies have used designs and analyses that are capable of providing satisfactory evidence for establishing a model.

Power. Also vital to the test of goodness of fit is its power (Sections 4.2 and 5.3). When the response scale is linear, adequate power may be readily available, as illustrated in the discussion of Figure 4.7. When the response scale is linear, therefore, even a small design may be sufficient basis for accepting a model.

The power problem changes radically when the response scale is not linear. Power may still be adequate for model rejection in special cases, as illustrated with the crossover tests. Model acceptance, however, is much more difficult for the reasons already discussed in Section 5.4.

The power problem is acute for two-variable models when response transformation is used. By themselves, two-factor designs of practicable size with a single score per cell seem generally unable to prevent invalid transformation to additivity. Similarly, multifactor designs that are treated as two-factor designs in the monotone analysis are generally inadequate for establishing a model.

Two-operation models seem generally able to prevent inappropriate monotone transformation, even with a single score per cell and with some empty cells, as shown in Section 5.6. In particular, the two-phase method can provide proper tests of fit that have adequate power even without replication within subjects. However, the number and spacing of the levels of the factors play important roles that need further study.

Verification by simulation may be generally necessary, at least in initial applications. This is straightforward. To illustrate, suppose that the transformed data obey an adding rule. These transformed data would be changed in some reasonable way although without introducing crossovers. The amount and pattern of change would be chosen so that, if they held in fact, they would represent an important violation of the model that ought to be detected. These changed data would be subjected to the same analysis as the original data, and this procedure would be repeated for a number of other altered data patterns. If these analyses eliminate the nonadditivity, this indicates that the original analysis had too little power to support the model.

Numerical Response. It may be worth repeating here that the rating scale methodology of Section 1.1 and the parallelism theorem of Section 2.1 can be considered monotone analysis. The linearity of the rating scale is not presupposed but assessed by the parallelism theorem (Section F5.5.1). The parallelism theorem is a stringent criterion, as shown by the failure of magnitude estimation (Section 1.1.7; see also Figures 4.6 and 4.7). The rating scale procedures of Section 1.1 may be considered an experimental method of response transformation.

There can be considerable advantages to making the response scale linear by experimental procedures rather than by statistical transformation. Indeed, the empirical studies with rating methods provided the initial foothold on cognitive algebra.

Cognitive Algebra. The base and frame for monotone analysis is provided by the algebraic integration models. These models can provide scale-free, or fundamental, measurement by virtue of their algebraic structure. This is the guiding theme of functional measurement.

But these algebraic models can provide measurement scales only if they are true empirically. A false model cannot yield true scales. Fortunately, the empirical work has revealed considerable success for these models. This seems sufficient to indicate the operation of a general cognitive algebra. It is this empirical work that, in the functional measurement view, forms the foundation of measurement theory.

Optimal Scaling. Cognitive algebra may provide a theoretical foundation for optimal scaling in relation to substantive theory. Optimal scaling requires some criterion, such as normality or additivity, as a scaling frame for response transformation. In the usual way, this criterion is imposed arbitrarily, especially from statistical considerations. This is appropriate when, for example, the purpose is to increase power for testing significance of main effects (Sections 1.1.9 and F5.6.1). For this statistical purpose, the additive model is appropriate even though it may be psychologically invalid.

But the situation is entirely different when optimal scaling is used for other purposes, such as measuring stimulus values. Unless the additive model is psychologically valid, stimulus values derived from it may not be meaningful. Cognitive algebra can be helpful in selecting a model for stimulus measurement that has substantive significance.

The averaging model, in particular, has been supported in a number of substantive areas. Averaging theory specifies conditions that are needed to obtain additivity and conditions that cause deviations from additivity. It thus provides a substantive base from which to assess appropriateness of optimal scaling with an additivity criterion. Moreover, approximate methods may be sufficient for some measurement problems. The averaging model is approximately additive when set size is constant and differential weighting is not too great, in which case bias introduced by transformation to additivity may not be serious. In this way, averaging theory may provide a theoretical foundation for additivity analysis.

Optimal scaling is less demanding than cognitive algebra. Markedly greater constraints are needed to establish a model than to use it for estimation. This was noted by Weiss and Anderson (1972), who found that a 5 × 5 design without replication, which is far too small to give serious support to an adding rule, provided sufficient constraint to recover the original stimulus and response metrics from the rank orders alone (see Figure 5.1). Of course, the validity of these estimated metrics rested on the validity of the model, which was established in prior analyses. As this example illustrates, cognitive algebra may justify substantive use of optimal scaling with rank data and other nonlinear response measures.

Further Work. From the standpoint of cognitive algebra, monotone analysis presents many statistical problems. One need is for computer programs that can handle nonadditive models, especially the averaging model. More information on power is also necessary. Another major need concerns estimation, both of weights and scale values. Some considerations that bear on bias and reliability of estimates have appeared throughout this chapter, but systematic study is needed.

A different direction lies in the study of stimulus integration in animal behavior and physiological psychology (Anderson, 1978a). Many investigators have speculated about the operation of algebraic rules of behavior, but the requisite measurement problems have not been resolved.

Monotone analysis with two-operation models may be helpful in these areas.

NOTES

5a. Monotone analysis automatically generalizes any integration model in an obvious way. For example, the two-factor adding model

$$R_{ij} = s_{Ai} + s_{Bj}$$

becomes

$$R_{ij} = \mathbf{M}[s_{Ai} + s_{Bj}],$$

where $\mathbf{M}$ is an arbitrary one-to-one monotone transformation. Similarly, if $\mathbf{I}$ is any integration rule for three variables, the model

$$R_{ijk} = \mathbf{I}(s_{Ai}, s_{Bj}, s_{Ck})$$

becomes

$$R_{ijk} = \mathbf{M}[\mathbf{I}(s_{Ai}, s_{Bj}, s_{Ck})].$$

These generalized models are not necessarily new models, of course, for they form a monotonically equivalent class. There is a tradeoff between $\mathbf{M}$ and $\mathbf{I}$, as noted in Section 5.9, and one model form may be preferred for simplicity. In addition, various restrictions on $\mathbf{M}$ and $\mathbf{I}$ may be operative, as discussed in Section 5.9.

5.2a. These acronyms are as follows. FUNPOT = FUNctional measurement with POlynomial Transformation. MONANOVA = MONotone ANalysis Of VAriance. ADDALS = ADDitivity analysis of Alternating Least Squares.

5.2b. The statistical analysis of the polynomial response scaling method, including the simplifying orthogonal decomposition of the interaction, was independently suggested by Edward Alf (personal communication, September, 1969).

5.2c. Additivity analysis and scaling of categorical response data can also be done using the canonical correlation program in the UCLA Biomedical P-series (Jennrich, 1977). This approach may be called *Fisher nominal scaling* after Fisher (1938, 1958), who introduced it.

5.2d. A proper test of fit depends on comparison of systematic discrepancies from the model with random discrepancies (error variability). The stress statistic does not separate these two sources of discrepancy—it lumps them together. Moreover, stress seems to be determined primarily by error variability, at least for the algebraic models under consideration, which makes it a poor index of systematic discrepancies. Stress also depends on the number of replications, the number of levels of each factor, and even on the closeness of spacing of the levels, all of which are determined by arbitrary choice of the investigator and are unrelated to the validity of the model. For these reasons, among others, stress values have very limited value in model analysis (see also Section 4.1).

5.3a. Problems of goodness of fit and power have also been discussed by Budescu and Wallsten (1979), who write from a background in conjoint measurement. Many of their points are well taken, but one of their main recommendations seems doubtful, namely, the use of normal score transformations; these transformations are based on nonessential statistical properties instead of the essential property of algebraic structure.

As Budescu and Wallsten (1979) say, "The uniqueness of FM [functional measurement] is in its realization that the hypothesized integration function could itself be used as the base and frame for scaling subjective values [p. 307]." Accordingly, the algebraic structure of the integration function is the sole criterion for monotone transformation, regardless of normality and other statistical properties.

Budescu and Wallsten are certainly justified in their concern with maintaining a proper significance level and obtaining adequate power. However, the methods of this chapter seem able to handle these problems in a practically effective way. If the assumptions of analysis of variance are not met, distribution-free tests may be used. The problem of power, which is more serious, is considered in Section 5.6.

5.3b. Krantz, Luce, Suppes, and Tversky (1971) suggested that standard analysis of variance could be applied to supplement the monotone transformation. With several scores in each cell, the transformation would be chosen to maximize additivity in the matrix of cell means. "The standard test for the significance of the interaction may, then, be used to test for the additivity of the data [p. 435]." The difficulty with this suggestion is that the transformed scores are all intercorrelated through their dependence on the same transformation, so the analysis of variance test is not valid. Weiss and Anderson (1972) found the same problem in an initial application of functional measurement to rank-order data. Following that, it was recognized that the replications method could provide a general error theory for monotone or nonmetric ordinal analysis (Anderson, 1975b; Leon & Anderson, 1974).

5.4a. The term *ordinal* is used here, as in mathematical measurement theory, to refer to qualitative analyses based on greater-than–less-than comparisons. *Monotone* analysis includes ordinal analysis as well as numerical analyses based on monotone transformation procedures. The term *scale free* may refer to ordinal tests or, as noted in the introduction to this chapter, to the response measure produced by monotone transformation with a valid model as the scaling frame, that is, to *fundamental* measurement.

5.4b. Many statistical niceties arise in making these ordinal tests. In the application of Dunnett's test to Table 5.2, for example, it would be reasonable to omit the top and bottom rows on the expectation that any crossover would appear in the middle range. This would increase power by the generally useful tactic of making a priori hypotheses as specific as prior information warrants. Strictly speaking, moreover, although not necessary in this case, the significance level for both separate tests would have to be adjusted to maintain a desired experimentwise significance level.

To complete this illustration of parametric multiple comparisons for ordinal tests, Tukey's HSD test was also applied to the complete set of 15 condition means. Error variance was taken as the average of the values listed for the Low and High photographs. All four critical differences in Table 5.2 remained significant.

The assumptions of normality and equal variance might be questionable in certain applications and would certainly need scrutiny in any attempt to employ multiple comparisons in a general way to establish, rather than reject, models. Moreover, repeated measurements designs and individual subject designs require somewhat different considerations. These and many other statistical problems need careful study.

5.4c. Parametric tests utilize metric information in the observable response measure without regard to its scale type, that is, without regard to the relation between the observable response and the underlying subjective response. At issue is the null hypothesis that a given pair of true means is equal. If the underlying response distributions have the same shape, as is generally required by distribution-free and parametric tests alike, then the observed response distributions will also have the same shape if the null hypothesis is true, regardless of the relation between the observed and underlying response. Hence the statistical test on the observed response provides a valid test of the null hypothesis. The parametric tests assume that the distributions of observable responses are normal with equal variance, but these statistical conditions can be assessed in the observed data and are logically independent of scale type (Section 1.1.9).

5.4d. Multiple comparisons procedures based on the standard Kruskal–Wallis and Friedman rank tests have the disadvantage that the test statistic for two conditions depends not only on the data for those two conditions but also on the data for the other conditions, although they are irrelevant to the given test. The Steel–Dwass and Nemenyi tests do not suffer from this problem, as noted in the cited references.

5.4e. A practical disadvantage of distribution-free tests arises in attempting to utilize all the data. The data actually analyzed were from the first replication for the less extreme of the two photographs at each value level, a conservative test that uses only part of the data. Data from both replications for each subject could presumably be pooled by taking their midpoint. However, pooling data from both photographs seems problematical because real differences between photographs must be expected. Parametric tests make pooling easy for both types of replications. The clearcut outcome in this test reflects the very strong crossovers in this experiment and should not be generally expected. It should be added that this signed-ranks test is only approximate and not strictly distribution-free (Hollander & Wolfe, 1973, p. 172).

5.4f. To disprove the additive model is no great empirical accomplishment and of itself confers little confidence on any other model. The crossovers of Table 5.2 are qualitatively consistent with an averaging-theoretical rationale and point to the operation of an averaging process. But the qualitative test is not adequate to establish the averaging model as a quantitative description. In general, the kinds of designs and analyses needed to establish a model differ from those that suffice to rule it out (see also Sections 4.2.3 and F2.3).

5.4g. Any investigator utilizes background knowledge in an attempt to select stimulus levels in some sensible way, for example, to cover some reasonable operating range at roughly equal intervals. In loudness studies, for example, equal dB spacing would be preferable to equal intensity spacing but not as good as equal spacing on the functional scale (Carterette & Anderson, 1979). This role of background knowledge is so obvious that it may not seem to need comment, but it deserves careful attention in the design stage.

The role of background knowledge in design is epistemologically interesting, for background knowledge is central in the inductive approach to measurement theory (Section F1.8.1). Here it may be noted that the use of background information about metric properties of the stimuli typically goes beyond rank orders to introduce supraordinal information. Although the importance of this supraordinal component may not be explicitly recognized, it shows that truly ordinal tests are not only rare but are generally to be avoided.

5.4h. This weakness of ordinal tests in establishing models also appears in the scale-free (ordinal) tests employed by Birnbaum (1974a, 1978). In a relevant instance, Birnbaum (1974a) studied person perception with the adding–subtracting model mentioned in Section 3.2. This model allows scale-free tests that indicated the adding and subtracting operations could not both be correct.

This outcome, of course, does not indicate which—if either—of the two operations is correct. Contrary to Birnbaum's claims, therefore, these tests are not scale-free tests of the adding model itself.

Previous scale-free tests had already ruled out the adding model, but these tests had a stronger logic that is illustrated in the text (e.g., Table 5.2). This ordinal approach had also shown that the constant-weight averaging model could not be the general case, but that differential weighting must be expected (e.g., Oden & Anderson, 1971; see Figure 6.1 and Table F2.5). However, the falsity of the adding model does not mean that the subtracting model may be assumed correct. Indeed, Birnbaum's (1974a) data appear to provide no basis for ruling out the constant-weight averaging model or even the adding model.

In an attempt to resolve this uncertainty, monotone transformation was applied to make the data parallel and obey the subtracting rule. This approach is only justified if the subtracting rule is valid, a question that faces the twin difficulties of goodness of fit and power.

As to goodness of fit, no proper test of the transformed data was presented. Percentage of variance accounted for, mean square error, and similar statistics are not proper tests of fit for the reasons given in Section 4.1 on weak inference. Accordingly, the monotone transformation was only optimal scaling, which is subject to the criticism by Krantz and Tversky (1971) and others that are cited in the text: Without a proper test of goodness of fit, the subtracting model is only presumed to be true.

The problem of power is also acute because the monotone transformation treated the data as a two-factor design with a single score per cell. This level of constraint seems inadequate to prevent invalid transformation, as shown by the results of Section 5.6. Monotone analysis has so much freedom to alter the data that it can readily distort the true model, incorrectly making nonsubtractive rules appear subtractive.

The seriousness of these twin problems of goodness of fit and power was noted by Weiss and Anderson (1972) and is discussed further in the text. This is no criticism of Birnbaum's attempts to establish the subtracting model, for only gradually have satisfactory methods become available for handling these problems. Nevertheless, the scale-free tests used by Birnbaum (1974a) allow only the weak conclusion that the adding and subtracting operations are not both correct. The further analyses rest on an essentially arbitrary assumption that the subtracting model was correct.

For similar reasons, the claim that these scale-free tests resolved the issue of model–scale ambiguity is not justified, even with the monotone transformation (Section F2.3.5). Later work on psychophysics has used the heuristic of stimulus invariance as well as two-operation models, which can provide additional constraint on monotone transformation (Sections 3.1–3.3). Moreover, as discussed in this chapter, satisfactory methods now appear to be available for handling the twin problems of goodness of fit and power.

It is desirable to establish the subtracting rule, but its present status is uncertain. Studies using metric tests have reported difficulties at the individual level, although these may reflect insufficient development of experimental procedure rather than flaws in the model (Carterette & Anderson, 1979; Shanteau & Anderson, 1969). However, the issue of ratio-versus-difference judgments, which has been the main focus of the subtracting model (Birnbaum, 1978), has been addressed with an either–or analysis; the possibility of a mixture of the two rules raises a power problem, as noted in Figure 5.3.

An additional difficulty with the scale-free tests used by Birnbaum is that they often involve judgments of difference between paired objects some of which are identical on one dimension. Subjects could discount the common dimension for these pairs, thereby violating the model. Evidence for partial discounting in an analogous task has been obtained by Anderson and Farkas (1975) and Farkas and Anderson (1979). Studies of choice tasks also suggest that difference judgments may involve processes other than in judgments of single objects (see Section 3.14 and Table F2.4).

5.5a. The idea of double cancellation as a necessary condition for additivity appears to be due to W. H. Kruskal (cited in Scheffé, 1959, p. 98). Its use as a sufficient condition appears in conjoint measurement, together with higher order cancellation conditions.

5.5b. The ordinal argument given by Sidowski and Anderson (1967) to show the validity of the interaction was also incorrect. However, an ordinal test can be applied as follows. In the observed rating data, the occupation of teacher was much preferred over accountant when the city was desirable, only slightly preferred when the city was undesirable. If the underlying process is truly additive, then a subject who prefers the occupation of teacher over accountant should do so equally for both cities. Reversals in occupation preference between the two cities should be symmetrical. If the observed interaction is real, however, the reversals should be asymmetrical. The data showed 27 reversals in one direction, 7 in the other, $\chi^2(1) = 9.03$, $p < .01$. The interaction is genuine, therefore, which verifies the original claim.

This kind of test is clearly not convenient or widely useful, in part because of the large number of subjects required for adequate power with binomial data. In the experiment in question, it should be noted, the linear nature of the rating scale was supported by previous work and also by the replicated parallelism for the three occupations other than teacher (an example of interlaced designs, Section 3.2). Hence the analysis of variance test is appropriate and no ordinal test is needed. This example emphasizes the importance and near-necessity of developing numerical response methods for the study of stimulus interaction and configural judgment.

5.5c. Very few crossovers or violations of conjoint axioms will be found with stimulus levels that are too few or too widely separated to provide effective constraint. Findings of very few violations perhaps speak less to the validity of the model than to lack of power in the design.

5.5d. Support for the conclusion that the monotone transformation approach is superior to the conjoint axiom approach for multilinear models is given by Emery and Barron (1979), who analyzed artificial, error-free data from a 4^3 design. Of 36 different cases of the model $A + BC$, the diagnostic procedures of Krantz and Tversky incorrectly diagnosed 21 to be of the form $A + B + C$, and none to be of the actual form $A + BC$. Optimal scaling using monotone transformation did substantially better, although its use rested on the assumption that one of three given models was correct and provided no basis for testing goodness of fit. Reanalysis of these examples using the two-phase method of the text would be of interest.

As a note on terminology, application by Emery and Barron (1979) of the terms *numerical conjoint measurement* or *conjoint scaling* to monotone transformation seems misleading. Their procedure "proceeds by assuming a *particular* composition rule and then scaling the data set to that model [p. 195]." and "always estimates scales consistent with an assumed model whether the model is valid or not [p. 204]." This is just optimal scaling. This seems exactly contrary to the spirit of conjoint measurement, for it is on exactly these grounds that the workers on conjoint measurement have criticized optimal scaling.

5.6a. All monotone transformations reported here were performed with the ADDALS 2 program of de Leeuw, Young, and Takane (1976). Stimulus and response variables were all treated as ordinal-continuous variables. Kruskal's least squares option was used, together with a between-replications comparison level. Special thanks are due Clifford A. Butzin for setting up this program for the UCSD computer. Thanks also to Joseph Kruskal, Yoshio Takane, and Forrest Young for their helpful comments on various aspects of monotone analysis.

All three-factor transformations were made using a three-factor adding model as the scaling frame. The two-phase transformations treated one pair of variables as a compound, single variable and accordingly used a two-factor adding model as the scaling frame. All data matrices were reduced to ranks before transformation, except when random error was added, in which case the numerical values were employed. A stress criterion of .0001 was often inadequate for error-free data, leaving clear nonparallelism that could be eliminated with a more stringent criterion. Accordingly, most of the work used a convergence criterion of .000001.

The two-phase transformation of the model $A(B + C)$, which is based on the two-factor adding model $(A \circledast B) + (A \circledast C)$, deserves a note. For two levels of A, this was treated as a factorial design with $2b$ rows and $2c$ columns. The upper left $b \times c$ subdesign consisted of the data for the first level of A; the lower right $b \times c$ subdesign consisted of the data for the second level of A; the upper right and lower left $b \times c$ subdesigns were empty. Two partial orders were used in ADDALS for each stimulus variable, one for each half of the total design. Convergence was slow.

5.6b. Inability of two-factor design to prevent unwarranted transformation to additivity has become a problem in psychophysics, in which recent work has placed increasing reliance on monotone transformation without recognition of its limitations. Empirical studies reported in Carterette and Anderson (1979, pp. 275–276) agree with the artificial examples presented in the text.

5.6c. An interesting statistical note is that certain sources of error variance can be reduced by smoothing the data with a monotone transformation. For illustration, an adding model was used to generate error-free data for a 6×6 design, with levels of A ranging from 1.1 to 6.6 in equal steps, and levels of B ranging from 1 to 6 in equal steps. Random replications were obtained by adding a random normal number with standard deviation .3 to each cell of the design. Each of eight independent replications was transformed separately with ADDALS, and a single analysis of variance was run on the group of eight replications. This process was repeated four times.

In the untransformed data, R (replications), $A \times R$, $B \times R$, $A \times B$, and $A \times B \times R$ all had about-equal mean squares, as they should since the listed interactions are zero except for random variability. In the transformed data, the mean squares for $A \times B$ and $A \times B \times R$ were about one-tenth the size of the mean squares for $A \times R$ and $B \times R$, which shows that the transformation smooths the data by selectively decreasing deviations from parallelism.

5.8a. The proof of the monotone additivity uniqueness theorem depends on two mild technical conditions. First, the ranges of x and y must include zero in order to apply a theorem of Pexider. Second, conditions are required on the domains and ranges of the various functions so that the needed inverse functions are well defined. Aczél requires that $\mathbf{M}_0$, g_0, and h_0 map some common domain D onto $(-\infty, \infty)$. Helmut Röhrl (personal communication) has pointed out that the same proof holds under the more general and more useful condition that $D_1 \cup D_2 \subseteq D_0$, where $D_0 = \mathbf{M}_0(D)$, $D_1 = g_0(D)$, and $D_2 = h_0(D)$.

5.8b. Empirical failure of a difference-plus-ratio model for length bisection is illustrated in Anderson (1977a; see also Carterette & Anderson, 1979, Note 1).

6

Importance Indexes and Self-Estimation Methodology

The first problem considered in this chapter concerns the concept of importance, especially in comparing importance of different kinds of information. Although widely used, the concept of importance has received little theoretical explication. Many applications seem unaware of the distinction between weight and magnitude indexes of importance; many use a confounded index. Generally, current methods for assessing importance seem inappropriate or applicable only under special conditions. The present discussion is intended to help clarify the concept of importance. It also shows how functional measurement can provide a theoretical base for conceptualizing and scaling importance.

The second problem concerns the method of self-estimation, in which subjects are asked to estimate their own weights or scale values. Self-estimation procedures have been widely used, especially in applications of multiattribute models to natural situations, but they have usually been taken for granted. Those investigators who have attempted to determine the validity of self-estimates, especially of weights, have nearly all reached pessimistic conclusions that self-estimation abilities are very poor. This poor showing, however, may reflect invalidity in the methods for assessing the self-estimates. The subjects may not be at fault, but rather the methods. The work on this problem within information integration theory, although not yet very extensive, presents a picture of cautious optimism about self-estimation capabilities.

6.1 Comparison and Measurement of Importance

Many investigators have felt the need to compare importance of two or more stimulus variables. Traditional scaling theory has given them little help; although enormous energy has been invested in the problem of scale value, the problem of importance or weight has been almost totally neglected. In the absence of a theoretical foundation, a variety of indexes of importance have been adopted. Some are appropriate in specific contexts, but virtually all have severe limitations. This section presents an overview of the concepts of importance and weight within the theoretical framework of information integration theory.[a]

Two different concepts of importance have been employed. One is a magnitude concept, the other is a weight concept. Both are useful, but they are not generally equivalent or interchangeable. The weight concept seems to be what is intended in most cases, but an inappropriate magnitude index is often used instead. The weight concept will be discussed first since it is needed to understand the various magnitude indexes.

6.1.1 WEIGHT DEFINITIONS OF IMPORTANCE

Weight definitions ordinarily represent importance as a parameter in some mathematical model, as in the ordinary regression model. A usual goal of a weight definition is to obtain a parameter that is independent of the scale range of the independent variable. The model analysis is necessary to this goal. Because the weights are model parameters, however, their validity depends on the validity of the model. Unless the model can be validated, weight estimates obtained from it may not be meaningful. Even when the model is valid, it is essential to allow for the identifiability or uniqueness properties of the estimation method.

Adding Model. Weights are not generally identifiable in adding or linear models because they are confounded with scale unit (Section 2.1.1). However, it is possible to compare weights when the scale unit is constant across stimulus variables. Although this case is special, it does have some important applications (see e.g., Section 3.6; Anderson, 1964c,d; Krantz, Luce, Suppes, & Tversky, 1971, pp. 303ff).

Averaging Model. The averaging model can provide weight estimates that are comparable even when the independent variables are qualitatively different and are unrelated to one another (Section 2.3). An interesting feature of this model is that the weight parameter is not tied to the stimulus dimension. Instead, it can have different values at different levels on the dimension and can also apply to stimulus factors that do not form a dimension in the usual sense. The averaging model thus provides a more useful concept of weight than the standard linear model, which assumes constant weighting along each dimension.

Regression Weights: Intercorrelation Problem. In ordinary regression models, the scale values of the predictor variables are given and the model analysis provides estimates of their weights. These regression weights have often been used to compare importance of different variables on the argument that, unlike the correlation coefficient, they are independent of the ranges of the variables.[a] Unfortunately, they have several properties that render them largely useless for this purpose.

The first problem pertains to the case in which the predictor variables are intercorrelated, the case that is typical of practical applications. In this case, each regression weight depends on the total set of predictor variables that is used. This problem has been considered in an important paper by Darlington (1968), who presents a striking example of a three-variable regression in which all pairwise correlations are nonnegative but the predictor with the highest single predictive power is forced by the other two variables to assume a zero weight (p. 166). This weight would even become negative with a slight change in the example. This result refers to the true parameter values; sampling error adds complications. As a consequence, regression weights for intercorrelated predictors are not very useful as measures of importance in any sense.

Darlington discusses five different measures of importance and concludes, "It would be better to simply concede that the notion of 'independent contribution to variance' has no meaning when predictor variables are intercorrelated [p. 169]." In what follows, therefore, intercorrelated predictors will not be considered further. Instead, regression weights will refer to single-variable regressions or to sets of independent predictors. Even in this case, regression weights are seldom proper indexes of importance.

Regression Weights: Scale Value Problem. The usual applications of regression analysis assume that the values of the predictor variables are known. If these values are not the true psychological values, then the weight estimates will be biased. This can be a serious problem in model analysis, especially when the weight estimate is used as an index of importance.

To illustrate, consider a regression analysis based on the two grayness scales of Figure 1.1. Suppose that the true regression is a linear function of the functional measurement scale of grayness with unit slope. If the magnitude estimation values are regressed on this scale, then the estimated weight for a linear regression will differ from unity. Moreover, its value will depend on the range of reflectance values employed. Over the lower half range of reflectance, the weight will be approximately .5; over the upper half range of reflectance, the weight will be approximately 10 times as large. Over the middle range, from 20% to 80%, the weight will be around 2.7. Unless the true psychological scale is known, therefore, the numerical value of the regression weight may mean very little.

Regression Weights: Prediction versus Understanding. In the usual applications, regression models are used as predictive equations. However, this predictive model is not generally appropriate for the study of psychological process. Instead, analysis as a structural, process model is usually needed. In general, the predictive model yields different weight values than the process model (Section 4.3.1).

Regression Weights: Unit Confounding. A seemingly unsolvable shortcoming of the regression model is that the weights are confounded with the unit of the scale. To illustrate, suppose that comfort is measured as a joint function of temperature and humidity and it is desired to say which is more important. The regression weight for temperature will change by a factor of five-ninths, depending on the arbitrary choice of Celsius or Fahrenheit scale. Temperature may seem to be more important than humidity with one scale, less important with the other. Since the unit of the physical temperature scale is arbitrary, this ambiguity is not resolvable (Anderson, 1974e, 1976b, p. 687).

This temperature–humidity example has used physical scales for simplicity. Exactly the same problem arises with psychological scales. In an integration model, it is true, the different stimulus variables are effectively reduced to common currency and so are comparable in principle. However, the linear model bypasses the comparison problem by confounding weight with scale unit (Section 2.1). This is an important advantage of the linear model, of course, but one that in general disallows psychologically meaningful comparisons of importance.

Standardized Regression Weights. The use of standardized regression weights is often proposed as a solution to the unit confounding problem. In principle, each value of a given predictor variable is divided by the standard deviation (or, more simply, the range) of values for that predictor. The regression is performed on these standardized scores.

Equivalently, the usual regression weights could be standardized by multiplying each by its standardization factor.

Two modes of standardization have been employed. In one, the standardization factor is computed from the scores of some subject population on the given predictor variable. Since between-individual variability on a given variable seems unrelated to the scale unit within any individual's head, this mode of standardization has no relevance to the present problem and will not be further considered.

In the other mode, the standardization factor is computed from the set of scale values of the given predictor variable. In the foregoing example, these would be the measured values of temperature and humidity. The attraction of standardization now becomes clear because it yields the same weight for Celsius and Fahrenheit scales and, indeed, for any other linearly related temperature scale. It might thus seem that the ambiguity of the unit can be resolved—if true linear scales of subjective value are available.

But if the investigator has any choice about the ranges of the predictor variables, then the standardization is arbitrary. Since the ordinary regression weight is itself independent of scale value range, the standardized weight perforce depends upon that range. This is clearly inappropriate.

If standardization is to be meaningful, therefore, it appears that the ranges of the variables cannot be subject to arbitrary choice. They must in some sense be natural. In psychophysical judgment, for example, it seems reasonable to speak of the total effective range of sensation in modalities such as loudness and taste. This maximal effective range can then be used as the standardization factor, even when only a part of the range is actually used.

This standardization, however, implicitly forces all stimulus variables to have the same effective range. In effect, all variables are reduced to a common percentile scale. This seems unsatisfactory to common sense, which tells us, for example, that loudness has a large sensory range but that taste has a small sensory range; and similarly that honesty has a larger subjective range than politeness. Of course, common sense could be wrong, as has been claimed in psychophysics by Teghtsoonian (1971). The issue is decidable because the averaging model can provide stimulus scales that have a common unit (Anderson, 1974a, p. 227).[b]

Self-Estimated Weights. An alternative approach is to ask the subject for direct numerical judgments of the weights. It would be desirable, as well as convenient, if subjects could make valid judgments of importance. Among other advantages, self-estimates are model-free. As yet, however, not much is known about the validity of self-estimated weights. This important problem is taken up in Section 6.2.

6.1.2 RELATIVE RANGE INDEX

In certain situations, the stimulus ranges of the variables may be required to be maximal, covering the entire practicable range; or the ranges may be required to be representative, covering some ecologically relevant range. Although the end points of the range may be somewhat ill defined, they may still be sufficiently definite for certain purposes. If the physical stimulus ranges of the variables are nonarbitrary, then it may be useful to compare importance of the variables in terms of the ranges of their effects on the actual behavior.

To illustrate the range concept, consider the experiment on meal preference shown in the left panel of Figure 6.1. In this graph, the main course appears to be considerably more important than the vegetable. This can be seen by comparing the vertical extent of a single curve, which represents the main course effect, to the vertical spread between the top and bottom curves, which represents the vegetable effect. In this experiment, both stimulus variables covered a reasonable ecological range. Within that frame of reference, it may be meaningful to speak of the relative importance of these variables in overall meal preference.

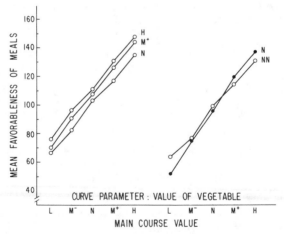

FIGURE 6.1. *Judgments of meals illustrate relative range index for comparing importance of main course and vegetable. Both panels show judgments of meals described by main course (horizontal axis) and vegetable (curve parameter). H, M⁺, N, M⁻, and L denote foods of high, moderately high, neutral, moderately low, and low taste value, respectively. Parallelism in left panel supports an adding-type model; crossover of one- and two-vegetable curves in right panel supports averaging over adding. (After Oden & Anderson, 1971.)*

Relative Range Index. The relative range index has the advantage of being defined in terms of the response, independent of stimulus scaling. Theoretical justification for comparing ranges can be obtained from the functional measurement analysis of the linear model (Section 2.1). Accordingly, it is assumed that the linear model holds and that the response scale is linear. For present purposes, the model is expressed in terms of the gross stimulus parameters since it is these that are being compared. For a two-way factorial design with I rows and J columns, the model is

$$R_{ij} = C_0 + \tilde{s}_{Ai} + \tilde{s}_{Bj} ,$$

and the marginal means are

$$\dot{R}_{i.} = C_0 + \tilde{s}_{Ai} + \tilde{s}_{B.} ,$$
$$\dot{R}_{.j} = C_0 + \tilde{s}_{A.} + \tilde{s}_{Bj} .$$

For simplicity, suppose that the levels of each stimulus variable are arranged in rank order on the basis of prior information. The range between the largest and smallest row means can then be written

$$\dot{R}_{I.} - \dot{R}_{1.} = C_0 + \tilde{s}_{AI} + \tilde{s}_{B.} - C_0 - \tilde{s}_{A1} - \tilde{s}_{B.}$$
$$= \tilde{s}_{AI} - \tilde{s}_{A1} .$$

Thus, the range of the row stimuli, $\tilde{s}_{AI} - \tilde{s}_{A1}$, is equal to the difference between the corresponding row means. By symmetry, a similar result holds for the column means

$$\dot{R}_{.J} - \dot{R}_{.1} = \tilde{s}_{BJ} - \tilde{s}_{B1} .$$

Since the effective stimulus ranges on the right sides of the last two equations are both expressed in terms of the response metric, they are directly comparable. Similar rationale applies to higher order factorial designs.

Although ranges can be compared directly in the response metric, a percentile index may be simpler. Let R_X be the range of variable X as already defined. Then the *relative range index* for X can be written

$$RRI_X = 100(R_X / \Sigma R_X) .$$

In this normalized form, the relative range indexes total 100 and are independent of the unit of the response scale. Furthermore, the ratio of two relative range indexes is independent of the number of other factors in the design.

It is worth noting that these range indexes do not require factorial design. To estimate the row range, it is sufficient to have one column in which the largest and smallest levels of the row stimulus are present. If this column is denoted by j, and the largest and smallest row stimuli are denoted by I and 1, then

$$R_{Ij} - R_{1j} = \bar{s}_{AI} - \bar{s}_{A1} .$$

The quantity on the left provides an unbiased estimate of the difference on the right. In this way, the range index can be applied fairly generally to nonfactorial design as well as to natural situations in which the stimulus attributes are not manipulated experimentally. It is, of course, essential that the linear model hold and that the response scale be linear.

Numerical Example. The meal judgments of Figure 6.1 are presented in Table 6.1 to illustrate calculations for the relative range index. From the row means, the vegetable range is $112 - 101 = 11$. The full main course range is $142 - 71 = 71$. The relative range index for the vegetable is then

$$RRI = 11/(11 + 71) = .13.$$

This value, however, seems inappropriately small. The two factors have different nominal ranges, from High to Neutral for vegetable, from High to Low for main course. If both factors are restricted to the High–Neutral range, as seems ecologically reasonable, then the relative importance of vegetables nearly doubles

$$RRI = 11/(11 + 35) = .24.$$

Within the context of this particular task, therefore, the main course seems to be about three times as important as a single vegetable.

This example provides a good illustration of the meaning and limitations of the range index. The High food items included the best that one normally gets, so the upper end of the range is reasonably well defined.

TABLE 6.1
Mean Preference Values of Meals

	Main course					
Vegetable	L	M$^-$	N	M$^+$	H	Mean
H	76	97	111	130	148	112
M$^+$	70	91	107	126	144	108
N	67	82	103	117	134	101
Mean	71	90	107	124	142	—

SOURCE: After Oden and Anderson (1971).
NOTE: Cell entries are preference values of meals defined by main course and vegetable.

The Neutral items were those prerated as neither liked nor disliked. These seem to provide an ecologically reasonable lower end to the range, one that is presumptively comparable between main course and vegetable. It is evident, however, that even in this case, the ends of the ranges are somewhat arbitrary and somewhat indefinite. If the relative range index is to be used, therefore, the basis on which it is obtained should be made clear.

Two or three statistical aspects of the relative range index deserve mention. As already noted, a complete factorial design is not necessary. Indeed, the foregoing calculation requires only three meals. From the H row, the main course range is $148 - 111 = 37$. From the H column, the vegetable range is $148 - 134 = 14$. These three data points then yield

$$RRI = 14/(14 + 37) = .27.$$

This and other similar calculations are equivalent, except for response variability, by virtue of the parallelism property of linear models.

An advantage of the relative range index is that it is independent of the number of factors in the design. If a salad factor is added to the meal, then the ranges of main course and vegetable will change, but their ratio will remain the same.[a]

Comments. Since the relative range index is calculated in terms of the response, it has the desirable property of being independent of any stimulus scaling. The range is defined as a difference in gross stimulus values, but these are the functional values obtained from the model analysis. As a consequence, of course, the relative range index is not theory-free. Unless the linear model holds, the index may not be very meaningful.

This limitation is shown clearly in the right panel of Figure 6.1. Although these two vegetable curves have nearly identical mean values, it is incorrect to conclude that the vegetable variable had zero effect. Because of the nonparallelism, a different vegetable effect is obtained from each column (main course) of the design. In practice, some real nonparallelism might be tolerated, but this example illustrates the need for substantive theory in any use of the relative range index. In the meals example, it should be noted, the averaging model can provide a theoretically appropriate index of weight.

Finally, it should be re-emphasized that range indexes are always arbitrary in that they depend on arbitrary choice of stimulus range. Keeney and Raiffa (1976), making this same point about a similar concept of scaling constant in multiattribute decision theory, state, "This may be overemphasizing the point that scaling constants *do not* indicate the relative importance of attributes, but because this misinterpretation is so common, we thought a little overindulgence might be in order [p. 273]." An arbitrary convention about stimulus range may be appropriate in certain situations, as illustrated in the meals example. Such conventions can be useful, but they are not substantive phenomena.

It may be added that many applications of multiattribute models seem to require a weight concept, not a magnitude concept. These applications involve tradeoffs in which some amount of one attribute is given up, or traded off, in return for some amount of another attribute. Tradeoff coefficients are intended to indicate how much of one attribute must be given up for a unit increment in another attribute. For this purpose, the weights of averaging theory seem appropriate.

Scaling constants and standardized weights, although arbitrary from the standpoint of substantive theory, need not be arbitrary from the standpoint of common sense. Their practical usefulness need not be doubted, especially in utilizing information in objective stimulus metrics. However, these indexes can no doubt be improved by relating them to substantive theory. Averaging theory, where it applies, offers one way to seek improvements in importance indexes.

6.1.3 OTHER MAGNITUDE DEFINITIONS OF IMPORTANCE

A major motivation for using magnitude definitions of importance is the felt need to obtain a simple index that goes beyond mere tests of significance. Unfortunately, these indexes seldom fulfill their promise. Most lead to merely verbal conclusions without substantive content.

The nature of magnitude definitions has already appeared in the previous discussion of the range index. These definitions do not attempt to separate weight from scale value, as separation would be inappropriate for their proper purpose. Instead, they attempt to represent importance directly in terms of the overt response. All these definitions are arbitrary, therefore, in that they depend on arbitrary choice of stimulus range. Each of the following three indexes suffers additional disadvantages.

Significance Level. Since significance level or p-value of the main effect of any variable depends on the range of that variable, it is subject to the range problem already noted. Since it also depends on sample size and error variance, it may well be smaller for the more important variable. And since it is calculated on the null hypothesis that the true effect is zero, it is logically irrelevant to measuring the size of nonzero effects. Although p-values are sometimes useful in an informal, ad hoc way, they have little merit as magnitude measures of importance.

Correlation Coefficient. The ordinary correlation coefficient provides a magnitude index of the strength of association between two variables. However, the correlation depends not only on the ranges of the two variables but also on their reliabilities. Accordingly, valid comparisons of two correlations are possible only under very special circumstances (see Section 7.9).

Percentage of Variance Accounted For. Percentage of variance indexes are discussed in standard statistics texts, and much attention has been devoted to developing formulas for various experimental designs. The range problem for this index can be illustrated with the temperature–humidity example. Suppose that two investigators used the same range of humidity but different ranges of temperature. Obviously, the two could reach opposite conclusions about the relative importance of temperature and humidity. Relative importance could vary from 0%, for a very small range of temperature, to 100%, for a very large range of temperature. This arbitrariness holds fairly often, so the percentage of variance statistic is often empty of substantive content.

The percentage of variance index has the further drawback of depending on the spacing of the stimulus levels within the range. A variable with a large effective range could be made to have an arbitrarily small percentage of variance index by choosing an arbitrarily large number of levels at the mean value of the range. Because of this arbitrary characteristic, the variable with the larger true range can easily yield a smaller percentage of variance index.[a]

It can be instructive to compare the proportion of systematic to error variance; this may be chasteningly low even when the results are highly significant. Beyond that, the percentage of variance statistic can occasionally be useful in an informal, ad hoc way. However, it carries the ever-present danger of making arbitrary statements seem like substantive conclusions.

Choice Importance Index. Choice tasks may involve a different concept of importance from that which has so far been considered. An attribute or dimension on which two objects are equal seems intuitively to have zero importance in the choice between them—even though it may be the most important attribute in the value of each separate object. This suggests that felt importance of any attribute in the choice process may be a direct function of the value difference between the objects on that attribute.

Because choices are common, it may be useful to consider developing an index for choice importance. An obvious candidate may be obtained by letting D_X be the magnitude of the value difference on attribute X and expressing the choice importance, CI_X, in relative form as

$$CI_X = 100w_X D_X / \Sigma w_X D_X.$$

The weight parameters allow for attentional factors as well as for importance weighting on the value scales.

Choice importance, as distinct from value importance, may deserve closer study. Of special concern is the likelihood that certain judgment–decision tasks involve a confounding of choice importance and value importance.[b]

6.1.4 EXAMPLES OF INVALID COMPARISONS OF IMPORTANCE

Comparisons of importance abound in the literature, but nearly all rest on invalid methods. Some specific examples will be considered here to illustrate some common pitfalls.

Arbitrary weights may be appropriate and useful for certain purposes. A prime example is the use of regression equations for predictive purposes. The fact that the weights are not comparable across qualitatively different variables does not affect predictive power. On the contrary; it is a great advantage of multiple regression that it does not require comparable weights.

Arbitrary weights may also allow valid comparisons within a single variable. For example, suppose that attention to some stimulus variable varies as a function of processing load and that this attentional factor is represented as a weight parameter in a regression equation. If the stimulus values remain constant, then the weights are comparable. Effects of different processing loads could thus be compared with no more than a monotone scale of weight.

But the situation is different when two variables are to be compared. Both weights must then be measured on ratio scales with a common unit. This point has already been discussed; it is illustrated in the following examples.

Personal Injury versus Property Damage. Studies of moral judgment frequently raise a question about the relative importance of two factors. In a typical study, the investigators concluded that children of all ages considered personal injury more worthy of condemnation than property damage. This conclusion seems so right that its relation to the design and data may escape scrutiny.

In the cited experiment, subjects were told two little stories about children who had done some harm and said which child should be punished more. Both story children were playing ball in the house, contrary to mother's orders. Upon throwing the ball into the air without specific harmful intent, one story child gave its sibling a bloody nose while the other broke its sibling's favorite record. Some 70% of the subjects considered personal injury to be more deserving of punishment.

No conclusion is possible from this result. The subject's response obviously depends on the experimenter's arbitrary choice of levels of damage. The effect could readily be reversed by increasing the amount of property damage or by decreasing the degree of personal injury (see, e.g., results by Leon, 1980). Since neither amount of injury nor damage have definite upper bounds, the relative range index is not appropriate. The cited conclusion seems intuitively reasonable, of course, and could perhaps be established using the qualitative scheme described in Section 2.3.3.[a]

Negativity Effect. A number of investigators have attempted to show that negative stimuli have greater effect than positive stimuli (Section F4.4.2). To demonstrate such negativity effects may seem straightforward. For example, responses could be obtained for a neutral stimulus, first by itself, then combined with a positive stimulus and with a negative stimulus. The positive or negative stimulus would be taken as more important according to whether it produced the greater shift in response from the neutral stimulus.

But this simple test is evidently inadequate to the true sense of the question. No one would doubt that a very negative stimulus would produce more change than a slightly positive stimulus, or vice versa. To be meaningful, the test must refer to the importance of the stimulus as distinct from its scale value.

To resolve this difficulty, various attempts have been made to select positive and negative stimuli that are equal and opposite in value. Most of these attempts have been plausible, but there is no way to determine whether they succeeded. For example, preliminary ratings have been used to select positive and negative stimuli equidistant from a neutral point. To be effective, this requires that the rating scale be linear and that the nominal neutral point be the true zero, preconditions that have been essentially ignored. Because of such measurement problems, most of the work on negativity and similar effects is difficult to interpret.

Actually, attempting to match positive and negative scale values is probably not a good idea, even assuming that the stimulus scaling problem could be solved (see also Section 7.7). Construction of paragraphs of equal and opposite value, for example, could be an extremely laborious trial of errors. Moreover, if weight varies with scale value, then it is inadequate to study just two points on the scale. Model analysis, when applicable, can provide a more penetrating and more flexible analysis than is possible with the more common approach.

Ill-Defined Weights. In a study of conflict over goals among members of an educational research institute, a multiple regression equation was used to measure relative amount of importance that each individual member placed on each of six goals or activities of the institute (e.g., advising, collecting data, etc.). Each member judged overall desirability of various profiles of activity for hypothetical institutes. In each profile, the levels of the six activities were presented on a scale of 1–10, but these levels were not further defined. These arbitrary numbers were used as stimulus values in a regression equation, and the resulting regression weights were presented to the members as a description of their policies.

The methodology employed in this research relies on arbitrary stimulus scales that are assumed to be common across individuals. Furthermore, the arbitrary scaling means that the regression weights are subject to all the problems previously listed. Scale values are therefore confounded with weights, and the meaning of the regression weights themselves is obscure.[b] Comparisons across individuals or across goal dimensions are thus uncertain.

An important aspect of this investigation was the use of subsequent bargaining sessions to reach a compromise set of weights. Reaching agreement can have great social usefulness even if the weights are not well defined. For this purpose, however, self-estimated weights (Section 6.2) would probably be more effective, and certainly simpler and more meaningful.

Causal versus Noncausal Cues. A subtle misuse of correlation arose in a test of the hypothesis that the subjective causal relation between a stimulus cue and the dimension of judgment affects the importance of the cue. Subjects judged expected grade point average (GPA) for hypothetical students who were characterized by two numerical stimulus cues. The first cue was either IQ score, which has a clear causal relation to GPA or weekly income in dollars, which has a much less definite causal relation. These two cue dimensions were chosen because the same numerical stimulus values could be assigned to each. The second cue was either hours of study per week or miles between home and campus, again showing strong and weak causal relations to GPA. For these two cue dimensions also, the same numerical values were assigned. Different subjects received the four possible combinations of first and second cues and predicted GPA for 10 hypothetical students.

The dependent measure was the correlation between the given cue values and the predicted GPA. Mean correlations were .78 for the causal cue, .47 for the noncausal cue. It was concluded that subjects depended more on causally significant cues than on noncausal cues.

This conclusion does not follow from the data. It rests on the implicit assumption that the specified numerical cue values are equivalent to their subjective values (or, more technically, that it is valid to compare standardized regression weights of the causal and noncausal cues). That each pair of cues had equal numerical, objective values is arbitrary and irrelevant. To see this, suppose that study time had been specified not as the given number of hours per week, but as the same number of minutes per week (or, more realistically, as 16 hours plus the same number of minutes). With a range of only 6–27 minutes, the time variable would have very little effect. Hence the very same analysis would show a very small correlation for study time and lead to the opposite conclusion. No one would doubt the cited conclusion, to be sure, but it cannot be verified with the design and analysis that were used.

In this case, integration theory can provide a correct analysis. The intuitive causal relation between any cue and the judgment dimension is part of the valuation operation that determines the weight parameter. The cue integration task itself is one to which averaging theory has been shown to apply. Accordingly, the methods of Section 2.3 can be used to obtain valid comparisons of the importance of causal and noncausal cues. The simplest way would use the qualitative scheme for estimating weights of Section 2.3.3.

Nonverbal Cues. Assessment of relative importance of diverse cues, especially of face and voice, has been a focal problem in the field of nonverbal cues. In one study of face–voice combinations, the stimuli were women's faces, photographed in attempts to use facial expressions to communicate three feelings—liking, neutrality, or dislike—toward another person. These photographs were paired with recorded voices of women attempting to say *maybe* to communicate liking, neutrality, or dislike toward an imaginary listener. Subjects rated these face–voice combinations on a 7-step scale of likableness.

To assess relative importance, the three levels of each factor were arbitrarily assigned values of −1, 0, and +1, and the marginal means of the design were regressed on these scale values to obtain regression weights of 1.50 and 1.03 for face and voice, respectively. These regression weights were treated as relative importance of face and voice. Relative importance of voice and verbal content was assessed with data from another study in which single words (e.g., *thanks, maybe, terrible*) were read in positive, neutral, or negative tones. These regression weights led to the model

Liking = .07 Verbal content + .38 Vocal tone + .55 Facial expression.

The investigator claimed that these relative importance values were general, not only for liking but for other feeling dimensions as well. This conclusion has had considerable currency in the field of nonverbal cues.

It should be clear that no conclusion can be drawn from these data. The regression coefficients are not proper weight parameters because they depend on the arbitrary scaling of the cue variables. Neither are they satisfactory magnitude measures, because they depend on arbitrary selection of the cues. Even within these experiments, the relative effect of verbal content could be greatly increased by changing from single words to longer passages. Because the selection of cue levels was arbitrary, so too is the conclusion.[c]

It may be added that the question of relative importance does not seem fruitful in itself. Although naturally attractive to investigators who desired to emphasize the role of nonverbal cues, this question is not meaningful apart from a theory of cue integration. Attempts to answer a theoretical question with common sense formulations have led to data and conclusions that do not seem meaningful. A number of investigators have stressed the importance of cue integration and this problem promises to be more productive (e.g., Bugental, 1974; Frijda, 1969; Lampel & Anderson, 1968). Even here, however, the relative importance question has had harmful effects, as illustrated by the relative shift ratio considered in the next subsection.

Relative Shift Ratio.   To assess the relative importance of two cues does not seem generally possible at a purely empirical level. The necessity for a theoretical base is brought out by analysis of the following relative shift ratio. This index was apparently first proposed by Frijda (1969) to assess the relative importance of facial and contextual cues on judgment of emotions.

Let A and B be the two cues, R_A and R_B the response to each single cue, and R_{AB} the response to the two together. The relative shift index is defined in terms of observed responses as

$$| R_{AB} - R_A | / | R_{AB} - R_B |.$$

At face value, this index seems reasonable. If A and B have equal importance, R_{AB} should seemingly lie halfway between R_A and R_B, so the index would equal 1. The more A increases in importance, the closer

R_{AB} approaches R_A and the lower the value of the index. Thus, the index might seem to provide a model-free measure of relative importance.[d]

However, the relative shift index is not model-free. On the contrary, its meaning depends on the integration rule for the two cues. The algebraic derivations for the adding and averaging rules are simple, so only the results are given here (Anderson, 1976d). If the adding rule holds (Eq. [1b] of Chapter 2), then the theoretical value of the index equals the ratio of the gross stimulus parameters, $\bar{s}_B/\bar{s}_A$. Since this depends on the scale values, it is not generally a proper measure of importance. It could, of course, be used as a magnitude index—if the adding model holds.

If the averaging model holds, then the index has a more complicated form, namely

$$w_B(w_0 + w_B)|w_0(s_B - I_0) + w_A(s_B - s_A)|$$
$$\div\ w_A(w_0 + w_A)|w_0(s_A - I_0) + w_B(s_A - s_B)|.$$

This also depends on the scale values, and numerical examples show that it is not even a monotone index of relative importance.

One special case is notable. If there is no initial impression, so that $w_0 = 0$, then the above expression reduces to the ratio of the weights, w_B/w_A. This is a proper index of importance.

This special case also makes clear that the relative shift ratio cannot be considered a model-free magnitude index of relative importance. The ratio constitutes a proper magnitude index if the adding model is valid; it then reduces to the ratio of the gross stimulus parameters, $\bar{s}_B/\bar{s}_A = w_B s_B/w_A s_A$, with sign ignored. But this ratio can yield opposite conclusions from the ratio w_B/w_A for the special case, depending on the magnitudes of the scale values. Something similar can happen in the averaging model even if w_0 is nonzero. Without knowledge about the operative integration rule, therefore, the relative shift ratio is not generally meaningful.

The foregoing approach is applicable to other proposed indexes of importance. One can usually analyze them similarly, by assessing them in terms of the adding and averaging models. It does not seem, however, that measurement of importance will be generally possible except within the context of some theoretical model.

6.2 Self-Estimated Parameters

A simple, attractive way to get parameter estimates is to ask the subject for them. If valid, such self-estimates would allow the use of the simplest experimental designs. Ideally, only one experimental condition or design cell would be needed to test a model. No less important, the self-estimated parameters would have substantive information that might not otherwise be obtainable. If a self-estimation methodology can be developed, therefore, it will provide an exceptionally useful tool. Such methods are essential for investigation in settings in which factorial-type design is difficult or impossible.

The main question about self-estimates concerns their validity. Subjects readily produce direct estimates of scale value and importance, but some way is needed to assess the validity of these estimates. In fact, self-estimates are subject to various biases that must be taken into account.

Cognitive algebra provides a validity criterion for assessing self-estimates. Where an algebraic model holds, the model-estimated parameters constitute a standard of comparison for the self-estimates. Moreover, the empirical studies show that subjects can use ratings as linear scales in many integration tasks. This work forms a promising basis for development of a self-estimation methodology. Not much is known about self-estimated parameters, however, and a number of problems need consideration.

6.2.1 VALIDATION OF SELF-ESTIMATED PARAMETERS

There are two main ways to assess validity of self-estimated parameters. Both rely on cognitive algebra, but in somewhat different ways.

Comparison of Self-Estimates with Functional Parameters. When both functional scales and self-estimates are available, the former provide a validational base for the latter. The first study of this kind obtained moderate differences between the two sets of estimates for preference judgments of foods (Shanteau & Anderson, 1969, pp. 321–323). However, later work in utility theory has yielded more promising results (Shanteau, 1970b, 1974). Shanteau used linear fan analysis to test the multiplying model

Subjective expected value = Subjective probability × Subjective value.

Subjects evaluated the worth of bets of the form, "_____ chance to win _____." The chances to win were specified by probability phrases listed in the upper half of Table 6.2. The lower half of the table lists the objects to be won.

Since the model did well in the test of goodness of fit, the marginal means of the factorial data table provide validated functional scales of both subjective probability and subjective value. Self-estimates for both classes of stimuli were obtained by ratings of the single stimuli. Both sets of estimates are listed in Table 6.2, where it can be seen that the self-estimates agree with the functional scaling. The importance of this out-

TABLE 6.2
Comparison of Functional and Self-Estimated Values of Subjective
Probability and Utility

	Functional value	Self-estimated value
Probability stimulus		
No chance	0	0
Unlikely	.19	.12
Not quite even	.47	.45
Better than even	.60	.59
Highly probable	.92	.90
Almost certain	.93	.92
Sure thing	1	1
Utility stimulus		
Nothing ($0)	0	0
Sandals	10.0	6.4
Camera	27.4	28.0
Radio	35.4	36.5
Suitcase	37.6	37.9
Bicycle	48.4	51.9
$75 cash	75	75

SOURCE: Data from J. Shanteau. Component processes in risky decision making. Journal of Experimental Psychology, 1974, *103*, 680–691. Copyright © 1974 by the American Psychological Association. Adapted by permission of the publisher and author.
NOTE: Values for first and last stimuli in each class set arbitrarily.

come is not that it validates the self-estimates, but that it provides validational support for the *method* whereby the self-estimates were obtained.

This comparison method provides a general basis for developing a self-estimation methodology. The magnitude and pattern of any discrepancies between the self-estimates and the functional scales can suggest improvements in the procedure for obtaining self-estimates. When good agreement is obtained, it provides confidence that the self-estimation method may be used alone. That is the desired end, for there are many situations in which factorial scaling is difficult or impossible.[a]

Joint Model–Parameter Validation. The other way to test self-estimated parameters is to employ them in the model analysis. If the model passes the test of goodness of fit, that provides simultaneous support for the validity of the self-estimates.

This method may be illustrated with the group discussion data of Figure 6.2. Each of three subjects received separate information about

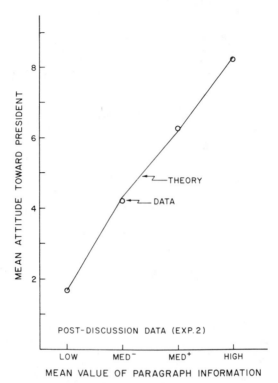

FIGURE 6.2. *Functional measurement test of multiattribute model for attitudes using self-estimated parameters. Open circles give observed attitudes toward United States presidents developed in group discussion. Solid line gives theoretical predictions from averaging model based on self-estimates of weight and scale value of other members in the group and of given stimulus information. Discrepancies from prediction not statistically significant, F(2, 45) = .25. (After Anderson & Graesser, 1976.)*

some United States president that they then discussed among themselves. Each subject made an overall attitudinal judgment about the president, based on the group discussion, and these data points are plotted in Figure 6.2. The subjects also made separate ratings of the scale values of the discussions of the other two group members and of the importance of the discussions in their own final judgments, together with similar ratings of themselves. These scale values and weights were substituted into the averaging model to obtain the theoretical predictions in Figure 6.2. The fit is good, and the differences between data and theory were not significant.[b] This agreement supports the averaging model for group discussion. More important for present purposes, this agreement also supports the validity of the self-estimated scale values and weights.

A more striking illustration of this approach is shown in Figure 6.3,

reproduced here from Section F1.7.3. Female subjects rated photographs of seven males on date preference (solid curve) and made self-
estimates of probability of acceptance (dashed curve at top of each panel)
and of physical attractiveness (which provided the spacing of the males
on the horizontal axis). These two attributes were hypothesized to multiply, and this multiplying rule was used to generate predicted date
preferences (dotted curves). Agreement between predicted and observed is excellent for each of these three representative subjects despite
the marked individual differences among them (see Shanteau & Nagy,
1976, 1979).

The method of joint model–parameter validation is more generally
applicable than is comparison of self-estimates with functional parameters. In the cited study of group discussion, factorial design would have
been barely practicable. In the study of date judgments, the two
stimulus attributes were only indirectly controllable by experimental
manipulation. Without the use of self-estimated parameters, these
studies would have been difficult or impossible.

However, there are two strong disadvantages to using self-estimates

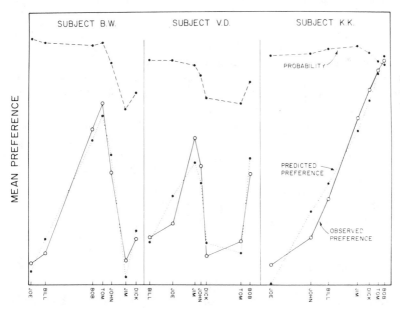

FIGURE 6.3. *Functional measurement test of multiattribute model for date-preference judgments*
using self-estimated parameters. Female subjects rate photographs of males on physical attractiveness
(horizontal axis), probability of acceptance (upper, dashed curve), and desirability as a date (solid
curve). Dotted curve gives theoretical predictions from Attractiveness × Probability model based on
self-estimated parameters. Note that the males have different rank order of attractiveness for different
females, as shown by their location on the horizontal axis. (After Shanteau & Nagy, 1976, 1979.)

directly in model analysis. The first is that correct statistical analysis can become rather complicated in order to allow for unreliability in the self-estimates and for scale adjustment parameters. Unless these problems have been thought through beforehand, the analysis may lack cogency and may even be impossible. For example, the most popular way of testing multiattribute models is almost guaranteed to produce systematic discrepancies from prediction even though the model is correct and the parameters are on linear scales (Section 4.3.6).

The other disadvantage is that the results may not be very informative when there are substantial discrepancies from prediction. In that case, the model, the self-estimates, and the linearity of the response scale are all in doubt. Discrepancies will then be generally difficult to interpret, especially without the patterning constraints of factorial design. Unless the self-estimation procedure is known to be adequate, therefore, this joint model–parameter method is mainly useful when the integration model and response scale are reasonably well established, as in the careful work of Shanteau and Nagy (1976, 1979). For developing and validating a self-estimation methodology, however, the comparison method seems generally preferable.

6.2.2 SELF-ESTIMATION OF SCALE VALUES

The need for a validational base for self-estimates of scale value is clear from the comparison of magnitude estimation and ratings in Section 1.1. Numerical judgments of sensory dimensions such as loudness and heaviness are presumptive scale values. Judgments of likableness of a person and other integrated responses may be viewed in the same way.[a] In the present context, therefore, the sharp difference between magnitude estimation and ordinary ratings re-emphasizes that self-estimates need more than face validity.

Of course, the success of the rating method in integration tasks is prima facie evidence that it can provide valid linear measures of self-estimated scale values. This does not avoid the need for validation, especially for unusual stimulus attributes or unusual dimensions of judgment. Nevertheless, previous work on integration tasks gives reason to expect that a fairly general method for self-estimation of scale values is within reach.

Two complications need to be kept in mind. The first is the obvious fact that even if the self-estimates are on true linear scales, the zero and unit may be different for different attribute dimensions. Zero and unit parameters would then be required to combine different dimensions (e.g., Sections 4.3.5 and 4.3.6).

The second complication is more subtle. According to averaging theory, the judgment of a single attribute is not generally its scale value, but rather a weighted average of that scale value and the prior attitude (see Section 2.3.4). When the equal-weight condition holds, prior attitude can be confounded with the zero and unit of the scale. The overt response can then be treated simply as a linear scale without considering prior attitude explicitly (e.g., Anderson & Graesser, 1976). The case of differential weighting has not been studied, but would be more complex. It would be desirable, therefore, to seek procedures that estimate the scale value itself.

Cognitive Structure. The importance of self-estimation may be emphasized by considering its role in measurement of cognitive structure. This may be treated as conditional judgment: Given certain information about some entity, judge that entity according to its location along some specified dimension or according to its membership in some category.

A simple example appears in the stereotypes. Given that a person is a doctor, nurse, or dentist, for example, judge the person on intelligence, annual income, probability of being female, and so forth. Such stereotype judgments represent a straightforward extension of the personality adjective task described in Section 1.2.1, and they are part of implicit personality theory (Sections 7.17, F1.8.3, and F4.1.8).

Category belongingness provides a second example. Given that an animal is a penguin, sparrow, or robin, for example, judge how well it belongs to the category of birds. As Oden (1977a,b; see Figure F1.15) has pointed out, integration theory provides a natural representation in terms of continuous variables of many concepts such as class belongingness and truth value that have been treated as all-or-none in the traditional normative view.

Such conditional judgments may be viewed as self-estimates, that is, as responses that index some stimulus value. The present approach provides a theoretical basis for obtaining valid numerical measures of such conditional judgments. Such judgments are in fact the basic data of integration theory, which are typically conditional on stimulus combinations from factorial designs.

Integration theory can provide a validational criterion even when the conditional judgments are of single stimuli or of stimulus combinations not in factorial design. Most important, perhaps, the rating methodology of Section 1.1 may be expected to provide true linear response measures for many such tasks, as noted in the previous subsection. In addition, the averaging and other integration rules can provide linear stimulus measures as validational criteria for the self-estimates.

Averaging theory brings out another aspect of the role of cognitive algebra in the study of conditional judgments. Given stimulus information S, the conditional judgment on dimension X may be written as an average of the given information and the prior information in the usual way as

$$R(X|S) = (ws + w_0 s_0)/(w + w_0).$$

When the averaging rule applies, therefore, conditional judgments may not be pure measures of the given information. This issue has been considered in the previous section and will not be pursued here. However, this result indicates that caution must be used in interpreting the response, for the face value meaning may not be entirely correct even in simple tasks.

6.2.3 SELF-ESTIMATION OF WEIGHTS

Earlier writers have generally concluded that people have little insight into the relative influence or importance of various pieces of information on their judgments. Studies reviewed by Slovic and Lichtenstein (1971) "all found serious discrepancies [p. 684]" between objective weights and subjective or self-estimated weights. Zeleny (1976) states, "Recent psychological studies indicate that an explicit importance-weighting process is unstable, suboptimal, and often arbitrary [p. 14]." In the same vein, Schmitt and Levine (1977) conclude, "Comparisons of objective and subjective weighting policies have consistently shown that statistical and subjective indices of judgment policy disagree [p. 16]." On the basis of these three evaluations, it might seem that there is little hope of obtaining a valid method for self-estimation of importance.

The fact is, however, that not one of the studies reviewed in the cited articles provided a valid criterion against which to compare the self-estimates. The most popular method compared self-estimates to weights obtained from regression equations. But regression weights have no validity as measures of psychological importance (Section 6.1). Despite the cited negative evidence, therefore, people may very well be able to self-estimate their weight parameters. The disagreement may reflect inadequacy of regression statistics, not of intuitive statistics. [a]

The quoted articles certainly make clear the necessity of a validity criterion for evaluation of the self-estimated weights. Integration theory can supply such a criterion, at least when the averaging model is applicable. Existing evidence shows some promise. Four studies have used some form of model–parameter validation. Of these, two have obtained mixed results (Anderson, Lindner, & Lopes, 1973; Farkas & Anderson, 1976) and two have obtained good results (Anderson & Alexander, 1971,

Figures 2–3; see also Figure F4.14; Anderson & Graesser, 1976; see Figure 6.2).

Only one study has compared self-estimated and functional weights. In Zalinski and Anderson (1977, in press), subjects judged their expected satisfaction from jobs defined by various levels of the four dimensions listed in Table 6.3, and also rated the importance of each dimension. These self-estimated weights are most appropriately compared to the functional weights obtained from the averaging model under the assumption that the three levels within each job dimension had equal weight. This comparison, given by the left and center columns of Table 6.3, shows moderate agreement.[b]

It seems more realistic, however, to allow unequal weights for the three levels within each job dimension. When this was done, the Low and High levels had substantially greater weight than the Average level, especially for the more important dimensions. Moreover, this differential-weight solution gives considerably larger values than the self-estimates, and the agreement is only monotone. The interpretation of these differential weight estimates is somewhat uncertain, however, in part because the self-estimates are not strictly comparable, since they were not obtained for the separate levels within each dimension and in part because of instability in the model-fitting for some individuals. At worst, however, this comparison demonstrates how alternative procedures for obtaining self-estimated weights can be evaluated.

One other approach is to study how self-estimated weights depend on various experimental variables. In Anderson (1964e), for example, subjects rated likableness of persons described by two, three, four, or six trait adjectives of homogeneous value and also rated the importance of each trait in their judgment.[c] Importance ratings showed an extremity

TABLE 6.3
Self-Estimated Weights Compared with Functional Weights

Job dimension	Weight estimates		
	Self-estimates	Equal weight	Differential weight
Management	1.00	1.00	1.00
Co-worker	1.68	1.53	2.36
Pay–promotion	1.99	2.11	3.43
Work enjoyment	2.28	2.72	5.67

SOURCE: After Zalinski and Anderson (1977, in press).
NOTE: Weight for Management dimension arbitrarily set equal to unity. All entries averaged over individual subjects. Entries in last column averaged over Lo, Ave, and Hi dimension levels.

effect; they were higher for more extreme adjectives, positive or negative, than for more neutral ones. In addition, importance judgments were essentially constant as a function of set size: Mean ratings were 15.9, 16.1, 15.8, and 15.6 for descriptions with two, three, four, and six adjectives, respectively.

Similar results have been obtained in subsequent work cited in Section F4.4.4, one graph of which is reproduced here as Figure 6.4. The left panel shows mean importance ratings as a function of adjective value in the personality adjective task. The bow shape represents an extremity effect with a positive–negative asymmetry. The same pattern appears for Conditions One and All, in which subjects judged only one or all of the adjectives in the description, respectively. The curves in the right panels are almost flat, independent of set size, indicating that subjects judge absolute rather than relative importance.

The extremity effect with personality adjectives in the two preceding experiments was also obtained in the attitude experiment of Figure 6.2 (see Anderson & Graesser, 1976, Table 2). This extremity effect in the importance ratings of the single stimuli is consistent with extremity effects that have been found in the overall judgment (Section F4.4.2). According to the averaging model, the former extremity effects will produce the latter.

For certain purposes, monotone scales of importance are adequate. Thus, the null hypothesis that importance ratings in Figure 6.4 are independent of number of adjectives in the description requires only a monotone scale. Self-estimated weights may thus be useful indexes for many experimental manipulations, as in studies of information salience or discounting. For exact model analysis, however, it is important to develop procedures that can yield linear or ratio scales of self-estimated weights.

6.2.4 SELF-ESTIMATION IN CONTEXT

Two different procedures can be used to obtain self-estimates. In the first, the component cues of any stimulus combination are presented individually and separately. In the second, the stimulus combination is presented as a whole, and each component cue is judged within that context. This second procedure is considered here.

Self-estimation in context has exceptional interest because it promises direct information on stimulus interaction. Inconsistency could cause the components to change in meaning and scale value. Inconsistency and redundancy both could cause the components to change in weight. Such interactions might be directly visible in the judgments of the components.

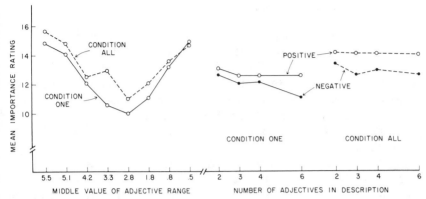

FIGURE 6.4. *Self-estimated importance of single adjectives contained in person descriptions. Bowing in left panel shows extremity effect, with rated importance least for adjectives in the neutral, middle range of value. Flat curves in right panel show that rated importance was largely independent of number of adjectives in description. Subjects in conditions One and All rated one and all the adjectives, respectively, in each description. (From N. H. Anderson, unpublished experiment, 1967.)*

Unfortunately, component judgments of scale value suffer from a substantial bias, as they are shifted from their normal value toward the overall value of the combination. This is the positive context effect noted in Section 1.1.5. This shift is not a true change in scale value, however, but a halo bias. The component seems to change value but does not really do so. Although this effect has only been studied in person perception, it is theoretically expected to hold in general. That restricts the usefulness of self-estimates of scale values in context.

Some use can still be made of component self-estimates of scale value. The evidence suggests that the halo bias obeys an averaging model, which provides a potential method of extracting the effective scale value. Under the equal weighting condition, in particular, the component estimates provide a linear function of true scale values, regardless of how the shift in component judgments is interpreted. This linear function constitutes a linear scale and will be adequate for some purposes. It was used in the cited study of group discussion, for example, in which the scale values were necessarily estimated in context.

Weight estimates, on the other hand, may be free of halo bias. In all the studies considered previously, the importance of individual components was estimated in context. No obvious signs of context effects were obtained, nor are any expected from the halo hypothesis. Although this information is far from adequate, it indicates a promising line of attack that deserves further study.

6.2.5 PREDICTION AND UNDERSTANDING

Any discussion of self-estimated parameters must take cognizance of the basic distinction between the two goals of prediction and understanding (Sections 4.3.1, F1.8.2). For practical prediction, it may not make any difference if the weight parameter is confounded with the scale unit. For practical prediction, approximate parameters may be entirely adequate. For practical applications of multiattribute models in particular, convenience may outweigh accuracy in obtaining self-estimates.

But the situation becomes quite different as soon as any attempt is made to go beyond bare prediction toward theoretical interpretation. The validity of the parameter estimates may then be crucial, as illustrated in the discussion of self-estimated weights. For this and other reasons discussed previously, it is important to work on developing a self-estimation methodology. That may be the most important current problem in the methodology of judgment theory.[a]

6.2.6 SELF-ESTIMATION AND CONSCIOUS KNOWLEDGE

The possibility of an effective self-estimation methodology has been challenged by the theoretical view of conscious knowledge proposed by Nisbett and Wilson (1977). In their view, people have little or no ability to report accurately on the effects of stimuli on their responses. Nisbett and Wilson refer to the literature on self-estimated importance cited earlier as the only area in which they found even meager accuracy of self-report. However, they denied that even this accuracy stemmed from private, introspective knowledge. Because of the importance of their view for self-estimation methodology, it requires separate consideration (see also Anderson, 1976d, Section 7.3.9, Self-perception).

Their theoretical position rests on the proposition that subjects are no more accurate than external observers in judging the influence of stimuli on their responses. As Nisbett and Bellows (1977) say in their experimental study of self-estimation capability, "The present analysis also leads to the expectation that observer predictions should be as accurate as subject reports. . . . Subjects gain little or nothing through private access to the operations of their own judgmental processes and base their reports exclusively on causal theories that are shared by observers [p. 615]."

If subjects cannot be more accurate than observers, their self-estimates cannot contain personal knowledge about their individual values. Since individual differences in value are often large, it would follow that subjects cannot know their own values. But this conclusion is phenomenologically false, for we are all aware that our tastes and opinions often differ from those of others. Accordingly, the experimental study by Nisbett and Bellows deserves careful scrutiny.

In this experiment, each subject judged one person, described by a 3-page job application folder in which physical appearance, academic credentials, a coffee-spilling incident during the alleged job interview, and two other stimulus variables were varied in a 2^5 design. The actual effects of each factor were taken as the differences between the two corresponding marginal means of this between-subject design. Subjects also rated how much each of the five factors influenced their responses on each of four judgment dimensions. Accuracy was defined as the correlation between these ratings and the actual effects. Similar ratings were made by observers who did not judge any applications but received only abbreviated descriptions of each stimulus factor.

From their analyses, Nisbett and Bellows concluded, "Subject reports about the effects of stimuli . . . bear little relation to the actual effects of the stimuli [p. 620]. . . . For the more subjective judgments, the accuracy of subject reports was nil and so was the accuracy of observer predictions [p. 621]. . . . Subject reports about the influence on their judgments were in general highly inaccurate [p. 622]," except for the intelligence cue, for which accuracy was attributed to public knowledge shared by the observers. If these conclusions were justified, they would virtually eliminate the possibility of a self-estimation methodology. Under scrutiny, however, it appears that the experimental design and the data analysis bear little relation to the conclusions.

The liking response illustrates one major problem in interpreting the results: None of the five stimulus variables had a significant effect on the overall judgment. Hence it was impossible for subjects' judgments of importance of the five stimulus variables to exhibit any accuracy; there was nothing to be accurate about. Much the same problem appeared in the other three response dimensions, for which only one of the five stimulus variables was significant. Almost necessarily, therefore, subject accuracy was nil and no greater than observer accuracy. This shortcoming should not be attributed to the subjects, however, because the experimental design and the data analysis were not adequate to assess any real self-estimation capabilities.

It is possible, of course, that Nisbett and Bellows are mainly correct in their basic claim that observers will be as accurate as subjects in judging the influence of stimuli on responses. This is a central issue for self-estimation methodology, for it would mean that individuals cannot reliably report on differences between their own values and weights and those of others. Fortunately, their claim allows a ready test: It implies that self-estimated parameters from different subjects can be used interchangeably. This seems incompatible with individual differences observed, for example, in rankings of physical attractiveness in date-preference judgments by Shanteau and Nagy, illustrated in Figure 6.3. It also seems clearly false on phenomenological grounds, for it denies personal knowledge of differences between own and others' values.[a]

Of course, phenomenology is not sufficient grounds for any definite conclusion about self-estimation capabilities. Severe limitations of conscious report have long been known and have been re-emphasized by Nisbett and Wilson (1977). A notable example arose in the work on person perception, in which subjects and experimenters alike gave confident, detailed reports about interactions among adjective traits in the person description. Under experimental analysis, however, it was found that the adjectives did not interact and that conscious report was a cognitive illusion (see *Foundations*, Chapter 3).

Accordingly, the validity of self-estimated parameters cannot be taken for granted, at least at the level of individual values. One advantage of the present approach is that it can provide a theoretical base for determining the actual effects of stimuli. This provides a criterion for assessing accuracy of self-report at the individual level.

NOTES

6.1a. The concept of importance, or weight, has caused controversy. Material of this chapter met with strenuous and near-total disapprobation as recently as a 1978 conference of prominent workers in judgment–decision theory. One main cause has been the traditional reliance on regression weights, without realizing their limitations. Associated with the traditional way of thinking has gone a lack of understanding of the role of weights in averaging theory. Some workers recognized the difficulties with linear regression models but developed invalid standardization procedures or declared the concept of weight to be meaningless. I do not regard the material of this chapter as problematical, but it should be noted that the concept of weight has occasioned considerable difference of opinion.

6.1.1a. Strictly speaking, the usual regression weights are not entirely independent of predictor range due to unreliability in the predictors (Section 4.3.3). This slight dependence may be ignored for present purposes.

6.1.1b. In psychophysics, the issue is whether all sensory dimensions have equal subjective ranges. Poulton (1968) observed that exponents of power functions obtained from magnitude estimation were inversely related to the intensity range of the physical stimulus. Poulton suggested an artifact interpretation in terms of one of several response biases in the method of magnitude estimation, namely, that subjects have a tendency to use a constant range of number responses, regardless of the range of sensory magnitude.

Teghtsoonian (1971) hypothesized instead that the maximum subjective range is the same for all sensory dimensions; this could cause a constant range of response. Although this hypothesis is considered to be "clearly an empirical question [Teghtsoonian, Teghtsoonian, & Karlsson, 1981, p. 93]," it evidently requires valid scales of subjective magnitude, which is an essentially theoretical question. The evidence for the hypothesis is the high negative correlation between the feasible range of physical intensities for various sense dimensions and the exponent of the power function fit to magnitude estimation data for each sense dimension. The value of this evidence, however, appears to rest entirely on the assumption that magnitude estimation is valid and unbiased, so that the exponent is a faithful reflection of subjective value. None of the evidence rules out the presence of the response bias tendency suggested by Poulton. If this tendency is present, then the exponents are biased, the obtained correlation is also biased, and the given interpretation is not warranted.

The crux of the issue is how to compare sensory magnitudes between different dimensions or qualities. Averaging theory makes such comparisons possible (Section 2.3; Anderson, 1974a, p. 227).

6.1.2a. If main course and vegetable had exactly equal true ranges, the ratio of their ranges in the observed data would be systematically greater than .5, due to bias from variable denominators. Furthermore, the ratio obtained from the mean group data would be systematically different from the mean of the individual ratios. For statistical test, therefore, it is generally preferable to compare differences rather than ratios.

6.1.3a. An interesting use of the percentage of variance statistic and of its interpretation as a weight index appear in Brehmer, Hagafors, and Johansson (1980). Subjects judged severity of disease in a fictitious medical task, given severity of two medical cue-symptoms. Each symptom was quantified at five numerical levels by the height of a vertical bar, and the two cues were combined in a 5 × 5 factorial design. In all conditions, both cues had the same five physical heights. In different conditions, however, subjects received different verbal instructions about the relative importance of the two symptoms and about the shape of the symptom–disease (cue–criterion) relation: either straight-line or U-shaped.

Application of the parallelism theorem by Brehmer *et al.* showed good support for an adding-type model across five experiments. This model provides a theoretical basis for interpreting the effect of the relative importance manipulation. It is assumed here that the subjects' judgments exhibited the straight-line or U-shaped form specified by the instructions; this would appear in plots of the marginal means of the factorial design. This information was not actually given, however; only the percentages of variance accounted for by each cue.

The main concern in Brehmer *et al.* was how subjects interpreted the verbal instructions about relative importance of the two cues. For conditions in which both cues had the same shape, it seems reasonable to assume that they also had the same scale values and that the instructions about relative importance affected only the weight. Accordingly, the methods of Section 3.6 may be applied to determine the weights.

When both cues are straight-line, weights may theoretically be evaluated as the slopes of the lines relating the functional scale values to the physical cue values. The functional scale values are estimated as the marginal means of the factorial design and plotted as a function of corresponding physical cue height. These physical heights may presumably be taken as the scale values for the straight-line condition on the grounds that subjective length is proportional to objective length (Note 4.3.3a). Hence the slopes are proportional to the weights and may be validly compared because the two cues had equal ranges.

Brehmer *et al.* used only the percentage of variance statistic but stated that the slopes should be proportional to the square root of this statistic. On this basis, they concluded that subjects instructed to use relative weights of 2:1, 3:1, 4:1, and 5:1 for the two cues did so. This appears to be a correct use of the percentage of variance statistic.

An interesting difficulty arises with the U-shaped stimulus cue. For this condition also,

Brehmer *et al.* (1980, p. 379) interpreted the square root of the percentage of variance as a slope and compared these values between the U-shaped and straight-line cues. But their approach is based on the physical cue values, in line with Brunswik's (1956) formulation. In terms of the physical values, of course, the slope is zero for the U-shaped cue; so their slope interpretation seems inappropriate.

Theoretical justification for comparing two U-shaped cues may be obtained from the foregoing integration theory analysis. Because both cues had the same physical values, they presumably had the same psychological scale values. Hence the analysis of Section 3.6 also applies, in much the same way as for the straight-line cues. This justifies the interpretation of the square root of the ratio of the percentages of variance as a relative weight.

It does not seem possible, however, to compare importance for two cues of different shape—because their psychological scale values cannot be compared. Even two straight-line cues with different physical ranges may not be comparable; instructions about relative importance may affect the scale unit as well as the weights. For example, a cue with a shorter physical range may be evaluated in terms of a smaller scale unit. The foregoing analysis depends on the assumption that the importance instructions affected only the weight and did not have differential effects on the units of the subjective stimulus scales.

A basic theoretical issue becomes manifest in this data analysis. In contrast to Brunswik's formulation, which requires physical cue values as a matter of principle, the theory of information integration employs subjective cue values. Hence the U-shaped relation is only relevant to the valuation function for the single cue, that is, to the relation between subjective and objective cue values. The weight, in contrast, refers to the relation between the subjective values of the single cues and the integrated response, which is linear by virtue of the adding rule. This integration-theoretical interpretation is discussed by Brehmer *et al.* (1980, p. 380) in terms of sequential processing, in which the stimulus variable is first rescaled in terms of the response metric, and these rescaled cues are weighted in the subsequent integration.

Even in this simple task, it appears that the concept of weight is basically theoretical, difficult to handle without a theoretical model (see also Note 2.3.2a). In contrast to the Brunswik model, which requires objective or physical metrics for the stimuli as a base for analysis, integration theory allows for subjective stimulus values through functional measurement methodology. In addition, there is considerable evidence that this class of tasks obeys an averaging model, not the linear regression model assumed in approaches based on Brunswik's formulation (Anderson, 1981a, pp. 282–283).

6.1.3b. Other discussions of the concept of weight are given by Luce (1980), McClelland (1980), and Shanteau (1980).

6.1.4a. In social attribution theory, attempts to compare relative importance of consensus and consistency information are invalid for similar reasons (Anderson, 1974b, p. 36).

6.1.4b. This obscurity of the concept of weight or importance in the cited application of multiple regression methodology is underscored by the fact that two subjects later decided to treat importance as the amount of time devoted to a given activity. That seems eminently reasonable, but the investigators considered it to be a questionable redefinition of the concept of importance. Unfortunately, their theory and procedure both left the concept of relative amount of importance vague and ill-defined.

6.1.4c. There do not appear to be any satisfactory studies of the relative importance of facial and contextual cues. The scholarly discussion by Frijda (1969) emphasizes that recognition of emotion represents complex information processing and presents many interesting results, but its treatment of the integration problem is handicapped by its reliance on the relative shift ratio considered in the text. The problem of discordant cue combinations, which is similar to the problem of inconsistency resolution (Section F3.4.1), cannot be handled with this ratio. Ekman, Friesen, and Ellsworth (1972) criticize previous conclusions as generally unwarranted and incorrect, but their analyses are not more satisfactory. In particular, their use of single-cue judgments seems unaware of any of the associated methodological problems.

Only two or three studies of facial cues (e.g., Bugental, 1974; Lampel & Anderson, 1968) have used a theory capable of assessing relative importance, but none of these has actually addressed this measurement question. Mehrabian (1968) has applied analysis of variance with the assumption that every interaction term can be given a psychological interpretation, but this approach suffers the shortcomings noted in Section 7.11. A study of face–word combinations by Friedman (1978, 1979) reported a negativity effect similar to that found by Lampel and Anderson (1968). However, Friedman did not consider the problem of response linearity, which is essential to his interpretation (see also Sections 7.11 and F4.4.2), and his index of importance is arbitrary, for it depends on arbitrary choice of stimuli. Apple (1979) obtained support for an adding-type rule for judgments of nervousness based on integration of voice pitch and posture–gesture cues, which replicates results on integration of personality traits (see Figure 1.4). If this rule is actually one of averaging, as may be expected from previous results on person perception, suitable design would yield valid comparisons of relative importance, using the exact procedures of Section 2.3.2 or the qualitative estimation scheme of Section 2.3.3.

6.1.4d. The relative shift ratio also depends on an implicit assumption that the responses to single cues and combined cues are all measured on linear scales with common zeros and common units. This assumption may not be satisfied if, for example, responses to single cues are measured in a different session than responses to combined cues (e.g., Section 1.1.8).

6.2.1a. Results on self-estimation of scale values will not be summarized here, but mention should be made of Brehmer and Slovic (1980), who obtained excellent agreement between judgments based on single stimulus cues and functional scales derived from judgments of cue combinations (see especially their Figure 3). The task involved decision making to which an adding-type model was shown to apply in three experiments, thereby validating the functional scales. The judgments based on the single stimulus cues may be treated as scale values, even though the averaging model actually holds, because the equal weighting condition (Section 6.2.2) was applicable. Brehmer and Slovic were primarily concerned with assessing invariance of scale values across tasks of different complexity. Their results supported invariance, even with a three-cue task in which two cue-valuation functions had nonlinear shapes.

6.2.1b. Besides the two studies of Figures 6.2 and 6.3, few if any others in the multiattribute literature have provided appropriate tests of goodness of fit. A few studies (e.g., Fischer, 1977) have given serious attention to this problem, but generally multiattribute studies rely on weak inference methods, which do not really test the model (Section 4.1).

6.2.2a. It may seem odd to treat integrated responses, such as likableness of a person, as scale values because that term is ordinarily associated with the separate stimulus cues rather than the overall response to the set of cues. Even for a description with a single trait adjective, the judgment of the person is theoretically different from the scale value of the adjective (Section 2.3.4). However, the person could be treated as one element in a superordinate integration task, such as group attractiveness, in which the judgment of the person would be the presumptive scale value.

6.2.3a. Similarly, Slovic and Lichtenstein (1971, p. 684) suggest that people strongly overestimate the importance they place on minor cues. This seems plausible but is difficult to test without valid and comparable measures of either of the two sets of weights. Tasks with unequal weighting within stimulus dimensions might provide an interesting basis for comparing intuitive statistics and regression statistics.

6.2.3b. Recent work by Birnbaum and Stegner (1981) also finds agreement between self-estimated and functional weights.

6.2.3c. Procedure in this study of importance ratings (Anderson, 1964e) was as follows: Each of 24 subjects preselected adjectives of equal likableness from each of six value ranges of the master list of 555 adjectives of Appendix B. Descriptions with 2, 3, 4, or 6 adjectives of homogeneous value were then constructed according to a 4 × 6, Set size × Value design for each subject. Subjects rated overall likableness for each person description as well as "how important each of his qualities was to you in influencing your impression of him." Responses for each description were recorded by the subject on an 8 ½ × 11 inch sheet on which were drawn a 5-inch line on the top half as a graphic rating scale for overall likableness and several 5-inch lines on the bottom half as graphic rating scales for the importance judgments.

6.2.5a. Self-estimation of weights is important in applications of multiattribute models, in which the overall value of an object is a weighted sum of its attribute values. Since the attributes may be entirely different in quality, they must be weighted in a way that makes their utility or value scales comparable and summable.

To handle this problem, the value ranges of the several attributes are generally standardized in some way. In a typical case (Einhorn & McCoach, 1977), the value scale of each attribute is standardized theoretically by division by the standard deviation of the attribute values. This forces all attributes to have the same range of (standardized) values. Einhorn and McCoach present a more detailed treatment, but the outcome is that their standardization forces the weight for each attribute to be variable, depending on whatever subset of objects is to be judged.

Two subsets of a homogeneous set of objects may be chosen so that one has a small range of values on a given attribute, whereas the other has a large range. Then the standardized weight for this attribute must be correspondingly small or large. This applies to any object common to both subsets: The weight of the given attribute in the overall value of that same object must be small in one subset, large in the other.

This kind of standardization implies that self-estimated weights must, if they are to be valid, vary across subsets of objects in the same way as the standard deviations. This prediction could readily be tested by varying the value range of a given attribute across different subsets and comparing the self-estimates for the different subsets. The prediction is that these self-estimates vary in direct proportion to the value ranges for the different subsets. This predicted outcome may be doubted for the reasons discussed in Section 6.1.

A theory-based analysis is possible with integration theory. Some multiattribute objects are known to obey an averaging model. Hence valid measures of value and weight are available as criteria for self-estimates. Any proposed method, such as that of Einhorn and McCoach, may readily be put to test.

The integration–theoretical approach may also help improve practical applications of multiattribute models. In any one investigation, it is true, moderate improvements may not be worth seeking. Rough approximations are often adequate, and accuracy may usefully be traded off for simplicity. But as Gilbert, Light, and Mosteller (1975) point out, "Because even small gains accumulated over time can sum to a considerable total, they may have valuable consequences for society [p. 40]." For practical prediction in multiattribute tasks, therefore, theory-based study of self-estimation methodology is important (Zalinski & Anderson, 1977, in press).

6.2.6a. Smith and Miller (1978) and White (1980) present general critiques of Nisbett and Wilson's (1977) view of conscious report. Both point out that Nisbett and Wilson provide no criterion for the essential process–product distinction, so their position may be circular and true by fiat. Both also point out the need to allow for individual differences in the experiment by Nisbett and Bellows (1977) considered in the text (see also Note F3.6.4b).

However, the reanalysis of Nisbett and Bellow's data by Smith and Miller is inconclusive because, in particular, it fails to test the difference between subjects and observers. Even had a reliable subject–observer difference been found, moreover, it would still have been inconclusive because of a confound in the design. Nisbett and Bellows (1977) presented observers only a "very abbreviated and impoverished [p. 618]" version of the stimulus information received by subjects; any difference between subjects and observers could thus be attributed to the difference in available information rather than to failure of their hypothesis. In other words, the design used by Nisbett and Bellows could not disconfirm their theoretical position.

The experiment reported by White represents a thoughtful attempt to obtain a cogent design, in particular, by avoiding the error of presenting different stimulus information to subjects and observers. However, the statistical analysis inappropriately pooled within- and between-subject variability by treating the four scores for each subject for each of the four response dimensions as independent (White, personal communication, March, 1981). With 14 subjects in each condition, there are only 26 df for the overall t test, not 446 as listed in the original article. Since the obtained t of 2.90 is inflated to the extent that the 16 scores for each subject are correlated across subjects, White's interpretation remains in doubt.

Sundry Problems in Method

This chapter takes up a miscellany of problems, partly conceptual, partly methodological. The section headings speak for themselves.

7.1 Objections to Cognitive Algebra

Among the objections that have been raised to cognitive algebra, one class has to do with various aspects of procedure and method. Most of these objections fall under the following headings.

Demand. Concern is sometimes expressed that the evidence for algebraic models might result from a demand implicit in the experimental situation.[a] In this view, the investigator's expectation or hope for some simple model becomes implicitly worked into the instructions and procedure. Subjects are assumed to be sensitive to such implicit demands and to behave to confirm the investigator's hope. The findings would not be general, therefore, only peculiarities of task and procedure.

Little or no evidence or theoretical rationale has been given to support this view. It is common in social judgment where, apparently, it stems largely from disbelief that a process as intuitively complex as person perception can really follow any simple algebraic rule. Subjects share this disbelief. When asked how they do the task, they give more or less complex protocols with no hint of simple integration rules. This is prima facie evidence against the demand interpretation.

A more direct line of evidence is that expectation and hope for a simple model are often disappointed. In the averaging–adding controversy, for example, many investigators have been strong adherents of the adding hypothesis. If demand were operative, these investigators would get results consistent with their adding hypothesis. In fact, the empirical results favor the averaging hypothesis fairly uniformly across investigators. Furthermore, a careful test of instructional demand by Gollob and Lugg (1973) provided strong support for the averaging hypothesis and no evidence for demand.

No less cogent is Shanteau's (1974) subadditivity effect in utility theory (see also Section F1.7.1). Theory, common sense, and simplicity all argue for an adding rule. The instructions to judge overall value of a commodity bundle can hardly avoid suggesting an adding rule. But subjects are deaf to these demands and show robust deviations from additivity.

Rating-scale methods typically do include a "demand" that subjects use the response scale in a linear way. This is proper, for linearity in the response function is independent of the form of the integration rule.[b] It should be noted, of course, that response linearity is easier to demand than to obtain (Section 1.1).

Superficial Processing. The superficial processing objection states that the experimental situation causes subjects to adopt a simple rule merely to get through the experiment. When faced with the prospect of making numerous judgments, subjects abandon their normal, presumably complex, processing mode and adopt an easy way to make the judgments with minimal mental strain.

This argument is plausible. Equally plausible is the argument that the formal experimental situation induces more careful processing with due attention to all aspects of the stimulus field. More extensive study of this matter is desirable, but available evidence does not support the objection. For example, an experimental condition that required more detailed processing obtained the same results as did the standard condition (Anderson, 1971c; Section F2.2.3, see also Section F1.5.2).

Form and Process. A third objection is that algebraic models may represent form but not process. This is sometimes the case. The data may exhibit a linear fan pattern, for example, even though no multiplication is involved (e.g., Sections F1.5.4 and F1.5.7). Even when the form reflects the process, the processing structure may still require elucidation (Section F4.5.4).

Nevertheless, cognitive algebra confers unique advantages for process analysis. The objection appears to rest on a misconception that the study of cognitive algebra sees models as ends in themselves. In fact, a major reason for interest in algebraic models rests on their role in cognitive analysis. Three classes of results from this research program may be cited (see also Anderson, 1968b, 1974a,b,d, 1978b, 1980a, 1981a,b, in press-a).

The first class refers to process results obtained directly from model analysis, which include the following:

(1) General theory of psychological measurement that applies at the level of individual values
(2) Solution of standing measurement questions, such as the question of the psychophysical law (e.g., Figure 3.1), simultaneous measurement of subjective probability and utility (Section F1.5.1), and definition and measurement of the weight parameter (Section 6.1)
(3) Successful experimental investigation of the averaging model
(4) Exact tests of multiattribute models with natural stimuli (Section 6.2)
(5) The general purpose adding rule in children's judgments (Section F1.3.6)
(6) Evidence for the hypothesis of meaning constancy, as given by parallelism analysis (Section F3.1.3)
(7) Exact treatment of continuous semantic representations and fuzzy set theory (Sections F1.8.2 and F4.5.4)

Behavior that deviates from the models is often more interesting than behavior that obeys the models, as illustrated by the following examples:

(1) Operation of discounting processes to handle inconsistent information (Section F3.4.1)
(2) Configurality in moral judgment (Section F4.4.4)
(3) Diverse instances of nonparallelism produced by differential weighting (Sections F2.2.4 and F4.4.2)

It may seem odd to credit models with usefulness in interpreting deviations from their own predictions, but this has occurred in two ways. First, the success of the models in some instances made it possible to develop methods for linear response scales; these can be most helpful for interpreting deviations from prediction. Second, model predictions can provide an appropriate baseline for interpreting any deviations—if the model has substantive relevance. The need for substantive relevance is well illustrated by examples of implicit additivity (Sections 7.5 and

7.13), in which the interpretations of deviations from the adding model were seen to be unwarranted after the averaging model had been established.

Finally, and most important, are qualitative conclusions that can be obtained from model-oriented analysis. These include the following.

(1) The importance of attentional processes in person perception (Section 7.14; Anderson, 1965b)

(2) The finding of separate memory systems for verbal materials and impressions or ideas (Anderson & Hubert, 1963; Section F4.2)

(3) The finding that valuation and integration processes are ordinarily independent in the personality adjective task (Section F1.8.3)

(4) The conclusion that a primary cognitive apparatus consists of a superstructure of operations acting on a semantic memory that plays a relatively passive role (Section F1.8.3)

(5) The halo conceptualization of the positive context effect (Anderson, 1966a; Section F3.2)

(6) The basal-surface, two-component hypothesis of attitude structure (Anderson, 1959c; Section F2.5.4)

(7) The demonstration that phenomenological reports about the influence of stimuli on perceptions of persons represent a cognitive illusion (Chapter 3 of the *Foundations* volume)

These results pass over numerous particular experimental studies that range from moral judgment in children to decision theory. The cited results, however, should suffice to illustrate both the usefulness of models in process analysis and the central concern with cognitive analysis in this research program.

Flexibility. A not infrequent objection is that cognitive algebra is so flexible that it can account for any outcome. In particular, the averaging model with differential weighting can fit nonparallel as well as parallel data.

This objection may be missing the point of cognitive algebra. The models are not of interest merely because they describe the data. They are of interest because they lead to understanding about processes underlying the observed behavior. One main theme of integration theory is the use of models as tools for cognitive analysis, a theme treated in more detail later.

It is true, to be sure, that ability to fit the data constitutes a validational test for a model. Unless the model can account for the observed behavior, it can hardly shed much light on the processes underlying that behavior. The crossover interactions of Sections 5.4 and F2.3 are a case in point. These crossovers are robust and provide strong tests of any model. The adding and summation models predicted no crossover and have been unable to give a coherent account of them. The averaging model predicted the crossovers—from conceptual analysis of the task.

This last point deserves emphasis. The averaging model accounts for the crossovers in terms of differential weighting, but the weights are not arbitrary parameters. The weights make conceptual sense, showing specifiable relations to amount of information, reliability of information, and other stimulus manipulations (Section F4.4). In this and many other ways, averaging theory embodies a different conceptual structure from that found in formulations based on adding and summation models. It is such conceptual structures that are at issue in the study of cognitive algebra.

Such supporting conceptual framework will be weak or absent in some cases. A good model fit may then not mean much. An example is in the first experiment on the Height + Width rule in children's judgment of rectangle area (Section F1.3.6). The fact that this adding rule fit the data did not confer much confidence on its validity. On the contrary, the natural reaction was that something was wrong. An extended series of experiments was needed to build up a framework within which this adding rule made conceptual sense (Anderson, 1980a; Cuneo, 1978, 1982).

Analysis of Variance and Cognitive Algebra. The great usefulness of analysis of variance in the study of information integration has been amply illustrated in the *Foundations* volume. It is striking how flexible and efficient this technique is and how adaptable to new needs. Nevertheless, these applications of analysis of variance have run into vigorous objections, beginning with the initial reports (Anderson, 1962a,b,c) and continuing to the present time. With these objections to method has sometimes gone an a fortiori rejection of the experiments and theory.

One group of objections is concerned with the problem of measurement. The usefulness of analysis of variance in the study of cognitive algebra is, of course, strongly dependent on possession of a linear response scale. Quite naturally, therefore, the rating method that was used in this work was subject to question (Section 1.1.1). However, the success of the algebraic rules simultaneously demonstrated that the rating method did yield linear response scales. Other work has shown how analysis of variance may be utilized in monotone analysis to provide a complete theory of measurement.

A second group of objections seems to stem from failure to recognize that analysis of variance is used differently in functional measurement from the way it is used in standard statistical practice. For example, response transformations that maximize additivity are often helpful in standard statistical analysis because they increase power for tests of main effects. This practice is not generally legitimate in cognitive algebra because response transformations may bias the response measure and misrepresent the operative model (e.g., Sections 5.2 and F5.6.1). More generally, standard statistical analysis imposes the general linear model of analysis of variance by fiat, whereas cognitive algebra seeks to establish the psychological validity of models (e.g., Sections 7.10 and 7.11). This difference is clear in the averaging model, which is in general nonlinear and not analyzable by ordinary analysis of variance.

A third group of objections seems to reflect failure to recognize the central concern with cognitive analysis in this research program. Since much of this research has been done in social cognition, it is fitting to quote a discussant's summary comments during a recent conference on this topic. Referring to the goal of explaining cognition in terms of information processes, Simon (1976) stated, [This goal] "is incompatible with the use of variance analysis as a principal analytic tool. The variance analysis paradigm . . . is largely useless for discovering and testing process models to explain what goes on between appearance of stimulus and performance of response [p. 261]."

Such statements are hard to fathom in view of the demonstrated prevalence of cognitive algebra; this is an important part of what goes on between stimulus and response. Relevant experimental applications are noted in the previous subsection and need not be repeated here. It may be re-emphasized, however, that cognitive algebra provides a powerful tool for cognitive analysis because it can dissect the observed response into its causal components. It also provides a novel basis for demonstrating psychological reality of the molar concepts represented by the terms of the model.

These results are not obtainable with protocols, which seem to be the primary data allowed in Simon's view of cognitive psychology. His view ignores a useful method for cognitive analysis; it thereby also ignores the boundary constraints that cognitive algebra imposes on any attempts at deeper process analysis. The need for such constraints is well illustrated by the work on person perception in which protocol analysis arrived at a cognitive illusion, not the true process (Chapter F3). One may have more confidence in protocol analysis when it has demonstrated its ability to account for the results provided by information integration theory. [c,d]

Structure of Operations. Cognitive algebra is sometimes wrongly identified with the mathematical formalism. The averaging rule, for example, is treated as mere mental arithmetic that could not represent the complex processes manifestly involved in various integration tasks. Since the averaging rule was discovered in person perception, it has never been viewed as mere mental arithmetic. A feature mixing operation, for example, will generate an averaging rule (Anderson, 1974d; Section F4.5.4). But whatever their complexity, some of these integration processes follow algebraic rules, and these rules can be useful for further analysis.

In a similar way, the possibility of algebraic rules has been rejected on the grounds that a single number cannot represent a complex stimulus, such as the president paragraph illustrated in Section 7.15. This criticism is incorrect, as shown in the discussion of valuation as a constructive operation. Theoretically, the stimulus may be treated as a molar unit, and its functional scale can provide sharp boundary conditions on more detailed structural analysis (Sections 7.14–7.17).

Relevance. The final objection is that results obtained in controlled laboratory situations may not generalize to natural settings. This objection reflects commendable concern with social action but an insufficient appreciation of the complementary roles of laboratory and field studies. One specific investigation that illustrates some pertinent considerations will be noted briefly.

In a study of bail-setting in the courts (Ebbesen & Konečni, 1974, 1975), judges set bail for realistic but hypothetical cases in the privacy of their chambers and also set bail for real cases from the bench. Both sets of data supported an averaging formulation. Ebbesen and Konečni found a paradoxical interaction in the courtroom data to which they gave an ingenious averaging-theoretical interpretation.

However, one major difference appeared between the results from the controlled stimulus design and the courtroom situation. In the privacy of their chambers, judges took into account nearly all the socially relevant factors, such as job–family ties and prior record. In the courtroom, however, their judgments were controlled largely by one factor, namely, severity of crime.

Two inferences were drawn from this difference in outcome. First, Ebbesen and Konečni (1975) suggested that the judges in their chambers "may have attempted to present themselves as unbiased [p. 810]," as though they were in some sense trying to conceal a courtroom bias. Second, they concluded that laboratory-type experiments, even in so realistic a situation as a judge's chambers, are misleading and invalid.

An alternative view is that the judge's mind worked much the same in chambers as on the bench. The two situations will still produce different outcomes, of course, owing to attention problems associated with the markedly more complex information field that prevails in the courtroom. One aspect of the information problem can be seen in the fact that some major item of information was actually missing in the courtroom situation in over one-third of the cases.

Such attentional factors can have marked effects on the parameters of the integration rule and hence on the actual response (Section 7.14). Nevertheless, the same value system and the same rule of information integration may operate in both situations.

In the present view, controlled experiments have a vital role: to establish the basic integration processes. This cannot generally be done in field situations because of insufficient control over the information field. Experimental control was essential to establishing averaging theory. In the bail setting study itself, Ebbesen and Konečni's use of averaging theory to interpret the paradoxical interaction rested directly on the body of evidence from controlled laboratory experiments.

Furthermore, the present view leads to two suggestions for reform in the field situation. First, contrary to Ebbesen and Konečni, judges' decision rules in their chambers are not considered an attempt at covering-up bias, but as their ideals of justice. As such, they can help interested judges improve their courtroom decisions. For example, a controlled design can help judges diagnose their operative ideal of justice. The response pattern in each judge's factorial graph can reveal that judge's functional values and judicial integration rule.

Second, if the lower quality of the courtroom decisions results from courtroom distractions and missing information, then the obvious step is to bypass these difficulties. Much might be done for justice, therefore, by the simple informational device of providing the judge with a standard form summarizing the facts in each case (Anderson, 1976d, pp. 111–121, 1976e, p. 129, 1981b; see also Pennington & Hastie, 1981).

7.2 Field Studies

Field-type studies are obviously important for obtaining results that have social relevance, especially for outcome generality. Less recognized is their cognitive relevance: It is in the long-practiced tasks of daily life that cognitive skills will be most highly developed. Investigations within field situations can thus be useful for many purposes.

One common problem in field-type investigations arises from the need to inject some degree of experimental control. Some relevant methodological problems are taken up in other sections of this chapter, but the general problem is outside the scope of this volume. However, the notable *Evaluation and Experiment*, edited by Bennett and Lumsdaine (1975), deserves mention because of its importance to anyone interested in field-type investigations.

A basic theme of most chapters in *Evaluation and Experiment* is the necessity of experimental control. The earlier optimism of Campbell and Stanley (1966) on the potential of quasi-experimental design has given way to the caution reflected in the title of the chapter by Campbell and Boruch (1975). Foremost among the six biases considered by Campbell and Boruch is the matching–regression artifact discussed in Sections 7.6 and 7.7. This long-known but ill-appreciated bias came into prominence when it was found that it tended to make compensatory education for disadvantaged groups look harmful.

In a truly impressive chapter, Gilbert, Light, and Mosteller (1975) survey and evaluate many past programs on social action and conclude that beneficial effects, if any, are typically of modest size. Modest effects can be very important socially, but are easily masked by noise and bias in the data. As a consequence, attempts to match natural groups rather than randomize introduce confoundings that render the results sometimes wrong and generally uncertain. The authors give many cogent comments on field-type investigations and reach the stern verdict that failure to use randomized design is often just *"fooling around with people* [p. 150]."

Applied decision making often involves problems to which the usual field-type experiments have limited relevance. As Edwards and Guttentag (1975) point out, the value systems of decision makers are central to their decisions. Experimental studies can provide useful, even vital, information about means to obtain valued ends, but these values are not themselves given by experiment. With their concern for applied decision making, therefore, Edwards and Guttentag quite reasonably downplay the usefulness of field experiments and emphasize Bayesian methods and multiattribute models. But with this emphasis, contrary to Edwards and Guttentag, experimental analysis of decision processes has a basic role not only for applied efficiency but also for theoretical analysis of cognitive skills. This requires, however, a different kind of experimental study from the usual field-type experiment, namely, experiments on judgmental processes of the kind considered in Edwards's (1968) earlier work and in the present research program. This latter work has provided a theoretical alternative to the Bayesian approach (Section F1.8.1), a theoretical foundation for multiattribute models (Section F1.7.3), and interesting results in field-type settings, as is illustrated next.

7.3 An Illustrative Field-Type Investigation

Extension of information integration theory to field situations is nicely exemplified in the work of Shanteau on livestock judging (e.g., Phelps & Shanteau, 1978). This task has great commercial importance, and Kansas State University has a special curriculum to train judges in various specialties of livestock evaluation. This situation provided many advantages and opportunities for research. Foremost was the depth of training and the wide range of skill development across the four college years and on through professional life. The stimuli are not overwhelmingly complex, and the training curriculum already embodied a delineation of relevant attributes. Moreover, there is an objective criterion for many judgments, for example, about meat quality in live animals.

One result concerning integrational capacity will be noted here for its general methodological interest. The prevailing opinion in decision theory has been that expert judges, contrary to their own firm beliefs, have very limited integrational capacity and take account of only a few stimulus cues. This prevailing opinion rested almost entirely on correlation–regression analysis. When Phelps and Shanteau applied these traditional methods, they found the same implication: Expert judges seemed to take account of only three dimensions of stimulus information.

Phelps and Shanteau suspected, however, that this poor showing was an artifact of the traditional methods. Because of natural intercorrelations, the first few variables in a stepwise regression will generally account for most of the effects of the remaining variables. The only effective way to break out of this confounding is to use controlled design. When this was done, a dramatically different picture emerged: Judges had high integrational capacity and could take account of 10 or more independent stimulus dimensions. Furthermore, it became possible to determine the form of the integration rule and to study its development over the course of training. By incorporating controlled design within a field situation, Phelps and Shanteau demonstrated that expert judges had much greater cognitive capacity than had previously been recognized.

7.4 Comparative Psychology

Comparisons are often sought between two individuals or two groups with different histories. This is a major problem in developmental psychology, for example, which emphasizes cross-age comparisons. Similar problems arise, even more acutely, in areas as different as personality and comparative animal behavior. The frequent complaint about lack of comparative animal studies reflects the difficulty of obtaining meaningful methods for comparison.

There may not be any problem when the response has absolute interest. Developmental curves of height or of vocabulary size, for example, have reasonably direct cross-age meanings. But when the response measure is considered an index of some unobservable state, such as loudness, intelligence, or moral obligation, then comparison between any two organisms becomes problematical. A useful survey of difficulties that relate to choice of stimulus materials and to statistical problems such as matching artifacts is given by Cole and Means (1980). The present section is mostly concerned with measurement, and later sections will take up some statistical problems.

Two examples from color perception will serve to emphasize the fundamental nature of the comparative problem. To a normal observer, comparison of black-and-white with color television suggests how different the visual worlds of color-normal and totally color-blind persons must be. Surprisingly, totally color-blind persons may be more or less unaware of their deficiency. They learn other cues, especially relative brightness, to determine usage of color names and do not appreciate that they are missing so vivid a visual experience as hue. Careful tests are required to detect such persons. Valid comparisons of color normal and color blind are possible, but not easy.

Now consider two presumably color-normal persons who are shown the same red patch. How can their individual sensations of redness be compared, say, in degree of saturation? Even if saturation could be measured on a linear scale for each individual, each scale must be allowed an individual unit parameter. Hence comparison of scale numbers may be no more meaningful than comparison of numerical readings from Celsius and Fahrenheit thermometers standing side by side. The thermometers, of course, can be intercalibrated because they both refer to the same observable state of nature. Similar intercalibration could be made for the two individual scales as measures of the physical saturation, but that merely evades the essential problem of comparing psychological sensations. It is tempting to argue that the two persons have similar physiological mechanisms and so should have similar sensations. Similarity is not identity, however, which is one reason for the difficulty of interpersonal comparison of sensation.

If interpersonal comparison is difficult for simple sensory experiences, it is even more difficult for more cognitive qualities. In one extensive published study of moral development, for example, children of varied race and age rated how much a character in a story should be rewarded or punished. It was concluded that whites are more punishing than blacks, and many similar comparisons were made involving age, sex, and so forth. But all these comparisons rest on the implicit assumption that a given number on the rating scale represents the same personal feeling about reward and punishment for white and black children and for younger and older children. This assumption is likely to be untrue and is seemingly not even testable. Accordingly, it is difficult to attach any meaning to the results. Many other studies could be cited to illustrate the same point.

This measurement problem fortunately is not present in all comparative analyses. Where this problem is present, however, it seems pointless to proceed with meaningless methods. One alternative is to shift from comparisons of single responses to comparisons of response patterns. Patterns of responses can sometimes be compared validly even when single responses cannot. Two examples will be given, one of interpersonal comparison of values, the other of interpersonal comparison of integration rules.

A method of value comparison is illustrated in the two left panels of Figure 1.4, in which the vertical elevations of the three curves represent the values of the three corresponding adjectives. It makes no sense to compare the elevations of the bottom curves and conclude that *ungrateful* has higher value for subject R. H. than for subject F. F.; that difference may merely reflect individual usage of the rating response. However, comparison of the patterns of the three curves shows that the two subjects do have truly different values, as noted in the discussion of the figure.

Integration rules, which are revealed by the pattern of the factorial plot, are independent of individual values. Study of response patterning thus provides one helpful approach to comparative analysis. One example is shown in Figure F1.9, in which 5-year-olds judged the area of rectangles by the Height + Width rule, whereas older children exhibited the normative Height × Width rule. This comparison between parallelism and linear fan patterns allows a true developmental conclusion, whereas comparison in terms of accuracy would mean little.

7.5 Change Scores

Interpretation of change scores is made difficult by the necessity of allowing for the baseline from which the change is measured. Two areas in which this problem arises will be discussed briefly to illustrate the need for model analysis.

Informational Learning. To illustrate the change-score problem in an informational learning task, suppose that two equivalent pieces of information are given on successive trials. Suppose that the response is measured on each trial so the change produced by each piece of information can be determined. Typically, the second piece of information produces less change than the first. Why should two equivalent pieces of information produce different effects?

An obvious reaction is to postulate some stimulus interaction to explain the diminished effect of the second piece of information. For example, the second piece of information may be partially redundant with the first, either semantically or affectively. This partial redundancy could lead to partial discounting and hence to decreased effect. Another interpretation is that the first piece of information sets up an expectancy for more information of the same type. This not only provides an expectancy mechanism for redundancy effects, but also suggests that unexpected information may have accentuated effects.

Such interaction explanations rest on some presupposition that both pieces of information should have equal observed effect. This represents an assumption, often implicit, that an adding model holds (see also Section 7.13). From the standpoint of averaging theory, the matter looks different.

The nature of the problem can be seen in the proportional-change form of the averaging model that was used in essentially this same context by Anderson and Hovland (1957). Suppose that the two informational stimuli have equal scale value, s, and equal relative weight, w. Let R_0 be the initial response, and let R_1 and R_2 be the responses after integration of the first and second pieces of information. Then the two change scores are

$$R_1 - R_0 = w(s - R_0),$$
$$R_2 - R_1 = w(s - R_1).$$

The second change score is less because R_1 is closer to s than is R_0. This difference would be accentuated if the two pieces of information had equal absolute weight, for then the relative weight would be less in the second equation than in the first.

The averaging model thus provides a simple account of the phenomenon. It is not necessary to assume any stimulus interaction. It is not necessary to postulate psychological processes such as redundancy or expectancy. On the contrary, such interaction explanations require explicit justification because of the extensive evidence for the averaging model (see also T. Anderson & Birnbaum, 1976; Bogartz, 1976; Harris, 1976; Himmelfarb, 1974).

Comparison of Different Populations. Essentially the same problem arises in attempts to compare populations that have systematic preexperimental differences. Subject populations that are naturally different are the most prominent instance. Subject populations that have been made systematically different by previous experimental treatment may also be included. Moreover, stimulus populations that are naturally different, such as familiar and unfamiliar words in memory studies, present similar problems. And the same holds for related response measures, such as measures of autonomic activity in different parts of the body or under different arousal states.

These diverse situations involve complicated problems that cannot be considered here, although the shape function method of Section 3.9 may be useful in some cases. The following example only shows that the essential point of the preceding subsection also applies to these comparison problems. In Figure 7.1, the two curves represent two different populations. Each population is evaluated under two stimulus conditions, I and II, listed on the horizontal axis. The problem at issue is to compare the change between I and II for the two populations.

The comparison is no problem, of course, if the response scale is absolute, for example, in studies of height or vocabulary size. If the physical measure is of sole concern, then the comparison of the change scores merely requires comparison of the actual physical measurements.

However, the matter is entirely different if the response measure is considered to be an index of some underlying state. Either height or vocabulary size might be so viewed, for example, in studies of health or educational method. In this case, comparison of the change scores is no longer merely empirical but rests on some theoretical assumption.

Suppose first that an additive model holds. Then the left panel, because it is parallel, agrees with the model, whereas the center panel, which is nonparallel, disagrees with the model. Interpretation of the center panel would therefore seek for some stimulus–organism interaction to explain the deviations from parallelism.

But there is a reasonable alternative to the additive model. To illustrate, suppose that 100 is the maximum possible response. In the center panel, the upper curve changes from 60 to 80 across the stimulus conditions; this is one-half the possible increase. The lower curve also shows one-half the possible increase, in this case, from 20 to 60. In proportion-

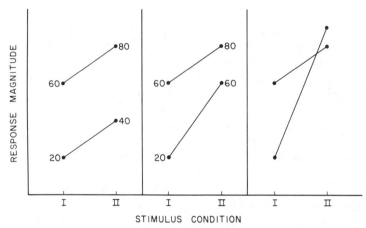

FIGURE 7.1. *Hypothetical data to illustrate problems of interpreting statistical interactions.*

ate terms, these two changes are equal. If the distance–proportional form of the averaging model is applied instead of the additive model, then the theoretical picture reverses: The center panel agrees with the averaging model, whereas the left panel, which is parallel, disagrees with the model. Interpretation of the left panel would therefore seek for some interaction to explain this deviation from proportionate change.

The lesson of this example holds in general: Comparison of change scores across different populations always requires some theoretical assumption. Unless that assumption is explicit and correct, the comparison may be unwarranted, incorrect, or both.

The case in the right panel might seem like an exception. Here the two curves cross over, so no theoretical model seems necessary to justify the conclusion that stimulus–organism interaction is present. The crossover certainly eases the interpretation, but it does so because of the recognition that reasonable noninteractive models would be generally unable to account for the result (Anderson, 1963, p. 169).

7.6 Selection–Regression Artifacts

Whenever stimuli are selected for further study on the basis of subjects' responses, care is needed to avoid *regression artifacts*. To illustrate this well-known artifact, suppose that a subject rates a set of stimuli on a 1–10 scale, in two successive replications. Suppose that the two replications are done under equivalent conditions, so there is no systematic difference between them. It might then seem that the stimuli rated 9 the first time should have an average rating of 9 the second time. This does not happen; the average on the second replication will typically be closer to the mean of the total set of stimuli. As the somewhat misleading term has it, there is a *regression toward the mean.*[a]

The actual cause of this regression artifact is unreliability in the response, coupled with the selection operation. Because of unreliability in the response, some stimuli will be rated 9 even though their true value is different from 9. The true value of these false 9's will typically be less than 9 more often than greater, merely because there are typically more stimuli below 9 than above. Hence the mean true value of those stimuli rated 9 the first time will be less than 9. On the second replication, the expected mean rating of the stimuli rated 9 the first time equals their mean true value and hence is less than 9. This is the regression artifact.

The regression artifact can be discerned in a published study of person impressions with children. Each child first rated single traits on a 1–7 scale, and the experimenter chose one H and one M^+ adjective with ratings of 7 and 5, respectively, or as close thereto as possible. In the next phase, this HM^+ pair was rated similarly, together with a number of other such pairs. The mean ratings of the separate H and M^+ adjectives were 6.98 and 5.03. Their average, namely, 6.00, was very close to the mean rating of 6.13 for the HM^+ pair. It was concluded that children form impressions of persons according to a simple averaging model.

This conclusion is not warranted. The ratings of the single traits are contaminated by the regression artifact and so are systematically too high. As far as these data go, therefore, they are actually evidence against the averaging model. In this particular experiment, the regression artifact could have been avoided by getting second ratings of the selected single traits at the same time that the paired combinations were judged (Section 1.1.8).

Selection–regression artifacts are a potential problem in learning studies whenever selection is made on the basis of some response criterion. In a probability learning study by Anderson and Grant (1957), for example, subjects predicted which of two random events would occur next in a sequence of trials on which either or both events could occur. One statistic was defined as a difference between two conditional probabilities of predicting Event 1, given that both events occurred on the previous trial, but conditional on which one of the two predictions occurred on the previous trial. This statistic was thought to be an index of learning rate within the learning model that was under test. However, the derivation failed to allow for the fact that knowledge of which response occurred on the previous trial conferred some knowledge about underlying response probability. Fortunately, it was possible to obtain a correct derivation for this particular model (Anderson, 1959a; Anderson & Grant, 1958). In general, however, response dependencies, as well as the use of criteria in learning–performance studies, always need scrutiny for selection–regression artifacts (e.g., Melton, 1936).

A regression artifact can also arise when two classes of stimuli are matched in some respect. To compare trait adjectives from intellectual and social dimensions, it might be desired to equate likableness across the two dimensions. Similar matching might be desired for comparing redundant and nonredundant trait pairs. The danger here is that the regression effect may have different magnitude for the two classes of traits, thereby vitiating the matching. Good procedure thus requires that the matching be verified with new ratings on the matching variable after the matching has been done.

The typical designs used in research on integration theory bypass the regression problem, even when stimuli are selected on the basis of preliminary ratings. In the meal judgments of Figure 6.1, for example, main course and vegetable were selected to lie within given value ranges on the basis of preliminary ratings for each subject. Stimulus selection was also used in the children's toy experiment of Figure F1.22. The exact values of the preliminary ratings are never at issue, however, because the design and analysis allow for the operative functional values.

7.7 Matching Artifacts

Sometimes it seems desirable to select two sets of stimuli so that they are matched in one property but differ in another property. Besides the regression artifact of the preceding section, stimulus matching can run aground on implicit assumptions about the measurement scale. The following six examples from published studies illustrate aspects of this problem.

Zero-Point Confounding. In a test between adding and averaging rules for group attractiveness, subjects made preliminary ratings of single faces on a 0–100 scale of friendliness. These ratings were reduced by 50 on the assumption that 50 represented the psychological zero of the scale. These revised ratings were used to construct paired groups, one with four faces, the other with three, to embody specified differences in mean and total value. In one illustrative pair, the four faces in one group had the values 17, 18, 17, and 16, and the three faces in the other group had the values 22, 19, and 22. The second group has a larger mean but a smaller total value than the first. Hence a choice of the second group as friendlier would seem to favor the averaging model.

This result was in fact obtained. But this theoretical rationale rests on the assumption that the psychological zero was indeed at 50. Suppose it was at 60. Then the values would be 7, 8, 7, and 6 for the first group of faces and 12, 9, and 12 for the second. In this case, the second group has larger mean and total, both. This possibility cannot reasonably be ruled out because the rating scale in question did not have even a nominal neutral point. Thus, the observed tendency to choose the second group is not serious evidence for the averaging model.

The implicit assumption about the scale zero is embarrassing when made explicit, but it is easy to overlook. Most analyses require only a linear scale. This experiment, however, required a ratio scale, that is, a linear scale with known zero, because the groups were of different size. It may be generally advisable, therefore, to include the C_0 term of Section 2.3 explicitly in any reasoning.

Variance of Subjective Values. The following study wished to determine how attractiveness of a social group is affected by heterogeneity among its members. Two groups of two photographs each were selected to have equal mean value on a prior normative scale but to differ by a factor of 10:1 in variance. For greater generality, the means were chosen from three scale ranges—high, medium, and low. Subjects chose the more attractive of the two groups. These choices favored the higher variance group, though only at the high scale range.

This result led to the following theoretical conclusions: Variability is a discriminable attribute of social groups to which subjects respond directly. This reflects a preference for stimulus complexity, in line with results from motivation theory, but only when the situation does not represent a threat, as in the low-value group of unpleasant photographs. More generally, this result suggests that stimulus attributes are hierarchically ordered in their control over behavior, with survival-related attributes dominant in the hierarchy.

This ingenious reasoning is hardly warranted by the design. The reasoning assumes that both groups of photographs were equated in attractiveness so that the difference in choice preference could be attributed to the difference in variance. However, the equating rests on two implicit assumptions, neither of which seems reasonable.

The first implicit assumption is that the normative preference scale for the single photographs was a true linear scale. The two photographs were about 2 units above and below their mean in the low-variance group, about 9 units above and below the mean in the high-variance group. These units, however, were actually percentages of 100 subjects who had made dichotomous, attractive–unattractive judgments for each of a large number of such photographs. For the high-value photographs, therefore, the usual normal distribution logic suggests that 9 units above represents a greater true difference than 9 units below. Hence the observed preference for the high-variance group could merely reflect a higher mean attractiveness value.

The second implicit assumption is that the integration rule for group attractiveness is an equal-weight average. If weight varies with scale value, however, matching does not produce groups of equal true attractiveness. For both reasons, therefore, the essential assumption that the groups were really matched on attractiveness is uncertain and undecidable.

Value Matching of Choice Alternatives. In decision theory, one popular hypothesis is that the choice between two alternatives is made on the basis of their net values. In buying a car, for example, the person would first integrate the various attributes of each car and then choose the one with the higher integrated value. An alternative hypothesis is that choices, at least when they are close, are resolved by selecting the alternative that is superior on the most important dimension.

To test between these two hypotheses, one investigator attempted to match two alternatives in value and then asked subjects to choose between them. The first hypothesis would predict random choice, whereas the second hypothesis would predict predominant choice of one alternative. The critical question with this test is whether the two alternatives are indeed equated in value.

In one attempt to resolve this problem, subjects were told that player A had a batting average of .273 and 26 home runs, whereas player B had a batting average of .287. In an initial session, they selected the number of home runs needed to make B equal to A in overall team value. In later sessions, they rank-ordered four players, including A and B. Of 41 subjects, 13 gave split ranks, while 22 favored player B with the higher batting average. This outcome agrees with the second of the two hypotheses.

This outcome, however, is somewhat disturbing. Since the subjects showed a predominant preference in the later sessions, the validity of the matching procedure in the first session comes under question. Despite its face validity, it may be subject to one or another of the biases that affect numerical response methods. In this study, the investigator was aware of the problem and attempted to resolve it in other ways.

However, none of those ways spoke to the basic question of the validity of the matching procedure.

Functional measurement may be able to provide the needed validational base for the matching procedure used in this investigation. In the example, batting average and home-run scores would be varied in factorial design. Subjects could judge the value of single players, judge the difference in value between two players, or adjust the value of one variable to equate values as was done in the cited experiment (see also Section 3.14). If any of these tasks lead to an algebraic model, the model will provide functional scales of stimulus and response as a basis for matching.

Correcting Group Differences. In a study of inconsistency effects, an investigator presented pairs of adjectives, one favorable and one unfavorable, to three different groups of subjects, each group serving under a different grammatical syntax condition that linked the two adjectives together as a person description. An appropriate procedure was used to match pairs so that the positive and negative adjectives had equal value across matched pairs but had high inconsistency in one pair, low inconsistency in the other pair. Subjects first rated likableness of persons described by the single adjectives, then of persons rated by the pairs. The aim was to study how degree of inconsistency and syntax influenced ratings of the persons described by the pairs.

Unfortunately, the three syntax groups differed in their initial ratings of the single adjectives, even before they had been treated differently, perhaps owing to lack of random assignment. In an attempt to correct for these systematic group differences, the mean rating of the two separate adjectives of each pair was subtracted from the rating of the pair. Positive and negative values of these corrected scores were considered to reflect greater relative influence of the positive and negative adjectives, respectively.

No justification was presented for this correction procedure. Apparently it rests on the implicit assumption that the simple average of the response to the two single adjectives provides an appropriate baseline. However, the appropriate baseline depends on the operative integration model. If the response to the pair is an average of the responses to the two single adjectives, then the correction procedure would indeed index the relative influence of the positive and negative adjectives. This integration model is known to be incorrect, however, since it does not account for the set-size effect (Section F2.4). Hence the corrected scores do not reflect the relative influence of the positive and negative adjectives.[a] For the same reason, it is difficult to understand how these scores can "correct" for the systematic, preexperimental differences between the three syntax groups. Instead of relying on uncertain correction procedures, it would have been preferable to rerun the experiment with improved procedure.

Effect of Unreliability. Unreliability in the matching variable means that matching can never be exact. Stimuli or subjects equated on some matching variable will not be truly equal. These inequalities should not be confounded with experimental variables.

An example of such confounding arose in a study in which subjects made various judgments of four persons, each described by three adjectives: HM^+H, $M^+M^+M^+$, $M^-M^+M^-$, and LM^+L. The main dependent variable was the likableness rating of the middle, M^+, trait in each description. This component rating varied directly with the value of the two surrounding traits, thereby showing the standard positive context effect. But a different M^+ trait was used in the each description. Although these four M^+ traits were matched in normative value, unreliability in these normative values is completely confounded with context value. Hence the observed differences in the ratings of the four M^+ traits is not a pure context effect, but is confounded with differences in their true values. In part because of such confounding, the data are unclear about one main purpose of this experiment, which was to compare the magnitude of the positive context effect across redundant and non-redundant conditions.

The confounding could have been eliminated by using each M^+ adjective in all four contexts, balanced across subjects. Alternatively, a larger sample of M^+ adjectives would have provided a basis for generalization (Section 1.3.6).

Unverified Matching. A good general rule is that matching should be verified by remeasuring the matching variable within the experimental context. To illustrate, consider the following study, which was intended to show that sociable-type adjectives have greater weight than intellectual-type adjectives in judgments of likableness. This hypothesis seems reasonable on the grounds that sociability is more relevant to the likableness response than is intellect. However, a test requires allowance for possible differences in scale values. Accordingly, two person descriptions were constructed, person A with three good sociable traits and one bad intellectual trait, person B with three good intellectual traits and one bad sociable trait. A standard list was used to equate each trait in one description with a corresponding trait in the other according to likableness value.

The outcome was striking. Person A was rated markedly more likable than person B. Since the single adjectives had presumably been equated across the two persons, it was concluded that the sociable adjectives had greater weight than the intellectual adjectives in judgments of likableness.

But this outcome seems almost self-contradictory. The standard list used for equating traits was actually a list of likableness of persons described by the single adjectives. If the sociable–intellectual quality affects weighting, that weighting is presumably already present in these list values. If the single adjectives were truly equated in likableness, it is hard to imagine how two sets of four could produce markedly different likableness judgments.

The simplest explanation is that the adjectives were not really equated. One possible problem is differential regression in equating across the sociable and intellectual dimensions (Section 7.6). This difficulty could easily have been avoided by getting judgments of persons described by the single adjectives within this same experiment. If the adjectives were truly equated, this would be verified by equality of these judgments. Without this verification, interpretation of the results is uncertain.

Other Limitations on Matching. Matching is a crude method. Aside from the pitfalls already considered, the method is limited to cases that can be matched. This may entail an undesirable restriction of the stimulus materials, as noted in the discussion of negativity effects (Section 6.1.4). Moreover, matching typically provides only limited information, that one variable is more important than another, for example, without much opportunity for quantification. In the last study discussed, the matching method would quickly reach a dead end because it could not compare importance of sociable traits of different value. Matching is sometimes appropriate and sometimes unavoidable, but it should not be used without seeking for less limited alternatives.[b]

7.8 Choice Data

Choice data suffer disadvantages that, although more or less obvious, are sometimes overlooked when an experiment is being planned. One major problem is that choices, being all or none, do not reflect degree of preference. This is inefficient because it loses information that would be available in a metric response. More seriously, it can lead to erroneous conclusions.

One prominent misuse of choice data occurs in developmental research. According to Piaget, the preoperational child, up to 6 or 7 years of age, is unable to integrate information from two or more dimensions. Faced with a choice between two two-dimensional alternatives, these children are claimed to "center" on one prominent dimension and use it as the basis for choice, completely neglecting the other dimension.

But choice data are not adequate evidence for centering. The choice may perhaps show which of the two dimensions was more important; it cannot eliminate the possibility that the other dimension had some effect. Use of a numerical response can reveal the actual effects of both dimensions, as illustrated in the area judgments of Figure 4.5. Extensive studies using the methods of integration theory have shown substantial integrational capacities in children as young as 4 years of age (e.g., Anderson, 1980a; Anderson & Butzin, 1978; Cuneo, 1980, 1982; Leon, 1980; Wilkening, 1979, 1980). The evidence that has been taken to support the concept of centering is an artifact of the choice response methodology.

A frequent practice with choice data is to pool choices across different individuals. Such pooling is sometimes justified, sometimes not. Paired-comparisons scaling of social values exemplifies unjustified pooling across individuals who may have quite different value systems (Section F5.3). Even when pooling may be justified, numerical response methods can offer advantages (e.g., Anderson, 1974b, pp. 37, 63). An application to signal detection is discussed in Section 3.10.

There is no question about the importance of choice tasks. Daily life is a sequence of yes–no decisions. Choice tasks have added theoretical interest since there is some evidence that explicit comparisons among alternatives may induce differential weighting strategies (see Shepard, 1964; Slovic & Lichtenstein, 1971). Even when choices are to be made, however, it may still be useful to obtain a numerical measure of degree of preference.

7.9 More Problems with Correlation

The inadequacy of the correlation coefficient for model testing, discussed in Section 4.1, is only one facet of a larger problem. Correlations are not merely limited in usefulness but generally treacherous.

Correlation is an instrument of the devil [Hilgard, 1955, p. 228].

Sweeping things under the rug is the enemy of good data analysis. Often, using the correlation coefficient is "sweeping under the rug" with a vengeance [Tukey, 1969, p. 89].

Some common problems in using correlation are noted briefly here.

Correlations Depend on Range and Reliability. The size of a correlation depends on the true relation between two variables; it also depends on their reliabilities and ranges. To compare two correlations, therefore, it is generally necessary first to demonstrate that corresponding variables are equated in range and reliability.

Figure 7.2 illustrates how correlation depends on range. The points in the left panel represent the square root relation, $y = \sqrt{x}$, with added variability. This variability was added in a systematic rather than a random way, but this simplification has no essential effect. The straight line was fit by standard regression procedure. The correlation between predicted and observed values is .981, and the mean absolute deviation from prediction is .094.

The right panel shows the very same data, but over a truncated range. Predictive accuracy increases, for the mean deviation is reduced to .072. The correlation does not increase, however, but instead decreases to .956. Either in terms of the true relation, therefore, or in terms of predictive accuracy, the two correlations give a misleading comparison between the two respective graphs.

It might be objected that this comparison is itself inappropriate because the true relation is nonlinear. Mild nonlinearity is not unrealistic,

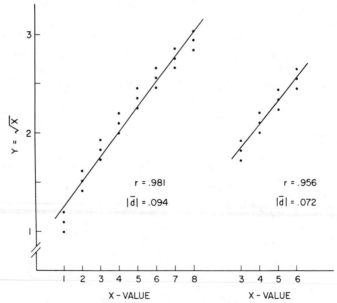

FIGURE 7.2. *Hypothetical data to illustrate that truncating range of predictor* x *decreases* y–x *correlation.*

however, and in any case does not affect the main argument. With a quadratic regression, the disparity between the two correlations would increase.

Even if ranges are equal, two correlations may differ merely because of differences in reliability. For example, one predictor may be based on more information than the other and therefore be more reliable. Because of such differences, the stronger relationship could yield the lower correlation.

One empirical illustration of the range–reliability problem comes from an attempt to study inference processes in person perception. Subjects were first read 12 trait adjectives that described a person. Then they were instructed to write down all the adjectives they could remember (the recalled adjectives). Next they were told to write down any other adjectives they thought might describe the person (the inferred adjectives). Finally, they rated the person on a scale of likableness.

The general hypothesis at issue was that subjects base their impression of the person not only on the given stimulus traits but also on additional inferred traits. In the data analysis, the likableness rating of the person correlated .47 with a weighted sum of good–bad values of the recalled adjectives; this correlation increased to .67 when the sum included both the recalled and the inferred adjectives. The investigators claimed that this substantial increase in correlation showed that inferred adjectives did indeed have a causal role in the impression.

This interpretation is not justified because the size of the correlation depends on the range and reliability of the predictor variables. Range and reliability could both be increased by inclusion of the inferred adjectives, even if they played no causal role. For example, the inferred adjectives might be merely synonyms of the recalled adjectives that were written down to satisfy the task requirement. The given interpretation may well be correct, to be sure, but the correlation analysis is incapable of demonstrating that.[a]

The dependence of correlation on range and reliability is well known but ill appreciated. Statisticians suggest the following standard: Two correlations may be compared only after it has been demonstrated that prevailing differences in range and reliability would not affect the conclusion.

Weights May Decrease Correlations. The unreliability problem in correlation-based analysis appears in attempts to apply multiattribute models to attitudes. Intuitively, it seems clear that some attributes are more relevant or more important than others in determining attitudes. Some theories have maintained the contrary, however, claiming that such weighting is not theoretically valid. The issue is thus between unweighted and weighted sum models. In present notation these models may be written as

$$\Sigma s_i \quad \text{and} \quad \Sigma w_i s_i.$$

Here s_i is the value of attribute i, and w_i is its hypothesized weighting factor.

If weights are psychologically real, including them in the formula should increase predictive power. This idea has been pursued with traditional regression analysis, which has relied on separate estimates of the value and weight parameters. These separate estimates were substituted into the two formulas, and the two respective sums were correlated with the actual attitude. Contrary to intuitive expectation, no benefit was gleaned from inclusion of the weights. This was generally taken as support for the theoretical unweighted sum formulation.

Unfortunately, this analysis is subject to the unreliability problem. Inclusion of the weight estimates adds unreliability to the weighted sum. This increases deviations from prediction and decreases the correlation. Even if the subjects do employ weighting factors, this method of analysis will tend to imply that they do not. This problem has often been overlooked in studies with multiattribute models, so these studies of the weighting problem are difficult to interpret (see also Section 4.3.6).[b]

Correlations Stay Constant under Linear Transformations. This property of correlation is desirable and useful, but it also can be misleading. In Figure 7.3, the curve represents predictions from a certain theoretical model of attitudes. The data points, represented by open circles, are clearly discrepant from theoretical prediction, but the correlation between the observed and predicted values is essentially perfect, .9999. Because the correlation neglects information about elevation and slope, it seems to imply near-perfect agreement even though the discrepancies are substantial. In this case, the inappropriateness of the correlation is clear from the graph. By themselves, however, correlations may have little meaning in model analysis.

Correlations Depend on Predictor Scaling. An odd property of the correlation is that it can be higher when computed from an incorrect regression equation than from the correct one. This paradox, pointed out by Birnbaum (1973), can arise when the scale values of the predictor are biased. Birnbaum used artificial examples, but they were not unrealistic, and they are relevant to standard applications of regression–correlation

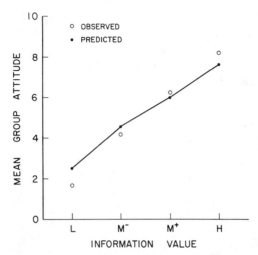

FIGURE 7.3. *Correlation of .9999 between observed values (open circles) and values predicted from summation model (filled circles) conceals the clear discrepancies between predicted and observed. Data from experiment on attitudes developed in group discussion (Anderson & Graesser, 1976). (From N. H. Anderson & J. Shanteau. Weak inference with linear models.* Psychological Bulletin, *1977, 84, 1155–1170. Copyright © 1977 by the American Psychological Association. Reprinted by permission of the publisher and authors.)*

analysis. As Birnbaum points out, this difficulty would not arise if functional measurement procedures were used for scaling.

Partial Correlation Does Not Imply True Relation. Partial correlations have often been used to infer the existence of a true relation between two variables, over and above any effect of a third variable. This inference is based on an incorrect belief that partial correlation somehow "partials out" or "controls for" the effects of the third variable. Brewer, Campbell, and Crano (1970) give a simple exposition that includes 10 empirical misuses from the psychological and sociological literature. One of their examples is noted here.

This investigation claimed to demonstrate a real relation between interpersonal attraction and objective similarity between two persons, over and above their perceived similarity. This hypothesis is plausible, but of a type for which meaningful evidence is difficult to obtain. The evidence actually presented was a significant partial correlation between attraction and objective similarity, with two measures of perceived similarity partialed out.

But suppose that objective similarity and perceived similarity both measure exactly the same thing. Their sum will be more reliable than either one alone and hence will yield a higher correlation than either one alone. It follows that the partial correlation will be nonzero, merely because of the measurement error or unreliability in the variables. The fact that the original hypothesis is likely to be true does not warrant the use of such evidence.[c]

7.10 Interaction and Related Terms

There are several terms, all relating to concepts of independence and interaction, that are used loosely or in more than one sense. This section attempts to delineate different usages and make clear the present usage. For simplicity and concreteness, a two-way factorial design will be taken as a basis of exposition. The same considerations apply more or less generally, even when there is no explicit experimental design.

Independence. The term *independence* is used in two basically different ways.[a] The more common refers to the surface form of the observed data. If the curve for the first row lies a constant amount above the curve for the second row, then it seems proper to say that the stimulus in the first row adds a constant amount, relative to the stimulus in the second row, independent of the column stimulus. More generally, parallelism in the factorial plot could be taken to mean that the row and column variables make independent contributions to the response. This is correct—if only the overt response is considered.

But this is not necessarily correct when there is any concern about underlying process and psychological meaning. Nonlinearity, or bias, in the overt response may misrepresent the underlying process and produce nonparallelism when independence holds or parallelism when independence fails. Even when the overt response is linear, the interpretation of the factorial graph is bound up with some theoretical model.[b]

In model analysis, *independence* refers to constancy of the model parameters, as discussed in the introduction to Chapter 2. This usage is not limited to specific models but applies generally to theoretical analysis. More properly put, the term independence in theoretical analysis always presupposes some model or class of models, even though that model may be implicit and not well defined.[b]

Interaction. Related to the two meanings of independence are two corresponding meanings of *interaction*. The surface meaning is the more prominent, namely, the interaction term in analysis of variance. Absence of interaction implies parallel curves, as though the row and column variables made independent, additive contributions to the response. The second meaning is defined in terms of the independence assumption used in model analysis. Independence means no interaction. A row stimulus interacts with column stimuli when its parameters are not constant but depend on the particular column stimulus.

The difference between these two meanings reflects two levels of analysis: the surface level of the observed response and the underlying level of theoretical representation. This difference is well illustrated by the multiplying model. The linear fan pattern yields a marked interaction term in the analysis of variance, but this interaction refers only to the surface level. Indeed, the linear fan pattern depends on the independence assumption, that is, absence of interaction in the theoretical model. The two meanings of interaction coincide only when the underlying model is additive—and the response scale is linear.

There is also a third, common language meaning of interaction, which may be illustrated by the concept of inconsistency. If a given row stimulus is inconsistent with some column stimulus, an attempt to integrate the two may evoke some interactive process, such as discounting, to reduce the inconsistency.[c]

The common language meaning is intimately related to the process model meaning. To say that two stimuli interact is to say that the response is different from what it would have been had there been no interaction. To demonstrate the interaction, therefore, it is necessary to specify what the response would have been without interaction. This requires some theoretical model, and the reference standard of no interaction corresponds to the independence assumption for that model. As a consequence, unfortunately, it is far more difficult to obtain evidence for interaction than is often recognized (e.g., Sections 7.11, 7.13, and F3.4).

In the present approach, the concept of interaction is used primarily in the theoretical sense. Although the surface meaning of analysis of variance cannot be avoided, especially in statistical discussions, the context should resolve any ambiguity.

Nonadditivity. The term *nonadditive* is also used on two different levels. The surface meaning is the same as for interaction and refers to nonparallelism in the observed data. The other meaning refers to nonlinearity in the algebraic form of the integration model, which is discussed in the next subsection.

Surface nonadditivity is often used as a clue to underlying nonadditivity. Data are said to be inherently nonadditive when they cannot be made additive by monotone transformation. This implies nonadditivity in the integration rule, as in the familiar crossover interaction (Section 5.4).

If observed data are monotonically additive, it does not follow that the integration rule is additive. In the first place, the integration rule may be monotonically additive without being additive. The multiplying rule, for example, is monotonically additive for positive stimulus values. In the second place, data generated by an inherently nonadditive rule may seem monotonically additive because of insufficient power in the design (Chapter 5).

Nonlinearity. The term *nonlinear* has three common uses that are conceptually distinct but are often confused. Each use corresponds to one of the three stages in the functional measurement diagram of Figure 1.2. On the stimulus side, the valuation function, V, may be nonlinear, that is, the psychological value, s, may be a nonlinear function of the physical stimulus value, S. This is a specialized usage, since it applies only to situations in which there is a physical metric on S, as in psychophysical judgment. Nonlinear valuation functions would be generally expected in psychophysics, of course, but they have limited psychological significance (Section F5.4).

On the response side, the response function, M, may be nonlinear, that is, the observed response measure, R, may not be a linear function of the underlying response, r. Linearity in the response function is equivalent to an equal-interval response scale and thus has central interest for measurement theory. Much of Section 1.1, for example, considers experimental procedures intended to make M linear.

Finally, the integration function, I, may be nonlinear. This is conceptually different from nonlinearity in the valuation and response functions, V and M, because the latter are functions of a single variable. In contrast, I is a function of two or more variables, and nonlinearity in I means that these variables are integrated by a nonadditive rule. Nonlinearity in the integration function is also conceptually different from interaction or configurality.[d]

Configurality. The term *configural* refers to response that depends on the pattern or configuration of stimuli. Interactions are thus configural, at least in form, because they refer to violations of independence. Configurality need not involve interaction, however, except in the sense that integration is interaction. Perception of a melody is configural, but that perception is formally equivalent to the rule governing the integration of the notes.

The term configural is sometimes used in a different sense to mean that the pattern of stimuli acts as a cognitive unit. This seems clear enough in the example of the melody, but it does not hold in general. It may or not hold for the multiplying model, for example, depending on the operative process (Section F4.5.4). In the averaging model, similarly, the response can depend on the pattern of weight parameters even though the integration may be routinely mechanical. It is necessary to be careful not to take advantage of surplus meaning when using the term configural.

7.11 Misuse of Analysis of Variance

Cognitive analysis requires a different orientation to analysis of variance than prevails in general experimental psychology. Some aspects of this matter have been discussed previously (e.g., Sections 4.2.1 and 7.10). Two related problems are considered here.

Locus of Nonlinearity. The term *nonlinearity* has three conceptually different meanings, as indicated in the preceding section, and failure to keep them distinct can lead to two problems of misinterpretation. The more serious problem arises from confusion between nonlinearity in the integration function, **I**, and nonlinearity in the response function, **M**. If the **I** and **M** functions are both linear, then statistical interactions will be absent, the data will exhibit parallelism, and the interpretation is more or less straightforward. Ambiguity arises when statistical interactions are present; they could stem from nonlinearity in either **I** or **M**, or in **I** and **M** together. Nonlinearity (nonadditivity) in **I** generally has psychological interest, whereas nonlinearity in **M** is often mere response bias. Unless response nonlinearity can be ruled out, therefore, the data may not be interpretable.

The seriousness of this problem is illustrated by the sharp difference between rating and magnitude estimation shown in Figures 1.1 and 1.3. Because these two response procedures are nonlinearly related, they yield very different patterns of statistical interaction. This disagreement between two plausible response procedures raises general doubt about the interpretability of interactions. This problem arose in the attempt by Hoffman, Slovic, and Rorer (1968) to employ analysis of variance to allow psychological interpretation of statistical interactions in decision theory. This is a desirable goal, but they failed to recognize the critical role of response linearity (Anderson, 1969c).

The other difficulty in interpreting statistical interactions arises from confusion between nonlinearity in **I** and in **V**, that is, between nonadditivity in the integration rule and nonlinearity in the function relating objective to subjective value. This problem can be serious when separate estimates of stimulus value are used, as in standard regression analysis. To illustrate, suppose that the integration rule is linear but that the valuation function is nonlinear. Then the regression analysis, forced to fit the data with biased stimulus values, forces the true linear rule into a nonlinear form. Applications of regression analysis have generally passed by the problem of stimulus scaling. As a consequence, reported nonlinearity in regression equations is seldom distinguishable from bias in stimulus or predictor values.

Analysis of variance proper, it should be noted, does not ordinarily require separate estimates of the stimulus values, in which case it is not subject to this difficulty. However, there is much work for which separate stimulus scales are useful or necessary, as in analysis of multiattribute models. This problem is considered in Section 6.2.

A Problem in Configurality. A number of writers have assumed that the general linear model underlying the analysis of variance is psychologically correct and that each statistical interaction term has psychological meaning. If this assumption were valid, it would certainly provide a powerful tool for cognitive analysis. However, there are three major reservations regarding this approach. First, as is well known, the analysis of variance model with interaction terms always fits the data perfectly, so its psychological validity is untestable. Second, the approach is invalid unless the response scale is linear; otherwise, response nonlinearity will be confounded with genuine statistical interaction, as already noted. Beyond these two problems is a third that relates to the issue of configurality.

This problem of configurality applies generally to applications of the analysis of variance model. However, present discussion is restricted for convenience to the following experimental task. Subjects judged likableness of persons described by sentences constructed from a 2^3 design schematized as follows:

The man is (*kind, cruel*); how probable is it
that he (*helps, harms*) (*physicians, criminals*)?

Each parenthesis is considered a two-level factor, so the design yields a total of eight sentences.

The essential issue is whether the analysis of variance, which breaks down the observed data into three main effects and four interactions, thereby provides a meaningful representation of the response as a sum

of seven corresponding cognitive processes. This claim has some plausibility for this particular task. Subject and verb, for example, would be
expected to show a statistical interaction on the ground that a man's
character predicts his actions. If the man is kind, he will probably be
helpful and not perform harmful acts; vice versa if he is cruel. If these
four expectations are written in 2 × 2 form, they will exhibit a strong
interaction.

The formal model, as proposed by Gollob (1974), Insko, Songer, and
McGarvey (1974), and by Wyer (1975b), represents the response to each
sentence as a sum of seven hypothesized cognitive processes. These
seven cognitive processes are assumed to correspond to the three main
effects and the four interactions of the 2^3 design. Each main effect and
interaction can be written algebraically as a single number using orthogonal comparisons in the standard way. The response, R_i, to the ith
sentence is given by the expression

$$R_i = \sum_{j=1}^{7} \omega_j B_{ij} + \text{constant.}$$

Here the B_{ij} are ±1, corresponding to coefficients in the standard orthogonal comparisons for the 2^3 design. The ω_j are the algebraic values of
the main effects and interactions, computed directly from the observed
data in the standard way. The essential hypothesis is that these analysis
of variance effects represent the strengths of seven underlying cognitive
processes.

The main trouble with this approach is that it rests on an implicit
assumption of independence that is not likely to hold. The response to
each given sentence depends on the meaning of that sentence, not on
the meaning of some other sentence. In the model representation of that
sentence, therefore, the strengths of the seven hypothesized cognitive
processes must depend only on that sentence, not on the other sentences in the design. If there is such a dependence, then the theoretical
representation is indeterminate.

It is easy to see that this independence assumption cannot hold in
general. Suppose that the given 2^3 design is replicated, but with *harms*
replaced by *hinders*. Four of the eight sentences in each design are the
same, namely, those with the positive verb. Theoretically, these four
sentences must each have the same cognitive representation in each
design, with equivalent values of the ω_j in one design as in the other.
But the response to the negative sentences is different in the two designs
because, in particular, harming criminals is quite different from hindering criminals. Hence the ω_j, which are calculated from the response to

all eight sentences, will not be equivalent across the two designs. In short, the theoretical representation of the four common sentences is indeterminate (Anderson, 1977c).[a]

This indeterminacy is general. Although the example rests on an ambiguity in the predicate, *hinders criminals,* a similar outcome may be expected if, for example, *physicians* is replaced by *children.* More generally, the choice of levels for each factor is arbitrary, so the theoretical representation is also arbitrary and indeterminate.

7.12 Stimulus and Response

A fundamental, difficult problem that arises in every area of psychology concerns the structure of the stimulus. Complex stimulus fields are the rule. Most responses represent joint action of a multiplicity of stimulus features or attributes that are uncontrolled and even unknown. All analysis depends in some way on identification of effective subfields of the total stimulus field.

Unfortunately, not much can be said about methods for identifying features or attributes. Techniques of factor analysis and multidimensional scaling have been designed for this purpose but they have not yet been very helpful in judgment theory (Section F5.6.5). Introspection seems to do reasonably well, at least in providing an opening wedge. In perception, for example, the existence of such qualities as loudness and brightness seems clear to common sense. Educated common sense can go further to reveal most of the cues to depth perception.

Cognitive theory is not the beneficiary of such natural perceptual cues. However, the concepts of subjective probability and value, for example, do have manipulable objective referents. This relates them to the external world and makes them easier to study. Other cognitive concepts, such as intent and blame, are almost entirely subjective, without clear physical counterparts. Yet these concepts seem almost as real as loudness and brightness. Common language may thus contain answers to some problems of attribute identification.

One-dimensional response measures are taken pretty much for granted in many experiments. Subjects obediently follow instructions to rate loudness, say, or likableness, and have no idea how remarkable their behavior is. Not only is the response being expressed on a numerical, one-dimensional scale, but it measures the qualitative concept intended by the instructions—or so the investigator presumes. If the question of response linearity is important, the question of the qualitative nature of the response is fundamental.

It seems generally accepted that there are some true one-dimensional qualities, especially for the usual sensory modalities. To the extent that this is true, it testifies to the exceptional advantage provided by introspective knowledge. However, face validity of instructions cannot be taken for granted, as shown by the following two examples.

The first example concerns adjective–noun combinations, such as *happy-go-lucky mother*. The initial work on such person descriptions attempted to test certain adjective–noun averaging rules by using judgments on the generalized good–bad scale of the semantic differential (Osgood, Suci, & Tannenbaum, 1957; Rokeach & Rothman, 1965). Closer consideration suggested that the semantic differential confounded three distinct evaluative dimensions of judgment: personal likableness, occupational proficiency, and social value (Anderson & Lopes, 1974). Conceptual clarity cannot be expected with such a confounded response.[a]

The second example comes from Shanteau (1970a), who showed subjects a sample of red and white beads and asked for one of two judgments about the urn from which the sample was drawn. The *inference* instructions asked for judgments of the probability that the urn contained more red than white beads. The *estimation* instructions asked for judgments of the proportion of red to white beads in the urn. These two instructions are logically quite different: As sample size increases, the inference judgment should approach 0 or 1 (except for a 50:50 urn), whereas the estimation judgment should approach the population proportion. In fact, Shanteau found that judgments under the two instructions were indistinguishable. This result was confirmed in a second experiment in which special care was taken to make clear the nature of the inference task.[b]

Shanteau's work was startling for it suggested that the experimental studies of the Bayesian model in decision theory were conceptually invalid. These studies had simply assumed that the subjects were making inferences, as the Bayesian model requires, whereas they actually appeared to be making estimation-type judgments. Thus, the experimental studies appeared to have limited bearing on the theoretical Bayesian formulation.

Problems of stimulus and response definition are in part methodological, in part theoretical. They have long been of concern throughout psychology, but working knowledge seems still close to the level of common sense. No general theory seems in sight, but an integration-theoretical approach can be of assistance in various ways. Thus, the unitization property of the averaging model allows some flexibility in choice of level of analysis. Furthermore, cognitive algebra can provide a strong form of construct validity. In the various experimental applications of the *Foundations* volume, for example, the success of the models helps to confer psychological reality on the concepts embodied in the stimulus and response terms of the model (Section F1.8).

7.13 Free-Floating Theory

Free-floating theory refers to theory that is deficient in relation to fact. One type of free-floating theory, commonly originating from a normative outlook, postulates processes to explain effects that do not exist or exist only relative to an epistemologically invalid standard. Another type, exemplified in many discussions of stimulus interaction, rests on explanations in terms of processes whose existence is not merely conjectural but contrary to available knowledge. Although basically a conceptual issue, free-floating theory deserves consideration from a methodological standpoint because such theory tends to engender inadequate experimental analysis.

Normative Theory. Normative theories provide rational prescriptions about how people "should" behave. They have been popular in decision theory, where they play a useful role in applications that seek for optimal behavior. Intuitive concepts about probability, for example, are often erroneous and may usefully be guided or replaced by normative, statistical calculation.

The normative standard often leads to postulation of psychological process. Deviations from the normative standard are considered clues to understanding the behavior and even a phenomenon to be explained. This is epistemologically dubious because it mixes two different conceptual frameworks, normative and descriptive. From a descriptive view, deviations from normative standards are not psychological phenomena, so attempts to give them psychological explanations are questionable.

An example is provided by the concept of conservatism, which refers to the finding that judgments of probabilities in certain decision tasks are typically less extreme than statistical theory would imply. Conservatism became the central issue in the Bayesian movement in psychological decision theory (see Slovic & Lichtenstein, 1971), where it was treated as a psychological phenomenon that needed psychological explanation. From a descriptive view, however, it is behavior that needs explanation, not its deviation from a nonpsychological standard.

The difference between these two outlooks is neither subtle nor pedantic. It has basic consequences for experimental design and data analysis. An earlier comparison of Bayesian theory with information integration theory pointed out two examples of associated differences in method (Anderson, 1974d):

> Unfortunately, there is an inevitable tendency to use the Bayesian model inappropriately. Considerable effort has been made to "explain" conservatism in terms of various psychological processes. But from the present view, conservatism is a noneffect. It has a purely nominal existence, by reference to a model that has no psychological content. It is such inappropriate usage that is subject to criticism.
>
> This criticism is underscored by the way that data are presented in typical Bayesian reports. The raw data are seldom given, but instead are transformed into statistical quantities, accuracy ratios or inferred log likelihood ratios, for example, by applying the Bayesian model to the data. Such data may have meaning within the Bayesian framework, but they are difficult to interpret in any other framework.
>
> The importance of a descriptive, process orientation is further emphasized by Shanteau's (1970a) finding that subjects in the Bayesian task seemed to be making estimations, basing their judgments directly on the proportion of sample beads. Estimation is a qualitatively different kind of behavior from the inferences assumed in the Bayesian model. Kahneman and Tversky (1972) provide further evidence for Shanteau's conclusion about the prepotence of the sample proportion [p. 270].[1]

The concept of weight provides another illustration of the hindering influence of normative frameworks. In serial integration, for example, the concept of weight allows representation of memory effects that are disallowed in signal detection theory, which rests on a normative base of optimal behavior (Section 3.10). In utility theory, similarly, extension of the concept of subjective probability to a more general concept of weight (Anderson & Shanteau, 1970, p. 450; Kahneman & Tversky, 1979; Payne, 1973, p. 449; Rapoport & Wallsten, 1972, p. 147) was accepted slowly because it did not fit the prevailing normative framework.

Cognitive Interaction. Free-floating theories are common in attempts to study interactive processes. One illustration has appeared in the discussion of contrast in Sections 1.1.5 and 1.1.6. Other illustrations may be found in the class of cognitive consistency theories that attempt to build on one or another assumption that the mind strives for consistency (Chapter F3).

The attractiveness of such interaction assumptions cannot be doubted. They are intuitively plausible, they make a good theoretical

---

[1]From *Contemporary developments in mathematical psychology* (Vol. 2), D. H. Krantz, R.C. Atkinson, R. D. Luce, & P. Suppes (Eds.). W. H. Freeman and Company. Copyright © 1974.

story, and in some tasks they might even be true. The problem is that most of them are known to be generally false in the tasks to which they have been applied. The well-known contrast artifacts discussed in Section 1.1.5 illustrate this problem. Without design that can rule out known artifacts and alternative explanations, contrast must be considered a free-floating explanatory process.

Free-floating theory hinders investigation in two ways: conceptually and experimentally. In the case of cognitive consistency theories, the interaction explanations, although reasonable speculation in the initial stages of investigation, became autonomous and interfered with the development of informational principles. Perhaps more serious has been the failure to adopt adequate experimental methods to study interaction processes. Interactions have great theoretical interest even though they are not as prevalent as once believed. However, they are by no means easy to study (Sections 7.10 and F3.4). Due to lack of attention to methodological problems, much work on interaction processes is uninterpretable.

Implicit Additivity. Theoretical interpretations in many areas rest on implicit assumptions that behavior should obey an additive rule. These implicit assumptions are usually descriptive, although many contain strong normative elements.

Examples of implicit additivity have appeared at several places in this volume. These include the relative shift index considered in Section 6.1.4, comparison of different populations (Section 7.4), and interpretation of change scores (Section 7.5). The problem in these cases is that investigators make theoretical interpretations on the basis of an implicit assumption of additivity without realizing that any assumption has been made. This can hinder progress, especially when the additivity assumption is not true.

This issue arose in the development of averaging theory. A well-known empirical finding is that neutral information causes the response to be less extreme and more resistant to change. Both effects are natural consequences of the averaging formulation that require no special explanation, even when they are paradoxical. An additive model obviously does not account for these effects and special processes have sometimes been invoked to explain them. Here again, the problem is that failure to recognize the operation of an implicit or questionable assumption often leads to experimental designs that are no longer interpretable once the assumption is made explicit.[a]

A different class of examples arises in connection with linear models, as in interpretations of the term *nonlinearity* (Section 7.10) and in misuses of analysis of variance (Section 7.11). Attempts to fathom the meaning of statistical interactions create the most trouble, for they often, if not usually, have no particular psychological meaning. This example also illustrates the free-floating power of words, for the term *interaction* inevitably gives rise to a feeling that something must be interacting, that some interaction process must be at work. Much might be done for conceptual clarity, not to mention statistics students, by replacing the term *interaction* with the term *residual.*

Objectivist View of Information. The last class of free-floating theories to be considered here may perhaps be characterized as stemming from an objectivist view of information. Two examples from social judgment will illustrate this issue.

Different persons given the same information will usually arrive at different judgments, judgments that tend to agree with their prior opinions. A popular interpretation is that people distort the given information to fit their preconceptions. Such interpretations stem, in part, from an inappropriate normative outlook that locates the information in the objective stimulus. From this normative view, there is a correct evaluation of the information; differing evaluations are therefore easily attributed to distorting processes such as motivated perception.

From a constructivist view, however, information is not in the objective stimulus per se, but results from interaction between person and stimulus (Section 7.15). Different individuals have differing background knowledge and value systems. They will necessarily evaluate the same stimulus differently, therefore, and these valuations will naturally reflect their prior knowledge and values. Calling this *distortion* is as inappropriate as saying that a person who disables some vegetable is distorting its taste.

Furthermore, apparent distortion can be obtained even when different individuals interpret the objective stimulus identically. This will happen when the response variable depends on an integration of given stimulus information and prior attitude, because different individuals have differing prior attitudes. This role of prior attitude is often overlooked, although it is obvious in some cases, for example, in so-called assimilation effects (Section 1.1.5; Anderson, 1974b, pp. 79–81). A more subtle case arises in person perception, in which the individual's general stereotypes of persons affect judgments of single trait adjectives (Section 6.2.2). A difficult case appears in the study of the positive context effect, which became a central problem in the initial stages of integration theory (Sections 1.1.5 and F3.2). This positive context effect also appears to result from an integration of the overall person attitude into the judgment of the single trait, not from distortion or change of meaning.

Much of the literature on distortion effects in social judgment has been done without adequate recognition of the conceptual problems (see e.g., Note 1.1.5b). Such terms as *distortion, assimilation, bias,* and *change of meaning* are attractive because they invoke the image of dynamic, interactive psychological processes. At present, however, they are largely free-floating theory.

A second, related example appears in the phrase, "going beyond the information given," which is used to refer to the ability of people to draw inferences. In person perception, for example, one may judge that a sensible person is likely to be friendly or that a man who sews buttons on his clothes is unlikely to be a police officer. The objection is that this phrase implies that the given information is in the objective stimulus. From a constructivist view, this phrase merely reflects the grip of normative thinking already described; the phrase is meaningless because the information is not simply given but results from a constructive process.

Method and Theory. The present discussion is not concerned with differences in theoretical views or with theoretical speculation. The term *free floating* is exact in that it refers to theory that lacks appropriate relation to fact.

The interaction interpretation of the primacy effect in the personality adjective task, discussed in Section 7.14, may help illustrate this distinction between proper and free-floating theory. In the initial stages of studying the primacy effect, the interaction interpretation was legitimate speculation and indeed the most plausible explanation. But subsequent experimental studies steadily ruled it out in favor of the attention decrement hypothesis. It is certainly reasonable to think that the interaction explanation may yet apply to other tasks. It is legitimate to speculate that some new way of conceptualizing the given task could resurrect the interaction explanation. What is questionable is the continued use of designs and methods that are incapable of ruling out likely alternative interpretations. Too often any value of such research depends entirely on dubious assumptions that are taken for granted. Too often such research is uninterpretable. The basic criticism of free-floating theory is that lack of due concern with methodology leads to needless waste by both the researcher and the public.

7.14 Attention

Attentional processes in social perception came into prominence in the studies of the primacy effect in the personality adjective task (e.g., Anderson, 1965b; Anderson & Barrios, 1961; Anderson & Norman, 1964; Hendrick & Costantini, 1970; Stewart, 1965). Besides illustrating an interesting interplay between theory and method, these studies also point up the importance of attentional processes in information integration.

A Miniature Case History. The studies of primacy (and recency) in the personality adjective task may be viewed as miniature case history of experimental inquiry. Empirically, these studies established that the same six adjectives, three favorable and three unfavorable, could have quite different effects in the favorable–unfavorable order than in the opposite, unfavorable–favorable order. Under certain conditions, the initial adjectives have greater influence on the overall person impression, a primacy effect.

This primacy effect was large, approaching a full point on an 8-point scale. That so large an effect could result merely from reversing the order of the same six words indicated that some important process was at work.

One attractive explanation of primacy was provided by the gestalt change-of-meaning hypothesis (Asch, 1946). The adjectives in the person description were assumed to undergo complex, semantic interactions. The initial adjectives were thought to set up a directed impression that caused the meanings of the later adjectives to change to agree better with the initial adjectives. The later adjectives in the favorable–unfavorable order would thereby become less unfavorable; the later adjectives in the unfavorable–favorable order would become less favorable. These meaning changes would yield the observed primacy effect.

An attentional hypothesis was suggested as an alternative explanation (Anderson & Barrios, 1961). Under this hypothesis, there is a progressive decrease in attention to successive adjectives, which lowers their weight parameters. Such changes in weighting would also yield the observed primacy effect. Under this attention decrement hypothesis, however, the later adjectives do not change in meaning; there is no interaction among the adjectives.

The experimental studies have uniformly favored the attention hypothesis and given little support to interaction hypotheses (see Section F3.3). The classic study by Hendrick and Costantini (1970) provided a perhaps definitive test. The unsuspected importance of attentional processes discovered in these studies has been supported by later work in other areas of person perception (see Nisbett & Ross, 1980; Taylor & Fiske, 1978).

The primacy–recency studies influenced the development of information integration theory in several respects. They provided one line of evidence against the then-popular theories of cognitive consistency and for an alternative formulation based on information principles. They buttressed the assumption that valuation and integration were ordinarily independent operations in this task, an important result for cognitive algebra and one that emphasized the constructive processes involved in valuation (Section 7.15). And at a more mundane level, the primacy–recency studies pointed up the importance of experimental procedures to control attentional processes (Section 1.3.4).

Theory–Method Duality. The primacy–recency problem also illustrates the duality of theory and method. This volume is mainly concerned with method, but method separated from theory cannot be well understood. The primacy–recency problem was perplexing because the primacy effect, although substantial under a standard set of conditions, was not robust. It vanished or changed to recency under other conditions. Taken altogether, the experimental outcomes were a jumble without apparent pattern. In retrospect, it is easy to understand this jumble in terms of attentional processes, but retrospective views seldom recapture the original uncertainties and misleading clues. Even the writer, who favored the attentional hypothesis, failed at one point to recognize its explanatory power (Section F3.3.4).

Methods for controlling attention are important also for model analysis. In particular, attentional factors will affect the weight parameters of the averaging model and, thereby, the pattern of data, in more than one way. The most obvious way is salience; more salient information will tend to have greater weight. The attention decrement already mentioned may be considered a salience factor.

Attentional processes are more general than salience, of course, for they reflect the momentary goal and purpose of the organism that control the dimension of response. The dimension of response affects the relevance of any given piece of information and thereby its weight parameter. In addition, attentional processes will control information search and hence the very information that enters into the integration (see also Section F4.4.1).

Innumerable aspects of procedure will affect attention and many must remain uncontrolled or unknown. Even in the brief president paragraph quoted in the next section, complete determination of attentional processes would be impossible. Nevertheless, exact analysis is possible with experimental designs based on the unitization principle.

7.15 Valuation as a Constructive Process

A basic tenet of information integration theory is that stimulus values depend on the prevailing motivational state and goal of the organism.

Values are not inherent properties of the stimulus; they emerge from stimulus–organism interaction.

Valuation as Inference. Valuation is typically constructive, operating on the stimulus field to process its implications for the goal and task at hand. As the personality adjective studies show, even single words can have very different weights and scale values in one task than in another (e.g., Anderson, 1968b, p. 732; Section F1.8.2). Such task dependence means that information is not so much given as inferred.

The valuation operation becomes more complicated with multiattribute stimuli because attentional processes begin to play a greater role. The following president paragraph from Appendix C (see Section 1.2.7) illustrates some relevant considerations.

> President Truman was a strong advocate of Civil Rights, and requested several important reforms be enacted by Congress. Although Congress failed to act, Truman was undaunted. By using his power to issue Executive Orders, Truman achieved major reforms single-handedly. Over the opposition of both admirals and generals, Truman's first order successfully integrated the armed forces. In addition, Truman established a committee to enforce non-discriminatory clauses contained in government contracts. By 1951, Truman's committee had made real progress toward eliminating job discrimination in large sections of the nation's economy [Anderson, Sawyers, & Farkas, 1972, p. 188].

A simple summary of this paragraph is that Truman was effective in extending civil rights. College students generally treat this as favorable information and place considerable importance on it. However, the admirals and generals mentioned in the paragraph evidently had a negative evaluation, not because they were opposed to civil rights in the abstract, no doubt, but because they felt that Truman's actions were premature and disruptive to service morale and efficiency.

A closer look at the paragraph reveals a more complicated structure. Two main actions by Truman are cited: integrating the armed forces and enforcing nondiscrimination in hiring by government contractors. Also there is an unsuccessful action of requesting Congress to act on civil rights. These three actions need separate consideration. One of the generals might favor nondiscrimination in civilian hiring while opposing integration in the army.

Analysis of the informational structure of the paragraph can be continued. It suggests without saying so that Truman was an effective administrator, for he found ways to achieve his aims despite lack of help from Congress. In addition, there is the positive tone conveyed by the words *single-handedly* and *undaunted.*[a] On the other hand, this same information may raise some question about Truman's ability to gain needed Congressional cooperation.

Even this short paragraph is seen to contain a number of different pieces of information. This information will vary in value, for a given subject will place positive value on some information, negative value on other information. This information will also vary in importance; *undaunted* may carry a very favorable value but it would not have anything like the importance of Truman's first executive order.

Unitization Principle. Valuation of the Truman paragraph is thus seen to rest on a complex of inference processes. The paragraph constitutes a stimulus field with multiple pieces of information. The effect of each piece of information will depend on attentional factors whose importance has already been noted in the preceding section. Furthermore, the weight and value placed on each piece of information are personal, unique to each individual. And, of course, the inference processes are intimately dependent on innumerable aspects of background knowledge about Congress and the armed forces, about the political structure of the United States, and about the state of the nation in 1951.

Analysis of this conglomeration of inference processes must remain largely incomplete in any instance. Attention may be uneven, haphazard, and difficult to study without thereby affecting it. Each individual has unique values and a cognitive background that is intricate, extensive, and largely unknown. Exact theory might thus seem impossible.

Nevertheless, exact theory is possible by virtue of the unitization principle (Sections 2.1.4, F1.1.5, and F1.6.5). This principle makes it possible to treat the paragraph as a molar unit. The molar w–s representation encapsulates the results of all the unobserved inference processes. Nothing need be assumed about these processes; they may be interactive or configural and may have any dependence on background knowledge. The molar representation makes complete and exact allowance for the operative effects of all this molecular processing—as shown empirically in the presidents experiment of Figure 4.3.

Cognitive Analysis. The unitization principle also provides a tool for more detailed cognitive analysis. One function of the unitization principle is as a method for mapping cognitive structure. This may be illustrated in the following discussion of inference networks in person perception (Anderson, 1981a):

> An alternative approach is to suppose that the stimulus and response adjectives both set up an image or schema of a person and that the inference results from a similarity comparison between the two. This allows

the various inference subprocesses to be treated as a molar unit, thereby avoiding sticky problems of attempting to isolate and verify what may, in part, be merely rationalizations for a more basic judgment of similarity. The similarity averaging formulation . . . would have two advantages. First, it would allow for the effects of a superposed schema, as when age, sex, or occupation of the person is specified. Second, it can account for stimulus–response asymmetry of inference, as in the *crafty* person being *intelligent* but the *intelligent* person being *not crafty*.

The network of inferential relations among the adjectives and other stimuli that can describe a person is known as *implicit personality theory*. Similar inference networks appear in other domains, but not a great deal is known about their structure. Multidimensional scaling, which might seem well suited for structural analysis, appears to have difficulties even with the fact of asymmetry. By recasting the task in an integrational format, it becomes possible, in principle, to get functional scales of the inferences that would be helpful in mapping out cognitive structure [pp. 300–301].

A second function of the unitization principle is to provide boundary constraints that must be obeyed by more molecular theory (Anderson, 1981a):

The concepts of valuation and integration may help elucidate this problem of cognitive units. Integration itself can be considered as a unitizing process. Recognition of words, for example, results from an integration of various cues, both focal and contextual. At higher levels, similarly, understanding meanings also results from integration of diverse cues. Moreover, the integration and valuation operations are interlinked: integration operations at one level constitute valuation operations with respect to the next level.

In this view, the processing chain is considered as a sequence of integration operations. At each level, integration has a simplifying effect, reducing a compound or complex stimulus field to a unitary resultant. By virtue of this simplification, integration at the next level can operate across a broader stimulus field.

Cognitive unitization has fundamental importance because valid analyses are possible at a molar level without immediate need to consider molecular detail. Moreover, this molar approach can provide boundary conditions for molecular analysis. When an algebraic model holds, it can be used to dissect an observed response into functional components and to measure each component on validated scales. These functional weights and scale values are complete and exact summaries of the molecular processing. Any molecular theory must obey these boundary conditions. They provide exact, quantitative constraints on molecular analysis that might otherwise be unavailable [pp. 8–9].

7.16 Schema Analysis

The purpose of this section is to show how integration theory provides a framework for experimental analysis of schemas. Popularized by

Bartlett's (1932) studies of memory, the concept of *schema* is attractive because it takes cognizance of the fact that knowledge exhibits organization. Many similar concepts are in current use. Here the concept of schema is used in a mainly neutral way; not as an explanation, but as what needs explanation.

Intuitive Physics. Intuitive physics, which refers to beliefs and expectations about physical events in everyday life, offers a rich field, not much explored, for schema analysis (Anderson, in press-a,b). For illustration, consider the collision task shown in Figure 7.4. If the pendulum mass, M, is released, it will strike the ball, B, driving it up the inclined plane. The subject's task is to predict how far the ball will roll up the incline. The starting point for discussion is that people can make sensible predictions in this collision task, prior to any specific experience with it. This is not surprising, for people have many background experiences with swinging objects, collisions, and rolling balls.

But the very ease with which people can make such intuitive predictions conceals an important problem. Although background knowledge may be considerable, it is usually partial, fragmentary, and indirectly related to the task at hand. Bits and pieces of previous knowledge acquired in diverse past experiences have to be assembled as a basis for response within the particular present situation. This problem is general, of course, not limited to intuitive physics.

The collision task exhibits a family of relatively simple schemas. Among these are the three obvious components of the physical event: the falling pendulum, the collision, and the uprolling ball. Each component event may be considered an integration schema, together with a set of valuation schemas that determine parameter values. The schema concept is appropriate here to emphasize that valuation and integration

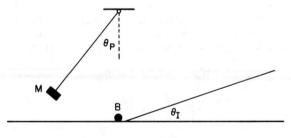

PENDULUM COLLISION TASK

FIGURE 7.4. *Pendulum-ball collision task. Weighted pendulum of mass M is released at angle θ_P to strike ball B driving it up plane inclined at angle θ_I. Subject predicts how far up the ball will roll for various combinations of task parameters.*

both involve knowledge organization. This approach may be useful for obtaining a theoretical and experimental base for schema analysis.

Ball Motion Schema. The focal schema, under the given instruction, concerns the ball motion after collision. The qualitative schema may be viewed as the progressive slowing of the ball as it rolls up the incline. The full, operative schema depends on incorporation of at least two schema parameters, namely, the initial impetus from the collision and the angle of incline.

With situational values for these schema parameters, the subject can make specific predictions. In terms of the focal schema, the task is one of integrating stimulus information, and the focal schema may accordingly be viewed as an integration rule. Available evidence suggests that the two cited schema parameters obey a multiplying rule (Anderson, in press-a,b; Note F4.5.3a). A similar analysis may be given for the falling pendulum schema.

Valuation Schemas. The parameters for the ball motion schema are associated with auxiliary schemas. These are the valuation operations that organize the background knowledge for utilization in the prevailing task and situation. Although some valuation operations are directly sensory or perceptual, many, perhaps most, involve constructive processes as discussed in Section 7.15. Such constructions embody organized, goal-directed processes and accordingly qualify as schemas. Here it may be re-emphasized that the methodology of integration theory can provide an exact approach to experimental analysis of the ill-defined mass of background knowledge that the subject utilizes in the task and goal of the moment.

Collision Schema. The main role of the collision schema is to represent the transfer of motion from pendulum to ball. This may also be viewed as an integration task, in the same way as outlined for the ball motion schema. Relevant stimulus variables include the mass of the pendulum, the mass of the ball, and the release angle of the pendulum. These variables must be integrated to determine the effect of the collision. This integration rule is a representation of the collision schema, although it may not exhibit a simple algebraic form.

If the ball motion schema itself obeys the hypothesized multiplying rule, then it provides a functional scale of the collision effect. This scale is a validated response measure of the collision effect—as it functions within the given task. Hence the integration rule for the collision schema is determinate. Moreover, this functional scale constitutes a molar boundary condition that any molecular analysis of the collision schema must obey (Section 7.15).

Coupling Variables. The transfer of motion from the pendulum to the ball depends on variables not yet mentioned. These are the coupling variables between the pendulum and ball. Different collision effects may be expected if the pendulum is made of rubber, glass, or iron. Different effects may be expected if the pendulum hits the ball head-on or glancing.

Coupling variables are present in the subject's interpretation of Figure 7.4 in the form of assumptions about the coupling. These assumptions are often implicit, but their presence may be demonstrated by contradicting them, for example, by saying that the pendulum is made of soap.

Such implicit coupling variables are inherent in the subject's judgment; they cannot be neglected merely because they are not known. Representation and analysis of the total task are thus by no means simple. Nevertheless, the unitization principle of Section 7.15 allows rigorous analysis even when all implicit aspects of the schema are unknown.

Assemblage View. The pervasive role of background knowledge deserves emphasis. The basic, three-component event schema is in part activated from prior knowledge, in part constructed from prior knowledge. Background knowledge is also involved in the valuation operation associated with each stimulus variable, for example, with the steepness of the incline. Of special interest are the valuation processes for the collision effect, which depend not only on quantitative variables such as the release angle and mass of the pendulum, but also on more qualitative variables that affect the coupling parameters.

This role of the background knowledge is constructive. The schema parameters, in particular, are not themselves stored in memory. Instead, they must be constructed on the spot (Anderson, 1974b, pp. 88–90). A diverse, diffuse field of background knowledge must thus be brought to bear on the basic schema of motion–collision–motion. In general, background knowledge will be loosely, often only analogically related to the prevailing goal. Utilization of this background knowledge requires organizational processes that jointly retrieve and relate it to the prevailing goal.

From this constructivist view, the full operative schema may be considered an *assemblage*. This term emphasizes the bringing together of diverse bits and pieces of background knowledge, which is a main cognitive activity in the task. The basic event schema of motion–collision–motion has perhaps the barest existence, serving as a frame for the assemblage.

The assemblage must be guided or organized in some way. It seems attractive to say that the organizer is the basic event schema. This may be true, but one aspect of the collision task has so far been taken for granted. This is the task goal, which requires separate discussion.

Goals as Organizers. An essential organizer for the collision task is the task goal, namely, predicting the travel distance of the ball up the incline. Other goals could be set: Subjects could be instructed to predict the post-collision behavior of the pendulum, in which case the steepness of the incline would lose salience. Or they could be instructed to describe what noise the collision would produce, in which case attention would focus on the material composition of the pendulum and ball. Each task goal sets up a somewhat different basic schema. Each task goal serves to organize a different assemblage of background knowledge.

This view of task goals as organizers reflects a familiar theme of information integration theory. This theme appears in cognitive algebra as the dependence of stimulus weight and stimulus value on the dimension of response. In general, stimulus parameters are not themselves stored in memory but are constructed for the operative goal, which serves to organize the constructive process. The conceptual framework and methodology of integration theory provide a window into these cognitive processes.

7.17 Memory Analysis

Integration theory embodies a functional approach that considers memory as an aid to judgment and action. Whereas traditional approaches to memory focus on reproduction of given stimuli, the functional approach is more concerned with how memory is utilized for attaining goals. The person's prevailing goal orientation affects the processing of prior memory; it also affects the storage of new memory. Accordingly, this functional approach is a useful supplement to a narrow concern with reproductive memory.

This section sketches some ways in which concepts and methods of integration theory may be applied to certain problems of memory analysis. This discussion rests on three principles from previous work that deserve explicit mention. First, judgment and action are constructive processes for which memory serves as a source of information. This follows directly from the principle of Section 7.15 that stimulus valuation is a constructive process and was illustrated in Section 7.16 on schema analysis.

Second, the construction of judgment and action involve an operational memory that includes, in particular, operations of valuation and integration. Semantic memory is accordingly viewed as a store of information that subserves a more active superstructure of operations (Sections F3.6.1 and F4.5.4).

Third, and most immediately relevant, is the failure of the verbal memory hypothesis that judgments are based directly on memory for the specific presented stimulus materials. Instead, the person's task goal affects the processing of the presented stimuli and leads to a memory store different from that for the verbal items themselves. This *two-memory hypothesis* (Anderson & Hubert, 1963; Section F4.2) means that traditional measures of recognition and recall, being concerned with reproductive memory, are not enough for memory analysis of judgment and action.

Judgment Memory. Functional measurement of memory content and organization may be possible by using memory-based judgments. Standard designs and methods could be used, except that some or all of the stimuli would be memorial. Functional scales of these memory effects could be obtained in the standard way. Although no magic key, this approach may be helpful in measuring cognitive structure.

These judgment–memory effects are in terms of the operative dimension of judgment. They are typically inferences or implications of the stimuli, which need not be equivalent to memory of the literal stimuli themselves. Indeed, they will not be equivalent according to the two-memory hypothesis. Hence, a method for measuring the operative elements of judgment memory is necessary.

A natural extension of previous work in this research program is to study memory effects in lists of adjectives that describe a person. Previous concentration on person perception provides a foundation of data and theory about person judgment that should be helpful in the study of judgment memory. For example, serial curves of judgment memory can be obtained as illustrated in Section F4.2, where they were used to assess attentional factors and memory structure. Other variables from memory theory that could be incorporated in integration designs include delay, repetition, redundancy, and context, as well as certain organizing processes (see Sections F4.5.4, F3.4, and F3.6).

Judgment theory emphasizes percept memory, of which person percepts are a prime cognitive example. Two kinds of schema are thus operative in judgment memory, one for the percept, another for the prevailing task goal. Memorial organization of a list of personality trait adjectives will no doubt differ depending on the person they describe and on the operative dimension of judgment. This matter seems important but not much is known about it.

Recognition Memory. Recognition memory is a special case of judgment memory in which the judgment dimension is familiarity. The present approach focuses naturally on familiarity integration, in which the familiarity judgment is an integrated resultant of two or more stimulus variables. Algebraic models of familiarity integration, if they can be established, have intrinsic interest and can provide functional measurement of familiarity.

Choice data, such as *new-old* responses, can be handled with the integration–decision model of Section 3.10. As implied in the discussion of this model, however, numerical indexes of familiarity may be more generally useful. In particular, it is desirable to develop rating procedures in the manner of Section 1.1 that can yield linear (equal-interval) scales of familiarity. Such linear response measures would facilitate the study of familiarity integration.

Memory Organization. Previous integration studies contain a number of results on memory organization. First, of course, is the meaning-constancy hypothesis: Stimuli do not interact or change meaning when being integrated. Directly related is the halo interpretation of the positive context effect: The strong introspective feeling that stimuli are assimilated to their context is a cognitive illusion. The extensive evidence on these issues is summarized in Chapter 3 of *Foundations*.

Other results on cognitive organization include the basal–surface structure of attitudes (Section F2.5.4), which is analogous to long term–short term memory; construct validity for cognitive units (Section 2.1.4); evidence on the role of conscious report (Sections 6.2.6 and F3.6.4); methods for studying redundancy, inconsistency, and other organizing processes (Sections F3.4, F4.1.8, and F4.5.4); and serial curves of percept memory as distinct from serial curves of item recall (Sections F2.5 and F4.2).

These results carry basic information about cognitive organization. They also illustrate the usefulness, even the necessity of a judgment–integration approach for certain questions of memory and organization. However, they have mainly been obtained with one task of person perception, and their generality needs to be assessed with other tasks and with retention times typical of memory studies.

Person Memory. Most of the results already cited pertain to person memory, inasmuch as most of the experiments employed a standard task of person perception. These results seem to be generally confirmed by work reported in Hastie, Ostrom, Ebbesen, Wyer, Hamilton, and Carlston (1980). This and other work on person memory will be reviewed elsewhere, together with a discussion of general memory theory. Two interrelated lines of further work are mentioned here.

Integration theory provides a direct approach to the structure of person memory. This has been illustrated in discussions of implicit personality theory, that is, the network of interrelations among the array of traits and behaviors that might characterize a person. This approach provides a useful, perhaps unique, basis for measuring organization of person memory (Sections 6.2.2, 7.16, F1.8.3, and F5.6.5). A similar approach may apply for assessing structure of other percepts.

A related line of inquiry concerns memory structure of real people. Judgments about a person one knows depend not only on the person's present behavior, but also on a prior general impression, perhaps supplemented by memory search for relevant incidents and events (Anderson, 1976e, Sections 3 and 4; 1981b). But this view and others like it present exceptionally difficult problems of dissecting cognitive structure because of lack of experimental control. The common tactic of having subjects list remembered incidents, other thoughts, or attributes of the person is treacherous because of causal confounding, halo effects, invalidity of the verbal memory hypothesis, and invalidities in conscious report.

Progress can be facilitated if some measure of experimental control is possible. One approach is to embed the person in a controlled experimental design (Sections F3.4.2 and F4.5.2). Judgments of the person conditional on the stimulus information in each cell of the design would be obtained and analyzed in the usual way. The functional values of the stimuli would provide information about the cognitive representation of the person. Within its limitations, this embedding method could provide structural information not otherwise available.

7.18 Methodology

This book may appropriately be ended with an apology.[a] Although methodological problems have been of central concern in the program of research on information integration theory, these problems have mostly been studied in the context of particular experimental investigations. There is much that remains unsystematic and uncertain, therefore, and attention to methodological problems should be a continuing matter. The present procedures have been productive, but they are only short steps on a long path that continue the work of many previous investigators.

Methodology is a bad word to many. Most investigators are truly concerned with methods, of course, but the term *methodology* suggests a dogmatic stance on standardization of procedure and correct data analysis. It connotes involvement in niceties and complexities of apparatus and especially statistics that are generally barren, often useless digressions, sometimes active hindrances to productive inquiry.

Properly considered, however, methodology is an organic part of substantive inquiry. Necessarily so, for the validity of methods derives from the empirical results that they bring in. There are some properly methodological problems that must be studied in their own right, abstracted from particular applications, including certain aspects of regression analysis, monotone transformation, and parameter estimation. However, methodological studies are dangerously subject to involutional development that rapidly loses empirical relevance. Steady feedback from empirical, substantive exploration is important for minimizing profitless digressions and keeping methodology on productive paths. The several preceding sections on cognitive organization are intended to illustrate this interdependence of method and theory.

This view toward methodology complements the inductive conception of scientific theory discussed in the *Foundations* volume (Section F1.8.1). Knowledge is not divorced from the methods by which it was acquired; those methods themselves constitute an integral part of knowledge.

NOTES

7.1a. The term *demand* is due to Orne (1962) and it and other problems of artifact and limitation have been of concern to many investigators. One part of this literature, on subject artifacts, was reviewed by Kruglanski (1975), who concluded that there was very little direct evidence, largely "because of the methodological difficulties present in those studies purporting to demonstrate the various artifacts [p. 142]."

A useful tactic for determining whether procedural variables have undesirable effects is to include them as minor variables in the experimental design (Anderson, 1968e). In a study of person perception, for example, Lampel and Anderson (1968) found that equal accuracy and naturalistic instructions gave similar results. This outcome supported other indications that judgments were not sensitive to this aspect of procedure.

7.1b. A related concern is that parallelism is somehow obtained because subjects rank order the stimulus combinations or space them at equal intervals on the response scale. This concern is groundless because the response scale is logically independent of the integration rule. Under the given hypothesis, moreover, the shape of the factorial plot would generally be nonparallel (Section 1.1.6).

7.1c. Theoretical and experimental comparisons between two methodologies for assessing rule development in children, one based on information integration theory, the other derived from protocol analysis, have been given by Wilkening and Anderson (1980, 1982, in press).

7.1d. Mention should also be made of a recent essay on functional measurement by Birnbaum (1982). The positions actually held in integration theory are mostly not those that are criticized, but rather like those supported as alternatives. This concerns various issues in measurement theory including context effects, stimulus generality and scale convergence, monotone transformation, and parallelism analysis. Nearly all the advocated positions have, with different emphases, long been standard in functional measurement. Birnbaum has made useful contributions to these issues, but his presentation gives an inappropriate portrayal of other work. This matter may be illustrated with one issue, namely, the parallelism property.

A major emphasis of Birnbaum's paper is that nonparallelism is often obtained in personality impressions. This is presented as a criticism of previous work on functional measurement and integration theory. But in fact the averaging model predicts systematic nonparallelism from experimental manipulations of the weight parameter. One such manipulation concerns reliability and expertise of the information source (see, e.g., Anderson, 1971a). The experimental work on source effects considered by Birnbaum is just as predicted by averaging theory (Section F4.4.3); it seems a criticism only because it is directed at the equal-weight case of the averaging model. The equal-weight case is not applicable, of course, because the source manipulation is expected to affect the weights. Instead, the differential-weight case is applicable, and it gives an excellent account of the results. It is inappropriate to present this work on source effects as a criticism without reference to the prior theoretical prediction or to prior experimental tests by others. Far from being a criticism of integration theory, these source effects provide strong support, both qualitative and quantitative, without requiring any new theoretical assumptions.

Another deviation from parallelism considered by Birnbaum is an interaction that has been interpreted as a negativity effect. It is not correct to say that previous work on integration theory failed to detect this effect or take it seriously. This effect was first reported in Anderson (1965a) and it has been replicated and given serious consideration (e.g., Anderson, 1974d, pp. 260–261; Sections F2.2.4, F2.3.5, and F4.4.2, Figure F4.14). There is a problem in eliminating the response bias interpretation, but the experimental report considered by Birnbaum does not resolve this problem (Section F2.3.5). It is inappropriate to present this effect as a criticism without reference to the work that discovered the effect and discussed its theoretical interpretation in terms of averaging theory.

There is one real disagreement—on an issue of methodology. Most workers on information integration theory have been concerned with controlling attentional factors because they affect the weights and hence the pattern of parallelism. Thus, the nonadditivity reported by Birnbaum (1974a) may merely reflect differential weighting from uncontrolled attentional processes in classroom experiments (Sections 1.2.6 and 7.14). Similarly, most workers on information integration theory have been concerned with developing procedures to avoid response biases and obtain true linear response measures. Birnbaum criticizes this approach and has instead relied heavily on monotone transformation to eliminate response biases. Monotone transformation is appropriate in principle, but in practice it involves the very difficult twin problems of goodness of fit and power that are discussed in Chapter 5.

7.6a. Regression *away* from the mean could be expected with a U-shaped distribution.

7.7a. The theoretical issue concerns the relation between the response to the two single adjectives and the response to their combination. For the averaging model of information integration theory, the regression analysis of Section 2.3.3 may be applied. Let w_P and w_N

denote the weights of the positive and negative adjectives, and let R_P, R_N, and R_{PN} denote the overt responses to the two single adjectives and their combination. Let w_0 and s_0 denote the weight and scale value of the initial impression and take $C_0 = 0$. Substitution into Eq. (48) of Chapter 2 yields

$$R_{PN} = [(w_0 + w_P)R_P + (w_0 + w_N)R_N - w_0 s_0]/(w_0 + w_P + w_N).$$

This relation may be normalized by taking the sum of the weights equal to 1

$$R_{PN} = (1 - w'_N)R_P + (1 - w'_P)R_N - w'_0 s_0,$$

where the primes denote relative weights.

The correction procedure cited in the text consists of subtracting the mean, $(R_P + R_N)/2$, from the preceding theoretical expression. This yields

$$(\tfrac{1}{2} - w'_N)R_P + (\tfrac{1}{2} - w'_P)R_N - w'_0 s_0.$$

Under the simple average model, $w_0 = 0$ and $w'_N + w'_P = 1$. Then, since R_P is greater than R_N, a negative score would indeed imply that the negative adjective had greater weight. But if $s_0 > 0$, then a negative score could also be obtained if positive and negative adjectives were equally weighted, or even if the positive adjective had greater weight. Since s_0 was unknown, the reported data are difficult to interpret. This case illustrates once more that comparison of importance depends on some theoretical model (Section 6.1.4).

7.7b. Although Section 7.7 is restricted to stimulus matching, some of these considerations also bear on the problem of matching subjects, especially across populations that are preexperimentally different (e.g., Sections 3.9 and 7.4). With a single but heterogeneous subject population, the standard technique of matching by stratification with subsequent random assignment within strata can be very effective (e.g., Note 1.2.5a).

Problems of matching seem in general to be poorly handled in psychology, as noted by Anderson (1959b) in an evaluation of all the articles in Volume 51 (1958) of the *Journal of Comparative and Physiological Psychology*. Although experimental expertise has steadily improved since then, even the knowledge that taking a difference score can increase error variability does not yet seem to be widely known (see, e.g., Anderson, 1968e, p. 6).

7.9a. This attempt to study inference processes also suffers a conceptual problem relating to the objectivist view of information (Section 7.13). In the functional measurement approach, the psychological effect of a given stimulus word is a resultant of the valuation operation. Valuation is a constructive process that involves the implications of the stimulus word for the prevailing dimension of judgment (Section 7.15). The stimulus word (and its specific internal representation, if one exists) are conceptually distinct from the resultant of the valuation operation. The same stimulus word has different w–s parameters for different tasks. These parameters are an exact, complete molar summary of all the implications and inferences from the given stimulus word.

From this functional measurement view, it is a conceptual error to identify the psychological stimulus with the external stimulus or with any rigid internal representation. It is also a conceptual error to use the normative ratings of the adjectives as their psychological values. Both problems result from an inadequate way of thinking engendered by traditional views of psychological measurement.

7.9b. A related problem arises in regression analysis, in which estimating weights from the data may be inferior to setting them all equal to unity even though they are not equal (see, e.g., Einhorn & Hogarth, 1975; Schmidt, 1971). Although estimation from the given data provides unbiased estimates of the population weights, their unreliability reflects random idiosyncrasies of the given data. Accordingly, this unreliability operates as bias in prediction to any new sample of data. This treatment of weights also provides another illustration of the difference between prediction and understanding.

7.9c. Structural equation analysis (Goldberger & Duncan, 1973) can in principle resolve some of the objections to partial correlations. This requires ideal conditions that may not be easy to satisfy in practice, as illustrated in the case discussed by Birnbaum and Mellers (1979a,b) and Moreland and Zajonc (1979).

7.10a. There is also a straightforward, factual meaning of independence. The response is said to be independent of a stimulus factor when it is constant, unaffected by variations in that factor. This meaning is not at issue here.

7.10b. The relation between independence and model parameters may be illustrated with the averaging model analysis given for Figure 7.1 (Section 7.5). In the center panel, which is nonparallel, the weight parameter is constant for both curves. In the left panel, which is parallel, the weight parameter is not constant, a violation of independence. If the additive model holds, of course, the interpretation reverses.

7.10c. The term *interaction* is sometimes used to refer to noninteractive integration, two stimuli being said to interact when both affect the response, even in an independent, additive fashion. Although this usage could perhaps be justified, it seems to trade on surplus meaning in the term interaction and can cause confusion.

7.10d. Confusion over the three meanings of *nonlinearity* is not infrequent in regression analysis of substantive problems. For example, one study of job preferences found that a nonlinear regression model yielded a higher correlation than did a linear regression model and concluded that use of interactions and complex configurations was widespread. This conclusion cannot be established with standard regression methods such as were used in this study. Among other problems, the predictor variables were quantified arbitrarily; hence the nonlinearity may have been merely nonlinear bias in the stimulus scale values employed by the investigator. The conclusion, however, refers to nonlinearity in the integration process, which is conceptually different.

Similar problems can arise on the response side. Nonlinearity in the response measure may merely be response bias, without substantive interest. Unless the observed response measure is known to be a true linear scale, nonlinearity in response may not be distinguishable from nonlinearity in integration. In this study, the observed response measure was defined arbitrarily so no interpretation is warranted. Indeed, for the nonlinear model in question, the logarithm of the theoretical response was additive or linear.

7.11a. Although this thought experiment seems clear in itself, empirical verification is given in Table 7.1. Each column lists the estimated values of the ω_j for the corresponding design. Five of the seven effects are significantly different for the two designs. Hence all four sentences that are common to the two designs have markedly different theoretical representations in each design. Since the cognitive process must be the same for each common sentence, the theoretical representation is indeterminate.

The use of such 2^3 designs arose in work on social balance theory by Gollob (1974), Insko et al. (1974), and Wyer (1975b). The result of Table 7.1 and the discussion of the text have occasioned some difference of opinion. Gollob (1979) admitted the indeterminacy but claims it is no objection, that the model was never intended to evaluate the cognitive processes involved in response to a single sentence. This seems to render the model analysis pointless (Anderson, 1979b). Wyer and Carlston (1979) differ from Gollob and agree with Anderson that the assumption of independence is essential. Wyer and Carlston remain optimistic about the model but they do not discuss any of the evidence against independence, such as illustrated in Table 7.1, nor indicate how any of the cited problems may be resolved.

7.12a. Analogous confounding may be present in work on distortion in social judgment: for example, confounding of social favorableness and personal preference (Note 1.1.5b).

TABLE 7.1
Indeterminacy of Analysis of Variance Applied to Balance Triad Model in Subject–Verb–Object Task

	Design	
Effect	Harms	Hinders
Subject	$-.92^{a,b}$	$-.03$
Verb	$1.30^{a,b}$	$.12$
Object	$.39^{a}$	$-.11$
S × V	$3.70^{a,b}$	2.50
S × O	$.79^{a,b}$	$.07$
V × O	1.09^{a}	$.78$
S × V × O	$1.05^{a,b}$	1.94

SOURCE: From N. H. Anderson. Some problems in using analysis of variance in balance theory. *Journal of Personality and Social Psychology*, 1977, 35, 140–158. Copyright © 1977 by the American Psychological Association. Reprinted by permission of the publisher and author.

NOTE: Entries are algebraic values of main effects and interactions for two 2^3 designs.

[a]Significantly different from 0, $p < .01$.

[b]Significantly different between the two designs, $p < .01$.

7.12b. Instructive examples in which subjects judge something other than prescribed appears in the illusion of nonparallelism of Note 1.1.7a and in other optical illusions. These examples show that failure to follow prescribed instructions does not necessarily reflect unclarity in the instructions. Some response systems are natural and may be elicited regardless of the investigator's intention and endeavors. In such cases, it may be advisable to respect the integrity of the response system.

7.13a. The paradoxical effect of neutral information appears in decision theory, in which sample information that is clearly nondiagnostic or irrelevant nevertheless moves the response toward neutral. This form of the effect, discussed by Shanteau (1975b; Troutman & Shanteau, 1977), disagrees not only with the additive model but more generally with the prevalent normative view in decision theory. Similar results have been reported by Nisbett and Ross (1980), who have similarly emphasized that this result creates difficulties for normative views. Nisbett and Ross also used the term *dilution effect* to replace Troutman and Shanteau's *water down effect* (see also Section F2.3.6).

7.15a. "Undaunted: courageous with an undiminished resolution [Webster's Seventh New Collegiate Dictionary, 1963]."

7.18a. I should add a personal apology, for my practice falls short of the ideals cited in the text, especially as regards sitting as a pilot subject. I always go over design, procedure, and outcome of successive pilot studies in great detail with my research assistants, this being part of my teaching as well as my research. I keep a file on procedural details for every experiment, although this is not as meticulous as it might be. However, I rarely sit as a pilot subject myself or observe subjects being run, as I ought to do.

Appendix A

Three sets of instructions are presented here, taken verbatim from the typescript read by the experimenter in the respective experiments. These instructions are not presented to set any standard, except hopefully in clarity and brevity. One purpose of presenting them is to show how simple and ordinary they are. This results in large part because the tasks are natural to the subjects; other tasks might require a more interactive practice period.

The first set of instructions (Anderson, 1965a) is included because this experiment was replicated by Gollob and Lugg (1973) with five different instruction conditions, including an essentially similar replication, as well as other conditions that were expected to produce support for adding rather than averaging (see Sections 7.1 and F2.3.3). As it happened, all five sets of instructions gave very similar results, in support of the averaging hypothesis.

The center-anchored response scale was used only in this one experiment, to avoid possible objections about floor and ceiling effects. It was found to be less desirable than the standard end-anchored response scale because, among other problems, it allowed various subjects to adopt quite different response ranges, thereby complicating the analysis in various ways. In addition, the use of booklets, which allowed two subjects to be run at once, is somewhat casual experimental procedure (which may be contrasted with the second set of instructions). The bracketed phrase [give card] in the second paragraph refers to an index card that contained the cited definition of the response scale and that lay in front of the subject throughout the experiment.

2-4 experiment
April 1964

INSTRUCTIONS

This is an experiment on how people form impressions of other people. Each page of these booklets has 2 or 4 adjectives that describe a certain person. Read each list of adjectives and then rate how much you think that you would like the person so described. There is no right or wrong answer. Simply give your own personal impression.

Here is how you make your ratings. [Give card.] Use 50 to rate a person you would neither like nor dislike. Use numbers *less* than 50 to rate persons you think you would *dislike*. Use numbers *greater* than 50 to rate persons you think you would *like*. Use larger or smaller numbers to indicate your *degree* of like or dislike. Exactly what numbers you use is up to you. Of course, you should spread your ratings out so you have room enough to rate everybody.

It is important that you pay equal attention to each adjective. Occasionally the adjectives may seem inconsistent, but you should consider each adjective as equally important in describing the person.

On each page of the booklet, begin by reading each adjective slowly to yourself. Be sure to read each adjective slowly to yourself so that you fully perceive all the adjectives. Try to form an impression of what the person is like. Don't rate until I say so. At the end of the specified time, I'll say, "Rate & Turn." You then mark down your rating on the line at the bottom of the page of the booklet, and turn to the next page.

Before we start, we'll go through this practice booklet to help you get used to the task. This will familiarize you with the adjectives, and give you practice in using the rating scale. Please realize this: you are free to change the way you use the rating scale at any time during these practice trials. The only purpose of this practice is to get you used to the task.

Instructions—Post-Practice

All right, are there any questions?

Did you have any trouble using the rating scale?

Did you have any trouble reading the adjectives slowly to yourself?

OK, here's the booklet for the regular experiment. The adjectives are the same as in the practice booklet, but they will appear in different combinations.

Remember to read the adjectives slowly to yourself, and to pay equal attention to each adjective. Don't rate until I say "Rate & Turn."

The second set of instructions comes from an experiment on inconsistency discounting (Anderson & Jacobson, 1965)[1] and includes four different instruction conditions that were intended to affect how the subjects handled the inconsistency. The typescript for these instructions did

[1]The following instructions are from N. H. Anderson & A. Jacobson. Effect of stimulus inconsistency and discounting instructions in personality impression formation. *Journal of Personality and Social Psychology,* 1965, 2, 531–539. Copyright © 1965 by the American Psychological Association. Reprinted by permission of the publisher and authors.

not explicitly mention the index card specifying the response scale that lay in front of the subject throughout the experiment, nor the transition from practice to the regular experiment. The first three paragraphs were common to all four conditions; the "second time" refers only to Condition 1.

Condition 1 represents our standard set of instructions, somewhat strained in this experiment in which the inconsistencies were deliberately chosen to be very strong, but included nevertheless for comparison purposes. The word elimination conditions represent a sorting task that could be useful for further experimental studies of inconsistency effects, a neglected area of great interest (Section F3.4).

I am doing research on how people form impressions of others. This is something that people do every day, but not a great deal is known about it. In this experiment, I am going to show you a card with 3 adjectives that describe a person. As you read the adjectives, try to imagine the type of person that the adjectives describe. Your task is to judge how much you think you would like such a person. There is no right or wrong answer; simply give your personal opinion.

I have a number of cards here, each with 3 adjectives. Each card describes a different person, so you will have a number of judgments to make. Make your judgments by using the numbers from 1 to 20. Use 1 to describe a person you would like least; use 20 to describe a person you would like most. Try to use all the numbers between 1 and 20. In other words, spread your judgments out over the whole 20-point scale. The first several trials are just practice to get you used to the task.

It is important that you pay close attention to each of the 3 adjectives on a card. Listen carefully while I read the words. Then I will give you the card and you are to read the adjectives aloud slowly in reverse order, so that all 3 will be fresh in your memory as you make your judgment. After you read the words, then make your judgment on the 20-point scale. [Second Time:] Now we are going to repeat the procedure. It is natural to find some changes in your impressions from time to time, so do not worry whether your new judgments are exactly the same as the first ones. Simply give your immediate impression.

[Condition 1] Imagine that 3 people have each contributed 1 word describing the person. These 3 people all know the person well, and each word is equally important in describing the person. Sometimes, of course, the 3 words may seem inconsistent. That's to be expected because each of the 3 people might see a different part of the person's personality. However all 3 words are accurate, and each word is equally important. You should pay equal attention to each of the 3. Sometimes this may seem hard, but just act naturally, and do the best you can.

[Condition 2] Imagine that 3 people have each contributed 1 word describing the person. These 3 people all know the person well. However, these 3 people might not all be equally good judges of personality. Consequently, the 3 words might not be equally important aspects of the person's personality. In order to decide what the person is really like, you might have to pay more attention to one word than another, at least in some cases. Sometimes this may seem hard, but just act naturally and do the best you can.

[Condition 3] Imagine that 3 people have each contributed 1 word describing the person. 2 of them know the person well and have described the person accurately. However, 1 of the words does not belong; it does not actually describe the person. You must decide which 2 words you think are correct and base your impression on those 2 words alone. Sometimes this may seem hard, but just act naturally and do the best you can.

[Condition 4] Subjects in Condition 4 were given the same instructions as those in Condition 3. In addition, they stated aloud the word that they had eliminated from consideration in each set.

The third set of instructions is from a psychological experiment on the weight–size illusion (Anderson, 1970a, Experiment 2; see Figure F1.10). This illustrates an explicit use of end anchors, as is appropriate with such stimuli. In this experiment, a line-mark response was used, each judgment being made on a separate slip of paper.

Your job in this experiment is to judge the heaviness of a series of blocks like these (show a couple). As you lift each block, you should judge how heavy it feels to you.

Here is how you lift the blocks. I will place the block here on this platform. Then you lift it by pulling down on this handle. Pull the block up once briefly and let it down. Keep your eyes on the block as you lift it. Do not jiggle the block, but just lift it briefly and let it down. You have ample time to lift the block, but you should set it down before the buzzer sounds. If the buzzer comes on, that means you are taking too long.

This is how you make your judgement. Just make a mark on this line. Mark near this end for the lightest weight; mark near this end for the heaviest weight. It is not important exactly where you mark, except that you should stay away from the ends of the line, even for the lightest and heaviest of the weights. For the other weights, mark at intermediate positions on the line so as to express how heavy each weight feels to you.

These two blocks are the standards for the experiment. This one is the heaviest; this one is the lightest. (Have S lift each standard three times alternately; the first time you give each standard, point to the appropriate region of the line lying in front of S and say, "This one should be marked around here," pointing about ½ or 1 inches from the light end, and 1 or 2 inches from the heavy end).

I'm going to start with a practice session. In this practice you should get used to the feel of the blocks, and how to mark your judgements on the line. It will take you a while to get used to the task, so you should feel free to change the way you make your judgements until you find the way that is most suitable. Remember, there is no right or wrong way to answer; your job is simply to tell how heavy each block feels to you. I will tell you when the practice is over.

All right, that ends the practice. Now there's a short rest before we continue.
                                                    .   .   .
All right, now it's time for another break.

Appendix B

Table B.1 presents the list of personality trait adjectives that has been standard in this research program (Anderson, 1964f, 1968d). The L value of each word is the mean likableness on a 7-point, 0–6 rating scale for 100 subjects. The s^2 values are the between-subject variances of the L values, and the M values are meaningfulness ratings on a 0–4 scale. Procedure and statistical detail, as well as references to related work on adjective lists, are given following the table.

The main function of this table is to serve as a handy source of trait adjectives with given normative values. This is often useful, although it should be recognized that these group means are not intended as scale values for any individual. There are 200 starred words that provide a representative sublist of higher quality (see following). In addition, four subranges have been found useful in experimental studies. Each subrange has 32 words with limits as follows:

H: 5.00 (*reasonable*)–5.45 (*truthful*)
M^+: 3.45 (*painstaking*)–3.74 (*persuasive*)
M^-: 2.22 (*unpopular*)–2.54 (*dependent*)
L: .72 (*spiteful*)–1.00 (*abusive*)

Procedure

There were three main phases of the list construction: selecting words, getting ratings of likability, and getting ratings of meaningfulness. All subjects were students in introductory psychology at the University of California, Los Angeles.

TABLE B.1
Ratings of Likableness, Meaningfulness, and Likableness Variances for 555 Common Personality Traits Arranged in Order of Decreasing Likableness

Number	Word	L	s²	M	Number	Word	L	s²	M
1*	sincere	573	.30	370	25	good-humored	507	.73	366
2*	honest	555	.47	384	26	honorable	507	.85	344
3*	understanding	549	.52	368	27*	humorous	505	.86	372
4*	loyal	547	.60	366	28*	responsible	505	.76	370
5*	truthful	545	.61	384	29*	cheerful	504	.83	372
6*	trustworthy	539	.62	370	30*	trustful	504	1.07	378
7*	intelligent	537	.62	368	31	warm-hearted	504	.62	360
8*	dependable	536	.66	386	32*	broad-minded	503	.80	364
9	open-minded	530	.56	354	33	gentle	503	1.00	368
10*	thoughtful	529	.47	376	34	well-spoken	501	.78	332
11	wise	528	.61	354	35	educated	500	.73	360
12*	considerate	527	.76	372	36	reasonable	500	.73	362
13	good-natured	527	.82	358	37	companionable	499	.88	314
14*	reliable	527	.66	374	38	likable	497	.78	368
15	mature	522	.66	344	39	trusting	497	1.20	378
16*	warm	522	.60	356	40*	clever	496	.56	370
17	earnest	521	.73	336	41*	pleasant	495	.86	372
18*	kind	520	.69	368	42*	courteous	494	.94	366
19*	friendly	519	.72	380	43	quick-witted	494	.78	356
20	kind-hearted	514	.87	354	44	tactful	494	.84	354
21*	happy	514	.77	370	45*	helpful	492	.74	374
22	clean	514	.99	350	46	appreciative	492	.78	364
23	interesting	511	.64	352	47*	imaginative	492	.96	364
24*	unselfish	510	.68	370	48	outstanding	492	1.00	334

49	self-disciplined	491	.75	366	79*	cooperative	476	.85	380	
50	brilliant	490	.96	366	80	ethical	476	1.15	336	
51*	enthusiastic	489	.72	382	81	intellectual	476	.91	358	
52	level-headed	489	.68	346	82	versatile	474	.66	358	
53*	polite	489	1.11	382	83*	capable	471	.63	370	
54	original	488	.75	338	84	courageous	471	.85	366	
55	smart	488	.65	362	85	constructive	468	.46	340	
56*	forgiving	486	1.03	370	86	productive	468	.81	362	
57	sharp-witted	486	1.01	368	87	progressive	468	.78	302	
58	well-read	486	.67	366	88	individualistic	467	1.50	360	
59*	ambitious	484	1.14	378	89*	observant	467	.81	374	
60	bright	483	.67	362	90	ingenious	466	.75	334	
61	respectful	483	1.17	360	91	lively	466	.75	360	
62*	efficient	482	.94	374	92*	neat	466	.93	382	
63	good-tempered	482	1.02	358	93*	punctual	466	1.26	382	
64	grateful	482	1.00	346	94*	logical	465	.76	370	
65	conscientious	481	.82	360	95*	prompt	465	1.16	380	
66	resourceful	481	.74	356	96	accurate	464	.98	336	
67*	alert	480	.65	370	97*	sensible	464	.84	368	
68	good	480	.99	330	98*	creative	462	1.15	366	
69*	witty	480	.81	370	99*	self-reliant	462	.96	368	
70	clear-headed	479	.69	340	100*	tolerant	461	.91	372	
71	kindly	479	1.06	362	101*	amusing	460	.89	376	
72	admirable	478	.78	344	102	clean-cut	460	1.49	338	
73*	patient	478	.70	376	103*	generous	459	.89	370	
74*	talented	478	.84	368	104	sympathetic	459	1.05	360	
75	perceptive	477	.84	366	105*	energetic	457	.81	384	
76	spirited	477	.64	342	106	high-spirited	457	.73	350	
77	sportsmanlike	477	1.11	352	107	self-controlled	456	.69	350	
78*	well-mannered	477	1.05	374	108	tender	456	1.30	344	

(continued)

TABLE B.1—*Continued*

Number	Word	L	s^2	M	Number	Word	L	s^2	M
109	active	455	.65	356	139	skillful	438	.80	364
110*	independent	455	1.32	374	140	enterprising	437	.76	322
111	respectable	455	1.10	354	141	gracious	437	1.04	350
112	inventive	453	.86	356	142	able	436	.68	354
113	wholesome	453	1.14	320	143	nice	436	1.28	354
114	congenial	452	.82	340	144	agreeable	434	.95	354
115	cordial	452	.96	330	145	skilled	433	.83	362
116	experienced	451	.76	356	146*	curious	432	1.13	372
117*	attentive	450	.84	372	147	modern	432	.93	302
118	cultured	450	.80	336	148	charming	430	.98	348
119*	frank	450	1.10	378	149*	sociable	429	.85	360
120	purposeful	450	.86	340	150*	modest	428	1.25	374
121	decent	449	1.00	318	151	decisive	427	1.03	360
122	diligent	449	.82	348	152	humble	427	1.51	354
123	realist	449	.94	362	153*	tidy	427	.82	382
124	eager	448	.80	368	154	popular	426	.98	362
125	poised	448	.78	342	155	upright	426	1.04	296
126*	competent	447	.82	374	156	literary	425	1.46	318
127	realistic	447	.90	362	157*	practical	425	.73	370
128	amiable	446	1.02	348	158	light-hearted	424	.99	324
129	optimistic	443	1.30	376	159	well-bred	423	1.13	332
130	vigorous	443	.81	354	160	refined	422	1.16	330
131	entertaining	442	.63	362	161*	self-confident	421	.81	376
132	adventurous	441	.90	350	162	cool-headed	420	.97	338
133	vivacious	440	.91	330	163*	studious	418	1.00	386
134	composed	439	.87	340	164	venturesome	417	.85	320
135*	relaxed	439	.99	378	165	discreet	416	1.29	310
136	romantic	439	1.19	348	166	informal	416	1.00	344
137	proficient	438	.70	322	167	thorough	416	.94	340
138	rational	438	1.37	364	168		414	.97	320

169*	inquisitive	413	1.47	380	199*	idealistic	384	1.35	350
170*	easygoing	412	1.20	366	200	soft-spoken	380	1.03	354
171*	outgoing	412	1.46	364	201	disciplined	379	1.24	346
172	self-sufficient	412	1.30	358	202*	serious	379	.89	366
173	casual	411	1.11	348	203	definite	375	.76	328
174	consistent	411	1.01	352	204	convincing	374	.76	346
175	moral	411	1.67	332	205*	persuasive	374	.92	378
176*	self-assured	411	.72	364	206*	obedient	373	1.67	380
177	untiring	410	.98	350	207	quick	373	1.33	326
178	hopeful	406	.92	328	208	sophisticated	372	.95	332
179*	calm	406	.84	366	209*	thrifty	372	.75	372
180	strong-minded	404	1.27	336	210*	sentimental	371	1.10	360
181	positive	403	1.28	342	211	objective	370	1.81	352
182*	confident	401	1.04	378	212*	nonconforming	369	1.33	370
183	artistic	400	1.58	348	213	righteous	369	2.24	312
184	precise	400	1.05	358	214	mathematical	367	1.01	326
185	scientific	400	1.05	340	215	meditative	366	1.52	324
186*	orderly	399	.84	360	216	fearless	366	1.12	358
187	social	398	1.05	338	217*	systematic	366	1.12	360
188	direct	396	1.07	338	218	subtle	365	1.00	320
189*	careful	390	.84	364	219	normal	362	1.21	324
190	candid	389	1.43	316	220*	daring	360	1.03	358
191	comical	389	1.09	360	221	middleclass	360	.99	328
192	obliging	389	1.53	334	222	lucky	358	1.30	348
193*	self-critical	389	1.55	360	223*	proud	358	1.66	368
194	fashionable	387	1.28	344	224	sensitive	358	2.00	354
195	religious	387	1.93	352	225	moralistic	357	2.13	310
196	soft-hearted	387	1.69	348	226*	talkative	352	1.32	390
197	dignified	386	1.05	358	227*	excited	351	.86	364
198	philosophical	386	1.78	326	228	moderate	351	.90	312

(continued)

TABLE B.1—*Continued*

Number	Word	L	s²	M	Number	Word	L	s²	M
229	satirical	351	1.18	324	259	solemn	289	.85	338
230	prudent	348	1.71	320	260	blunt	287	1.63	352
231	reserved	348	1.00	356	261	self-righteous	287	2.46	310
232*	persistent	347	1.66	382	262	average	284	.90	320
233	meticulous	346	1.38	348	263	discriminating	283	3.48	350
234*	unconventional	346	.92	344	264*	emotional	283	1.23	376
235	deliberate	345	1.40	344	265	unlucky	280	.52	360
236	painstaking	345	1.44	334	266*	bashful	279	.65	380
237*	bold	336	1.22	366	267	self-concerned	279	1.64	334
238	suave	335	1.40	322	268	authoritative	274	1.81	334
239*	cautious	334	.77	364	269*	lonesome	274	1.06	366
240	innocent	332	1.27	342	270*	restless	274	.76	362
241	inoffensive	332	.91	330	271	choosy	272	1.62	334
242	shrewd	328	2.47	346	272	self-possessed	272	2.53	284
243	methodical	325	1.54	336	273	naive	270	1.06	360
244	nonchalant	324	1.23	356	274	opportunist	270	2.47	342
245	self-contented	324	2.04	324	275	theatrical	269	1.59	326
246*	perfectionistic	322	1.69	380	276	unsophisticated	267	1.23	332
247	forward	318	1.12	346	277	impressionable	266	.91	346
248*	excitable	317	1.15	366	278	ordinary	266	.77	332
249	outspoken	313	1.77	362	279	strict	266	1.30	348
250	prideful	313	1.99	350	280	skeptical	264	1.52	348
251*	quiet	311	.91	376	281	extravagant	263	.88	360
252*	impulsive	307	1.58	380	282	forceful	263	1.65	358
253*	aggressive	304	1.43	372	283	cunning	262	2.18	344
254	changeable	297	1.08	356	284	inexperienced	262	.66	344
255	conservative	295	.92	352	285	unmethodical	262	.86	310
256*	shy	291	.89	376	286	daredevil	261	1.23	344
257	hesitant	290	.76	358	287	wordy	261	1.05	350
258*	unpredictable	290	1.26	378	288*	daydreamer	260	.95	368

#	Word			
289	conventional	260	.95	322
290*	materialistic	260	1.66	370
291	self-satisfied	260	2.00	346
292*	rebellious	258	1.40	370
293	eccentric	257	1.58	336
294	opinionated	257	1.98	356
295	stern	257	1.10	356
296*	lonely	256	1.02	364
297*	dependent	254	1.97	360
298	unsystematic	253	.92	344
299*	self-conscious	249	.92	366
300	undecided	249	.86	342
301	resigned	248	1.22	320
302	clownish	247	1.73	348
303	anxious	246	.90	338
304	conforming	246	1.26	362
305*	critical	243	1.46	378
306*	conformist	241	1.15	372
307	radical	241	1.80	340
308	dissatisfied	239	1.65	356
309	old-fashioned	239	1.39	340
310	meek	238	1.37	346
311	frivolous	237	1.55	314
312	discontented	237	1.00	358
313	troubled	235	.71	360
314	irreligious	234	1.74	308
315	overcautious	229	.55	360
316*	silent	228	.83	368
317	tough	228	1.74	336
318	ungraceful	228	.87	350
319*	argumentative	227	1.25	354
320	withdrawing	227	.78	342
321	uninquisitive	225	.94	358
322*	forgetful	224	.83	386
323	inhibited	224	.87	342
324	unskilled	224	.71	360
325	crafty	223	1.98	342
326	passive	223	.97	348
327	immodest	222	1.61	340
328	unpopular	222	.80	362
329*	timid	222	.78	380
330	spendthrift	221	.73	354
331	temperamental	221	1.10	360
332*	gullible	219	.88	366
333*	indecisive	219	.90	376
334	silly	219	1.53	350
335	submissive	219	.90	336
336	unstudious	218	1.06	338
337	preoccupied	216	1.12	358
338	tense	215	.90	356
339*	fearful	214	.69	370
340	unromantic	214	1.33	334
341*	absent-minded	213	1.00	382
342*	impractical	213	1.12	364
343	withdrawn	213	.80	356
344	unadventurous	212	.93	356
345*	sarcastic	210	1.30	370
346	sad	209	.93	358
347*	unemotional	209	1.50	366
348	worrying	209	.71	366

(continued)

TABLE B.1—Continued

Number	Word	L	s^2	M		Number	Word	L	s^2	M
349	high-strung	208	1.57	334		379	illogical	186	.97	354
350	unoriginal	207	.81	350		380	rash	186	.59	342
351	unpoised	206	.76	332		381	unenthusiastic	186	1.05	356
352	compulsive	205	1.20	320		382	inaccurate	185	.59	318
353*	worrier	205	1.00	376		383	noninquisitive	184	.90	358
354	demanding	203	.94	362		384	unagreeable	184	1.08	340
355*	unhappy	203	.98	376		385	jumpy	183	.73	344
356*	indifferent	202	1.31	372		386*	possessive	183	1.62	378
357	uncultured	201	1.00	342		387	purposeless	183	1.90	344
358*	clumsy	199	.92	376		388*	moody	182	1.36	370
359*	insecure	198	.75	370		389	unenterprising	180	.81	320
360	unentertaining	198	.65	338		390	unintellectual	180	1.17	332
361	imitative	198	1.17	330		391	unwise	180	.79	358
362	melancholy	198	1.13	342		392*	oversensitive	179	.77	364
363	mediocre	197	1.10	336		393	inefficient	178	.68	358
364	obstinate	197	.94	348		394	reckless	178	1.42	362
365*	unhealthy	197	1.42	364		395	pompous	177	1.43	326
366	headstrong	196	1.17	336		396	uncongenial	175	.69	304
367*	nervous	196	.83	380		397*	untidy	175	.92	386
368	nonconfident	196	.87	344		398	unaccommodating	174	.68	312
369*	stubborn	196	1.31	380		399*	noisy	173	.88	378
370*	unimaginative	195	1.06	368		400	squeamish	172	.97	316
371	down-hearted	194	.97	288		401	cynical	171	1.26	334
372*	unobservant	194	.90	366		402*	angry	169	.90	374
373*	inconsistent	193	.91	372		403	listless	169	.72	332
374*	unpunctual	192	.96	366		404	uninspiring	169	.64	336
375	unindustrious	191	.81	354		405*	unintelligent	168	1.07	364
376	disturbed	189	.97	312		406*	domineering	167	1.52	382
377*	superstitious	189	1.33	376		407	scolding	166	.67	346
378	frustrated	188	.93	350		408*	depressed	166	1.01	370

409	unobliging	165	.86	322	439	unsporting	152	.80	334
410*	pessimistic	164	1.06	376	440	finicky	150	.68	316
411*	unattentive	164	.74	364	441	resentful	150	.90	352
412	boisterous	163	1.10	352	442	unruly	150	.88	324
413	suspicious	163	.88	362	443*	fault-finding	148	.96	358
414	inattentive	162	1.13	356	444	messy	147	.78	370
415*	overconfident	162	.88	376	445	misfit	147	1.28	322
416	smug	161	.68	304	446*	uninteresting	146	.78	372
417*	unsociable	161	1.13	354	447	scornful	145	.88	350
418	unproductive	160	.65	346	448	antisocial	144	1.24	358
419*	wasteful	160	.67	366	449*	irritable	143	.85	378
420	fickle	159	1.13	330	450	stingy	143	.69	368
421	neglectful	159	.59	356	451	tactless	142	.85	356
422*	short-tempered	159	.85	376	452*	careless	140	.91	374
423	hot-headed	158	1.09	362	453	foolish	140	.83	348
424	unsocial	158	1.16	332	454	troublesome	140	.73	364
425*	envious	157	.77	364	455	ungracious	140	.71	344
426*	overcritical	157	.85	374	456	negligent	139	.68	360
427	scheming	156	1.50	348	457	wishy-washy	139	1.17	328
428	sly	156	1.58	346	458	profane	137	1.65	312
429	weak	155	1.02	338	459*	gloomy	136	.84	376
430	foolhardy	154	1.00	330	460	helpless	136	1.12	358
431	immature	154	.88	352	461*	disagreeable	134	.67	372
432*	dominating	153	1.28	372	462	touchy	134	.83	362
433	showy	153	.92	354	463	irrational	130	.70	354
434*	sloppy	153	.96	376	464	tiresome	130	.70	340
435*	unsympathetic	153	1.32	366	465*	disobedient	128	1.23	378
436	uncompromising	153	1.26	358	466*	complaining	127	.74	374
437*	hot-tempered	152	1.06	366	467	lifeless	127	.68	354
438	neurotic	152	1.34	300	468	vain	127	.99	350

(continued)

TABLE B.1—Continued

Number	Word	L	s²	M	Number	Word	L	s²	M
469*	lazy	126	.88	380	499*	irresponsible	106	1.17	372
470*	unappreciative	126	.84	372	500*	prejudiced	106	1.33	376
471	maladjusted	123	1.07	314	501	bragging	104	.72	370
472	aimless	122	1.16	342	502*	jealous	104	.77	372
473*	boastful	122	.74	380	503*	unpleasant	104	.81	372
474	dull	121	.81	352	504*	unreliable	104	.93	386
475*	gossipy	119	.96	376	505*	impolite	103	.72	374
476	unappealing	119	1.04	332	506	crude	102	1.29	360
477	hypochondriac	118	.88	356	507*	nosey	102	.67	378
478*	irritating	118	.67	372	508	humorless	101	.82	362
479	petty	118	.73	336	509*	quarrelsome	101	.72	370
480	shallow	118	1.00	332	510	abusive	100	.83	330
481	deceptive	117	1.01	358	511*	distrustful	99	1.24	378
482	grouchy	117	.61	366	512	intolerant	98	.97	362
483*	egotistical	116	1.25	372	513	unforgiving	98	.71	368
484	meddlesome	116	.62	344	514*	boring	97	.76	374
485	uncivil	116	.96	300	515	unethical	97	.90	342
486*	cold	113	.94	360	516	unreasonable	97	.86	370
487	unsportsmanlike	113	.72	356	517*	self-centered	96	1.13	380
488	bossy	112	.89	370	518	snobbish	96	.87	356
489	unpleasing	112	.71	342	519	unkindly	96	.64	358
490*	cowardly	110	.82	374	520*	ill-mannered	95	.76	374
491*	discourteous	110	.80	370	521	ill-tempered	95	.62	362
492	incompetent	110	.68	364	522*	unfriendly	92	.80	386
493	childish	109	.81	360	523*	hostile	91	.77	372
494	superficial	109	.95	330	524	dislikable	90	.78	340
495*	ungrateful	109	.71	370	525	ultra-critical	90	.98	348
496	self-conceited	108	1.14	304	526	offensive	88	.83	362
497	hard-hearted	107	1.00	328	527	belligerent	86	.79	332
498	unfair	107	1.00	364	528	underhanded	86	1.19	330

529	annoying	84	.66	358
530	disrespectful	83	.79	360
531*	loud-mouthed	83	.87	376
532*	selfish	82	.65	384
533*	narrow-minded	80	.58	374
534	vulgar	79	1.10	354
535	heartless	78	.92	350
536	insolent	78	.88	322
537	thoughtless	77	.76	366
538*	rude	76	.79	376
539*	conceited	74	.84	378
540*	greedy	72	.61	374
541	spiteful	72	.61	338
542	insulting	69	.86	370
543*	insincere	66	.65	364
544*	unkind	66	.71	378
545*	untrustworthy	65	.63	376
546	deceitful	62	.96	360
547	dishonorable	52	.47	342
548*	malicious	52	.49	346
549*	obnoxious	48	.60	376
550*	untruthful	43	.43	380
551*	dishonest	41	.51	386
552*	cruel	40	.54	376
553*	mean	37	.48	356
554*	phony	27	.30	360
555*	liar	26	.36	392

SOURCE: Adapted from N. H. Anderson. Likableness ratings of 555 personality-trait words. *Journal of Personality and Social Psychology*, 1968, 9, 272–279. Copyright © 1968 by the American Psychological Association. Adapted by permission of the publisher and author.

NOTE: Decimal points omitted on L and M values.

*Starred sublist of 200 high meaningful words; see text.

WORD SELECTION

Step 1. As the first step in the list construction, the writer went through the approximately 18,000 trait-names compiled by Allport and Odbert (1936). An effort was made to extract all entries that were at all likely to be useful, and about 3500 selections were made in this way.

Step 2. These 3500 words were then screened to about 2200 by the writer and an assistant. Words in the following categories were eliminated: (*a*) extreme words, such as *ferocious* and *majestic;* (*b*) words denoting temporary states such as *aghast* and *hurt;* (*c*) words pertaining to physical characteristics such as *emaciated* and *hairy;* (*d*) strongly sex-linked words such as *beautiful* and *alluring;* and (*e*) other words not considered suitable for the impression-formation task, such as *honey-tongued, anal,* and *fond.*

Step 3. Many of the 2200 words retained at Step 2 would be relatively unfamiliar to college students. To weed out unfamiliar words, the list was next rated by 20 subjects who were instructed: (*a*) to mark the word with an X "unless the word is quite meaningful to you"; and (*b*) to mark the remaining words 0, 1, 2, or 3 according to their appropriateness for describing college students. Considerable emphasis was given to this last aspect of the instructions. The writer went over the instructions with the subjects who then rated a practice sheet of words. Some difficulty was experienced in this rating procedure and considerable pilot work was required, apparently because of a strong affinity in some subjects to rate along a favorableness dimension. This difficulty also arose in the pilot work for the meaningfulness ratings below.

Words with more than two Xs were first eliminated. An arbitrary cutoff was then chosen for the sum of the appropriateness ratings to yield the final set of 555 words.

LIKABLENESS RATINGS

The final list of 555 words was now rated by 100 subjects on a 7-point scale. They were instructed to use the numbers 0–6 about equally often, with 0 being defined as "least favorable or desirable" and 6 as "most favorable or desirable." The intermediate numbers were listed on the sheet, but not verbally defined.

The subjects were told to think of a person as being described by each word and to rate the word according to how much they would like the person. It was emphasized that each subject should rate according to his own personal opinion. There were five pages of words, and 8 minutes were allotted each page. Subjects were run one, two, or three at a time. Half of the subjects were of either sex, and the two experimenters were balanced over sex of subject.

MEANINGFULNESS RATINGS

The list of 555 words was also rated on meaningfulness by 50 subjects, half of each sex. The scale ranged from 0 ("I have almost no idea of the meaning of this word") to 4 ("I have a very clear and definite understanding of the meaning of this word"). The intermediate steps were also verbally categorized in an attempt to get a reasonably large spread of ratings.

The subjects were instructed to rate the words on how well they knew their meanings as descriptions of people, and encouraged to spread their ratings "over the whole scale as much as you reasonably can." Subjects were run one or two at a time. The same word booklets and timing were used as for the likableness ratings (Anderson, 1968d, pp. 272, 277).

Results

The frequency distribution of L values, given in Figure B.1, is notable for its bimodality. The subjects tended to consider the adjectives positive or negative, with a paucity of neutral words. Other evidence shows that this bimodality is real, not a response-scale artifact (see Figure F2.2). It is tempting to speculate that the bimodality represents a general polarizing tendency in evaluative judgment, perhaps a consequence of the prevailing ecological need to make yes–no decisions.

Nearly two-thirds of the M values are 3.50 or larger, considered highly meaningful. This skewing reflects the preliminary screenings in

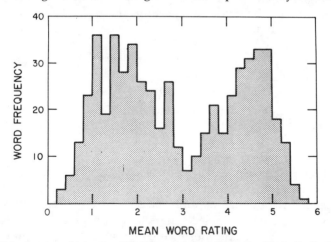

FIGURE B.1. *Frequency histogram of likableness values of 555 personality trait adjectives. (From N. H. Anderson. Likableness ratings of 555 personality–trait words. Journal of Personality and Social Psychology, 1968, 9, 272–279. Copyright © 1968 by the American Psychological Association. Reprinted by permission of the publisher and author.)*

the list construction procedure. The M values tend to be larger near the extremes than in the center, in agreement with direct ratings of importance (Figure 6.4). It may be worth noting that some subjects had an extreme tendency to rate on likableness rather than meaningfulness. Despite considerable pains, the meaningfulness instructions were never completely satisfactory and the cause was never determined. However, this problem did not recur with the importance ratings in the later experiment of Figure 6.4.

The s^2 values largely reflect between-subjects differences. This becomes prominent in the most variable words, such as *discriminating* ($s^2 = 3.48$) and *sensitive* ($s^2 = 2.00$), which have two distinct meanings. The same holds for most of the 11 words with $s^2 \geq 2.00$, namely, *cunning, discriminating, moralistic, opportunistic, righteous, self-contented, self-possessed, self-righteous, self-satisfied, sensitive,* and *shrewd.*

The 200 starred words include the 16 words with the highest and lowest L values; these words are useful as end anchors. The remaining range of L values was split into 10 subranges, and words were chosen from each subrange in approximate proportion to their total frequency. Words were mainly selected to have high M values within each subrange, and words with high s^2 were generally omitted. A small number of words were included or excluded for other reasons. For example, the criterion cutoff on M in the highest subrange was 3.70, but *warm* at 3.56 was retained for historical reasons. Again, *imaginative* at 3.64 was included to provide an opposite for *unimaginative*.

Data on reliability have been obtained by Edwards at Ohio State University and by Schmidt and Rosenbaum at the University of Iowa (Anderson, 1968d, p. 278). Edwards obtained ratings of 554 of the words in Table B.1 on a 7-point scale from 80 male and 80 female students in introductory psychology classes. Schmidt and Rosenbaum obtained ratings of 140 of the words in Table B.1 on a 7-point scale from 53 males and 76 females. The correlation with the mean L-scores of Table B.1 was .98 in both cases. It should be recognized, of course, that these correlations of mean ratings do not reflect the substantial individual differences.

In another reliability analysis, 20 adjectives were chosen by stratified sampling, and 10 males and 10 females at the University of California, San Diego, rated each adjective four times, twice on each of 2 days, 1 week apart. To minimize memory effects across successive ratings, a graphic scale was used. Subjects marked a 2-inch line labeled "Dislike" and "Like" at its ends, and these were read to the nearest .1 inch. These mean ratings had a product-moment correlation of .992 with the entries in Table B.1.

TABLE B.2
Summary Analysis of Variance: Reliability Analysis of
Likableness Ratings

Source	df	MS
*Subjects	18	200.35
Sex (X)	1	4.00
*Words	19	1875.10
*W × X	19	13.37
*W × Ss	342	29.62
Day	1	.20
D × X	1	3.06
D × Ss	18	6.20
*Run	1	25.50
R × X	1	.00
R × Ss	18	3.24
Day × Run	1	1.69
D × R × X	1	.01
D × R × Ss	18	2.70
Day × Words	19	4.01
D × W × X	19	3.86
D × W × Ss	342	4.98
Run × Words	19	2.57
R × W × X	19	2.96
R × W × Ss	342	2.57
Day × Run × Words	19	3.05
D × R × W × X	19	2.05
D × R × W × Ss	342	2.47

Of more interest for the reliability analysis are the results of the five-
way analysis of variance summarized in Table B.2, where the five
sources with mean squares greater than 10 are starred. The highest, of
course, is for Words. The Subjects source is next, but this main effect
merely signifies that the grand mean ratings were different for different
subjects. More pertinent are the Word × Subject and the Word × Sex
interactions, which show that the responses for different subjects cannot
be accounted for by differences in scale zero points. These interactions
do not prove real differences in individual value systems, however,
since they can arise if the subjects have identical values but different
units in their usage of the rating scale.

The final source is Runs within Days. This mean square reflects a drop
in overall mean rating from 9.56 to 9.31 from the first to the second run

of the day. This effect is small, only 1% of the total response range. It has little practical significance, but it does testify to the high intraindividual reliability that allows so small an effect to be detected.

F ratios are not included in Table B.2 since they depend on which sources are assumed to be random factors. It may be noted, however, that the results imply that the Run factor, which would ordinarily be considered a random factor, is actually a fixed factor.

Related Work

A number of articles related to the above list can only be mentioned briefly here. Similar studies in other nations have been reported for 100 German personality trait words (Schönbach, 1972), for 455 Japanese personality trait words (Aoki, 1971), and for 557 Chinese personality trait adjectives (Yang & Yang, 1971). The last study also obtained bimodality even more pronounced than in Figure B.1 above.

Several articles have been concerned with the question of whether the 555 adjectives of Table B.1 have changed their meanings or values since 1964 (Conolley & Knight, 1976; Conolley & Maruyama, 1976; Lück, Regelman, & Schönbach, 1976; McKillip, 1978; Rosnow, Wainer, & Arms, 1969). This question is interesting because it bears on temporal trends in the culture, but it presents exceptional methodological difficulties. First, 555 adjectives provide 555 opportunities for Type I error, a problem that is severely compounded by selection–regression effects. This problem was considered by McKillip, who argued that the changes claimed by Conolley and Knight were largely a result of statistical regression. Second, comparison of ratings of single adjectives across different populations or time periods is largely meaningless (Sections 1.1.8, 7.4). Even the Word × Subject interaction in the present data is not adequate evidence for real individual differences in value. The use of trait clusters or syndromes by Lück et al. may be a helpful step toward a methodology for comparative analysis.

Appendix C

President Paragraphs

This appendix presents the 220 biographical paragraphs about United States presidents mentioned in Section 1.2.7. This material is reproduced from *Behavior Research Methods & Instrumentation*, 1972, 4, 177–192. (Copyright 1972 by the Psychonomic Society. Reproduced by permission.)

NORMAN H. ANDERSON, BARBARA K. SAWYERS
and ARTHUR J. FARKAS
University of California, San Diego, La Jolla, California 92037

A collection of 220 paragraphs of graded value about U.S. presidents is given. The collection includes 16 paragraphs about each of nine presidents and 8 paragraphs about each of eight presidents. For each president, the paragraphs have one of four rough values for judgments of statesmanship, H, M⁺, M⁻, and L. These paragraphs have proved useful in experimental applications of integration theory to attitude change. Other advantages of U.S. history as a source of issues and material for research on attitudes are also pointed out.

This report makes available a collection of paragraphs about U.S. presidents that we have found useful in applications of integration theory to attitude change (Anderson, 1971). Each paragraph contains information about some president, usually on his performance in office though sometimes on other actions and accomplishments. In the experiments, the S reads a set of paragraphs about some president and then judges him on statemanship and how well he did his job.

Three experiments have used these paragraphs in successful tests of information integration theory (Anderson, 1972; Anderson & Farkas, 1972; Sawyers & Anderson, 1971). Good support has been found for the parallelism prediction in all three experiments. The second cited study has particular interest since it obtained the first serial position curve in attitude research. That was possible only because of this collection of stimulus materials.

The main body of the collection contains 16 paragraphs about each of nine presidents and 8 paragraphs about each of eight presidents. In each case, there are equally many paragraphs at each of four levels of favorableness: very favorable, H; mildly favorable, M+; mildly unfavorable, M−; and very unfavorable, L. There are also paragraphs about three presidents that serve as end-anchors, and a short history summary.

One advantage of the collection is methodological. The paragraphs are fairly homogeneous across presidents, and each president can be considered as a separate "issue." It is possible, therefore, to use each S in several

*This work was supported by the United States Office of Education, Project No. 9-0399 and Contract No. OEC-9-71-0031(508). The opinions expressed herein do not necessarily reflect the position or policy of the United States Office of Education. The work was facilitated by a grant from the National Institute of Mental Health to the Center for Human Information Processing, University of California, San Diego. We wish to thank Alice Bird, Karen Fiegener, Gertrude Helmstetter, Betty Johnson, Delores McKinnon, Rosemary Painter, and Jane Ward for their assistance on this project.

different experimental conditions. Each S serves as his own comparison. The error term is then "within" rather than "between," which markedly reduces error variance. That makes possible experiments that would otherwise hardly be feasible.

The paragraphs are based on biographies and other standard historical sources. Any single paragraph is necessarily a partial version of a complex set of events, but we have tried to avoid serious historical inaccuracies. Actually, historians and biographers themselves are often in considerable disagreement. Evaluations of presidential actions often rest on a complex set of assumptions about the motivations of the president and on uncertain facts.

An extreme example is the "midnight judges" of John Adams, who served a single term between Washington and Jefferson. Adams had a prickly and sometimes pompous personality, and for that, as well as for political reasons, he has often received a bad press. The story of the "midnight judges," which still has some historical currency, tells of the new judgeships rushed through and confirmed by a colluding Federalist Senate in the last few hours of Adams's administration. But apparently Adams had been pushing judiciary reform for some time, and the judgeships were filled at a normal pace over the last month of Adams's administration after the judiciary bill was finally passed. That the judges were good Federalists was only in the spirit of the times, and that they all lost their posts in the subsequent administration is more a reflection on the then Democratic-Republican party than on their fitness for office.

We must apologize for this example, which we have included as a very unfavorable paragraph. The paragraph was written from an older source and the error was detected late. Unfortunately, it is hard to get 16 adequate paragraphs on a one-term president. Adams caused great difficulty and left little choice. Truman, who was avoided initially because of his recency, has been added as an alternative since the experiments cited above.

For each president, there are two or four paragraphs of each of four favorableness values. Each paragraph is a restricted block of information, often a general trait illustrated by one or more incidents. Redundancy and contradictions between paragraphs were kept to a minimum. Inclusion of positive and negative information within the same paragraph was avoided. In addition, the paragraphs were constructed to have roughly equal importance or weight, an important consideration for the averaging hypothesis of integration theory.

After blocking out the main incidents for a given president, several revisions and shakedowns were needed to reach a reasonable first approximation. These were then checked over by two or three undergraduates, who gave detailed comments. The paragraphs were again rewritten, and a somewhat larger sample of undergraduate reaction was obtained. The final revision was then made.

We had hoped to construct paragraphs such that H, M^+, M^-, and L were roughly equally spaced in value. But, despite considerable attention to this matter, the M^+ paragraphs seem to be too near the H paragraphs in actual use (Sawyers & Anderson, 1971, Fig. 1, upper right panel). One possible cause is that many high paragraphs deal with important but somewhat uninteresting or distant problems, such as tariff reform or foreign policy. Ss seem to evaluate these less highly than their historical worth, though they place high value on evidence of personal integrity. At the same time, since the M^+ paragraphs were intended to have the same weight as the H paragraphs, they could not be uninformatively neutral.

We hope that these paragraphs will be useful to others as they stand. We also hope that they will stimulate further interest in U.S. history as a source of materials for research on social judgment. There are numerous other possibilities, including ethical judgments and problems of resolving conflicting information and opinions. U.S. presidents constitute an ideal set of issues. Ss find the task interesting, the material is relevant to their roles as citizens, and their prior specific knowledge is typically very small. Large amounts of material are available that have in most cases been worked over from several points of view by historians.

These characteristics are particularly important in view of the need for studies of long-term integration of large masses of information. Much traditional work on attitude change deals with such small amounts of stimulus information that it might more appropriately be considered as impression formation. Such work is certainly interesting and useful, but a realistic study of social attitudes must employ a larger scale, both in duration of exposure and in amount of material. U.S. history provides an ideal vehicle for such investigations.

The various annual "almanacs" give brief lives of each president, references to more complete biographies, as well as summaries of U.S. history. Somewhat more detailed lives can be found in the *Dictionary of American Biography* and similar compilations. *The Presidents of the United States*, by M. E. Armbruster, contains a set of portraits as well as short lives. Also of interest is *Presidential Portraits*, published by the Smithsonian Institution Press, which includes a portrait and short appreciation of each president.

REFERENCES

ANDERSON, N. H. Integration theory and attitude change. Psychological Review, 1971, 78, 171-206.
ANDERSON, N. H. Information integration theory applied to attitudes about U.S. presidents. Journal of Educational Psychology, 1972, in press.
ANDERSON, N. H., & FARKAS, A. J. New light on order effects in attitude change. Technical Report No. 23, Center for Human Information Processing, University of California, San Diego, March 1972.
SAWYERS, B. K., & ANDERSON, N. H. Test of integration theory in attitude change. Journal of Personality & Social Psychology, 1971, 18, 230-233.

PARAGRAPHS

Paragraph Arrangement

Each paragraph is preceded by a letter-number code. The letter denotes the favorableness value, and the number denotes the number of that paragraph within its value class. For bookkeeping purposes, the letters A, B, C, and D are used instead of H, M^+, M^-, and L. When there are four paragraphs at a given value, the numbers have been assigned so that 1 and 2 go together, and also 3 and 4, in such a way as to minimize redundancy within each set of two paragraphs.

The presidents are listed in chronological order, first for the 16-paragraph presidents, then for the 8-paragraph presidents. They are listed here, together with their years in office, a piece of information that is ordinarily included in the S's booklet (see Table 1).

A history summary and four paragraphs each on Washington, Lincoln, and Harding are also included. The history summary, part of the instructions of the experiments, is intended to provide a better frame of reference and to make the task more real. It also has the two more specific purposes of defusing the slavery issue and of amplifying the importance of issues such as tariff reform. The paragraphs on Harding can serve as a low end-anchor, and the paragraphs on Lincoln and Washington as high end-anchors. They can be used as practice and to define the usage of the response scale.

Table 1

Presidents With 16 Paragraphs		Presidents With 8 Paragraphs	
John Adams	1797-1801	James Madison	1809-1817
Thomas Jefferson	1801-1809	Martin Van Buren	1837-1841
James Monroe	1817-1825	John Tyler	1841-1845
Andrew Jackson	1829-1837	James Knox Polk	1845-1849
Grover Cleveland	1885-1889; 1893-1897	Franklin Pierce	1853-1857
Theodore Roosevelt	1901-1909	Rutherford B. Hayes	1877-1881
William Howard Taft	1909-1913	Chester A. Arthur	1881-1885
Woodrow Wilson	1913-1921	Benjamin Harrison	1889-1893
Harry S. Truman	1945-1953		

BRIEF HISTORY SUMMARY

During the early years of the nation, around 1800, the major problem confronting the government was the development of a foreign policy. Our relations with both England and France were fragile at this time and treaties of commerce and friendship were of utmost importance. Problems of expansion of the Western frontier also existed at this time, and continued well into the 1800s.

During this period, the country established her final independence from England in the War of 1812. But then problems between the North and South began to cause dissent at home. Further adding to domestic strife was the financial disruption caused by the War of 1812. Throughout the 1800s and well into the 1900s, the question of an equitable tariff plagued each President in turn. This issue was vital because the newly developed industries in the nation could be aided or broken by the tariff.

Toward the end of the 1800s, the country faced many new foreign problems. As a leader in this hemisphere the United States was looked to by Latin America for aid in solving her internal strife. The Indian problem was still plaguing the United States on her own soil. Difficulties were arising as labor unions began to form and as large government departments made civil service reforms necessary.

The early 1900s saw the United States involved for the first time in a major world conflict, World War I. Breaking a tradition of isolationism, the United States now became a world power. The same general domestic problems persisted also; tariff, regulation of industry, and economic difficulties.

All of these "growing pains" confronted each Chief Executive in turn, and they were solved sometimes satisfactorily, sometimes not. The problems of the first 150 years of our country may seem small compared to the problems of today, but at the time, problems such as the tariff and Western expansion were as vital to the public welfare as any problem we face today.

GEORGE WASHINGTON 1789-1797

1. George Washington's great desire in life was to live quietly on his farm in Richmond, Virginia. He was not personally or politically ambitious, and only with reluctance did he take on his political duties, first as delegate from Virginia to the Continental Congress, then as general of the revolution, and later as President of the United States. He was personally reserved, only moderately intelligent, and he had a fierce temper which he kept under strict control, but which occasionally erupted like a volcano. Nevertheless, he was far-sighted and practical, resolute and persistent in action, and always fair and magnanimous. Because of his personal qualities, other men respected him, and turned to him for leadership in times of stress. His successes, often achieved under the most difficult conditions, truly entitle him to be called "the Father of his Country."

2. It is not easy for us today to comprehend the difficulties that George Washington faced as general of the Revolutionary troops. A large minority of the colonists openly supported the British, and many more were totally indifferent. There was no central government, only a loose confederation of often quarrelling colonies, each jealous of its own rights and privileges. Money and supplies were scarce. The soldiers were ill-fed, ill-armed, poorly trained, and could return to their homes virtually at will. Washington's leadership and planning, his "poise, sense, and resolution," so admired by his contemporaries, were the key to the final success of the American Revolution.

3. George Washington had a vital role in the adoption of the Constitution of the United States. After the Revolution had been won, he had retired to private life at his beloved farm in Richmond. Tired and ill, he reluctantly accepted the responsibility of representing the state of Virginia at the Constitutional Convention. Arriving in Philadelphia, he threw himself into the work and played a predominant role in ironing out the many disputed issues underlying the new Constitution. When the Constitution was submitted to the separate states for ratification it barely passed; only the general belief that Washington would become the first Chief Magistrate of the United States caused it to be accepted.

4. The Whiskey Rebellion, which occurred toward the end of Washington's first term as President, was a small but important event in U.S. history, and it illustrates Washington's character and wisdom. In 1791, Congress passed an excise tax on whiskey, but the farmers of western Pennsylvania persistently refused to pay the tax, and even tarred and feathered some of the federal officers. Finally, in 1794, 500 armed farmers joined in revolt, and burned the home of the Regional Collector of the Excise. Washington called into federal service the state militia of Virginia, Maryland, New Jersey, Pennsylvania and, when negotiations with the rebels failed, sent 15,000 soldiers into the region. At 30-1 odds, the farmers faded away and no blood was shed. Two rebel leaders were captured and convicted of treason, but Washington pardoned them. By his actions in this affair, Washington did much to establish the authority of the new federal government to enforce its laws.

ABRAHAM LINCOLN 1861-1865

1.   Behind his awkward manners and taste for bucolic anecdotes, Lincoln was a man of rare political skills. Although he lost the race for U.S. Senator in 1858, his debates with Douglas and his "House Divided" speech brought him national prominence and led to his nomination for the Presidency two years later. As President, Lincoln moved at once to unite the warring factions within his own party by offering his most able opponents posts in his Cabinet. Lincoln's strongest opponent, an extremely capable man, was made Secretary of State. Historians all admire Lincoln's ability to smooth over differences and keep his Cabinet and party working together amid the strains and dissensions of the Civil War.

2.   Abraham Lincoln was born and raised as a woodcutter and farmer on the American frontier in Kentucky and Indiana. Like everyone else, the Lincolns lived in a log cabin with a packed earth floor. Lincoln had to educate himself. Schools were almost nonexistent and he had less than a year of formal schooling all his life. Even books were scarce. Lincoln once walked twenty miles and back to borrow one book. The books he had, he studied deeply. As one of his neighbors later said, "It didn't seem natural, nohow, to see a feller read like that." Lincoln thought more deeply than other people, and he was able to see the main issues more clearly. This was one of the qualities that made him a great leader.

3.   President Lincoln's famous Emancipation Proclamation was only a wartime measure, and it did not even apply to the border states because Lincoln knew that would cause them to secede. Lincoln also knew that his proclamation would become ineffective when the war was over, so he placed utmost importance on getting the 13th Amendment through Congress. But many Congressmen were against freeing the slaves. Even after he arranged for Nevada to become a new state, Lincoln still lacked two votes of the necessary 2/3 majority in Congress. Finally, he sent for two leading Congressmen of his party and said: "The abolition of slavery by constitutional provision settles the fate, for all coming time, not only of millions now in bondage, but of unborn millions to come—a measure of such importance that those two votes must be procured." Lincoln got the Amendment through Congress, though he was assassinated before it was ratified by the states.

4.   Abraham Lincoln was a man of great compassion and magnanimity. A Southern writer said: "He loved mankind, and that meant all men. He was for the underdog, for the poor and downtrodden, white or black." Lincoln favored generous treatment toward the South. He vetoed the Wade-Davis bill which favored harsh punitive reconstruction measures, though he was roundly denounced by his own party who sought to override his veto. Lincoln's view was outlined in his second inaugural address: "With malice toward none; with charity for all; . . . let us strive on to bind up the nation's wounds."

WARREN HARDING 1921-1923

1. Warren Harding was nominated as a compromise candidate whose main attraction was his sociable, gladhanding character, good looks, and easy-going nature. He fulfilled all the expectations of the party bosses. His domestic policy was one of acquiescence to cronies, Congress, and big business. The excess profits tax was repealed, immigration quotas were imposed for the first time in U.S. history, and tariffs were raised to all-time highs as the nation plunged into isolationism.

2. Warren Harding could not be called a scholarly man. His inaugural address was so weak that it was characterized as "the most illiterate statement ever made by the responsible head of a civilized government." Harding realized his limitations, and sought advice from others. Unfortunately, he often took bad advice, and as a consequence he made several very foolish decisions.

3. Warren Harding was a sociable man, and he gave highly placed federal jobs to many personal friends. Unfortunately, he was gullible and many people took advantage of this. One example arose in the Congressional investigation of the Veterans Bureau which was headed by a personal selection of Harding. Of the total amount budgeted by Congress to go into this government bureau, over one-half had gone for graft. When this was uncovered, the man who headed the bureau was sent to Leavenworth Federal Prison. Harding's short administration was filled with such incidents.

4. President Warren Harding was involved in several schemes to defraud the government. The most famous of these became known as the Teapot Dome Scandal. The Teapot Dome was a naval oil reserve belonging to the government. Harding signed an unconstitutional executive order which allowed this valuable oil to be transferred to a privately owned oil company. The Secretary of the Interior in Harding's cabinet received a bribe of $223,000 for this transaction, and was later convicted and sent to prison.

381

A1. John Adams was the first Vice-President of the United States, and he played an effective role as the presiding officer of the new U.S. Senate. The Senate was small and split politically, and Adams used his tie-breaking vote to support President Washington on several important issues. This legislation was especially significant since it helped set the course of events in the newly-formed nation. In his second term as Vice-President, he worked very hard to improve international relations. His firm support helped ratify an important treaty with Great Britain, and he also worked for peaceful settlement of differences with the French government.

A2. John Adams played several important roles in the American Revolution. As a young lawyer of humble origin, he became known for his forthrightness and integrity. Adams was a strong advocate of economic freedom in the Colonies. When Britain passed the oppressive Stamp Act, Adams became one of its most forcible opponents; his article questioning the legal validity of the Stamp Act had widespread influence throughout the Colonies. From this beginning, he was soon completely absorbed in the Revolutionary struggle. As a member of the Provincial Congress of Massachusetts, and later as a delegate to the Continental Congress, Adams continued his efforts to set up an effective democracy.

A3. The Declaration of Independence, which begins with the revolutionary words, "All men are created equal," is one of the basic documents of this country. Much of the credit for the Declaration of Independence goes to John Adams. He worked hard on the drafting of this important document, clarifying ideas and resolving differences of opinion. Then, in a brilliant speech to the Continental Congress, he did much to win its acceptance. This accomplishment began his long career of public service. He became the first Vice-President, and followed George Washington to become the second President of the United States.

A4. Probably the most difficult problem that faced President John Adams was in our relations with France. The French were then at war with the British and sometimes harassed American vessels on the high seas for their support of the British. This produced a great deal of war feeling, in the public, in Congress, and even in Adams' own Cabinet. However, Adams believed that war with France was unnecessary and undesirable. He pursued negotiations abroad with

the French while attempting to keep the war party under control at home. The negotiations were long and there were many complications. However, Adams persevered with great skill, outwitting the war party, and reached an honorable agreement with the French. The resulting treaty of Morfontaine began a long-lasting peace between our nation and France.

B1. Early in his political career, John Adams was chosen by the Congress to be the American envoy to Holland. Negotiations were difficult and prolonged over a two-year period, but he was successful in obtaining a treaty of amity and commerce with the government in Amsterdam, and smoothed relations between this country and the Dutch leaders. Adams also obtained a much-needed loan from the Dutch government and returned to this country encouraged by the warm reception an envoy of the new nation had received.

B2. In an attempt to negotiate a treaty of commerce and friendship, President John Adams sent a commission to France. The agents representing the French government demanded not only a large official loan to France, but also wanted sizable personal bribes. President Adams refused, and in his report of this incident the French agents were referred to as X, Y, and Z to protect their identity. The "X Y Z Affair," as it became known, stirred up much patriotic excitement in this country, and the citizens were pleased that the President refused to be a part of it.

B3. In the riots and agitation resulting from the British Stamp Tax, an unfortunate series of circumstances led to the arrest of a group of British soldiers. Then a young lawyer, John Adams was against the Stamp Tax, but he believed that every man deserved a fair trial. Accordingly, Adams volunteered to serve as defense lawyer for the British troops although he knew that many American colonists would criticize him for this.

B4. As President of the United States, John Adams put forth a number of recommendations to Congress. Among the measures that were subsequently passed into law was a provision which decreased the size of the army, releasing many officers and men from the service. Adams also set forth guidelines for judiciary reform. The bill that was passed created new judgeships, freeing the Supreme Court Justices from the time-consuming task of sitting as circuit judges.

D1. Among the most detested legislation ever passed by an American Congress were the Alien and Sedition Laws, enacted during the administration of John Adams. These laws gave the President power to seize or deport resident aliens in war or threat of war, and they also established penalties for "printing, writing, or speaking in a scandalous or malicious way against the government of the United States." President Adams favored the passage of the Alien and Sedition Laws and later caused the prosecution of one Thomas Cooper who had published a pamphlet strongly criticizing Adams. These laws were used in many instances as political weapons by frightened or vindictive men and they caused much injustice. In later years, they were declared unconstitutional.

D2. President John Adams' bluntness and lack of tact, and his self-willed character seriously handicapped his administration. He was unable to inspire loyalty in his subordinates, and he was often inept in his dealings with Congress. Often hot-tempered, and always unbending, Adams had made many enemies in public life, and was consequently defeated in his bid for a second term. Disappointed and bitter, Adams finished his packing in the night and left town before dawn on the day his successor was inaugurated.

D3. President John Adams' "Midnight Judges" have been considered one of the black marks of his administration. In his last days in office, Adams nominated 18 new United States judges. These men were given their posts as rewards for political support, and many were ill-qualified for the job. Adams' judiciary law, which allowed this to occur, was repealed after Adams was defeated for reelection, and all the Midnight Judges lost their offices.

D4. When President John Adams took office, he had very few friends he could trust. His popularity in his own party was low, and he did not know which men to choose for his Cabinet. For some reason, he decided to retain the previous Cabinet members, although he must have realized that many of them opposed his policies. This decision, which has puzzled historians ever since, caused many of the difficulties he experienced in his administration. Lack of loyal support in his own Cabinet hindered Adams at every turn, yet it was only late in his administration that he did anything about it.

C1. When he was Vice-President, John Adams published an anonymous series of political-philosophical articles entitled, "Discourses on Davila." Among other things, these articles warned against the dangers of a pure democracy, and criticized the French Revolution, then a popular idol. It soon became known, of course, that Adams was the author, and the articles were interpreted as an attack on the Secretary of State. Public criticism was more severe than was really justified, but Adams had furnished his political enemies with ammunition that they later used against him.

C2. John Adams was much taken by the ceremonies and customs of the royal courts during his stay as American envoy in Europe, and he affected courtly manners and dress upon his return. As Vice-President, Adams would lecture the Senate at great length on the virtues of following parliamentary customs of the House of Lords. In consequence, Adams was mockingly called "His Rotundity," because he was fat as well as pompous. These manners were politically unwise in the immediate aftermath of the Revolutionary War and did much to isolate Adams from his party as well as from the people.

C3. President John Adams has been held responsible for the demise of the Federalist Party. This political party, the first in the country, was fragmented by disagreements between Adams and other prominent party members. Adams' opponents were no less to blame, but Adams did little to heal the split. The disunity was a significant factor in Adams' defeat for reelection, and the Federalist Party never again played an important role in American politics.

C4. John Adams had a long-standing feud with Alexander Hamilton in which both men acted badly at times. Although Hamilton supported Adams for President in 1796, he disagreed with and opposed many of Adams' Presidential policies. Adams in turn deeply distrusted Hamilton, considering him "a man devoid of moral principle," and repeatedly insinuated that he was a member of the pro-British faction. When he was President, Adams tried to prevent Hamilton from being made second-in-command in the army and only gave in at the insistence of George Washington.

A1. At a time when most men in this country saw the institution of slavery as essential to the American economy, Thomas Jefferson spoke out strongly against this practice. Although he realized that immediate abolition was not possible, he continually wrote and spoke of the national disgrace that slavery was imposing on this country. His opinions made him many enemies, particularly in the South, but he held to them. When he became President, Jefferson partially fulfilled his goal by sponsoring and signing an important bill strictly forbidding any future traffic in slavery in the U.S.

A2. After Thomas Jefferson left the Presidency, he set out to accomplish one of the great ambitions of his life, that of setting up a university in his home state of Virginia. Jefferson had always been vitally interested in education, and he made extensive studies of several European university systems to draw the best features from each. After this university was built, Jefferson served as the first rector. Jefferson's achievement was a great asset to the state of Virginia. It also served as a blueprint for the state universities which are so important in our educational system today.

A3. When the American colonies were ruled by England, one of the major complaints was the enforced taxation to support the state church. Thomas Jefferson strongly disapproved of this practice. After U.S. independence was won, he fought for complete separation of church and state. In his native state of Virginia, he was able to obtain the passage of the Bill for Religious Freedom which asserted that "civil rights have no dependence on our religious opinions." This legislation provided that members of churches themselves would pay for the maintenance of the church, and that these payments would be voluntary rather than compulsory.

A4. Thomas Jefferson was one of the most versatile men ever to ascend to the Presidency, an acknowledged scholar, inventor, lawyer, and naturalist. Nicknamed "The Sage of Monticello," he had interests that ran the gamut from literature to astronomy to agriculture. While an ambassador abroad, Jefferson sent home many seeds and plants along with carefully gathered information on new farming methods which might improve U.S. agriculture. Jefferson's inventions were varied also, from the invention of the swivel chair to the design of a plow which won an international prize. Jefferson refused to patent any of his inventions, desiring to make these items useful to the people of the country without restrictions.

B1. Thomas Jefferson, as a delegate to the first Continental Congress, drew up the original draft of the Declaration of Independence. This document welded philosophic principles with practical explanations which justified America's desire for independence. In the Declaration, Jefferson did not put forth new or revolutionary ideas; rather he incorporated those ideas present in the country at the time. For this reason, the points put forward in the document were truly "self-evident." The Declaration was carefully reviewed and edited by the Congress, and was adopted on July 4th, 1776.

B2. During the administration of Thomas Jefferson the great Louisiana Purchase was made. Early in his Presidency, Jefferson had been interested in exploring the unknown areas of the West, and had personally selected two well-known men, Lewis and Clark, to traverse and chart this territory. When he made an offer to France to buy a portion of this land, France unexpectedly offered all the Louisiana Territory. Jefferson immediately seized the opportunity. This transaction doubled the area of the U.S. and provided land from which 13 of our states were developed.

B3. When an independent system of government was established in this country, Thomas Jefferson was sent abroad as the first American minister to France. His difficult assignment was to try to negotiate treaties of commerce with several European nations. Because the U.S. was a very new and unproved nation, the large European countries were reluctant to enter into agreements with it. Jefferson, however, was able to secure a treaty with Prussia, and finally, after a great deal of hard diplomatic work, France also signed an important trade agreement with the U.S.

B4. Thomas Jefferson was a student of government and considered the study of political matters to be a science. He was opposed to the strong concentration of power in the central government. However, adhering to this philosophy in actual practice was not always possible. When he became Secretary of State, Jefferson often found that a government run entirely "by the people" was difficult to achieve. He persevered, however, in his ideals, and lent the balance which helped maintain the spirit of the Constitution during the early years of the new government.

C1. President Thomas Jefferson sometimes became so personally involved with an issue that he let emotion rather than reason guide his actions. For example, in the trial of Aaron Burr for treason, Jefferson publicly declared Burr guilty "beyond all doubt" even before a jury had heard the case. Such a statement from the President himself suggested that he considered a conviction more important than a fair trial. The Burr trial was poorly handled by the administration, with their chief witness being a man himself implicated as a traitor. Burr was finally acquitted of the charges, due mainly to a complete lack of evidence.

C2. When Thomas Jefferson was Secretary of State he got into an unpleasant feud with the Secretary of the Treasury. At that time there were severe financial problems in the country, and the Secretary of the Treasury proposed a bank bill which provided for certain economic reforms. However, Jefferson fought the measure stubbornly, and when the bill was passed into law, he attacked the Treasury Secretary on a personal basis. This dispute caused a great deal of dissension within the administration.

C3. During the time he was Governor of Virginia, Thomas Jefferson was involved in an unfortunate incident dealing with the handling of certain prisoners of war. Three prisoners were brought to him, including an important British general. By diplomatic custom, prisoners of high rank were paroled and exchanged. However, Jefferson had received reports that this general had indulged in cruel practices and he became emotionally involved. He had the prisoners put in chains and denied them all privileges of communication. National leaders protested to Jefferson, fearing reprisals from the British. Jefferson refused to reverse his decision, but finally after a year of imprisonment the men were paroled in accordance with usual practice.

C4. Thomas Jefferson took office as the third President of the U.S. in one of the most contested elections in American history. Jefferson's backers tried to arrange electoral votes to assure his winning the election, but Jefferson and his opponent wound up in a tie. The decision then had to be made in the House of Representatives, and ballot after ballot was cast without a decision being reached. Finally, representatives from three states contacted Jefferson through an intermediary and promised him their votes in return for certain pledges of action, although he believed Jefferson. The terms were reported agreed upon, although Jefferson later denied that he had made any such bargain. Nevertheless, on the next ballot, the 35th, Jefferson received the needed votes to win the election.

D1. Shortly after taking office, President Thomas Jefferson began a long fight to remove district and Supreme Court judges who were not of his political party. After successfully impeaching one district judge, Jefferson moved directly against a Supreme Court member. Jefferson was defeated in this attempt, however, and the judge was finally absolved of all Jefferson's charges. Throughout his administration he attempted to take away the powers granted to the Supreme Court by the Constitution. At one time he even tried to get Congress to impeach the entire Court, planning to appoint his own men to the positions. Fortunately, Jefferson's moves were blocked in every case, and the Court remained an important and essential part of the check and balance system of our government.

D2. In his inaugural address, President Thomas Jefferson pledged that he would remove no one from government office for political purposes. However, he immediately began to do just that, thus beginning the spoils system in government. In one glaring example, Jefferson removed a competent employee from an important job and installed in his place a 77-year-old man who was feeble in mind and body, with absolutely no qualifications for the office except that he belonged to Jefferson's political party. In response to public protest, Jefferson issued a statement to the effect that just as soon as a political balance was reached, men would be put in office on the basis of their qualifications, but not before.

D3. As Governor of Virginia, Thomas Jefferson proved to be an extremely weak leader. Jefferson was unable to handle state financial matters, and as a consequence the Virginia militia was left without guns, bullets, food, or even shoes, at a time when British troops were attempting to overrun the country. After several disasters, the militia was completely demoralized and refused to respond to the call to arms. The British met little resistance and easily invaded the state capitol which they burned and looted. For the rest of his term, Governor Jefferson was unable to get the state assembly to meet and no reconstruction of the government could be begun. Finally, Jefferson resigned from office, turning the job over to a stronger leader.

D4. During his last term in office, Thomas Jefferson put into force an embargo which caused great economic hardship in this country. Jefferson was warned by his Secretary of the Treasury and several other national leaders that the embargo would be a financial disaster, and that it would impose unconstitutional controls on individual states and private citizens. Jefferson ignored their warnings. The months went by and conditions in the country became rapidly worse as ports were closed and food supplies diminished. Protests came from the citizens, the state governors, and even Jefferson's Cabinet revolted against his stubborn pursuit of the embargo. Finally, after 15 months, Congress repealed the embargo over Jefferson's strong protests.

JAMES MONROE 1817-1825

A1. As a very young man, James Monroe fought for independence in this country, becoming a colonel in the Revolutionary army by the time he was 21. After independence was won, he was elected to the Congress of Confederation and played a leading role in establishing guidelines for the new government. Monroe was appointed to head the committee to deal with commerce in the new nation, which he did with much success. James Monroe became one of the most active "founding fathers" when debate began over the ratification of the Constitution. He strongly believed that basic rights of the individual citizen should be incorporated in the document, and he led the fight which gave us the Bill of Rights.

A2. Few Presidents have been as popular as James Monroe, both when he took office and when he left office two terms later. Political and sectional rivalries were nearly non-existent, as party jealousies were forgotten for the first, and last, time in U.S. history. Monroe's administration has been called the "Era of Good Feeling." Monroe's popularity with the people was heightened by his extended tour across the country when he was the first took office. Wanting first-hand information about the problems he was to face as President, Monroe inspected various government installations and made innumerable speeches. In those days, before the radio or even the telegraph, Monroe gave people their first personal contact with their elected leader.

A3. As President, James Monroe proved to be an extremely able administrator. This was illustrated by his choosing experienced and capable men as Cabinet members and advisors. President Monroe's Cabinet was one of the strongest in this nation's history, and included such outstanding men as Adams and Calhoun. Monroe sought the advice of these men often, never reaching important decisions without hearing the opinions of the most capable men the country could offer. It is a tribute to President Monroe's ability to work in close collaboration with such strong figures that his entire Cabinet served with him continuously through both his terms as President.

A4. Throughout his two terms in office, President James Monroe was concerned for the welfare of the American Indians. In his first annual message to Congress, he urged legislation which would secure the Indians in their lands, and provide grants which would ease the bad conditions under which they were living. During the rest of his term, President Monroe continued to push for needed legislation in this area. He was successful in securing for the Indians

the establishment of the Indian Territory. In addition Monroe set in motion plans which were to provide for the self-governing of Indian tribes, and the establishment of schools and churches.

B1. When Russia threatened to push her territorial claims southward along the Pacific coast through the Oregon Territory, President James Monroe took immediate action. Monroe protested to the Russian government that this area, claimed jointly by the U.S. and England, could not be taken over in this manner. After lengthy deliberation, a treaty was finally concluded which established definite boundary lines between Russian-settled Alaska and the Northwest Territory. Russia agreed to form no establishments south of this boundary and the U.S. agreed to make no establishments north of it.

B2. As Secretary of State, James Monroe showed courage and level-headedness during the attack of Washington, D.C. in the War of 1812. When the Secretary of War ignored the peril of a British invasion, Monroe personally scouted the enemy's position and brought back intelligence reports. There was no U.S. army to speak of in the capitol at the time, and so British troops were virtually unresisted as they approached the city. Monroe, however, had the foresight to advise the removal of all public records from the city, thus preserving them from destruction when the British burned nearly every public building.

B3. James Monroe took a very active interest in the westward development of the U.S. As a Congressman from the state of Virginia, he personally surveyed the lands which lay between the Alleghanies and the Mississippi, then reported to the legislature on the importance of gaining free navigation rights on the Mississippi. As head of an important committee, Monroe spent long months dealing with representatives of Spain who then controlled this territory. Finally agreements were reached and free navigation of the Mississippi was established from the source to the ocean.

B4. After he left the Presidency, James Monroe continued to serve his country in many ways, as the President of the Virginia Constitutional Convention, for example. Because of his concern with public service, Monroe neglected his own affairs and finances. As a consequence, he had to sell his home and spend the last few months of his life with his children in New York City. Even there, however, Monroe continued to be active, presiding over public meetings and ceremonies whenever called upon.

C1. When James Monroe held the office of Secretary of State, he was involved in a strange incident which caused the administration some embarrassment. A French informer offered to sell the U.S. some secret papers which allegedly proved certain actions by Great Britain against the U.S. Monroe arranged for the purchase of these papers for several thousand dollars. However, after the affair had been made public, Monroe had to admit that the papers were essentially worthless. The names of involved persons had been deleted from the papers and very little actual evidence of intrigue could be found.

C2. When James Monroe was a member of the Senate, a feud developed between him and another Senator who had previously been a close friend. The issue was one of personal morality in which the Senator had previously admitted a somewhat unsavory affair to Monroe. When Monroe went abroad as ambassador, he left all of the correspondence and written reports about the incident with a friend. Soon thereafter, the entire story was exposed and published in a small book. Although it appears that Monroe himself was not guilty of betraying the confidence, his handling of the matter was indiscreet and unfortunate for all persons concerned.

C3. As ambassador to England, James Monroe displayed a lack of diplomatic ability which caused the U.S. government some embarrassment. The incident occurred when an American warship was fired upon by a British cruiser because she would not allow the British aboard to search for deserters from the British navy. Ambassador Monroe sent an official note of protest; however, he made the mistake of protesting the general principle of searching for deserters rather than demanding an apology for the incident itself. Although his action was quickly reversed by the U.S. government, England took advantage of the matter to refuse a redress of grievances.

C4. During the administration of James Monroe, a Seminole Indian uprising began in the Spanish territory of Florida. When the Spanish government failed to stop the rebellion, Monroe sent U.S. troops into the area, even though the incident occurred on foreign soil. Partly as a direct result of Monroe's poor handling of the matter, American troops attacked Spanish forts and also killed two British citizens.

D1. When James Monroe was U.S. Ambassador to France, he committed a series of diplomatic blunders. Monroe was strongly in favor of the French government, although the U.S. was attempting to remain neutral, particularly in France's disputes with other European nations. Acting completely without authorization from Washington, Monroe made promises to French officials which this government could not keep without starting a war with England. After a number of such unwise and imprudent actions, Monroe was recalled from France by an American government which voiced its "uneasiness and dissatisfaction" with the diplomatic errors he had made.

D2. President James Monroe stuck strictly to the letter of the Constitution on some occasions, and stretched it to fit his needs at other times. When he wanted to acquire the Spanish territory of Florida, Monroe managed to find sanction for this in the Constitution. But when Congress attempted to pass laws which would provide for building roads and canals, Monroe vetoed the measure on the grounds that he could find no justification for this in the Constitution. New roads, bridges, and canals were badly needed at this time. Only after Monroe left office was Congress able to act on these problems.

D3. Immediately upon taking the office of President, James Monroe began a financial policy which ultimately plunged the country into a serious economic depression. Monroe drastically reduced federal income by repealing all federal internal taxes. This action was popular but showed no foresight and led to financial difficulties. The problem was intensified by Monroe's inaction on protective tariffs. Although badly needed to protect infant U.S. industries, Monroe took no action to alleviate the situation. Finally, Monroe made a tour of the South and saw the depth of the national crisis. He then asked Congress for the needed tariffs; however, it was too late in the session and Congress adjourned without taking action.

D4. James Monroe's erratic nature did much to decrease both his popularity and his political effectiveness. After failing to perform satisfactorily as a U.S. ambassador, he was recalled to the U.S. Thereupon, he published a five-hundred-page pamphlet defending his own behavior and vigorously criticizing the administration. While mainly factual, the pamphlet omitted many important points which were unfavorable to Monroe. Monroe unwisely used this pamphlet as an outlet for his hostility against the leaders who had recalled him, and in so doing he defeated his own purposes. The article concluded with an all-out attack on administration policy, claiming that "our national honor is in the dust . . . and our government and people branded as cowards."

ANDREW JACKSON 1829-1837

A1. When Andrew Jackson was President, relations between the United States and Britain were still precarious. Jackson was remarkable for his ability to maintain harmony between the two countries. He smoothed over difficulties which arose, and acted in a statesman-like manner to resolve conflicts of interest between the two countries. One such conflict arose over the question of trade between the British colonies and the United States. Britain had always taken advantage of her Caribbean possessions, blocking any trade which would have benefited the small American colonies. President Jackson moved quickly and decisively and was able to secure a reciprocity agreement with Britain which halted this injustice and opened up the desired avenues of trade.

A2. When Andrew Jackson took office as President, the territory now known as Texas was part of Mexico and controlled by the Mexican government. A group of American settlers in the territory began a revolt against the Mexican government and begged Jackson for federal support. President Jackson spent long months investigating the issue while remaining unprejudiced about the dispute. He refused to ratify a treaty which would have proved unfair to Mexico and faithfully maintained the neutrality of the United States. For this wise diplomatic policy, President Jackson earned a great deal of respect both at home and abroad.

A3. Andrew Jackson had a distinguished record in public service even before he reached the White House. As a young lawyer he was appointed district attorney, then promoted to a position on the bench of the Supreme Court of Tennessee. Later he became a delegate to the constitutional convention of Tennessee where he aided in the admission of the state to the Union. After his state joined the Union, he went to Washington as its first Congressman, then served twice as its United States Senator. In this capacity, Jackson secured the passage of two important measures which provided protection for his home state and protected the rights of the private soldier.

A4. President Andrew Jackson did a great deal to further the economy of the nation and to initiate internal improvements. After completely paying off the national debt, President Jackson distributed the excess left in the treasury to the individual states "for purposes of education and internal improvement..." When a

group of politicians, under the pressure of a small group of profiteers, urged an unwise road and canal building project, President Jackson felt that the project was an unnecessary and illegal use of government funds. Although great political pressure was put on him, he vetoed the bill. This illustrated Andrew Jackson's strong personal integrity, which he demonstrated on many other occasions.

B1. Andrew Jackson had a deep interest in the people of the nation as individuals, not just as voters. He always responded to the desires of the common man to whom, he felt, the President must be a servant. Shortly after he took office he was approached by a woman, begging for a government job. She said her children were starving and she pleaded with the new President with tears in her eyes. Deeply moved, President Jackson knew that he could not give the woman a job in this manner. Though he was very poor himself at this time, he gave her half of the money he had with him, thus alleviating her immediate problems until she could find a position.

B2. During Andrew Jackson's campaign for the Presidency his opponents engaged in some extreme mud-slinging. Unable to attack the popular Jackson on political grounds, they resorted to scandal about the events surrounding his marriage. Jackson was deeply in love with his wife, and he was angered by these attacks. He refused, however, to use this type of politicking himself. To his antagonists Jackson replied, "I have nothing in my political creed to keep secret ... I have no secrets, nor do I wish to conceal my opinions..."

B3. President Jackson's popularity, which gave him two terms in office, was even greater when he left the White House than when he entered it. One reason for this popular admiration was Jackson's talent for identifying with the desires and needs of the common man. He was truly a man "with his hand on the pulse of the nation."

B4. In the last military battle ever fought between the United States and Britain, General Andrew Jackson led the American troops to victory in the Battle of New Orleans. Jackson won the battle, fought against great odds, because he was able to inspire and lead men. Jackson's success, which signalled the final independence of the American colonies from Britain, won him great popularity throughout the nation.

C1. Andrew Jackson was a hot-headed person whose stormy character often involved him in unpleasant incidents. As a young lawyer he challenged an opposing attorney to a duel after he felt that he was insulted in the courtroom. Jackson similarly challenged the Governor of Tennessee when he felt that the Governor had insulted his wife. Fortunately friends interceded and reasoned with the duelers, and both of these duels ended with all participants firing their pistols into the air. These incidents illustrate Jackson's impetuous nature, which sometimes interfered with the execution of his Presidential duties.

C2. Realizing the potential value of parcels of land during the early years of the nation, Andrew Jackson let no opportunity go by. As a lawyer on the Western frontier he soon became a large landowner, collecting fees "at the rate of an acre for ten cents of service." Later, as a military commander, Jackson acquired under questionable circumstances three square miles of land originally inhabited by the Creek Indians.

C3. The United States had a hostile interlude with France during the administration of Andrew Jackson. This was caused by Jackson's unreasonable demands that France pay for damages to American shipping which had occurred many years earlier, during the Napoleonic wars. France broke off diplomatic relations, and Jackson immediately began to prepare for war. Fortunately France had more sense than to go to war over such a trivial matter. She made a token payment, after which the matter was forgotten.

C4. Andrew Jackson lost control of his Cabinet during his first term due to a curious incident which became known as the "Affair of Mrs. Eaton." Jackson's campaign manager became involved with a young married girl whom he later married when her husband committed suicide. The girl, however, was not accepted by Washington society, and Jackson took up her cause in an unfortunate manner. He called a Cabinet meeting and asked for the resignation of any member whose wife would not treat the girl with respect. This unwise use of Presidential pressure eventually resulted in the resignation of five of Jackson's Cabinet members.

D1. Andrew Jackson did much to spread the spoils system in government. When he took office he replaced more than one-sixth of the government officeholders, filling their jobs with personal friends and using the system to pay off political debts. An extreme case was his appointment of a close friend of questionable character to the lucrative post of Collector of Customs at New York. After nine years in this post, Jackson's "friend" fled to England taking with him a million and a quarter dollars belonging to the United States government. This was not an isolated incident; many of the men that Jackson appointed were opportunists seeking power and wealth and used their positions for personal gain.

D2. Andrew Jackson handled the Nullification issue very badly late in his first term as President. At that time, Congress was dominated by the New England states, and the Southern states had little or no representation. As a result, a tariff was levied against them that was extraordinarily unfair and punitive. When the South Carolina legislature voted to nullify this tariff, Jackson quickly got the Force Bill passed which gave him the power to use government troops to collect the taxes. This was an unwise move, and Jackson's own Vice-President resigned his office in order to uphold the rights of the South. When South Carolina threatened to secede if the tariff was not lowered, Jackson was forced to back down and lower the tariff before open hostilities could lead to a civil war.

D3. Andrew Jackson was an old Indian fighter, having led military troops against Indian braves in many battles. He continued in this attitude when he became President, and had little regard for Indian rights. Jackson refused to honor the terms of Indian treaties, even those that he himself had drawn up while a general in the army. Most of the eastern tribes were forced to give up their lands to white settlers during his administration, and the dispossessed Indians were shoved further and further west, into Indian Territory as it came to be known.

D4. Before becoming President, Andrew Jackson was involved in a business transaction in which he lost $7000. This affair left him with a fanatic distrust of all banks. Indeed, when he became President he seemed determined to crush the Bank of the United States, disregarding warnings that this action would probably lead to financial crisis in the country. When Jackson ordered federal funds transferred from the Bank he was vigorously opposed by his Cabinet, particularly his Secretary of the Treasury, an expert economist. Jackson removed the Secretary from office and replaced him with a man who would bow to the President's wishes. As a result, credit tightened up and there was great financial distress in the nation.

A1. Grover Cleveland was elected Governor of New York after a vigorous campaign in which he promised political reform to the voters. During his two years in office, Cleveland did bring the promised reforms, much to the surprise and chagrin of the political machine in the state. Governor Cleveland was very interested in the work of the state legislature, and read every word of every law passed by this body. This meant that often he had to stay up all night before he felt that he could either sign or veto a proposed bill. Cleveland's reputation for honesty and concern with the law did much to win him the Presidential nomination at the next national convention.

A2. President Grover Cleveland was an able and effective administrator of foreign affairs. As one example, he tackled vigorously a longstanding fisheries dispute between the United States and Canada. After many long months of study and careful consideration, a draft of the treaty was concluded that was fair to both countries and acceptable to Great Britain. The treaty provided that the United States fleet would honor the three-mile limit off the Canadian coast, yet would have rights to purchase supplies and fuel from Canadian ports. Because the treaty was fair and based on mutual understanding, it was accepted without reservation by all parties and insured harmonious relations.

A3. President Grover Cleveland supported civil service reforms, and took legislative steps to help eliminate the spoils system. Cleveland deplored the practice of giving government jobs as payment for political support, and he refused to expel anyone from his job without just cause. As a result of his adherence to these standards, before Cleveland left office about one-half of all government offices were under the civil service system and were filled by competitive examinations. Cleveland's reforms did much to eliminate the spoils system of political patronage in our government.

A4. In his inaugural address, President Grover Cleveland made a promise to the American Indians. As soon as he took office he began legislation that would deal fairly with them. Cleveland revoked an earlier order that had allowed settlers to take over land belonging to the Winnebago and Crow Creek Indians in Oklahoma. He ordered the white trespassers to leave the Indian territory, and

the cattlemen who had been defrauding the Indians were punished. Various steps also were taken toward the civic assimilation of the Indian nations.

B1. Early in his second term, President Grover Cleveland was called upon to seek arbitration in a boundary dispute between Venezuela and British Guiana. Cleveland, on the authority of the Monroe Doctrine, urged a commission be appointed to settle this dispute. Great Britain initially protested, but finally came to an agreement with Venezuela. Although the Monroe Doctrine is not seen today as an appropriate means to settle such disputes, at the time Cleveland acted appropriately.

B2. President Grover Cleveland advocated tariff reductions on raw materials needed for the development of American industry. He felt that the existing tariff was harmful and unnecessary, and he used his influence and energies to get reforms enacted. Cleveland's labors were rewarded when Congress passed a tariff bill which corrected the injustices, and paved the way for the economic growth of the country.

B3. After he retired from the Presidency, Grover Cleveland performed a valuable public service by working to salvage and reorganize the Equitable Life Assurance Society. The Society was made up of three large life insurance companies supposedly operating for the benefit of policy holders alone. In truth, though, a few insiders were making a great profit from its operation. Grover Cleveland was asked to lead a board of directors which would clean up the corruption and put the Society back in the hands of the people. Cleveland accomplished this goal and thereby helped promote public confidence in all insurance companies.

B4. When he chose his Cabinet, President Grover Cleveland kept an inaugural promise to "abandon all sectional prejudice and distrust" left over from the Civil War. Well-qualified men who had once served the Confederate cause were appointed to important Cabinet posts, including the post of Attorney General. In integrating the Cabinet in this manner Cleveland provided that all sections of the country would be represented in matters of national importance.

C1. Grover Cleveland was a very conservative President, using his power of veto more often than any other President in history. Cleveland vetoed all Civil War pensions unless he was able to verify the merits of each individual case. This was an insurmountable task in view of the large number of these pensions requested. His administration lost much support because of this, yet Cleveland was unwilling or unable to change his policies to better reflect public needs.

C2. Grover Cleveland was unable to accept the fact that the daily actions of the President were of great interest and concern to the nation. Secretive in his manner, Cleveland closed and locked the White House gates to visitors. When he required a serious operation, all knowledge of it was withheld from the public until long afterwards. The public resented this, and Cleveland enjoyed less popularity than might otherwise have been the case.

C3. After Grover Cleveland had served as President for one term, he was defeated in a bid for reelection. One reason for his defeat was the fact that he chose the tariff revision as a campaign issue. The tariff problem was extremely complicated and technical, and Cleveland showed poor judgment in using the tariff matter for political purposes. Inevitably, the end result was that the public was misinformed about the need for reforms of this nature, and subsequently suffered as inadequate tariff bills were passed.

C4. Grover Cleveland wrote all of his own speeches and was unreasonably sensitive to press criticism when it came. On one occasion, when his style was described as "ponderous," Cleveland was openly outraged. He attacked the ethics of the press in a letter to the editor of Puck: "I don't think that there ever was a time when newspaper lying was so general and mean as at present." The President was denounced for this, but stubbornly refused to "take anything back." He did amend his statements to "not include all the newspapers," but he had hurt himself politically.

D1. When Grover Cleveland was President, a severe economic crisis gripped the nation. Against the warnings of his economic advisors, and contrary to the wishes of a large part of his party, President Cleveland proposed a repeal of the Sherman Silver Purchase Act. Cleveland was obstinate and, after a long and heated fight in Congress, the repeal bill was finally passed. However, Cleveland's bill did not accomplish its purpose and the economy grew worse. Moreover, the controversy over the bill had divided the nation into two opposing camps, and had caused a fatal split in Cleveland's own party.

D2. President Grover Cleveland mishandled labor-management problems, and this did much to make his administration unpopular. Cleveland ordered military troops into Chicago when a strike was called by the Pullman workers, who had a real grievance. The Governor of Illinois protested that the presence of the troops would lead to violence, which in fact happened. Rather than withdraw the troops, Cleveland immediately extended federal warnings to nine other western states, prohibiting sympathetic activity. Cleveland's military power won out over the civilian protests, and the strikers were finally forced back to work.

D3. During Grover Cleveland's second term in office, an economic panic seized the nation. Cleveland did not alleviate the problems, and conditions grew progressively worse. An "army," of unemployed marched to Washington to demonstrate their plight, but their leader was promptly arrested. With farm prices falling and unemployment rising, Cleveland's party was ousted from Congress by a landslide vote. Cleveland's philosophy was that "natural laws" would cure the ills of the country, and he still did not take action to provide employment or relieve distressed businesses.

D4. As President, Grover Cleveland attempted to reestablish the monarchy in Hawaii. Prior to Cleveland's election, a bloodless revolution had swept the island of Hawaii and the queen and her monarchy had been overthrown. The native Hawaiians then set up a democratic government and petitioned for annexation to the United States. Cleveland rejected their pleas and attempted to put the old queen back on the throne. The queen, however, insisted on beheadings and exile for all the popular participants of the revolt, and she would not settle for anything less. In the end, Cleveland was forced to abandon his attempts to overthrow the people's government.

A1. During President Roosevelt's administration many urgent domestic reforms were achieved. Two important measures dealt with protecting the American consumer from impure and dangerous foods and drugs. President Roosevelt became intensely involved with this issue after reading an exposé of the deplorable sanitary conditions in the meat-packing houses. Although influential meat-packer groups fought his reforms, Roosevelt persisted in his efforts, realizing the necessity of protecting the public from the unsanitary and dangerous methods used in preparing meat for consumption. Very soon a bill was passed which required regular government inspections of these facilities.

A2. The rights of the workingman were vigorously protected by Theodore Roosevelt. As a young assemblyman, he began to champion the workingman's rights by sponsoring bills which regulated working conditions of women and children and established safety measures in factories. When he became President, Roosevelt continued to be concerned with labor problems. He saw the need for labor unions to protect the workers, and to this end he encouraged the growth of the labor movement. Roosevelt proposed legislation to support the eight-hour working day, and fought for workmen's compensation laws which would protect the worker in cases of accident or disability.

A3. President Theodore Roosevelt was awarded the Nobel Peace Prize for his energetic and successful efforts in settling and avoiding international conflicts in Europe. Roosevelt was largely responsible for arranging a mediation of the Russo-Japanese War by setting up a delicate meeting of delegates of both sides aboard the Presidential yacht, Mayflower. Later, when open conflict between France and Germany threatened, President Roosevelt interceded and persuaded the two nations to meet at the conference table. When the peace talks deadlocked and war seemed imminent, Roosevelt offered a compromise which was accepted by both sides, ending the threat of open conflict.

A4. President Theodore Roosevelt was the first national leader to be concerned with the problem of conservation on a large scale. He took many measures to halt the destruction of the country's wilderness areas. During his two terms as President, the National Forest Service was established, and acreage for national forests was greatly increased. In addition, 5 national parks and 13 national monuments were opened. The first federal bird reservation was established by Roosevelt, with 50 opened before he left office.

Fervently believing in conservation, President Theodore Roosevelt publicly stated: "As a people we have a right and a duty, second to none, to protect ourselves and our children against the wasteful development of our natural resources."

B1. Theodore Roosevelt served as Civil Service Commissioner in Washington, D.C. for six years before he became President. During this time many jobs were placed on the merit system and examination procedures were revised. After reaching the Presidency, Roosevelt continued to promote improvements in the Commission, placing additional jobs under the civil service system.

B2. For two years, Theodore Roosevelt served as Assistant Secretary of the Navy. Roosevelt was familiar with the construction and running of ships, and he often made personal inspection tours of naval installations. During his term as Assistant Secretary, he made several improvements and administrative reforms within the Navy Department. As President, Roosevelt's interest in the improvement of the Department continued. He was able to get passage of a bill which, among other things, ruled against the advancement of naval officers on the basis of tenure rather than ability.

B3. As a young man, Theodore Roosevelt was appointed a member of the New York Board of Police Commissioners, then was elected by the other members to head the Commission. During his term in this office, an examining board was set up and examinations were designed to be similar to the federal civil service examinations. The merit system for promotions was also begun, and improvements were also made to insure fairness in eligibility for jobs.

B4. Theodore Roosevelt read and wrote on many different subjects. Among his writings were biographies, accounts of his early days as a farmer and a rancher, and historical narratives. Theodore Roosevelt's four-volume Winning of the West, written when he was very young, was favorably received by historians. This large account of the early American push westward is still considered to be one of the best written descriptions of this period of U.S. history. After leaving the Presidency, Roosevelt continued writing, focusing attention on the continent of Africa with his African Game Trails, and remaining politically concerned with a group of essays on the first World War.

C1. President Theodore Roosevelt often alienated Congress with his attempts to dominate it. On one occasion, Roosevelt used the secret service in an attempt to gather information against Congressmen regarding abuses of franking privileges for mailing. Further disapproval from Congress came over an issue involving the country of Santo Domingo. Roosevelt ordered American agents to take charge of Dominican customs receipts when the country got into financial difficulty. This action put Santo Domingo on its financial feet, but Congress felt they should have been consulted more closely before measures of this sort were taken.

C2. Outspoken and often tactless, Theodore Roosevelt on one occasion attacked several nature writers. One nature writer in particular had written a book in which he attributed human characteristics to wild animals. Roosevelt took the author to task, although admitting at the time, "I know that as President I ought not to do this." His outburst angered many naturalists, and only a retaliated by pointing out the fact that Roosevelt was only a big-game hunter and not qualified to criticize them in this manner.

C3. Theodore Roosevelt was a skilled politician. However, this characteristic is not always necessarily good in a national leader. One example occurred as the time for Roosevelt's reelection drew near. In order to secure enough votes for himself at the national convention, Roosevelt found it necessary to give a public office to a man whom he had justly denounced as an enemy of the civil service system at an earlier time. Roosevelt excused this action, saying, "In politics we have to do a great many things that we ought not to do."

C4. Theodore Roosevelt believed in a strong federal government, and this belief carried into the area of the private morality of citizens. In an address to Congress a year after he took office, Roosevelt recommended "that the whole question of marriage and divorce should be relegated to the authority" of the federal government. This action, he realized, would require a Constitutional amendment, but Roosevelt felt it was worth the effort. Roosevelt spoke out against population control also, feeling that when "quantity falls off, the quality will go down too." This strange type of reasoning came at a time when already sociologists were pointing to the need for slowing down our population growth.

D1. As Assistant Secretary of the Navy, Theodore Roosevelt favored a war with Spain to free Cuba from Spanish rule. He felt that Cuba should belong to the U.S., and that the prospect of a war

with Spain was good because of "the benefit done our military forces by trying both the Army and Navy in actual practice." When an American warship, the Maine, blew up in Havana harbor, Roosevelt issued a public statement that the Spanish had destroyed the vessel, although he did not have adequate proof of the source of the explosion. Public opinion was inflamed over the issue, and the U.S. was soon plunged into an unnecessary war with Spain.

D2. As President, Theodore Roosevelt sometimes made hasty and unwise decisions. One example involved three companies of Negro soldiers stationed near Brownsville, Texas. A riot was reported, and the accusation made that several soldiers had shot up the town and killed one citizen. Although preliminary evidence strongly disputed this charge, Roosevelt, acting on a hasty report from the Inspector General's Office, ordered all three companies dishonorably discharged en masse. A later investigation showed the probable innocence of the men, but Roosevelt would not reinstate them unless they could prove their own innocence. Few of the men ever were reinstated and none were ever given the opportunity to defend themselves in a civil or a military court.

D3. Theodore Roosevelt was intensely attracted by military action. When he was Assistant Secretary of the Navy, he stated in a prepared address, "No triumph of peace is quite so great as the supreme triumph of war." When the U.S. went to war with Spain in Cuba, Roosevelt immediately quit his post as Assistant Secretary to join the battle. He led his troops in a reckless charge up San Juan Hill, causing heavy casualties to both sides. After the battle, Roosevelt conducted tours of the battlefield to show off the Spanish dead, and felt that the number of American casualties was positive proof that he was in the heat of battle.

D4. During the administration of Theodore Roosevelt, the U.S. decided to construct a canal across the Colombia-ruled territory of Panama. Roosevelt strongly felt that the U.S. should control the canal, but Colombia rejected this proposal. Roosevelt became very angry, calling Colombia's leaders "jack rabbits" and "Dagos." Shortly thereafter, rebels in Panama overthrew the Colombian government, an act Roosevelt was accused of fomenting. There is no direct evidence of this, but American warships did keep Colombia out of Panama at that time. Shortly after the revolution, Roosevelt attained his goal; the U.S. was given perpetual "use, occupation, and control" of the Panama Canal Zone.

393

WILLIAM HOWARD TAFT 1909-1913

A1. As President of the Philippines Commission, William Howard Taft earned respect and praise both at home and in the Philippines. He set up a judicial system, improved public works and harbors, and established a system of free public education for the natives. Called "Saint Taft" by the inhabitants of the Philippines, Taft devoted all of his efforts to improving living conditions there. He was concerned only for the welfare of the people and he left when the governing of the Islands could be turned over to the native Philippinos.

A2. President William Howard Taft was an able and efficient administrator in domestic matters. He set up the Department of Labor as a separate Cabinet post, and enlarged the national health bureau which expanded federal programs for health and welfare of the people. President Taft also set up the Budget Bureau, making the first important revision of federal finances in history. He personally directed budget cuts and instigated several efficiency measures. By up-dating procedures and eliminating waste, Taft was able to show a surplus of money instead of a deficit by the end of his first year in office.

A3. President William Howard Taft was very successful in giving the country many domestic reforms and improvements. He greatly extended the civil service system, thus reducing political patronage. President Taft also reduced the working day of government employees from 10 to 8 hours. The postal savings bank was established during his term in office, as was the parcel post system. This system provided efficient, low-cost transportation of goods for the ordinary citizen. In addition, President Taft got legislation enacted that required campaign expenditures to be made public and strongly backed the adoption of the 17th Amendment which provided for the direct election of U.S. Senators.

A4. As a Cabinet member, William Howard Taft performed a great service to this country in Panama. Sent to the Canal Zone to negotiate a treaty with the new government there, Taft soon became actively involved in labor, political, engineering, and sanitation problems. He became an able and enthusiastic troubleshooter for the administration, reducing many sources of friction between the U.S. and Panama. In addition to actually supervising construction of the Canal, Taft successfully established health jurisdiction and defined harbor boundaries to the satisfaction of both governments.

B1. President William Howard Taft carried on his predecessor's work in the area of conservation. He enlarged the program, withdrawing acreage from public lands and establishing wildlife sanctuaries. The program also provided for the selection of a number of national park sites, and helped protect many fast-diminishing species of birds, wildlife and plant life.

B2. President William Howard Taft was concerned with the plight of the American farmer. When he took office, farmers were paying interest rates which were higher than those paid by any other business group in the country. To provide a financial system which would reduce farm interest rates, Taft proposed the establishment of credit unions. This remedy was designed to cut operating costs for the farmers, with the ultimate result being greater productivity.

B3. When he took the office of President, William Howard Taft was shocked at the number of requests he received for jobs from so-called "party faithfuls." He took steps to reduce the spoils system, carrying on the efforts of previous presidents in this area. Taft was also instrumental in bringing assistant postmasters into the civil service system, and attempted to get passed a law that would insure merit advancement of people in the diplomatic service.

B4. Before he was elected President, William Howard Taft had held public office nearly continuously for 29 years. Appointed to the bench as a judge at 31, Taft went on to become a Solicitor General, a member of the Cincinnati Superior Court, a U.S. circuit judge, U.S. Commissioner and finally a member of the President's Cabinet. The experience he received at all of these posts stood him in good stead when he became President.

C1. Toward the end of his Presidency, William Howard Taft became involved in a situation which continues to puzzle historians. A certain Senator had consistently opposed Taft's efforts at social reforms for workers and farmers, and had also fought Taft's attempts to reduce tariffs. Since this Senator controlled a powerful committee, he was able to block much of Taft's proposed legislation. Now Taft developed close relations with this Senator, speaking favorably of him in public speeches, and inviting him to the White House. Naturally, this relationship alienated many of Taft's supporters. At the same time, there is no evidence that it did Taft the slightest good in getting his legislation through the Senate.

C2. By his last year in office, William Howard Taft had alienated certain segments of his own party, and the friction between Taft and the ex-President had become an open conflict. Taft came out badly in this clash of personalities. Although ordinarily without malice, Taft now called his old friend a "political emotionalist or neurotic," and even passed on unfounded rumors about him. It was several years before the two men met face-to-face again, and the old ties of friendship were never reestablished.

C3. President William Howard Taft had little talent at guiding public opinion, and often chose to say nothing rather than defend his policies to the public. The White House correspondents complained that Taft withheld the news from them, and he was much criticized in the newspapers. Taft resented this criticism, and finally stopped reading almost everything but the headlines saying, "I don't think their reading will do me any particular good . . . and would only be provocative of anger."

C4. William Howard Taft was not happy in the role of a politician. He was urged to run for President by an ambitious and socially brilliant wife, but upon reaching the White House called it "the lonesomest place in the world." Taft was himself ill-equipped to handle political life, and experienced many problems in his relations with Congress. Only when he left the White House and returned to public service as a judge was he content again.

D1. President William Howard Taft made a serious error in judgment in dealing with a reciprocity treaty with Canada. This treaty would have been of great benefit to trade and commerce in the U.S. However, Taft in public and in private, referred to Canada as "only an adjunct of the U.S." Then, one of Taft's supporters in the House of Representatives made a speech in which he expressed the wish that "the American flag will float over every square foot of the British North American possessions." Unfortunately, Taft failed to deny these aims for several months. The Canadians, naturally enough, were irritated and seriously alarmed. This threat of American imperialism was one of the main factors in the defeat of the treaty in Canada.

D2. William Howard Taft was not a leader of men nor a changer of policy, and this carried over to his position as Chief Justice of the Supreme Court. Most other Chief Justices have been concerned with the spirit of justice; however, to Taft, expediency was important even when it might mean forfeiting principle. As Chief Justice, Taft refused to dissent from the majority view even when it meant he had to abandon previously held beliefs. He felt that dissension caused too many delays in Court action. For example, Taft had been strongly opposed to prohibition. As leader of the Supreme Court, however, he supported the Prohibition Amendment, saying "law was law whether it worked or not."

D3. President William Howard Taft, upon taking office, made the tariff problem his first cause, and it was his first failure. The bill that Taft finally got passed through Congress kept tariff rates high instead of lowering them, as Taft had originally promised. But instead of vetoing the bill, Taft ineptly praised it as "the best tariff law ever passed." With this maneuver Taft not only lost face, but he also lost control of Congress. The country was given a very poor piece of legislation instead of a major reform, and in general Taft's administration policies were stalemated due to his inability to influence Congress.

D4. President William Howard Taft had a disappointing record in the area of foreign affairs. He failed in his attempt to bring peace to the Latin American countries and was unable to persuade Congress to continue his Russian commercial treaty. Taft was also unsuccessful in China when he tried to establish good relations with that country by introducing American dollars into the Chinese economy. This "dollar diplomacy," as it came to be known, failed mainly because Taft plunged into the scheme without first obtaining adequate and up-to-date information on treaties between China and other countries and on the nature of the Chinese economy.

WOODROW WILSON 1913-1921

A1. President Woodrow Wilson believed very strongly in the concepts of democracy, feeling that the nation should truly have a "government by the people." In office only 11 days, he held the first Presidential press conference in history, in accord with his belief in the rights of the public to regularly hear from the President on the state of affairs of the nation. Wilson's precedent has been followed by every President since his time. During his terms in office, President Wilson repeatedly took issues directly to the people. He felt the need to explain government policy personally to the people he governed. In return, the people of the nation supported him on several critical occasions with letters and telegrams to their Congressmen.

A2. It was Woodrow Wilson's goal to make the motto "The New Freedom", a reality. President Wilson was very active in backing many laws dealing with social justice. Two particularly important pieces of legislation dealt with working conditions for children, and safety provisions for sailors. This latter legislation, the Seaman's Act, protected merchant sailors against unsafe working conditions aboard vessels, and also gave them greater freedom in their relations with private shipowners. The law dealing with children's working conditions corrected a particularly bad situation that then prevailed. It set up reasonable employment regulations, and eliminated unfair practices in hiring and exploiting child labor.

A3. President Wilson was deeply concerned with freedom of economic opportunity, and was personally instrumental in getting Congress to pass some far-reaching laws to protect opportunity for the individual. This legislation included an anti-trust law that prevented monopolistic combines, and especially the establishment of the Federal Trade Commission. The Federal Trade Commission offered guidance and education to businessmen, but its main purpose was to eliminate unfair and deceptive business practices. It was very beneficial to consumers and even today remains one of the main safeguards against dishonest business practices.

A4. Woodrow Wilson hated war and did everything in his power to establish the League of Nations which would work for a lasting world peace. At the end of World War I, he went to France personally to negotiate for the League, the first United States

President to attempt such a diplomatic feat. The League of Nations was a far-sighted idea which helped pave the way for the United Nations Organization. President Wilson was awarded the Nobel Peace Prize for his efforts in setting up the League. He was one of only two United States Presidents ever to receive this high award.

B1. When the railroad unions threatened a nationwide strike, President Woodrow Wilson was able to get the unions to accept arbitration, but the railroad companies refused to participate. President Wilson realized the potential danger of a large-scale strike, and he also saw justification for some of the workers' demands. A week before the strike deadline, he called a joint session of Congress and petitioned for legislation that would give the workers some of their demands. Congress acted swiftly and the measure became law, thus avoiding a costly national strike.

B2. Shortly after he took office, President Woodrow Wilson began a campaign for reforms in the currency and banking systems. The legislation which was enacted was the Federal Reserve Bill. It established twelve Federal Reserve Banks which replaced the antiquated central banking system. New currency, Federal Reserve notes, was also created.

B3. Before he became President, Woodrow Wilson distinguished himself as a teacher and a writer. After receiving a Ph.D. degree from Johns Hopkins University, Wilson served as professor of history and politics at Wesleyan University. He then received an appointment as professor of jurisprudence and history at Princeton where he wrote a five-volume History of the American People. Woodrow Wilson later became president of Princeton University and brought about various educational reforms such as higher standards of scholarship.

B4. At the end of his first term as President, Woodrow Wilson tackled the problem of agricultural credit. Wilson began to realize the pressing needs of the farmers who had been neglected by the government in the past. One need was for long-term loans that could be paid off when crops were harvested. President Wilson's administration put its weight behind legislation which provided these loans at reasonable interest rates.

C1. Woodrow Wilson desired a third term in office although he was partially paralyzed from a stroke and suffered other disabilities. For over a year his illnesses had kept him out of touch with the public. However, in a last minute try for reelection he attempted to inform the voters of his policies, but it was too little and much too late. Wilson's attempt to run again when he was physically unable to hold office left his own party defeated and disorganized.

C2. Woodrow Wilson was an opportunistic politician from his earliest beginnings. He used his connections as a lecturer at Princeton to preach his politics, then stepped out of this position when the political bosses decided they could make him President. An orator who knew how to manipulate opinion, Wilson attempted and often succeeded in persuasive arguments to gain a point or cover an error. Wilson campaigned for reelection under the slogan "He Kept Us Out of War." Then when World War I broke out shortly after, he led the country into war with the slogan "The World Must Be Made Safe for Democracy."

C3. Woodrow Wilson did not like to ask or take advice from any man, and on occasion this tendency became ludicrous. Once an interested and concerned leader cornered the President in an attempt to advise him on important matters. Wilson tried to change the subject and avoid hearing things that would upset him or cause him to face an unpleasant situation. The man was determined, however, and persisted. Finally, unable to wave the man aside, Wilson stuck his fingers in his ears and ran from the room.

C4. Woodrow Wilson returned to this country from the Versailles Peace Convention with an unacceptable compromise treaty. He was widely criticized for giving in to foreign pressures, and he soon found that the American people would not accept the document. Stubbornly clinging to his ill-fated treaty, he tried in vain to win public and Congressional acceptance for it. Wilson, with his high ideals, may have been a man ahead of his time, but he failed as a leader to deal with the problems of the moment. The treaty that decided important issues after World War I was never accepted by this country.

D1. When a civil war broke out in Mexico, Woodrow Wilson interfered and sent in armed troops. The lives of many American soldiers were uselessly lost when a punitive force was ordered into Vera Cruz by Wilson to compel the new government there to salute the American flag. This mishandling of the whole situation nearly led to a war between the United States and Mexico, but Wilson was forced to pull out American troops when trouble arose in Europe. When foreign interference was withdrawn, Mexico quietly settled her problems herself. The entire incident could have been avoided if Wilson had listened to informed advisors rather than blundering into the situation.

D2. Woodrow Wilson was responsible to a large degree for the deadlock at the Versailles Peace Convention after World War I, and the subsequent failure of the League of Nations. Wilson refused to take anyone knowledgeable about foreign affairs to Versailles, but went himself accompanied by "yes-men." This was the main cause of his failure at the peace negotiations at Versailles. Back in this country, he refused to compromise to save the League of Nations, stubbornly saying "anyone who opposes me I'll crush." At a time when diplomacy and skill at handling men and situations were imperative, Wilson failed in a costly display of stubbornness and vanity.

D3. When Woodrow Wilson reached the Presidency, he carried into office a strictly Southern viewpoint on issues and policy, including social prejudices against the Negro. Although favoring social justice in other areas, Wilson failed in the matter of racial justice. Southern political leaders began to gain power during his administration, and they began to impose segregation rules in federal departments and agencies. Wilson refused to prevent this, and these segregation policies became entrenched in the government.

D4. Woodrow Wilson showed many extreme inconsistencies in his handling of issues and in his Presidential policies. Although he was a strict moralist, he twice ordered the armed invasion of Mexico. Wilson urged neutrality in World War I, and refused to ready the defenses of the country. Then, when the German submarine threat came, the country was unprepared to defend itself. In another instance, Wilson advocated self-determination for Europe, yet denied this to marine-occupied Haiti and Santo Domingo. These inconsistencies reflected an unsoundness in the foreign policy of this country at a critical period in history.

HARRY S. TRUMAN 1945-1953

A1. In his first inaugural address, President Harry S. Truman enunciated the four major goals of his administration. His fourth goal, which became known as the Point Four Program, was to share American scientific and industrial knowledge with underdeveloped nations. Point Four aimed to increase food supplies, institute public health programs, and establish primary and vocational education. Within six months after Congress enacted Truman's program, 350 technicians were at work in 27 countries. In north Burma, Point Four technicians had reduced the number of people afflicted by malaria from 50% to 10%. In many places throughout the Middle East, Latin America and Asia, Truman's Point Four technicians were the first to establish public school systems.

A2. When Harry Truman was elected County Judge, Jackson County was in miserable condition. Truman's predecessors had built several hundred miles of shoddy roads, and had left the county $2,400,000 in debt. In his first two years, Judge Truman reduced the debt by $700,000 and repaired many of the roads. He successfully persuaded the banks to reduce the county's interest payments from 6% to 2¼%, and this further reduced the county debt. Truman then convinced the voters to pass a $7,000,000 bond issue. With this money, Truman built many public works that created jobs for the unemployed of the Great Depression. When Truman left office, the county was in excellent financial condition and possessed many well-built roads and public works. As judge, Truman was both honest and efficient.

A3. President Truman was a strong advocate of Civil Rights, and requested several important reforms to be enacted by Congress. Although Congress failed to act, Truman was undaunted. By using his power to issue Executive Orders, Truman achieved major reforms single-handedly. Over the opposition of both admirals and generals, Truman's first order successfully integrated the armed forces. In addition, Truman established a committee to enforce non-discriminatory clauses contained in government contracts. By 1951, Truman's committee had made real progress toward eliminating job discrimination in large sections of the nation's economy.

A4. Early in 1941, Senator Harry S. Truman was appointed chairman of an important Senate committee to investigate the procurement and construction of all supplies, munitions, vehicles, and facilities connected with war against Nazi Germany. Truman dedicated himself to this work and did an outstanding job. Through fair and comprehensive investigations, Truman exposed many costly acts of mismanagement and corruption. Through such actions, the Truman Committee, as it came to be known, soon developed a formidable reputation. In many cases all that was required to correct an abuse was Truman's announcement that he would investigate. It is estimated that the Truman Committee produced a direct saving of 15 billion dollars for the American taxpayer. In addition, the committee's reputation probably kept countless other problems from ever developing.

B1. Because Truman was only a high school graduate, he worked hard to overcome what he felt were his intellectual limitations. He read as much as he could about the problems that confronted his administration. He tried to appoint good advisors, and then consulted with them extensively. Once President Truman had gathered the facts and advice, he would make a clear-cut decision. Then he would delegate authority to his associates so that they could put Truman's decision into action. When he left office, Truman prided himself on having been a "clean desk" administrator.

B2. In the aftermath of World War II, the Turkish government faced bankruptcy and Greece was torn by civil strife. President Truman persuaded Congress to appropriate 250 million dollars for Greece and 150 million dollars for Turkey. Truman's use of American money restored stability and helped both nations rebuild their weakened economies. Truman's policy of economic aid became known as the Truman Doctrine, and formed the basis of Truman's foreign policy.

B3. President Truman helped improve relations with Latin America by various actions including his good will tours. On a trip to Mexico, Truman's warmth and simplicity reduced some of the tensions in Mexican-American relations. In an honest gesture of respect, Truman laid a wreath before the monument to Mexican heroes of the Mexican-American War. He later made a trip to Rio de Janeiro to attend an important conference of Western Hemisphere countries and afterwards endorsed the mutual-assistance treaty drafted by the conferees.

B4. During his last months in office, President Harry S. Truman worked to ensure an easy transition from his administration to that of his successor. Truman briefed the President-elect on foreign policy and taxes, and also ordered his Cabinet members to prepare the incoming officials for their new responsibilities. In addition, Truman wrote to members of Congress suggesting that they lower the tax liability of future Presidents. By these and other actions, President Truman eliminated some of the difficulties that faced the President-elect.

C1. President Truman prided himself on "shooting from the lip," as he put it. But his hasty answers and snap judgments at press conferences promoted domestic opposition to his programs, and offended foreign countries. Once Truman told a reporter that he had just sent an "ultimatum" to Stalin. This remark caused an immediate uproar, and the White House quickly issued a correction.

C2. Truman began his political career as the protege of T. J. Pendergast, the boss of the Kansas City political machine. On account of Senator Truman's close association with Pendergast, the White House shunned him as Pendergast's "office boy in Washington." When Boss Pendergast was convicted of bribery and income tax evasion, Senator Truman failed to disassociate himself. This marred Truman's reputation and lessened his effectiveness as a Senator.

C3. President Truman was inept and undiplomatic in his relations with Congress. When he had decided on a course of action, he expected Congress to support him obediently, and he made little or no effort to compromise or consult with Congressional leaders. Truman's methods alienated support even when his party controlled Congress. In domestic affairs, Truman got very little constructive legislation through Congress.

C4. President Harry S. Truman was often intemperate and coarse in his use of language. When several newspaper columnists urged him to fire certain members of his Cabinet and staff, Truman publicly replied, "No s.o.b. is going to dictate to me." On another occasion, a respected music critic panned a vocal performance by Truman's daughter, who wanted to be a singer but lacked talent. Truman wrote the critic a blistering note, threatening him with a black eye and a broken nose if they ever met. Although such public displays of temper did no real harm, they lowered the dignity of the Presidency and reduced Truman's effectiveness in office.

D1. President Truman often resorted to dictatorial methods in his treatment of labor unions. Although he was friendly to labor, he thought they had to accept the government's terms. In one major episode, Truman's negotiations failed to end a nation wide rail strike. Truman then threatened to order the army to run the railroads, but this threat failed to end the strike. Finally, Truman called a special session of Congress and demanded Congressional authorization to draft all the strikers into the army. There is no doubt Truman would have done so. However, this final threat crushed the strike though Truman's high-handed methods were widely criticized.

D2. In 1950, a Congressional committee began finding evidence of bribery and corruption in the Reconstruction Finance Corporation. President Truman immediately declared the committee report to be asinine, and obstructed the investigators while refusing to do anything about the problem. Nevertheless, Congress pursued the investigation. This led into the Department of Internal Revenue, where both the Commissioner and the Assistant Commissioner had cheated on their income taxes, and where more than 200 people later lost their jobs, and into the Justice Department which was failing to prosecute these cases. This all became known as the "Truman scandals." However, President Truman refused for a long time to clean up his administration until forced to act by public opinion.

D3. Truman sometimes compromised his moral principles for political expediency. When he ran for his first elective office, the racist Ku Klux Klan still had a great deal of political influence in Missouri. Truman's campaign workers kept insisting that if he wanted to win the election, he would have to join the Klan. For a while, Truman refused to do so, but he finally gave way and sent in his entrance fee. After his initiation into the Klan, Truman was a full-fledged member, though he never took any part in Klan affairs.

D4. When a steel strike threatened to cause a critical shortage of steel, President Truman tried unsuccessfully to negotiate between labor and management. When management rejected Truman's compromise, Truman became so angry that he ordered the Secretary of Commerce to seize and operate every steel mill in the United States. Truman's advisers were almost unanimously against this, but Truman persisted, hoping to force the steel companies to accept his proposal. The steel companies filed suit, of course, and the Supreme Court quickly declared Truman's act to be completely unconstitutional.

JAMES MADISON 1809-1817

A1. James Madison played a leading role as a delegate to the Continental Congress and was called "Father of the Constitution." He was instrumental in framing the Constitution and played an important role in its adoption by his writings in the *Federalist* papers. James Madison's records of the debates became the principal record of the Constitutional Convention. Published after his death as the *Journal of the Federal Convention*, they serve as the sole existing record of this monumental event in American history.

A2. After the War of 1812, President James Madison sought to promote the growth of new industry in a nation which was then primarily agricultural. He urged Congress to take steps to preserve the manufacturing which had sprung up during the war years and to help new businesses get a start. Responding to Madison's recommendations, an important tariff bill was passed by Congress which gave needed protection to American businessmen. In addition, a new United States Bank was chartered which promoted prosperity and business growth in the new nation.

B1. When he was the Secretary of State, James Madison promoted the purchase of the Louisiana Territory from France. Shrewdly calculating that the French government would need money at this particular time, Secretary Madison, by his transactions, enabled the country to expand into the rich delta lands of the South. Madison continued the policy of promoting national growth after he became President. During his two terms in office the Missouri Territory was organized and the states of Louisiana and Indiana were admitted to the Union.

B2. As a member of Congress, James Madison was instrumental in the passage of legislation which formed many new departments of the young government. His most remembered effort, however, was the preparation and sponsoring of the first group of amendments to the Constitution. This set of amendments incorporated approximately twenty-four additional guarantees of liberties for the citizens of the United States.

C1. James Madison was a very conservative President, believing in a strict interpretation of the Constitution. One of his last acts in office was the vetoing of the "Bonus Bill." This bill would have provided federal aid for the building of much needed roads and canals. Madison vetoed this bill on the grounds that he could find nothing in the Constitution which expressly said that the government should build roads and canals.

C2. James Madison was a man of contradictions. Though very conservative in his political views, his personal life was lavish and he was often deeply in debt. When he went to Washington as Secretary of State, he began to spend large sums of money on housing and furnishings. This extravagance led him into complete bankruptcy in a few years. On slavery, Madison was again paradoxical. He was opposed to slavery in principle, yet he refused to free his own personal slaves even when he could ill afford to keep them financially.

D1. In his first month as President of the United States, James Madison secretly sent messages to both England and France. In these messages Madison promised each country that if it would stop molesting American vessels on the high seas, he would urge Congress to declare war on the other country. Both countries soon found out about this underhanded tactic, and became very hostile. The United States averted war with France but finally fell into armed conflict with England. This conflict was aptly named "Mr. Madison's War."

D2. Partly in an attempt to bring together a disunited country, James Madison led the United States into the unnecessary and humiliating War of 1812. Personally leading the troops, Madison failed in an attempt to invade Canada. While he was absent from Washington, British troops captured the city and burned the White House. The war fortunately ended when Britain agreed to withdraw her troops. This war, for which Madison was directly responsible, accomplished nothing. Moreover, it put the country deeply in debt and in grave financial difficulty.

MARTIN VAN BUREN 1837-1841

A1. A major accomplishment of President Martin Van Buren was the establishment of an independent federal treasury system. At that time, federal funds were handled by private banking interests and corruption was widespread. President Van Buren worked for a treasury system that would be independent of political influence. His proposal, which was made into law just before the end of his term, was carefully worked out and had far-reaching importance. It essentially eliminated corruption in the handling of government funds in the treasury, and basically the same system remains in effect today.

A2. During the administration of Martin Van Buren, U.S. relations with Canada and Great Britain were still precarious. An unfortunate incident developed when a band of Canadian rebels seized and burned an American steamer, killing an American seaman. Given the temper of American public opinion at that time, this easily could have developed into a full-scale war between the United States and Canada. However, President Van Buren took decisive action to prevent open conflict, and finally the Webster-Ashburton Treaty was signed. Because of President Van Buren's cool-headed handling of the situation, war was averted and peaceful relations were reestablished between the United States and Canada.

B1. Martin Van Buren began to prepare himself for a life of public service at a very early age. At fourteen he began to study law, and at twenty-one was admitted to the bar and began practicing law. Van Buren served his country in many capacities throughout his years in public office. He was a state senator, United States Senator, and Governor of the state of New York. Later he went to Washington as Secretary of State, and was finally elected President.

B2. Martin Van Buren's administration made various reforms but did not "rock the boat." Among the changes that were brought about during Van Buren's term in office were such things as the organization of an express service, and the provision that no federal employee would be asked to work on a government project more than 10 hours a day. This was one of the first improvements officially made by any President in the area of labor reforms.

C1. Shortly after Martin Van Buren's election as President of the United States, the country's first economic panic began. Van Buren was not involved in causing the panic. However, he believed in a passive federal government, and so did not attempt to interfere with the economy. The panic, together with Van Buren's unwillingness to take governmental action, was probably the main factor in his defeat when he ran for a second term in office.

C2. The continuing friction and struggle between the pro- and anti-slavery factions became potentially explosive during the Presidency of Martin Van Buren. Van Buren sought to avoid the entire issue, making no promise to either faction except the pledge of noninvolvement. Following this policy, Van Buren refused to back the abolition of slavery in the District of Columbia.

D1. Martin Van Buren did much to institutionalize the "spoils system" in government. This system allowed those who got political power to reward their supporters with jobs in government. Van Buren attempted to convert the Post Office Department into a spoils machine, and was also influential in the organization of one of the first political machines in the state of New York. Because of his adroit behind-the-scenes political maneuvers, Van Buren earned the nickname "The Little Magician."

D2. Martin Van Buren's presidency was marked by a period of civil unrest. Van Buren refused to take any stand on the slavery problem in the South and maintained a political status quo attitude. Also, the war with the Seminole Indians was allowed to continue for many years, costing countless lives and great misery. Van Buren did nothing to promote an end to this war. Following his policy of minimal government involvement, he failed to protect those minorities who could not alone bring about needed changes in the country.

A1. As President of the United States, John Tyler proved to be very capable in handling foreign affairs. He brought to the Presidency a wealth of training and discipline that made him effective in obtaining harmony with other nations. He initiated a treaty that provided for free trade between the United States and China, and reaffirmed an atmosphere of peaceful relations. President Tyler also effected the Webster-Ashburton Treaty which finally put to rest a long-standing boundary dispute between Canada and Maine. This important treaty ended hostilities with Britain along that border.

A2. President John Tyler worked very hard to get various nonpartisan measures approved by Congress. During his earlier career of public service he had earned the reputation of an independent thinker, and his extensive experience made him effective in pushing bills through Congress. His reform measures included a much needed reorganization of the navy, the distribution of proceeds from the sale of government lands, and the establishment of a national bank. Tyler's Presidency also saw the fortunate end of the long and often ugly Seminole Indian War.

B1. Long before becoming President, John Tyler was active in public service. He was elected to the Virginia State Legislature five times, and later served as a U.S. Senator. In addition, against great odds, he was twice elected Governor of Virginia. He was then elected Vice-President of the United States and succeeded to the Presidency when his predecessor died in office.

B2. After John Tyler's retirement from the office of President of the United States, he became the chancellor of William and Mary College, a position he had held before his election. Tyler's active interest and concern for the future of his country precluded a leisurely retirement. Although he did not run for public office, John Tyler was appointed president of the Peace Convention which was attempting to head off a war between the North and the South.

C1. When Vice-President John Tyler succeeded to the duties of the Presidency by the death in office of his predecessor, he took over the title of President as well. At that time, this move was unprecedented and shocked many people who felt that he was only serving out a term of duty and should not enter the Presidency as though he had been the people's choice. Tyler immediately made it clear who was boss, warning his Secretary of State, "I can never consent to being dictated to." His administration was stormy and Tyler welcomed its end. As he left the White House, he described his term in office as a bed of thorns.

C2. The Presidency of John Tyler was marked by dissension between him and his Cabinet. After he twice vetoed a bill that Congress had passed, Tyler's entire Cabinet, save one, resigned. This was only the beginning of a long Cabinet procession. Altogether, 32 men served in the six available Cabinet posts during Tyler's term of office.

D1. Popular feeling was strongly against John Tyler when his term as President drew to a close. His stubborn refusal to submit to the will of the people led to such public acts of revolt as the stoning of the White House and the burning of the President in effigy. When he vetoed an important tariff bill, Tyler was threatened with impeachment, though the vote fell short and he served out his full term. Tyler's conservative position was not changed by these demonstrations of displeasure. One of his last official acts as President reflected his strong advocacy of slavery by laying the groundwork for the addition of yet another slave state to the Union.

D2. John Tyler believed in a strict interpretation of the Constitution, and therefore opposed most internal improvements in government. His refusal to reorganize the financial structure of the nation allowed the great economic panic to continue unabated throughout his term. Congress, finally exasperated and frustrated by Tyler's stubborn conservatism, overrode Tyler's veto in order to pass a necessary reform bill. This was the first Presidential veto ever to be overridden. Feelings were running high against Tyler by this time, and were intensified when he sponsored a joint resolution for the annexation of Texas, which led directly to the war with Mexico.

A1. James Knox Polk began serving his country at an early age. Elected to the Tennessee State Legislature at 28, by 30 he had moved to Washington as a United States Representative. Polk became a leader of great force as chairman of the powerful Ways and Means Committee, and as majority leader of his party. After being elected Speaker of the House, James Polk served as the Governor of Tennessee for one term. Called "Young Hickory," by his supporters, Polk was an astute political leader, who was sensitive to the public's needs. For these reasons, before he reached the age of 50 he was elected to the office of President of the United States.

A2. James Knox Polk served his term as President of the United States with understanding and vigor. He demonstrated his belief in a free society when he announced in his inaugural address that those who disagree with the President are "entitled to the full and free exercise of their opinions and are entitled to respect and regard." President Polk also handled foreign affairs ably, reducing import duties on important items such as coal and steel, and effecting an important treaty with Latin America. This treaty was the basis for the later construction of the Panama Canal, a vital waterway access from the East to California before the days of modern transportation.

B1. James Knox Polk worked very hard as President of the United States. During his four years in office, he was away from Washington only six weeks. President Polk spent many hours carefully studying each piece of legislation that he sent to Congress. He also handled the problems of his office personally, willing to give attention to even the smallest administrative detail.

B2. Many economic reforms were established through the efforts of James Knox Polk. As President of the United States, he settled a long-standing tariff dispute between the North and the South. Polk also established a badly needed new treasury system which protected and promoted national economy. Because of his efforts in advancing these reforms, Polk has been called by his biographers an efficient and industrious President.

C1. James Knox Polk sought to claim the Oregon Territory for the United States although Great Britain had settlements in that area. This caused considerable hostility and war was threatened. In the end, a compromise was effected but it displeased the United States citizens living in the territory. They believed the territory should not have been given up so easily. Polk handled the entire affair poorly and the settlement was unsatisfactory to all parties involved.

C2. After losing two bids for reelection as Governor of Tennessee, the political future of James Knox Polk looked bleak. Only because of a schism in the political party was he even nominated to run for President. The other candidates were deadlocked and finally, on the 9th ballot, Polk emerged as a "dark horse" candidate. He won the election by a scant 38,000 votes, one of the smallest margins in history.

D1. As President, James Knox Polk broke off diplomatic relations with Mexico his first month in office. He was determined to annex California and the New Mexico Territory to the Union. When it became apparent that force was necessary, he declared war on Mexico. United States troops captured the capital of Mexico and forced the Mexican government to sign a treaty which gave up one-half of Mexico's territory to the United States. This one million square miles of land taken from Mexico included the area now California, Nevada, Utah, western Colorado, western New Mexico, and much of Arizona and Texas.

D2. James Knox Polk had little faith in his Cabinet members, although he had chosen them himself. He was said to be constantly suspicious of their ulterior motives and demanded that they disavow any Presidential aspirations while they served in his administration. Polk felt that he alone was competent to make judgments and decisions on even minor issues. Polk was, therefore, kept very busy with routine matters that could have been handled by assistants. This suspicion and egotism made it difficult for Polk to accomplish meaningful legislation during his administration.

A1. Developing and preserving good relations between Canada and the United States was a primary goal of President Franklin Pierce. Long-standing differences between the two countries welled up in a dispute over offshore fishing rights shortly after Pierce took office. Pierce immediately began negotiations, with the aim of maintaining American rights and interests, while being fair to Canada as well. After careful study, the Fisheries-Reciprocity Treaty was put into effect. This solved the immediate conflict and also laid down far-reaching guidelines that were important in developing future friendly relations between the two countries.

A2. President Franklin Pierce was an extremely able administrator. Economic prosperity was a pressing problem at this time and President Pierce began positive action as soon as he took office to expand American commerce as rapidly as possible. New areas of foreign trade were opened with Japan, Brazil, and Peru. In addition, Pierce continually studied and prepared needed reforms for the tariff laws. A wave of economic prosperity spread over the country largely as a result of President Pierce's efforts.

B1. President Franklin Pierce felt that the federal pension system badly needed study and revision. In too many cases the needy were refused aid while those who were less in need received support. When Pierce took office nearly 14 thousand persons were drawing pensions, an extremely large proportion of the population at that time. The reforms that Pierce advocated eliminated pensions for those who did not need them, and only granted aid on the basis of need.

B2. President Franklin Pierce was not afraid to tackle the unpleasant aspects of his office. One particularly unpleasant problem was the need to reduce the number of staff officers in the naval service. Many of these officers were near retirement or serving in "figurehead" positions and could reasonably be relieved of duty. President Pierce put a final stamp of approval on legislation which retired or dismissed over 200 top naval officers who were found to be not "up to standard." Protests from influential politicians did not dissuade Pierce, although he knew that he would lose many influential backers by this action.

C1. From his early days as a politician, Franklin Pierce advocated a strict interpretation of the Constitution. Later, when he became President, Pierce continued in this conservative attitude, believing that the federal government should not consider any actions not specifically laid down by the Constitution. This position was unfortunate at this period in history; the rapid growth of the country required changes in government that Pierce failed to provide.

C2. Franklin Pierce was a "dark horse" candidate for the Presidency, winning support mainly because he was considered a "safe man", by the South. He believed that slavery was guaranteed by the Constitution and should therefore be maintained. Pierce was an amiable and probably honest man, but his leanings toward Southern viewpoints promoted sectional strife in the country.

D1. In his inaugural address, President Franklin Pierce clearly stated his intentions to carry out a policy of expansionism. The first target was to be the annexation of Spanish-owned Cuba. Under Pierce's direction, the Ostend Manifesto was drawn up, in which Spain was notified that the United States was "justified in wresting it (Cuba) from Spain as we possess the power," The world was shocked when this document was published, and Pierce was forced to back down on his threats. In a second incident, attempts were made to forcefully set up a government in Nicaragua under direct United States rule. The purpose of this type of colonialism was to extend American power into other areas of the continent.

D2. President Franklin Pierce felt that slavery should be continued because the Southern economic structure depended on slavery. The territories of Kansas and Nebraska were made slave states after Pierce strongly supported legislation to this end. In the Northwest, Pierce also supported a measure which opened the territory up to slavery and removed the Indians living on the land to reservations. These policies became increasingly unpopular, but Pierce stubbornly clung to his opinions. Even after leaving office, Pierce condemned Lincoln's Emancipation Proclamation which freed the slaves.

RUTHERFORD B. HAYES 1877-1881

A1. President Rutherford B. Hayes worked very hard to obtain legislation for the welfare of the nation, particularly in the area of education. He proposed the first bills which would provide free public education in the country, finally allowing rich and poor alike the opportunity of obtaining schooling. President Hayes' interest in the educational welfare of the nation's youth continued after he left office. His chief interest in these later years was the establishment of well-equipped manual training schools which would teach skills to those who wished to become craftsmen.

A2. During his term as President, Rutherford B. Hayes worked tirelessly for reforms in government hiring policies. At that time, the spoils system was in effect, and Hayes' reforms were opposed by political leaders whose power depended on the spoils system. However, President Hayes would not be swayed from his purpose, and continued to try to liberate jobs from partisan political control. After many struggles, civil service legislation was passed which definitely reformed the system. Much of the credit for these reforms must go directly to President Hayes who took the initiative and personally influenced the legislation.

B1. President Hayes believed in a "sound money" policy, that is, money that was backed by government security. To keep the country on a sound money basis, President Hayes vetoed a silver bill which he felt was inflationary. A substitute bill was then passed by Congress which was much sounder economically. Business picked up, farm prices rose and there was a general increase in prosperity.

B2. Rutherford B. Hayes had been long concerned over the Indian problem in the country, and his administration saw many reforms in the Department of Indian Affairs. Steps were taken to eliminate the plundering of Indian lands, and the mistreatment of Indians by settlers was reduced. President Hayes himself opened an Indian school in Pennsylvania. Altogether, his actions did much to help this long-abused minority.

C1. Shortly after Rutherford B. Hayes was sworn in as President, the country's first great labor strike began. The railroad workers, in an effort to secure better wages and better working conditions, walked off their jobs across the country. Hayes was determined to break the strike at any cost, and he quickly sent in federal troops. The strike was finally broken, but not before a number of lives were lost. Hayes' actions began a long policy of government interference in labor problems.

C2. Rutherford B. Hayes entered the office of President owing political favors to a great number of men. He repaid these favors by doling out federal jobs, too often to men who should not have been in positions of authority. In one incident a man known publically to be particularly corrupt had to be given a job because he had backed Hayes in his campaign. Hayes gave him a lighthouse to keep, hoping this would keep the man isolated from public scrutiny. Fortunately for Hayes, the man was accidentally drowned in a storm.

D1. During Rutherford B. Hayes' administration there occurred one of the great injustices inflicted upon minority groups in this country. The Chinese had long been a welcome source of labor in the West, especially in building the transcontinental railroads. But as the West became more settled, it was decided that their presence threatened "American labor." These groups began persecutions of the Chinese, with hundreds of families driven from their homes, terrorized, and killed. Hayes did nothing to stop these injustices; to do so would have been ill-timed politically because of the strength of the labor unions in the country at that time. As a result of his inaction, the Chinese were sacrificed to political expediency and a treaty was arranged which excluded further immigration from China.

D2. Rutherford B. Hayes took the office of President in one of the most disputed elections in the history of the country. Hayes' political party refused to accept the legality of some electoral representatives, and for three months secret meetings were held with politicians from the four critical Southern states. Finally the politicians of both parties agreed to a deal to give the Presidency to Hayes, although he had fewer votes than his opponent. In return, Hayes agreed to end Reconstruction in the South, thus allowing the restoration of "white supremacy." This deal left the Southern Negroes disenfranchised for many years to come, and denied them basic rights as citizens of the United States.

CHESTER A. ARTHUR 1881-1885

A1. President Arthur's most important achievement was his successful reform of the civil service system. He convinced Congress to enact the first major civil service law, and then appointed a strong, reform-minded Civil Service Commission to enforce the new law. With Arthur's complete support and cooperation, the Commission administered open, competitive examinations for federal jobs. On the basis of these examinations, President Arthur awarded federal jobs solely to competent applicants. Moreover, these federal office holders were no longer forced by political bosses to make political contributions in order to keep their jobs. President Arthur's reforms did much to eliminate the spoils system in the federal government. It also substantially raised the efficiency of government employees.

A2. Before becoming President, Chester A. Arthur was an extremely effective abolitionist lawyer. When a family of Virginia slaves sought freedom in New York, their owners invoked the Fugitive Slave Law and demanded that New York return their "property." Arthur quickly came to the defense of the family and helped prepare a Supreme Court challenge of the detested Fugitive Slave Law. In addition, Arthur personally convinced the Attorney General of New York to enter the case on behalf of the family. He thus transformed a local lawsuit into an important national case. Later, when a black woman was forcibly evicted from a moving trolley car, Arthur prosecuted the company, won substantial damages for his client, and successfully enjoined the trolley company from further discrimination.

B1. By use of his veto power, President Chester A. Arthur forced Congress to rewrite several poorly written pieces of legislation. When Congress passed the Rivers and Harbors bill, President Arthur vetoed it as being unconstitutional and also wasteful of federal funds. Although Congress overrode this veto, Arthur later vetoed several immigration bills. He showed that those bills not only violated U.S. treaty provisions, but were largely unenforceable. This time Congress heeded his advice and rewrote the measures accordingly. Arthur used the veto sparingly but effectively.

B2. Chester A. Arthur was both an able administrator and a cultured gentleman. As Quartermaster-General for the State of New York, he was commended for the efficiency and economy with which he discharged his difficult war-time duties. Earlier, as an undergraduate at Union College, he majored in humanities, and graduated Phi Beta Kappa. For his deep interest in literature, he was elected to several important literary societies. During his term as President, Chester A. Arthur greatly enhanced the cultural and

C1. President Arthur was unwilling to negotiate with Congress and that led to the rejection of his foreign policy. Under Arthur's close direction, his representatives negotiated trade treaties with Spain, Mexico, and the Dominican Republic for the reciprocal admission, duty free, of many products. Nevertheless, although Arthur expended much effort on these treaties, he did nothing to persuade the Senate to ratify them. Consequently, the Senate refused outright to ratify the Spanish and Dominican treaties. And although the Senate did ratify the Mexican treaty, Congress did not enact the legislation that was necessary to implement it.

C2. During President Arthur's administration, excessive tariffs withdrew such large amounts of money from circulation that the U.S. was threatened with a severe monetary shortage. To rectify this condition, Arthur appointed a commission to set up extensive tariff reforms. But later, Arthur failed to endorse the commission's report, and then did nothing to persuade Congress to enact the commission's proposals. Without Presidential leadership, Congress substituted a patchwork tariff bill that failed to solve the monetary problem.

D1. In his first year in office, President Arthur made the curious nomination of Roscoe Conkling to the U.S. Supreme Court. Not only was Conkling the discredited boss of the New York political machine, but his character and nasty temper rendered him unfit to be a judge. Actually, Arthur knew that Conkling would decline the nomination, as indeed he did, so that no harm was done. Arthur made the nomination because he was indebted to Conkling for political favors; he hoped that the honor of being nominated to the Supreme Court would help repay his obligations without any real cost. President Arthur's scheme was quickly recognized, of course, and many people criticized him for misusing the office of the Presidency.

D2. As Vice-President, Chester A. Arthur continued to consider himself primarily as the boss of New York City politics. He bitterly fought with President Garfield to insure that his machine got the lion's share of the patronage. When Garfield refused to go along with Arthur's schemes, Arthur used his position as president of the Senate to obstruct all of Garfield's appointments. As Vice-President-elect, Arthur engaged openly in much dubious back-room politicking to ensure that his handpicked candidate was elected to the U.S. Senate. Arthur's tenure as Vice-President was an

A1. As President of the United States, Benjamin Harrison promoted growth within the nation, and peace abroad. Primarily due to his urgings as chairman of the Committee on Territories, six new states were admitted to the Union, the most states admitted under any one President. President Harrison firmly defended American interests in foreign affairs also, while avoiding any major conflict with foreign powers. His organization of the Bering Sea arbitration was important for continued friendly relations with Great Britain. President Harrison also furthered harmony with the Latin American countries by convening the Pan-American Congress in Washington.

A2. During Benjamin Harrison's term as President of the United States, two important acts were passed through Congress—the famous Sherman Anti-Trust Act and the Silver Purchase Act. The Silver Purchase Act was designed to protect agrarian interests in the country by the addition of 54 million dollars a year to the currency in circulation. The Anti-Trust Act gave protection against business monopolies that were exploiting the consumer. Much modified and elaborated, it remains today one of the basic laws of the land.

B1. During the Civil War, Benjamin Harrison put aside a profitable law career to serve his country as the commander of a regiment of volunteer infantrymen. Affectionately called "Little Ben" by his men, Harrison was an efficient military leader. After showing unusual brilliance in an important battle, he was promoted to the rank of brigadier general. Later, as Senator from Indiana and as President, he was concerned with improving conditions in the army and navy.

B2. After his term as President, Benjamin Harrison returned to his law practice. He gave a series of lectures on political science at Stanford University, and later was appointed the United States representative to the Peace Conference at The Hague. In his final years, Benjamin Harrison wrote many magazine articles, as well as two books. The first, *This Country of Mine*, discussed the role of the federal government. In the second book, Harrison reflected upon the joys and pains of the Presidency.

C1. As a politician, Benjamin Harrison had met with many failures. Before becoming President he had unsuccessfully run for Governor of Indiana and had reached the Senate only by appointment to fill an unexpired term. A delegate to the National Convention, Harrison was nominated as the presidential candidate of his party on the eighth ballot, primarily because he was a "safe" candidate who would follow a status quo policy as dictated by the political machine. Benjamin Harrison won the presidential campaign, but did not win the popular vote. Only his vote-getting in important states, such as New York, enabled him to capture the majority of the votes in the electoral college.

C2. Benjamin Harrison has been described by historians as a drab and cold President. While in office, he was nicknamed "The White House iceberg," because he was standoffish and snobbish when dealing with others. Harrison's administration has been termed mediocre, serving more or less to preserve the status quo. The measures passed through Congress during Harrison's term in office were generally conservative.

D1. Benjamin Harrison was hesitant, even after his election, to take any firm stand on national issues or to state specific government policies. His administration was marked by economic difficulty and civil strife which he was unable to handle. Partly to resolve these conflicts, Harrison opened up the territory of Oklahoma to homesteaders. This reversed an earlier edict which had set this land aside for five Indian tribes. The settlers displaced the Indians from their land, adding further to the injustices suffered by the Indians.

D2. The economic policies of Benjamin Harrison were narrow and near-sighted and led to the economic panic of 1893. Harrison was ill-informed when he supported and got the passage of the unfortunate Tariff Act of 1890. This Act was designed to raise duties on imports but instead it caused inflation and destroyed many businesses and industries in the country. This Tariff Act was extremely unpopular, and was fortunately repealed by the next administration when Harrison was voted out of office.

References

Aczél, J. *Lectures on functional equations and their applications*. New York: Academic Press, 1966.

Addelman, S. Orthogonal main-effect plans for asymmetrical factorial experiments. *Technometrics*, 1962, *4*, 21–46. (a)

Addelman, S. Symmetrical and asymmetrical fractional factorial plans. *Technometrics*, 1962, *4*, 47–58. (b)

Addelman, S., & Kempthorne, O. *Orthogonal main-effect plans* (Tech. Rep. ARL-79). Wright-Patterson Air Force Base, Ohio, 1961.

Adelman, L., Stewart, T. R., & Hammond, K. R. A case history of the application of social judgment theory to policy formulation. *Policy Sciences*, 1975, *6*, 137–159.

Ajzen, I. Intuitive theories of events and the effects of base-rate information on prediction. *Journal of Personality and Social Psychology*, 1977, *35*, 303–314.

Alf, E. F., Jr. Parameter estimation and hypothesis testing for integration theory models. Unpublished paper, San Diego State University, California, September 1971.

Allport, G. W., & Odbert, H. S. Trait-names: A psycho-lexical study. *Psychological Monographs*, 1936, *47* (1, Whole No. 211).

Anderson, N. H. *Effect of first-order conditional probability in a two-choice learning situation*. Unpublished doctoral dissertation, University of Wisconsin, Madison, 1956.

Anderson, N. H. An analysis of sequential dependencies. In R. R. Bush & W. K. Estes (Eds.), *Studies in mathematical learning theory*. Stanford, California: Stanford University Press, 1959. (a)

Anderson, N. H. Education for research in psychology. *American Psychologist*, 1959, *14*, 695–696. (b)

Anderson, N. H. Test of a model for opinion change. *Journal of Abnormal and Social Psychology*, 1959, *59*, 371–381. (c)

Anderson, N. H. Effect of first-order conditional probability in a two-choice learning situation. *Journal of Experimental Psychology*, 1960, *59*, 73–93.

Anderson, N. H. Group performance in an anagram task. *Journal of Social Psychology*, 1961, *55*, 67–75. (a)

Anderson, N. H. Scales and statistics: Parametric and nonparametric. *Psychological Bulletin,* 1961, *58,* 305–316. (b)

Anderson, N. H. Two learning models for responses measured on a continuous scale. *Psychometrika,* 1961, *26,* 391–403. (c)

Anderson, N. H. Application of an additive model to impression formation. *Science,* 1962, *138,* 817–818. (a)

Anderson, N. H. On the quantification of Miller's conflict theory. *Psychological Review,* 1962, *69,* 400–414. (b)

Anderson, N. H. *Application of an additive model to impression formation.* Paper presented at the third annual meeting of the Psychonomic Society. St. Louis, Missouri, August 1962. (c)

Anderson, N. H. Comparison of different populations: Resistance to extinction and transfer. *Psychological Review,* 1963, *70,* 162–179.

Anderson, N. H. An evaluation of stimulus sampling theory: Comments on Prof. Estes' paper. In A. W. Melton (Ed.), *Categories of human learning.* New York: Academic Press, 1964. (a)

Anderson, N. H. Linear models for responses measured on a continuous scale. *Journal of Mathematical Psychology,* 1964, *1,* 121–142. (b)

Anderson, N. H. Note on weighted sum and linear operator models. *Psychonomic Science,* 1964, *1,* 189–190. (c)

Anderson, N. H. Test of a model for number-averaging behavior. *Psychonomic Science,* 1964, *1,* 191–192. (d)

Anderson, N. H. Unpublished experiment. University of California, Los Angeles, 1964. (e)

Anderson, N. H. *Likableness ratings of 555 personality-trait adjectives.* Unpublished manuscript, University of California, Los Angeles, 1964. (f)

Anderson, N. H. Averaging versus adding as a stimulus-combination rule in impression formation. *Journal of Experimental Psychology,* 1965, *70,* 394–400. (a)

Anderson, N. H. Primacy effects in personality impression formation using a generalized order effect paradigm. *Journal of Personality and Social Psychology,* 1965, *2,* 1–9. (b)

Anderson, N. H. Component ratings in impression formation. *Psychonomic Science,* 1966, *6,* 279–280. (a)

Anderson, N. H. Test of a prediction of stimulus sampling theory in probability learning. *Journal of Experimental Psychology,* 1966, *71,* 499–510. (b)

Anderson, N. H. Application of a weighted average model to a psychophysical averaging task. *Psychonomic Science,* 1967, *8,* 227–228. (a)

Anderson, N. H. Averaging model analysis of set-size effect in impression formation. *Journal of Experimental Psychology,* 1967, *75,* 158–165. (b)

Anderson, N. H. Application of a linear-serial model to a personality-impression task using serial presentation. *Journal of Personality and Social Psychology,* 1968, *10,* 354–362. (a)

Anderson, N. H. A simple model for information integration. In R. P. Abelson, E. Aronson, W. J. McGuire, T. M. Newcomb, M. J. Rosenberg, & P. H. Tannenbaum (Eds.), *Theories of cognitive consistency: A sourcebook.* Chicago, Illinois: Rand McNally, 1968. (b)

Anderson, N. H. Averaging of space and number stimuli with simultaneous presentation. *Journal of Experimental Psychology,* 1968, *77,* 383–392. (c)

Anderson, N. H. Likableness ratings of 555 personality-trait words. *Journal of Personality and Social Psychology,* 1968, *9,* 272–279. (d)

Anderson, N. H. Partial analysis of high-way factorial designs. *Behavior Research Methods & Instrumentation,* 1968, *1,* 2–7. (e)

Anderson, N. H. Application of a model for numerical response to a probability learning situation. *Journal of Experimental Psychology,* 1969, *80,* 19–27. (a)

Anderson, N. H. A search task. In J. F. Voss (Ed.), *Approaches to thought.* Columbus, Ohio: Merrill, 1969. (b)

Anderson, N. H. Comment on "An analysis-of-variance model for the assessment of configural cue utilization in clinical judgment." *Psychological Bulletin,* 1969, *72,* 63–65. (c)

Anderson, N. H. Variation of CS–US interval in long-term avoidance conditioning in the rat with wheel turn and with shuttle tasks. *Journal of Comparative and Physiological Psychology,* 1969, *68,* 100–106. (d)

Anderson, N. H. Averaging model applied to the size–weight illusion. *Perception & Psychophysics,* 1970, *8,* 1–4. (a)

Anderson, N. H. Functional measurement and psychophysical judgment. *Psychological Review,* 1970. *77,* 153–170. (b)

Anderson, N. H. Integration theory and attitude change. *Psychological Review,* 1971, *78,* 171–206. (a)

Anderson, N. H. Test of adaptation-level theory as an explanation of a recency effect in psychophysical integration. *Journal of Experimental Psychology,* 1971, *87,* 57–63. (b)

Anderson, N. H. Two more tests against change of meaning in adjective combinations. *Journal of Verbal Learning and Verbal Behavior,* 1971, *10,* 75–85. (c)

Anderson, N. H. Cross-task validation of functional measurement. *Perception & Psychophysics,* 1972, *12,* 389–395. (a)

Anderson, N. H. Looking for configurality in clinical judgment. *Psychological Bulletin,* 1972, *78,* 93–102. (b)

Anderson, N. H. *Algebraic models in perception* (Tech. Rep. CHIP 30). La Jolla: Center for Human Information Processing, University of California, San Diego, November 1972. (c)

Anderson, N. H. Functional measurement of social desirability. *Sociometry,* 1973, *36,* 89–98. (a)

Anderson, N. H. Information integration theory applied to attitudes about U.S. presidents. *Journal of Educational Psychology,* 1973, *64,* 1–8. (b)

Anderson, N. H. Serial position curves in impression formation. *Journal of Experimental Psychology,* 1973, *97,* 8–12. (c)

Anderson, N. H. Algebraic models in perception. In E. C. Carterette & M. P. Friedman (Eds.), *Handbook of perception* (Vol. 2). New York: Academic Press, 1974. (a)

Anderson, N. H. Cognitive algebra. In L. Berkowitz (Ed.), *Advances in experimental social psychology* (Vol. 7). New York: Academic Press, 1974. (b)

Anderson, N. H. Cross-task validation of functional measurement using judgments of total magnitude. *Journal of Experimental Psychology,* 1974, *102,* 226–233. (c)

Anderson, N. H. Information integration theory: A brief survey. In D. H. Krantz, R. C. Atkinson, R. D. Luce, & P. Suppes (Eds.), *Contemporary developments in mathematical psychology* (Vol. 2). San Francisco, California: Freeman, 1974. (d)

Anderson, N. H. *Methods for studying information integration* (Tech. Rep. CHIP 43). La Jolla: Center for Human Information Processing, University of California, San Diego, June 1974. (e)

Anderson, N. H. *Algebraic models for information integration* (Tech. Rep. CHIP 45). La Jolla: Center for Human Information Processing, University of California, San Diego, June 1974. (f)

Anderson, N. H. On the role of context effects in psychophysical judgment. *Psychological Review,* 1975, *82,* 462–482. (a)

Anderson, N. H. Invited talk presented at the Japanese–American conference on multidimensional scaling. Center for Human Information Processing, University of California, San Diego, August 1975. (b)

Anderson, N. H. Equity judgments as information integration. *Journal of Personality and Social Psychology*, 1976, *33*, 291–299. (a)

Anderson, N. H. How functional measurement can yield validated interval scales of mental quantities. *Journal of Applied Psychology*, 1976, *61*, 677–692. (b)

Anderson, N. H. Integration theory, functional measurement and the psychophysical law. In H.-G. Geissler & Yu. M. Zabrodin (Eds.), *Advances in psychophysics*. Berlin: VEB Deutscher Verlag, 1976. (c)

Anderson, N. H. *Social perception and cognition* (Tech. Rep. CHIP 62). La Jolla: Center for Human Information Processing, University of California, San Diego, July 1976. (d)

Anderson, N. H. *Integration theory applied to cognitive responses and attitudes* (Tech. Rep. CHIP 68). La Jolla: Center for Human Information Processing, University of California, San Diego, December 1976. (e)

Anderson, N. H. Failure of additivity in bisection of length. *Perception & Psychophysics*, 1977, *22*, 213–222. (a)

Anderson, N. H. Note on functional measurement and data analysis. *Perception & Psychophysics*, 1977, *21*, 201–215. (b)

Anderson, N. H. Some problems in using analysis of variance in balance theory. *Journal of Personality and Social Psychology*, 1977, *35*, 140–158. (c)

Anderson, N. H. Measurement of motivation and incentive. *Behavior Research Methods & Instrumentation*, 1978, *10*, 360–375. (a)

Anderson, N. H. Progress in cognitive algebra. In L. Berkowitz (Ed.), *Cognitive theories in social psychology*. New York: Academic Press, 1978. (b)

Anderson, N. H. Algebraic rules in psychological measurement. *American Scientist*, 1979, *67*, 555–563. (a)

Anderson, N. H. Indeterminate theory: Reply to Gollob. *Journal of Personality and Social Psychology*, 1979, *37*, 950–952. (b)

Anderson, N. H. Information integration theory in developmental psychology. In F. Wilkening, J. Becker, & T. Trabasso (Eds.), *Information integration by children*. Hillsdale, New Jersey: Erlbaum, 1980. (a)

Anderson, N. H. Reply to Lawless. *American Scientist*, 1980, *68*, 8. (b)

Anderson, N. H. *Foundations of information integration theory*. New York: Academic Press, 1981. (a)

Anderson, N. H. Integration theory applied to cognitive responses and attitudes. In R. E. Petty, T. M. Ostrom, & T. C. Brock (Eds.), *Cognitive responses in persuasion*. Hillsdale, New Jersey: Erlbaum, 1981. (b)

Anderson, N. H. Cognitive algebra and social psychophysics. In B. Wegener (Ed.), *Social attitudes and psychophysical measurement*. Hillsdale, New Jersey: Erlbaum, 1982.

Anderson, N. H. Intuitive physics: Understanding and learning of physical relations. In T. Tighe & B. E. Shepp (Eds.), *Interactions: Perception, cognition, and development*. Hillsdale, New Jersey: Erlbaum, in press. (a)

Anderson, N. H. Cognitive algebra in intuitive physics. In H.-G. Geissler (Ed.), *Current issues in perception*. Hillsdale, New Jersey: Erlbaum, in press. (b)

Anderson, N. H., & Alexander, G. R. Choice test of the averaging hypothesis for information integration. *Cognitive Psychology*, 1971, *2*, 313–324.

Anderson, N. H., & Barrios, A. A. Primacy effects in personality impression formation. *Journal of Abnormal and Social Psychology*, 1961, *63*, 346–350.

Anderson, N. H., & Butzin, C. A. Performance = Motivation × Ability: An integration-theoretical analysis. *Journal of Personality and Social Psychology*, 1974, *30*, 598–604.

Anderson, N. H., & Butzin, C. A. Integration theory applied to children's judgments of equity. *Developmental Psychology*, 1978, *14*, 593–606.

Anderson, N. H., & Clavadetscher, J. Tests of a conditioning hypothesis with adjective combinations. *Journal of Experimental Psychology: Human Learning and Memory*, 1976, *2*, 11–20.

Anderson, N. H., & Cuneo, D. O. The Height + Width rule in children's judgments of quantity. *Journal of Experimental Psychology: General*, 1978, *107*, 335–378. (a)

Anderson, N. H., & Cuneo, D. O. The Height + Width rule seems solid: Reply to Bogartz. *Journal of Experimental Psychology: General*, 1978, *107*, 388–392. (b)

Anderson, N. H., & Farkas, A. J. New light on order effects in attitude change. *Journal of Personality and Social Psychology*, 1973, *28*, 88–93.

Anderson, N. H., & Farkas, A. J. Integration theory applied to models of inequity. *Personality and Social Psychology Bulletin*, 1975, *1*, 588–591.

Anderson, N. H., & Graesser, C. C. An information integration analysis of attitude change in group discussion. *Journal of Personality and Social Psychology*, 1976, *34*, 210–222.

Anderson, N. H., & Grant, D. A. A test of a statistical learning theory model for two-choice behavior with double stimulus events. *Journal of Experimental Psychology*, 1957, *54*, 305–317.

Anderson, N. H., & Grant, D. A. Correction and reanalysis. *Journal of Experimental Psychology*, 1958, *56*, 453–454.

Anderson, N. H., & Hovland, C. I. The representation of order effects in communication research. In C. I. Hovland (Ed.), *The order of presentation in persuasion*. New Haven, Connecticut: Yale University Press, 1957.

Anderson, N. H., & Hubert, S. Effects of concomitant verbal recall on order effects in personality impression formation. *Journal of Verbal Learning and Verbal Behavior*, 1963, *2*, 379–391.

Anderson, N. H., & Jacobson, A. Effect of stimulus inconsistency and discounting instructions in personality impression formation. *Journal of Personality and Social Psychology*, 1965, *2*, 531–539.

Anderson, N. H., & Jacobson, A. Further data on a weighted average model for judgment in a lifted weight task. *Perception & Psychophysics*, 1968, *4*, 81–84.

Anderson, N. H., & Lampel, A. K. Effect of context on ratings of personality traits. *Psychonomic Science*, 1965, *3*, 433–434.

Anderson, N. H., & Leon, M. Direct test for context effects in two judgmental integration tasks. Unpublished experiment, University of California, San Diego, 1970.

Anderson, N. H., Lindner, R., & Lopes, L. L. Integration theory applied to judgments of group attractiveness. *Journal of Personality and Social Psychology*, 1973, *26*, 400–408.

Anderson, N. H., & Lopes, L. L. Some psycholinguistic aspects of person perception. *Memory & Cognition*, 1974, *2*, 67–74.

Anderson, N. H., & Nakamura, C. Y. Avoidance decrement in avoidance conditioning. *Journal of Comparative and Physiological Psychology*, 1964, *57*, 196–204.

Anderson, N. H., & Norman, A. Order effects in impression formation in four classes of stimuli. *Journal of Abnormal and Social Psychology*, 1964, *69*, 467–471.

Anderson, N. H., & Rollins, H. A. Two failures to prevent avoidance decrement. *Psychological Reports*, 1966, *19*, 71–78.

Anderson, N. H., Rollins, H. A., & Riskin, S. R. Effects of punishment on avoidance decrement. *Journal of Comparative and Physiological Psychology*, 1966, *62*, 147–149.

Anderson, N. H., Sawyers, B. K., & Farkas, A. J. President paragraphs. *Behavior Research Methods & Instrumentation*, 1972, 4, 177–192.

Anderson, N. H., & Shanteau, J. C. Information integration in risky decision making. *Journal of Experimental Psychology*, 1970, 84, 441–451.

Anderson, N. H., & Shanteau, J. Weak inference with linear models. *Psychological Bulletin*, 1977, 84, 1155–1170.

Anderson, N. H., & Weiss, D. J. Test of a multiplying model for estimated area of rectangles. *American Journal of Psychology*, 1971, 84, 543–548.

Anderson, N. H., & Whalen, R. E. Likelihood judgments and sequential effects in a two-choice probability learning situation. *Journal of Experimental Psychology*, 1960, 60, 111–120.

Anderson, T., & Birnbaum, M. H. Test of an additive model of social inference. *Journal of Personality and Social Psychology*, 1976, 33, 655–662.

Aoki, T. A psycho-lexical study of personality trait words—Selection, classification and desirability ratings of 455 words. *Japanese Journal of Psychology*, 1971, 42, 1–13.

Apple, W. L. *Perceiving emotion in others: Integration of verbal, nonverbal, and contextual cues.* Unpublished doctoral dissertation, Columbia University, New York, 1979.

Asch, S. E. Forming impressions of personality. *Journal of Abnormal and Social Psychology*, 1946, 41, 258–290.

Atkinson, R. C., & Estes, W. K. Stimulus sampling theory. In R. D. Luce, R. R. Bush, & E. Galanter (Eds.), *Handbook of mathematical psychology* (Vol. 2). New York: Wiley, 1963.

Bartlett, F. C. *Remembering: A study in experimental and social psychology.* London: Cambridge University Press, 1932.

Bechtel, G. G. F tests for the absolute invariance of dominance and composition scales. *Psychometrika*, 1967, 32, 157–182. (a)

Bechtel, G. G. The analysis of variance and pairwise scaling. *Psychometrika*, 1967, 32, 47–65. (b)

Beier, E. M. *Effects of trial-to-trial variation in magnitude of reward upon an instrumental running response.* Unpublished doctoral dissertation, Yale University, Connecticut, 1958.

Bennett, C. A., & Lumsdaine, A. A. (Eds.) *Evaluation and experiment.* New York: Academic Press, 1975.

Binder, A. Further considerations on testing the null hypothesis and the strategy and tactics of investigating theoretical models. *Psychological Review*, 1963, 70, 107–115.

Birnbaum, M. H. The devil rides again: Correlation as an index of fit. *Psychological Bulletin*, 1973, 79, 239–242.

Birnbaum, M. H. The nonadditivity of personality impressions. *Journal of Experimental Psychology*, 1974, 102, 543–561. (a)

Birnbaum, M. H. Using contextual effects to derive psychophysical scales. *Perception & Psychophysics*, 1974, 15, 89–96. (b)

Birnbaum, M. H. Intuitive numerical prediction. *American Journal of Psychology*, 1976, 89, 417–429.

Birnbaum, M. H. Differences and ratios in psychological measurement. In N. J. Castellan & F. Restle (Eds.), *Cognitive theory* (Vol. 3). Hillsdale, New Jersey: Erlbaum, 1978.

Birnbaum, M. H. Reply to Eisler: On the subtractive theory of stimulus comparison. *Perception & Psychophysics*, 1979, 25, 150–156.

Birnbaum, M. H. Controversies in psychological measurement. In B. Wegener (Ed.), *Social attitudes and psychophysical measurement.* Hillsdale, New Jersey: Erlbaum, 1982.

Birnbaum, M. H., & Elmasian, R. Loudness "ratios" and "differences" involve the same psychophysical operation. *Perception & Psychophysics*, 1977, 22, 383–391.

Birnbaum, M. H., & Mellers, B. A. Measurement and the mental map. *Perception & Psychophysics*, 1978, *23*, 403–408.

Birnbaum, M. H., & Mellers, B. A. Stimulus recognition may mediate exposure effects. *Journal of Personality and Social Psychology*, 1979, *37*, 391–394. (a)

Birnbaum, M. H., & Mellers, B. A. One-mediator model of exposure effects is still viable. *Journal of Personality and Social Psychology*, 1979, *37*, 1090–1096. (b)

Birnbaum, M. H., & Mellers, B. A. *Credibility of sources and base rates in judgment.* Paper presented at the annual meeting of the Psychonomic Society, Philadelphia, Pennsylvania, November 1981.

Birnbaum, M. H., & Stegner, S. E. Measuring the importance of cues in judgment individuals: Subjective theories of IQ as a function of heredity and environment. *Journal of Experimental Social Psychology*, 1981, *17*, 159–182.

Birnbaum, M. H., & Veit, C. T. Scale convergence as a criterion for rescaling: Information integration with difference, ratio, and averaging tasks. *Perception & Psychophysics*, 1974, *15*, 7–15.

Blankenship, D. A. Unpublished paper, University of California, San Diego, September 1974.

Blankenship, D. A., & Anderson, N. H. Subjective duration: A functional measurement analysis. *Perception & Psychophysics*, 1976, *20*, 168–172.

Bock, R. D., & Jones, L. V. *The measurement and prediction of judgment and choice.* San Francisco, California: Holden-Day, 1968.

Bogartz, R. S. On the meaning of statistical interactions. *Journal of Experimental Child Psychology*, 1976, *22*, 178–183.

Bogartz, R. S. Comments on Anderson and Cuneo's "The Height + Width rule in children's judgments of quantity." *Journal of Experimental Psychology: General*, 1978, *107*, 379–387.

Bogartz, R. S. Line ratio judgments yield subjective lengths proportional to physical lengths: Reanalysis of Engen's data. *Perception & Psychophysics*, 1979, *26*, 247–249.

Bogartz, R. S. Proportional effects in experimental designs. *Psychological Bulletin*, 1982, in press.

Bogartz, R. S., & Wackwitz, J. H. Polynomial response scaling and functional measurement. *Journal of Mathematical Psychology*, 1971, *8*, 418–443.

Bohrnstedt, G. W., & Marwell, G. The reliability of products of two random variables. In K. F. Schuessler (Ed.), *Sociological methodology 1978.* San Francisco, California: Jossey-Bass, 1977.

Bradley, R. A., & Terry, M. E. Rank analysis of incomplete block designs. I. The method of paired comparisons. *Biometrika*, 1952, *39*, 324–345.

Brehmer, B., Hagafors, R., & Johansson, R. Cognitive skills in judgment: Subjects' ability to use information about weights, function forms, and organizing principles. *Organizational Behavior and Human Performance*, 1980, *26*, 373–385.

Brehmer, B., & Slovic, P. Information integration in multiple-cue judgments. *Journal of Experimental Psychology: Human Perception and Performance*, 1980, *6*, 302–308.

Brewer, M. B., Campbell, D. T., & Crano, W. D. Testing a single-factor model as an alternative to the misuse of partial correlations in hypothesis-testing research. *Sociometry*, 1970, *33*, 1–11.

Brunswik, E. *Perception and the representative design of psychological experiments.* Berkeley: University of California Press, 1956.

Budescu, D. V., & Wallsten, T. S. A note on monotonic transformations in the context of functional measurement and analysis of variance. *Bulletin of the Psychonomic Society*, 1979, *14*, 307–310.

Bugental, D. E. Interpretations of naturally occurring discrepancies between words and intonation: Modes of inconsistency resolution. *Journal of Personality and Social Psychology*, 1974, *30*, 125–133.

Burke, C. J., Estes, W. K., & Hellyer, S. Rate of verbal conditioning in relation to stimulus variability. *Journal of Experimental Psychology*, 1954, *48*, 153–161.

Busemeyer, J. R. Importance of measurement theory, error theory, and experimental design for testing the significance of interactions. *Psychological Bulletin*, 1980, *88*, 237–244.

Bush, R. R., & Mosteller, F. *Stochastic models for learning*. New York: Wiley, 1955.

Butzin, C. A., & Anderson, N. H. Functional measurement of children's judgments. *Child Development*, 1973, *44*, 529–537.

Byrne, D., & Griffitt, W. Similarity and awareness of similarity of personality characteristics as determinants of attraction. *Journal of Experimental Research in Personality*, 1969, *3*, 179–186.

Campbell, D. T., & Boruch, R. F. Making the case for randomized assignment to treatments by considering the alternatives: Six ways in which quasi-experimental evaluations in compensatory education tend to underestimate effects. In C. A. Bennett & A. A. Lumsdaine (Eds.), *Evaluation and experiment*. New York: Academic Press, 1975.

Campbell, D. T., Hunt, W. A., & Lewis, N. A. The effects of assimilation and contrast in judgments of clinical materials. *American Journal of Psychology*, 1957, *70*, 347–360.

Campbell, D. T., Lewis, N. A., & Hunt, W. A. Context effects with judgmental language that is absolute, extensive, and extra-experimentally anchored. *Journal of Experimental Psychology*, 1958, *55*, 220–228.

Campbell, D. T., & Stanley, J. C. *Experimental and quasi-experimental designs for research*. Chicago, Illinois: Rand McNally, 1966.

Carterette, E. C., & Anderson, N. H. Bisection of loudness. *Perception & Psychophysics*, 1979, *26*, 265–280.

Carterette, E. C., Friedman, M. P., & Cosmides, R. Reaction-time distributions in the detection of weak signals in noise. *Journal of the Acoustical Society of America*, 1965, *38*, 531–542.

Chandler, J. P. STEPIT—Finds local minima of a smooth function of several parameters. *Behavioral Science*, 1969, *14*, 81–82.

Clark, H. H. The language-as-fixed-effect fallacy: A critique of language statistics in psychological research. *Journal of Verbal Learning and Verbal Behavior*, 1973, *12*, 335–359.

Clavadetscher, J. E. *Two context processes in the Ebbinghaus illusion*. Unpublished doctoral dissertation, University of California, San Diego, 1977.

Clavadetscher, J. E., & Anderson, N. H. Comparative judgment: Tests of two theories using the Baldwin figure. *Journal of Experimental Psychology: Human Perception and Performance*, 1977, *3*, 119–135.

Cochran, W. G., & Cox, G. M. *Experimental designs* (2nd ed.). New York: Wiley, 1957.

Cohen, J. *Statistical power analysis for the behavioral sciences*. New York: Academic Press, 1969.

Cole, M., & Means, B. *Comparative studies of how people think: A cautionary introduction*. Cambridge, Massachusetts: Harvard University Press, 1980.

Collyer, C. E. Discrimination of spatial and temporal intervals defined by three light flashes: Effects of spacing on temporal judgments and of timing on spatial judgments. *Perception & Psychophysics*, 1977, *21*, 357–364.

Connor, W. S., & Young, S. *Fractional factorial designs for experiments with factors at two and three levels* (Applied Mathematics Series 58). Washington, D.C.: National Bureau of Standards, 1961.

Conolley, E. S., & Knight, G. P. Anderson's personality-trait words: Has their likableness changed? *Personality and Social Psychology Bulletin*, 1976, *2*, 303–306.

Conolley, E. S., & Maruyama, G. M. The "likableness" of 555 personality trait words ten years later. JSAS *Catalog of Selected Documents in Psychology*, 1976, *6*, 69. (M. No. 1291)

Coombs, C. H. *A theory of data*. New York: Wiley, 1964.

Coons, E. E., Anderson, N. H., & Myers, A. K. Disappearance of avoidance responding during continued training. *Journal of Comparative and Physiological Psychology*, 1960, *53*, 290–292.

Cox, E. P., III. The optimal number of response alternatives for a scale: A review. *Journal of Marketing Research*, 1980, *17*, 407–422.

Cuneo, D. O. *Children's judgments of numerical quantity: The role of length, density, and number cues*. Unpublished doctoral dissertation, University of California, San Diego, 1978.

Cuneo, D. O. A general strategy for judgments of quantity: The Height + Width rule. *Child Development*, 1980, *51*, 299–301.

Cuneo, D. O. Children's judgments of numerical quantity: A new view of early quantification. *Cognitive Psychology*, 1982, *14*, 13–44.

Curtis, D. W. Magnitude estimations and category judgments of brightness and brightness intervals: A two-stage interpretation. *Journal of Experimental Psychology*, 1970, *83*, 201–208.

Curtis, D. W., & Mullin, L. C. Judgments of average magnitude: Analyses in terms of the functional measurement and two-stage models. *Perception & Psychophysics*, 1975, *18*, 299–308.

Darlington, R. B. Multiple regression in psychological research and practice. *Psychological Bulletin*, 1968, *69*, 161–182.

de Leeuw, J., Young, F. W., & Takane, Y. Additive structure in qualitative data: An alternating least squares method with optimal scaling features. *Psychometrika*, 1976, *41*, 471–503.

Dixon, W. J., & Brown, M. B. DMDP-77: Biomedical computer programs, P-series. Los Angeles: University of California Press, 1977.

Dixon, W. J., & Massey, F. J., Jr. *Introduction to statistical analysis* (3rd ed.). New York: McGraw-Hill, 1969.

Drake, S. *Galileo at work*. Chicago, Illinois: University of Chicago Press, 1978.

Durlach, N. I., & Colburn, H. S. Binaural phenomena. In E. C. Carterette & M. P. Friedman (Eds.), *Handbook of perception* (Vol. 4). New York: Academic Press, 1978.

Ebbesen, E. B., & Konečni, V. J. *Cognitive algebra in legal decision making* (Tech. Rep. CHIP 46). La Jolla: Center for Human Information Processing, University of California, San Diego, September 1974.

Ebbesen, E. B., & Konečni, V. J. Decision making and information integration in the courts: The setting of bail. *Journal of Personality and Social Psychology*, 1975, *32*, 805–821.

Edwards, W. Tactical note on the relation between scientific and statistical hypotheses. *Psychological Bulletin*, 1965, *63*, 400–402.

Edwards, W. Conservatism in human information processing. In B. Kleinmuntz (Ed.), *Formal representation of human judgment*. New York: Wiley, 1968.

Edwards, W. Bayesian and regression models of human information processing—A myopic perspective. *Organizational Behavior and Human Performance*, 1971, *6*, 639–648.

Edwards, W., & Guttentag, M. Experiments and evaluations: A reexamination. In C. A. Bennett & A. A. Lumsdaine (Eds.), *Evaluation and experiment*. New York: Academic Press, 1975.

Egan, J. P., Schulman, A. I., & Greenberg, G. Z. Operating characteristics determined by binary decisions and by ratings. *Journal of the Acoustical Society of America*, 1959, *31*, 768–773.

Einhorn, H. J. Use of nonlinear, noncompensatory models as a function of task and amount of information. *Organizational Behavior and Human Performance*, 1971, *6*, 1–27.

Einhorn, H. J., & Hogarth, R. M. Unit weighting schemes for decision making. *Organizational Behavior and Human Performance*, 1975, *13*, 171–192.

Einhorn, H. J., & McCoach, W. A simple multiattribute utility procedure for evaluation. *Behavioral Science*, 1977, *22*, 270–282.

Eiser, J. R. Enhancement of contrast in the absolute judgment of attitude statements. *Journal of Personality and Social Psychology*, 1971, *17*, 1–10.

Eiser, J. R. *Cognitive social psychology*. New York: McGraw-Hill, 1980.

Eisler, H. On the ability to estimate differences: A note on Birnbaum's subtractive model. *Perception & Psychophysics*, 1978, *24*, 185–189.

Ekman, P., Friesen, W. V., & Ellsworth, P. *Emotion in the human face*. New York: Pergamon, 1972.

Elkind, D., & Dabek, R. F. Personal injury and property damage in the moral judgments of children. *Child Development*, 1977, *48*, 518–522.

Ellis, B. *Basic concepts of measurement*. London and New York: Cambridge University Press, 1966.

Emery, D. R., & Barron, F. H. Axiomatic and numerical conjoint measurement: An evaluation of diagnostic efficacy. *Psychometrika*, 1979, *44*, 195–210.

Eriksen, C. W., & Hake, H. W. Anchor effects in absolute judgments. *Journal of Experimental Psychology*, 1957, *53*, 132–138.

Estes, W. K. Probability learning. In A. W. Melton (Ed.), *Categories of human learning*. New York: Academic Press, 1964.

Estes, W. K., & Burke, C. J. A theory of stimulus variability in learning. *Psychological Review*, 1953, *60*, 276–286.

Estes, W. K., & Suppes, P. Foundations of linear models. In R. R. Bush & W. K. Estes (Eds.), *Studies in mathematical learning theory*. Stanford, California: Stanford University Press, 1959.

Farkas, A. J., & Anderson, N. H. Integration theory and inoculation theory as explanations of the "paper tiger" effect. *Journal of Social Psychology*, 1976, *98*, 253–268.

Farkas, A. J., & Anderson, N. H. Multidimensional input in equity theory. *Journal of Personality and Social Psychology*, 1979, *37*, 879–896.

Farley, J., & Fantino, E. The symmetrical law of effect and the matching relation in choice behavior. *Journal of the Experimental Analysis of Behavior*, 1978, *29*, 37–60.

Fischer, G. W. Convergent validation of decomposed multi-attribute utility assessment procedures for risky and riskless decisions. *Organizational Behavior and Human Performance*, 1977, *18*, 295–315.

Fischhoff, B., Slovic, P., & Lichtenstein, S. Subjective sensitivity analysis. *Organizational Behavior and Human Performance*, 1979, *23*, 339–359.

Fisher, R. A. *Statistical methods for research workers* (7th ed.). London: Oliver and Boyd, 1938.

Fisher, R. A. *Statistical methods for research workers* (13th ed.). New York: Hafner, 1958.

Fiske, S. T. Attention and weight in person perception: The impact of negative and extreme behavior. *Journal of Personality and Social Psychology*, 1980, *38*, 889–906.

Friedman, H. S. The relative strength of verbal versus nonverbal cues. *Personality and Social Psychology Bulletin*, 1978, *4*, 147–150.

Friedman, H. S. The interactive effects of facial expressions of emotion and verbal messages on perceptions of affective meaning. *Journal of Experimental Social Psychology*, 1979, *15*, 453–469.

Friedman, M. P., Burke, C. J., Cole, M., Keller, L., Millward, R. B., & Estes, W. K. Two-choice behavior under extended training with shifting probabilities of reinforcement. In R. C. Atkinson (Ed.), *Studies in mathematical psychology.* Stanford, California: Stanford University Press, 1964.

Friedman, M. P., Carterette, E. C., & Anderson, N. H. Long-term probability learning with a random schedule of reinforcement. *Journal of Experimental Psychology,* 1968, *78,* 442–455.

Frijda, N. H. Recognition of emotion. In L. Berkowitz (Ed.), *Advances in experimental social psychology* (Vol. 4). New York: Academic Press, 1969.

Gallant, A. R. Nonlinear regression. *The American Statistician,* 1975, *29,* 73–81.

Garner, W. R. *Uncertainty and structure as psychological concepts.* New York: Wiley, 1962.

Garner, W. R., & Morton, J. Perceptual independence: Definitions, models, and experimental paradigms. *Psychological Bulletin,* 1969, *72,* 233–259.

Gilbert, J. P., Light, R. J., & Mosteller, F. Assessing social innovations: An empirical base for policy. In C. A. Bennett & A. A. Lumsdaine (Eds.), *Evaluation and experiment.* New York: Academic Press, 1975.

Goldberger, A. S. Structural equation models: An overview. In A. S. Goldberger & O. D. Duncan (Eds.), *Structural equation models in the social sciences.* New York: Seminar Press, 1973.

Goldberger, A. S., & Duncan, O. D. (Eds.) *Structural equation models in the social sciences.* New York: Seminar Press, 1973.

Gollob, H. F. The subject–verb–object approach to social cognition. *Psychological Review,* 1974, *81,* 286–321.

Gollob, H. F. A reply to Norman H. Anderson's critique of the subject–verb–object approach to social cognition. *Journal of Personality and Social Psychology,* 1979, *37,* 931–949.

Gollob, H. F., & Lugg, A. M. Effect of instruction and stimulus presentation on the occurrence of averaging responses in impression formation. *Journal of Experimental Psychology,* 1973, *98,* 217–219.

Graesser, C. C., & Anderson, N. H. Cognitive algebra of the equation: Gift size = Generosity × Income. *Journal of Experimental Psychology,* 1974, *103,* 692–699.

Grant, D. A. Analysis-of-variance tests in the analysis and comparison of curves. *Psychological Bulletin,* 1956, *53,* 141–154.

Grant, D. A. Testing the null hypothesis and the strategy and tactics of investigating theoretical models. *Psychological Review,* 1962, *69,* 54–61.

Grant, D. A., & Hake, H. W. Acquisition and extinction of the Humphreys' verbal response with differing percentages of "reinforcement." *American Psychologist,* 1949, *4,* 226. (Abstract)

Graybill, F. A. *An introduction to linear statistical models* (Vol. 1). New York: McGraw-Hill, 1961.

Green, D. M., & Swets, J. A. *Signal detection theory and psychophysics.* New York: Wiley, 1966.

Greenwald, A. G. Within-subjects designs: To use or not to use. *Psychological Bulletin,* 1976, *83,* 314–320.

Guilford, J. P. *Psychometric methods* (2nd ed.). New York: McGraw-Hill, 1954.

Hahn, G. J., & Shapiro, S. S. *A catalog and computer program for the design and analysis of orthogonal symmetric and asymmetric fractional factorial experiments* (Report 66–C-165). Schenectady, New York: General Electric Co., 1966.

Hake, H. W., & Hyman, R. Perception of the statistical structure of a random series of binary symbols. *Journal of Experimental Psychology,* 1953, *45,* 64–74.

Hamilton, D. L., & Fallot, R. D. Information salience as a weighting factor in impression formation. *Journal of Personality and Social Psychology,* 1974, *30,* 444–448.

Hammond, K. R., McClelland, G. H., & Mumpower, J. *The Colorado report on the integration of approaches to judgment and decision making* (Tech. Rep. No. 213). Boulder: Institute of Behavioral Science, University of Colorado, October 1978.

Hammond, K. R., McClelland, G. H., & Mumpower, J. *Human judgment and decision making*. New York: Praeger, 1980.

Hammond, K. R., Stewart, T. R., Brehmer, B., & Steinmann, D. O. Social judgment theory. In M. F. Kaplan & S. Schwartz (Eds.), *Human judgment and decision processes*. New York: Academic Press, 1975.

Hammond, K. R., & Summers, D. A. Cognitive dependence on linear and nonlinear cues. *Psychological Review*, 1965, *72*, 215–224.

Harris, R. J. The uncertain connection between verbal theories and research hypotheses in social psychology. *Journal of Experimental Social Psychology*, 1976, *12*, 210–219.

Hastie, R., Ostrom, T. M., Ebbesen, E. B., Wyer, R. S., Jr., Hamilton, D. L., & Carlston, D. E. *Person memory: The cognitive basis of social perception*. Hillsdale, New Jersey: Erlbaum, 1980.

Helson, H. *Adaptation-level theory*. New York: Harper, 1964.

Helson, H., & Kozaki, A. Anchor effects using numerical estimates of simple dot patterns. *Perception & Psychophysics*, 1968, *4*, 163–164.

Hendrick, C., & Costantini, A. F. Effects of varying trait inconsistency and response requirements on the primacy effect in impression formation. *Journal of Personality and Social Psychology*, 1970, *15*, 158–164.

Hendrick, C., Franz, C. M., & Hoving, K. L. How do children form impressions of persons? They average. *Memory & Cognition*, 1975, *3*, 325–328.

Herr, D. G., & Gaebelein, J. Nonorthogonal two-way analysis of variance. *Psychological Bulletin*, 1978, *85*, 207–216.

Herrnstein, R. J. On the law of effect. *Journal of the Experimental Analysis of Behavior*, 1970, *13*, 243–266.

Hilgard, E. R. Discussion of probabilistic functionalism. *Psychological Review*, 1955, *62*, 226–228.

Himmelfarb, S. "Resistance" to persuasion induced by information integration. In S. Himmelfarb & A. H. Eagly (Eds.), *Readings in attitude change*. New York: Wiley, 1974.

Himmelfarb, S., & Anderson, N. H. Integration theory applied to opinion attribution. *Journal of Personality and Social Psychology*, 1975, *31*, 1064–1072.

Hodges, B. H. Adding and averaging models for information integration. *Psychological Review*, 1973, *80*, 80–84.

Hoffman, P. J., Slovic, P., & Rorer, L. G. An analysis-of-variance model for the assessment of configural cue utilization in clinical judgment. *Psychological Bulletin*, 1968, *69*, 338–349.

Hollander, M., & Wolfe, D. A. *Nonparametric statistical methods*. New York: Wiley, 1973.

Hommers, W., & Anderson, N. H. Moral algebra of recompense. In N. H. Anderson (Ed.), *Contributions to information integration theory*, in press.

Huynh, H. Some approximate tests for repeated measurement designs. *Psychometrika*, 1978, *43*, 161–175.

Huynh, H., & Mandeville, G. K. Validity conditions in repeated measures designs. *Psychological Bulletin*, 1979, *86*, 964–973.

Insko, C. A., Songer, E., & McGarvey, W. Balance, positivity, and agreement in the Jordan paradigm: A defense of balance theory. *Journal of Experimental Social Psychology*, 1974, *10*, 53–83.

Isaac, P. D. Linear regression, structural relations, and measurement error. *Psychological Bulletin*, 1970, *74*, 213–218.

Jaccard, J. J., & Fishbein, M. Inferential beliefs and order effects in personality impression formation. *Journal of Personality and Social Psychology*, 1975, *31*, 1031–1040.

Jennrich, R. I. Asymptotic properties of non-linear least squares estimators. *The Annals of Mathematical Statistics*, 1969, *40*, 633–643.

Jennrich, R. I. Scaling for minimum interaction using BMDP6M. In W. J. Dixon & M. B. Brown (Eds.), *Biomedical computer programs, P-series*. Los Angeles: University of California Press, 1977.

Jones, L. V. Some invariant findings under the method of successive intervals. In H. Gulliksen & S. Messick (Eds.), *Psychological scaling*. New York: Wiley, 1960.

Jones, M. R. From probability learning to sequential processing: A critical review. *Psychological Bulletin*, 1971, *76*, 153–185.

Judd, C. M., & Harackiewicz, J. M. Contrast effects in attitude judgment: An examination of the accentuation hypothesis. *Journal of Personality and Social Psychology*, 1980, *38*, 390–398.

Kahneman, D., & Tversky, A. Subjective probability: A judgment of representativeness. *Cognitive Psychology*, 1972, *3*, 430–454.

Kahneman, D., & Tversky, A. Prospect theory: An analysis of decision under risk. *Econometrica*, 1979, *47*, 263–291.

Keeney, R. L., & Raiffa, H. *Decisions with multiple objectives*. New York: Wiley, 1976.

Kendler, H. H., & Kendler, T. S. Vertical and horizontal processes in problem solving. *Psychological Review*, 1962, *69*, 1–16.

Keppel, G. *Design and analysis*. Englewood Cliffs, New Jersey: Prentice-Hall, 1973.

Kinchla, R. A., & Collyer, C. E. Detecting a target letter in briefly presented arrays: A confidence rating analysis in terms of a weighted additive effects model. *Perception & Psychophysics*, 1974, *16*, 117–122.

Kirk, R. E. *Experimental design: Procedures for the behavioral sciences*. Belmont, California: Brooks/Cole, 1968.

Kirk, W. L., Jr. *An analysis of the mediational approach to reversal and nonreversal shifts in concept formation*. Unpublished doctoral dissertation, University of California, Los Angeles, 1964.

Klitzner, M. D. Hedonic integration: Test of a linear model. *Perception & Psychophysics*, 1975, *18*, 49–54.

Klitzner, M. D. *Small animal fear: An integration-theoretical analysis*. Unpublished doctoral dissertation, University of California, San Diego, 1977.

Klitzner, M. D., & Anderson, N. H. Motivation × Expectancy × Value: A functional measurement approach. *Motivation and Emotion*, 1977, *1*, 347–365.

Krantz, D. H. Threshold theories of signal detection. *Psychological Review*, 1969, *76*, 308–324.

Krantz, D. H., Luce, R. D., Suppes, P., & Tversky, A. *Foundations of measurement* (Vol. 1). New York: Academic Press, 1971.

Krantz, D. H., & Tversky, A. Conjoint-measurement analysis of composition rules in psychology. *Psychological Review*, 1971, *78*, 151–169.

Krantz, D. L., & Campbell, D. T. Separating perceptual and linguistic effects of context shifts upon absolute judgments. *Journal of Experimental Psychology*, 1961, *62*, 35–42.

Kruglanski, A. W. The human subject in the psychology experiment: Fact and artifact. In L. Berkowitz (Ed.), *Advances in experimental social psychology* (Vol. 8). New York: Academic Press, 1975.

Kruskal, J. B. Analysis of factorial experiments by estimating monotone transformations of the data. *Journal of the Royal Statistical Society* (*B*), 1965, *27*, 251–263.

Lampel, A. K., & Anderson, N. H. Combining visual and verbal information in an impression-formation task. *Journal of Personality and Social Psychology*, 1968, *9*, 1–6.

Lane, J., & Anderson, N. H. Integration of intention and outcome in moral judgment. *Memory & Cognition*, 1976, *4*, 1–5.

Lee, W. *Decision theory and human behavior*. New York: Wiley, 1971.

Lehman, E. L. *Nonparametrics*. San Francisco, California: Holden-Day, 1975.

Leon, M. Integration of intent and consequence information in children's moral judgments. In F. Wilkening, J. Becker, & T. Trabasso (Eds.), *Information integration by children*. Hillsdale, New Jersey: Erlbaum, 1980.

Leon, M., & Anderson, N. H. A ratio rule from integration theory applied to inference judgments. *Journal of Experimental Psychology*, 1974, *102*, 27–36.

Leon, M., Oden, G. C., & Anderson, N. H. Functional measurement of social values. *Journal of Personality and Social Psychology*, 1973, *27*, 301–310.

Levin, I. P. Information integration in numerical judgments and decision processes. *Journal of Experimental Psychology: General*, 1975, *104*, 39–53.

Levin, I. P. Information integration in transportation decisions. In M. F. Kaplan & S. Schwartz (Eds.), *Human judgment and decision processes in applied settings*. New York: Academic Press, 1977.

Levin, I. P., Kim, K. J., & Corry, F. A. Invariance of the weight parameter in information integration. *Memory & Cognition*, 1976, *4*, 43–47.

Levine, M. V. Transformations that render curves parallel. *Journal of Mathematical Psychology*, 1970, *7*, 410–443.

Levy, L. H. Group variance and group attractiveness. *Journal of Abnormal and Social Psychology*, 1964, *68*, 661–664.

Lichtenstein, S., Earle, T. C. & Slovic, P. Cue utilization in a numerical prediction task. *Journal of Experimental Psychology: Human Perception and Performance*, 1975, *1*, 77–85.

Lichtenstein, S., & Slovic, P. Reversals of preference between bids and choices in gambling decisions. *Journal of Experimental Psychology*, 1971, *89*, 46–55.

Lichtenstein, S., & Slovic, P. Response-induced reversals of preference in gambling: An extended replication in Las Vegas. *Journal of Experimental Psychology*, 1973, *101*, 16–20.

Lindman, H. R. Inconsistent preferences among gambles. *Journal of Experimental Psychology*, 1971, *89*, 390–397.

Logan, F. A., Beier, E. M., & Kincaid, W. D. Extinction following partial and varied reinforcement. *Journal of Experimental Psychology*, 1956, *52*, 65–70.

Lopes, L. L. A unified integration model for "Prior expectancy and behavioral extremity as determinants of attitude attribution." *Journal of Experimental Social Psychology*, 1972, *8*, 156–160.

Lopes, L. L. Individual strategies in goal-setting. *Organizational Behavior and Human Performance*, 1976, *15*, 268–277. (a)

Lopes, L. L. Model-based decision and inference in stud poker. *Journal of Experimental Psychology: General*, 1976, *105*, 217–239. (b)

Lord, F. M. On the statistical treatment of football numbers. *American Psychologist*, 1953, *8*, 750–751.

Luce, R. D. *Individual choice behavior*. New York: Wiley, 1959.

Luce, R. D. Remarks on the theory of the measurement and its relation to psychology. In *Les modèles et la formalisation du comportement*. Paris: Editions du Centre National de la Récherche Scientifique, 1967.

Luce, R. D. *Axioms for the averaging and adding representations of functional measurement* (Unpublished manuscript). Cambridge: Department of Psychology and Social Relations, Harvard University, February 1980.

Luce, R. D., & Galanter, E. Psychophysical scaling. In R. D. Luce, R. R. Bush, & E. Galanter (Eds.), *Handbook of mathematical psychology* (Vol. 1). New York: Wiley, 1963.

Luce, R. D., & Green, D. M. Detection, discrimination, and recognition. In E. C. Carterette & M. P. Friedman (Eds.), *Handbook of perception* (Vol. 2). New York: Academic Press, 1974.

Lück, H. E., Regelmann, S., & Schönbach, P. Zur sozialen Erwünschtheit von Eigenschaftsbezeichnungen Datenvergleiche: Köln 1966—Bochum 1971—Köln 1972. *Zeitschrift für experimentelle und angewandte Psychologie*, 1976, *23*, 253–266.

Malinvaud, E. *Statistical methods of econometrics*. Chicago, Illinois: Rand McNally, 1966. (Originally published in French, 1964.)

Malinvaud, E. The consistency of nonlinear regressions. *The Annals of Mathematical Statistics*, 1970, *41*, 956–969.

Mandel, J. *The statistical analysis of experimental data*. New York: Wiley, 1964.

Manis, M., & Armstrong, G. W. Contrast effects in verbal output. *Journal of Experimental Social Psychology*, 1971, *7*, 381–388.

Mansfield, R. J. W. Psychophysics and the neural basis of information processing. In H.-G. Geissler & Yu. M. Zabrodin (Eds.), *Advances in psychophysics*. Berlin: VEB Deutscher Verlag, 1976.

Marks, L. E. *Sensory processes*. New York: Academic Press, 1974.

Marks, L. E. A theory of loudness and loudness judgments. *Psychological Review*, 1979, *86*, 256–285. (a)

Marks, L. E. Sensory and cognitive factors in judgments of loudness. *Journal of Experimental Psychology: Human Perception and Performance*, 1979, *5*, 426–443. (b)

Marks, L. E. Psychophysical measurement: Procedures, tasks, scales. In B. Wegener (Ed.), *Social attitudes and psychophysical measurement*. Hillsdale, New Jersey: Erlbaum, 1982.

Massaro, D. W., & Anderson, N. H. A test of a perspective theory of geometrical illusions. *American Journal of Psychology*, 1970, *83*, 567–575.

Massaro, D. W., & Anderson, N. H. Judgmental model of the Ebbinghaus illusion. *Journal of Experimental Psychology*, 1971, *89*, 147–151.

McClelland, G. H. *Axioms for the weighted linear model* (Tech. Rep. 227). Boulder: Center for Research on Judgment and Policy, University of Colorado, July 1980.

McGuire, W. J. Inducing resistance to persuasion. In L. Berkowitz (Ed.), *Advances in experimental social psychology* (Vol. 1). New York: Academic Press, 1964.

McKillip, J. Comment on "Anderson's personality trait words: Has their meaning changed?" *Personality and Social Psychology Bulletin*, 1978, *4*, 289–291.

Mehrabian, A. Inference of attitudes from the posture, orientation, and distance of a communicator. *Journal of Consulting and Clinical Psychology*, 1968, *32*, 296–308.

Mehrabian, A. *Nonverbal communication*. Chicago, Illinois: Aldine-Atherton, 1972.

Mehrabian, A., & Ferris, S. R. Inference of attitudes from nonverbal communication in two channels. *Journal of Consulting Psychology*, 1967, *31*, 248–252.

Melton, A. W. The end-spurt in memorization curves as an artifact of the averaging of individual curves. *Psychological Monographs*, 1936, *47*, (No. 212), 119–134.

Miller, R. G., Jr. *Simultaneous statistical inference*. New York: McGraw-Hill, 1966.

Montgomery, H., & Eisler, H. Is an equal interval scale an equal discriminability scale? *Perception & Psychophysics*, 1974, *15*, 441–448.

Moreland, R. L., & Zajonc, R. B. Exposure effects may not depend on stimulus recognition. *Journal of Personality and Social Psychology*, 1979, *37*, 1085–1089.

Myers, J. L. Probability learning and sequence learning. In W. K. Estes (Ed.), *Handbook of learning and cognitive processes* (Vol. 3). Hillsdale, New Jersey: Erlbaum, 1976.

Nakamura, C. Y., & Anderson, N. H. Avoidance behavior differences within and between strains of rats. *Journal of Comparative and Physiological Psychology*, 1962, *55*, 740–747.

Nakamura, C. Y., & Anderson, N. H. Avoidance conditioning in wheel box and shuttle box. *Psychological Reports*, 1964, *14*, 327–334.

Nakamura, C. Y., & Anderson, N. H. Test of a CER interpretation of the avoidance decrement phenomenon. *Journal of Comparative and Physiological Psychology*, 1968, *66*, 759–763.

Nisbett, R. E., & Bellows, N. Verbal reports about causal influences on social judgments: Private access versus public theories. *Journal of Personality and Social Psychology*, 1977, *35*, 613–624.

Nisbett, R. E., & Ross, L. *Human inference: Strategies and shortcomings of social judgment.* Englewood Cliffs, New Jersey: Prentice-Hall, 1980.

Nisbett, R. E., & Wilson, T. D. Telling more than we can know: Verbal reports on mental processes. *Psychological Review*, 1977, *84*, 231–259.

Norman, K. L. Dynamic processes in stimulus integration theory: Effects of feedback on averaging of motor movements. *Journal of Experimental Psychology*, 1974, *102*, 399–408. (a)

Norman, K. L. Rule learning in a stimulus integration task. *Journal of Experimental Psychology*, 1974, *103*, 941–947. (b)

Norman, K. L. A solution for weights and scale values in functional measurement. *Psychological Review*, 1976, *83*, 80–84. (a)

Norman, K. L. Effects of feedback on the weights and subjective values in an information integration model. *Organizational Behavior and Human Performance*, 1976, *17*, 367–387. (b)

Norman, K. L. SIMILE: A FORTRAN program package for stimulus-integration models. *Behavior Research Methods & Instrumentation*, 1979, *11*, 79–80.

Oden, G. C. *Semantic constraints and ambiguity resolution.* Unpublished doctoral dissertation, University of California, San Diego, 1974.

Oden, G. C. Fuzziness in semantic memory: Choosing exemplars of subjective categories. *Memory & Cognition*, 1977, *5*, 198–204. (a)

Oden, G. C. Integration of fuzzy logical information. *Journal of Experimental Psychology: Human Perception and Performance*, 1977, *3*, 565–575. (b)

Oden, G. C. Semantic constraints and judged preference for interpretations of ambiguous sentences. *Memory & Cognition*, 1978, *6*, 26–37.

Oden, G. C. A fuzzy logical model of letter identification. *Journal of Experimental Psychology: Human Perception and Performance*, 1979, *5*, 336–352.

Oden, G. C., & Anderson, N. H. Differential weighting in integration theory. *Journal of Experimental Psychology*, 1971, *89*, 152–161.

Oden, G. C., & Anderson, N. H. Integration of semantic constraints. *Journal of Verbal Learning and Verbal Behavior*, 1974, *13*, 138–148.

Oden, G. C., & Massaro, D. W. Integration of featural information in speech perception. *Psychological Review*, 1978, *85*, 172–191.

Oden, G. C., & Wong, S. GEP: A generalized experimental package. (Distributed by Digital Equipment Users Society, Maynard, Massachusetts), 1973.

Orne, M. T. On the social psychology of the psychological experiment: With particular reference to demand characteristics and their implications. *American Psychologist*, 1962, *17*, 776–783.

Osgood, C. E., Suci, G. J., & Tannenbaum, P. H. *The measurement of meaning.* Urbana: University of Illinois Press, 1957.

Ostrom, T. M., Werner, C., & Saks, M. J. An integration theory analysis of jurors' presumptions of guilt or innocence. *Journal of Personality and Social Psychology*, 1978, *36*, 436–450.

Parducci, A. Category judgment: A range–frequency model. *Psychological Review*, 1965, *72*, 407–418.

Parducci, A. Contextual effects: A range–frequency analysis. In E. C. Carterette &

M. P. Friedman (Eds.), *Handbook of perception* (Vol. 2). New York: Academic Press, 1974.

Parducci, A. Category ratings: Still more contextual effects! In B. Wegener (Ed.), *Social attitudes and psychophysical measurement*. Hillsdale, New Jersey: Erlbaum, 1982.

Parducci, A., & Perrett, L. F. Category rating scales: Effects of relative spacing and frequency of stimulus values. *Journal of Experimental Psychology*, 1971, *89*, 427–452.

Parducci, A., Thaler, H., & Anderson, N. H. Stimulus averaging and the context for judgment. *Perception & Psychophysics*, 1968, *3*, 145–150.

Payne, J. W. Alternative approaches to decision making under risk: Moments versus risk dimensions. *Psychological Bulletin*, 1973, *80*, 439–453.

Pennington, N., & Hastie, R. Juror decision-making models: The generalization gap. *Psychological Bulletin*, 1981, *89*, 246–287.

Person, H. B., & Barron, F. H. Polynomial psychophysics of group risk perception. *Acta Psychologica*, 1978, *42*, 421–428.

Phelps, R. H., & Shanteau, J. Livestock judges: How much information can an expert use? *Organizational Behavior and Human Performance*, 1978, *21*, 209–219.

Pollack, I. Neutralization of stimulus bias in the rating of grays. *Journal of Experimental Psychology*, 1965, *69*, 564–578.

Poulton, E. C. The new psychophysics: Six models for magnitude estimation. *Psychological Bulletin*, 1968, *69*, 1–19.

Poulton, E. C. Unwanted range effects from using within-subject experimental designs. *Psychological Bulletin*, 1973, *80*, 113–121.

Poulton, E. C. Models for biases in judging sensory magnitude. *Psychological Bulletin*, 1979, *86*, 777–803.

Rapoport, A., & Wallsten, T. S. Individual decision behavior. *Annual Review of Psychology*, 1972, *23*, 131–176.

Restle, F. Visual illusions. In M. H. Appley (Ed.), *Adaptation-level theory*. New York: Academic Press, 1971.

Rock, D. A., Werts, C. E., Linn, R. L., & Jöreskog, K. G. A maximum likelihood solution to the errors in variables and errors in equations model. *Multivariate Behavioral Research*, 1977, *12*, 187–197.

Rokeach, M., & Rothman, G. The principle of belief congruence and the congruity principle as models of cognitive interaction. *Psychological Review*, 1965, *72*, 128–142.

Ronis, D. L., Baumgardner, M. H., Leippe, M. R., Cacioppo, J. T., & Greenwald, A. G. In search of reliable persuasion effects: I. A computer-controlled procedure for studying persuasion. *Journal of Personality and Social Psychology*, 1977, *35*, 548–569.

Rosnow, R. L., & Arms, R. L. Adding versus averaging as a stimulus-combination rule in forming impressions of groups. *Journal of Personality and Social Psychology*, 1968, *10*, 363–369.

Rosnow, R. L., Wainer, H., & Arms, R. L. Anderson's personality-trait words rated by men and women as a function of stimulus sex. *Psychological Reports*, 1969, *24*, 787–790.

Sawyers, B. K., & Anderson, N. H. Test of integration theory in attitude change. *Journal of Personality and Social Psychology*, 1971, *18*, 230–233.

Scheffé, H. An analysis of variance for paired comparisons. *Journal of the American Statistical Association*, 1952, *47*, 381–400.

Scheffé, H. *The analysis of variance*. New York: Wiley, 1959.

Schmidt, C. F., & Levin, I. P. Test of an averaging model of person preference: Effect of context. *Journal of Personality and Social Psychology*, 1972, *23*, 277–282.

Schmidt, F. L. The relative efficiency of regression and simple unit predictor weights in applied differential psychology. *Educational and Psychological Measurement*, 1971, *31*, 699–714.

Schmidt, F. L. Implications of a measurement problem for expectancy theory research. *Organizational Behavior and Human Performance*, 1973, *10*, 243–251.

Schmitt, N., & Levine, R. L. Statistical and subjective weights: Some problems and proposals. *Organizational Behavior and Human Performance*, 1977, *20*, 15–30.

Schönbach, P. Likableness ratings of 100 German personality-trait words corresponding to a subset of Anderson's 555 trait words. *European Journal of Social Psychology*, 1972, *2*, 327–334.

Searle, S. R. *Linear models*. New York: Wiley, 1971.

Shannon, C. E. A mathematical theory of communication. *Bell System Technical Journal*, 1948, *27*, 379–423.

Shanteau, J. C. An additive model for sequential decision making. *Journal of Experimental Psychology*, 1970, *85*, 181–191. (a)

Shanteau, J. C. *Component processes in risky decision judgments.* Unpublished doctoral dissertation, University of California, San Diego, 1970. (b)

Shanteau, J. Descriptive versus normative models of sequential inference judgment. *Journal of Experimental Psychology*, 1972, *93*, 63–68.

Shanteau, J. Component processes in risky decision making. *Journal of Experimental Psychology*, 1974, *103*, 680–691.

Shanteau, J. An information-integration analysis of risky decision making. In M. F. Kaplan & S. Schwartz (Eds.), *Human judgment and decision processes.* New York: Academic Press, 1975. (a)

Shanteau, J. Averaging versus multiplying combination rules of inference judgment. *Acta Psychologica*, 1975, *39*, 83–89. (b)

Shanteau, J. POLYLIN: A FORTRAN IV program for the analysis of multiplicative (multilinear) trend components of interactions. *Behavior Research Methods & Instrumentation*, 1977, *9*, 381–382.

Shanteau, J. *The concept of weight in judgment and decision making: A review and some unifying proposals* (Tech. Rep. 228). Boulder: Center for Research on Judgment and Policy, University of Colorado, July 1980.

Shanteau, J. C., & Anderson, N. H. Test of a conflict model for preference judgment. *Journal of Mathematical Psychology*, 1969, *6*, 312–325.

Shanteau, J., & Anderson, N. H. Integration theory applied to judgments of the value of information. *Journal of Experimental Psychology*, 1972, *92*, 266–275.

Shanteau, J., & Nagy, G. Decisions made about other people: A human judgment analysis of dating choice. In J. S. Carroll & J. W. Payne (Eds.), *Cognition and social behavior.* Potomac, Maryland: Erlbaum, 1976.

Shanteau, J., & Nagy, G. F. Probability of acceptance in dating choice. *Journal of Personality and Social Psychology*, 1979, *37*, 522–533.

Shepard, R. N. On subjectively optimum selection among multiattribute alternatives. In M. W. Shelly & G. L. Bryan (Eds.), *Human judgments and optimality.* New York: Wiley, 1964.

Sherif, M., & Hovland, C. I. *Social judgment: Assimilation and contrast effects in communication and attitude change.* New Haven, Connecticut: Yale University Press, 1961.

Sidowski, J. B., & Anderson, N. H. Judgments of City–Occupation combinations. *Psychonomic Science*, 1967, *7*, 279–280.

Siegel, S. *Nonparametric statistics for the behavioral sciences.* New York: McGraw-Hill, 1956.

Simon, H. A. Discussion: Cognition and social behavior. In J. S. Carroll & J. W. Payne (Eds.), *Cognition and social behavior.* Potomac, Maryland: Erlbaum, 1976.

Simpson, D. D., & Ostrom, T. M. Contrast effects in impression formation. *Journal of Personality and Social Psychology*, 1976, *34*, 625–629.

Singh, R., Gupta, M., & Dalal, A. K. Cultural difference in attribution of performance: An integration-theoretical analysis. *Journal of Personality and Social Psychology*, 1979, *37*, 1342–1351.

Sjöberg, L. Studies of the rated favorableness of offers to gamble. *Scandinavian Journal of Psychology*, 1968, *9*, 257–273.

Slovic, P., & Lichtenstein, S. Relative importance of probabilities and payoffs in risk taking. *Journal of Experimental Psychology*, 1968, *78*, Monograph Supplement (3, Pt. 2).

Slovic, P. Choice between equally valued alternatives. *Journal of Experimental Psychology: Human Perception and Performance*, 1975, *1*, 280–287.

Slovic, P., & Lichtenstein, S. Comparison of Bayesian and regression approaches to the study of information processing in judgment. *Organizational Behavior and Human Performance*, 1971, *6*, 649–744.

Smith, E. R., & Miller, F. D. Limits on perception of cognitive processes: A reply to Nisbett and Wilson. *Psychological Review*, 1978, *85*, 355–362.

Speed, F. M., Hocking, R. R., & Hackney, O. P. Methods of analysis of linear models with unbalanced data. *Journal of the American Statistical Association*, 1978, *73*, 105–112.

Sternberg, S. Stochastic learning theory. In R. D. Luce, R. R. Bush, & E. Galanter (Eds.), *Handbook of mathematical psychology* (Vol. 2). New York: Wiley, 1963.

Stevens, S. S. On the psychophysical law. *Psychological Review*, 1957, *64*, 153–181.

Stevens, S. S. Adaptation-level vs. the relativity of judgment. *American Journal of Psychology*, 1958, *71*, 633–646.

Stevens, S. S. Issues in psychophysical measurement. *Psychological Review*, 1971, *78*, 426–450.

Stevens, S. S. Perceptual magnitude and its measurement. In E. C. Carterette & M. P. Friedman (Eds.), *Handbook of perception* (Vol. 2). New York: Academic Press, 1974.

Stevens, S. S. *Psychophysics*. New York: Wiley, 1975.

Stevens, S. S., & Galanter, E. H. Ratio scales and category scales for a dozen perceptual continua. *Journal of Experimental Psychology*, 1957, *54*, 377–411.

Stewart, R. H. Effect of continuous responding on the order effect in personality impression formation. *Journal of Personality and Social Psychology*, 1965, *1*, 161–165.

Surber, C. F. Developmental processes in social inference: Averaging of intentions and consequences in moral judgment. *Developmental Psychology*, 1977, *13*, 654–665.

Takahashi, S. Effect of information redundancy on context effects in personality impression formation. *Japanese Psychological Research*, 1975, *17*, 155–166.

Taylor, S. E., & Fiske, S. T. Salience, attention, and attribution: Top of the head phenomena. In L. Berkowitz (Ed.), *Advances in experimental social psychology* (Vol. 11). New York: Academic Press, 1978.

Teghtsoonian, R. On the exponents in Stevens' law and the constant in Ekman's law. *Psychological Review*, 1971, *78*, 71–80.

Teghtsoonian, R., Teghtsoonian, M., & Karlsson, J.-G. The limits of perceived magnitude: Comparison among individuals and among perceptual continua. *Acta Psychologica*, 1981, *49*, 83–94.

Thurstone, L. L. Fechner's law and the method of equal-appearing intervals. *Journal of Experimental Psychology*, 1929, *12*, 214–224. (Reprinted in *The measurement of values* 1959.)

Thurstone, L. L. *The measurement of values*. Chicago, Illinois: University of Chicago Press, 1959.

Torgerson, W. S. *Theory and methods of scaling*. New York: Wiley, 1958.

Torgerson, W. S. Distances and ratios in psychological scaling. *Acta Psychologica*, 1961, *19*, 201–205.

Troutman, C. M., & Shanteau, J. Inferences based on nondiagnostic information. *Organizational Behavior and Human Performance,* 1977, *19,* 43–55.

Tukey, J. W. One degree of freedom for non-additivity. *Biometrics,* 1949, *5,* 232–242.

Tukey, J. W. Analyzing data: Sanctification or detective work? *American Psychologist,* 1969, *24,* 83–102.

Ulehla, Z. J., Canges, L., & Wackwitz, F. Signal detectability theory applied to conceptual discrimination. *Psychonomic Science,* 1967, *8,* 221–222.

Upshaw, H. S. The personal reference scale: An approach to social judgment. In L. Berkowitz (Ed.), *Advances in experimental social psychology* (Vol. 4). New York: Academic Press, 1969.

Volkmann, J. Scales of judgment and their implications for social psychology. In J. H. Rohrer & M. Sherif (Eds.), *Social psychology at the crossroads.* New York: Harper, 1951.

Warburton, D. M., & Greeno, J. G. General shape function model of learning with applications in psychobiology. *Psychological Review,* 1970, *77,* 348–352.

Ward, L. M. Category judgments of loudness in the absence of an experimenter-induced identification function. *Journal of Experimental Psychology,* 1972, *94,* 179–184.

Ward, L. M. Heuristic use or information integration in the estimation of subjective likelihood? *Bulletin of the Psychonomic Society,* 1975, *6,* 43–46.

Warren, R. D., White, J. K., & Fuller, W. A. An errors-in-variables analysis of managerial role performance. *Journal of the American Statistical Association,* 1974, *69,* 886–893.

Watson, C. S., Rilling, M. E., & Bourbon, W. T. Receiver-operating characteristics determined by a mechanical analog to the rating scale. *Journal of the Acoustical Society of America,* 1964, *36,* 283–288.

Weiner, B., & Peter, N. A cognitive–developmental analysis of achievement and moral judgments. *Developmental Psychology,* 1973, *9,* 290–309.

Weiss, D. J. Averaging: An empirical validity criterion for magnitude estimation. *Perception & Psychophysics,* 1972, *12,* 385–388.

Weiss, D. J. *A functional measurement analysis of equisection.* Unpublished doctoral dissertation, University of California, San Diego, 1973. (a)

Weiss, D. J. FUNPOT: A FORTRAN program for finding a polynomial transformation to reduce any sources of variance in a factorial design. *Behavioral Science,* 1973, *18,* 150. (b)

Weiss, D. J. Quantifying private events: A functional measurement analysis of equisection. *Perception & Psychophysics,* 1975, *17,* 351–357.

Weiss, D. J. Note on choosing a response scale. *Perceptual and Motor Skills,* 1980, *50,* 472–474. (a)

Weiss, D. J. ORPOCO: Orthogonal polynomial coefficients. *Behavior Research Methods & Instrumentation,* 1980, *12,* 635. (b)

Weiss, D. J., & Anderson, N. H. Subjective averaging of length with serial presentation. *Journal of Experimental Psychology,* 1969, *82,* 52–63.

Weiss, D. J., & Anderson, N. H. Use of rank order data in functional measurement. *Psychological Bulletin,* 1972, *78,* 64–69.

Weiss, D. J., & Shanteau, J. Group–Individual POLYLIN. *Behavioral Research Methods & Instrumentation,* 1982, in press.

White, P. Limitations on verbal reports of internal events: A refutation of Nisbett and Wilson and of Bem. *Psychological Review,* 1980, *87,* 105–112.

Wike, E. L., & Church, J. D. Comments on Clark's "The language-as-fixed-effect fallacy." *Journal of Verbal Learning and Verbal Behavior,* 1976, *15,* 249–255.

Wilkening, F. Combining of stimulus dimensions in children's and adults' judgments of area: An information integration analysis. *Developmental Psychology,* 1979, *15,* 25–33.

Wilkening, F. Development of dimensional integration in children's perceptual judgment: Experiments with area, volume, and velocity. In F. Wilkening, J. Becker, & T. Trabasso (Eds.), *Information integration by children*. Hillsdale, New Jersey: Erlbaum, 1980.

Wilkening, F. Integrating velocity, time, and distance information: A developmental study. *Cognitive Psychology*, 1981, *13*, 231–247.

Wilkening, F., & Anderson, N. H. *Comparison of two rule assessment methodologies for studying cognitive development* (Tech. Rep. CHIP 94). La Jolla: Center for Human Information Processing, University of California, San Diego, June 1980.

Wilkening, F., & Anderson, N. H. Comparison of two rule-assessment methodologies for studying cognitive development and knowledge structure. *Psychological Bulletin*, 1982, *92*, 215–237.

Wilkening, F., & Anderson, N. H. Representation and diagnosis of knowledge structures. In N. H. Anderson (Ed.), *Contributions to information integration theory*, in press.

Wilson, W., Miller, H. L., & Lower, J. S. Much ado about the null hypothesis. *Psychological Bulletin*, 1967, *67*, 188–196.

Winsberg, S., & Ramsay, J. O. Monotonic transformations to additivity using splines. *Biometrika*, 1980, *67*, 669–674.

Winer, B. J. *Statistical principles in experimental design* (2nd ed). New York: McGraw-Hill, 1971.

Wyer, R. S., Jr. A quantitative comparison of three models of impression formation. *Journal of Experimental Research in Personality*, 1969, *4*, 29–41.

Wyer, R. S., Jr. Effects of information inconsistency and grammatical context on evaluations of persons. *Journal of Personality and Social Psychology*, 1973, *25*, 45–49.

Wyer, R. S., Jr. Functional measurement methodology applied to a subjective probability model of cognitive functioning. *Journal of Personality and Social Psychology*. 1975, *31*, 94–100. (a)

Wyer, R. S., Jr. Some informational determinants of one's own liking for a person and beliefs that others will like this person. *Journal of Personality and Social Psychology*, 1975, *31*, 1041–1053. (b)

Wyer, R. S., Jr., & Carlston, D. E. *Social cognition, inference, and attribution*. Hillsdale, New Jersey: Erlbaum, 1979.

Yang, K.-S., & Yang, P.-H.L. Desirability, meaningfulness, and familiarity ratings of 557 Chinese personality-trait adjectives. *Acta Psychologica Taiwanica*, 1971 (No. 13), 36–57.

Young, F. W., de Leeuw, J., & Takane, Y. Regression with qualitative and quantitative variables: An alternating least squares method with optimal scaling features. *Psychometrika*, 1976, *41*, 505–529.

Zalinski, J., & Anderson, N. H. Measurement of importance in multiattribute judgment models. *Journal of Applied Psychology*, Submitted for publication, December 1, 1977.

Zalinski, J., & Anderson, N. H. Measurement of importance in multiattribute judgment models. In J. B. Sidowski (Ed.), *Conditioning, cognition, and methodology: Contemporary issues in experimental psychology*. Hillsdale, New Jersey: Erlbaum, in press.

Zeleny, M. The attribute-dynamic attitude model (ADAM). *Management Science*, 1976, *23*, 12–26.

Index